Bioremediation of Pollutants

Bioremediation of Pollutants

Editors
D.K. Maheshwari
R.C. Dubey

I.K. International Publishing House Pvt. Ltd.
NEW DELHI • BANGALORE

Published by

I.K. International Publishing House Pvt. Ltd.
S-25, Green Park Extension
Uphaar Cinema Market
New Delhi – 110 016 (India)
E-mail: info@ikinternational.com
Website: www.ikbooks.com

ISBN 978-93-81141-05-2

10 9 8 7 6 5 4 3 2 1

Published by Krishan Makhijani for I.K. International Publishing House Pvt Ltd., S-25, Green Park Extension, Uphaar Cinema Market, New Delhi – 110 016 and Printed by Rekha Printers Pvt. Ltd., Okhla Industrial Area, Phase II, New Delhi – 110 020

Preface

Advances and advantages of the use of biological including microorganisms over other processes and procedure are not only eco-friendly but also have long lasting effects due to their sustainable approaches. Microbes and their interactions with innate microbial community dynamics greatly influence natural bioremedial processing occurring in soil and water. Due to the efficacy of selected microbial strains or microbial consortia together with molecular manipulations, it has now become a cost-effective and more eco-friendly approach for restoring better environmental quality. Nowadays, Government legislation is forcing the industrial houses to use more environment-friendly approaches so as to protect our ecosystem. Thus, the changing climate and environment has led to the need of sustainable use of natural resources.

Bioremediation is an important process nowadays used for abatement of toxic pollutants undesirable to different types of ecosystem. Petroleum and its hydrocarbons products in the form of waste, industrial plastic wastes, phenol and cyanide from industrial wastewater, azo textile dyes in the form of discharge from textile industries, heavy metal pollutants, chemical fertilizers, pesticides, etc. are a few of them hazardous to various components of ecosystem. Microorganisms are ubiquitous due to their versatile habit and habitat. Many species of microbes are responsible for bioconversion and biotransformation of waste into various value-added products for the betterment of life of human beings, while urbanization, industrialization and increase in population are responsible for degradation of environment. Various microorganisms are involved and are able to degrade solid waste, liquid effluents generated in industries containing heavy metals pollution, arsenic in groundwater and petroleum products entering as oil pollutants due to oilspills in the marine environment. Microorganisms have a major role in the management of pathogens and parasites besides acting as source for providing sustainable benefits. Thus, the microorganisms in the form of bacteria, fungi, cyanobacteria, etc. are of prime importance in strengthening our knowledge on environment.

This book covers the current developments in the field of environmental microbiology with emphasis on their emergence in industries. Expert scientists have contributed the chapters based on their long-term researches. All the chapters included in this book are devoted to management of environment through microbial actions. This book deals with various facets of bacteria, fungi, lichens and other forms, bestowed if exploited around the world in the maintenance of a healthy environment.

We would like to express our sincere thanks to all the authors, without their contributions this book would not have been possible. The contributions are indeed excellent.

D.K. Maheshwari
R.C. Dubey

Contents

The Editors

D.K. Maheshwari started his teaching carrier as a lecturer in the Department of Botany, D.A.V. (PG) College, Muzaffarnagar and thereafter served as Reader in the Department of Microbiology, Barkatullah University, Bhopal. He joined Gurukul Kangri University, Haridwar as Professor in the year 1990 and served as Dean, Faculty of Life Science (2004-2006). Prof. Maheshwari is an active member of several scientific bodies of international repute and in the board of panels of various academic and administrative bodies including UPSC and NAAC of Govt. of India. He has been the Editor of the *Journal of Indian Botanical Society* and he was awardee of young scientist "Prof. Y.S. Murthy Medal" for his outstanding contribution.

As a young scientist, he was selected under UNESCO programmes and worked in Biological Research Center, Szeged (Hungary) in the year 1983-84 and also visited Czechoslovakia, Belgium, Holland, Germany, Japan and S. Korea. He was visiting Professor in Science University of Tokyo, in 1993 and 1998, and Guest Professor, in the University of Ulm (Germany). Prof. Maheshwari visited S. Korea in the year 2000, 2003 and 2006 and 2010 under bilateral scientific exchange programmes sponsored by Indian National Science Academy (INSA), New Delhi and National Research Foundation, Korea.

Prof. Maheshwari has many research papers (90) in leading peer-reviewed journals both Indian as well as foreign. More than 35 candidates have been awarded Doctorate (Ph.D.) degree under him. He has completed 12 major research projects sponsored by various funding agencies. Prof. Maheshwari is the editor of *Microbes: Agriculture, Industry and Environment* (2000) and *Innovative Approaches in Microbiology* (2002). He is co-author of *Practical Microbiology* (2004) and *A Textbook of Microbiology* (3rd edn., 2010) *Biotechnological Applications of Microorganisms: A Techno-Commercial Approach* (2006); *Potential Microorganisms for Sustainable Agriculture* (2008); *Industrial Exploitation of Microorganisms* (2009), *Microbiology Monographs* (V-16). *Bacteria and Plant Health* (2010). Springer, Heidelberg, Germany Book (volume), I. *Bacteria in Agrobiology : Crop Ecosystem, II. Bacteria in Agrobiology : Plant Growth, Response III. Bacteria in Agrobiology : Plant Nutrient Management, IV. Bacteria in Agrobiology: Stress Management, V. Bacteria in Agrobiology : Disease Management and VI. Bacteria in Agrobiology : Plant Probiotics*, has accepted their publications in the year 2010-2011 and member, Editorial Board, *Korean J. Agric, Chem. and Biotechnology*.

He is a Fellow of the Indian Botanical Society and Indian Phytopathological Society and Life Member of Indian Science Congress; Phytopathological Society of India; Botanical Society and Association of Microbiologists in India. He is nominated as Convenor "Science forum" from Uttarakhand Council for Science and Technology, Govt. of India, Dehradun.

Professor R.C. Dubey, Dept. of Botany & Microbiology, earned M.Sc. and Ph.D. degrees from the Banaras Hindu University in 1981 and 1986, respectively. He served Kumaun University (Nainital) as lecturer from 1987 to 1996; thereafter, he joined Gurukul Kangri University (Haridwar) in 1996 as Reader. He joined as Professor in 2004.

His field of interest is soil microbiology and microbial biotechnology having expertise in biological control of soil-borne plant pathogens, mycorrhizae, Rhizosphere microbiology and botanical pesticides, besides enzymology and heavy metal toxicity. He has published more than 82 research and review papers in the national and international journals of repute. He has produced 16 Ph.Ds and is supervising several research students on varied aspects of microbiology. He has handles Research Projects sponsored by UGC, UCOST and CSIR. He has authored three books, viz., *Practical Microbiology* (2004), *A Text Book of Biotechnology* (4th edn., 2006) and *A Textbook of Microbiology* (3rd edn., 2010). He is also co-editor of *Himalayan Microbial Diversity* (1997); *Microbes: Agriculture, Industry and Environment* (2000); *Innovative Approaches in Microbiology* (2002); *Biotechnological Applications of Microorganisms, A Techno-Commercial Approach* (2006); *Potential Microorganisms for Sustainable Agriculture* (2008); *Industrial Exploitation of Microorganisms* (2009).

He was the Organizing Secretary of the national seminar on Bioinoculants for Holistic Sustainable Rural Development jointly organized by the Department of Botany & Microbiology and DDU state Institute for Rural Development (U.P. Govt.) (1998). He was the Co-coordinator of the Workshop on Molecular Biology and Applied Microbiology, and Hands-on-Training on Microbial Fermentation and Inoculants Production (2008).

He is the Life Member and Fellow of the Indian Botanical Society; Indian Phytopathological Society and the International Society for Conservation of Natural Resources. He was Associate Editor of the *Journal of the Indian Botanical Society* (2000-2004), and at present he is in the Editorial Board of the *Journal of Environmental Biology and Conservation.*

Contributors

Agrahari, D., *Department of Environmental Science, B.B. Ambedkar University (A Central University), Lucknow (UP)-226025*

Ajungla, T., *Dept. of Botany, Nagaland University, Nagaland. 798627*

Ali, A. S., *Postgraduate Department of Biotechnology, Saifia College of Science and Education, Bhopal (MP), 462001*

Ali, S. A., *Postgraduate Department of Biotechnology, Saifia College of Science and Education, Bhopal (MP), 462001*

Arti *Department of Microbiology, College of Basic Sciences and Humanities, G.B. Pant University of Agriculture & Technology, Pantnagar-263145, US Nagar, Uttarakhand*

Bajpai, R., *Department of Environmental Science, B. B. A. University, Lucknow-226025*

Bose, A., *Yeast and Mycorrhiza Biotechnology Laboratory, Department of Biosciences, R.D. University, Jabalpur (M.P.)*

Dalal, S. *Department of Botany and Microbiology, Gurukul Kangri University, Haridwar-249404*

Das, R., *School of Biotechnology, Guru Ghasidas University, Bilaspur (C.G.) 495009*

Dhanasekaran, D., *Department of Microbiology, School of Life Sciences, Bharathidasan University, Tiruchirappalli-620024*

Dixit, S., *Department of Environmental Science, B.B. Ambedkar (Central) University, Raibarely Road, Lucknow-226025, U.P.*

Dkhar, M. S., *Dept. of Botany, NEHU, Shillong-22, Meghalaya*

Dubey, R.C., *Department of Botany and Microbiology, Gurukul Kangri University, Haridwar-249404*

Dwivedi, S.K., *Department of Environmental Science, B.B. Ambedkar University (A Central University), Lucknow (UP)-226025*

Gautam, S.P., *Yeast and Mycorrhiza Biotechnology Laboratory, Department of Biosciences, R.D. University, Jabalpur (M.P.) Central Pollution Control Board, New Delhi-110032*

Goel, R., *Department of Microbiology, CBSH, G.B. Pant University of Agriculture & Technology, Pantnagar-263145, US Nagar, Uttarakhand*

Gupta, A., *Central Institute of Medicinal and Aromatic Plants, (Council of Scientific and Industrial Research), P.O. CIMAP, Lucknow-226015*

Jagadeesh, K.S., *Dept. of Agricultural Microbiology, University of Agricultural Science, Dharwad-580005*

Kalra, A., *Central Institute of Medicinal and Aromatic Plants, (Council of Scientific and Industrial Research), P.O. CIMAP, Lucknow-226015*

Khan, I., *Postgraduate Department of Biotechnology, Saifia College of Science and Education, Bhopal (MP), 462001*

Kumar S., *Department of Botany and Microbiology, Gurukul Kangri University, Haridwar-249404*

Kumar, P., *Department of Botany and Microbiology, Gurukul Kangri University, Haridwar-249404*

Kushwaha, R.K.S. *Department of Botany, Christ Church College, Kanpur-208001*

Maheshwari, D.K. *Department of Botany and Microbiology, Gurukul Kangri University, Haridwar-249404*

Marihal, A.K. *Dept. of Agricultural Microbiology, University of Agricultural Science, Dharwad-580005*

Mishra, A., *Central Institute of Medicinal and Aromatic Plants, (Council of Scientific and Industrial Research), P.O. CIMAP, Lucknow-226015*

Nayaka, S. *Lichenology Laboratory, National Botanical Research Institute (CSIR), Rana Pratap Marg Lucknow-226001*

Pandey, R.R., *Department of Life Sciences, Manipur University, Canchipur, Imphal-795003*

Pandey, R., *Central Institute of Medicinal and Aromatic Plants, (Council of Scientific and Industrial Research), P.O. CIMAP, Lucknow-226015*

Pradeep, S.M., *Dept. of Agricultural Microbiology, University of Agricultural Science, Dharwad-580005*

Saini, J., *Department of Microbiology, College of Basic Sciences and Humanities, G.B. Pant University of Agriculture & Technology, Pantnagar-263145, US Nagar, Uttarakhand*

Sharma, G.D., *Pro. Vice-chancellor, Assam University, Silchar-788011*

Shukla, A. *Department of Environmental Science, B.B. Ambedkar University (A Central University), Lucknow (UP)-226025*

Singh, D.P., *Department of Environmental Science, B.B. Ambedkar (Central) University, Raibarely Road, Lucknow-226025, U.P.*

Singh, I., *Department of Applied Microbiology and Biotechnology, Dr. H.S. Gour University, Sagar-470003*

Singh, J. S., *Department of Environmental Science, B.B. Ambedkar (Central) University, Raibarely Road, Lucknow-226025, U.P.*

Sinha, S., *Ecotoxicology and Bioremediation Group, National Botanical Research Institute, Lucknow-226001*

Soni, R., *Department of Microbiology, CBSH, G.B. Pant University of Agriculture & Technology, Pantnagar-263145, US Nagar, Uttarakhand*

Tewari, L., *Department of Microbiology, College of Basic Sciences and Humanities, G.B. Pant University of Agriculture & Technology, Pantnagar-263145, US Nagar, Uttarakhand*

Tiwari, S. *Yeast and Mycorrhiza Biotechnology Laboratory, Department of Biosciences, R.D. University Jabalpur (M.P.)*

Tiwary, B.N., *School of Biotechnology, Guru Ghasidas University, Bilaspur (C.G.)-495009*

Upreti, D.K., *Lichenology Laboratory, National Botanical Research Institute (CSIR), Rana Pratap Marg, Lucknow-226001, India*

1

Bacterial Degradation of Phenol and Cyanide from Industrial Wastewater

Shailu Dalal[1], R.R. Pandey[2] and R.C. Dubey[1]

[1]*Department of Botany and Microbiology, Gurukul Kangri University, Haridwar-249 404*

[2]*Department of Life Sciences, Manipur University, Canchipur, Imphal-795 003*

E-mail: profrcdubey@gmail.com

Phenols and cyanides may be present in minute concentrations in many natural products, but their large-scale presence in the environment is attributed to the human activities as these compounds are extensively used in industries. Phenols being antioxidants in nature are found in almost all the plants. Lima beans, almonds and cassava have been reported to be rich sources of cyanides. A large amount of phenol is produced by various industries involved in the synthesis of phenol and its substituents, particularly by pharmaceutical ones that are involved in production of many drugs. Cyanides are released in the environment in bulk by metal finishing and mining industries. Phenols and cyanides can be removed and recovered by several physico-chemical processes, but the biological treatment stands more economical and cost-effective as compared to other methods. Several microbial species have the ability to degrade these hazardous compounds into less toxic byproducts. The microorganisms use phenols and cyanides either as a source of carbon or nitrogen during the metabolic processes. Biological treatment of these under anaerobic and aerobic conditions is quite possible. The present review illustrates the advances and advantages of the use of biological treatment over other treatment procedures involved in removal of such toxic pollutants.

INTRODUCTION

Industrialization has provided mankind a comfortable life and may be quoted as a characteristic of the present age. A serious aspect, which had earlier been overlooked but recently has attracted much attention in the course of modernization, is the increased pollution levels in the environment. Among the hazardous pollutants often found in most of the industrial effluents, frequently released in the surroundings, are phenols and cyanides.

Phenol is an aromatic compound discovered in 1834 by Runge from coal tar. Sir Joseph Lister used phenol for the first time in 1865. With the development of its industrial applications, the use of phenol as an antiseptic faded. In pure form phenol is used as a disinfectant. For its local anesthetic and antiseptic properties, phenol has become an important component of shaving soaps and creams. It is also used in veterinary medicine and as an anesthetic for gastric troubles. In the manufacture of glue, phenol plays a major role as a peptidising agent. It is a primary petrochemical intermediate product which is used as a solvent for extraction in many chemical analyses. This aromatic compound is largely used in industries that are involved in the manufacture of phenol-formaldehyde resin (Busca *et al.*, 2008). Such thermosetting resins are highly economical and primarily used in adhesion of plywood, construction of automotives and manufacturing of appliances. A wide range of industrial applications of phenol has been a major factor of environmental pollution which ultimately affects the aquatic and terrestrial lives. In human beings, direct exposure to phenol results in severe skin burns that can further extend upto coma, convulsions and death.

Cyanide, another important constituent of industrial effluents, was first discovered by Scheele, a Swedish chemist, in 1782. Cyanide pollution is caused by both natural and anthropogenic sources, latter being more frequent. Industrial waste, basically from electroplating operations, contains 0.5 to 20% w/v of cyanide. Other sources of cyanide occurred from petrochemical emissions, tobacco smokes, plastics burnings, fumigants and industries involved in the manufacture of synthetic fibers, paints, pesticides and pharma products (Dubey and Holmes, 1995). Large sources of cyanide in the environment are the metal mining and processing industries, the effluents of which contain 0.1 to 0.5 $\mu g\ ml^{-1}$ cyanide, whereas tailing impoundment water may contain 7.0 to 30.0 μg cyanide ml^{-1}.

In nature, cyanide exists in various forms of complexes such as NaCN, KCN, HCN, $Zn(CN)_2$, out of which KCN and NaCN are among the most lethal complexes. Cyanides form strong metallic complexes with Fe, Ni, Zn and Cu that are common components of industrial wastewater. This is probably due to the fact that cyanides are neither absorbed nor retained in soil and prefer mainly to remain in an aqueous phase. Cyanide inhibits the enzyme cytochrome oxidase. Apart from this it also inhibits the activity of many other enzymes in the cellular systems.

PROPERTIES, SOURCES AND APPLICATIONS OF PHENOL

Chemical and Physical Properties

Phenol in pure form is a white crystalline solid with a melting point of 40.9°C. It liquefies upon contact with water and has a characteristic pungent odor with a prickly burning taste. It is soluble in most organic solvents such as ether, ethanol and benzene; however, its solubility in water is 9.8% at room temperature, while above 68°C it becomes entirely water-soluble. Phenol acts as a weak acid when dissolved in water and is moderately volatile at room temperature (Busca *et al.*, 2008).

Sources and Applications

Natural sources: Phenol occurs naturally in many substances such as tea, wine, smoked foods, etc. Phenol is a main constituent of coal tar. Its level increases in the environment due to forest fires. It has been detected among the volatile components from liquid manure at concentrations ranging between 7-55 $\mu g\ kg^{-1}$ dry wt and has an average concentration in manure as 30 $\mu g\ kg^{-1}$ dry wt (RIVM, 1986).

Artificial sources: The most important source of phenol is chemical synthesis by Hock process (Jordan *et al.*, 2002). It is also produced from benzole and coal tar during coal coking, by extraction with caustic solutions. Phenol was introduced into medical arena by Sir Joseph Lister who pioneered its application as an antiseptic agent. Nowadays, it is widely used in manufacturing of drugs like aspirin and is also an active ingredient of disinfectants, antiseptics, ear and nasal drops and oral analgesics like chloraseptic spray. Industrially, it is used in manufacturing of phenolic resins like bakelite (phenol-formamide resin) and bisphenol (monomer of epoxy resins). It also acts as a starting material in the synthesis of nylon-6, nylon-66, polyphenoxy and polysulphone polymers, and corrosion of resistant polyesters. Phenol is being used in the production of fertilizers, herbicides, explosives, paints and paint removers. Various sources of phenol in water are shown in Fig. 1.1.

Different concentrations of phenol released into the environment through wastewater are summarized in Fig. 1.2.

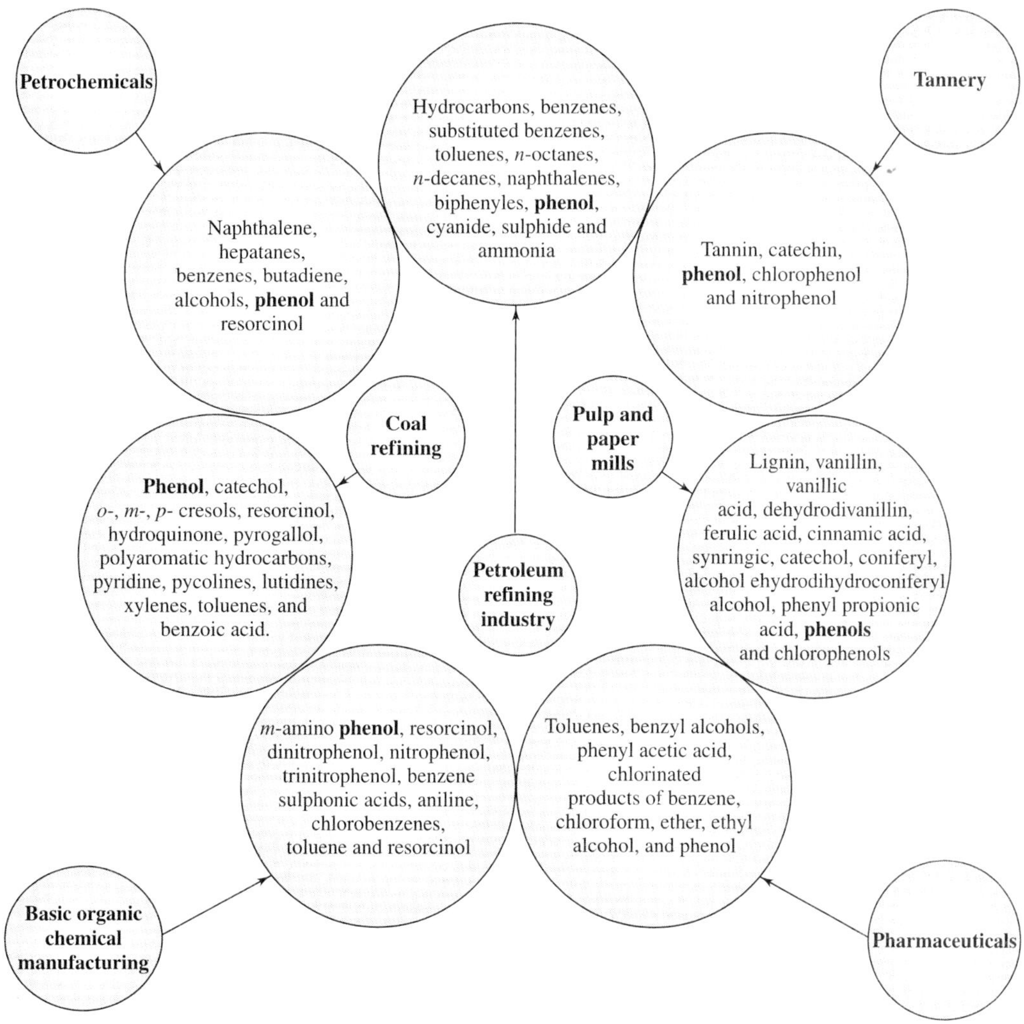

Fig. 1.1 Sources of phenol in water (Adapted from Kumaran and Paruchuri, 1997).

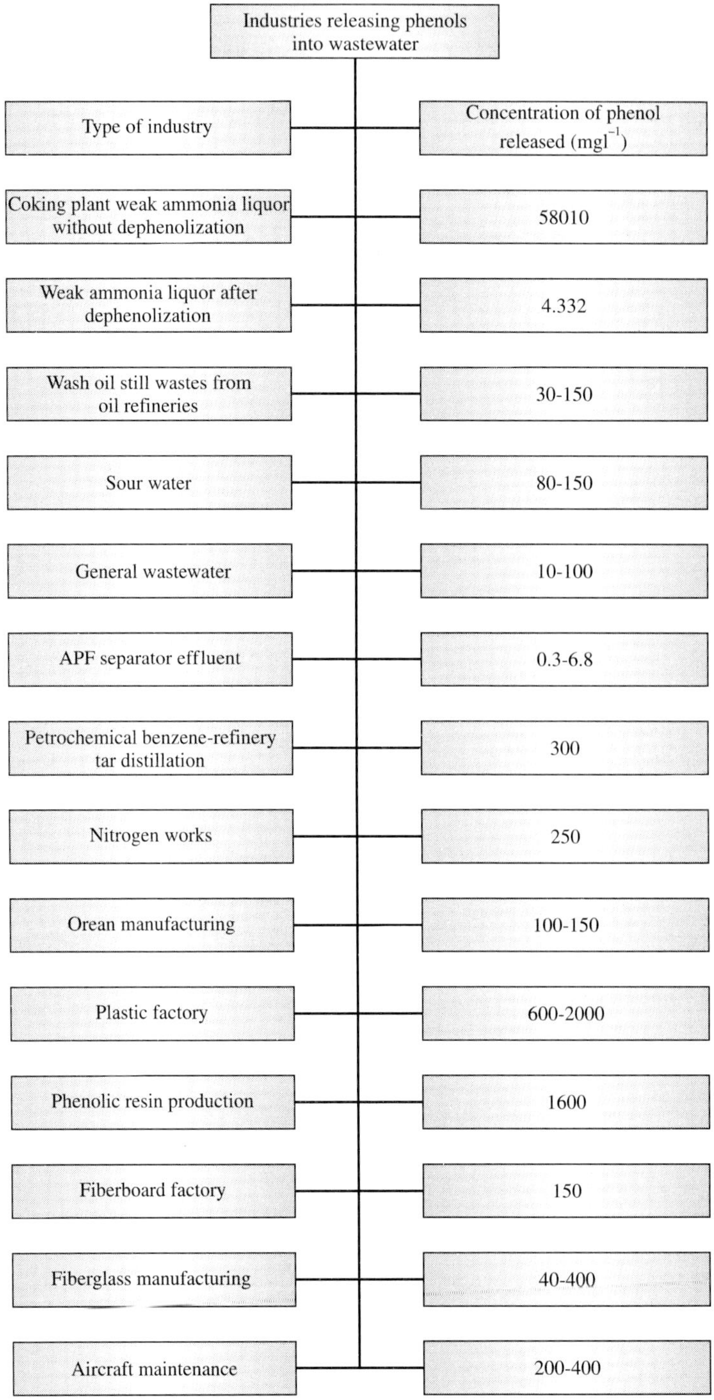

Fig. 1.2 Various concentrations of phenol released in the environment by different types of industries (*Source:* Singh and Srivastava, 2002).

Endogenous sources: An additional source of phenol in the surroundings has been recorded due to the formation of xenobiotic such as benzene under the influence of light. Other sources include combustion of fossil fuels and tobacco, and decomposition of organic materials (Busca *et al.*, 2008). It is also present in the dung of many animals. Around 1.25×10^9 kg of phenol is estimated to be produced annually.

PROVIDENCE OF PHENOL IN NATURE

No data is available related to the wet and dry deposition of phenol. The same is expected to be negligible as phenol occurs in the air in almost gaseous phase. The theoretical deposition rates for phenol were estimated assuming a behavior similar to SO_2. By comparing the rate of phenol reaction with hydroxyl radicals, it was concluded that most of the phenol in the atmosphere gets chemically degraded and is not transported (RIVM, 1986).

Phenol absorbs light in the region of 290-330 nm, and therefore, a major part in the atmosphere is degraded directly by photochemical reactions. It may react in air with hydroxyl and NO_3 radicals and undergo other photochemical reactions to form dihydroxy-benzenes, nitrophenols, and ring cleavage products. The gas-phase reaction of phenol with photochemically produced hydroxyl radicals is probably the removal mechanism in the atmosphere. The half-life of phenol in air is 5 h based on its estimated reaction rate with hydroxyl radicals (RIVM, 1986). A half-life of 15 h for phenol reaction with hydroxyl radicals in the air. It has been reported to react at night with radicals of nitrate ensuing a considerable removal process and a half-life of 15 min has been predicted at an atmospheric concentration of 2×10^8 nitrate radicals cm^{-3}. The half-life of phenol in polluted atmospheres decreases during smog. A minor part of phenol is removed by rain thus a moderately high concentration has been found in rainwater. The fact that it has been detected in rainwater, some phenol may wash out of the atmosphere in limited amounts because of its short atmospheric half-life (ATSDR, 1998). Thus, the transport of phenol from air to water and soil is much expected (RIVM, 1986).

Soil

The rate of phenol degradation in soil is more rapid, thus the probability of groundwater contamination is low in soil as compared to water. This may alter in case of oil spills or continuous release such as leaching from landfills. On the basis of sorption coefficient, the organic matter present in the soil probably acts as a sorbing material for phenol. The volatilization of phenol near dry surface soil is relatively rapid. It has been found that phenol in the soil has a half-life of less than 5 days, while that of acidic soils and some other surface soil types may reach a half-life between 20 and 25 days (HSDB, 1998).

Water

Phenol gets much absorbed in the water because it has 9.8% solubility and relatively low vapor pressure. With these properties, phenol probably ends up largely in water phase and might directly photodegrade on water surfaces because of its tendency to absorb light in the region of 290-330 nm. In the presence of sunlight, phenol reacts with the phytochemically produced hydroxyl and peroxy radicles.

Phenol was detected from groundwater as a result of leaching from phenol-spills and landfill stations as well as from hazardous waste sites. Its meager concentration in natural water is readily biodegradable, but at higher concentrations the inhibition of the microbial community may take place. However, degradation of phenol was reported to be slower in salty water, and a half-life of 9 days has been reported in an estuarine river. Hence, it is evident that a rapid degradation of phenol may occur in natural water, however, it still persists in the environment because the exact conditions under which phenol can rapidly get degraded may not be present at all junctures.

POLLUTION AND HEALTH HAZARDS OF PHENOL

United State-Environmental Policy Act and World Health Organization have recognized phenol as a priority pollutant released in the environment. Ecological investigations have reported phenol as a toxic substance. The release of industrial wastewater into lakes, rivers and ponds usually alters the characteristics, particularly the odor of such water bodies. Approximately 0.005 mg l^{-1} of phenol is capable of imparting obnoxious odor by combining with chlorine to make chlorophenols. Various standards have been fixed by the Government of India (1993) for the disposal of wastewater containing phenolic compounds. According to general standards for discharge of pollutants issued by Environmental (Protection) Third Amendment Rule (1993), 5 mg/l of phenol is permissible to be discharged in public sewers and marine coastal areas. This rule allows the discharge of 1.0 mg/l phenol in inland surface water. Therefore, the permissible limits for discharging phenolic wastes by the industries in the public sewers should not exceed 5 mg/l. In water bodies at a concentration of 2 mg/l, phenol becomes toxic to fishes. Its presence can be estimated in fish flesh in a much lower concentration.

The health hazards have been well documented in reports of US-Environmental Protection Agency (1994). The human exposure to phenol is negligible through air. Occupational exposure may occur during the manufacturing of phenol related substances. A vast amount of exposure comes from drinking water and food contaminated with phenol, which is readily absorbed through skin and can cause skin and eye burns upon contact and extends into comas and convulsions. It also affects the kidney, liver, lungs and vascular system.

METHODS OF PHENOL DETOXIFICATION

Limited standards for the discharge of phenol in water bodies have imposed great demands on the various methods for the removal of phenolics from water (Ibrahim *et al.*, 2001). The various methods available for the separation of phenol from wastewater include physico-chemical and biological analyses. Some of the physico-chemical methods used to separate or degrade phenol from the wastewater are as follows:

1. **Separation by Steam Distillation:** This method is based on the principle of steam volatilility of phenols. This is a commercial process during which complete separation may occur, however, it is not cost effective.
2. **Electrical Discharges for Phenol Degradation:** In this method the degradation of phenol takes place by applying electric charges in a discharge reactor. The electrodes used in the process are very costly, and moreover, the feasibility of this process was questioned while applying in salty wastewater.
3. **Supercritical Water Gasification of Phenol:** In this method water containing pollutants is heated above its critical temperature. Phenol, on such a treatment, gives rise to H_2, O_2, CO_2 and CH_4.
4. **Adsorption:** This is a widely used method for the removal of many pollutants. Treatment of wastewater containing phenol involves steps such as saturation, loading, desorption and

regeneration. Apart from activated carbon, the use of activated resins such as amberlite XAD-4 and acrylate divinylbenzene has also been studied. Main drawbacks of this method are the disposal of adsorbent beds and release of secondary pollutants in the environment.

5. **Extraction:** The process is based on the miscibility of phenol in an organic solvent such as benzene, n-hexane, cyclohexane, toluene, etc. Phenol is extracted by an organic solvent and, thereafter, separated by water. This method is commercial but costly.
6. **Membrane Pervaporation:** It has been suggested that the separation of phenol can be performed by a membrane i.e., polyether-polyamide block copolymer (PEBA), which is much effective for the separation of aromatic hydrocarbons. As the mixture of phenol and water enters the reactor, it is separated by the PEBA membrane. Water is present on the feed side and vapor remains on the other side, which evaporates the flowing compound. This method is used commercially.
7. **Membrane Based Solvent Extraction:** Polypropylene membranes have been employed for the separation of phenol from water. Emulsion liquid membrane has also been used efficiently in the method.
8. **Wet Air Oxidation:** This method is useful for the wastewater, which contains highly toxic pollutants to incinerate or biodegrade. In this method, phenol is oxidized and it breaks down into various components such as acetic acid, malic acid, oxalic acid, succinic acid and formic acid. However, complete mineralization of phenols by this process becomes impossible as some intermediates such as propionic acid, ethanol or methanol do not get oxidized. This method, therefore, has limitations for the commercial application.

BIOREMEDIATION

Use of microorganisms such as bacteria, fungi and algae for the removal of pollutants from the environment is termed bioremediation. The process of cleaning-up of toxic materials from the environment using plants is called phytoremediation. A large number of phenol degrading bacterial and fungal species have been isolated from contaminated sites by various workers and subsequently used in phenol bioremoval. However, the structure of any compound plays an important role in its bioremediation. Phenol is one of the simplest derivatives of benzene and is toxic to microorganisms at higher concentrations, which can inhibit their growth and development. For such reasons, phenol should be used in calculative quantities. Jiang *et al.* (2006) have used co-aggregative cells and suggested a consortium to be more advantageous over the use of single bacterial genera. Various species of *Pseudomonads, Commamonas, Rhizobium* and *Bacillus* have been reported to degrade phenol. Biological abatement of phenol is more advantageous over any other physico-chemical techniques because of its cost-effectivity, complete mineralization and thereby non-releasing of any secondary byproducts in the environment.

Phytoremediation

US-Environmental Policy Act (US-EPA) (2001) suggests the superiority of phytoremediation over many other processes because of its biological nature with no risk of any secondary pollutant. The method requires less manpower and the groundwater levels can be cleaned up easily without digging out the soil or pumping out the polluted water. This ensures safety to the workers without any risk of exposure. Phytoremediation cannot be applied to a highly contaminated site, as the plants have a limited capacity to decontaminate the toxicants of a site. The plants clean up the contaminated soil and water as far as their roots reach (US-EPA, 2001). There are two methods of phytoremediation e.g., phytostabilization and phytoextraction. The former includes growing of vegetation to prevent wind and water erosion, while the later involves absorption of hazardous materials through root and accumulation in the top organs.

Degradation of Phenol by Microorganisms

Microorganisms have been introduced for the degradation of phenols since long. Successful isolation of a phenol degrading bacteria was performed in early 1932. Thereafter, the overuse of synthetic phenols has led to serious environmental threat and imposed scientists to work more in this direction. Numerous microbes with their efficiency to degrade phenol have been unearthed, which include bacteria, fungi, yeasts and algae. Bacterial systems have been studied extensively that include the strains of different genera e.g., *Pseudomonas aeruginosa* and *P. pseudomallei*, *Bacillus*, *Acinetobacter* XA05 and *Sphingomonas* FG03 *Cupriavidus*, *Commamonas*, *Burkholderia*, *Alcaligenes faecalis* and *Rhodococcus* and *Rhizobium*. The yeasts and fungi include *Candida tropicalis*, *Aspergillus awamori* and *Aureobasidium pullulans*.

Mechanism of Phenol Degradation in Microbes

Microbes have acquired inherent mechanisms of phenol degradation. With the advent of modern technology, mechanisms of phenol degradation have been studied in details, both on enzymatic and genetic parameters. Based on the use of molecular oxygen, mechanism of phenol resistance has been classified into two types: anaerobic and aerobic degradation.

Anaerobic Degradation

Anaerobic degradation of phenol has been studied in many bacterial strains such as denitrifying *Pseudomonas* strain K172, *Clostridium* sp. and *Thauera aromatica*. Lack and Fuches (1994) suggested that the anaerobic breakdown starts with phosphorylation of phenol by a phosphate moiety from an unidentified phosphoryl donor. This reaction is catalyzed by phenyl phosphate kinase to give rise to the first intermediate product i.e., phenyl phosphate which consecutively proceeds to the formation of 4-hydroxybenzoate with the help of enzyme phenyl phosphate carboxylase. This enzyme is susceptible to oxygen and radical trapping agents. Unlike other carboxylases, it does not depend upon biotin or thiamine diphosphate and uses carbon dioxide as a substrate and a metal as a co-catalyst. The 4-hydroxybenzoate breaks down to provide 4-hydroxybenzoyl-CoA via the intermediate benzoyl co-enzyme A under the catalyzation of 4-hydroxybenzoyl-CoA ligase. The 4-hydroxybenzoyl-CoA becomes dehydroxylated to give benzoyl-CoA, which is found as an intermediate in many microorganisms. 4-hydroxybenzoate decarboxylase catalyzes the conversion of phenol to 4-hydroxybenzoate via anaerobic decarboxylation in *Clostridium* species. A postulated pathway of anaerobic phenol biodegradation by a denitrifying bacterium i.e., *Thauera aromatica* is presented in Fig: 1.3.

During 1980s, anaerobic breakdown of many mononuclear aromatic compounds was studied in detail, and it was found that the mononuclear aromatic compounds are fed by three intermediates i.e., benzoyl-CoA, resorcinol, and phloroglucinol. The similarity of the three pathways is that the aromatic nucleus is undermined via a reductive attack. The benzoyl-CoA pathway emerges to be the most important one because an extensive range of compounds including phenol, hydroxybenzoates, phenylacetate, aniline, certain cresols and even the hydrocarbon toluene are metabolized through this pathway.

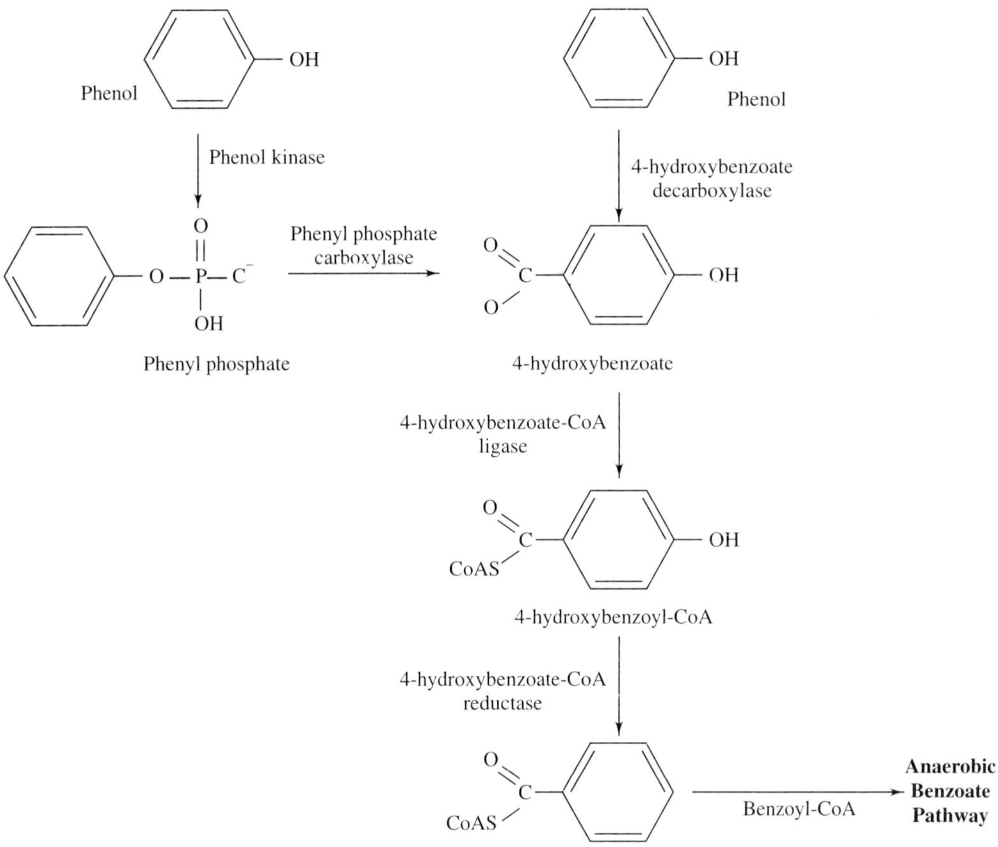

Fig. 1.3 Postulated pathway for anaerobic biodegradation of phenol by a denitrifying bacterium, i.e., *Thauera aromatica.*

Aerobic Degradation

In aerobic degradation pathway, phenol is first hydroxylated at *ortho* position by phenol hydroxylase to form catechol. The phenol hydroxylase was first purified from the yeast *Trichosproron cutaneum*. Since then this enzyme has been isolated from several bacterial species like *Acinetobacter*, *Pseudomonas picketti*, *Bacillus stearothermophilus* BR219 and characterization was done. In these organisms the enzyme is a flavoprotein hydroxylase. But phenol hydroxylase is a multicomponent enzyme in *Acinetobacter radioresistens* and *Pseudomonas* CF600. Catechol is a common intermediate in the catalytic pathway of many aromatic compounds, which then bifurcates into either *ortho* or *meta* catalytic pathway depending on the ring cleavage of catechol at *ortho* or *meta* position.

(i) Ortho cleavage pathway

In *ortho* catalytic pathway, the catechol is cleaved at *ortho* position by catechol 1, 2-oxygenase (C120) and finally gets converted into succinate and acetyl CoA as shown in Fig. 1.4.

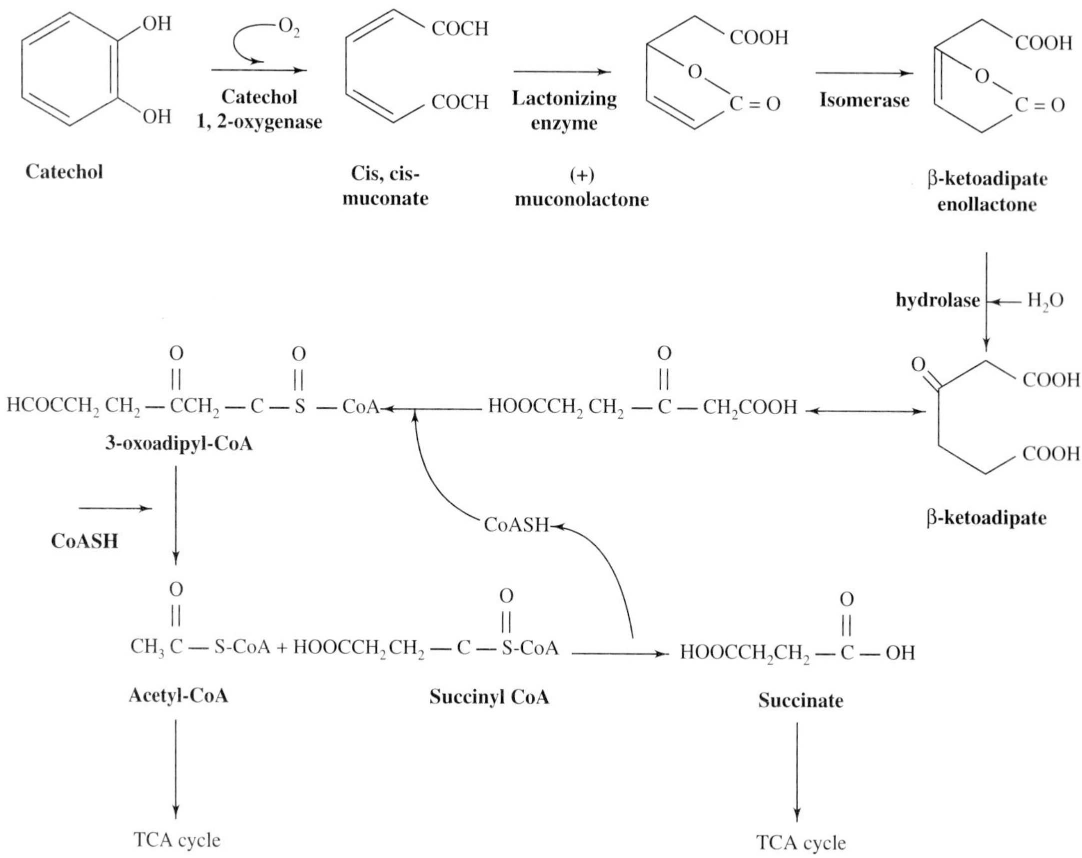

Fig. 1.4 Ortho cleavage pathway.

Genes Involved in the Process

Pseudomonas putida has been extensively studied for the genetics involved in the *ortho* pathway. Ornston (1966) assessed that in *P. putida, cis, cis-* muconate is inducer for the enzymes of *ortho* pathway namely catechol 1, 2-oxygenase, mucono lactonizing enzyme and muconolactone isomerase, which are encoded by the genes *cat*A, *cat*B and *cat*C respectively. Further, Aldrich *et al.* (1987) have worked out that the *cat*B and *cat*C genes are closely linked on the chromosome forming an operon. On the contrary, *cat*A is separated from *cat*BC operon, whereas the *cat*R gene is responsible for regulation and has been mapped upstream to the *cat*BC operon and its transcription is divergent from the operon (Rothmel *et al.*, 1990). The binding site of *cat*R includes both its own promoter and the regulatory region of *cat*BC operon. Thus, its binding leads to autoregulation and activation of the *cat*BC genes. The binding of *cat*R to *cat*R-*cat*BC promoter control region takes place both in the presence and absence of inducer *cis, cis*-muconate, but activates *cat*BC operon only in the presence of *cis, cis*-muconate (Rothmel *et al.*, 1990). Parsek *et al.* (1992) have showed that the inducer *cis, cis*-muconate permits the binding of *cat*R to different site in *cat*BC promoter region forming a functional transcription initiation complex.

Meta Cleavage Pathway

In *meta* cleavage pathway, catechol is cleaved at the *meta* position catalyzed by the enzyme catechol 2, 3- oxygenase and leads to the formation of acetaldehyde and pyruvate as shown in Fig. 1.5. The pathway was studied by Feist and Hegeman (1969) in *Pseudomonas putida.* However, there are many organisms in nature that possess both the pathways for the degradation of phenol. Feist and Hegeman (1969) have projected that the induction of *ortho* or *meta* pathway depends upon the nature of primary aromatic substrate. When phenol is used as a substrate, it induces the growth of catechol 1, 2-oxygenase apparently after the bacterial cells are grown at the expense of primary substrate such as cresols, salicylate, benzosulphate, etc. and the *meta* pathway is induced.

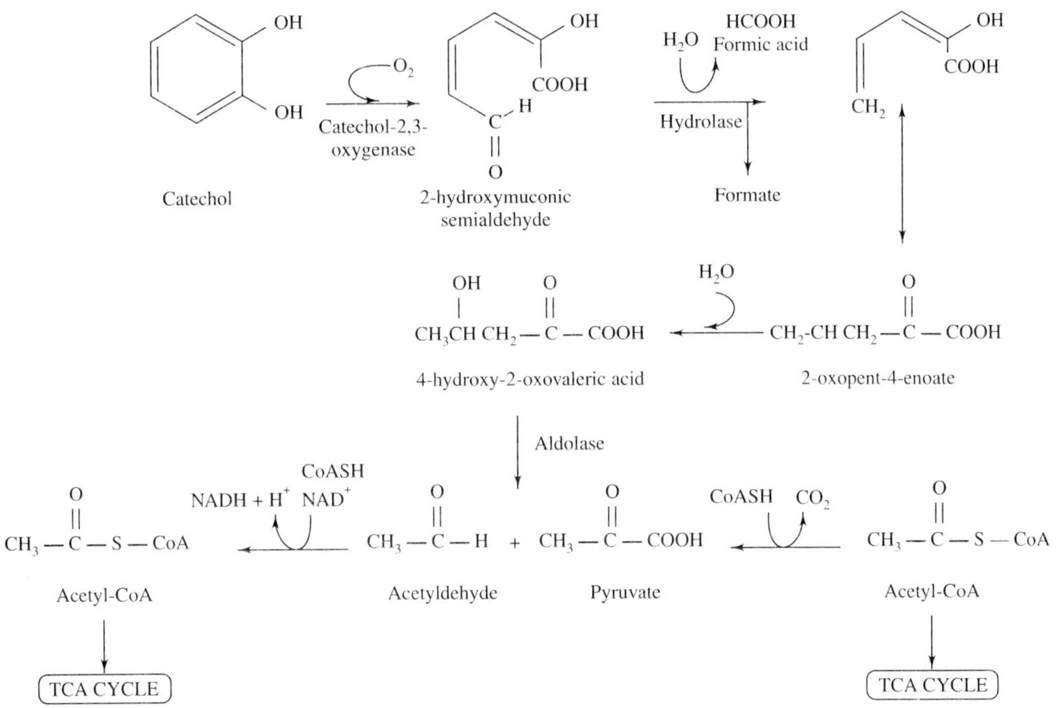

Fig. 1.5 Meta cleavage pathway.

Genes Involved in the Pathway

Different workers have reported that the genes encoding the enzymes of the *meta* cleavage pathway are located in a single operon. Hughes and Bayley (1983) studied the mutants of *Alcaligenes eutrophus,* which were blocked for each of the *meta* cleavage pathway enzyme and further confirmed that the enzymes of this pathway are synthesized only in the presence of phenol or *p*-cresol. Kukor and Oslen (1991) showed that the genes responsible for encoding the enzymes of *meta* cleavage pathway in *Pseudomonas pickettii* PKO1 are arranged in a single operon. The promoter for its operon lies nearest to *tbuE* gene, which is responsible for encoding the enzyme, catechol 2, 3-oxygenase. With the help of deletion subcloning, they suggested that the genes for *meta* pathway lie in the order *tbuEFGKIHJ* in the operon.

Table 1.1 Some common phenol degrading bacteria

Type of phenol to be removed	*Bacteria involved*	*Gene/Enzyme*	*Reference*
Phenol	*Bacillus stearothermophilus*	Phenol hydroxylase	Kim and Oriel, 1995.
Phenol, 2-chloro-ethanol	*Pseudomonas putida*	Phenol hydroxylase	Allsop *et al.* (1993)
Phenol	*Pseudomonas putida*	Phenol hydroxylase	Bodzek *et al.* (1996).
Phenol	*Bacillus* sp.	Phenol hydroxylase	Ali *et al.* (1998).
Phenol	*Ralstonia eutropha*	Catechol 2,3-dioxygenase	Leonard *et al.* (1999).
Phenol	*Acinetobacter calcoaceticus*	Phenol hydroxylase	Nakamura and Sawada (2000).
Phenol	*Streptomyces setoni*	Catechol 1,2-dioxygenase	An *et al.* (2001).
Phenol	*Alcaligenes* sp.	Phenol hydroxylase	Baek *et al.* (2001).
Phenol	*Pseudomonas putida* H	plasmid encoaded pPGH1 encoading for catechol 2,3-dioxygenase and phenol hydroxylase	Gonzalez *et al.* (2001)
Phenol	*Acinetobacter* sp.	Phenol hydroxylase	Hao *et al.* (2002).
Ortho-nitrophenol	*Alcaligenes* sp. NyZ215	Catechol 1,2-dioxygenase (encoaded by onpABC)	Xiao *et al.* (2007).
Phenol	*Pseudomonas* sp.	Phenol hydroxylase	Prpich and Daugulis (2005).
Phenol	*Pseudomonas pickettii*	Phenol hydroxylase/ *tbuD gene*	Kukor and Olsen (1991).
Phenol	*Bacillus thermoleovorans* (A2)	Phenol hydroxylase, Catechol, 2-3-dioxygenase pathway (*phe*B, *phe*C, *phe*E, *phe*D)	Duffner *et al.* (2000).
Phenol	*Geobacillus stearothermophilus*	Phenol hydroxylase, Catechol 2,3-dioxygenase (*Phe*A and *Phe*B)	Omokoko *et al.* (2008).
Phenol	*Bacillus subtilis*	Catechol 2,3-dioxygenase	Tam le *et al.* (2006).
Phenolic acids	*Bacillus subtilis*	*Pad* C encodes phenolic acid dicarboxylase.	Tran *et al.* (2008).
Phenolic acids	*Lactobacillus lantarum*	Phenolic acid dicarboxylase (encoaded by *pad A*)	Gury *et al.* (2009).
Phenolic acids	*Pediococcus pentosaceus*	Phenolic acid dicarboxylase	Barthelmebs *et al.* (2000).
Para nitrophenol	*Pseudomonas* sp. PDS-7	Hydroxyquinol 1,2-dioxygenase encoding gene *pnp*C	Dong *et al.* (2008).
Phenol	*Pseudomonas fluoresence*	Catechol 2,3-dioxygenase /Phenol hydroxylase/ *Phe*BA operon	Merimaa *et al.* (2006).

Contd.

Contd.

Alkyl phenol	*Pseudomonas putida* MT4	*bupA1A2A3A4A5A6* codes for henol hydroxylase and *bupBCEHIFG* encodes for *meta* cleavage pathway genes	Takeo *et al.* (2006).
2,4,6-Trichlorophenol	*Ralstonia eutropha* JMP134 (pJP4)	Operon tcp*RXABCYD*	Matus *et al.* (2003).
Phenol	*Commamonas testosterone* R5	Phenol hydroxylase encoaded by gene cluster *phcKLMNOP*	Teramoto *et al.* (1999).
Phenol, chloro and methyl substituted Catechols	*Rhodococcus opacus*	3-chlorocatechol 1,2-dioxygenase	Ferraroni *et al.* (2006).
Phenol	*Corynebacterium efficiens* YS-314	Catechol 1,2-dioxygenase	Nishio *et al.* (2003).
Phenol	*Rhodococcus* sp. AN-22	Catechol 1,2-dioxygenase	Matsumura *et al.* (2006).
Phenol	*Rhodococcus rhodochrous*	Catechol 1,2-dioxygenase	Strachan *et al.* (1998).
Phenol	*Rhodococcus jostii* RHA1	Catechol 1,2-dioxygenase	McLeod *et al.* (2006).
Phenol	*Rhodococcus opacus*	Catechol 1,2-dioxygenase	Strachan *et al.* (1998).
Phenol	*Rhodococcus erythropolis*	Catechol 1,2-dioxygenase	McLeod *et al.* (2006).
Phenol	*Rhodococcus gordoniae*	Catechol 1,2-dioxygenase	Tancsics *et al.* (2008).
Phenol	*Arthrobacter* sp. BA-5-17	Catechol1,2-dioxygenase	Murakami *et al.* (2004).
p-Cresol	*Corynebacterium glutamicum*	Protocatachuate, 3, 4-dioxygenase/ *ncg12314* and *ncg12315*	Shen and Liu (2005).
Phenol	*Halomonas campisalis*	Catechol, 1, 2-dioxygenase	Alva and Peyton (2003).

Consecutively, they encode the enzymes catechol 2, 3-oxygenase, 2-hydroxymuconate semialdehyde hydrolase, 2-hydroxymuconate semialdehyde dehydrogenase, 4-hydroxy-2-oxovalerate aldolase, 4-oxalocrotonate decarboxylase, 4-oxalocrotonate isomerase and 2-hydroxypent-2, 4-dienoate hydroxylase. In contrast to the product induced pathway of *Pseudomonas aeruginosa,* the enzymes of *meta* cleavage pathway are molded differently.

Kukor and Oslen (1991) gave a model for the regulation of pathway. According to them, the regulator TbuS, the product of the *tbuS* regulator gene of *meta* cleavage operon, acts both as an activator and a repressor. In the presence of phenol or *p*-cresol, the TbuS protein forms the transcription activator complex, which enhances the process of mRNA production and translation of the genes of *meta* cleavage pathway. But in the absence of phenol or *p*-cresol, the TbuS protein blocks the transcription of *tbuEFGKIHJ* operon.

FACTORS INFLUENCING MICROBIAL DEGRADATION OF PHENOL

There are various factors that affect microbial degradation of phenol, which is determined either by preventing or invigorating the growth of microbes or affecting gene expression. The major factor that affects the process of phenol bioremediation and other xenobiotic compounds is the chemical structure and compound toxicity. Structural parameters normally involve number, type and position of substituents and the degree of branching. More the number of substituents in the structure, more toxic, recalcitrant and less degradable the compound. In phenols, mono, di-, tri- and penta-chlorophenol are reported to be more toxic and less degradable than unsubstituted phenol. On the contrary, *ortho*- and *para*-substituted phenols are more degradable than *meta*-substituted phenols.

Toxicity of any compound may prevent or make the metabolic reaction much sluggish and delayed. The amount of toxicity is precise and varies with the toxicants and their specific concentration as well as the microorganisms performing the task of degradation. Microbial cells do not work even if one of the essential steps in their metabolic mill is obstructed. This obstruction may result due to disorderness of cell physiology or inactivation of a single enzyme or pathway essential for metabolizing the toxicant (National Research Council, 1993).

Microbial growth is easily inhibited at pH values lesser than 3 or greater than 9. Their physiology also gets altered when there is a sudden fluctuation in pH values. Temperature is another criterion for the growth of microbes in phenol contaminated sites. Different bacteria have their own optimum range of temperature for the growth and multiplication. Psychrophilic bacterial strain such as *Pseudomonas putida* has been fruitfully applied to degrade phenol at a temperature of 10°C. Similarly, thermophilic bacterium *Bacillus stearothermophilus* has also been used to degrade phenol effectively at a higher temperature of 65°C. The nutritional requirements of microorganisms normally include nitrogen, phosphorus, potassium, sodium, calcium, magnesium, iron, trace elements and carbon. Aerobic microbes require oxygen dissolved in the medium along with other nutrient factors for respiration. Some microorganisms carrying out the tedious task of bioremediation of such recalcitrant compounds also require an additional source of carbon such as yeast extract that not only helps the cells to acclimatize in higher phenolic concentrations, but also enhance the tolerance of the cells to substrate inhibition. Lob and Tar (2000) have reported that the addition of 0.2 to 2.0 g l^{-1} of yeast extract has increased the rate of phenol degradation, lowered the toxicity of phenol in the medium and built up more cell mass. Apart from yeast extract, alternative carbon sources such as *o-cresol*, toluene and naphthalene have also been used.

CYANIDE

Cyanide is another toxic pollutant, which is an important constituent of industrial effluents. Cyanides are the compounds containing CN^- as their functional group. In nature, the CN^- combines with various metals and non-metals to form complexes like KCN (potassium cyanide), $Ca(CN)_2$ (calcium cyanide) and CuCN (copper cyanide). The most common form of cyanide in nature is hydrogen cyanide (HCN), which is found in almost 2000 plant species in the form of cyanogenic glycosides.

PHYSICAL AND CHEMICAL PROPERTIES OF HYDROGEN CYANIDE

The relative molecular mass of the compound is 27.03, while its boiling point is 25.70°C. It is miscible with water at 30°C and highly soluble in ethanol. The vapor pressure (kPa) of HCN is 35.2 and 107.2 at 0°C and 27.2°C, respectively (WHO, 2007). It has a bitter almond odor with a magnitude of 0.7 mg/m^3 and 0.17 mg/l.

SOURCES AND APPLICATION

The wide application of cyanide has enhanced the production of HCN, which was calculated to be around 1.4 million tonnes throughout the world. HCN is an important compound used for the production of sodium cyanide, potassium silver cyanide and calcium cyanide. Sodium cyanide is further used for introducing the cyano-group to the organic halides to obtain nitriles, which are processed to various compounds containing amide, esters and amine moieties. Apart from the chemical synthesis of the above, some salts of cyanides such as those of copper, zinc and cadmium are used for the electroplating of iron, steel, zinc, respectively. In jewellery industries, they are required for cyanidation of gold and silver from their respective ores. Potassium cyanide is used in the process of refining of platinum by electrolysis and separation of gold, silver and copper from platinum (ECETOC, 2004). They are widely used in coal gasification units, hardening of metals, flour mills, seeds in vacuum chambers, emissions of petrochemicals and fumigation of ships. The complex salt of calcium cyanide is used as a fumigant for the process of fumigation, as it readily gives HCN in contact with air. It is also widely used in the manufacture of herbicides, rhodenticide and fertilizers. When applied in small amount, it steadies the cement and is used in the processing of stainless steel (ACGIH, 2001).

POLLUTION

Such a wide applicability of cyanide has led to its overproduction, and hence, it is over used. Since 1975, as many as 30 accidental cases have been recorded due to bad transportation, leaching of pipelines and tailings. Major sources of cyanide pollution in nature are found from the industries involved in chemical synthesis, while the release of cyanide occurred from the industrial effluents involved in the process of gold extraction from cheap ores, where the requirement for cyanide is much higher. Apart from the anthropogenic activities of human beings, there are many plants that are cyanogenic in nature. The industries manufacture cassava starch from cassava plants, and this process requires the hydrolysis of cyanoglycogen by plant enzymes releasing 200 mg l^{-1} of cyanide in the wastewater released from these factories. Moreover, there are various microorganisms that release HCN to kill their competitors, e.g., *Pseudomonas putida*, *Bacillus pumilus*, *Klebsiella oxytosa,* etc. The various sources of cyanide in nature are shown in Fig. 1.6.

POLLUTION LEVELS OF CYANIDE

In air the levels of cyanide as a pollutant are much lower as compared to that in water and soil. According to general standards laid by environment protection third amendment rules for discharge of pollutants (1993), in India, the permissible limit for cyanide discharge in inland surface water, irrigation land and marine coastal areas is 0.2 mg/l, whereas the limit is relaxed upto 2.0 mg/l for public sewers (Environment Protection Rule, 1993). The US-Environmental Protection Agency (US-EPA) has proposed a limit for drinking and aquatic-biota waters regarding total cyanide to be 200 and 50 ppb, respectively, where total cyanide refers to free and metal-complexed cyanides (Dash *et al*., 2008). Discharge of excessive amount of cyanide in natural water bodies enhances its levels in them. Cyanide gets destroyed by various methods used for the treatment of drinking water. On the contrary, if any residual moiety of cyanide remains, it quickly combines with chlorine to give cyanogen chloride, which further disintegrates to give cyanide (WHO, 2007).

CYANIDE POISONING

HCN is a readily absorbable compound in human beings, both orally and through skin (ATSDR, 1997). The symptoms of cyanide poisoning are slower to occur when ingested orally as compared to its inhalation and absorption by the lungs. Potent salts of cyanide such as potassium cyanide (KCN) and sodium cyanide (NaCN) upon ingestion release free cyanide radicals, which are highly reactive in nature, and in the acidic pH of the stomach bind to the hydrogen ions to form hydrogen cyanide (HCN) that is readily absorbed by the bloodstream.

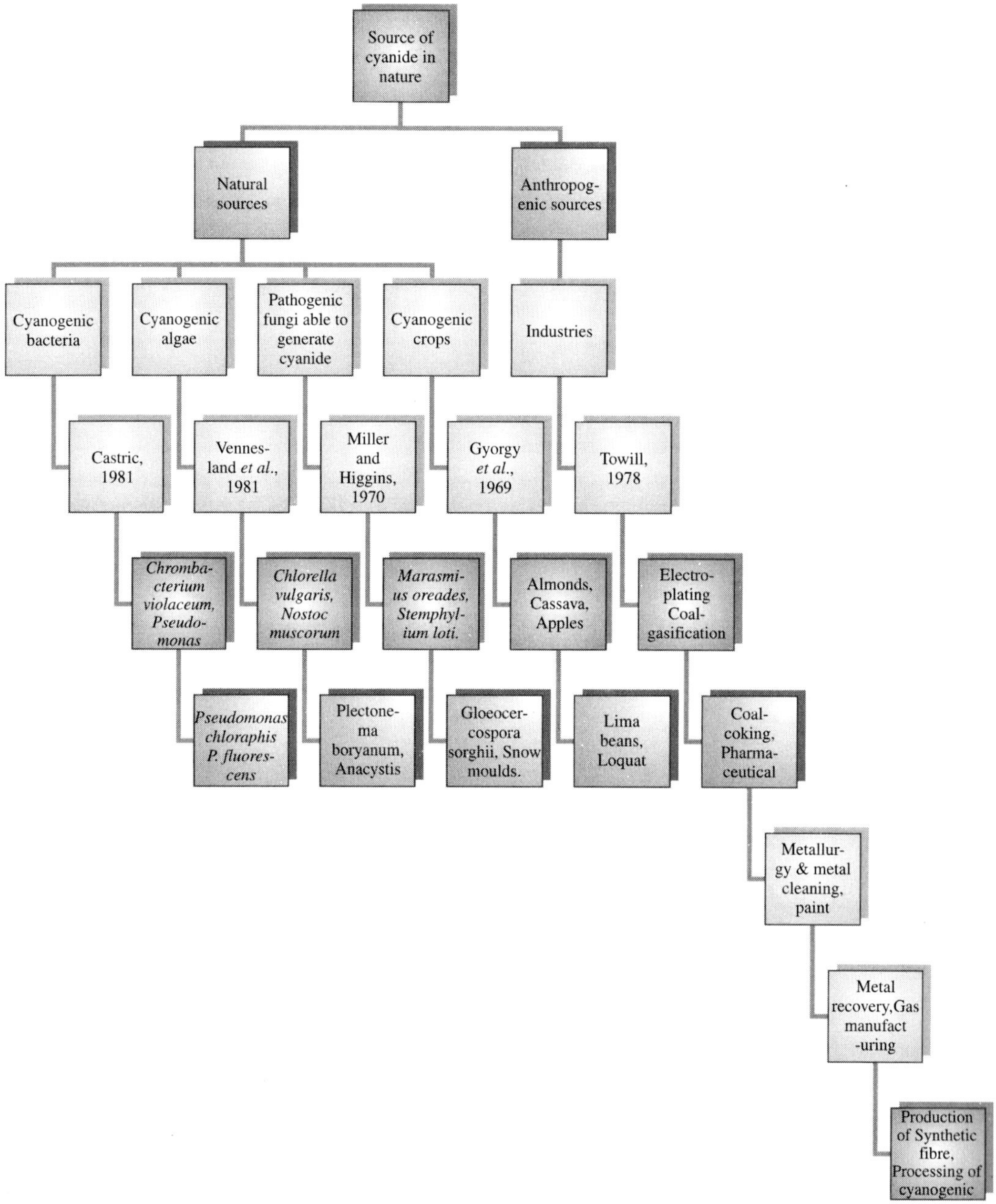

Fig. 1.6 Sources of cyanide released in the environment (Source: Dubey and Holmes, 1995).

Cyanide not only inhibits the growth and metabolism, but also affects the respiration, nitrogen and phosphate metabolism of the cells. The presence of cyanide in the growth medium has improved the generation time in *Escherichia coli*. Cyanide has a capability to change the morphology of the cells of *Bacillus pumillus*. Exposure to cyanide results in mutations in *Neurospora crassa*. The enzyme cytochrome oxidase of mitochondrial origin is entirely destroyed by cyanide. Other enzymes in the cell, which are destroyed fully by cyanide, are peroxidases, tyrosinases, catalases, ascorbic oxidases, and phosphatases. The mechanism of enzyme inhibition by the cyanide is due to the fact that cyanide moiety binds to the metallic cofactors of the metalloenzymes and inactivates them. CN^- also restrains the mechanism of DNA repair in *Chlamydomonas reinhardii* and DNA replication in *Escherichia coli*.

Interestingly, where cyanide is such a persuasive inhibitor of the cellular system, there are many cyanogenic microorganisms that release cyanide as their defence mechanism. These include bacteria like *Pseudomonas fluorescens*, *Achromobacter* and fungi such as *Trametes versicolor* and *Phanerochaete chrysosporium.*

METHODS FOR CYANIDE TREATMENT

There are many commercial methods available for the treatment of cyanide. Dubey and Holmes (1995) reviewed the methods used for the treatment of wastewater cyanide, which include ferrocyanide precipitation, prussion-blue and copper catalyzed H_2O_2 precipitation, ozonation, incineration, alkaline chlorination, electrolysis and biological degradation. Out of these, only three methods are used commercially and are regarded efficient for the complete removal of cyanide from wastewater. The first method, alkaline chlorination, though a commercially employed technique, is inefficient in the removal of iron cyanide. The other one is electrolytic decomposition, which efficiently removes strong concentrations of cyanide (3.5 mg/ml), but is inefficient when the cyanide concentrations are weak (0.1 mg/ml) probably due to the accumulation of cyanate in the electrolyte. The third method is ozonation, which has a negative aspect that it cannot treat cobalt cyanides, but is quite easy with other metallic salts like copper, zinc and nickel. Moreover, these processes are costly. Hence, the biological treatment is one of the methods, which is cost effective and efficient for complete mineralization of the compounds and also a safe method for the treatment of cyanide-rich waste. Various bacteria found in nature and also involved in the degradation of cyanide are shown in Table 1.2.

Table 1.2 Most commonly used cyanide degrading bacteria

Types of cyanide to be removed	*Bacteria involved*	*Gene/ Enzyme*	*References*
(Cyanides) WAD	*Pseudomonas stutzeri*	Cyanidase	Watanabe *et al.* (1998a, b)
Ferrous(II) cyanide complex	*Pseudomonas fluorescens*	Undefined	Dursun and Aksu (2000)
Cyanate	*Pseudomonas fluorescens*	Cyanase	Kunz and Nagappan (1989)
Potassium cyanide	*Klebsiella oxytoca*	Nitrogenase	Kao *et al.* (2006)
Cyanate	*Chromobacterium violaceum*	Cyn operon	Carepo *et al.* (2004)
Sodium cyanide, cyanates and thiocyanates	*Pseudomonas putida*	Undefined	Chapatwala *et al.* (1998)
Cyanides	*Methylobacterium* sp.	Undefined	Campos *et al.* (2006)
Phenol and cyanides	*Pseudomonas fluorescens* NCIMB 11764	Cyanide oxygenase	Kitisa *et al.* (2005)

Contd.

Contd.

Copper and zinc cyanide	*Citrobacter* sp., *Pseudomonas*	sp.Undefined	Patil *et al.* (2000)
Potassium cyanide	*Burkholderia cepacia* C-3	Cynidase	Adjei and Ohta (2000)
Potassium cyanide	*Bacillus magaterium*	Undefined	Castric and Strobel (1969)
Thiocyanate	*Pseudomonas stutzeri*	Cyanase	Grigor'eva *et al.* (2006)
Potassium cyanide	*Bacillus pumilis*	Cyanide dihydratase *cyn*D.	Jandhyala *et al.* (2003)
Potassium cyanide	*Klebsiella oxytoca*	Undefined	Chen *et al.* (2008)
Potassium cyanide	*Pseudomonas stutzeri* AK61	Cyanidase (cyanide dihydratase)	Watanabe *et al.* (1998a, b)
Sodium cyanide	*Pseudomonas pseudoalcaligenes* CECT5344	Cyanase/*cyn*S	Luque-Almagro *et al.* (2008)
Nickel-complexed Cyanide	*Rhizobium daejeonense*	Undefined	Quan *et al.* (2005)
Cyanide	*Pseudomonas pseudoalcaligenes* CECT5344	Cyanase coaded by *cyn*S	Luque-Almagro *et al.* (2008)
Cyanase	*Escherichia coli*	Cyanase/*Cyn*S	Anderson *et al.* (1990)
Metal complexed-	*Chryseobacterium caeni*	Undefined	Quan *et al.* (2007)Cyanide

Pathways of Cyanide Degradation

There are many pathways for the degradation of cyanide in microorganisms. Various enzymes and the respective microorganisms are listed in Table 1.3.

Table 1.3 Different pathways of cyanide degradation carried out by bacteria and fungi

Enzymes involved	*Microorganism (Bacteria/Fungi)*	*Reaction*	*Reference*
Cyanide mono-oxygenase	*Pseudomonads*	$HCN+O_2+H^+ +NADPH \rightarrow HOCN+NADP^+ +H_2O$.	Dorr and Knowles (1989).
Cyanide dioxygenase	*P. fluorescens* *B. pumillus* *P. cereus*	$HCN+O_2+2H^+ +NADPH \rightarrow CO_2+NH_3+NADP^+$	Harris and Knowles (1983).
Cyanase	*E. coli*	$HOCN+H_2O \rightarrow CO_2+NH_3$	Kunz and Nagappan (1989).
Cyanide hydratase	Snow moulds and some pathogenic fungi	$HCN+H_2O \rightarrow HCONH_2$	Fry and Myers (1981).
Cyanidase	*Alcaligenes* *Xylosooxidans* *denitrificans*	$HCN+2H_2O \rightarrow HCOOH+NH_3$	Ingvorsen *et al.* (1991).
Nitrilase	*Klebsiella ozaenae,* *Nocarida* sp., *Arthrobacter* sp.	Bromoxynil (nitrile)→3, 5-bromo, 4-hydroxy benzoic acid.	Bandyopadhyay *et al.* (1986).
Rhodanese	*B. subtilis,* *B. stearothermophilus,* *Thiobacillus denitrificans*	Cyanide→Thiocynate + Sulphite	Bowen *et al.* (1965).
Cyanoalanine synthetase	*B. megaterium*	Cyanide→β- Cyanoalanine.	Castric and Strabel (1969).

ENVIRONMENTAL FACTORS AFFECTING CYANIDE BIODEGRADATION

Cyanides are widely degraded in nature by several microorganisms. Like any other toxicants, cyanide degrading organisms inhabiting the soil or water show their competence based on the concentrations of cyanides. At higher concentration, acetonitrile inhibited the nitrile degrading enzyme i.e., nitrile hydroxylase in *Klebsiella oxytoca*, thereby ceasing the biodegradation of the compound.

Nutrient accessibility is also a common factor responsible for cyanide degradation and its complexes. Carbon has been identified as a limiting factor in the microbial degradation of metal-cyanides. Cyanides are toxic to *methanogens,* which are anaerobes, since oxygen is consumed in most of the cyanide degradation pathways. Thus, the availability of oxygen may prove to be an important factor in the microbial mineralization of cyanide. An inhibition of cyanide biodegradation due to the presence of many additional pollutants and a greater concentration of co-contaminants has been observed.

Temperature and pH are two important parameters in the degradation of cyanide. The enzymes of the metabolic mill for cyanide get activated at a temperature range of 20 to 40°C and at an optimum pH of 6 to 8. At acute pH the rate of biodegradation gets affected. Bacterial strains can degrade cyanide at a neutral pH range, while many fungal strains such as *Fusarium solani, F. oxysporum* and *Trichoderma polysporum* have the ability to degrade cyanide at an acidic pH range of 4 to 5 (Dash *et al*., 2008). The pH may be a particularly important factor in the bioremediation of soils contaminated with cyanide.

CONCLUSION

The development and application of biological methods for phenol and cyanide biodegradation is limited primarily by physical and economic factors. Most organisms with efficiency to degrade these toxic compounds get inhibited by their higher concentrations. Industrial effluents have toxicants in concentrations, which may be several times greater than the permissible range for most of the microorganisms. This may provide a hindrance for the biological treatment of wastewater and may not be a practical option in all cases. Formation of some secondary by-products such as ammonia and presence of other contaminants may also limit the efficacy of biological treatments.

Conceivably research should emphasise more on pilot scale treatment of effluents rather than laboratory scale treatments, as possibly there may be a notable difference in small scale laboratory and field degradation. A self-designed large-scale effluent treatment system has been represented in Fig. 1.7 which can be set up in the field for the biological treatment of waste streams.

Additionally, there may be certain other factors such as high alkaline or acidic nature of the waste stream that may cause damage to the microbes. Besides this, conditions such as temperature and sudden chemical shock may lead to cell arrest, and hence, inhibit cell function. Phenol has a tendency to make the environment anaerobic by consuming all the oxygen present in water, thus posing a threat to the aerobic microbes.

A single microbe may not be capable enough to degrade different substituents of phenol or cyanide present in the same waste stream. For example, a bacterium which degrades phenol effectively may not degrade alkyl or halide substituted phenols. A consortium of microorganisms in such cases can prove more supportive and may enhance the rate of bioremediation.

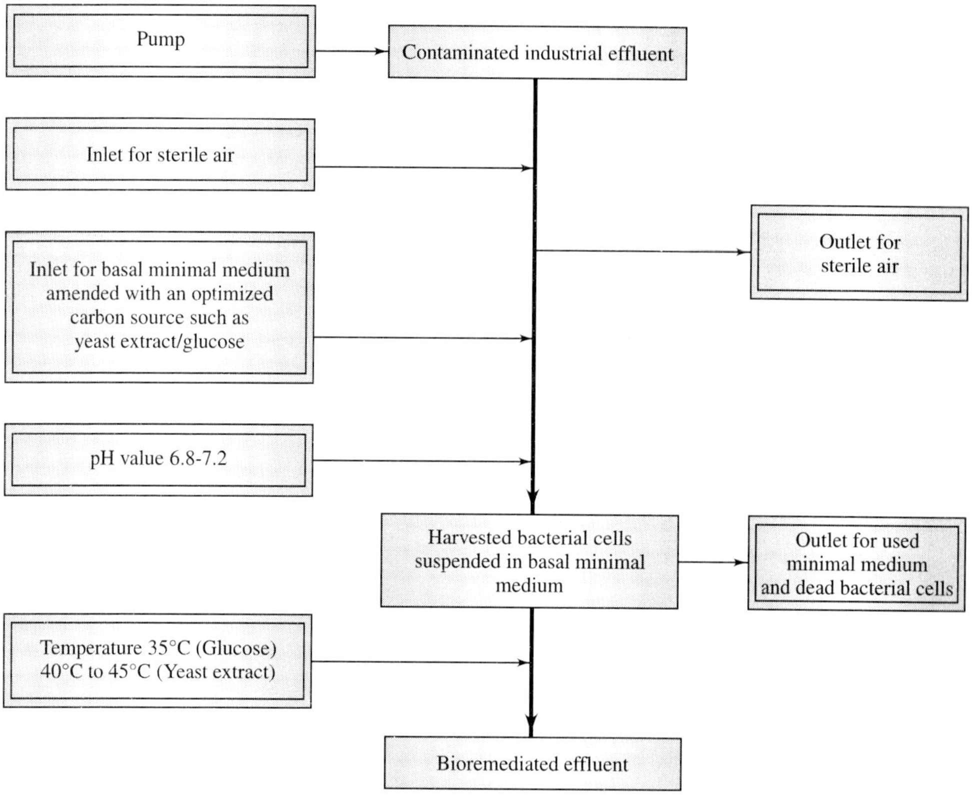

Fig. 1.7 Flow chart proposing set up for the treatment of large-scale effluent *in vivo*. Conditions like temperature, pH, and carbon source may vary with the organism used in the process of remediation.

REFERENCES

ACGIH. (2001). *In*: Documentation of the threshold values and biological exposure indices, 8th eds., Cincinnatti, OH, American Conference of Governmental Industrial Hygienists. 1-6.

Adjei, M.D. and Ohta, Y. (2000). *World J. Microbiol. Biotechnol.* **16:** 171–175.

Aldrich, T.L., Franz, J., Gill, J.F., Kilbane, J.J and Chakraborty A.M. (1987). *Gene* **52:** 185-195.

Ali, S., Roberto, F., La, Fuente and Dona, A.C. (1998). *Enzyme Microbial. Technol.* **23:** 462-468.

Allsop, P.J., Chisti, Y., Moo-Young, M. and Sullivan, G.R. (1993). *Biotechnol. Bioeng.* **41:** 572-580.

Alva, V.A. and Peyton, B.M. (2003). *Environ. Sci. Technol.* **37:** 4397-4402.

An, H., Park, H. and Kim, E. (2001). *FEMS Microbiol. Lett.* **195:** 17-22.

Anderson, P.M., Sung, Y.C. and Fuches, J.A. (1990). *FEMS. Microbiol. Rev.* **7:** 247-52.

ATSDR. (1998). Toxicological profile for phenol. U.S. Department of Health and Human Services. Agency for Toxic Substances and Disease Registry, Division of Toxicology/Toxicology Information Branch, Atlanta, Georgia.

ATSDR. (1997). Toxicological profile for cyanide. Atlanta, GA, United States Department of Health and Human Services, Public Health Service, Agency for Toxic Substance and Disease Registry.

Baek, S., Yin, C. and Lee, S. (2001). *Biotechnol. Lett.* **23:** 627-630.

Bandyopadhyay, A.K., Nagasawa, T., Asano, J., Fujishiro, K.T. and Yamada, H. (1986). *Appl. Environ. Microbiol.* **51:** 302-306.

Bodzek, M., Jolanta, B. and Malgorzata, K. (1996). *J. Membrane Sci.* **113:** 373-384.

Bowen, T.J., Butler, P.J. and Happold, F.C. (1965). *Biochem. J.* **97:** 651 - 657.

Busca, G., Berardeneilli, S., Resini, C. and Arrighi, L. (2008). *J. Hazard. Matter.* **7:** 263-288.

Campos, M.G., Pereira, P. and Roseiro, J.C. (2006). *Enzyme Microb. Technol.* **38**: 848–854.

Carepo, M.S, Azevedo, J.S., Porto, J.I., Bentes-Sousa, A.R., Batista Jda, S., Silva, A.L. and Schneider, M.P. (2004). *Genet. Mol. Res.* **31**:181-194.

Castric, P.A. (1981). *In:* Cyanide in Biology, Vennesland, B., Com, E.E., Knowles, C.J., Westley, J. and Wissing, F. eds. London: Academic Press. pp. 233-261.

Castric, P.A. and Strobel, G.A. (1969). *J. Bio. Chem.* **244:** 4083-4094.

Chapatwala, K.D., Babu, G.R.V., Vijaya, O.K., Kumar, K.P. and Wolfram, J.H. (1998). *J. Ind. Microbiol. Biotechnol.* **20**: 28-33.

Chen, C.Y., Kao, C.M. and Chen, S.C. (2008). *Chemosphere* **71:** 133–139.

Cyanide in drinking water. Background document for development of WHO guidelines for drinking water quality. 2007. www.who/sde/wsh/07.01/2.

Dash, R.R., Gaur, A. and Balomajumder, C. (2008). *J. Hazard. Mater.* **163:** 1–11.

Dong, X., Hong, Q., He, L., Jiang, X. and Li, S. (2008*). Int. Biodeter. Biodegrad.* **62:** 257-262.

Dorr, P.K. and Knowles, C.J. (1989). *FEMS Microbiol. Lett.* **60:** 289-294.

Dubey, S.K and Holmes D.S. (1995). *World. J. Microbiol. Biotechnol.* **11:** 257-267.

Duffner, F.M., Kirchner, U., Bauer, M.P. and Müller, R. (2000). *Gene.* **256:** 215-221.

Dursun, A.Y. and Aksu, Z. (2000). *Process Biochem.* **35:** 615–622.

ECETOC. (2004). Hydrogen cyanide, sodium and potassium cyanides and acetone cynohydrin. Brussels, European Centre for Ecotoxicology and Toxicology of Chemicals (ECETOC joint assessment of commodity chemicals.)

Feist, C.F. and Hegeman, G.D. (1969). *J. Bacteriol.* **100:** 869-877.

Ferraroni M, Kolomytseva, M.P., Solyanikova, I.P., Scozzafava, A., Golovleva, L.A. and Briganti, F. (2006). *J. Mol. Biol.* **360:** 788-799.

Fry, W.E. and Myers, D.F. (1981). *In:* Cyanide in Biology. (Eds. Vennesland, B., Conn, E.E., Knowles, C.J., Westley, J. and Wissing, F.), London: Academic Press. pp. 322-334.

Gonzalez, G., Herrera, G., Ma, T. and Garcia, P.M. (2001). *Biores. Technol.* **80:** 137-142.

Grigor'eva, N.V., Kondrat'eva, T.F., Krasil'nikova, E.N. and Karavako, G.I. (2006). *Mikrobiologiia.* **75:** 320-328.

Gury, J., Seraut, H., Tran, N.P., Barthelmebs, L., Weidmann, S., Gervais, P. and Cavin, J.F. (2009). *Appl. Environ. Microbiol.*

Gyorgy, B., Andre, L., Stehli, L. and Pungor, E. (1969). *Anal. Chim. Acta.* **46:** 318-321.

Hao, O.J., Kim, M.H., Seagren, E.A. and Kim, H. (2002*). Chemosphere*, **46:** 797-807.

Harris, R. and Knowles, C.J. (1983). *FEMS. Microbiol. Lett.* **20**: 337-341.

HSDB (Hazardous Substances Data Bank). (1998). National Library of Medicine, National Toxicology Information Program, Bethesda, M.D.

Hughes, E.J.L. and Bayly, R.C. (1983). *J. Bacteriol.* **154:** 1363-1370.

Ibrahim, M.S., Ali, H.I., Taylore, K.E., Biswas, N. and Bewtra. J.K. (2001). *Water. Environ. Res.* **73:** 1685-172.

Ingvorsen, K., Hojer-Peddersen, B. and Godtfredsen, SE. (1991). *Appl. Environ. Microbiol.* **57:** 1783-1789.

Jandhyala, D., Berman, M., Meyers, P.R., Sewell, B.T., Willson, R.C., and Benedik, M.J. (2003). *Appl. Environ. Microbiol.* **69:** 4794-4805.

Jiang H.E., Hwatay, J., Maszenan, A.M. and LeeTay, S.T. (2006). *Environ. Sci. Technol.* **40:** 6137–6142.

Jordan, W., Barneveld van, H., Gerlich, O., Kleine-Boymann, M. and Ullrich, J. (2002). *Can. J. Microbiol.* **42:** 519–523.

Kao, C.M., Chen, K.F., Liu, J.K., Chou, S.M. and Chen, S.C. (2006). *Appl. Microbiol. Biotechnol.* **71:** 228–233.

Kitisa, M., Karakayaa, E., Yigita, N.O., Civelekoglua, G. and Akcilb, A. (2005). *Water. Res.* **39:** 1652–1662.

Kumaran, P. and Paruchuri, Y.L. (1997). *Wat. Res.* **31:** 11-22.

Kunz, D.A. and Nagappan, O. (1989). *Appl. Environ. Microbiol.* **55:** 256-258.

Lack, A. and Fuches, G. (1994). *Arch. Microbiol.* **161:** 132-139.

Leonard, D., Ben, C.Y., Destnehaut, C., Lindley, N.D. and Queinnec, I. (1999). *Biotechnol. Bioeng.* **65(4):** 407-414.

Lob, K.C. and Tar, P.P. (2000). *Bull. Environ. Contam. Toxicol.* **64:** 756-763.

Luque-Almagro, V.M., Blasco, R., Huertas, M.J., Martínez-Luque, M., Moreno-Vivia, C., Castillo, F. and Rolda, M.D. (2008). *Biochem. Soc. Trans.* **33:** 168–169.

Matsumura, E., Sakai, M., Hayashi, K., Murakami, S., Takenaka, S. and Aoki, K. (2006). *Biochem. J.* **393**: 219-226.

Matus, V. Sánchez, M.A., Martínez, M. and González, B. (2003). *Appl Environ Microbiol.* **69:** 7108-15.

McLeod, M.P., Warren, R.L., Hsiao, W.W., Araki, N., Myhre, M., Fernandes, C., Miyazawa, D., Wong, W., Lillquist, A.L., Wang, D., Dosanjh, M., Hara, H., Petrescu, A., Morin, R.D., Yang, G., Stott, J.M., Schein, J.E., Shin, H., Smailus, D., Siddiqui, A.S., Marra, M.A., Jones, S.J., Holt, R., Brinkman, F.S., Miyauchi, K., Fukuda, M., Davies, J.E., Mohn, W.W. and Eltis, L.D. (2006). *Proc. Natl. Acad. Sci.* U.S.A. **103 (42):** 15582-15587.

Merimaa, M., Heinaru, E., Liivak, M., Vedler, E. and Heinaru, A. (2006). *Arch. Microbiol.* **186:** 287-96.

Miller, R.L. and Higgin, V.J. (1970). *Phytopathol.* **60:** 104-110.

Murakami, S., Kodama, N., Shinke, R. and Aoki, K. (1997). *Gene* **185 (1):** 49-54.

Nakamura, Y. and Sawada, T. (2000). *J. Chem. Technol. Biotechnol.* **75**: 137-142.

National Research Council. (1993). *In situ* Bioremediation: When does it Work? National Academy Press, Washington DC.

Nishio, Y., Nakamura, Y., Kawarabayasi, Y., Usuda, Y., Kimura, E., Sugimoto, S., Matsui, K., Yamagishi, A., Kikuchi, H., Ikeo, K. and Gojobori. T. (2003). *Genome. Res.* **13:** 1572–1579.

Omokoko, B., Jäntges, U.K., Zimmermann, M., Reiss, M. and Hartmeier, W. (2008). *BMC Microbiol.* **8:** 197.

Ornston, L.N. (1966). *J. Biol.Chem.* **241:** 3800-3810.

Parsek, M.R., Shinabarger, D.L., Rothmel, R.K. and Chakrabarty A.M. (1992). *J. Bacteriol.* **174**: 7798-7808.

Patil, Y.B. and Paknikar, K.M. (2000). *Process Biochem.* **35:** 1139–1151.

Prpich, G.P. and Daugulis, A.J. (2005). *Biodegradation.* **16:** 329-339.

Quan, Z.X., Bae, H.S., Baek, J.H., Chen, W.F., Im, W.T. and Lee, S.T. (2005). *Int. J. Syst. Evol. Microbiol.* **55:** 2543-9

RIVM. (1986). [Criteria Document: Phenol]. Bilthoven, The Netherlands, Nat. Inst. Public Health and Environ. Protect. Docum. No. 738513002) (English).

Rothmel, R.K., Aldrich, T.L., Houghton, J.E., Coco, W.M., Ornston, L.N. and Chakrabarty A.M. (1990). *J. Bacteriol.* **172**: 922-931.

Singh, D.K. and Srivastava, B. (2002). *J. Sci. Indust. Res.* **61**: 208-218.

Strachan, P.D., Freer, A.A. and Fewson, C.A. (1998). *Biochem. J.* **333:** 741-747.

Takeo, M., Prabu, S.K., Kitamura, C., Hirai, M., Takahashi, H., Kato, D. and Negoro, S. (2006). *J. Biosci. Bioeng.* **102:** 352-61.

Tam le, T., Eymann, C., Albrecht, D., Sietmann, R., Schauer, F., Hecker, M. and Antelmann, H. (2006). *Environ. Microbiol.* **8:** 1408-27.

Tancsics, A., Szoboszlay, S., Kriszt, B., Kukolya, J., Baka, E., Marialigeti, K. and Revesz, S. (2008). *J. Appl. Microbiol.* **105**: 1026-1033.

Teramoto, M, Futamata, H, Harayama, S and Watanabe, K. (1999). *Mol. Gen. Genet.* **262:** 552-558.

Tran, N.P., Gury, J., Dartois, V., Nguyen, T.K., Seraut, H., Barthelmebs, L. Gervais, P and Cavin, J.F. (2008). *J. Bacteriol.* **190:** 3213-3224.

US-EPA (United States Environmental Protection Agency). (2001). A citizen's guide to phytoremediation. www.epa.gov/superfund/sites.

Vennesland, B., Conn, E.E., Knowles, C.J., Westley, J. and Wissing, F. (Eds) (1981). Cyanide in Biology. London: Academic Press.

Watanabe, A., Yano, K., lkebukuro, K. and Karube l. (1998a). *Microbiology* **144:** 1677-1682.

Xiao, Y., Zhang, J.J., Liu, H. and Zhou, N.Y. (2007). *J. Bacteriol.* **189:** 6587-6593.

Kim, I. and Oriel, P.J. (1995). *Appl. Environ. Microbiol.* **61**: 1252-1256.

Kukor, J.J and Oslen R.H. (1991). *J. Bacteriol.* **173**: 4587-4594.

Towill, Le., Drury I.S., Whitefield, B.L., Lewis, E.B., Galyan, E.L., and Hammons, A.S. (1978). Review of environment effects of pollutants, Vol. 5. Cyanide, EPA-600/1-78-027. Springfield, VA: National Technical Information Service.

2

Bioremediation of Pesticides by Microorganisms: General Aspects and Recent Advances

Lakshmi Tewari, Jitendra Saini and Arti

Department of Microbiology, College of Basic Sciences and Humanities, G.B. Pant University of Agriculture & Technology, Pantnagar-263 145, US Nagar, Uttarakhand

E-mail: lakshmi_tewari@yahoo.co.in

With the advent of Green Revolution, there had been a quantum jump in the use of synthetic pesticides to protect crops from various pests and diseases and to enhance the productivity throughout the world, and have now become a part of modern agriculture. Although they play a significant role in augmenting food production, their large scale and indiscriminate use in India has resulted in highly unstable ecosystem, development of resistance by insects, elimination of parasites, predators and pollinators, resurgence of minor pests and destruction of useful insects. Thus, looking towards the environmental concerns and health hazards resulting due to the continuous use of these noxious xenobiotic pesticides. It is highly desirable to detoxify them. Traditional methods of pesticide detoxification have relied on landfills and incineration, which generate secondary contamination problems due to leaching of pesticides into surrounding soil and groundwater supplies and production of potentially toxic by-product emissions. By contrast, bioremediation may be viewed as a more effective and environmentally benign clean-up technology since it results in partial or complete bioconversion of the organic pollutants to microbial biomass and stable non-toxic end-products. Rhizosphere harbours a variety of beneficial microorganisms having the potential for degradation of these pollutants. These indigenous rhizosphere competent microbial strains are being exploited these days for the degradation of organic pollutants through bioremedial processes. Microbial interactions and innate microbial community dynamics greatly influence natural bioremedial processes occurring in soil. Microorganisms involve various biochemical mechanisms for degradation of pesticides such as oxidative transformations by synthesizing various enzymes, hydrolytic transformations, aromatic nitroreductive processes, carbon–phosphorus bond cleavage reactions, pesticide conjugation reactions and formation of bound pesticide residues. Chemicals released by plants may also enhance xenobiotic degradation, and it may therefore be beneficial to use plants in the remediation of contaminated soils. There is potential to use enzymatic treatment also in bioremediation, however, enzymatic treatments are not ideal for complete xenobiotic mineralization because mineralization usually requires many enzymes and several cofactors. By selecting an effective indigenous strain or by developing a recombinant pesticide degrading microorganism together with optimized environmental conditions, bioremediation becomes a cost-effective and more ecofriendly approach for restoring environmental quality.

INTRODUCTION

Rapid industrialization and urbanization during the past decades has revolutionized and affected the society and environment in many ways. With the advent of Green Revolution, there has been a quantum jump in the use of synthetic herbicides and pesticides throughout the world to sustain high yielding crop varieties as they get easily attacked by pests. They have now become a part of modern agriculture. Chemical pesticides have played an important role in increasing the food production. A considerable large number of insects, fungi, bacteria, viruses, nematodes and weeds cause severe loss in agricultural yields. In India, 20-30 per cent of crops are estimated to be damaged by pests, diseases and weeds in fields and storage conditions, accounting to a loss of approximately $ 25 billions. The estimated crop losses affected by just one single insect pest *Helicoverpa armigera,* which damages several crops, exceeds 300 million dollars. Therefore, chemical pesticides play a significant role in augmenting food production all over the world. But the large scale and indiscriminate use of pesticides in India has resulted in highly unstable ecosystem, development of resistance by insects, elimination of parasites, predators and pollinators, resurgence of minor pests and destruction of useful insects. Moreover, most of the pesticides are highly toxic, carcinogenic and non-biodegradable in nature and persist in the environment for a long period of time. Rejection of Indian agricultural exports by the western countries is more than 10,000 million rupees per annum due to high amount of pesticide residues in them.

Thus, looking towards the environmental concerns and health hazards resulting due to the continuous use of these noxious xenobiotic pesticides, it is highly desirable to either stop their use or to find some way to detoxify them. But since protection of crops from insect pests and pathogen damage is a must in order to get adequate food supply, their application cannot be stopped. The other alternatives left are: (i) their partial replacement by biological control agents (biopesticides) in the integrated pest management (IPM) system and (ii) their detoxification through degradation by biological means, a process known as bioremediation. Both legislation and technology aimed at cleaning up and preventing further damage to the environment have prominent developments in the late twentieth century and have supported the birth of bioremediation technology (Atlas and Bartha, 1998). Technologies using microorganisms with extensive biodegradative capacities have been developed for use in both pollution prevention and site remediation. Bioremediation, as defined by the American Academy of Microbiology is, "*the use of living organisms to reduce or eliminate environmental hazards resulting from accumulation of toxic chemicals or other hazardous wastes*" (Gibson and Sayler, 1992). Bioremediation is not a new technology; it is evident in that humankind has practiced composting, sewage treatment and fermentation since the beginning of recorded history.

PESTICIDES—TOXIC XENOBIOTIC ENVIRONMENTAL POLLUTANTS

There has been an enormous increase in the use of various synthetic pesticides that contribute to the spectacular increase in the crop yield. Soil, groundwater and sediments are the ultimate sinks for these pollutants, where they are either broken down to simpler forms or remain persistent. Some of the pesticides are susceptible to biomagnification and cause more danger to the environment. The safe and economical disposal of excess pesticide waste is a problem of considerable magnitude. Pesticides are considered *Xenobiotic* (*xenos* means "foreign" in Greek) compounds. These are synthetic foreign (man-made) organic compounds produced chemically and have no obvious counterpart in the natural world. Most of them are *recalcitrant* and resist their biodegradation. Over 1000 pesticides have been marketed for chemical pest control purposes. Pesticides include herbicides, insecticides, bacteriocides and fungicides etc. (Shah and Dhaliwal, 2006). Chemically, pesticides are of a wide variety, including chlorinated compounds, aromatic rings, nitrogen- and phosphorous-containing compounds and others. Toxicity and bio-accumulation potential of chlorophenol increases with the degree of chlorination and lipophilicity. The constituents of many pesticides are generally derivatives of benzene. The major groups of pesticides, their target organisms and common examples are given below (Table 2.1). The aromatic ring has large negative resonance energy, therefore, benzene and its derivatives are stable group of compounds.

Table 2.1 Major groups of pesticides, their target organisms and common examples

Group of Pesticide	*Target organisms*	*Common examples*
Insecticides	Insects	Carbamyl, DDT, aldrin, endosulfan, HCH, malathione, Lindane
Fungicides	Fungi	Bordeaux mixture, captan, dinocap, sulphur, thiram, Pentachlorophenol (PCP)
Herbicides/weedicides	Weeds	Atrazine, 2,4D, dinoseb, isoproturon, maleichydrazide, MCPA, Simazine, 2,4,5-T, Decamba
Nematicides	Nematodes	DBCB, ECB, methyl bromide, methy isocyanate
Rodenticides	Rodents	Aluminium phosphide, methyl bromide, sodium fluoroacetate, zinc phosphide
Avicides	Birds	Endrin, methyl parathion, fenthion, thallium
Bacteriocides	Bacteria	Bordeaux mixture, cupric hydroxide, streptomycin, tetracycline
Molluscides	Molluscs	Carbonyl, metaldehyde, methicarb, PCP, phorate
Acaricides	Mites	Chlorenthol, chlorfenson, cyhexatin, dicofol, dinoseb, DNOC

Toxic effects of organophosphate and carbamate pesticides occur in the nervous system where chemicals disrupt the enzyme that regulates acetyl-cholinesterase, a neurotransmitter. The pyrethroids are functional toxins that produce adverse effects in a secondary way as a consequence of neuronal hyper excitability. World Health Organization (WHO) estimates that one million pesticide poisoning cases occur every year globally. Not only this, a long term professional exposure to these pesticides also results in increased risk of several chronic and fatal diseases such as cancer. About 100 active ingredients in pesticides have been found to cause cancer in experimental animals or humans (Encyclopedia of Pest Management, 2002).

PERSISTENCE AND BIOMAGNIFICATION OF PESTICIDES

Most of the pesticides are *recalcitrant* in nature and resist their biodegradation, while some are metabolized incompletely, and as a result, accumulate in the environment (Table 2.2).

Table 2.2 Duration of environmental persistence of some common pesticides

Biocides	*Time for 75-100% disappearance*
1. Chlorinated insecticides	
DDT (1,1,1-tricholro-2,2-bis-(p-cholorophenyl) ethane)	4 years
Alarin	3 years
Chlordane	5 years
Heptachlor	2 years
Lindane (hexachloro-cyclohexane)	3 years
2. Organophosphate insecticides	
Diazinon	12 weeks
Malathion	1 week
Parathion	1 week
3. Herbicides	
2,4-D (2,4-dichlorophenoxyacetic acid)	4 weeks
2,4,5-T(2,4,5-trichlorophenoxyacetic acid)	20 weeks
Dalapon	8 weeks
Atrazine	40 weeks
Simazine	48 weeks
Propazine	1.5 year

(Source: Madigan and Martinko, 2006)

Some common examples of biodegradable and recalcitrant pesticides are given in Fig. 2.1.

Hexachlorohexane (HCH), endosulfan, parathione and methyl parathione, which were banned or restricted in US and Europe several years ago, are still applied in India to control insect pests affecting pulses and wheat. Unfortunately, the above-mentioned insecticides are not only very toxic but also poorly biodegradable. In the past, organochlorine pesticides were commonly used, but due to their persistence in nature and adverse effects on human health and the environment, most have been banned or taken off the market (e.g., DDT and chlordane). The chlorinated pesticides are relatively resistant to microbial attack. In general, the more extensive the chlorine substitution, the more persistent the pesticide.

Mirex ($C_{10}Cl_{12}$) and Kepone ($C_{10}Cl_{10}O$) are extensively chlorinated insecticidal compounds (Fig. 2.2).

The extensive application of pesticides in Indian agriculture results in residual concentrations in almost every environment, drinking water and food. The term *biodegradation* has been used to describe transformations of every type, including those that yield products more complex than the starting material as well as those responsible for the complete oxidation of organic compounds to CO_2, H_2O, NO_3^- and other inorganic components. Occasionally, microbial transformations result in residues that are more stable than the parent compound, yet this phenomenon is sometimes called *degradation* because the parent compound disappears, while some call it *mineralization*.

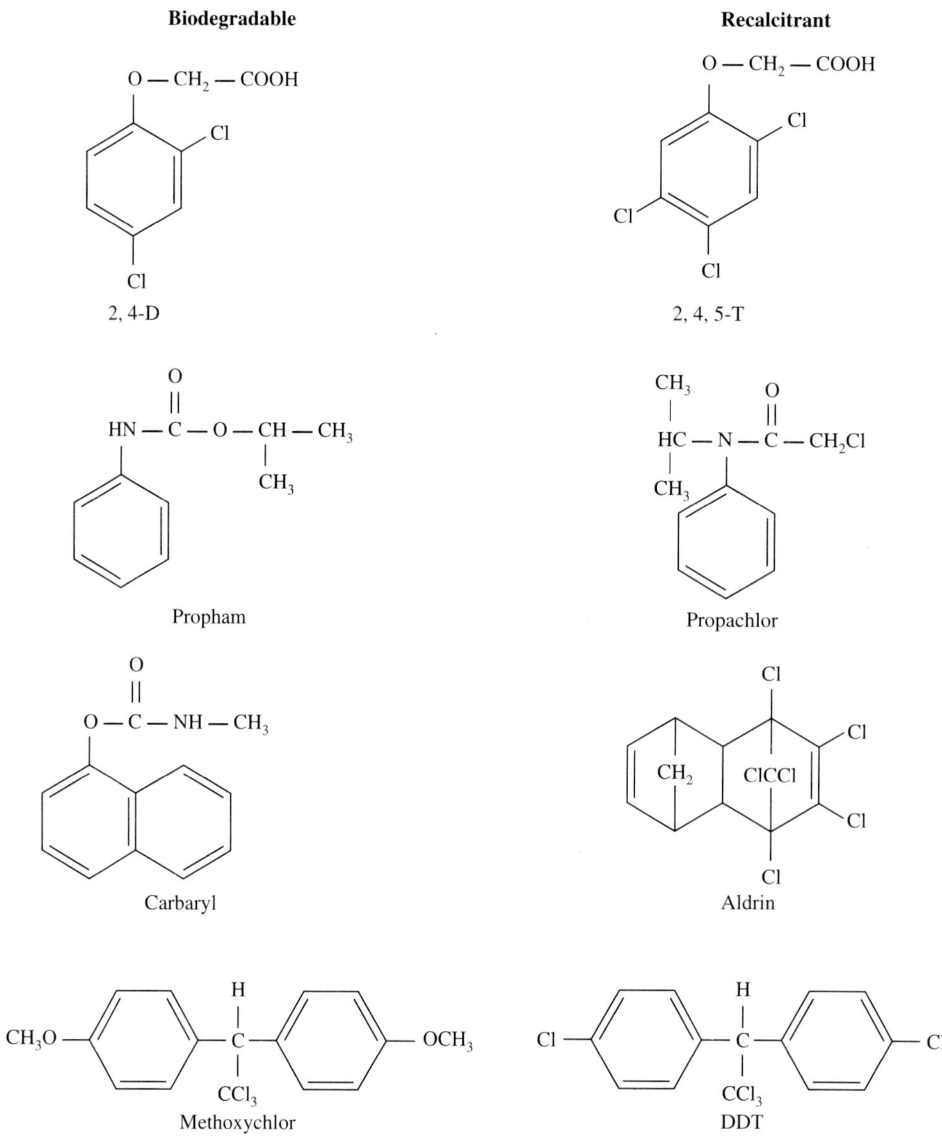

Fig. 2.1 Some examples of biodegradable and recalcitrant pesticides *(Source: Atlas & Bartha* ,1998).

What happens if a persistent pesticide is introduced into the ecosphere? It accumulates in the environment, not only at the place where it is applied but also at far distant places. The chlorinated hydrocarbon insecticides have been detected in remote and even arctic regions, thousands of miles away from the application site. It is important, therefore, to keep in mind that assessing the effect of a persistent organic chemical only on the environment to which it is directly applied is insufficient. Distribution tends to dilute, and in the environments only indirectly exposed, they are generally present in the low parts per billion (ppb) ranges such as organochlorines. Then, how these low concentrations make so harmful effects? It is only because of a phenomenon called *biological magnification* or

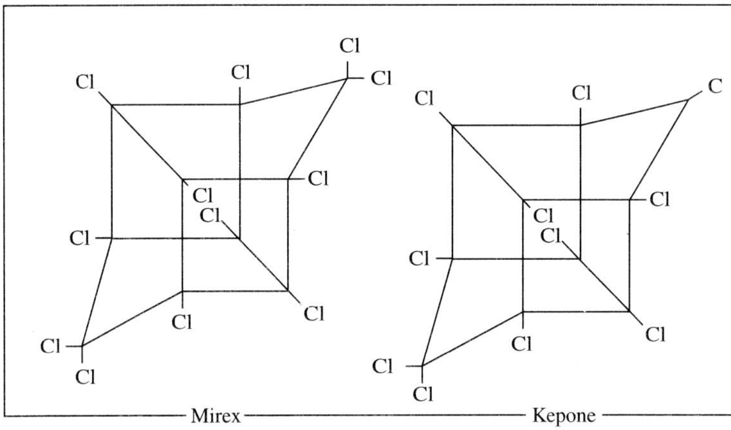

Fig. 2.2 Structural formulae of the extensively chlorinated insecticides, Mirex and Kepone (*Source:* Atlas and Bartha, 1998).

biomagnification. However, for a pollutant to be biomagnified, it must be both persistent and lipophilic. Because of their lipophilic character, minute dissolved amounts of these substances are partitioned from the surrounding water into the lipids of both prokaryotic and eukaryotic microorganisms. Their concentrations in the cells, compared to the surrounding medium, may increase by one to three orders of magnitude. Members of the next higher trophic level then ingest the microorganisms. Only 10-15% of the biomass is transferred to the higher trophic level, but the persistent lipophilic pollutant is neither degraded nor excreted to a significant extent and is preserved practically without loss in smaller biomass of the second trophic level, and consequently, its concentration increases. The same thing occurs at successively higher trophic levels. The top trophic level, composed of birds, mammalian carnivores and large predatory fish, may carry a body burden of the environmental pollutant that exceeds the environmental concentration by a factor of $10^4 – 10^6$. If the pollutant is a biologically active substance, such as a chlorinated hydrocarbon insecticide, DDT, at such levels it may cause death or serious damage to the affected organism (Fig. 2.3).

MICROBIAL POTENTIAL FOR DEGRADATION OF PESTICIDES

Microbial degradation of pesticides has been long recognized. Recent research has revealed a number of microbial systems capable of biodegradation of organic compounds. The natural capacity of microorganisms to degrade a large variety of synthetic herbicides and pesticides is the essence of microbial method for the degradation of soil contaminants (bioremediation) —the basis for green technologies. Another very interesting feature of microorganisms is that they can degrade some of the organic substances that are produced only synthetically. Although microbial degradation of pesticides does not always lead to detoxification, in many cases the products are much less hazardous and/or become susceptible to further degradation. The microbes having the potential for pesticide degradation are mainly bacteria, especially actinomycetes and cyanobacteria, algae and fungi. Twenty-eight of the bacterial genera that can utilize aliphatic hydrocarbons have been isolated (Encyclopedia of Pest Management, 2002), and most common among them are the species of *Pseudomonas, Alcaligenes, Bacillus, Arthrobacter, Brevibacterium, Flavobacterium, Klebsiella, Methylococcus, etc.* Several fungi having pesticide degrading potential have also been identified, such as the species of *Aspergillus, Candida, Fusarium, Penicillium, Trichoderma,*

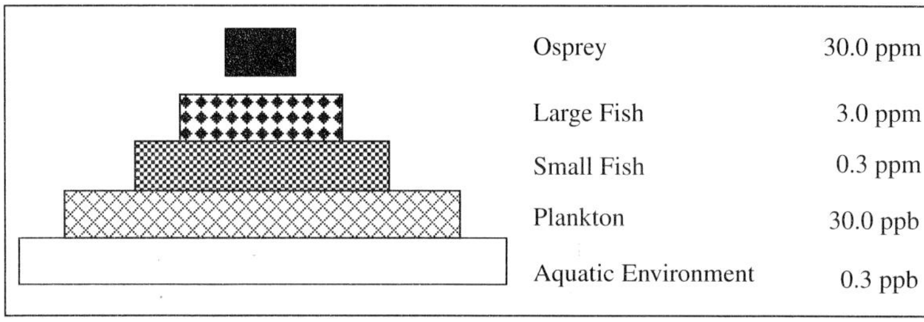

Fig. 2.3 Biomagnification of chlorinated hydrocarbon insecticide, DDT, to different trophic levels. (*Source:* Atlas and Bartha, 1998).

Rhodotorula, Pleurotus, Phaenerochaete, etc. (Table 2.3). A relatively enormous catalytic power, large surface-volume area and rapid rate of reproduction of microorganisms contribute to the major role they play in the chemical transformation. Some organisms require an adaptation period for the constitutive synthesis of pesticide degrading enzymes before attacking it. Some, through random mutation, acquire this ability, while in others, the synthesis of degrading enzymes is induced in the presence of a particular pesticide.

The biochemical processes induced by microorganisms under aerobic and anaerobic conditions are mineralization, detoxification, cometabolism and activation. Unlike organochlorine pesticides, organophosphate, carbamate and pyrethroid pesticides are biodegradable. The main detoxification processes are hydrolysis and oxidation, with hydrolysis being the most efficient route for all three types of pesticides.

Table 2.3 Microorganisms capable of degrading organic compounds, pesticides or their metabolites

S.No.	*Degrading Microorganisms*	*Organic compound or pesticide*
I. Bacteria:		
1.	*Alcaligenes denitrificans*	Fluoranthene (PAH)
2.	*Alcaligenes faecalis*	Arylacetonitrils
3.	*Arthrobacter sp.*	Carbofuran, Parathion
4.	*Arthrobacter sp.*	EPTC, Pentachlorophenol, glyphosate
5.	*Bacillus sphaericus*	Urea herbicides, Parathion
6.	*Brevibacterium oxydans* DH35A	Cyclohexylamine
7.	*Burkholderia sp.* P514	1,2,4,5-T.e CB
8.	*Clostridium*	Quinoline, Glyphosate
9.	*Corynebacterium nitrophilus*	Acetonitril, Carboxylic acid
10.	*Dehalococcoides ethanogenes*	Trichloroethylene (TCE)
11.	*Desulfovibrio sp.*	Nitroaromatic compounds
12.	*Flavobacterium sp.*	Pentachlorophenol, Parathion
13.	*Geobacter sp.*	Aromatic compounds
14.	*Klebsiella pneumoniae*	3&4 Hydrobenzoate
15.	*Methylococcus capsulatus*	Trichloroethylene
16.	*Nitrosomonas europaea*	1,1,1-Trichloroethane
17.	*Nocardia*	Quinoline
18.	*Pseudomonas stutzeri*	Parathion, Methyl parathion

Contd.

Contd.

19.	*Pseudomonas capaciea* *Pseudomonas sp.*	2,4,5-T Diazinon
20.	*Rhodococcus chlorophenolicus*	Pentachlorophenol (PCP)
II. Fungi and Yeast:		
1.	*Aspergillus flavus*	DDT
2.	*Aspergillus paraceticus*	DDT
3.	*Aspergillus niger*	2,4-D
4.	*Candida tropicalis*	Phenol
5.	*Chrysosporium lignorum*	3,4-Dichloroaniline
6.	*Fusarium oxysporum*	DDT
7.	*Phaenerochaete chrysosporium*	Lindane, DDT, Pentachlorophenol,
8.	*Pleurotus ostreatus*	DDT
9.	*Trichoderma viride*	DDT
III. Ectomycorrhizal Fungi:		
1.	*Paxillus involutus*	Mefluidide
2.	*Scillus luteus*	Mefluidide

(*Source:* Mateen *et al.*, 1994 ; *Encyclopedia of Pest Management*, 2002)

BIOREMEDIATION: AN EMERGING TECHNOLOGY FOR ENVIRONMENT CLEAN-UP

The manufacturing and use of pesticides has been rising tremendously in India, and the waste generated by the pesticide industry has become a serious environmental problem due to the present insufficient and ineffective waste treatment technology involving physico-chemical and biological treatments. As a result, recalcitrant pesticide residues remain in surface soil, leading to the toxicity of soil-water environment. Considering the toxic effects of pesticides, it is essential to remove these chemo-pollutants from the environment. Bioremediation including phytoremediation and rhizoremediation is expected to be a useful clean-up method for soil contaminated with persistent organic pesticides including dieldrin and endrin (Matsumoto *et al.*, 2009). Traditional methods of pesticide detoxification have relied on landfills and incineration, which generate secondary contamination problems due to leaching of pesticides into the surrounding soil and groundwater supplies and production of potentially toxic by-product emissions. Moreover, incineration, although approved by US EPA, is a very costly process requiring large amounts of energy (Chen and Mulchandani, 1998). From this point of view, biodegradation is a much safer and economical process for detoxifying pesticides. Many techniques of dispersal, collection, removal, landfill disposal and incineration simply dilute or sequester the contaminants or transfer them to another environment. By contrast, bioremediation may be viewed as a more effective and environmentally benign clean-up technology, since it results in the partial or complete bioconversion of the organic pollutants, such as pesticides, to microbial biomass and stable non-toxic end-products (Baker and Herson, 1994). It is a relatively recent addition to the battery of clean-up strategies currently employed to restore and rehabilitate contaminated sites.

Bioremediation has been defined as a "*biological response to environmental abuse*". Thus by definition, *it is the use of living organisms, primarily microorganisms, to degrade the environmental contaminants into less toxic forms*. Bioremediation is a combination of two words — *bio* for biological, and *remediation* which means to remediate or eliminate. Depending upon the type of organism used in the process, bioremediation may be of different types:

Phytoremediation: The use of plants to clean-up the environment.

Mycoremediation: The use of fungi for the clean-up of contaminated environment. Bioremediation is often characterized as environment-friendly and cost-effective approach for the removal of contaminants from the environment. The application of fungal technology (mycoremediation) for the clean-up of contaminated soil holds promise since 1985 when the white-rot fungus *Phanerochaete chrysosporium* was found to be able to degrade a number of important environmental pollutants (Bumpus *et al.*,1985). Since then several strains of white-rot fungi have been demonstrated to attack many organopollutants.

There are many advantages of bioremediation technology:

(a) It harnesses natural biogeochemical processes.
(b) It is a cost-effective alternative.
(c) Toxic chemicals are destroyed or removed from the environment and not merely separated.
(d) Low capital expenditure.
(e) Less energy required when compared with other technologies.
(f) Less manual supervision requirement.

TYPES OF BIOREMEDIATION TECHNOLOGIES

Bioremediation technologies have been broadly divided into two categories based on whether biodegradation is stimulated *in situ* or carried out *ex situ* in compost heaps or bioreactors. Organic pollutants can be bioremediated using either *in situ* or *ex situ* systems (Fig. 2.4).

I. *In situ* Bioremediation Techniques

In situ bioremediation techniques involve enhancement of the biodegradation rate of organic contaminants within the affected area (soil, sediment and surface water or groundwater environments). In Latin, *in situ* means "in the origin place". It is the clean-up approach that directly involves the contact between microorganisms and the dissolved and sorbed contaminants for biotransformation (Alcalde *et al.*, 2006). These types of technologies are less expensive, create less dust and cause less release of volatile contaminants. Potential advantages of *in situ* bioremediation methods include minimal site disruption, simultaneous treatment of contaminated soil and groundwater, minimal exposure of public and site personnel and low cost. But these techniques have some disadvantages also such as: time consuming method as compared to other remedial methods, seasonal variation of microbial activity under the influence of changing environmental conditions and problematic application of treatment additives (nutrients, surfactants and oxygen). When native microorganisms lack biodegradable capacity, genetically engineered microorganisms (GEMs) may be added to the surface during *in situ* bioremediation, although stimulation of indigenous microorganisms is always preferred over GEMs. The subject of pesticide bioremediation has been considered in several excellent recent reviews covering bioaugmentation, biostimulation and enzymatic bioremediation (Jorgensen, 2007). There are two types of *in situ* bioremediation: intrinsic and engineered *in situ* bioremediation.

(a) **Intrinsic *in situ* bioremediation**: The conversion of environmental pollutants (pesticides) into harmless forms through the innate capabilities of naturally occurring indigenous microbial flora is called intrinsic bioremediation. However, the inherent capacities of indigenous microbes to metabolize the pollutant should be tested at laboratory and field levels before using it for *in situ* bioremediation, and site monitoring programs should be run for analysing the progress of the remedial technique (Dubey, 2002). The factors that influence the biodegradation of pollutant through this technique at contaminated sites include groundwater flow throughout the year, supply of nutrients and electron acceptors for microbial growth and absence of toxic compounds. The other environmental factors such as pH, pesticide concentration, temperature, aeration and nutrient availability determine whether biotransformation takes place or not.

(b) Engineered *in situ* bioremediation: Intrinsic bioremediation is a slow process due to poor adapted microorganisms, limited availability of electron acceptor and nutrients, cold temperature and high concentration of pollutants. Therefore, when site conditions are not suitable, bioremediation requires construction of engineered systems to supply materials that stimulate microbial growth. It accelerates the desired biodegradation reactions by encouraging the growth of more microorganisms via optimizing physico-chemical conditions. Oxygen and other electron acceptors (e.g., NO_3^{1-} and SO_4^{2-}) and nutrients promote microbial growth on the surface of contaminated site. In some processes, both water injection and extraction wells are used in combination to control the flow of contaminated groundwater combined with above-ground bioreactor treatment and subsequent reinjection of nutrient spiked effluents are done. Bioremediation of organic compounds *in situ* requires stimulation of the degradative activities of indigenous (endogenous) microbial populations by the provision of nutrients or/and external electron acceptors. Alternatively, it may involve the addition of competent, exogenous microbial inocula, with or without nutrient and electron acceptor supplementation (Colleran, 1997). The most important *in situ* bioremediation techniques used for land treatments are described below:

1. **Bioventing:** This technique is widely used at sites that are contaminated by light organic pollutants (e.g., petroleum hydrocarbons) and where contamination is deep under the surface. In this technique, air and nutrients are introduced through injection wells in order to stimulate the growth of indigenous and exogenous microorganisms (Hinchee *et al.*, 1995). Air flow rate is carefully controlled that stimulates aerobic biodegradation of contaminants and minimizes volatilization. The resulting vapour by-product is then treated and atmospherically discharged. H_2O_2 has also been used widely as an alternative oxygen source in percolation trials.
2. **Bioaugmentation:** This process involves the introduction of an efficient indigenous or exogenous microorganism or enzyme into a contaminated soil to stimulate the degradation of organic pollutants present in the soil. This process is usually used for the removal of by-products of raw materials and wastes. Bacteria are the most commonly used agents in these biodegradation processes.
3. **Bio-stimulation:** Bio-stimulation involves the introduction of nutrients or substrates such as fertilizers, to stimulate the growth and metabolism of the indigenous species performing biodegradation of pollutants.
4. **Biosparging:** Biosparging involves the injection of air under pressure below the water level to increase groundwater oxygen concentrations and enhance the rate of biological degradation of contaminants by indigenous microorganisms. Biosparging increases the mixing in the saturated zone and thereby increases the contact between the soil and groundwater. The ease and low cost of installing small-diameter air injection points allows considerable flexibility in the design and construction of the system.

II. *Ex situ* Bioremediation Techniques

Ex situ bioremediation techniques are usually aerobic and involve the treatment of contaminated soil or sediments using solid or slurry phase systems. It actually involves the removal of waste material from polluted area and their collection at a place distant from the contaminated site to facilitate microbial degradation. There are certain limitations and disadvantages of this technology besides being a costly process. Based on the physical nature of the contaminant under treatment, this technology is classified into two types: (i) Slurry phase bioremediation systems involving treatment of solid liquid suspensions in bioreactors and (ii) Solid phase bioremediation system including land farming (soil treatment units) and soil piles, compost heaps and engineered bio piles. Composting techniques are used for the remediation of highly contaminated sites and have proved successful for military sites contaminated with explosives such as TNT, RDX and Tetryl.

(a) **Slurry phase bioremediation:** Slurry phase bioremediation is a controlled batch treatment technique in which excavated soil or sediments are mixed with water and treated in bioreactor vessels or contained ponds or lagoons. Processing of the soil involves separation of stones and rubbles from the contaminated soil to provide a low viscosity. Then the soil is mixed with a predetermined amount of water to form slurry. Thus, slurry phase treatment is a triphasic system involving three major components: water, air and suspended particulate matter including the desired microorganism. The concentration of water added depends on the concentration of pollutants, the rate of biodegradation, and the physical nature of the soil (USEPA, 2006). In addition to the provision of adequate aeration and mixing, nutrients are universally added, together with surfactants or dispersants as required. Optimum pH and temperature conditions are also provided in bioreactor vessels. Effective bioremediation has been obtained with slurry phase systems for soil and sediments contaminated with a wide range of organic compounds including pesticides, petroleum hydrocarbons, pentachlorophenol, polychlorinated biphenyls, (PCBs), etc.

Biologically, there are three types of slurry phase bioreactors: *Aerated lagoons, low-shear airlift reactor* and *fluidized-bed soil reactor.* A slurry bioreactor may be defined as a containment vessel and apparatus used to create a three-phase (solid, liquid, and gas) mixing condition to increase the rate of bioremediation of soil bound and water-soluble pollutants as a water slurry of the contaminated soil and biomass (usually indigenous microorganisms) capable of degrading target contaminants. In general, the rate and extent of biodegradation are greater in a bioreactor system than *in situ* or in solid-phase systems because the contained environment is more manageable and hence more controllable and predictable. Despite the advantages of bioreactor systems, there are some disadvantages, such as the contaminated soil requires pre-treatment (e.g., excavation) or alternatively, the contaminant can be stripped from the soil via soil washing or physical extraction (e.g., vacuum extraction) before being placed in a bioreactor.

(b) **Solid phase bioremediation:** Solid phase system includes organic wastes, manures, sewage sludge and municipal solid wastes. The traditional clean-up practices involve the informal processing of organic materials and production of compost, which may be used as soil amendment. In solid phase bioremediation, contaminated soil is excavated and placed into piles. Bacterial growth is stimulated through a network of pipes that are distributed throughout the piles. By pulling air through pipes, the necessary ventilation is provided for microbial respiration. Moisture is introduced by spraying the soil with water. Solid-phase systems require a large amount of space, and clean-ups require more time to complete than with slurry-phase processes.

Some solid-phase treatment processes include land farming and composting. *Land farming* is suggested for oil sludges as a low cost disposal method in which contaminated soil is spread on a thin surface and nutrients and minerals are added to promote the growth of indigenous microorganisms. Tilting is done periodically for aeration and mixing. This practice is limited to the treatment of superficial 10-35 cm of soil. This technique requires more land space and time. *Composting* involves mixing of contaminated soil with non-hazardous organic amendments such as manure, straw, hay, or corncobs to enhance the bacterial growth. After mixing, the soil is covered to protect it from erosion and to maintain proper moisture and temperature necessary for bacterial growth.

Advantages of *in situ* over *ex situ* Bioremediation Techniques

- *In situ* bioremediation can be used to completely degrade and detoxify some organic contaminants, thereby permanently removing liability for the contaminants.

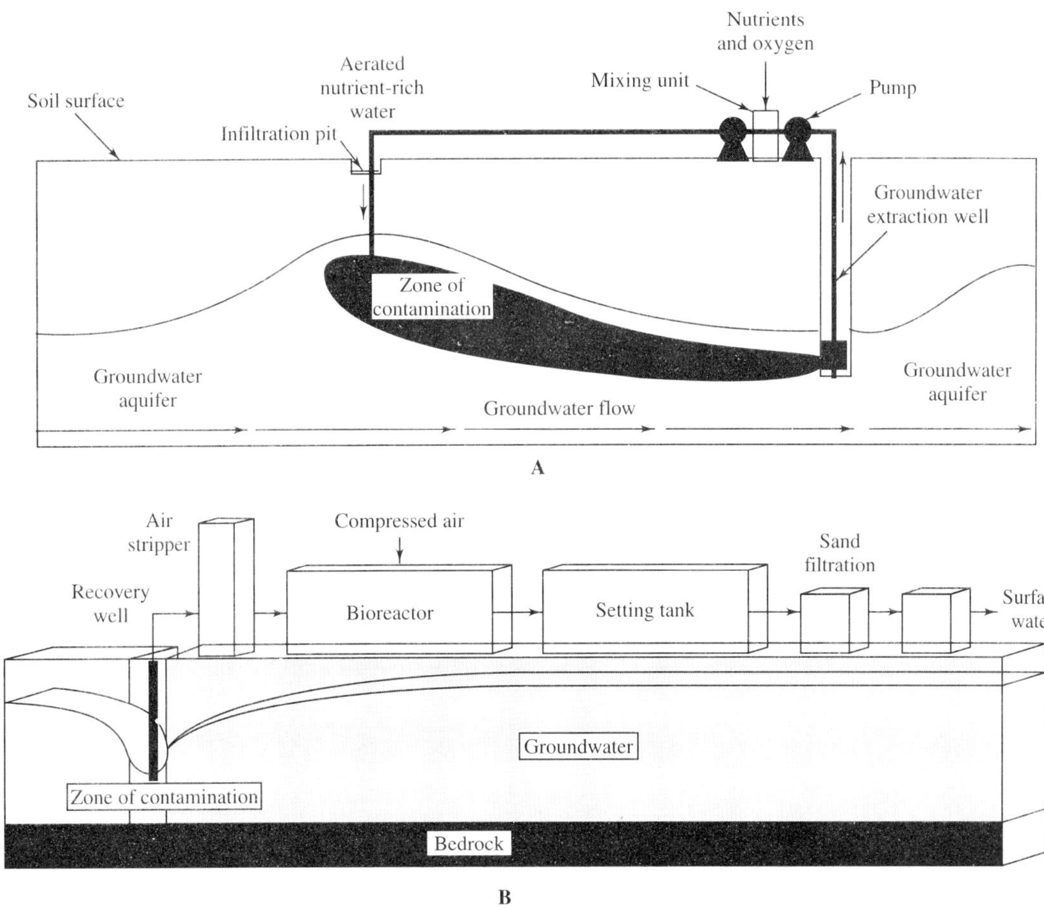

Fig. 2.4 Bioremediation of subsurface contaminated soil and groundwater by (A) *in situ* and (B) *ex situ* bioremediation technology (Source: Atlas and Bartha, 1998).

- For deep, widely dispersed plumes of heavy metals and radionuclide, *in situ* bioremediation and immobilization may be the only viable solution.
- For some types of contaminants, physical and chemical methods of remediation may not completely remove the contaminants, leaving residual concentrations that are above regulatory guidelines. Bioremediation can be used as a cost-effective secondary treatment scheme to decrease the concentration of contaminants to acceptable levels. In other cases, bioremediation can be the primary treatment method, followed by physical or chemical methods for final site closure.
- In some cases, natural attenuation (including natural bioremediation) of the contaminant plumes may be the only cost-effective solution.
- For complex mixtures of contaminants requiring a combination or sequence of physical and chemical remediation methods, bioremediation techniques that use microbial consortia to concurrently address all contaminants may be faster and more cost-effective.
- The ultimate degradation of organic chemicals (e.g., pesticides) in polluted agricultural and industrial areas is mainly the result of microbial activity. Biological removal of chemo-pollutants becomes the method of choice since microorganisms can use a variety of xenobiotic compounds for their growth and mineralize and detoxify them.

The recent advances in bioremediation technology using *microbial consortium* have been found effective for the treatment of pesticides in soil. Biodegradation and bioremediation are matching processes to an extent that both of these are based on the conversion and metabolism of pesticides by microorganisms. The difference between these two is that, *biodegradation* is a natural process, whereas *bioremediation* is a technology.

MICROBIAL BIOREMEDIATION INVOLVING AEROBIC/ANAEROBIC MICROORGANISMS

Recent advances made in the area of catalytic breakdown and metabolic pathways used by both aerobic and anaerobic bacteria for degradation of complex aromatic and aliphatic compounds are of great advantage in designing appropriate *in situ* or *ex situ* bioremediation protocols. Pesticides are subjected to both biotic and abiotic transformation processes. In general, abiotic transformations result in the partial degradation; however, the results of partial degradation are chemicals that are more easily degraded by microorganisms. The most significant abiotic processes are the hydrolytic reactions. These transformations occur through interactions with reactive chemical groups on mineral surfaces, reactive organic compounds, and inorganic metals. The exact mechanism for microbial adaptation to pesticides is not well understood. Microorganisms may acquire genetic material to encode the biochemical mechanisms necessary to deal with a potential substrate. Microbial bioremediation can take place under *aerobic* as well as *anaerobic* conditions. In aerobic conditions, microorganisms use the available atmospheric oxygen for their metabolic functions in order to produce carbon dioxide and water through pesticide degradation. However, under anaerobic conditions, due to the absence of oxygen, microorganisms use these chemical compounds in the soil as substrate, breaking them down to obtain the energy they need. Field *et al.* (1995) reviewed the intrinsic chemical considerations that limit the biodegradability of aromatic pollutants in aerobic and anaerobic environments.

Pesticide-Bioremediation under Aerobic Conditions

The use of *oxygenase* enzyme by aerobic species to initiate electrophilic attack on aromatic molecules is seriously hindered by the presence of numerous electron-withdrawing substituents, such as chloro, nitro and azo groups. Co-metabolism by the organisms allows the microbe to catalyze the hydrolysis reaction. An important factor in the bioremediation of pesticide contaminated soil is the availability of the contaminant to the microorganisms. This availability is a function of the affinity of adsorption of the organic compound to the soil. Moisture content also plays a significant role in microbial degradation of pesticides. Availability of the pesticide to the organism is dependent upon the solubility of the compound in water. A moisture content of 50% will give good degradation rates. The concentration of pesticide in soil also contributes to the rate of degradation. Often, when specific compounds such as pesticides are present in soil, significant populations of microbes that degrade these compounds are not present. Remediation of these soils is generally done with the aid of bio-augmentation, the development of specific seed cultures and inoculation of the soil or bioreactor. For some pesticides such as DDT, lindane and heptachlor, anaerobic degradation works better than aerobic degradation. (Fathepure *et al.*, 1995).

Pesticide-Bioremediation under Anaerobic Conditions

Under anaerobic conditions, aromatic compound degradation is usually initiated by nucleophilic attack. Consequently, presence of chloro, nitro or azo ring substituents will favour initial reductive attack on aromatic pollutant by anaerobic bacteria. On the other hand, electron donating functional groups, such as amino groups, tend to reduce the susceptibility of aromatic compounds to anaerobic transformation, while increasing their susceptibility to aerobic degradation. Furthermore, the lack of any functional group has been associated with the observed recalcitrance of hydrocarbons in anaerobic environment. There are many degradation reactions that characterize the breakdown of pesticide anaerobically, such as: (i) addition of hydroxyl group replacing the hydrogen atom, (ii) oxidation of sulphur to SO_2. This is a common reaction that results in the formation of an epoxide group. The epoxide group may be resistant to microbial degradation and toxic to the cell material of the microorganisms, (iii) addition/removal of a methyl group. It is common in the methylation of arsenic pesticides, (iv) removal of chlorine. It is common among halogenated compounds. In this process a hydrogen atom or hydroxyl group replaces the chlorine atom, (v) chlorine migration. It is the movement of chlorine from one position to another position on the ring, (vi) reduction of a nitro (NO_2^-) group to amino group (NH_3), (vii) replacement of sulphur with oxygen. It may occur when an insecticide contains a sulphur-phosphorous double bond, (viii) cleavage of an ether linkage, (ix) metabolism of side chains. It occurs through the cleavage of two carbon atoms by oxidation, (x) hydrolysis, degradation of a compound through the addition of water (Dolfing & Harrison, 1993).

ENVIRONMENTAL FACTORS INFLUENCING *IN SITU* BIOREMEDIATION RATES

Bioremediation processes are highly dependent on the potential of microorganisms used for degradation purposes. However, both the rate and extent of remediation (*in situ*) of organic contaminants by potential microbes are highly affected by a variety of environmental factors, some of which may be manipulated whereas others are difficult to modify within the contaminated site. It is dependent on abiotic environmental conditions such as temperature, moisture, soil pH, etc, microbial community or plant species (or both), pesticide characteristics and biological and chemical reactions. Abiotic degradation is due to chemical and physical transformations of the pesticide by processes such as photolysis, hydrolysis, oxidation, reduction, and rearrangements. Further, pesticides may be biologically unavailable because of compartmentalization that occurs as a result of pesticide adsorption to soil and soil colloids without altering the chemical structure of the original molecule. However, enzymatic transformation, which is mainly the result of biotic processes mediated by plants and microorganisms, is by far the major route of detoxification. The metabolism of pesticides may involve a three-phase process (Shimabukuro, 1985). In phase I metabolism, the initial properties of a parent compound are transformed through oxidation, reduction, or hydrolysis to generally produce a more water-soluble and usually a less toxic product than the parent. The second phase involves conjugation of a pesticide or pesticide metabolite to a sugar, amino acid, or glutathione, which increases the water solubility and reduces toxicity compared with the parent pesticide. The third phase involves the conversion of phase II metabolites into secondary conjugates, which are also non-toxic (Hatzios, 1997).

Most of the microorganisms exhibit growth optima at or near neutral pH (pH-7.0) values. Most laboratory based biodegradation studies have, therefore, been carried out in this pH range. However, the pH values for the soil throughout the world may vary from highly acidic to highly alkaline (pH-11.0) values. Therefore, adjustment of soil pH can significantly alter bioremediation rates. Liming therefore is done by addition of finely ground agricultural limestone, calcium hydroxide or calcium carbonate to the acidic soil for optimizing the process. But an increase in soil pH tends to decrease the availability of calcium, magnesium and phosphorus, whereas a decrease in soil pH results in decreasing availability of nitrate and chloride. Fungi are known to tolerate more acidic conditions and are consequently likely to play a more significant role than bacteria in the bioremediation of acidic soil. The vast majority of *in situ* bioremediation applications have been carried out under mesophilic conditions (typically between 20° and 40°C). The use of *in situ* bioremediation techniques for soil in tropical countries where the soil temperature may exceed 50°C, requires the use of a thermophilic microbe. A strain of *Bacillus stearothermophilus*, capable of growing optimally at 60°C, was shown to degrade hydrocarbon in such soils during bioremediation processes (Colleran, 1997).

INFLUENCE OF MICROBIAL INTERACTIONS AND INNATE MICROBIAL COMMUNITY DYNAMICS ON NATURAL BIOREMEDIAL PROCESSES OCCURRING IN SOIL

As a general rule, organic compounds are more effectively degraded in environments containing many microorganisms than in a pure culture of single organism. This is due to several factors. Natural microbial communities are complex assemblages in which various microorganisms are highly interdependent. The range of degradative capabilities represented in a complex community of many bacteria and fungi is far greater than the capabilities of any single organism alone. Further, the product of partial degradation of a xenobiotic by one organism may serve as a substrate for another organism. The concerted action of several different organisms may lead to complete mineralization of the xenobiotic. A microbial community is also likely to be more resistant than a solitary species to a toxic product of biodegradation, because one of its members may be able to detoxify it. Thus, composition of a microbial community responds to environmental conditions coming over time to exploit the nutrients in the most effective manner. The fate of organic compounds introduced into the soil is determined by a combination of physical, chemical and biological factors. A particular molecule may be removed by volatilization, leaching, adsorption, photochemical degradation or it may undergo abiotic oxidation or hydrolysis. Finally, the molecule may undergo biodegradation through the action of microorganisms. In some instances, the products of biological and nonbiological degradation may be identical. The laboratory studies of the fate of a single organic compound do not provide clear and accurate results for the persistence of xenobiotics in the environment, because in the natural habitats microbial communities are likely to be exposed to mixtures of several organic compounds and heavy metals. Many organisms are unable to grow in the presence of heavy metals. Thus, the bacteria that are able to degrade certain persistent organic pesticides such as polycyclic aromatic hydrocarbons or chlorinated organic compounds are likely to disappear from the environment when heavy metals are also present.

In this way microbial interactions in natural microbial communities greatly influence biodegradation or biotransformation of a particular pesticide. There are three key factors influencing microbial degradation of pesticides: (i) commensalism and mutualism, (ii) cometabolism and (iii) phenomenon of gratuitous biodegradation. *Commensalism* is an interactive association between two populations of different species that live together in which one population benefits from the association and the other is not affected. *Mutualism* is a symbiosis, an interaction in which two organisms of different species live in close physical association for their mutual benefits. *Gratuitous biodegradation* occurs when an enzyme is able to transform a compound other than its natural substrate. But transformation of unnatural substrate requires its binding to the active site of the enzyme without affecting its catalytic activity. There are several bacteria and fungi, which are of diverse metabolic potential and produce several enzymes able to act on a wide range of molecules. *Cometabolism* is the ability of an organism to transform a non-growth substrate as long as the growth substrate or other transformable compound is also present. A non-growth substrate is one that cannot serve as a sole source of carbon and energy for a pure culture of bacterium, and hence cannot support cell division. Some of the pesticides may appear as recalcitrants, but can be degraded by the process of cometabolism. A number of microbial cell bound and extracellular enzymes can catalyze the breakage of bonds in herbicide molecules, e.g., cometabolism of MCA (monochloroacetate) and the herbicide MCPA (monochloropropionate). *Pseudomonas putida* strain PP3 as such cannot metabolize MCA, but while metabolizing MCPA, the organism catalyzes dehalogenation of MCA (Chatterji, 2007).

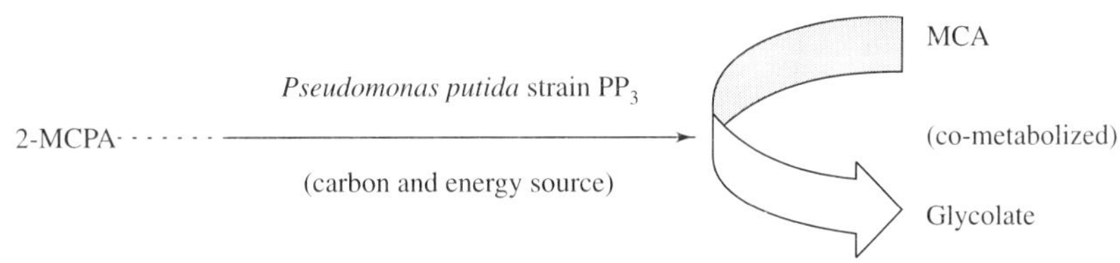

BIOCHEMICAL MECHANISMS INVOLVED IN MICROBIAL DEGRADATION OF PESTICIDES

1. Oxidative Transformations

(a) *Reactions by cytochrome P450*

Oxygenation is the most frequent first step in the biotransformation of pesticides and other organic xenobiotics. Many of these reactions are mediated by oxidative enzymes, e.g., cytochrome P450s. These are the most extensively studied oxidative enzymes and are the most important enzymes in Phase I pesticide metabolism (Barrett, 2000). Cytochrome P450s are hemethiolate proteins that have been characterized in animals, plants, bacteria, and filamentous fungi. Cytochrome P450s often catalyze monooxygenase reactions, usually resulting in hydroxylation. Agrochemicals can influence cytochrome P450 systems by acting as effectors, thereby modifying pesticide metabolism, or by modulating overall metabolism of an organism. These effects can increase or decrease physiological activities, which may affect the growth and development.

(b) *Transformation by peroxidases, phenoloxidases, and related oxidoreductases*

In addition to P450s, microorganisms produce other oxidative enzymes (e.g., peroxidase, polyphenol-oxidase, laccase, and tyrosinase) that catalyze polymerization of various anilines and phenols (Dec and Bollag, 2001). White-rot fungi (*Phanerochaete chrysosporium*) offer high potential for xenobiotic transformation because they possess lignin peroxidase and manganese dependent peroxidases that can degrade a wide range of pollutants such as polychlorinated biphenyls (PCBs) and nitroaromatic explosives.

Some pesticides like propanil (herbicide) are partially biodegraded to form azo-compounds, which are carcinogenic and thus their biodegradation may lead to another problem. In most instances, polymerization products have reduced toxicity compared with the substrate, whereas polymerization of 3, 4-dichloroaniline (metabolite of propanil) by soil microorganisms results in the formation of carcinogenic tetrachloroazobenzene (Pothuluri *et al.*, 1991) (Fig. 2.5).

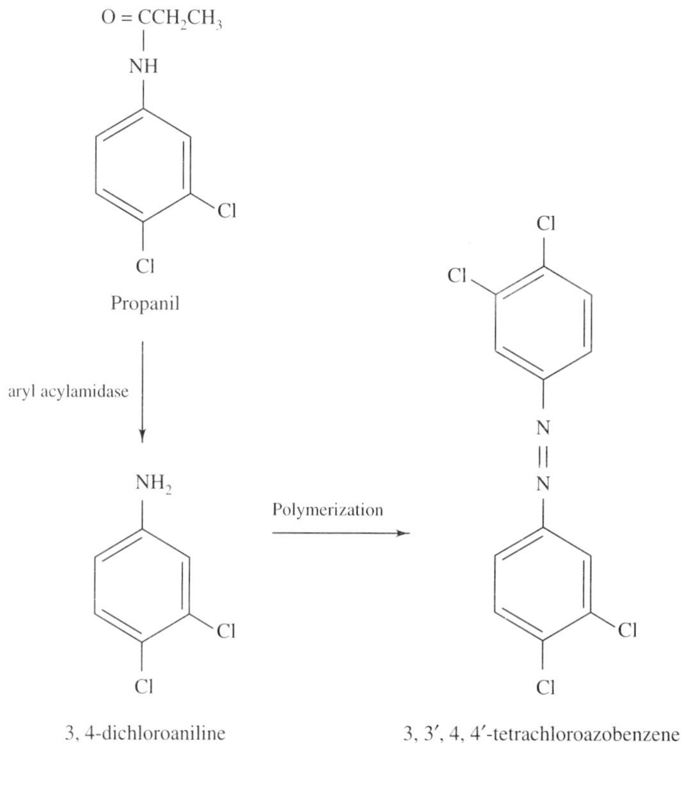

Fig. 2.5 Amide hydrolysis of propanil by aryl acyl-amidase in plants and microorganisms and its polymerization by microbial peroxidases.

(c) *Oxidative transformations of pesticides by oxygenases*

Few microorganisms, especially aerobic bacteria, are able to transform various nitro-aromatic compounds by carrying out oxidative reactions catalyzed by numerous enzymes from many different pathways. Bacteria produce different types of oxygenases, flavin monooxygenases, and dioxygenases, which are generally involved in the initial oxidation of nitro-aromatic pesticides, e.g., 2, 4-dinitrophenol can be metabolized by these three enzymes (Cassidy *et al.*, 1999). Depending on the compound, nitrite can be released before, or after ring cleavage. Overall, these diverse microbial nitro-aromatic degradative pathways allow for ring hydroxylation, ring cleavage, and subsequent mineralization of several xenobiotics, e.g., nitrobenzene, nitrobenzoic acid, nitrophenols, and nitrotoluene. Similar to halogen substituents, nitro-substitution of aromatic rings has a strong negative effect on biodegradability. Both halogen and nitro-substituents are electron withdrawing and tend to deactivate the aromatic ring. Compounds with several nitro-substituents tend to be recalcitrant. The biodegradation of nitro-aromatic compounds tends to be slow and often leads to bound or polymerized residues in soil and sediments. Similar to chloro-aromatics, extensively nitro-substituted aromatics are more easily transformed under reductive than under oxidative conditions. The oxidative and reductive pathways of nitrobenzene biodegradation by *Comamonas* sp. and *Pseudomonas pseudoal caligenes* respectively, are shown in Fig. 2.6.

2. Hydrolytic Transformations

Hydrolytic enzymes cleave the bonds of a substrate by adding -H or -OH group from H_2O to each product. There are many hydrolytic enzymes that are capable of metabolizing a variety of substrates, particularly those containing amide, carbamate or ester functional groups. These enzymes may be compartmentalized or extracellular reactions can occur under aerobic and anaerobic conditions. Ester hydrolysis is commonly carried out by *esterase* and to a much lesser extent by *lipases* and *proteases*. Four types of esterases have been characterized in *Pseudomonas fluorescens*, each differing in protein structure, cellular localization, and substrate specificity. Atrazine was traditionally considered to be moderately persistent, but now bacteria are known that can completely mineralize atrazine. The gene regions encoding the first three enzymes of atrazine degradation have been isolated and characterized from *Pseudomonas* sp. strain ADP. This bacterium mineralizes high concentrations of atrazine under both growth and non-growth conditions, using the herbicide as the sole nitrogen source. The *atzA* gene encodes atrazine chlorohydrolase, which dechlorinates atrazine hydrolytically to the nonphytotoxic metabolite hydroxyatrazine (Fig. 2.7). The next step in the degradation pathway is hydrolytic removal of the aminoethyl group from hydroxyatrazine by *atzB* gene product, hydroxyatrazine ethyl amidohydrolase. Finally, the *atzC* gene encodes for another amidohydrolase that converts *N*-isopropylammelide to cyanuric acid. Wackett *et al.* (2002) have recently sequenced the complete catabolic plasmid pADP-1 from this strain and have identified three additional genes *atzD, atzE,* and *atzF* encoding for cyanuric acid amidohydrolase, biuret hydrolase, and allophanate hydrolase, respectively, mineralizing atrazine completely to urea. Propanil is the most widely studied pesticide with regard to amide hydrolysis by microbial aryl acylamidases.

Many microbes are capable of amide hydrolysis of propanil. Aryl acylamidases have been purified from several bacterial genera including *B. sphaericus*, *Pseudomonas pickettii*, *P. fluorescens*, *P. aeruginosa*, *Nocardia globerula*, and a coryneform-like bacterium. However, there is evidence that sulfatases in the fungi *Trichoderma harzianum* and *P. chrysosporium* hydrolyze the insecticide, endosulfan. The herbicide 2, 4-Dichlorophenoxyacetic acid (2, 4-D) is biodegraded within days, while 2, 4, 5-Trichlorophenoxyacetic acid (2, 4, 5-T) differs only by one additional chlorine substitution in the meta position, yet this compound persists for many months. The additional substitution interferes with the hydroxylation and cleavage of the aromatic ring (Fig. 2.8). Biodegradation of 2, 4-D occurs via modified *ortho* cleavage pathway.

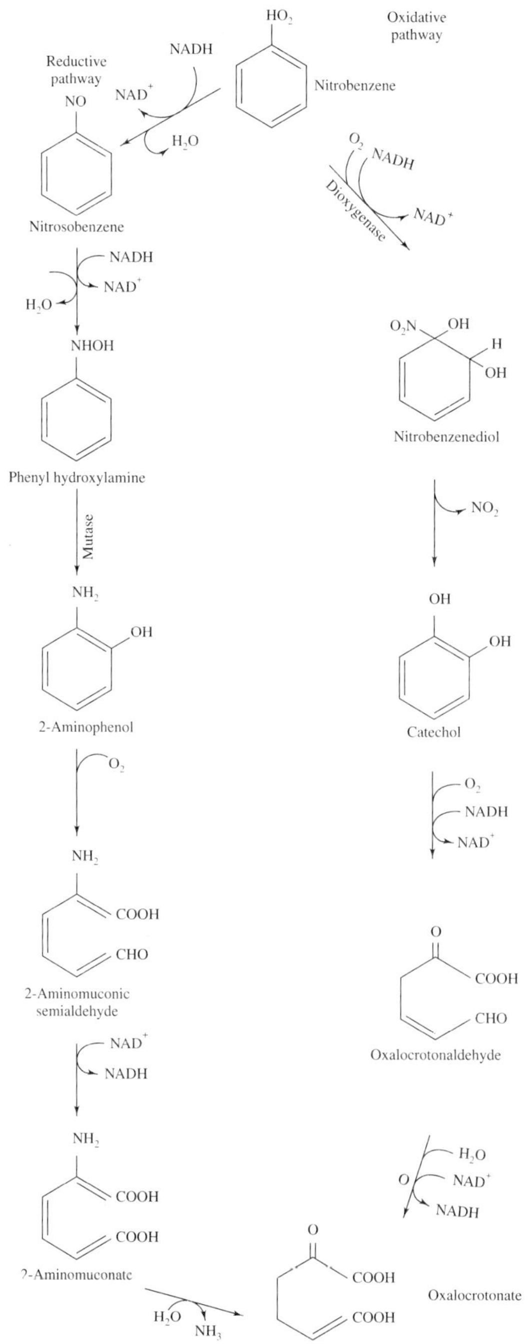

Fig. 2.6 The oxidative and reductive pathways of nitrobenzene biodegradation by *Comamonas* sp. and *Pseudomonas pseudoalcaligenes*. *(Source:* Atlas & Bartha, 1998*)*

3. Aromatic Nitroreductive Processes

In bacteria, three pathways of reductive metabolism of nitroaromatics have been characterized: aromatic nitroreduction, partial nitroreduction, and hydrogenation. Reductive metabolism of nitroaromatic xenobiotics is mediated by *nitroreductase* enzymes found in aerobic and anaerobic bacteria, and several genera of fungi that have varying sensitivities to O_2 concentrations. There is a potential to develop transgenic crops that express a bacterial nitroreductase gene to metabolize diphenyl ether herbicides, thereby providing crop tolerance to these herbicides (Hoagland and Zablotowicz, 2001). Numerous bacteria are capable of partial nitroreduction, resulting in NH_3 release and subsequent ring cleavage.

4. Carbon-Phosphorus Bond Cleavage Reactions

Organophosphonates used as pesticides have a carbon-to-phosphorus(C–P) bond, which does not undergo photochemical, hydrolytic, thermal, or chemical degradation. However, many organophosphonate compounds do not persist in the environment because of microbial degradation. Degradation of C–P bonds has been extensively studied in bacteria. For instance, a gene cluster designated *phn*, consisting of 17 genes from *Escherichia coli*, is responsible for the degradation of a wide range of phosphonates and is likely to encode for a C–P lyase (Kim *et al.*, 1993). The enzyme(s) responsible for direct cleavage of organophosphonate C–P bonds is known by the general name *C–P lyase*.

5. Pesticide Conjugation Reactions

Pesticide conjugation has recently been defined as the "*metabolic process whereby an exogenous or endogenous natural compound is joined to a pesticide or its metabolite(s) facilitating detoxification, compartmentalization, sequestration, and/or mineralization.*" (Hall *et al.*, 2001). Conjugation of pesticides often involves utilization of the existing enzymatic machinery and is therefore called a *cometabolic process*. Uridine diphosphate-glucosyl (UDPG) transferase, an enzyme involved in cellulose

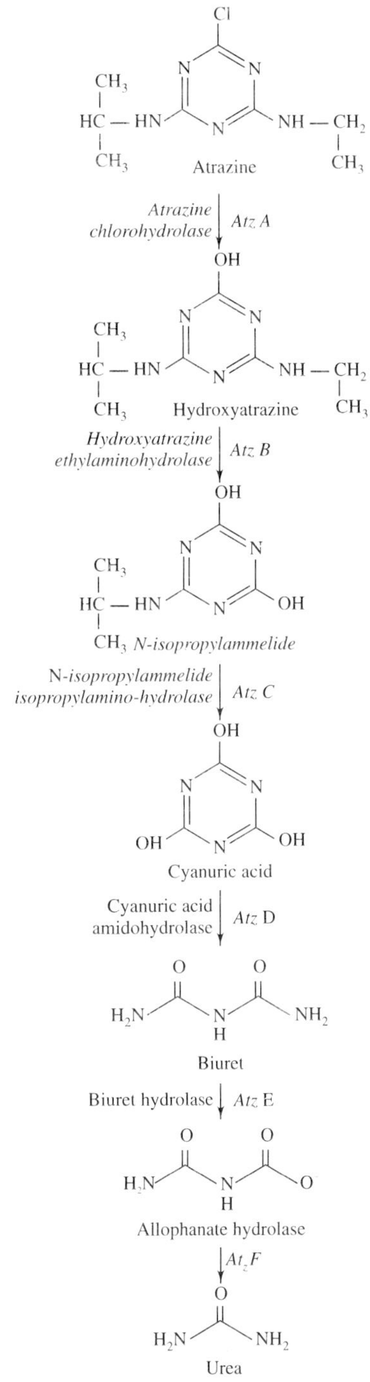

Fig. 2.7 Metabolic pathway for degradation of Atrazine by *Pseudomonas* sp. strain ADP *(Source:* Wackett *et al.*, 2002; Martinez *et al.*, 2001*)*.

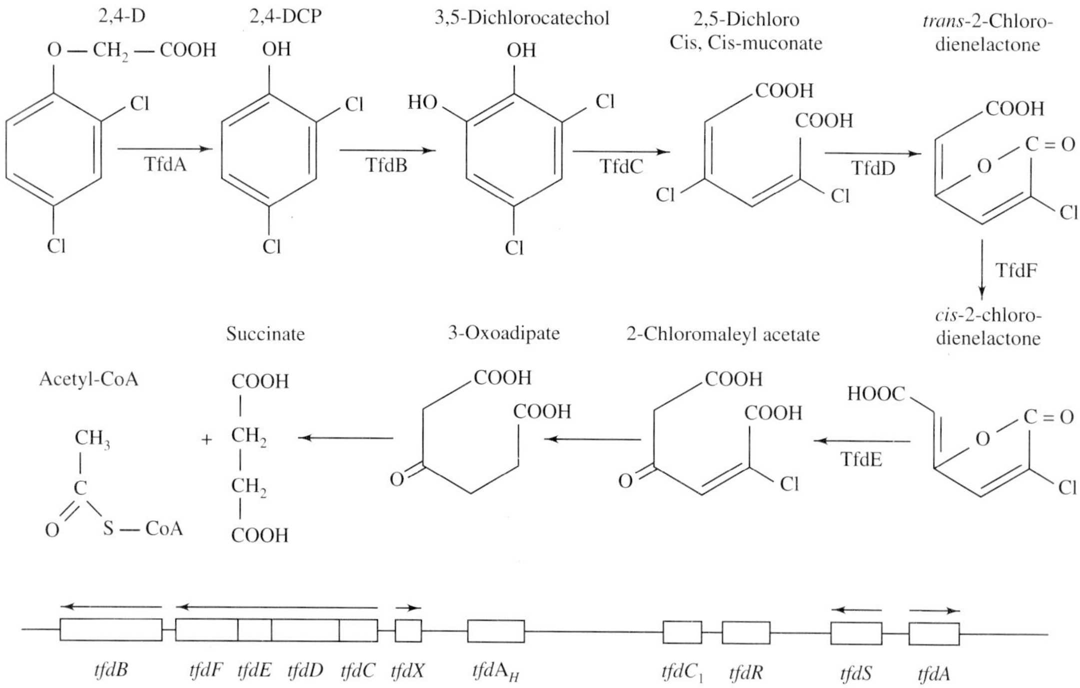

Fig. 2.8 Biochemical pathway of 2, 4-D biodegradation and the genetic organization of *tfd* genes that encode metabolism of 2, 4-D in *Alcaligenes eutrophus*. The plasmid encoded gene products (Tfd enzymes) and the reactions they catalyze are indicated in the biochemical pathway. The final metabolic steps are encoded by chromosomal genes (*Source:* Atlas and Bartha, 1998).

biosynthesis, mediates pesticide-glucose conjugation and pesticide-glucose ester conjugation reactions. As mentioned above, glucose esters of pesticides are cleaved by esterases, often resulting in the release of the pesticide.

Microbial pesticide conjugation reactions include *xylosylation, alkylation, acylation*, and *nitrosation* and can occur intra- or extracellularly. During fungal degradation of lignin, carbohydrates are generated, but toxic phenols are also concomitantly released. These phenols are extracellularly conjugated to xylose as a detoxification mechanism. The biotransformed pesticide is released into the soil, where it is susceptible to further metabolism by bacteria. Both fungi and bacteria use methylation as a common conjugation reaction to detoxify xenobiotics. For example, formation of *O*-methylated pentachlorophenol by fungal cultures of *Trichoderma virgatum* results in a less toxic, but more recalcitrant, pentachloroanisole. *Phanerochaete chrysosporium* methylates chlorophenoxyacetic acid via a manganese-lignin peroxidase, which is an extracellular degrading enzyme system (Joshi and Gold, 1993). Phenols and anilines in soil are often acylated by fungi. For example, the herbicide metobromuron is metabolized by microbes to 4-bromoaniline, which is then acylated to form 4-bromoacetaniline (Fig. 2.9). Glutathione-*S*-transferases that function as reductive dehalogenases from *Sphingomonas* strains are involved in the dechlorination of pentachlorophenol and lindane.

6. Formation of Bound Pesticide Residues

Pesticides (mainly conjugated pesticides) are often bound to plant cell walls. Bound pesticide residues are generally considered as those that cannot be extracted with aqueous and organic solvents, however, a more precise definition has been provided: *"a bound xenobiotic residue is a residue associated with one or more classes of endogenous macromolecules. It cannot be dissociated from the natural macromolecule using exhaustive extraction or digestion without significantly changing the nature of the associated endogenous macromolecules"* (Skidmore *et al.*, 1998). On the basis of reports in literature, it appears that xenobiotics are incorporated randomly into different cell wall components; however, little is known about the type of linkages involved in this binding. *Phanerochaete chrysosporium* has been shown to mineralize bound chloroaniline and 2, 4-dichlorophenol, indicating that these compounds may become bioavailable. However, the biological relevance of typically low concentrations of bound pesticide residues is not known. Presently, the U.S. Environmental Protection Agency requires no characterization of bound pesticide residues if concentrations are less than 0.05 ppm of the parent equivalents or 10% of the total pesticide residue. If concentrations exceed these levels, determination of the bioavailability is required.

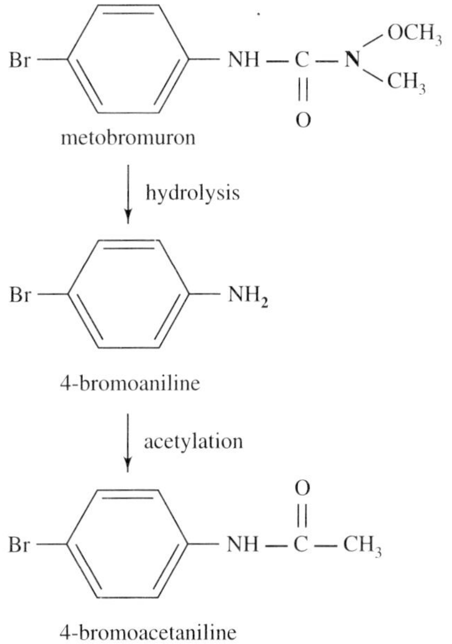

Fig. 2.9 Biotransformation of the herbicide metobromuron by microorganisms.

BIOREMEDIATION OF PESTICIDE IN THE RHIZOSPHERE

Chemicals released by plants may enhance xenobiotic degradation, and it may therefore be beneficial to use plants in the remediation of contaminated soils. There are three general mechanisms by which rhizosphere may act to enhance co-metabolism of anthropogenic contaminants:

(i) Rhizosphere may allow selective enrichment of degrader organisms that have densities too low to significantly degrade xenobiotics in root-free soil.

(ii) The rhizosphere may enhance growth-linked metabolism or stimulate microbial growth by providing a natural substrate when the concentration of xenobiotics is low or unavailable.

(iii) Rhizosphere is rich in natural compounds that may induce cometabolism of xenobiotics in certain microorganisms that carry degradative genes or plasmids. This may permit initial degradation of xenobiotics that would otherwise be unavailable as carbon sources. Bioremediation including phyto- and rhizo-remediation is expected to be a useful clean-up method for soil contaminated with persistent organic pesticides including dieldrin and endrin (Matscumoto *et al.*, 2009).

Rhizosphere effects on xenobiotic biotransformation have been studied for a variety of compounds, although the mechanisms by which certain plants enhance biodegradation are still poorly understood. Research on *phytoremediation*, through trial and error, has focused on densely rooted, fast growing grasses and plants, such as *Brassica* sp., with fine root systems. Mulberry (*Morus alba* L.) and poplar (*Populus deltoides*) trees have been used successfully in the phytoremediation of chlorophenols and chlorinated solvents such as trichloroethylene (TCE). Salicylic acid, flavonoids, and monoterpenes are structurally analogous to many anthropogenic compounds in that they are small, mobile chemicals that are amenable to cellular uptake and may interact through signal transduction pathways to induce the production of specific degradative enzymes. Salicylic acid is an effective inducer of many different enzymes that may be involved in the cometabolism of xenobiotics such as polyaromatic hydrocarbons (PAHs) and PCBs. Degradation of xenobiotics by plants have been used in the phytoremediation of PAH contaminated soils, suggesting the involvement of rhizosphere microorganisms in PAH degradation. A microbial community-based approach may be useful for screening different plant chemicals to find inducers of xenobiotic-degrading enzymes. Bioremediation of lindane-contaminated soil with fungi like *P. chrysosporium* is possible. The use of filamentous fungal systems for bioremediation is more advantageous as compared to other microbes because of the following reasons:

(i) Fungi are in direct contact with solid, liquid, and vapour portions of the soil.

(ii) Fungi are capable of transforming a large number of structurally dissimilar compounds.

(iii) Fungi are able to withstand toxic effects of many xenobiotics.

(iv) Fungi release metabolites, making them available for further degradation by other microorganisms (Mougin *et al.*, 1996).

USE OF ENZYMES IN BIOREMEDIATION

There is potential to use enzymatic treatment in bioremediation. Advantages of enzymatic treatment over microbial bioremediation include (1) no requirement for acclimatization phase; (2) use over a wider range of environmental conditions (pH, moisture, temperature); (3) effectiveness at high and low pollutant concentrations; (4) movement of enzymes readily into soil micropores and their protection from inactivation; and (5) little effect of inhibitors of microbial metabolism on enzymes (Dec and Bollag, 2001). The enzymatic basis for pesticide bioremediation has been well reviewed (Colin *et al.*, 2008). Disadvantages of enzymatic treatment in bioremediation include high cost of isolation and storage, difficulty in maintaining enzyme stability, requirement for expensive cofactors, and lack of xenobiotic mineralization. Microbial enzymes with potential for pesticide metabolism include *oxidoreductases, hydroxylases, amidases*, and *esterases*. However, enzymatic treatments are not ideal for complete xenobiotic mineralization because mineralization usually requires many enzymes and several cofactors such as NAD(P)H and FAD.

Oxidoreductases, such as laccase, tyrosinase, and horseradish peroxidase can be used to decontaminate soil and water. These enzymes oxidize the substrate to free radicals, which are susceptible to chemical coupling, forming oligomers. For enzymatic treatment to be effective in bioremediation, enzymes must be stabilized. The most effective way to stabilize enzymes is by immobilization. Immobilization can be accomplished by enzyme linkage to organic or inorganic solid supports by adsorption on solid surfaces such as glass, entrapment in polymeric gels, encapsulation, or intermolecular cross-linking. Although preparing supports can be time-consuming and expensive, the support can generally be reused. Enzymatic treatment holds great promise in bioremediation of contaminated soil and water. Reductive dehalogenation (RDE), is the only significant mechanism for the breakdown of halogenated aromatic, aliphatic, and heterocyclic compounds like PCBs, TCE, hexachlorobenzene, and halogenated pesticides such as heptachlor and aldrin. In theory, certain micro-sites within the rhizosphere are favourable (anaerobic conditions, low redox potentials, and available electron acceptors) for RDE, thus facilitating the transformation of halogenated compounds. Spatial and temporal heterogeneity in O_2 distribution in the rhizosphere environment usually (but not always) provides microbes with localized environments that are anaerobic and have low redox potential, thereby favouring RDE reactions (Barkovskii, 2001). Moreover, most of the terminal electron acceptors, such as nitrate, ferric iron, sulphate, and quinones are abundant in the rhizosphere. The bioavailability of hydrophobic contaminants determines the rate of xenobiotic transformation and mineralization.

CONCLUSION

Technologies using microorganisms with extensive biodegradative capacities have been developed for use in both pollution prevention and site remediation. Bioremediation, the technology employing living organisms, especially microorganisms, for the removal of pollutants from the environment is one of the several technologies that may be applied. For bioremediation to be effective, the pollutant must be subject to microbial attack or microbial transformation, the metabolic product must be safe and the process must not cause adverse ecological side effects. Environmental conditions must permit *in situ* growth of the microorganism capable of bioremediation or transformation of the pollutant so that it can be biodegraded *ex situ* in bioreactors. By selecting an effective indigenous strain or by developing a recombinant pesticide degrading microorganism together with optimized environmental conditions, bioremediation becomes a cost effective and more ecofriendly approach for restoring environmental quality. In many cases, especially for pesticides which are being used today extensively for enhancing crop productivity, bioremediation can biodegrade, detoxify or immobilize hazardous pollutants and is becoming a widely used technology for environmental clean-up. Moreover, the use of biological control agents replacing (partially or completely) synthetic chemical pesticides under integrated pest management system (IPM) appears to be more helpful in minimizing environmental pollution.

REFERENCES

Alcalde, M., Ferrer, M., Plou, F.J. and Ballesteros, A. (2006). *Trends Biotechnol.*, **24**:281-287.

Atlas, M.R. and Bartha, R. (1998). *In*: Microbial Ecology, Fundamentals and Applications, IV edition, Benjamin/Cummings Science Publishing California, USA. pp. 511-555.

Baker, K.H. and Herson, D. S. (1994). *In: Bioremediation*. (Eds. Baker, K.H. and Herson, D.S.), McGraw-Hill, New York, pp. 1-7.

Barkovskii, A.L. (2001). *In:* Pesticide Biotransformation in Plants and Microorganisms: Similarities and Divergences. (Eds. J. C. Hall, R. E. Hoagland, and R. M. Zablotowicz), ACS Symposium Series 777.Washington, DC: American Chemical Society. pp. 40–56.

Barrett, M. (2000). *In:* Herbicides and Their Mechanisms of Action. (Eds. A. H. Cobbs and R. C. Kirkwood), Sheffield, Great Britain: Sheffield Academic. pp. 25–37.

Bumpus, J.A., Tien, M., Wright, D. and Aust, S.D. (1985). *Science*. **228** (4706) : 1434-1436.

Cassidy, M. B., Lee, H., Trevors, J. T. and Zablotowicz, R. M. (1999). *J. Ind. Microbiol. Biotechnol.* **23:** 232–241.

Chatterji, A.K. (2007). *In*: Introduction to environmental biotechnology, 2nd ed., Prentice-Hall of India Pvt. Ltd. India, pp. 124-144.

Chen, W. and Mulchandani, A. (1998). *Trends Biotechnol.* **16**: 71-76.

Colin, S., Pandey, G., Hartley, C.J., Jackson, C.J., Cheesmen, M.J., Taylor, M.C., Pandey, R., Khurana, J.L., Teese, M., Copping, C.W., Wein, K.M., Jain, R.K., Ruplal, Russel, R.J., and Oakeshott, J.G., (2008). *Indian J. Microbiol.,* **48**: 65-79.

Colleran, E. (1997). *In:* Methods in biotechnology– Bioremediation Protocols. (Eds. Sheehan, D.). Humana Press, NJ. pp. 3-22.

Dec, J. and Bollag, J. M. (2001). *In:* Pesticide Biotransformation in Plants and Microorganisms: Similarities and Divergences. (Eds. J. C. Hall, R. E. Hoagland, and R. M. Zablotowicz), ACS Symposium Series 777. Washington, DC: American Chemical Society. pp. 182–193.

Dolfing, J. and Harrison, B.K. (1993). *FEMS Microbiol.*, Ecol. **13**: 23-30.

Dubey, R. C. (2002). A Textbook of Biotechnology. S. Chand and Co. Ltd. New Delhi, India. pp 364-382.

Fathepure, B.Z, Youngers, G.A, Richter, D. L. and Downs, C.E. (1995). *In:* Bioremediation of chlorinated solvents. (Eds., R.E. Hinchee, A. Leeson, and L. Semprini), Batelle, Columbus, OH, US, pp.169-187.

Field, J.A., Stams, A. J. M., Kato, M. and Schraa, G. (1995). *Antonie van Leuwenhoek.* **67**: 47-77.

Gibson, D.T. and Sayler, G.S. (1992). Scientific foundation for bioremediation: Current status and future needs. American Academy of Microbiology, Washington, D.C.

Gothalwal, R and Bisen, P.S. (2002). *In:* Encyclopedia of Pest Management, Eds. David Pimentel, Marcel Dekker Inc., India.

Hall, J. C., J. S. Wickenden, and Yau, K.Y.F. (2001). *In:* Pesticide Biotransformation in Plants and Microorganisms: Similarities and Divergences. (Eds. J. C. Hall, R. E. Hoagland, and R. M. Zablotowicz), Washington, DC: American Chemical Society. pp. 89–118.

Hatzios, K. K. (1997). *In:* Regulation of Enzymatic Systems Detoxifying Xenobiotics in Plants. NATO ASI Series. Zablotowicz, (Eds). Pesticide Biotransformation in Plants and Microorganisms: Similarities and Divergences. K. K. Hatzios, (Ed.), Washington, DC: American Chemical Society. pp. 275–288.

Hinchee, R. E., Miller, R. N. and Johnson, P. C. (1995). *In situ* aeration: air sparging, bioventing and related remediation processes, Battelle Press, Columbus, Ohio.

Hoagland, R. E. and Zablotowicz, R. M. (2001). *In:* Pesticide Biotransformation in Plants and Microorganisms: Similarities and Divergences. (Eds. J. C. Hall, R. E. Hoagland, and R. M. Zablotowicz), ACS Symposium Series 777. Washington, DC: American Chemical Society. pp. 58–88.

Jorgensen, K.S. (2007). *Adv. Appl. Microbiol.* **61**: 285-305.

Joshi, D. K. and Gold, M. H. (1993). *Appl. Environ. Microbiol.* **59**: 1779-1785.

Kim, S. K., Makino, K., Amemura, M., Shinagawa, H. and Nakata, A. (1993). *J. Bacteriol.* **175**: 1316–1324.

Mateen A., Chapalamadugu, S., Kaskar, B., Bhatti, A. R., and Chaudhry, G. R. (1994). *In:* Biological degradation and bioremediation of toxic chemicals. G. R. Chaudhry (Eds.), Dioscorides Press, Portland, Oreg. pp. 198-233.

Matsumoto, E., Kawanka, Y., Yun, S. and Oyaizu, H. (2009). *Appl. Microbiol. Biotechnol.,* **84** :205-216.

Mougin, C., Pericaud, C., Malosse, C., Laugero, C. and Asther, M. (1996). *Pestic. Sci.* **47**:51–59.

Pothuluri, J. V., Hinson, J. A. and Cerniglia, C. E. (1991). *J. Environ. Qual.* **20:** 330–347.

Saha, L.R. and Dhaliwal, G.S. (2006). Handbook of plant protection, 2nd ed., pp. 59-102.

Shimabukuro, R.H. (1985). *In:* Weed Physiology. S. O. Duke, (Eds.) Vol. 2. Boca Raton, FL: CRC Press. pp. 215–240.

Skidmore, M.W., Paulson, G.D., Kuiper, H.A., Ohlin, B. and Reynolds, S. (1998). *Pure Appl. Chem.* **70:** 1423–1447.

USEPA. (2006). *In situ* and *Ex situ* biodegradation technologies for remediation of contaminated sites. EPA/625/R-06/015. http://www.epa.gov/nrmrl/pubs/625r06015/625r06015.pdf.

Wackett, L.P., Sadowsky, M.J., Martinez, B., and Shapir, N. (2002). *App. Microbiol. Biotechnol.* **58**(1): 39-45.

3

Microbial Biodegradation—An Approach to Remediate Industrial Plastic Waste

Ravindra Soni and Reeta Goel
Department of Microbiology, CBSH,
G.B. Pant University of Agriculture & Technology, Pantnagar-263 145, India
E-mail: rg55@rediffmail.com

It is not as if only large industries depend on plastics for their sustenance, small homes too extensively use plastic materials. Plastics are disadvantageous as they are resistant to biodegradation, thus leading to pollution and harmful to the natural environment. The widespread use and high volume conception of plastic mainly in industries obviously results in generation of large amount of waste amounting for more than 30 percent of total waste generated in urban societies. The degradation of polymers may proceed by one or more mechanisms, including microbial degradation in which microorganisms such as fungi and bacteria can degrade the material. Research on plastic biodegradation depicted that it can be biodegraded if the right microbial consortium is used.

INTRODUCTION

There is a single voice coming from each corner of the earth that "Avoid plastic based material, use less plastics". Governments of several countries of the world have already banned the use of polythene bags. Now question arises that why plastic is so popular among the new generation and what can be the alternative to this most utilized polymer? An attempt is hereby made to answer these questions in most satisfactory way.

THE WORLD OF PLASTIC AND POLYMER

Poly means *many*, which is translated to accumulation of units. Polymers are therefore a collection of smaller units into many linked units. A polymer can be very large, ranging from few thousands to million units. This small unit, which we are going to refer to as the base unit, is called the monomer. These base units join together to form a polymer. Plastic refers to man-made polymer materials (Scott, 1999).

The official definition of plastics is any or numerous organic, synthetic or processes materials of high molecular weight capable of being molded. There are different types of plastic (polymeric) materials; some are natural, other are man-made.

These polymers consist of long chains without any cross linkages between the chains viz., polyethylene, polypropylene, polyvinyl chloride, and polystyrene etc (Allen, 1995). Generally, polymer is a compound of high molecular mass, which is made up by the addition of a large number of molecules by subjecting them to heat and/or pressure, and defined as polymerization. Polymerization is mainly of two types i.e., addition and condensation.

Big Six

Different monomers were used to make polymers having different characteristics. Today, over 6000 plastic products are known. The application of these products range from frying pan coating to space shuttle consul. The majority of polymer products are produced from six major stock polymers:

1. High Density Polyethylene (HDPE)
2. Low Density Polyethylene (LDPE)
3. Polypropylene (PP)
4. Polystyrene (PS)
5. Polyurethane (PU)
6. Polyethylene terephthalate (PET or PETE)

The "Big Six" plastics are all thermoplastics, i.e., they can be melted and shaped to whatever is desired, and they all tend to be flexible. Three of them, LDPE, HDPE, and polypropylene have both crystalline and amorphous regions. The crystalline regions with the structural regularity impart toughness and resistance to mechanical abrasion and this makes them opaque.

Polyethylene: The Most Common Plastic

Ethylene is made up from petroleum. At room temperature and pressure, ethylene gas can be made to react using a special catalyst.

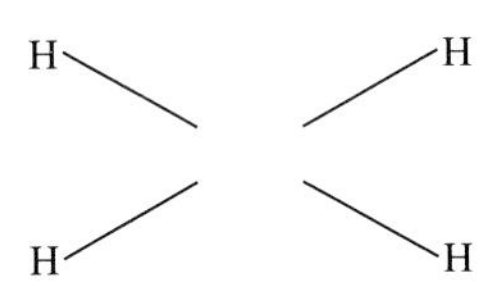

Fig. 3.1 Ethylene molecule.

Ethylene contains a sigma (single) bond and a Pi bond between the two carbon atoms (Fig. 3.1). This combination of bonds makes the molecule reactive. Where ethylene reacts to form polymer, the double bond is converted to single bonds.

Low and High Density Polyethylene: Chain Branching

Low density means less mass per volume and high density indicates more mass per volume.

$$\text{Density (D)} = \text{mass (g)/volume (ml)}$$

In polyethylene, if we can get more strands (polymer chain) per given volume, we get the LDPE (Low Density Polyethylene). It was observed that a branched polyethylene can be made, which produces branching of the molecule as tree trunks (Fig. 3.2). This is the product that has a soft, clear, plastic that is used for grocery bags and other shopping bags, etc.

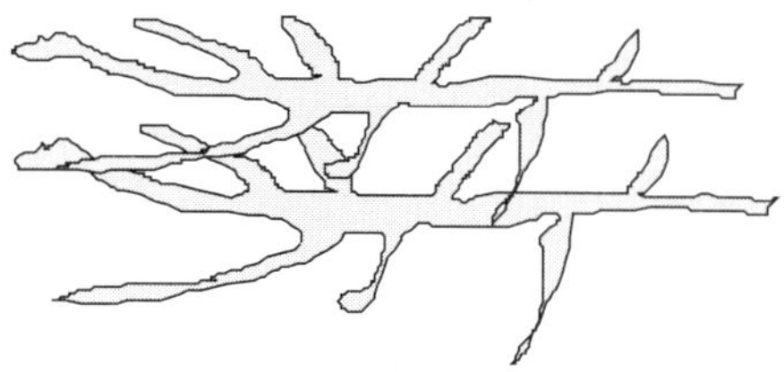

Fig. 3.2 LDPE, a branched polyethylene.

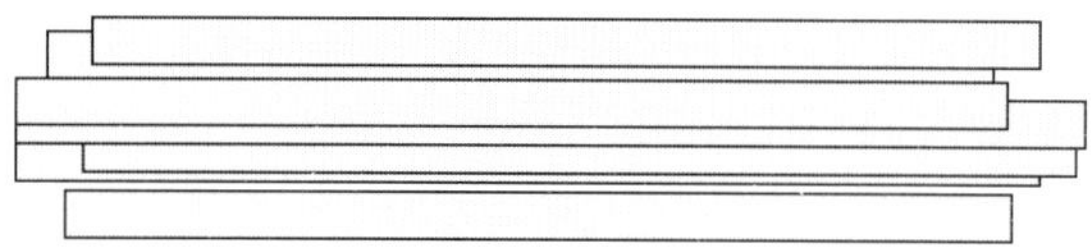

Fig. 3.3 HDPE, a unbranched polyethylene.

High Density Polyethylene (HDPE) is the other type of polyethylene polymer. In this type of polymer the strands are not branched (Fig. 3.3). They are cleanly stacked to give more strands (polymer chain) per volume. Polyethylene represents 64% of the produced synthetic plastics, which is produced in approximately equal amounts of high-density polyethylene (HDPE) and low-density polyethylene (LDPE) (Gadd, 1992; Chain, 1992).

PROPERTIES OF PLASTICS

It is the uniqueness and distinctiveness in the properties and characteristics of plastics that spurs their use in various fields. Plastic exhibits wide range of properties. Some of these properties, in turn, are due to the following:

1. The length of the chain (the number of monomer units).
2. The three-dimensional arrangement of the chain in the solid.
3. The branching of the chain.
4. The chemical composition of the monomer units.
5. The bonding between the chain.
6. The orientation of the monomer units within the chain (www.mhhe.com/chemistry/text9.htm).

APPLICATIONS OF PLASTICS

Plastics are the raw materials for various key industries as analyzed individually in the following paragraphs:

Building and Construction Industry

The use of plastics in this sector abounds in plumbing fixtures, siding, flooring, insulation, panels, doors, windows, glazing, bathroom units, gratings, railings and a growing list of both structural and interior and/or decorative purposes.

Electronics

In almost all electrical and electronic uses, plastics are playing one role or the other and lending safety and cost effectiveness. Lightweight, durable, attractive and cost-effective plastics are used in nearly all the small appliances, including coffee makers, irons, mixers, can openers, hair dryers and shavers. Bigger appliances such as microwave ovens and food processors also use plastic components. All refrigerators today are insulated with thermal-efficient plastic foam, and their interiors are made up of durable, easy to-clean plastics.

Packaging

Plastics are often the answer and sometimes the only answer to packaging problems. They are capable of meeting all kinds of packaging needs. Plastics are available in different forms and each form offers different qualities. Rigid plastics can be chosen when protection is needed and flexible plastics when convenience is paramount.

Transportation

On land, sea, in the air and space, plastics are on the move. Plastics are used in everything from automobiles and light trucks to trailers and motorcycles, from marine craft and canoes to minesweepers and trains, from buses and air planes to space shuttles.

Aeronautics

During the past 50 years, the aeronautics technology has soared and plastics have played a major role in this.

Extensive Application in Households

It is not as if only large industries depend on plastics for their sustenance, small homes too extensively use plastic materials. Plastics may help domestic households, save energy, and thereby economise on their heating and cooling bills (www.plasticindustry.org/industry).

These widespread applications are not only due to their favourable mechanical and thermal properties, but also due to stability and durability of plastics, which make them suitable for many applications (Witt *et al.*, 1997). Plastics have use in all sectors of the economy—infrastructure, construction, agriculture, consumer goods, telecommunications and packaging (Tang *et al.*, 2003).

Ecological Impact of Plastic Waste

Plastics are disadvantageous as they are resistant to biodegradation thus leading to pollution, and are therefore harmful to the natural environment (Kathiresan, 2003). The widespread use and high volume conception of plastic mainly in industries obviously results in generation of large amount of waste accounting for more than 30 per cent of the total waste generated in urban societies (*The Hindu*, 2003). Plastics are so versatile in their use that their impact on the environment is extremely wide ranging (Tang *et al.*, 2003). There are 3 places where plastics wastes can end up—in landfills, incinerators and/ or elsewhere. The pollution that occurs in the disposal stage is largely during incineration and when plastic wastes fail to reach landfills or incinerator. Given the limited re-cyclability of plastics, a large amount of plastic wastes is burnt in incinerators. Even in the villages in India, plastic and other portions of the wastes are frequently burnt in backyard fires. But burning of these chlorine containing substances releases toxic heavy metal(s) and emits noxious gases like dioxins and furans. The latter two are the most toxic and poisonous substances on the earth and can cause a variety of health problems including damage to the reproductive, respiratory, and immune systems. In fact, dioxin has been shown to have hormonal activity and is an endocrine disruptor (Chaturvedi, 2002). Plastic waste disposal by burying it in the soil is also not a safe option as it blocks the natural supply of air and water to the soil. It directly affects plant life and may become a cause for landslides in mountainous regions. It also reduces water retaining capacity of the soil and hence affects the water level (Harsha, 2001).

The polythene is the most common solid waste that has been recently recognized as a major threat to marine life. The polythene could sometimes cause blockage in the intestines of fish, birds and marine mammals (Spear *et al.*, 1995; Secchi and Zarzur, 1999). Degradation of polythene is a great challenge as the materials are increasingly used. A general estimate of worldwide plastic waste generation is annually about 57 million tonnes (Bollag *et al.*, 2000).

Recycling has emerged as the most practical method to deal with this problem, yet the difficulty of sorting wide variety of plastics and the changes in the material over time showed considerable disadvantages. Besides the new technology for recycling is more expensive than the existing one (Fiecther, 1990; Becerra, 1998; Griffin, 1994). Thus designing ecofriendly biodegradable plastic is the need of hour. The successful production and marketing of biodegradable plastics will help to alleviate the problems of environmental pollution. In the past 10 years, several biodegradable plastics have been introduced into the market, however, none is efficiently biodegradable in landfills (Anonymous, 1999).

BIODEGRADATION OF POLYTHENE

Biodegradation

Biodegradation is considered a subset of degradation, which is defined here as any physical or chemical change in a material caused by any environmental factor, including light, heat, moisture, wind, chemical conditions and/or biological activity.

Polyethylene and its Biodegradation

The field tests burying plastic samples in soil have been widely conducted for their biodegradation because of the similarity to actual conditions of use or disposal. The degradation of polymers may proceed by one or more mechanisms, including microbial degradation in which microorganisms such as fungi and bacteria can degrade the material. The degradation mechanisms vary depending on the polymers environment and desired applications. The biodegradability of plastics is desirable to be estimated in natural environment, where the wasted plastics are exposed as such (Orhan *et al.*, 2004). The growth of microorganisms on plastic polymers can be related to their capability to cause changes in the polymer molecular weight and some of their measurable physical and chemical properties (Gadd, 1992).

From a chemical perspective, we would expect polyethylene to be biodegradable, as linear alkenes are usually subject to biodegradation. However, for polyethylene, there is an inverse relationship between the molecular weight and biodegradability. Linear hydrocarbon oligomers with molecular weights lower than 620 support microbial growth, while those having higher molecular weights are not utilized (Haines and Alexander, 1974). It is widely accepted that the resistance of polyethylene to biodegradation is correlated from its high molecular weight, three-dimensional structure and hydrophobic nature, all of which interfere with its availability to microorganisms. Nevertheless, several studies have demonstrated partial biodegradation of polyethylene after U.V. irradiation (Cornell *et al.*, 1984), thermal treatment (Albertsson *et al.*, 1998; Volle-Speclveda *et al.*, 2002), physico-chemical treatment (Manzur *et al.*, 2004), and oxidation with nitric acid (Brown *et al.*, 1974). Furthermore, a synergistic effect has also been found between photo-oxidation and biodegradation of polyethylene. Apparently, the biodegradation of polyethylene is enhanced by oxidation pretreatment, which increases surface hydrophilicity by the formation of carbonyl groups that can be utilized by microorganisms (Albertsson 1978, 1980; Cornell *et al.*, 1984).

Biodegradation may be resulting from the utilization of polyethylene as a nutrient (i.e. a carbon source) which can be more efficient if the degrading microorganism forms a biofilm on the polyethylene surface. However, the hydrophobicity of the polyethylene interferes with the formation of a microbial biofilm. Attempts to facilitate colonization of polyethylene by adding non-ionic surfactants to the culture medium promoted the biodegradation of polyethylene (Albertsson *et al.*, 1993; Ehara *et al.*, 2000). Presumably, the surfactant increased the hydrophilicity of the polyethylene surface and thus facilitated the adhesion of bacteria to the polymer.

Role of Plasticizers

Plasticizers are added to polyethylene to enhance its biodegradability. With the aim of decreasing the plastic wastes in the environment, additive like polyamides, polyester, polysulfone and polycarbonate, different starches, adipate are added to LDPE matrix, which aid in obtaining partially biodegradable product (Nakamura *et al.*, 2005).

Role of Temperature

Lotto *et al.* (2005) studied the correlation of biodegradation rate and temperature. In most of the cases, higher temperature accelerates the rate of biodegradation, and the biodegradation was found to be greater at 46°C than at room temperature (24°C). Hadad *et al.* (2005) reported thermophilic bacteria, *Brevibacillus borstelensis* strain 707, which can degrade the low density polythene. They further confirmed that this organism used LDPE as the sole carbon source.

Techniques to Detect Biodegradation of Polyethylene

To detect morphological and structural changes in polymers, some physico-chemical (thermal analysis, X-ray diffraction, gel permeation chromatography) and spectroscopic (infrared and Raman spectroscopy, nuclear magnetic resonance and mass spectroscopy) methods are commonly being used in literature (Volke-Spulveda *et al.*, 1999).

Our Ongoing Efforts

To reduce the load of plastic waste on the environment, two main efforts have generally been pursued: one is to synthesize biodegradable plastics and the other to isolate selected microorganisms to biodegrade plastic wastes. Different strains have been isolated that have the biopotential to degrade various plastic based polymers. These bacterial isolates are listed in Table 3.1 and research is going on at Microbiology Department of G.B. Pant University of Agriculture and Technology, Pantnagar, and will be discussed in the coming paragraphs.

Table 3.1 Different strains and their characterized biopotential at Pantnagar

Name of the strains	*Biopotential*
Arthrobacter strain zzCNA2	Polycarbonate
Enterobacter strain LNA3	Polycarbonate
Acinetobacter sp strain GB1	Polysulfone
Sphingobacterium sp. strain GB2	Polysulfone
Bacillus pumilus strain S2	LDPE-g-PMH and LDPE-g-PMMA.
B. cereus strain PN15	LDPE-g-PMH and LDPE-g-PMMA.
Arthrobacter luteolus strain LNR3	LDPE
Bacterium Te68R strain PN12	LDPE
Bacillus cereus strain R GR10	LDPE

Degradation of Polycarbonate

Two bacterial strains that are identified as *Arthrobacter* strain CNA2 (Ac.No.DQ205429) and *Enterobacter* strain LNA3 (Ac.No.DQ205431) have shown their ability to utilized polycarbonate as a carbon source in 1/10 diluted nutrient agar medium. Both the strains can tolerate polycarbonate up to a concentration of 5-10 mg/ml, respectively. Thin layer chromatography (TLC) and λ max determination of degraded and undegraded compound shows that polycarbonate gets biodegraded with the formation of some new products. The red shift in λ max (243-279 nm) is due to the formation of phenolic and carboxylic compounds (Fig. 3.4).

Degradation of Polycarbonate

Acinetobacter sp. strain GB1 (Accession No.DQ118019) and *Sphingobacterium* sp. strain GB2 (Acc. No. DQ118020) were able to degrade polysulfone in 1/10 diluted nutrient agar medium. Both GB1 and GB2 were showing maximum degradation activities at concentration of 2 and 8 mg/ml of polysulfone, respectively. The results were also confirmed with TLC and λ max determination (Fig. 3.5).

Biodegradation Study for Grafted Polyester and Polyamide of Low Density Polyethylene

The isolates have been screened for their tolerance towards grafted polymer of LDPE such as LDPE-g-PMH and LDPE-g-PMMA. Strain identification for polymer degradation shows that the two strains, *Bacillus pumilus* strain S2 (Acc. No. DQ209209) and *B. cereus* strain PN15 (DQ209210) have the capacity to degrade the above-mentioned polymers (Fig. 3.6). Among these isolates, *Bacillus pumilus* had maximum tolerance towards all the three polymers (10 mg/ml).

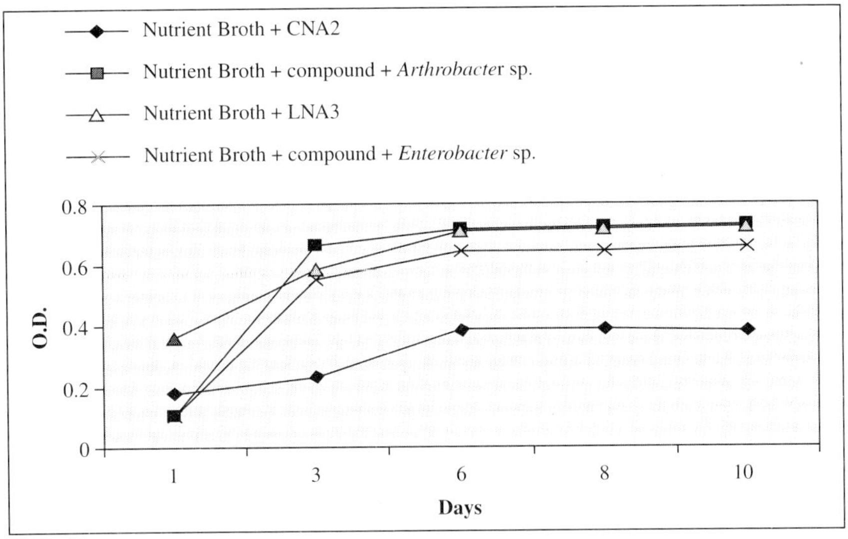

Fig. 3.4 Growth of *Arthrobacter* sp. and *Enterobacter* sp. in the presence of polycarbonate (Kusumlata, 2004).

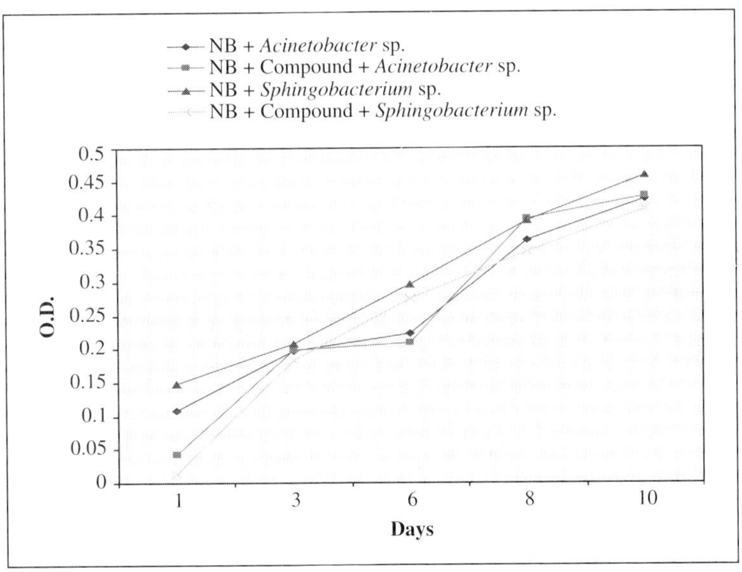

Fig. 3.5 Growth of *Acinetobacter* sp. and *Sphingobacterium* sp. in the presence of polysulfone.

The *in vitro* degradation studies conducted for a trial period of 11 days have shown *Bacillus pumilus* as an ideal candidate for degradation of polyester and polyamide. These results were further evident when FTIR spectra of undegraded polymers were compared with spectra of degraded polymers (Fig. 3.6).

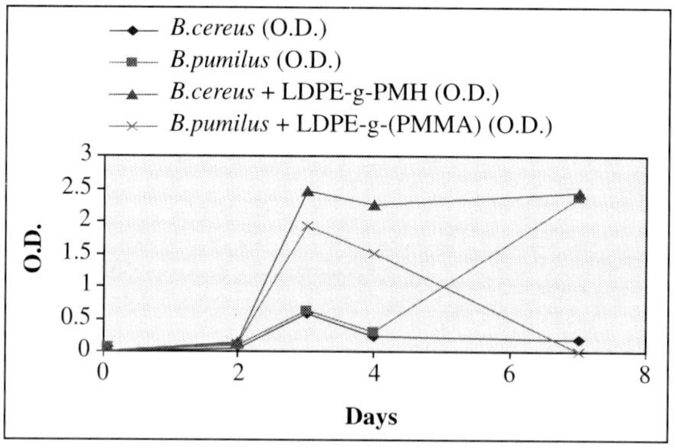

Fig. 3.6 Growth of *Bacillus pumilus* and *Bacillus cereus* in the presence of LDPE-g-PMMA & LDPE–g-PMH respectively (Sarita Kumari, 2005).

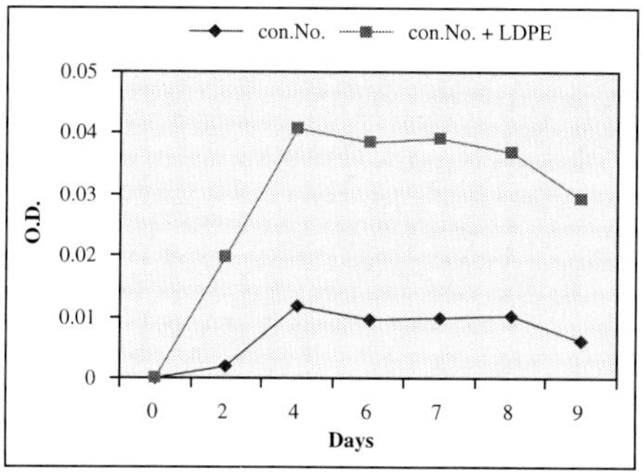

Fig. 3.7 Growth of consortium in the presence of low density polythene (Soni, 2006).

Moreover, a consortium was developed and used to degrade the low density polyethylene (LDPE) too (Fig. 3.7). Later all the strains were characterized as *Arthrobacter luteolus* strain LNR3 (DQ486130), *Bacterium Te68R* strain PN12 (DQ423487) and *Bacillus cereus* strain RGR10 (DQ423486). These results are also supported by comparative FTIR spectra and thermal gravimetric analysis of the biodegraded LDPE in references to control undegraded LDPE.

In FTIR spectra, significant shifting in CH_2 stretching and C-O stretching frequencies was observed due to microbial degradation of LDPE. LDPE did not show any C-O stretching frequency, whereas its biodegradation in the presence of all consortium showed C-O stretching frequency at $1161 cm^{-1}$ (Fig. 3.8).

Thermal analysis data of the microbially degraded LDPE with reference to pure LDPE as control is summarized in Table 3.2. The consortium has intensified the decomposition of LDPE to 21.7 % weight loss with greater number of DTG peak temperature (400°C) at lower rates (Figs. 3.9 and 3.10).

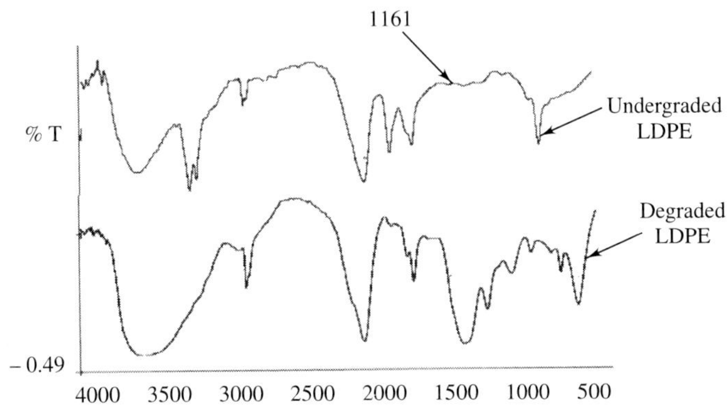

Fig. 3.8 FTIR spectra of degraded and undegraded LDPE by consortium (Soni, 2006).

Table 3.2 Thermal data of the microbially degraded LDPE with reference to pure LDPE

Sample	*DTG*		*DTA*				*TG Wt.*
Name	*Peak Temp.*		*Exotherm*		*ΔH*		*loss(%) at*
	Cel	*rate*	*Cel*	*mJ/min*	*Cel*	*mJ/min*	*400°C*
LDPE	451	1.79 mg/min	457	14.6	107	129	4.5
					467	53	
LDPE	43	93.5 g/min			44	42.7	
	177	29.5 g/min			118	6.66	21.7
	438	38 μg/min			176	17.1	
	527	25.8 μg/min					

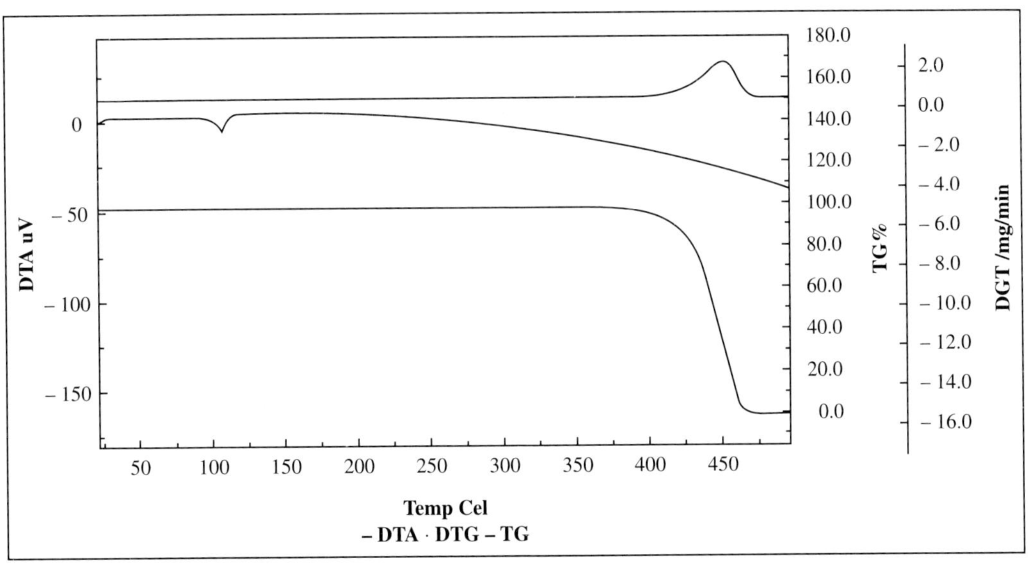

Fig. 3.9 Thermal analysis of pure LDPE.

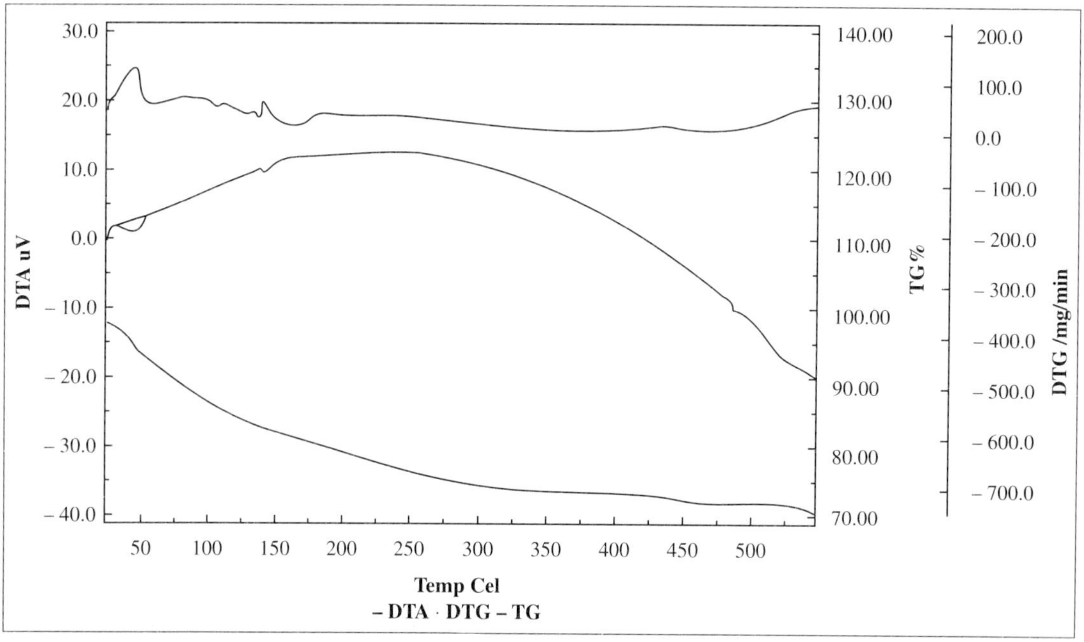

Fig. 3.10 Thermal analysis of biodegraded LDPE (dissolved in growth medium) with consortium.

CONCLUSION

At last, as we all know that several industries, mainly the plastic based industries, create a huge amount of plastic waste that is either disposed of with effluents or as solid waste, thus creating pollution in the environment. It is clear from the above discussed content that the only eco-friendly way to get rid of this industrial and other plastic waste is the use of microorganisms. The selection of strains or a group of strains (consortium), which have the potential to completely degrade the plastic, is the need of hour. With more and more research on plastic biodegradation, environmental pollution caused by non-biodegradable plastics could be reduced.

ACKNOWLEDGEMENTS

This work is supported by DBT grant to R.G. We also thank CDRI, Lucknow, IIT Roorkee and NCCS, Pune for FTIR DTA-DTG-TG and 16S rRNA sequencing, respectively.

REFERENCES

Albertsson, A.C., Sares, C. and Karlsson, S. (1993). *Acta Polymerica.* **44:** 243-246.

Albertsson, A.C. (1978). *J. App. Poly. Sci.* **22:** 3419-3433.

Albertsson, A.C. (1980). *Eur. Por. J.* **16:** 623-630.

Albertsson, A.C. Andersson, S.O. and Karlsson, S. (1998). *Poly. Degrade. Stability.* **18:** 73-87.

Allen, A.B., Hilliard, N.P., and Howard, G.T. (1999). *Int. Biodeterioration & Biodegradation* **43**:37-41.

Amass, W., Amass, A. and Tighe, B. (1998). *Polymer International*. **47**: 89-144.

Anonymous, (1999). *Report by Chem Risk-A service of Mclaren hart Inc. Ohio*. pp. 14.

Becerra, E. (1998). (http://www.bact.bact.wisc.edu/sciencesEd/BacterialPlastics.html).

Bergey's Manual of Determinative Bacteriology (Eleventh Edition). (2001). (Eds. Holt, J.G., Krieg, N.R., Sneath, P.H.A., Staley, J.T. and Williams, S.T.) Williams & Wilkins: A Waverly Company.

Bollag, W.B., Jerzy, Dec and Bollag, J.M. (2000). *In. J. leaderberg* (ed.) Academic, New York pp. 461-471.

Chaturvedi, B. (2002). Director, Chintan Environmental Organization in New Delhi, made this letter available to Environment (Centre for Civil Society).

Chain, R.B. (1992). *In*: Microbial Control of Pollution; (Eds. Fry, J.C., Gadd, G.M., Herbert, R.A., Jones, C. W. and Watson-Craik, I.A.,) Cambridge University Press: Cambridge, pp. 293.

Cornell, J.H., Kaplan, A.M. and Rogers, M.R. (1984). *J. App. Poly. Sci.* **29:** 2581-2597.

Crabbe, J.R., Campbell, J.R., Thompson, L., Walz, S.L. and Schultz, W.W. (1994) *Int. Biodeterioraion & Biodegradation*. **33:** 103-113.

Ehara, K., Lioyshi, Y., Tsutsumi, Y. and Nishida, T. (2000). *Journal of wood Science* **46:** 180-183.

Ferguson, J.D., Weimer, A.W. and George, S.M. (2004). *Chem. Mater.* **16:** 5602-5609.

Fiechter, A. (1990). Plastics from bacteria and for bacteria: poly (β-hydroxyalkauoetcs) as natural, biocompatible and biodegradable polyesters. pp. 77-93.

Gadd, J.C., Herbert, G.M., Jones, R.A., Watson-Craik, I.A., (1992). Cambridge UniversityPress: Cambridge, pp. 293.

Griffin, G. L. (1994). *Chemistry and technology of biodegradable polymers*. Ist ed. London: Blackie Academic and Professional.

Hadad, D., Geresh, S. and Sian, A. (2005). *J. Appl. Microbiol.* **98:** 1093-1100.

Haines, J. R. and Alexander, M. (1974). *Appl. Microbio.* **28:** 1084.

Harsha, T.P. (2001). *Plastic problems*. CEE-NFS. Vol. 02. (http://www.americanplasticscouncil.org/s_apc/docs/1700/1678.pdf) American Plastics Council Year End Statistics for 2004.

Kathiresan (2003). *Rev. Biol. Trop.* **51(3):** 629-634.

Kusumlata, (2004). *Thesis G.B. Pant University of Agriculture &. Technology, Pantnagar, India.*

Lotto, N. T., Calil, M.R., Guedes, C.G.F. and Rosa, D.S. (2005). *Material Science and Engineering*. (In press).

Malik and Pryank Jain. "*Carbon and Its Compounds*" (Third Edition). Essentials of sciences. Dhanpat Rai Publishing Company (P) Ltd, pp.391.

Manzur, A., Limon-Gonzalez, M., and Favela-Torres, E. (2004). *J. Appl. Pol. Sci.* **92:** 265-271.

Nakamura, E.N., Cordi, L., Almediar, G.S.G., Duran, N. and Mei, L.H.I. (2005). *J. Mat. Proc. Tech.* **27:** 489-492.

Orhan Y., Hrenoviae, A. J. and Kgungora H. B. (2004). *Acta Chim. Slov.* **51:** 579-588.

Sarita K. (2005). M.Sc. Thesis G.B. Pant University of Agriculture and Technology, Pantnagar, India.

Scott, G. (1999). *In: Polymers and the Environment*. The Royal Society of Chemistry, Cambridge, UK.

Secchi, M.E.R. and Zarzur, S. (1999). *Aquat. Mammal* **25(1):** 21-24.

Shivram, (2001). International Symposium on Biodegradable Polymers *on* 17th Nov. 2001, at IICT, Hyderabad.

Soni, R. (2006). M.Sc. Thesis G.B. Pant University of agriculture and technology, Pantnagar, India.

Spear, L.B., Ainley, D.G. and Ribii, C.A. (1995). *Mar. Environmen. Res.* **40:** 123-141.

Tang, Y.W., Labow, R.S. and Santerre, J.P. (2003). *Biomaterials.* **24(12)**: 2003-2011.

The Hindu (2003). God's own plastic wasteland. Online Edition of India's National Newspaper. 05 Jun.

Volke-Spulveda, T. (1999). *J. Appl. Pol. Sci.* **79:** 1435-1440.

Vollee-Speclveda, T., Sauccdo-Castaneda, G., Gutrierrez-Rojas, M., Manzur, A. and Favela-Torres, E. 2002. *J. App. Poly. Sci.* **83:** 305-314.

Witt, V., Muller, R.J. and Klein, J. (1997). 15BN, 3-00-0015299. www.mhhe.com/chemistry/text9.html. www.plasticindustry.org/industry

Zheng, Y., Ernest, K.Y. and Bassi, A.S. (2005). *Crit. Revi. Biotechnol.* **25:** 243-250.

4

Lichen Biodeterioration Studies in India: An Overview

Rajesh Bajpai, D.K. Upreti,[1] S. Nayaka[1] and S.K. Dwivedi

Department of Environmental Science, B. B. A. University, Lucknow-226 025, India

[1]Lichenology Laboratory, National Botanical Research Institute (CSIR), Lucknow-226001, India

E-mail: upretidk@rediffmail.com

Biodeterioration may be defined as any undesirable change in the properties of a material caused by the vital activities of living organisms. Biodeterioration of stone monuments and buildings is a well recognized problem in tropical regions, where environmental factors such as high temperature, high relative humidity levels, and heavy rainfall favor the growth and sustenance of a wide variety of living organisms on stone surfaces. The organisms that are capable of causing biodeterioration are called biodeteriogens. These organisms can cause direct or indirect damage to many kinds of stone monuments, lichens are one of them. In Indian context, in the last two decades, a fairly good number of research work was carried out dealing with lichen growth on monuments and historical buildings. The account of lichens growing on the monuments in the states of Karnataka, Madhya Pradesh, Orissa and Uttar Pradesh is available. In the present overview, an attempt has been made to elucidate and compile the information available on the lichen taxa growing on different monuments and buildings of India and causing damage to their surfaces.

INTRODUCTION

As the earliest colonizers of terrestrial habitats on the earth, lichens are amongst the most successful forms of symbiosis (Galloway, 1994; Seaward, 1997). It is estimated that around 8% of the terrestrial surface of the earth is covered by lichen-dominated vegetation (Larson, 1987). According to Ahmadjian (1993), a lichen may be described as "an association between a fungus, usually an ascomycetes but in a few cases a basidiomycetes or deuteromycetes, and one or more photosynthetic partners, generally green alga or cyanobacteria. In lichens, the fungus forms a thallus or lichenized stroma that may contain unique secondary compounds. The role of the alga in the lichen partnership is producing food for itself and its partner, the fungus. The fungi in a lichen partnership cannot live independently. The fungus partner is able to obtain and hold water, which is essential for every living thing. The mycobiont is firmly attached to phycobiont and cannot be easily washed away by water or blown by wind. Though fungi are generally deteriorative, yet in the lichens they do not destroy the algal partner. Instead, they obtain their nourishment from the algae without destroying them.

Due to this peculiar physiology, lichens are eminently successful and enjoy a worldwide distribution. They occur in every conceivable habitat, growing on a variety of substrata, including most natural substrata as well as a host of human manipulated or manufactured substrata. Common natural substrata include all categories of rock (saxicolous), bark (corticolous), wood (lignicolous), soil (terricolous) and evergreen leaves (folicolous). Common man-made substrata supporting lichens include rubber, plastics, glass, stone work, concrete, plaster, ceramic, tiles, brick and various types of metals.

The lichens occupying rocks as their substrates, generally known as saxicolous species, can be divided into three distinct groups: crustose, foliose and fruticose, on the basis of modes of attachment to the substrates (Jones and Wilson, 1985). Crustose lichens may be subdivided into epilithic (living on the surface of the rock) and endolithic (living in the interior of the rock) types. The latter may differ by mode of entry; cryptoendolithic forms occupy structural cavities and chasmoendolithic forms inhibit fissures and cracks within rocks, while euendolithic forms actively bore into rocks (Golubic *et al.,* 1981; Bell, 1993).

Throughout the history, humans have used the most beautiful and durable stones for building monumental buildings. The use of stone as a medium for artistic expression has ranged from the construction of ancient monuments, historical buildings to small-scale statues. While the weathering of rock for soil formation is unquestionably essential for the evolution of life on the earth, the decay of culturally significant stone artifacts represents an irretrievable loss of our heritage, monuments and history. The wind, sunlight and temperature as well as rain, snow and moisture are the agents that induce both physical and chemical weathering processes. The first affects the stability of the rock substratum, while the second acts through chemical corrosion of the stone-forming minerals, such as oxidation and hydration reactions as well as dissolution of carbonates and solubilization of some elements from silicate bearing minerals. Mankind, as part of the natural environment, contributes to the decay of exposed monumental stone materials. Air pollution resulting from anthropogenic sources such as electric utilities, domestic heating, road and air transportation has increased the atmospheric concentration of inorganic and organic compounds in the form of gases, aerosols or particulate matter and their deposition on stone surfaces. The complex physical and chemical interactions of these agents with the mineral material have dramatically accelerated the decay of building stones (Arnold, 1981; 1993; Johanson *et al.,* 1988; Rodriques, 1991; Baedecker and Reddy, 1993).

In addition, the negligence of historic sites and their consequent deterioration and improper restoration and conservation treatments have aggravated the preservation of cultural properties worldwide (Charola, 1993). A considerable number of investigations have begun to elucidate the essential role biological agents play in the deterioration of monumental stone (Paine *et al.,* 1993; Strzelczyk, 1981; Caneva and Salvadori, 1989). Physical, chemical and biological agents act in co-association, ranging from synergistic to antagonistic to deteriorate monumental stone (Valentin, 1993).

LICHEN BIODETERIORATION STUDIES IN INDIA

The investigation of lichens and monuments in India has been initiated recently. It was Gayathri (1980), who for the first time described the effects of lichens on granite statues in India. Singh and Upreti (1991) provided a detailed account of lichens growing on different monuments of Lucknow city and listed the occurrence of eleven species of lichens found growing on different monuments and historical buildings. Singh and Dhawan (1991) studied the qualitative assessment of damage caused by three lichen species to a 16th century monument, Yogarsimha Swami temple, Baggavalli, Karnataka.

Bajpai *et al.* (1992) suggested a technique for investigating the effect of biocides on lichens. The technique is based on the measurement of the total number of ultra weak photons emitted by living systems in the visible range. The individual organism, such as thalli of algae, fungi and lichens or any part of it or of other group of plants in the form of living tissues emit ultra weak photons, the flux of which exhibits an interesting structure lasting for a few minutes. The structure, a light induced and reproducible, can characterize the metabolic activities of a system. It can thus be used to quantify the efficiency of various biocides on different organisms. Singh and Sinha (1993) provided a detailed account of the corrosion of natural and monumental stone with special reference to lichens, the kind of rock damage, together with the list of lichen substances.

Chatterjee *et al.* (1995) enumerated 18 genera and 40 species of lichens from some Indian monuments in Karnataka and Orissa, and mentioned the taxonomic account and key for their identification. The monuments exhibit a distributional pattern of lichens depending on the microclimate created at different niches by their architectural designs.

Bajpai *et al.* (1999) studied the effect of some biocides (Butachlor and Propachlor) on *Pertusaria velata, Lecanora* sp., *Thelenella* sp., *Diploschistes scruposus, Cladia aggregata* and *Heterodermia* sp. Among various biocides, Butachlor is known to interfere with protein synthesis, while Propachlor interferes with DNA synthesis as well as blocks the Hill reaction in photosynthesis of photobiont.

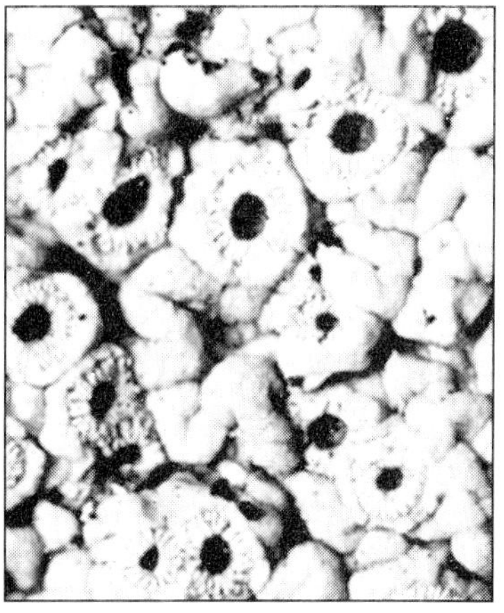

Diploschistes sp.

Singh *et al.* (1999) enumerated 40 lichen species belonging to 18 genera and 14 families, found growing on certain monuments of Karnataka and Orissa. For the eradication of lichens from monuments, the detail of the chemical treatments was also provided. Twelve laboratory chemicals and agricultural pesticides, herbicides and fungicides were tested. Crustose lichens were found to be the most resistant to chemical treatment, followed by foliose and fruticose forms. Some chemicals such as Paraquant dichloride (PDC) and Butachlor impart their own colours to stone materials. Jain (2001) listed ten species of algae and five species of lichens found growing on Gwalior Fort in Madhya Pradesh.

Upreti (2002) studied the lichen flora of Khajuraho group of temples and rocks of nearby area and listed the occurrence of ten taxa of lichens. It was observed that the type of stone, architectural design and climatic conditions determine the composition of the lichen flora. The walls near the ground level were more shaded and moist, bearing the luxuriant growth of some moisture loving lichen species of *Endocarpon, Buellia,* and *Peltula.*

Upreti *et al.* (2004) studied the lichens growing over the rock shelters of Bhimbetka world heritage zone, Madhya Pradesh. A total of 14 species of lichens growing over rocks in different localities of the area were listed together with their thallus character and chemical products.

Saxena *et al.* (2004) provided a detailed account of the lichens growing on different artifacts in the Indian subcontinent. Some interesting distributional and ecological patterns of lichens growing on historical monuments and buildings were also provided. Ayub (2005) surveyed the lichen flora of some major historical monuments and buildings of Agra, Allahabad, Faizabad, Kanpur, Lucknow and Varanasi district of Uttar Pradesh, and reported above 14 species belonging to six genera of six families. Bajpai (2007) conducted the taxonomic and ecological studies on lichens of Bhimbetka world heritage zone in Raisen district of Madhya Pradesh, and reported 42 species belonging to 17 genera and 11 families. Out of the 42 species of lichens recorded from the shelter, 32 species produced the lichen substances having chelating properties.

Bajpai *et al.* (2007) discussed the diversity of rock inhabiting lichens in some districts of Madhya Pradesh and mentioned the maximum diversity of lichens on sandstone followed by siliceous, bauxite and calcareous substrates. Bajpai *et al.* (2008) provided an account of lichen distribution on some major monuments of Madhya Pradesh and enumerated 95 species belonging to 34 genera of 17 families, of which 65 species have the lichen substances with chelating properties.

MECHANISM OF LICHEN BIODETERIORATION

The colonization of lichens on building material and biodeterioration are usually linked to environmental conditions. Guillitte (1995) reported the concept of bioreceptivity as the aptitude of a material to be colonized by one or several groups of living organisms. The bioreceptivity is related to the totality of material properties that contribute to the establishment, anchorage and development of flora and fauna. In stony materials, the bioreceptivity is related to surface roughness, moisture content, and chemical composition of the outer layer and texture of the rock.

The appearance of a lichen mosaic may be viewed as a natural feature of ancient monuments. Many building materials are prone to colonization by lichens, and this causes changes in the colour and chemical or physical properties of the materials.

According to Salter (1856); Bachmann (1911); Smith (1921); Schatz *et al.* (1954), the lichens are primary agents in monument deterioration as well as soil formation. Evaluation by early workers of the role of lichens in the weathering of rocks was based on field observations, whereas in the latter part of the nineteenth century major emphasis was placed on the ability of carbon dioxide and oxalic acid produced by lichens (Uloth, 1861) to function as corrosive agents of the substratum. Although the mechanical action of lichen hyphae and rhizines was recognized by early workers (Smith, 1921), subsequent studies by Fry (1927) provided a rational explanation of the mechanism involved and the effect on the substratum.

1. Biogeophysical Weathering of Substratum by Lichens

The biogeophysical weathering of the substratum on which saxicolous lichens grow can be described conveniently in terms of the mechanism involved.

(a) Penetration of Rhizines

Rhizines are bundles of fungal hyphae present on the lower side of the thallus that can penetrate the substratum on which the lichens grow. The depth of penetration is thought to be influenced by the chemical and physical composition of the rock and the nature of the thallus. The ability of rhizines to penetrate the substratum and cause mechanical disintegration was recognized by several early workers. Rhizines originating from the medulla may penetrate down to 15 mm in the limestone (Smith, 1921). The high solubility of calcium carbonate compared to that of the minerals of other rocks, facilitates this deep penetration. The length of individual hyphae varies according to the species of lichen, and it ranged from 400 μm to 20 mm.

Sometimes the morphology, growth form of the lichens, size shape of rhizinae or other organs of attachment play an important role in the colonization of lichens. *Peltula,* a squamulose lichen is attached to the substratum with the help of bundle of hypha at the centre of the thallus, while *Endocarpon* and *Phylliscum* form thick mat of rhizines and hyphae respectively on their lower surface. The crustose lichens (*Caloplaca subsoluta, Diploschistes candidissimus*) attached tightly with their rhizinae are the most effective biodeteriorant than foliose (*Phaeophyscia hispidula, Parmotrema presorediosum*) forms, whereas squamulouse (*Phylliscum indicum*) seems to have no effect on the rock surface.

(b) Expansion and Contraction of Lichen Thallus

The epilithic crustose lichens growing on rocks have a medullary zone that is attached directly to the substratum. When the cortical tissue at the marginal fringe of the thallus contracts during drying, it creates a pulling strain that may tear the thallus and leave the extreme margins attached to the substratum. The greater contraction of the upper surface of the thallus on drying, coupled with the firm attachment of the haptera to the substratum, caused either detachment of particles of the substratum, removal of a very thin film of substratum or tearing of the thallus. With respect to their morphology, crustose lichens are closely attached to the substratum and are more significant in stone weathering than foliose and fruticose lichens. Among crustose lichens, the epi and endolithic strains are very important for stone biodeterioration (Richardson, 1973).

The hyphae present on the lower side of the thallus are attached to the substrate surface by gelatin or mucous. A wet thallus absorbs large amount of water as the photobiont is a mucilaginous cyanobacteria. When the thallus starts drying up gradually, it shrinks due to loss of water. The upper cortex of thallus exhibits stronger response to drying process resulting in greater degree of shrinkage. The lower part of the thallus stuck to the substratum with gelatin or mucous also dries up and starts peeling off along with the chips of the substratum.

2. Biogeochemical Weathering of Substratum by Lichen Substrates

Lichens produce a variety of chemical compounds, which play an important role in the biogeochemical weathering of minerals and rock substratum. Lichen absorbs water either in the form of liquid or as vapor and can withstand extremes of desiccation. The relative rates of respiration and photosynthesis of lichen thalli are dependent on the temperature and water content and lichen tissue usually has an appreciably lower photosynthetic rate per unit surface area than the leaves of higher plants (Gannutz, 1970). The CO_2 produced by respiration dissolves in water and produces H^+ ions, which participate in the chemical reaction with minerals of the substratum and deteriorate it. According to Zopf (1907), insoluble extracellular oxalic acid produced by lichens is the principle agent in the disintegration of rocks. Calcium oxalate occurs on the outer surface of the fungal hyphae in the thallus or on the surface of the upper cortex.

That many of the lichen compounds have high molecular weight would argue against their solubility in water. These compounds frequently contain polar donor groups in ortho position, for example, as –OH and –COOH in evernic and lobaric acid; -OH and –CHO in salazinic acid and atranorin, which favor the complexing of cations. In addition, water-soluble phenolic units may be important in metal-complexing reactions. The low solubility and weak acidity of lichen compounds largely produce their effectiveness as biogeochemical weathering agents. Lichen compounds are extracellular and usually present in the medulla, which in crustose lichens are in direct contact with the substratum and may act as a primitive water reservoir.

FACTORS AFFECTING THE GROWTH OF LICHENS OVER MONUMENTS

The growth of lichens on monuments and historical buildings of an area depends on a number of factors.

1. Climatic Condition

The relative humidity and temperature are the two most important factors of climate, responsible for the growth of lichens on monuments. Generally, a temperature range between 20-35°C is considered optimum for the growth of most of the species of lichens, but there are species that are capable of withstanding a much wider range of temperature. The majority of lichens grow on an open or well-lighted site, having a higher range of temperature. Species of cyanolichen (*Collema, Phylliscum and Peltula*) prefer a shady place with more moisture to grow. In more moist habitats, the lichen thalli of *Lepraria, Lecanora* sometimes only produce sorediate structures and have a powdery appearance.

2. Dispersal

The dispersal of lichen spores or the vegetative propagules (soredia and isidia) plays a vital role in the development of lichens. The dispersal is mostly through air. However, at times, the spores may be dispersed through the person visiting the monuments and during conservation treatment. During mechanical removal of the sorediate or isidiate forms of lichen from the surface of monuments, the soredia, isidia may disperse on nearby habitats.

3. Environmental Pollution

The lichen species growing on calcareous substrates have an inbuilt tolerance to fight against acidic gases present in the environment. Thus the monuments having lime or cement plaster, being alkaline in nature, provide a suitable substrate for the growth of many lichen taxa on them. Depending upon the growth form, type of substrate, photobiont type and lichen substances present in the thallus, different lichen taxa may be grouped as sensitive or tolerant to the pollution. The members of the lichen family, Physciaceae (*Phaeophyscia hispidula*, *Pyxine* and *Dirinaria*) are considered toxitolerant lichens and are common on the monuments of tropical India. Similarly, *Lecanora muralis,* a temperate lichen, has become widespread in the polluted urban environment all over Europe. The toxitolerant species exhibit an aggressive behavior toward rock building materials.

4. Nature of Substrates

The rough surface helps the lichen propagules or diaspores to anchor than the smooth one, where they are easily blown away or washed off by wind or rain water, respectively. The soft rocks are more easily colonized than the hard ones.

5. Water Holding Capacity

Different types of rocks have different degree of water absorbing and holding capacities. The water holding capacity of rocks depends on the porosity of rock. The non-porous rocks have hardly any water holding capacity, while rocks with large pores do not absorb water in greater amount and are also poor in retaining it. Thus, the rocks with smaller pores are more efficient retainers, and because of effective capillary action and lesser surface exposure of water to the air, they retain the water for a longer time. The leprose lichens with thin medullary crust over rock have less water intake capacity, whereas crustose lichens colonize on rocks having moderate water holding capacity. Among the foliose lichens, the taxa with thin thallus grow on rocks having maximum water holding capacity.

Upreti *et al.* (2006) studied the correlation between water uptake capacity of rocks and the type of lichen growth in Bhimbetka rock shelter. The leprose lichen *Lepraria* and *Cryptothecia* species with a thin medullary crust spreading over rocks had the lowest water uptake capacity ranging from 100-160 ml. The uptake capacity in crustose (*Buellia, Rinodina, Staurothele*) species ranged from 160-220 ml. *Caloplaca, Endocarpon, Peltula* and *Phylliscum,* the squamulose taxa with thick medullary zone, exhibit the uptake capacity ranged between 180-250 ml. *Collema* and *Dirinaria,* the foliose species with thin thalli growing on rocks, have water capacity ranged between 170-250, while the rocks colonized by *Parmotrema* and *Pyxine* having thick thallus show water holding capacity between 260-320 ml.

6. pH

The chemical composition of substrates due to the presence of various minerals determines the pH values. Lichen communities thriving on calcareous rocks due to alkaline substrates receive a chemical protection against the adverse effect of acidic gases in atmospherically polluted areas. The lime plaster or cement plaster, a common construction material in India, being alkaline in nature is preferred by a large number of lichen taxa to grow. The lime and cement plasters have excellent water holding capacity too, further supporting the colonization of different lichen propagules.

7. Rock Composition

The lichen thalli exhibit selective enrichment of Ca, Na, K, Zn and Mg. Generally, carbonate and ferromagnesium silicate minerals weather easily leading to total decomposition. The morphology, growth form, type of lichen substance in thallus and environmental condition of the area play an important role in the accumulation of different metals in lichens. The accumulation of Ca and Mg in lichens collected from Bhimbetka rocks shelter was found maximum in *Dirinaria aegialita,* a foliose sorediate lichens followed by *Peltula euploca,* a squamulose lichens lacking rhiziniae on the lower surface and *Endocarpon subrosettum* with thick rhizinal matt on lower side.

A comparative account of the Ca and Mg accumulation in lichen thallus and substrates clearly indicates that both Ca and Mg accumulated in much higher amounts in thallus than substratum. The crustose lichen (*Caloplaca* and *Diploschistes*) accumulates greater amount of both the salts followed by squamulose (*Peltula* and *Phylliscum*), foliose (*Parmotrema* and *Phaeophyscia*) and leprose (*Lepraria*) one. The probable reason for wide range of variation in accumulation of Ca and Mg may be the varied morphology, anatomy and chemistry of the lichen thallus.

The calcium and magnesium in the form of oxalate accumulate on the surface of the substrate leaving significant and often unsightly white deposits. This can be a problem for delicate and intricate stone monuments because white calcium oxalate deposits often obscure the detail and historical significance of the structure. *Peltula euploca* and *Phylliscum indicum* with maximum dominance on the rock appear to be the most effective biodeteriorant as they accumulate maximum Ca and Mg content compared to leafy as well as powdery form of lichens like *Phaeophyscia hispidula*, *Parmotrema presorediosum* and *Lepraria lobificans*.

8. Architectural Designs

Apart from the physical and chemical properties of the monuments, the architectural design of the monuments and buildings also play an important role in determining the type of lichen vegetation. The monuments with their diverse architectural design and directional orientation of their different faces create a number of niches that receive varying amounts of light, moisture and other growth controlling factors. Such niches develop their own micro-environmental conditions. Each of them is manifested by its own characteristic lichen flora, which differs to some or a great extent from the general flora of the area.

The monuments, depending upon the direction and orientation, receive different intensity of sunlight and can be categorized into three zones depending on the height and exposure.

The plinth area and lower strata of monuments generally show dominance of moisture loving lichen species such as *Lepraria* and *Collema*. Sometime the species grow quite luxuriantly and cover the whole area by coalescing thalli.

The vertical height upto 2-3 feet near the plinth is comparatively exposed to more wind and sun and is preferred by species of *Buellia, Dirinaria, Physcia, Pyxine* together with *Diploschistes,* and *Endocarpon.*

The higher strata (middle) of monuments apparently have meager or no moisture for the greater part of the day. They are exposed to harsher light and wind conditions and are drier than the plinth area. Here lichen flora largely consists of the genus *Caloplaca, Dimelaena* and *Peltula* together with *Parmotrema* species.

The top most strata consists generally the most xeric niche of the monuments. Most of the areas at height have hardly any moisture as it is exposed to strong sunlight almost for the whole day. Some xeric squamulouse lichen community taxa of *Caloplaca, Endocarpon, Peltula,* and *Staurothele* having inherent xerophytic character are able to thrive on such habitats.

The species of lichen genera *Parmotrema, Dirinaria, Pyxine, Physcia, Dimelaena* and *Endocarpon* mostly prefers to grow on horizontal face while *Caloplaca, Phylliscum, Peltula* and *Diploschistes* grows on both the vertical and horizontal face. The horizontal face, that is exposed to direct sunlight for the greater part of the day provide more uniform growth condition to lichens but the vertical face exposed to a plethora of light/ moisture/ wind gives rise to a variety of microclimate and different lichen communities make their appearance there.

CONCLUSION

Sometimes the types of tree vegetation in and around the monuments also influence the growth and colonization of different lichens on the monuments. In Bhimbetka area, the rock shelter under *Ficus* trees has more shady niches suitable for the growth of many shade loving lichen taxa such as *Lepraria, Collema* and some members of cyanolichens. The rock shelters in the cluster of many rock outcrops have narrow passage between them. The vertical faces of the passage remain moist and shady, thus providing suitable habitat for the growth of many lichens taxa such as *Buellia, Chrysospora, Dirinaria, Diploschistes, Staurothele, Physcia* and *Pyxine.*

Lichens not only play a role in deterioration, but are also used more frequently as indicators of environmental quality. A close relationship has been found between the growth and the distribution of the identified lichenic species and some environmental characteristics of an examined area. In fact, these lichen species have been proposed and used as biomonitors. The biomonitoring with lichens is a low cost technique and can help to achieve the goal of sustainable development because they can focus risk assessment and management efforts where they are needed and demonstrate the effectiveness of voluntary or regulatory control measures.

The floristic account of lichens available from the monuments not only helps in conducting ecological studies, but is also useful in improving our knowledge of the lichen biodiversity of the area. So far little is known about the lichen flora of Indian monuments. Thus, there is a tremendous scope to carry out such studies in Indian context.

Little is known about the impact of biodeteriorative processes on monuments in India and other developing countries. We have not yet developed all the scientific analysis that may be important in the future and do not know what kind of chemical treatment (easy and risk free biocides) method may protect our monuments and historical buildings.

A number of powerful tools such as F-T Raman spectroscopy, powder X- ray diffraction (XRD), polarized microscopy, environmental scanning electron microscopy (ESEM) imaging can be utilized to study the lichen and substratum interface.

In India, the problem of lichen biodeterioration is under research and much of the work published is limited to few states of north and south India. The systematic and ecological, lichen-substratum relationship, calcium oxalate film, method of prevention and control studies in context to Indian monuments are not available so far.

The lichen biodeterioration studies involve the multidisciplinary effort, as the biologist alone cannot assess the damage and treatment methods without the cooperation of ecologist, environmentalist, geologist, geochemist, crystallographers, cultural property conservators, archaeologist and historians in order to recommend the most effective management scheme.

ACKNOWLEDGEMENTS

We are thankful to Director, Dr. R. Tuli, National Botanical Research Institute (CSIR), Lucknow, for providing necessary facilities.

REFERENCES

Ahmadjian, V. (1993). *In:* The Lichen Symbiosis. Wiley, New York, pp. 1-6

Arnold, A. (1981). *In:* The conservation of stone II, (Ed., Rossi-Manaresi, R.) Centro per la Conservazione delle Sculture all' Aperto, Bologna, Italy. pp. 13-23.

Arnold, A. (1993). *In:* Congres International sur la conservation de la Pierre et autres Materiaux, UNESCO, Paris, pp. 23-29.

Ayub, A. (2005). Lichen flora of some major historical monuments & buildings of Uttar Pradesh. Ph.D. Thesis, Dr. R. M. L. Avadh University, Faizabad.

Bachmann, E. (1911). *Ber. Deut. Bot. Ges.* 27: 261-273.

Baedecker, P. A. and Reddy, M. M. (1993). *J. Che. Edu.* 70 (2): 104-115.

Bajpai, A. (2007). Taxonomic & Ecological Studies on Lichens of Bhimbetka World Heritage zone, Raisen district, M.P. Ph.D. Thesis, Lucknow University, Lucknow.

Bajpai, P.K., Bajpai R.P. and Sinha, G.P. (1992). *Intl. Biodet. Biodeg.* 30: 1-8.

Bajpai, P.K., Bajpai, R.P., Chaterjee, S., Singh, A. and Sinha, G.P. (1999). *In:* Biology of lichens. (Eds. Mukerji, K. G. Chamola, B.P. Upreti, D.K. and Upadhyaya, R.) Aravali Book International, New Delhi. pp. 57-67.

Bajpai, R., Upreti, D.K. and Dwivedi, S.K. (2008). *Geophytology* (accepted).

Bajpai, R., Dwivedi, S.K., and Upreti, D.K., (2007). *In:* abstracts of the National conference on biodiversity conservation & sustainable development at New Science College, Rewa, Madhya Pradesh pp.-15.

Bell, R.A. (1993). *J. Phycol.* 29:133-139.

Caneva, G. and Salvadori, O. (1989). *In:* The Deterioration and Conservation of stone (Eds., Larraini, L. and Pieper, R.) UNESCO, Paris, pp. 182-234.

Charola, A.E. (1993). *In:* Actes of the Congres International sur la Conservation de la Pierre et autres Materiaux, UNESCO 29.06.-1.07, Paris, pp. 65-68.

Chatterjee, S., Singh, A. and Sinha, G.P. (1995). *Geophytology* 25: 81-88.

Fry, E.J. (1927). *Annl. Bot.* (London) 41: 437-460.

Galloway, D.J. (1994). *In: Ascomycetes systematic. Problems and Perspectives in the Nineties.* (Eds. Hawksworth, D.L) Plenum, New York, pp. 175-184.

Gannutz, T.P. (1970). *Ant. J.* 5: 49-51.

Gayathri, P. (1980). *Res. Bull.* 2: 41-52.

Golubic, S., Friedmann, E.I. and Schneier, J. (1981). *J. Sedi. Petr.* 51: 475-478.

Guillitte, O. (1995). *Sci. Tot. Envt.* 167: 215-220.

Jain, A.K. (2001). *In: Studies in biodeterioration of material*, (Eds. Agarwal, O.P. Dhawan, S., and Pathak, N) ICCI & ICBCP, Lucknow pp. 59-68.

Johanson, L.G., Lindqvist, O, and Mangio, R.E. (1988). *In:* Air Pollution and Conservation, (Ed. Rosvall, R.) Elsevier Applied Science, London, New York, pp. 255-265.

Jones, D. and Wilson, M.J. (1985). *Intl. Biodet. Biodeg.* 21: 99-104.

Larson, D.W. (1987). *Biolith. Lichen.* 25: 351-360.

Paine, S.G., Linggood, F.V., Schimmer, F., and Thrupp, T.C. (1993). The Relationship of microorganisms to the decay of stone. Philosophical Transactions of the Royal Society, London, Vol. CCXXII-, B486, B 97-127.

Richardson, B.A. (1973). *Stone Indut.* 8(2): 2-6.

Rodrigues, J.D, (1991). *In:* Proceedings of the European Symposium (Science, Technology, and European Cultural Heritage), (Eds. Baer, N.S., Sabbioni, C., and Sors, A.I.,) pp. 124-137, Butterwort- Heinemann Ltd., Oxford.

Salter, J.W. (1856). *Cheml. Gaztt.* 14: 130-131.

Saxena, S., (Upreti, D.K., Singh, A. and Singh, K.P., (2004). *In:* Biodeterioration of stone surface (Eds., Clair, St. L. and Seaward, M.) Kluwer Academic Publishers, Netherland, pp. 181-193.

Schatz, A., Cheronis, N.D., Schatz, V., and Trelawany, G.S. (1954). *Proce. Pa. Acad. Sci.* 28: 44-51.

Seaward, M.R.D. (1997). *Intl. Biodet. Biodeg.* 40: 269-273.

Singh, A. and Dhawan, S., (1991). *Geophytol.* 21: 119-123.

Singh, A. and Sinha, G.P. (1993). *In: Recent Advance in Biodeterioration and Biodegradation* (Eds. Garg, K.L. and Mukerji, K.G.) Naya Prakashan, Kolkata, pp: 355-377.

Singh, A. and Upreti, D.K. (1991). *In:* Biodeterioration of cultural property, (Eds., Agarwal O.P., and Dhawan S.) Mac Millan, India. New Delhi pp. 219-231.

Singh, A., Chatterjee, S. and Sinha, G.P. (1999). *In:* Biology of lichens, (Eds. Mukerjee, K.G. Chamola, B.P., Upreti, D.K. and Upadhyaya, R.K.) Aravali, Book International. New Delhi, pp. 115-151.

Smith, A.L. (1921). "Lichens", Cambridge University Press, Lodon and New York, pp. 10-56.

Strzelczyk, A.B. (1981). *Micro. Biodet.* 6: 61-80.

Uloth, W. (1861). *Flora* (Jena) 44: 565-560.

Upreti, D.K. (2002). *In:* Proceedings of National Seminar on biodeterioration of material- 2. (Eds. Srivastava, R.B. Mathur, G.N. and Agarwal, O.P.) DMSRDE, Kanpur, pp. 123-127.

Upreti, D.K., Bajpai, A. and Joshi, Y. (2006). *Brit. Lich. Soci. Bull.* 98: 36-37.

Upreti, D.K., Nayaka, S. and Joshi, Y. (2004). The 10th Congreee of the International Fedration of Rock Art Organization (IFRAO) & federation of Rock Art (28th Nov- 2nd Dec. 2004) Rock Art Society of India. pp. 30-31.

Valentin, N. (1993). *In:* Congres International sur la Conservation dela Pierre et autres Materiaux UNESCO, Paris, pp. 30-34.

Zopf, W. (1907). "Die Flectenstoffe in chemischer, botanischer, pharmakologischer und technischer, Beziehung" Fischer, Jena.

5

Bioremediation of Contaminated Soils using Earthworms

Ayesha S. Ali, Iram Khan and Sharique A. Ali
Postgraduate Department of Biotechnology, Saifia College of Science and Education, Bhopal (MP)-462 001, India.
E-mail: drshariqueali@yahoo.co.in

Earthworms are excellent bio-indicators of relative health of ecosystems and possess a number of qualities that predispose them for use in environmental monitoring and remediation of soils. Due to their unique living habits, they are exposed to chemicals present in their environment released from various industrial and agricultural sources, which can accumulate in their tissues. A wide range of potential biomarkers have been developed in earthworms like behavioral, reproductive, enzymological, lysosomal, genetic, immunological, neurological and histopathological, including the effect of both organic and inorganic substances. Earthworms have been used in bioremediation of agricultural and industrially contaminated soils where they ingest it and convert it into humus-like substance which is highly useful and retain a significant portion of toxic substances like heavy metals and pesticides in their tissues, thereby reducing their concentration in the soil. Due to low cost and ease of management, soil bioremediation using earthworms finds great scope specially in developing countries like India.

INTRODUCTION

For many years, soil was considered simply the loose fraction of the earth's crust and it was not until the 1880's that soil was recognized as a natural body—worthy of study in its own right—by the Russian scientist Dokuchaev (Krasilnikov, 1958). Soil is a complex mixture of mineral matter, organic matter and living organisms. It is a product of the environment, constantly changing, evolving and developing over time, sometimes very slowly in dry desert areas or more quickly in wet tropical regions. It can well be thought of as the "skin" of the land; without it the land would die. Like skin, the soil is constantly being eroded at its surface by wind, water and man's activities, and being renewed at its base by weathering of its parent material (Nikiforoff, 1959). A single gram of soil (about 1/5 teaspoon) can contain over

100 million bacteria, 1 million actinomycetes and 100,000 fungi with hyphae if strung together would measure 5 metres in length.

Hazardous organic materials such as heavy metals like lead, mercury, copper as well as pesticides are used or generated widely in domestic, municipal, agricultural, industrial, and military activities. From agricultural, home, and industrial usage, pesticides can enter into crop residues, municipal sludges, farm manures, and soils. Insects, diseases, and weed control in farming may lead to accumulation of pesticides in soils, in which decomposition of these materials may occur slowly (Fryer *et al.*, 1979). Metallic contaminants in organic materials and land arise from pesticides and farm manures (Mullins *et al.*, 1982). Organic contaminants (e.g., polychlorinated biphenyls [PCBs], polycyclic aromatic hydrocarbons [PAHs]) other than pesticides can enter into the soil from fuel combustion or sewage sludge and other feedstocks. These contaminants from sludge additions to land may persist in soils or contaminate forage on which the livestock graze. The spillage of fuel oil hydrocarbons can contaminate soils. These hydrocarbons will inhibit seed germination and plant growth, but plants do not appear to accumulate the hydrocarbons (Williams and Keehan, 1993). Major inputs of metals into the environment also occur from municipal and industrial sludges and by-products.

IMPACT OF SOIL CONTAMINATION ON SOIL QUALITY

Soil flora and fauna account for 90% of total transformative capacity of soil, and therefore soil biota are particularly sensitive towards the presence of contaminants in their habitat. Soil organisms are assumed to be directly responsible for soil ecosystem processes, especially the decomposition of soil organic matter and the cycling of nutrients (Wardle and Giller, 1997). These processes are regarded as major components in the global cycling of materials, energy and nutrients. For example, the soil biomass (25 cm topsoil layer) is known to process over 100,000 kg of fresh organic material each year per hectare in many agricultural systems. This processing includes the decomposition of dead organic matter by the microbes as well as the consumption and production rates in the soil community food web. An exposure to a surplus of heavy metals can occur during various stages of the life history of a plant, from germination through vegetative growth up to reproduction, affecting its various parts such as bark, leaves, flowers etc. Heavy metals with high affinity for sulfhydryl groups such as As, Cd, Cu, Hg and Pb, can block the enzyme and thus hamper chlorophyll synthesis. Not only plants, but even soil invertebrates such as microbial communities (Duxbury, 1985; Visser and Parkinson, 1992), nematodes (Bongers, 1990; Laszczyca *et al.*, 2004) are also significantly affected by the presence of contaminants in soil. For example, Hunter *et al.* (1987a) found a decrease in earthworm abundance in soils near a copper refinery containing 52000 μg Cu per g. A reduction in total population or any undesirable effect on the physiology of soil biota will therefore affect the total productivity as well as other principal soil processes, which will ultimately create a negative impact on soil health, reducing the total soil biomass as well as affecting the recycling of mineral and energy in the soils.

ROLE OF EARTHWORMS IN DETECTION OF SOIL CONTAMINATION

Due to their essential functions in ecosystems, soil invertebrates, specifically earthworms, are useful for assessing the ecological effects of chemicals. Earthworms are saprotrophic invertebrates, which contribute to the overall structure, drainage, and aeration of soil ecosystems. In addition, earthworms directly and indirectly influence soil microbial communities, mainly through the processes of feeding, burrowing, and fecal (cast) deposition. These are large, relatively immobile, numerous, easy to sample and easily identified. As they are in full contact with the substrate in which they live and consume large volumes of this substrate, earthworms are exposed to chemicals present in their terrestrial environment, which not only kill them but their growth, fecundity and behavior is also affected. Earthworms accumulate some chemicals in their tissues at higher levels than that of the substrate in which they live (Hillel, 1971). These characteristics make earthworms attractive for monitoring the impact of contaminants in soils. Earthworms, are also prey to many vertebrates and provide a route through which the contaminants may be transferred to higher tropic levels. For this reason, and because of their importance as stimulators of microbial decomposition process, they are widely used as indicators of soil contamination. (Fischer and Koszorus, 1992; Edwards and Bohlen, 1996).

BIOMARKERS USED IN THE STUDY OF SOIL CONTAMINATION

More recently, the use of biomarkers to estimate either exposure or resultant effects of chemicals has received considerable attention. A biomarker can be defined as functional response to toxicant-induced stress measured at physiological, cellular, biochemical or molecular levels. Biomarkers, in theory, offer two outstanding advantages in ecotoxicological investigations. First, by their very nature they are responsive only to the bio- or toxico-active fraction of the accumulated body burden of one or more potential toxicants. To this extent they reflect, albeit indirectly, the analytically elusive bioavailable fraction of environmental chemicals within chosen test organisms. Second, they integrate the interactive effects of several chemicals in complex mixtures. However, in the past, some molecular biomarkers have been criticized because of the lack of relevance to key higher ecological functions (Weeks, 1995).

The biomarker response reflects only the bioactive fraction, which may or may not increase or decrease in the same way as the external dose of the pollutant. Biomarkers are sensitive indicators that reveal these changes. They are therefore also indicators that toxicants have entered the organism and, as such, provide information about the bioavailability of the toxicant. Furthermore they indicate that the toxicant(s) have been distributed within the organism and have initiated a toxicological effect at certain critical targets. As measures of toxic effects in organisms at the below individual (molecular or cellular) level (Van Gestel and Van Brummelen, 1996), they represent early or initial responses to environmental perturbations and contamination. Therefore, they are generally taken as being more sensitive than tests measuring effects at higher levels of biological hierarchy, such as the organ, individual, or population. In contrast to the simple measurement of contaminants accumulating in body tissues, biomarkers can offer more complete and biologically relevant information on the potential impact of toxic pollutants on the health of organisms.

Earthworm biomarkers, especially physiological and non-specific markers, have been used extensively to document and quantify the effects of environmental pollutants. Earthworms are virtually ubiquitous and ecologically important soil organisms, and are valuable for assessing biological risks of hazardous and toxic compounds in terrestrial environments due to which they have been used in numerous toxicity and bioaccumulation studies. Many researchers have considered earthworm biomarkers as one of the most useful tools for assessing heavy metal pollution in soils because earthworm biomass and abundance have been found to be more sensitive to pollution in comparison with other indicator taxa. Ali (1997) reported significant reduction in earthworm biomass after exposure to low concentrations of lead (0.05 μg/g) for short and long durations of exposure. The presence and abundance of earthworms can be a determining factor for the occurrence of higher organisms. Behavioral changes have also been observed in a diverse range of earthworm species following exposure to chemicals. Massive trembling of the worm following exposure to carbaryl has been reported, rendering it impossible to re-enter the soil. Frequent episodes of whole body spasms have also been observed, following exposure to contaminants

(Ander Lan and Aspock, 1962; Stenersen *et al.*, 1973). Induced surfacing of earthworms has been considered as a side effect of agrochemicals. Avoidance of contaminated soil has also been observed as an avoidance behavior of earthworms. Avoidance behavior is species dependent and is also influenced by the characters of chemoreceptors (Stenersen, 1992; Lukkari and Haimi, 2004).

Spurgeon *et al.* (2003) grouped the major earthworm biomarkers into four major categories namely cellular markers, markers involving measurement of activity of certain enzymes and proteins, molecular markers and metabolic responses. Cellular biomarkers have been used to measure the effects of cellular function and integrity, which include the measurement of lyosomal membrane stability using Neutral Red Retention Assay (Weeks and Svendsen, 1996), immune activity assays for measuring the effects of organic pollutants and metals, comet assays to measure the breakage of DNA strands (Salagovic *et al.*, 1996) and assessment of sperm number and morphology (Cikutovic *et al.*, 1993; Luo *et al.*, 1999). Measurement of activity of detoxification enzymes and proteins form an important class of biomarkers, and involves measuring phase I cytochrome P-450 enzymes (Eason *et al.*, 1998), phase II enzymes such as glutathione-S-transferase (Booth and Halloran, 2001), activity of antioxidants such as superoxide dismutase, catalase and peroxidase and expression of metallothioneins (Sturzenbaum *et al.*, 2001). Several biomarkers have been evolved, which include molecular responses such as heat shock family of protein chaperones, lysosomal membrane linked genes and metal containing enzymes (Sturzenbaum *et al.*, 2001). Some of the molecular biomarkers like annetocin have been found to exhibit a likely link to reproduction (Oumi *et al.*, 1996). A last group of biomarkers records responses within a full or partial transcription, proteome or metabolome and involves comprehensive metabolic profiling H^1 NMR spectroscopy, and has been used to identify low molecular weight metabolite changes in earthworms exposed to copper (Gibb *et al.*, 1997), metal mixtures and fluorinated organic compounds.

SOIL REMEDIATION USING SOIL ORGANISMS AND EARTHWORMS

The environmental fate of a large number of organic chemicals is controlled by *abiotic transformation processes*, which include various hydrolytic and redox chemical reactions occurring in the soil systems. *Biotic transformations or biodegradation* changes the original molecular structure of a compound and ultimately yields inorganic products like carbon dioxide, water, ammonia, methane, etc. Naturally occurring biodegradation may be a suitable remedial action at sites where the contaminants of concern are readily biodegradable, site conditions are favorable, and the time necessary for naturally occurring biodegradation to effect clean-up is reasonable considering the site-specific circumstances. Naturaliy occurring biodegradation is a long-term remediation option. It may require years or decades to affect adequate clean-up of a site, depending on the site conditions.

Bioremediation is the use of living organisms to degrade the environmental contaminants into less toxic forms. It uses naturally occurring bacteria and fungi or plants to degrade or detoxify substances hazardous to human health and/or the environment. The organisms may be indigenous to a contaminated area or they may be isolated from elsewhere and brought to the contaminated site. Contaminant compounds are transformed by living organisms through reactions that take place as a part of their metabolic processes. Biodegradation of a compound is often a result of the actions of multiple organisms. When organisms are imported to a contaminated site to enhance degradation, the process is known as bioaugmentation. For bioremediation to be effective, organisms must enzymatically attack the pollutants and convert them to harmless products. As bioremediation can be effective only where environmental conditions permit growth and activity, its application often involves the manipulation of environmental parameters to allow growth and degradation to proceed at a faster rate.

Like other technologies, bioremediation has its limitations. Some contaminants, such as chlorinated organic or high aromatic hydrocarbons, are resistant to microbial attack. They are either degraded slowly or not at all, hence it is not easy to predict the rates of clean-up for a bioremediation exercise; there are no rules to predict if a contaminant can be degraded. Bioremediation techniques are typically more economical than traditional methods such as incineration, and some pollutants can be treated on site, thus reducing exposure risks for clean-up personnel, or potentially wider exposure as a result of transportation accidents. Since bioremediation is based on natural attenuation, the public considers it more acceptable than other technologies.

Composting is applied in bioremediation as a means of degrading toxic organic compounds and perhaps lessening the toxicity of metallic contaminants in organic residues, wastes, and by-products. In addition, composting stabilizes wastes for ultimate disposal in traditional manners in landfills or on farmland. Composting has been practiced to reduce the volume and water content of feedstock, to destroy pathogens, and to destroy odor-producing nitrogenous and sulfurous compounds (Barker, 1997). Nitrate leaching can occur from unlined landfills. Composting of nitrogen-rich materials with other feed stocks may lead to stable materials, which are less likely to contaminate water, than the addition of nitrogen-rich material alone to land or landfills. Zach *et al.* (1999) considered composting as a remediation method for handling contaminated soil, sediment, and organic wastes. Mechanical treatment by grinding, mixing, and sieving out nondegradable or disturbing materials (metals, plastics, glass, stones) gives good conditions for the biological treatment of compostable materials. The biological treatment builds up stable organic compounds through humification, and reduces the concentration of organic pollutants. Composting can be used to lower the level of chemical contaminants in residues or soils to which polluted residues have been added.

Vermicomposting is the process by which worms are used to convert organic materials (usually wastes) into a humus-like material known as *vermicompost*. The goal is to process the material as quickly and efficiently as possible. Epigeic species like *Eudrilus eugeniae, Eisenia foetida* and *Perionyx excavatus* are appropriate for vermicomposting. The ancient Greeks considered earthworm to have an important role in improving the quality, fertility and productivity of the soil. Aristotle (384-322 before J.C.), a student of Plato's, called worms the "bowels of the earth". Charles Darwin (1881), the naturalist famous for his ideas on evolution, estimated that 10.6 tonnes of materials are brought to the soil surface of each acre by earthworms (or approximately St/hectare). Due to their direct interaction with soil and major role in degradation of various substances, earthworms have been largely used in composting techniques for soil remediation. Vermicompost appears to be generally superior to conventionally produced compost in a number of important ways, such as it is superior to most composts as an inoculant in the production of compost; worms have a number of other possible uses on farms, including value as a high quality animal feed; and vermicomposting and vermiculture offer potential to organic farmers as sources of supplemental income.

Vermicompost has many advantages over chemical fertilizers. It restores microbial population, which includes nitrogen fixers, phosphate solubilizers, etc. and provides major and micro-nutrients to the plants. It also improves the soil texture and water holding capacity of the soil, provides good aeration to soil, thereby improving root growth and proliferation of beneficial soil microorganisms. It decreases the use of pesticides for controlling plant pathogens, improves structural stability of the soil, thereby preventing soil erosion, and enhances the quality of grains/fruits due to increased sugar content. At the same time, the beginning of vermicomposting is a more complicated process than traditional composting. It can be quicker, but to make it so generally requires more labour, and space because worms are surface feeders and would not operate in material more than a meter in depth. It is more vulnerable to environmental pressures, such as temperature, freezing conditions and drought and perhaps, most importantly, it requires more start-up resources, either in cash (to buy the worms) or time and labour (to grow them).

Environmental concerns in case of vermicomposting of sewage sludge and municipal refuse include the fate of heavy metals, the major pollutants of sludge. For example, in North America, 50-60% of municipal sludges cannot be applied on agricultural land because the cadmium (Cd) content exceeds the permissible heavy metal limit (of 25 ppm) (Tyagi and Couillard, 1991). Different earthworm species deal with heavy metals in different ways, immobilisation and excretion being the most important strategies employed to minimize the toxic effects. This implies that the choice of earthworm species depends the particular task required of it and the range of products anticipated: protein preparation would best be done using species that egest cadmium, rather than accumulate it.

Recently Tharakan *et al.* (2005) conducted a study on the biological transformation of polychlorinated biphenyls (PCBs) in sludge from the Ralston Street Lagoon (RSL) using the red worm *Eisenia foetida*. Sample analyses demonstrated total PCB reductions ranging from 55 to 66 % in sludge inoculated with earthworms, which showed an increase in PCB levels in the earthworm biomass, with concentrations reaching as high as 313 ppm, indicating that most of the PCB was bioaccumulated in the earthworm tissues.

USE OF EARTHWORM BIOMARKERS IN SOIL REMEDIATION

Soil biological investigations such as soil respiration, biomass, enzyme activities, and population count can give information on the presence of viable microorganisms, as well as the intensity and the kind and duration of the effects of pollutants on the metabolic activity of the soil, and are thus well suited to measure the impact of pollution on soil health (Schinner *et al.*, 1996; Van Beelen and Doelman, 1997). Various soil biological methods have been used to describe metabolic activities in the course of bioremediation such as soil respiration, dehydrogenase activity and population counts (Song and Bartha, 1990; Janke *et al.*, 1992; Margesin and Schinner, 1997).

Earthworm behaviour such as locomotion, feeding, burrowing, and surface migration can be used as a biomarker for pollutant effects. Capowiez *et al.* (2002) conducted a study on the burrowing behaviour of two earthworm species of different ecological types (the anecic *Aporrectodea nocturna* and the endogeic *Allolobophora icterica*) using 2D terraria, by taping imidacloprid as a model pesticide. The activity of two classical biochemical markers (AchE and GST activities) was also measured. Imidacloprid had no effect on the biochemical markers in either earthworm species whatever the concentration (0.01, 0.1 and 1 ppm). In contrast, the behaviour of earthworm changed dramatically in the presence of imidacloprid. Following one week of exposure to the pesticide at two different concentrations (0.5 and 1 ppm), burrow length, the rate of burrow reuse and the distance covered decreased for both the species. It was concluded that earthworm behaviour is a sensitive biomarker that can be studied.

Very recently Khan *et al.* (2008) investigated the changes in biomass and certain behavioral responses of earthworm *Lumbricus terrestris* exposed to copper chloride for a total period of 60 days. Reduction in biomass was observed at all concentrations above 100 mg copper chloride/kg dry weight of soil, which became more significant above 450 mg copper chloride /kg dry weight of soil ($p < 0.05$), while responses to prick reflex weakened at these concentrations. Coiling and impaired movement was observed in earthworms exposed to maximum concentration of 750 mg of copper chloride/kg dry weight of soil for a period of 30 days, while a lower concentration of 450 mg copper chloride/kg dry weight of soil also induced coiling and impaired movement after 60 days of exposure.

The emergence of new technologies from the genomics revolution will transform the potential application of biomarkers to assess how pollutants impact people, animals, and ecosystems. Genetic databases provide a huge resource from which candidate molecular biomarkers can be identified and, subsequently, exploited to address these issues. However, a major challenge is to link these novel molecular indices to ecologically relevant whole-organism life cycle traits (such as reproduction and growth). Such a functional link is provided by annetocin, previously characterized as a member of the vasopressin/oxytocin superfamily of neuropeptides. It is expressed in annelid worms within the neurons of the central nervous system and has been shown to be involved in the induction of egg-laying behavior. *Ricketts et al.* (2003) used annetocin as a novel biomarker of reproductive fitness in the earthworm, *Eisenia fetida*. The design of primer pairs targeted toward oligochaete annetocin has facilitated the isolation of a full-length annetocin cDNA from this species. Optimization of a real-time quantitative PCR procedure exploiting the fluorescent DNA-binding molecule, Sybr Green, has allowed the measurement of annetocin transcript levels over a range covering six orders of magnitude. Using this approach, gene expression was measured in earthworms exposed to soils polluted with high concentrations of zinc and lead. Traditional growth and reproductive indices, including cocoon production, were also recorded and related to the molecular parameter.

Earthworm populations can be modified by a range of factors, which include soil conditions, food availability (Fraser *et al.*, 1994), altered predator abundance (Churchfield *et al.*, 1991) and climate (Lofs, 1992). However if a population is exposed to an additional stress through elevated metal concentrations, this may be sufficient to amplify natural variation and reduce numbers so that recovery is no longer possible. Earthworm populations are known to be reduced by high concentrations of metals in soil. Bengtsson *et al.* (1983) found a lower total number and biomass of earthworm at sites close to a brass mill. All worms were absent in soils containing 600 μg Cu per g and 2200 μg Zn per g of NH4 Ac extractable copper and zinc. Hunter *et al.* (1987a) found a decrease in earthworm abundance in soils near a copper refinery containing 52000 μg Cu per g, while Bisessar (1982) noted the absence of worms in soils around a lead smelter containing 230 μg As per g, 33 μg Cd per g, 287 μg Cu per gram and 4800 μg Pb per g.

Effects on the digestive system of earthworm species have been reported in response to toxicity generated by many agrochemicals such as pesticides. Reduction or abnormal increase in the activity of these enzymes has been reported in many cases in response to pesticide toxicity. In an earlier study by Mishra *et al.* (1988), protease activity was found to be significantly reduced in worms exposed to carbaryl, while a heavy reduction in activities of cellulase, amylase and invertase enzymes was reported in earthworms flourishing in soils sprayed with carbaryl. Patnaik and Dash (1993) reported reduction in the activity of cellulase and other carbohydrases in earthworms exposed to various concentrations of malathion, while urease activity was reported to increase with increased concentration of pesticide, which was due to the higher rate of excretion in the pesticide exposed worms as compared to that of controls.

Laboratory experiments were conducted by Cancio (1995) to study the effects of exposure to a sublethal concentration (500 p.p.m.) of lead on the ultrastructure and acid phosphatase compartmentalization of chloragogenous tissue of the earthworm, *Eisenia foetida*. For the cytochemical demonstration of acid phosphatase activity, lead and cerium were used as capturing agents. In both cases there was a change in the compartmentalization of acid phosphatase, the enzyme activity being localized within the chloragosomes in controls, but distributed throughout the cytosol in treated animals. In addition, acid phosphatase activity increased following lead exposure. At the ultrastructural level, disruption of the chloragosomal membranes, an increase in chloragosomal fusion processes and vesiculation of the cytoplasm were evident. Moreover, an enhanced release of chloragosomes to the extracellular space was found in lead-exposed worms.

The importance of reproduction as a key life cycle parameter that determines the long-term status of earthworm populations has led to the formulation of guidelines on the use of earthworm reproduction for the testing of chemicals (ISO, 1998). Numerous reproductive parameters have been studied in earthworms exposed to various contaminants. Sperm count seems to be a very sensitive biomarker. The number and integrity of sperms in earthworms have been studied using *L. terrestris, E. fetida* and *Eudrilus eigeniae*. Cikutovic *et al.* (1993) observed a reduction in the number of sperm cells and seminal vescicles on exposure to chlordane and cadmium. Marked abnormalities in earthworm's sperm ultrastructure were reported on exposure to contaminants. The normal sperm of earthworm such as *Eisenia foetida* consists of a bacillary head and a flagellum with a mean total length of about 50 μm as measured by light microscopy. Reinecke *et al.* (1995) observed abnormalities in nuclear and flagellar regions on exposure to dieldrin. Several metal salts also damage the earthworm sperm cells (Reinecke and Reinecke, 1996). Luo *et al.* (1999) reported abnormalities in sperm structure like apical loop and head bending, while some of the sperms showed tail folding and swelling of head on exposure to two novel pesticides, Imidacloprid and RH-5849. Very recently Espinoza-Navarro and Bustos-Obreg (2005) reported reduction in spermatic viability, alteration of cell proliferation and modification in DNA structure of spermatogonia of worms exposed to malathion. The spermatheca of exposed worms showed vacuolization of basal epithelium and anomalous disposition of spermatozoa, which were concentrated in the center without contacting the basal epithelium, indicating that the pesticide had affected spermathecal content, eliciting phagocytosis of spermatozoa or modifying the anchorage sites between spermatozoa and microvilli in the basal epithelium.

Cocoon production is one of the most sensitive parameters for toxicity test. Reduction in cocoon production on exposure to various contaminants like Zn (Spurgeon and Hopkin, 1996), Cd (Lock and Janssen, 2002), Mn (Reinecke and Reinecke, 1997; Kuperman *et al.*, 2003), Cu (Malecki *et al.*, 1982; Holmstrup *et al.*, 1998, Helling, 2000), Pb (Davies *et al.*, 2003) has been reported. Significant effects of RDX on the reproduction of *Eisenia andrei* were observed at very low concentrations (Robidoux *et al.*, 2000; Simini *et al.*, 2003). Organophosphate pesticides like parathion, malathion, diazonin and chloropyrifos have been reported to reduce the earthworm cocoon production and cocoon viability (Booth and Halloran, 2001; Bustos-Obregon and Goichcochea, 2002).

Venables *et al.* (1992) measured a suppressed spreading of coelomocytes, phagocytosis and reduction of NBT. Total immune activity was found to be declined on exposure to certain pesticides like carbamates and organophosphorus compounds, while inhibition of phagocytosis was reported in *E. andrei* on exposure to carbaryl and 2,4-D (Ville *et al.*, 1997). Metal contaminants can also affect the immune system, e.g., methyl mercuric chloride toxicity reduced the phagocytosis in *E. andrei* (Sauve and Fournier, 2000). A dose-response relationship between various xenogenic compounds and concomitantly the immunological response has been observed (Rodriguez-Grau *et al.*, 1989; Chen *et al.*, 1991). The immunological response also appears to be species dependent, tissue dependent and dependent on the time of sampling (Fitzpatrick *et al.*, 1992; Goven *et al.*, 1994; Diogene *et al.*, 1997; Massicotte *et al.*, 2003). Cytotoxic effects of cement kiln dust were analysed in *L. terrestis*. Coelomocyte viability and phagocytosis were reported to be affected by kiln dust emissions (Massicotte *et al.*, 2004).

Immunoactive coelomocytes and their viability is one of the most promising surrogate assays to assess immunotoxic risks (Bunn *et al.*, 1996; Burch *et al.*, 1999). Several studies concerned the effects of environmental pollution, including heavy metals, on earthworm immune functions mediated by coelomocytes (Scott-Fordsmand and Weeks, 2000). Fugere *et al.* (1996) recorded the inhibition of phagocytic activity of coelomocytes exposed *in vitro* to heavy metal (Cd, Zn) solutions. Homa *et al.* (2003) studied the effects of heavy metal toxicity on the coelomocytes of earthworm *A. chlorotica* and reported that coelomocyte viability and activity was significantly reduced. This was explained as a result of accumulation of heavy metals in body tissues of earthworms including coelomocytes, which in turn affects their health and viability.

FUTURE PROSPECTS AND RECOMMENDATIONS

The bioremediation treatments are effective in the degradation of various polluted compounds where the compost treatments stimulate soil metabolic processes and help in preserving the biochemical quality of the soil. Biodegradation of xenobiotic organics using various earthworm species is much faster than in unamended soils on site. Metallic pollutants are not degraded during vermicomposting but may be converted into organic species that are less bioavailable. Degradation of organic contaminants in soils is facilitated by the addition of composted or raw organic matter, thereby increasing the substrate levels for metabolism of the contaminants. Recalcitrant materials, such as organochlorines, may not undergo degradation in composts or soils, and the effects of forming organic complexes with metallic pollutants may be nonpermanent or short-lived.

As a processing system, bioremediation of organic waste using earthworms is very simple as the worms ingest material, break it up in their rudimentary gizzards, consume the digestible/putrefiable portion, and then excrete a stable, humus-like material that has a variety of documented benefits as well as they retain a significant part of the different contaminants in their body tissues reducing their quantity in the soil. Bioremediation of soils using vermitechnology can be a promising technique having a great potential in certain challenging areas of terrestrial pollution. In a developing nation like India, where on one side pollution is increasing due to accumulation and cycling of contaminants in the environment, and on the other side there is a shortage of resources for their removal due to which our environment and its resources have become endangered, there is a need for a proper remediation technology, which is cost effective and simple to use. Therefore bioremediation of soil using earthworms or vermitechnology finds great scope in future. Earthworms are increasingly used as indicator species for monitoring soil pollution as well as find great use in soil bioremediation.

Recent studies have shown that vermicomposting operations can benefit a variety of industries including viticulture. Logsdon (1994) reported a study made in Pune, India by Jhambekar from Matarasha Agriculture Bioteka that grapes fertilized with two tonnes of vermicompost per acre, per year, for a period of five years increased yield to 15 tonnes per acre, which was much higher than the yields under conventional fertilization. In Australia, clear benefits have been derived from organic amendments in vineyard management.

In recent years, there has been increasing interest in developing *in situ* techniques for the remediation of oil-contaminated soil. Biodegradation by naturally occurring populations (consortia) of soil organisms is a major mechanism for the degradation of petroleum contaminants from the environment. Soil microorganisms which degrade these organic pollutants using their own enzymatic pathways; the end-products of aerobic hydrocarbon mineralization are microbial biomass, CO_2 and water.

A major obstacle in the use of soil bioremediation techniques is the need to prove that the products are completely safe, reliable and acceptable, as well as caution is required in promoting the potential benefits as overstated claims may damage this industry in its infancy. Rigorous scientific studies indicate that bioremediation of soils contaminated with municipal and farm waste may be a suitable option for the production of beneficial products. Composition and consistency of these products would largely depend on their initial composition as well as the composition of substances added to them. Treatment of soils contaminated with sewage sludge would require constant monitoring of nutrients and contaminants as well as prevention of pathogen regrowth. There is a concurrent need for more extensive investigation on the range and rates of application of soil bioremediation so that restrictions and recommendations can be formulated.

ACKNOWLEDGEMENTS

The authors are thankful to Mr. Zainuddin Shah, Secretary, Saifia Education Society and Prof. Nasir Ali, Principal, Saifia College of Science and Education, for providing necessary facilities and encouragement.

REFERENCES

Ali, S.A. (1997). *Ind. J. Z. Spect.* **8(2):** 47-49.

An der Lan von, H. and Aspock, H. (1962). Zur wirkung von sevin auf regenwhurmer. Aus dem Zoologischen Institut der Universitat Insbruck, Univ-Prof. Dr. O. Steinback, Vorsatnd. pp.180-182.

Barker, A.V. (1997). *In: Agricultural Uses of By-products and Wastes.*

Bengtsson, G., Nordstrom, S. and Rundren, S. (1983). *Environ. Pollut.* 30: 87-108.

Bisessar S. (1982). *Water Air Soil Pollut.* **17:** 305-308.

Bongers, T. (1990).*Oecologia.* **83:**14-19.

Booth, L.H. and Halloran, K. (2001). *Environ. Toxicol. Chem.* **20(11):** 2494-2502.

Bunn K.E., Thompson T.M. and Tarrant K.A (1996). *Bull. Environ. Contam. Toxicol.* **57:** 632-639.

Burch, S.W., Fitzpatrick, L.C., Goven, A.J., Venables, B.J. and Giggleman, M.A. (1999). *Bull. Environ. Contam. Toxicol.* **52:** 547-554.

Bustos-Obreg, E. and Goichcochea, R.I. (2002). *Asian J. Androl.,* **4:** 195-199.

Cancio, I., Gwynn, I., Ireland, M.P., Cajaraville, M.P. (1995). *Histochem J.* **27(12):** 965-73.

Capowiez, Y., Rault, M., Mazzia, C. and Belzunces, L. (2002). *Pedobiologia.* **47:** 542-547.

Chen, S.C., Fitzpatrick, L.C., Goven, A.J., Venables, B.J. and Cooper, E.L. (1991). *Environ. Toxicol. Chem.* **10:** 1037-1043.

Churchfield, S. (1991). *In:* The biology of the Soricidae, (Eds. Findley, J.S. and Yates, T.L.) Albuquerque: The Museum of Southwestern Biology, University of New Mexico. Pp. 23-34.

Cikutovic, M.A., Fitzpatrick, L.C., Venables, B.J. and Goven, A.J. (1993). *Environ. Pollut.* **81:** 123-125.

Darwin, C. 1881 (1945 reprint). Darwin on humus and the earthworms: the formation of vegetable mould through the action of worms with observations on their habits, 153 pp. Faber and Faber, London.

Davies, N.A., Hodson, M.E. and Black, S. (2003). *Environ. Pollut.* **121:** 49-54.

Diogene, J., Dufour, M., Poirier, G.G. and Nadeau, D. (1997). *Lab Anim.* **31:** 326-336.

Duxbury, T. (1985). *In:* Advances in microbial ecology. (Eds. Marshall, K.C.,) New York, Plenum Press, pp. 185-235

Eason, C.T., Booth L.H., Brennan, S. and Ataria, J. (1998). *In:* Advances in Earthworm Ecotoxicology. (Eds. Sheppard, S., Bambridge, J., Holmstrup, M., Posthuma, L.,) SETAC Press, Pensacola, FL, pp. 191-198.

Edwards, C.A. and Bohlen, P.J. (1996). *In:* Ecotoxicology of Earthworms. (Eds. Edwards, P.J. and Heimbach, F.) Chapman and Hall London. Intercept Ltd, Andover, UK, pp.197-206.

Espinoza-Navarro, O. and Bustos-Obreg, E. (2005). Effect of malathion on the male reproductive organs of earthworms, *Eisenia foetida*.

Fitzpatrick, L.C., Sassani, R., Venables, B.J. and Goven, A.J. (1992). *Environ. Pollut.* **77:** 65-69.

Fraser, P.M., Haynes R.J. and Williams, P.H. (1994). *Biol. Fertil. Soils,* **17:** 185-190.

Fryer, J.D., Smith, P.D., and Ludwig, J.W. (1979). *J. Environ. Qual.* **8:** 83-86.

Fugère, N., Brousseau, P., Krzystyniak, K., Coderre, D. and Fournier, M. (1996). *Toxicol.* **109:**157-166.

Gibbs, J.O.T., Svendsen, C., Weeks, J.M. and Nicholson, J.K., (1997). *Biomarkers* **2:** 295-302.

Goven, A. J., Chen, S.C., Fitzpatrick, L. C. and Venables, B.J. (1994). *Environ. Toxicol. Chem.* **13:** 607-613

Helling, B., Reinecke, S.A. and Reinecke, A.J., (2000) *Ecotoxicol. Environ. Saf.* **46:** 108-116.

Hillel, D. (1971). Soil and Water. Academic Press New York and London. pp. 288.

Holmstrup, M., Petersen, B. Larsen, M. (1998). *Environ. Toxicol. Chem.* **17:** 897-901.

Homa, J., Niklinska, M. and Plytycz, B. (2003). *Pedobiologia.* **47(5 – 6):** 640-645.

Hunter, B.A., Johnson, M.S. and Thompson, D.J. (1987). *Invertebrates. J. App. Ecol.,* **24:** 587-599 ISO, (1998). Determination of Acute Toxicity Using Artificial Substrate.International Standards Organisation, Geneva.

Janke, S., Schamber, H. and Kunze, C. (1992). *Angrew. Botanik.* **66:** 42-45.

Khan, I., Ali, A.S. and Ali, S.A. (2007). *Japanese J. Environ. Ttoxicol.* (In Press).

Krasilnikov, N.A. (1958). Soil Microorganisms and Higher Plants.

Kuperman, K.G, Checkaj, R.T, Simini, M., Phillips, C.T, Kolakowski, J.E, Kurnas, C.W. and Sunahara, G.I. (2003). *Pedobiologia* **47:** 651-656.

Laszczyca, P., Augustyniak, M., Babczynska, A., Bednarska, K., Kafel, A., Migula, P., Wilczek, G. and Witas, I. (2004). *Environ Int.* **30(7):** 901-10.

Lock, K. and Janssen, C.R. (2002). *Ecotoxicol Environ Safety.* **52(1):** 1-7.

Lofs, A. (1992). *In:* Ecotoxicology of earthworms. P.W. Greig- Smith *et al.* Intercept, Hants. 85-89.

Logsdon, G (1994) Biocycle 35: 63-65

Lukkari, T. and Haimi, J. (2004). *Ecotox. Environ. Saf.,* In Press.

Luo, Y., Zang, Y., Zhong, Y. and Kong, Z. (1999). *Chemosphere* 39: 2347-2356.

Malecki, M.R., Neuhauser, E.F. and Loehr, R.C. (1982). *Pedobiologia.* **24:** 129-137.

Margesin, R. and Schinner, F. (1997). *Appl. Microbiol. Biotechnol.* **47:** 462-468.

Massicotte, R., Robidoux, P.Y., Sauve, S., Flipo, D., Fournier, M. and Trottier, B. (2003). *J. Environ. Monit.* **5(5)**:774-9.

Massicotte, R., Robidoux, P.Y., Sauve, S., Flipo, D., Fournier, M. and Trottier, B. (2004). *Ecotoxicology and Environmental Safety* **59:** 10-16.

Mishra, P.C., Pradhan S.C., Mishra P.K. and Sahoo S. (1988). *Poll Res.* **7(1-2):** 13-15.

Mullins, G.L., Martens, D.C., Kornegay, E.T. and Hallock, D.L. (1982). *J. Environ. Qual.* 17: 740–746.

Nikiforoff, C. C. (1959). *Science* **129:** 186-196.

Oumi, T., Ukena, K., Matsushima, O., Ikeda, T., Fujita, T., Minakata, H. and Nomoto, K. (1996). *J. Exp. Zool.* **276:** 151-156.

Patnaik, H.K. and Dash, M.C. (1993). *Bull. Environ. Contam. Toxicol.* **51:** 780-786.

Rechcigl, J.E. and MacKinnon, H.C., Eds. American Chemical Society, Washington, DC. pp. 140-162.

Reinecke, A.J. and Reinecke, S.A. (1997). *Biol. Fertil. Soils* **24:** 27-31.

Reinecke, A.J., Reinecke, S.A. and Froneman, M.L. (1995). *Environ. Toxicol. Chem.* **14:** 961-965.

Reinecke, A.J. and Reinecke, S.A. (1996). *Pedobiologia* **40:** 439-448.

Ricketts H.J, Morgan A.J., Spurgeon D.J. and Kille, P. (2002). *Ecotoxicology and Environmental Safety* **57:** 4-10.

Robidoux, P. Y., Svendsen, C., Caumartin, J., Hawari, J., Ampleman, G., Thiboutot, S., Weeks, J.M. and Sunahara, G.I. (2000). *Environ. Toxicol. Chem.* **19:** 1764-1773.

Rodriguez-Grau, J., Venables, B.J., Fitzpatrick, L.C. and Goven, A.J. (1989). *Environ. Toxicol. Chem.* **8:**1201-1207.

Salagovic, J., Gilles, J., Berschaeve, L. and Kalina, I. (1996). *Folia Biol (Praha)* **42:**17-21.

Sauve, S. and Fournier, M. (2000). *Ecotoxicol. Environ. Saf.,* **60(1):** 67-72.

Schinner, F., Ohlinger, R., Kandeler, E. and Margesin R. (1996). Methods in Soil Biology. Springer, Heidelberg.

Scott-Fordsmand, J.J. and Weeks, J.M. (2000). *Rev. Environ. Contam. Toxicol.* 165: 117-159.

Shugart, L.R. (1990). *In*: Biomarkers of environmental contamination. McCarthy, J.F., Shugart, L.R. eds. Lewis, Boca Raton, FL, pp. 217-227.

Simini, M., Checkai, R.T., Kuperman, R.G. and Phillip, C. (2003). *Pedobiologia* **47:** 657-662.

Song, H.G. and Bartha, R. (1990). *Appl. Environ. Microbiol.* **56:** 646-651.

Spurgeon, D.J., Svendsen, C., Weeks, J.M., Hankard, P.K., Stubberud, H.E. and Kammenga, J.E. (2003). *Environ Toxicol Chem.* **22(7):**1465-72.

Spurgeon, D.J. and Hopkin, S.P. (1996). *Pedobiologia,* **40:** 80-96.

Stenersen, J., Gilman, A. and Vardanis, A. (1973). *J. Agric. Food Chem.* **21:** 166-171.

Stenersen, J., Brekke, E. and Engelstad, F. (1992). *Soil Biol. Biochem.* **24(12):** 1295-1307.

Sturzenbaum, S.R., Winters, C., Galay, M., Morgan, A.J. and Kille, P. (2001). *J.Biol.Chem.* **276:** 34013 -34018.

Tharakan, J., Tomlinson, D., Addagada, A. and Shafagati, A. (2005). *Engineering in Life Sciences.* **6(1):** 43-50.

Tyagi, R.D., Couillard, D. and Tran, F.T. (1991). *Process Biochem.* (Oxford) **26:**47–54.

Van Beelen, P.V. and Doelman, P. (1997). *Chemosphere.* **34:** 455-499.

Van Gestel, C.A.M. and Van Brummelen, T.C. (1996). *Ecotoxicology* **5:** 217-225.

Venables, B.J., Fitzpatrick, L.C. and Goven, A.J. (1992). Earthworms as indicators of ecotoxicity. In: Greig-Smith, P.W., Becker, H.

Ville, P., Roch, P.,Cooper, E.L. and Narbonne, J. (1997). *Arch. Environ.Contam.Toxicol.* **32:** 291-297.

Visser, S. and Parkinson, D. (1992). *American Journal of AlternativeAgriculture* **7:** 3-37.

Wardle, D.A. and Giller, K.E. (1997). *Soil Biol. Biochem.* **28:** 1549-1554.

Weeks, J.M. and Svendsen,C. (1996). *Environ. Toxicol. Chem.* **15:** 1801-1805.

Weeks, J.M. (1995). *J. Appl. Ecol.* **2:** 215-216.

Williams, R.T. and Keehan, K.R. (1993). *In:* Science and Engineering of Composting. (Eds. Hoitink, H.A.J. and Keener, H.M.,) Renaissance Press, Worthington, OH. pp. 363-382.

Zach, A., Latif, M., Binner, E. and Lechner, P. (1999). *Compost Sci. Util.* **7(4):** 25-33.

6

Bioremediation and Cyanobacteria: An Overview

Kaushal Kishore Choudhary[1] and Rajan Kumar Gupta[2]
[1]Department of Botany, Banaras Hindu University, Varanasi-221 005, U.P., India
[2]Pt. L.M.S. Government Postgraduate College, Rishikesh-249 201, Uttarakhand
E-mail: kkc1970@gmail.com

Significant elevation in toxic and hazardous substances of the atmosphere and their unhealthy effect on humans and other biosystems is of increasing concern of the present-day environmental biotechnology programme. The rapid expansion and increasing sophistication of various industries in the past century has remarkably increased the amount and complexity of toxic waste effluents and have modified the sustainable physico-chemical behavior of air, water and soil. Conventional approaches of removal of soil from contaminated site by excavation and transportation to elsewhere for treatment or to cap and contain the contaminated areas of site designed for removal or detoxification was cost-sensitive, required a large new area for final disposal and also posed a significant risk in excavation, handling and transportation. With advancement in understanding of microbial metabolism and their habitat diversity, remediation of contaminants or pollutants by microorganisms, i.e., bioremediation was proposed due to low-cost, easily available germplasms, high public acceptance and ecofriendly nature. Bioremediation might be processed in *in situ* or *ex situ* conditions with fungi, bacteria or cyanobacteria. Among them, cyanobacteria provide better option as some of them can fix atmospheric nitrogen along with atmospheric carbon, thereby enhancing the fertility of the water and soils. Cyanobacteria are capable of detoxifying or removing or destroying a wide range of contaminants by modifying their metabolic processes and producing or secreting a variety of stress-tolerant metabolites inside their cells or in the environment. Cyanobacteria can significantly remediate the contaminated sites incorporated with high levels of metals like Fe, Mo, Mn, Zn, Ni, Cu, V, Co, Cr, As, Hg, Cd and Pb, polycyclic aromatic hydrocarbons (PAHs) and dyes. The present article is a brief account of bioremediation and significant contribution of cyanobacteria in remediation of polluted environments.

INTRODUCTION

Indiscriminate utilization of natural resources to fulfill the unlimited demand of ever-increasing human population in terms of food, fuel and fodder has instigated widespread pollution of the natural global environment. Application of excessive inorganic chemical fertilizer, acquisition of land for agriculture practices, rapid industrialization and burning of fossil fuels is leading to the introduction of pollutants (foreign substances or energies) and contaminants (naturally occurring) into the environment, thereby generating significant enhancement in contaminated sites globally (Zhu and Chen, 2002). The accumulation of undesired substances in the atmosphere is negatively affecting the productivity and fertility of the air, water and soil, thereby causing a potential health threat to humans and other living systems (Pimentel *et al.*, 2005).

Nature has developed balanced ecosystems with respect to oxygen, hydrogen, nitrogen, carbon dioxide, argon and water vapor for the sustenance of diverse flora and fauna. But, encroachment of earth by humans and their activities in terms of urbanization, industrialization and uncontrolled utilization of natural resources have badly disrupted natural equilibrium (environmental pollution) leading to environmental instability, disorder, harm or discomfort to physical systems (Acho-Chi, 1998). Maintenance of productive and fertile ecosystem is the urgent need of present-day environmental biotechnology programme. In view of the detrimental effects of heavy metal accumulation in the diverse ecosystem, removal of toxic substances accumulating in natural ecosystems is the increasing concern worldwide (Lombi *et al.*, 2001). To continue the sustainable practices, biological system mediated removal of toxic substances (bioremediation) from air, water and soil has been widely recognized.

The removal of toxic substances from polluted sites is in practice for long time (Vidali, 2001). Traditional approach of remediation involved the removal of polluted soils and their transport to a landfill (Powrie and Robinson, 2000). The transport of polluted soil has many disadvantages as it does not degrade or transform the pollutants, rather it is simply the transport of contaminants from one place to another (Duggan, 2005). Additionally, it creates significant risk in excavation, handling and transport of hazardous material. Also, the approach is expensive in that it requires new landfills sites for final disposal of the hazardous material. The cap and contain method was only a reliable traditional approach for the removal of hazardous material, as it involved the isolation of contaminated sites and their monitoring and maintenance (Vidali, 2001). Because of less efficacy of cap and contain method, recent approach has been aimed towards complete degradation of pollutants or at least transformation of hazardous material into innocuous substances. Some chemical technologies were also developed and applied, but due to their cost-sensitivity, technological complexity and increased risk of exposure to contaminants for both workers at the site and nearby residents, these approaches were not widely accepted. Hence, bioremediation seems to be the only better option for the remediation of polluted sites (Matsunaga *et al.*, 1999; Ribeiro *et al.*, 2008).

Bioremediation using oxygen evolving cyanobacteria is a cost-effective and ecofriendly approach to environment management. Cyanobacteria are capable of degrading or detoxifying many gaseous, solid and liquid recalcitrant pollutants including those of natural and xenobiotic origins viz., carbon dioxide, nitrogen, phosphorous, phenolics, pesticides, antibiotics, melanoidin, lignin and detergents (Kertesz *et al.*, 1994; Subramanian and Uma, 1999). Metals can be removed from effluents by the processes of bioaccumulation and biosorption (Mohamed, 2001). The present article has been aimed to discuss the general strategies involved in bioremediation and cyanobacterial potential in removal of toxic substances from polluted sites.

BIOREMEDIATION

Bioremediation is the combination of two words viz., *bio* meaning *biological*; and *remediation* meaning *to remedy*. Bioremediation is commonly used to define the removal of toxic wastes from contaminated sites by microorganisms. The removal of toxic substances by higher plants is referred to as phytoremediation. Bioremediation can be defined as "any process that uses microorganisms, fungi, green plants or their enzymes to return the natural environment altered by contaminants/pollutants to its original productive and fertile condition". Bioremediation may be employed to attack specific soil contaminants, such as degradation of chlorinated hydrocarbons by bacteria.

Bioremediation is a technology-based process that aims towards the removal of toxic wastes/effluents released from industries or accumulated in the fields along with chemical fertilizers. The removal of toxic wastes may be achieved by suitable plants or microbes, either natural occurring or tailor-made for the specific purpose (Ripp *et al.*, 2000; Sayler and Ripp, 2000; Seidel *et al.*, 2004). Bioremediation is an eco-friendly, cost-effective and natural technology targeted to remove heavy metals, radionuclides, xenobiotic compounds, organic waste, pesticides etc. from contaminated sites or industrial discharges through biological means (Kertesz *et al.*, 1994; Subramanian and Uma, 1999).

Bioremediation Strategies

There are two main approaches for the degradation or transformation of pollutants from polluted sites:

***In situ* bioremediation**—*In situ* technique defines the application of techniques to remediate the polluted soil and water at the site with minimal disturbances.

***Ex situ* bioremediation**—*Ex situ* techniques define the application of techniques to polluted soil and water at the site which has been removed from contaminated site via excavation (soil) or pumping (water).

Bioaugmentation—This is the degradation of pollutants by adding microorganisms to the polluted sites.

In situ Bioremediation

In situ bioremediation techniques are the most viable and reliable options for the removal of hazardous wastes from contaminated sites as these are cost effective and less disturbing to the system and avoid costly excavation and transport of contaminants (Ellis *et al.*, 2000). *In situ* bioremediation of contaminated soil and groundwater can be undertaken in one of the following ways using naturally occurring microorganisms:

Bioventing

This is the most common *in situ* treatment of pollutants that involves the supply of oxygen and nutrients through wells to contaminated soils to enhance the proliferation of indigenous microbes. Actually, addition of contaminants into the soil decreases the availability of dissolved oxygen and nutrients, thereby limiting the growth of naturally degrading microbes that can degrade or transform the pollutants. Supply of controlled oxygen and nutrients accelerates the growth of indigenous microbes and subsequent destruction of contaminants at higher rate. Bioventing process stimulates *in situ* biodegradation of aerobically degradable compounds of soils contaminated with hydrocarbons, non-chlorinated solvents, some pesticides, wood preservatives and other organic chemicals (Dupont, 2006; Khan *et al.*, 2004). Bioventing process has some limitations such as high and extremely low moisture contents and low temperature may reduce the efficacy of this process.

Biosparging

Biosparging is an *in situ* biodegradation approach that uses indigenous microorganisms to biodegrade organic constituents in the saturated zone. In this process of bioremediation, air particularly oxygen and nutrients are injected into the saturated zone to increase the biological activity of the indigenous microorganisms. Biosparging is commonly used to reduce the concentrations of petroleum constituents that are dissolved in groundwater, adsorbed to soil below the water table, and within the capillary fringe (Norris *et al.*, 1993, 1994). The effectiveness of biosparging is governed by the physico-chemical properties of soil and water. These include intrinsic permeability of soil, groundwater temperature, pH levels, microbial population density, nutrient concentration, iron concentration etc.

Bioreactors

This method involves flushing of contaminants from the soil, so that the same can be treated in bioreactors, where a continuous supply of nutrients, oxygen and microorganisms is maintained. Polycyclic aromatic hydrocarbons (PAHs) and diesel-contaminated soil constitute a group of priority pollutants which are present at high concentrations in the soils of many industrially contaminated sites. Bioreactors have been designed for degradation of a wide variety of pollutants (Kozliak *et al.*, 2000; Mueller *et al.*, 1993). Gallego *et al.* (2001) have described the biostimulation of bioremediation of diesel-contaminated soil with addition of activated sludge from a domestic waste water plant, inorganic nitrogen and phosphorus into the bioreactors more than 90% after 45 days. Bioreactors have proved most effective for soil remediation, since conditions for enhanced degradation can be achieved most readily.

Bioaugmentation

Bioaugmentation can be defined as the addition of pregrown microbial cultures to enhance microbial populations at a site to improve contaminant clean-up and reduce clean-up time and cost. The approach involves the study of contaminant degrading capability of indigenous microbes for bioremediation. If indigenous microbes are unable to perform the biostimulation, non-indigenous or genetically modified microbes capable of degrading the contaminants are inoculated into the field. Bioaugmentation is generally applied for the bioremediation of soil and water contaminated with chlorinated ethenes such as tetrachloroethylenes and trichloroethylenes, which are transformed into non-toxic forms of ethylene and chloride. Bioremediation is typically performed by the addition of electron donor (biostimulation) to promote the prolific growth of dechlorinating microbes in bioaugmentation culture (Gentry *et al.*, 2004; Barbeau *et al.*, 1997; Boon *et al.*, 2002).

Ex situ Bioremediation

These techniques involve the removal of contaminated soil from the polluted sites through excavation and its treatment for bioremediation elsewhere. Although, *ex situ* bioremediation is a costlier approach, it showed advancement over *in situ* bioremediation in requiring little time for bioremediation and more certainty about the uniformity of the treatment because of the ability to homogenize, screen and continuous mixing of soil. The following approaches have been developed for *ex situ* bioremediation.

Landfarming

Ex situ landfarming has been proven most successful in treating petroleum hydrocarbons. This technique is a full-scale bioremediation technology that incorporates liners and other methods to control leaching of contaminants. Contaminated soils, sediments, or sludges are excavated and applied into lined beds and periodically turned over or tilled to aerate the waste. *Ex situ* landfarming bioremediation is generally associated with controlling the moisture content, aeration, pH and nutrients. In spite of successful application, this technique has several limitations such as requirement of large space, uncontrolled condition of rainfall and temperature, and inability to biodegrade inorganic contaminants. Landfarming technique of *ex situ* bioremediation has been applied for the biodegradation or biotransformation of petrochemical wastes like anthracene, phenanthrene, pyrene, and hydrocarbons (Rodrigo *et al.*, 2007). Hezaji and Husain (2004) described the effect of moisture content, microbial density and composition, nutrients and tilling on the degradation processes in landfarming operations. Petroleum sludges high in PAHs have been treated through landfarming in which soil is mixed with sludge, kept bare of vegetation, tilled, and fertilized to encourage microbial degradation of the contaminants (Reilley and Banks, 1996).

Role of Cyanobacteria in Bioremediation

Cyanobacteria have recently been raised as experimental organisms of environmental biotechnology programme not only because of their role in soil fertility, but also due to their potential to remove heavy metals from polluted sites and their active participation in reclamation usar soils. Cyanobacteria, in addition to enrichment of soil, play a significant role in suppressing weeds, degradation or transformation of heavy metals into less or non-toxic forms. Cyanobacteria are also capable of degrading naturally occurring hydrocarbons (Ellis, 1977; Narro *et al.*, 1992) and xenobiotics (Megharaj *et al.*, 1987) present at the contaminated sites. Some of the cyanobacterial potential in reclamation of usar soils and degradation or transformation of several toxic and hazardous substances present in the soil and water have been discussed below.

Cyanobacteria in Reclamation of Usar Soils

Usar soils that occur widely in certain parts of India exhibit extreme ecological conditions for the proliferation of microbial growth. Usar soils are characterized by high pH, high salinity, unproductive, impermeable and hard due to the presence of undesirable salts on the surface. The presence of excess sodium salt in soils disperses the soil aggregates resulting into increase in soil pore size through which air and water move otherwise. Usar soils are generally classified into saline and alkaline. Saline soils are termed 'solonchak' and alkaline soils are called 'solonetz'. Saline soils are distributed in more than 7 Mha of land in India. The reclamation of usar soils is of increasing concern due to their unproductive and unfertile nature.

Earlier attempts were centered on the application of gypsum, pyrite, sulphur to modify chemical structure of the soil and excessive irrigation for the removal of dissolved salt, but problem was still challenging. Therefore, reclamation of usar soils through microorganisms including cyanobacteria was proposed. The first report on reclamation of usar soils using cyanobacteria was proposed by Singh (1950). Later studies by Thomas and Apte (1984) suggested the reduction of 12-35 percent soil salinity of 'kharland' soils after the introduction of salt tolerant cyanobacterium *Anabaena torulosa*. Recent advances in metabolic adaptation of cyanobacteria in diverse habitats have revealed the salt and salinity tolerance potential of cyanobacteria. A number of halotolerant/alkalotolerant and halophilic/alkalophilic cyanobacteria have been reported (Singh, 1961; Kaushik, 1983). Some of the examples of cyanobacteria inhabiting salt affected soils are *Nostoc*, *Calothrix*, *Plectonema*, *Scytonema*, *Cylindrospermum*, *Westiellopsis* and *Hapalosiphon*.

Cyanobacteria have developed adaptive mechanisms in response to salinity. Jha *et al.* (1987) reported the synthesis of biopolymers and increased heterocyst and nitrogen fixation in response to stress. Increased demand for the nitrogen during salt stress might be confined to the synthesis of nitrogenous osmoregulatory compounds like amino acids (Measures, 1975) and quarternary ammonium compounds (Galinsky and Trueper, 1982). Additionally, production of extracellular polysachharides in response to high sodium concentration was reported by Roychoudhury *et al.* (1985) that bind free sodium radicals preventing the organisms by cell injury. The presence of anionic polysachharide in their mucilaginous sheath provides support against desiccation. Cyanobacteria have been reported to withstand the high level of salinity and alkalinity by of accumulating K^+ and proline (Bhargava, 2005) inside their cells. Further adaptation of cyanobacteria under salt and alkalinity stress is associated with accumulation of osmoregulatory proteins i.e., proline (Stewart and Lee, 1974), carbohydrate i.e., trehalose (Reed and Stewart, 1983) and sucrose (Blumwald and Tel-Or, 1982).

Algalization of salt affected soil with cyanobacteria enhances the soil aggregation property by adding polysachharidic material to the soil that helps in binding the soil. Improvement in soil aggregation enhances increased air and water movement in the soil, ultimately supporting better root penetration and increased uptake of nutrients from soil by plants which are limiting in sodic and saline-sodic soils. Moreover, establishment of cyanobacteria in saline soils supplements carbon and nitrogen to the soil. Not only this, cyanobacteria mobilize unavailable sources of phosphorus fixed in saline-sodic soils due to its high pH making them available for growing plants (Kaushik, 1983). Successful amelioration of usar soils by cyanobacteria have supported the successful establishment of crop plants with high yields (Kaushik, 1989). Hence, the application of cyanobacteria in saline soils may enhance the productivity and crop yield by maintaining the physico-chemical properties of the soil.

Cyanobacteria Mediated Bioremediation of Polluted Ecosystems

Human encroachment of the earth surface and development in terms of industrialization and urbanization for their comfort have completely modified the environment by incorporating toxic substances into air, soil and water, making the environment and life unhealthy. Removal of these toxic substances from the environment or their transformation into non-toxic forms are urgently required. With the advancement in environmental biotechnology programme, removal of toxic wastes from contaminated sites using biological system particularly microorganisms including cyanobacteria has been considered advantageous over traditional approaches, which require large spaces and produce large amount of wet bulky sludge. Also, restoration of polluted environments using cyanobacteria has manifold advantages over chemical treatment, as cyanobacteria are widespread in all conceivable systems and are also able to accumulate high levels of metal or pollutants. Some of the metal or pollutant accumulation, degradation and transformation potential of cyanobacteria have been discussed below.

Heavy metals are defined as metals with a density higher than 5 g cm^{-3}. Weast (1984) has defined 53 elements as heavy metals out of 90 naturally occurring metals. He further categorized that 17 heavy metals are available for living cells and are important for organisms and ecosystems. Among these metals, Fe, Mo and Mn are important as micronutrients, Zn, Ni, Cu, V, Co, W and Cr are toxic elements with high or low importance as trace elements and As, Hg, Ag, Sb, Cd, Pb and U have no known functions in plant metabolisms and are more or less toxic to plants and microorganisms (Schützendübel and Polle, 2002; Nies, 1999; Breckle, 1991).

Use of microorganisms including cyanobacteria in removal of heavy metals from contaminated sites has a number of potential advantages: (i) rapid kinetics of the metal removal, (ii) the capability of the microbial biomass to remove metallic ions, (iii) the utilization of naturally abundant renewable biomaterials, and the possibility to treat water containing multiple metals. Cyanobacteria capable of fixing atmospheric nitrogen along with atmospheric carbon make them suitable bioremediating agents.

Removal of Cu(II) under laboratory condition has been reported by De Philippis *et al.*, (2003) using two capsulated, exopolysachharide-producing cyanobacteria, *Cyanospora capsulata* and *Nostoc* PCC 7936. They reported the biosorption of Cu from the first minutes of contact with metals and attained equilibrium state after 5 to 6 hours when no more copper removal was evident (De Philippis *et al.*, 2003). Verma and Singh (1990) also reported Cu uptake by a diazotrophic cyanobacterium, *Nostoc calcicola*. Micheletti *et al.* (2008) showed sorption of Cu by exopolysachharide producing cyanobacteria *Cyanothece* and *Nostoc* sp. The metal uptake was observed to be dependent on various nutritional factors and tolerance to the intracellular detoxification mechanism (Verma and Singh, 1995). El-Enany and Issa (2000), while performing an experiment for remediation of sewage water using *Nostoc linckia* (metal tolerant) and *Nostoc rivularis* (metal sensitive), showed the increased heterocyst frequency and enhanced nitrogen fixation grown at low and moderate levels (25 % and 50 %) over those grown at high levels (75%). Further observation made by them showed the enhanced accumulation of 30-fold and 10-fold of Zn and 10-fold and 2-fold of Cd by *N. linckia* and *N. rivularis* respectively grown in growth medium with 75% sewage water over growth medium with 25 and 50% sewage water.

Lead is one of the most toxic substances accumulating in the ecosystems. The removal of lead by cyanobacteria was reported by Raungsomboon *et al.*, (2008) under laboratory condition. They reported that a cyanobacterium, *Gloeocapsa* is capable of growing in the range of 0-20 mg L^{-1}, but with reduced Pb^{+2} removal efficiency when the concentration was increased from 2.5 to 20 mg L^{-1}. The maximum accumulation of Pb^{+2} by *Gloeocapsa* was reported to be 232.56 mg g^{-1}. Roy *et al.* (2008) reported the growth of cyanobacterium, *Synechocystis* sp PCC6803 up to 300 mg L^{-1} Pb^{+2}, and the growth was inhibited at concentration 400 mg L^{-1} Pb^{+2}. They also reported that the increased superoxide dismutase (SOD) and catalase (CAT) activity of the organism was associated with exposure to toxic lead compounds. The ability of cyanobacteria to accumulate biologically important microelements (B, Mo, Se, and Zn) and to optimize technological processes for producing biologically active substances was reported by Sedykh *et al.* (2005).

Certain cyanobacteria produce bioflocculants (Bender *et al.*, 1994) that protect them from toxic effects of heavy metals (Kaplan *et al.*, 1987; Kureck *et al.*, 1991). Bioflocculants are extracellular macromolecules capable of clarifying turbid water and may remove dissolved nutrients from water column, thereby accelerating the heterotrophic activity in the sediment region. Bioflocculants are characterized by the presence of numerous negatively charged binding sites that empowered the cyanobacteria in removal of heavy metals from polluted sites. Bender *et al.* (1989, 1991a, 1991b) showed that *Oscillatoria* sp. are effective in removing Pb, Cd, Cu, Zn, Co, Cr, Fe, and Mn from water by producing extracellular bioflocculants when exposed to heavy metals stress. Bar-Or and Shilo (1987) reported the production of bioflocculants by *Phormidium* sp. strain J-1characterized by sulfated polysachharides with attached fatty acids and proteins. The uptake of metal ions (Cu, Pb, Zn, Ni, Cd and Cr) in *Spirulina platensis* was accompanied by liberation of protons, suggesting an ion exchange mechanism (Greene *et al.* 1987). The removal of mercury and lead by *Spirulina platensis* has been reported by Slotton *et al.* (1989). Cyanobacteria have developed multiple strategies for combating the toxic metal stress. Cyanobacteria are endowed with carboxyl groups on cyanobacterial cell biomass that help in the binding of various ions (Gardea-Torresdey *et al.*, 1990), possess intracellular polyphosphates, which participate in metal sequestration, and the presence of extracellular polysachharides that serve to chelate or bind metal ions (Zhang and Majidi, 1994; Kaplan *et al.*, 1987).

Reports on immobilization of cyanobacteria in silica gel matrix and their potential application in removal of heavy metals have also been reported. Gardea-Torresdey *et al.* (1998) have experimentally worked out the potency of cyanobacterium, *Synechococcus* sp., to uptake copper(II), lead(II), cadmium(II), nickel(II), chromium(III), and chromium(VI) under batch conditions, as well as uptake of copper (II), lead (II), cadmium (II), and nickel (II) by silica immobilized cells under flow conditions. Biosorption of Cr(VI) using *Nostoc calcicola* HH-12 and *Chroococcus* sp. HH-11 immobilized in Ca-alginate was reported (Anjana *et al.,* 2007). Many of the cyanobacteria synthesize metal binding proteins 'metallothioneins' that help organisms in the sequestration of toxic metal ions. Metallothioneins contain a number of thiol containing cysteine residues that are involved in metal binding. These proteins act as defense mechanisms employed by the organism by binding metal ions intracellularly (Gardea-Torresdey *et al.*, 1998).

Some other possible applications of cyanobacteria are the degradation of polycyclic aromatic hydrocarbons. PAHs are also called polynuclear aromatics (PNAs) that constitute a class of hazardous organic chemicals made up of two or more fused benzene rings in linear, angular, or cluster arrangements, containing carbon and hydrogen (Cerniglia, 1992). PAHs are hydrophobic and lipophilic in nature, which makes them persistent in environment. The lipophilicity, environmetal persistent and xenotoxicity increase as the molecular size increases with fusion of four or five benzene rings. A major source of PAHs contamination in environment is the petroleum products. Some of the PAHs are anthracene, benzo(a) pyrene, benz(a)anthracene, fluoranthene, phenanthrene, perylene, pyrene, and fluorine. The degradation or transformation of PAHs is on the priority pollutant list because of their carcinogenic and mutagenic nature (Keith and Telliard, 1979). Cyanobacteria are capable of oxidising PAHs contained in crude oil pollutants (Cerniglia, 1984). Reghukumar *et al.* (2001) reported the degradation of crude oil containing aliphatics (hexadecane), waxes and bitumen and aromatics (anthracene and phenantherene) by mixture of cyanobacterial species viz., *Oscillatoria salina* Biswas, *Plectonema terebrans* Bornet ex Flahault and *Aphanocapsa* sp. In view of the above discussion, it might be suggested that the future of cyanobacteria mediated maintenance of polluted soil and water productive and fertile is promising and may hold good if suitable and sustainable approaches are developed.

FUTURE PROSPECTS

Complete dependency on physical and chemical sources of environment for the developmental processes adopted by humans and ignorance of living resources in the past have compelled humans to live in a threatened, dreadful and depleted atmosphere of the present. Rapid destruction in natural resources have stimulated scientists engaged in environmental programme to use the living system, particularly microbes, to clean-up the degraded soil and water. Cyanobacteria, among microbes, are better candidates that can be utilized for different human-oriented developmental processes including agriculture, industrial or environmental programme. Cyanobacteria diversifying all conceivable habitats provide diverse gene pools and metabolites and require concerted efforts for genetic or biochemical manipulation for their application in production of metabolites and degraded environment for sustainable practices of water and soil.

ACKNOWLEDGEMENTS

Author wishes to thank, Head, Department of Botany, Banaras Hindu University, Varanasi. Author (KKC) is thankful to CSIR, (RKG) is thankful to UGC, New Delhi and UCOST, Uttarakhand for the financial support.

REFERENCES

Acho-Chi (1998). *Environ Urban* **10:** 161-174.

Anjana, K., Kaushik, A., Kiran, B. and Nisha, R. (2007). *J. Hazard Mater* **148:** 383-386.

Barbeau, C., Deschenes, L., Karamanev, D., Comeau, Y. and Samson, R. (1997). *Appl Microbiol. Biotechnol.* **48:** 745.

Bar-Or, Y. and Shilo, M. (1987). *Appl. Environ. Microbiol.* **53:** 2226-2230.

Bender, J., Archibold, E.R., Ibeanusi, V. and Gould, J.P. (1989). *Water Sci. Technol.* **21:** 1661-1665.

Bender, J., Rodriguez-Eaton, S., Ekanemesang, U.M. and Phillips, P. (1994). *Appl. Environ. Microbiol.* **60:** 2311-2315.

Bender, J., Vatcharapijarn, Y. and Gould, J.P. (1991a). *In*: Proceedings of the 15th Annual Army Environmental R&D Symposium, June 1991, Williamsburg, Va, pp. 25-27.

Bender, J.A., Gould, J.P., Vatcharapijarn, Y. and Saha, G. (1991b). *Water Air Soil Pollut.* 59: 359-367.

Bhargava, S. (2005). *J. Basic Microbiol.* **45:** 171-181.

Blumwald, E. and Tel-Or, E. (1982). *Arch. Microbiol.* **132:** 168-172.

Boon, N., De Gelder, L., Lievens, H., Siciliano, S.D., Top, E.M. and Verstraete, W. (2002). *Environ. Sci. Technol.* **36:** 4698.

Breckle, C.W. (1991). *In:* Plant roots: the hidden half. Waisel, Y., Eshel, A., Kafkafi, U. eds. New York, NY: Marcel Dekker, pp. 351-373.

Cerniglia, C.E. (1984). *Adv. Appl. Microbiol.* **30:** 31-71.

Cerniglia, C.E. (1992). *Biodegradation* **3:** 351-168.

De Philippis, R., Paperi, R., Sili, C. and Vincenzini, M. (2003). *J. Appl. Phycol.* **15:** 155-161.

Duggan, J. (2005). *Resour. Conserv. Recy.* **45:** 97-113.

Dupont, R.R. (2006). *Environ. Prog.* **12:** 45-53.

El-Enany, A.E. and Issa, A.A. (2000). *Environ. Toxicol. Pharmacol.* **8:** 95-101.

Ellis, B.E. (1977). *Plant Sci. Lett.* **8:** 213–216.

Ellis, D.E., Lutz, E.J., Odom, J.M., Buchanan, Jr. R.J. and Bartlett, C.L. (2000). *Environ. Sci. Technol.* **34:** 2254-2260.

Galinski, E.A. and Trueper, H.G. (1982). *FEMS Microbiol. Lett.* **13:** 357-360.

Gallego, J.L.R., Loredo, J., Llamas, J. F., Vázquez, F. and Sánchez, J. (2001). *Biodegradation* **12:** 325-335.

Gardea-Torresdey, J.L., Arenas, J.L., Francisco, N.M.C., Tiemann, K.J. and Webb, R. (1998). *J. Hazard Subst. Res.* **1:** 1-18.

Gardea-Torresdey, J.L., Becker-Hapak, M.K., Hosea, J.M. and Darnell, D.W. (1990). *Environ. Sci. Technol.* **19:** 1372-1379.

Gentry, T.J., Rensing, C. and Pepper, I.L. (2004). *Crit. Rev. Env. Sci. Tech.* **34:** 447-494.

Greene, B., McPherson, R. and Darnall, D. (1987). Algal sorbants for selective metal ion recovery Patterson JW and Passion R (eds). Lewis Publishers, Chelsea, MI, pp. 315–338

Hejazi, R.F. and Husain, T. (2004). *Environ. Sci. Technol.* **38:** 2457–2469.

Jha, M.N., Venkataraman, G.S. and Kaushik, B.D. (1988). *Mircen. J.* **3:** 307-317.

Kaplan, D., Christiaen, D. and Arad, S.M. (1987). *Appl. Environ. Microbiol.* **53:** 2953-2956.

Kaushik, B.D. (1983). *J. Biol. Res.* **3:** 99-103.

Kaushik, B.D. (1989). *Phykos.* **28:** 101-109.

Keith, L.H. and Telliard, W.A. (1979). *Environ. Sci. Technol.* **13:** 416-423.

Khan, F.I., Husain, T. and Hejazi, R. (2004). *J. Environ. Manage* **71:** 95-122.

Kozliak, E.I., Ostlie-Dunn, T.L., Jacobson, M.L., Mattson, S.R. and Domack, R.T. (2000). *Bioremediation J.* **4:** 81-96.

Kurek, E., Francis, A.J. and Bollag, J.M. (1991). *Arch. Environ. Contam. Toxicol.* **20:** 106-111.

Lombi, E., Zhao, F.J., Dunham, S.J. and McGrath, S.P. (2001). *J. Environ. Qual.* **30:** 1919-1926.

Matsunaga, T., Takeyama, H., Nakao, T. and Yamazawa, A. (1999). *J. Biotechnol.* **70:** 33-38.

Measures, J.C. (1975). *Nature* **257:** 398-400.

Megharaj, M., Venkateswarlu, K. and Rao, A.S. (1987). *Bull. Environ. Contam. Toxicol.* **39:** 251–256.

Micheletti, E., Colica, G., Viti, C., Tamagnini, P. and De Philippis, R. (2008). *J. Appl. Microbiol.* **105:** 88-94.

Mohamed, Z.A. (2001). *Water Res.* **35:** 4405-4409.

Mueller, J.G., Lantz, S.E., Ross, D., Colvin, R.J., Middaugh, D.P. and Pritchard, P.H. (1993). *Environ. Sci. Technol.* **27:** 691–698.

Narro, M.L., Cerniglia, C.E., van Baalen, C. and Gibson, D.T. (1992). *Appl. Environ. Microbiol.* **58:** 1351-1359.

Nies, D.H. (1999). *Appl. Microbiol. Biotechnol.* **51:** 730-750.

Norris, R.D., Hinchee, R.E., Brown, R.A., McCarty, P.L., Semprini, L., Wilson, J.T., Kampbell, D.H., Reinhard, M., Bower, E.J., Borden, R.C., Vogel, T.M., Thomas, J.M. and Ward, C.H. (1994). Handbook of Bioremediation. Boca Raton, FL:CRC Press.

Norris, R.D., Hinchee, R.E., Brown, R.A., McCarty, P.L., Semprini, L., Wilson, J.T., Kampbell, D.H., Reinhard, M., Bower, E.J., Borden, R.C., Vogel, T.M., Thomas, J.M. and Ward, C.H. (1993). *FEMS Microbiol. Rev.* **15:** 195-215

Pimentel, P., Hepperly, P., Hanson, J., Douds, D. and Seidel, R. (2005). *Bioscience* **55:** 573-582.

Powrie, P. and Robinson, J.P. (2000). *In:* Sustainable solid waste management in the Southern Black Sea region, (Eds. Nath, B., Pelovski, Y. and Stoyanov, S.K.), Kluwer Academic Publishers, The Netherlands, pp. 113-140.

Raghukumar, C., Vipparty, V., David, J.J. and Chandramohan, D. (2001). *Appl. Microbiol. Biotechnol.* **57:** 433-436.

Raungsomboon, S., Chidthaisong, A., Bunnag, B., Inthorn, D. and Harvey, N.W. (2008). *Bioresource Technol.* **99:** 5650-5658.

Reed, R.H. and Stewart, W.D.P. (1983). *New Phytol* **95:** 595-603.

Reilley, K.A. and Banks, M.K. (1994). *J. Environ. Qual.* **25:** 212-219.

Ribeiro, J.P., Lopes, J. and Fachini, A. (2008). *J. Environ. Analyt. Chem.* **88:** 701-710.

Ripp, S., Nivens, D.E., Ahn, Y., Werner, C., Jarrell, I.V.J., Easter, J.P., Cox, C.D., Burlage, R.S. and Sayler, G.S. (2000). *Env. Sci. Technol.* **34:** 846-853.

Rodrigo, J., Benedict, O., Fatima, B., Maria, P. and Flávio, C. (2007). *Bioremediation J.* **11:** 1-11.

Roy, S., Ghosh, A.N. and Thakur, A.R. (2008). *Biometals* **21:** 515-524.

Roychoudhury, P., Kaushik, B.D. and Venkataraman, G.S. (1985). *Curr. Sci.* **54:** 1181-1183.

Sayler, G.S. and Ripp, S. (2000). *Curr. Opin Biotechnol.* **11:** 286-289.

Schützendübel, A. and Polle, A. (2002). *J. Exp. Bot.* **53:** 1351-1365.

Sedykh, E., Lyabusheva, O., Tambiev, A. and Bannykh, L. (2005). *J. Anal. Chem.* **60:** 29-33.

Seidel, H., Löser, C., Zehnsdorf, A., Hoffmann, P. and Schmerold, R. (2004). *Environ. Sci. Technol.* **38:** 1582-1588.

Singh, R.N. (1950). *Nature* **765:** 325-326.

Singh, R.N. (1961). Role of blue-green algae in nitrogen economy of Indian Agriculture. Indian Council of Agricultural Research, New Delhi, pp. 175.

Slotton, D.G., Goldman, C.R. and Frank, A. (1989). *Nutr. Rep. Int.* **40:**1165-1172.

Stewart, W.D.P. and Lee, J.A. (1974). *Planta* **120:** 279-289.

Subramanian, G. and Uma, L. (1999). *Bulletin de l'Institut océanographique* **2:** 599-606.

Thomas, J. and Apte, S.K. (1984). *J. Biosci.* **6:** 771-794.

Verma, S.K. and Singh, S.P. (1990). *Curr. Microbiol.* **21:** 33–37.

Verma, S.K. and Singh, S.P. (1995). *Bull. Environ. Contam.* **54:** 614-619.

Vidali, M. (2001). *Pure Appl. Chem.* **73:** 1163-1172.

Weast, R.C. (1984). CRC Handbook of chemistry and physics, 64th edition. Boca Raton, CRC Press.

Zhang, W. and Majidi, V. (1994). *Environ. Sci. Technol.* **28:** 1577-1581.

Zhu, Z.L. and Chen, D.L. (2002). *Nutr. Cycl. Agroecosys.* **63:** 117-127.

7

Role of Microbes in Bioremediation Technology

Ankita Shukla, S.K. Dwivedi and Deepak Agrahari

Department of Environmental Science

B.B. Ambedkar University, Lucknow (UP)-226 025, India.

E-mail: skdwivedibbau@gmail.com

The increase in industrialization and urbanization leads to environment contamination and causes pollution and adverse health effects. For removal of these pollutants, some biogents are used and this process is known a bioremediation. Bioremediation is most effective and recent technology and mainly helps in the removal of heavy metals from the soil. Microorganisms (primarily bacteria and fungi) are nature's original recyclers and transform natural and synthetic chemicals into sources of energy and raw materials for their growth. Bioaugmentation, biofilters, bioreactors, biostimulation, bioventing, composting and landfarming are the techniques used in bioremediation. Plant Growth Promoting Rhizobacteria (PGPR) include a diverse group of free living soil bacteria that help in the removal of heavy metals from soil and uptake by the plant. The plants that grow on metal contaminated soil are generally iron deficient. Rhizobacteria produce metal chelating agents called siderophores and help the plants to obtain sufficient iron, enhancing the bioavailability of soil bound iron. Antibiotics released by some rhizobacteria increase root absorption of heavy metals. Fungi, especially white-rot fungus, produce an enzyme laccase, Mn peroxidase and lignin peroxidase (LiP) causes lignin degradation of lignocellulosic substrates. *Phanerochaete chrysosporium,* a major wood rotting fungus, is capable enough to degrade a wide range of xenobiotic compounds including azo dyes. Bioremediation is a safe and eco-friendly process, but it is time taking and enhances the microbial population. Despite some disadvantages, by understanding of microbial communities and their response to natural environment and pollution, some new techniques are introduced which are cost-effective and safer for the environment.

INTRODUCTION

Environmental pollution owing to anthropogenic and natural sources is growing day by day due to increasing population, industrialization and urbanization. The difficulty for the community, scientists, and academicians is how to deal with the pollutants that degrade the environment. Advancements in science and technology have also allowed humans to take advantage of natural resources. Huge figure of pollutants and dissipate resources contain heavy metals to be thrown into the surroundings yearly. According to Third World Network reports, more than one billion pounds (450 million kilograms) of toxins are on the loose worldwide into atmosphere and hydrosphere. The environmentalists around the world are trying to prevail over it by numerous ways. Despite the fact that they are raising their voices at global platforms concerning the exhaustion of natural resources. The perfect explanation for check on contamination is bioremediation—an efficient, inventive tools to arrive along in this century that uses biological systems for dealing with contaminants. Though the latest machinery is a multidisciplinary approach, its main driving strength depends on microbiology. It includes biostimulation (stimulating viable native microbial population), bioaugmentation (artificial introduction of viable population), bioaccumulation (live cells), biosorption (dead microbial biomass) and phytoremediation (plants).

"Remediate" means to solve a trouble, and "bio-remediate" means to use biological organisms to solve an environmental problem such as polluted soil or groundwater. Bioremediation is the use of existing microorganisms to degrade ecological pollutants or check contamination. In other words, it is a tool for removing pollutants from the environment, thus restoring the novel natural environment and preventing supplementary contamination. The fast extension and rising complexity of the chemical industries during the last century has intended that there have been rising levels of complex noxious effluents being released into the surroundings. A lot of major incidents have occurred in the earlier period, which disclose the requirement to check the run off of effluents into the surroundings, such as the Exxon Valdez oil spill, the Union-Carbide (Dow) Bhopal disaster, large scale contamination of the Rhine River, the progressive decline of the aquatic habitats and conifer forests in the Northeastern US, Canada, and parts of Europe or the release of radioactive material in the Chernobyl accident etc.

Bioremediation is a sustainable policy that utilizes the metabolic perspective of microbes and vegetation to clear the impure environment. It achieves pollutant disintegration or restriction by exploiting the existing metabolic perspective of microorganisms with novel catabolic functions resulting from assortment or by introduction of genes encoding such functions. Certain plants functioning mutually with soil organisms can alter the contaminants into nontoxic and frequently valuable forms. In addition to this rhizospheric consequence, plants themselves are capable to passively take up a broad series of organic wastes from soil through their roots. One significant trait of bioremediation is that it is carried out in unsterile open environments, which contain a variety of organisms. This tool can be applied for the exclusion of xenobiotic compounds from agrochemical and petrochemical industries, oil spills, heavy metals in sewage, sludge, marine sediments, a variety of chemicals, pesticides, excessive nutrients, phenols, hydrocarbons and the wastewater arising from dye manufacturing. The bioremediation skill is cost valuable, eco-friendly and substitute to conventional treatments, which rely on incineration, volatilization or immobilization of the pollutants. The conservative management technologies simply relocate the pollutants, creating a new dissipate like incineration residues and do not eliminate the problem. However, the universal approval of bioremediation as a management equipment requires the manifestation of its efficiency, consistency and inevitability, and its advantages are greater than conservative management technologies. The victorious achievement of a bioremediation process and manifestation of its efficiency require an interdisciplinary, organized monitoring and assessment policy at each process-scale stage. A suitable action, procedure and optimization throughout the scale-up depends on five interrelated criteria: chemical and engineering aspects; economics; eco-toxical aspects; biological nature; and aesthetic aspect. Bioremediation is principally explored for purifying metal infected wastes. The ultimate goal is to transfer lab technology to the field to make it a common approach to take away pollutants and to build a world free of contaminants.

TYPES OF BIOREMEDIATION

Bioremediation is of two types:
(i) *in situ* bioremediation
(ii) *ex situ* bioremediation

In situ Bioremediation

In situ bioremediation means that there is no need to excavate or remove soils or water in order to accomplish remediation. In situ bioremediation is functional in degradation of contaminants in saturated soils and groundwater. It is an advanced process for cleaning polluted surroundings, as it is cheaper and uses risk-free microorganisms to degrade the chemicals. *Chemotaxis* is significant in the study of *in situ* bioremediation because microbial organisms with chemotactic abilities can shift into a region containing contaminants. So by enhancing the chemotactic abilities of cells, *in situ* bioremediation will become a safer process in degrading hazardous compounds. *In situ* bioremediation methods have many possible advantages:

1. It does not need digging of the infected soil and therefore proves to be price valuable.
2. There is least place distraction, so the quantity of dust produced is of lesser amount and instantaneous management of soil and groundwater is feasible.

In situ bioremediation also has some disadvantages:

1. The method is time taking compared to other remedial methods.
2. Seasonal variant of the microbial action owing to direct exposure to changes in ecological factors that cannot be restricted and problematic application of action additives.
3. Microbes take action well only when the waste materials present permit them to generate nutrients and power for the expansion of supplementary cells. When these circumstances are not favourable, their ability to degrade is reduced. In such cases genetically engineered microorganisms have to be used.

(a) Types of in situ Bioremediation

Intrinsic bioremediation

It deals with the encouragement of native or naturally occurring microbial populations by feeding them with nutrients and oxygen to enhance their metabolic action.

Engineered in situ bioremediation

It involves the introduction of certain microorganisms to the site of pollution. When site situation is not appropriate, the engineered system has to be introduced to that fastidious site. Engineered *in situ* bioremediation accelerates the degradation process by enhancing the physico-chemical conditions to promote the expansion of microorganisms. Oxygen, electron acceptors and nutrients (e.g., nitrogen and phosphorus) encourage microbial growth.

Ex situ Bioremediation

Ex situ bioremediation processes necessitate the digging of infected soil or pumping of groundwater to make the microbial degradation possible. This technique has many disadvantages.

Methods Involved in the Treatment of Waste Materials

Ex situ bioremediation can be classified as:

1. Solid phase system (including land treatment and soil piles)
2. Slurry phase system (including solid-liquid suspensions in bioreactors)
   (i) Solid phase treatment: It includes organic wastes (e.g., leaves, animal manures and agricultural wastes) and problematic wastes (e.g., domestic and industrial wastes, sewage sludge and municipal solid wastes). Solid phase soil treatment processes consist of landfarming, soil biopiles and composting.
   (ii) Slurry phase bioremediation: Slurry phase bioremediation is a comparatively more quick procedure compared to supplementary action processes. In this the contaminated soil is combined with water and other additives in a large tank called bioreactor and mixed to keep the microorganisms, already present in the soil, in contact with the contaminants in the soil.

Nutrients and oxygen are added and situation in the bioreactor is controlled to generate the most favorable environment for the microbes to degrade the contaminants. When the treatment is done, the water is detached from the solids that are disposed of or treated further if they still contain pollutants.

The bioremediation process depends upon many factors. These factors include:

1. microbial population capable of degrading the pollutants;
2. the availability of contaminants to the microbial population; and
3. the environment factors (type of soil, temperature, and pH, the presence of oxygen or other electron acceptors, and nutrients).

MICROORGANISMS INVOLVED IN BIOREMEDIATION PROCESS

Microorganisms can be isolated from almost any environmental conditions. Because of their ability to adapt themselves according to environmental conditions, microbes are of following types:

Aerobic microbes degrade the pollutants in the presence of oxygen. Examples are *Pseudomonas*, *Alcaligenes*, *Sphingomonas*, *Rhodococcus*, and *Mycobacterium*. Aerobic microbes mainly degrade pesticides and hydrocarbons, both alkanes and polyaromatic compounds.

Anaerobic microbes degrade the pollutants in the absence of oxygen. Anaerobic bacteria are not as frequently used as aerobic bacteria. These are mainly used for the bioremediation of polychlorinated biphenyls (PCBs) in river sediments, dechlorination of the solvent trichloroethylene (TCE), and chloroform.

Lignolytic fungi: Fungi such as white-rot fungus *Phanaerochaete chrysosporium* have the ability to degrade lignin containing substrates e.g., straw, saw dust, or corn cobs.

Methylotrophs are aerobic bacteria that utilize methane for carbon and energy for their growth. They produce an enzyme, methane monooxygenase, which degrades the chlorinated aliphatic trichloroethylene and 1, 2-dichloroethane. Microbes (primarily bacteria and fungi) are nature's innovative recyclers. Their ability to convert natural and artificial chemicals into sources of power and untreated resources for their own development suggests that costly chemical or physical remediation processes might be replaced with natural processes that are lesser in expenditure and more environmentally pleasant. Microbes therefore symbolize a promising, largely available reserve for latest environmental biotechnologies. Investigation continues to confirm the bioremediation potential of microorganisms. For example, a current addition to the emergent list of bacteria that can reduce metals is *Geobacter metallireducens,* which removes uranium, a radioactive waste, from drainage waters in mining operations and infected groundwater. These discoveries propose that additional investigation of microbial diversity is likely to lead to the detection of a lot of supplementary organisms with distinctive properties valuable in bioremediation. The exploitation of microorganisms is not restricted to individual field of study of bioremediation. It has a widespread use. Petroleum and its products and oils constitute hydrocarbons, and if present in the surroundings, these cause pollution. An oil slick caused by oil tankers and petrol leakage into the marine environment is currently a frequently happening event. A number of microorganisms can consume oil as food, and many of them produce effective surface-active compounds that can emulsify oil in water and make its subtraction possible. Unlike chemical surfactants, the microbial emulsifier is non-hazardous and biodegradable. The microorganisms capable of degrading petroleum include pseudomonads, various *Corynebacteria, Mycobacteria* and some yeasts. Apart from degrading hydrocarbons, microbes also have the ability to remove industrial wastes, and reduce the toxic cations of heavy metals (such as selenium) to a much less toxic soluble form. For example, plants like locoweed remove large amounts of the toxic element, selenium. The selenium is stored in plant tissues where it poses no harm until and unless the plant is eaten. Many algae and bacteria release secretions that absorb metals toxic in high levels. By this, metals are removed from the food chain. Degradation of dyes is also brought about by some anaerobic bacteria and fungi. Due to the increase in population, the major problem towards the world is to increase food production. To increase food production rate, several pesticides are used. The utilization of these pesticides in crops has resulted to accumulation of artificial complex compounds known as xenobiotics, and these can be degraded by genetically altered microbes. Heavy metals are usually defined as elements with metallic properties (ductility, conductivity, stability as cations, ligand specificity, etc.) and atomic number > 20. The most common heavy metal contaminants are Cd, Cr, Cu, Hg, Pb and Ni. Metals are usual components in soil with a number of heavy metals being required by plants as micronutrients. The pollution of biosphere by noxious metals has accelerated noticeably since the beginning of the industrial revolution such as mining and smelting of metals, electroplating, gas exhaust, energy and fuel production, fertilizer, sewage and pesticide application, municipal waste generation, etc.(Kabata and Pendias,1989). Metal pollution has become one of the most rigorous environmental troubles at present. Excessive buildup of heavy metals is toxic to most of the plants. Heavy metal ions, when present at a high level in the environment, are absorbed by roots and translocated to shoot leading to impaired metabolism and reduced growth (Bingham *et al.,*1986; Foy *et al.,*1978*).*Heavy metal contamination in water and soil poses a key environmental and human health trouble. Excessive metal absorption in polluted soil results in decreased soil microbial action and soil productiveness and yield losses (McGrath *et al.,*1995).

Cadmium is a non-essential, heavy metal toxic to plants and can inhibit root and shoot growth, affect nutrient uptake and homeostasis and is habitually accumulated by agriculturally significant crops (Sanità and Gabrielli,1999). Thus, when Cd-enriched crop products are consumed by animals and humans, they cause diseases. The contamination of soil with Cd can negatively affect the biodiversity and action of soil microbial communities (McGrath, 1994). Experiments by Burd *et al.* (1998) showed that canola seeds developed normally in the presence of up to 1 mmol/L nickel chloride, but plant root and shoot elongation were inhibited at higher levels.

Heavy metals cannot be destroyed biologically, but are only transformed from one oxidation state or organic complex to another (Garbisu and Alkorta, 2001). Excavation and landfill, thermal treatment, acid leaching and electroreclamation are not suitable practically due to their high cost, low efficiency, destruction of soil structure and fertility and soil properties, etc. Thus, the development of phytoremediation strategies for soils contaminated with heavy metals is necessary (Chaney *et al.*, 2000; Cheng *et al.*, 2002 ; Lasat, 2002).

In phytoremediation, the use of plants to pull out or detoxify pollutants through physical, chemical, and biological processes (Cunningham and Ow, 1996; Saxena, 1999; Wenzel *et al.*, 1999) has been reported to be a valuable, non-intrusive, inexpensive, aesthetically pleasurable, ecologically caring, communally accepted tools to remediate contaminated soils (Alkorta and Garbisu, 2001; Garbisu *et al.*, 2002; Weber *et al.*, 2001). It also helps in preventing landscape devastation and enhances action and variety of soil microorganisms to sustain vigorous environment, which is accordingly well thought out to be a more gorgeous choice than conventional methods that are presently in use for dealing with heavy metal contamination (Bogardt and Hemmingsen,1992; Cunningham and Berti, 1993; Cunningham *et al.*, 1995; Salt *et al.*, 1995).

Phytoremediation of heavy metals may take one of the several forms: phytoextraction, rhizofiltration, phytostabilization and phytovolatilization. Phytoextraction refers to processes in which plants are used to concentrate metals from the soil into the roots and shoots of the plant; rhizofiltration is the use of plant roots to absorb, concentrate or precipitate metals from effluents; phytostabilization is the use of plants to reduce the mobility of heavy metals through absorption and precipitation by plants, thus reducing their bioavailability; phytovolatilization is the uptake and release of volatile materials such as mercury- or arsenic-containing compounds into the atmosphere. The ideal plants for phytoextraction should grow rapidly, produce a high amount of biomass, should be able to tolerate and accumulate high concentration of metals in shoots. Most of the commonly known heavy metal accumulators belong to the *Brassicaceae* family. (Kumar *et al.,* 1995).

Although hyperaccumulator plants have exceptionally high metal accumulating capacity, most of these have a slow growth rate and often produce limited amounts of biomass when the concentration of available metal in the contaminated soil is very high. An alternative is to use species with a lower metal accumulating capacity but higher growth rates such as Indian mustard (*Brassica juncea*). The another alternative is to provide them with an associated plant growth-promoting rhizobacteria, which is also considered to be an important component of phytoremediation technology (Glick, 2003; Wenzel *et al.*, 1999). Obviously, the rhizosphere contains a large number of microbial population with high metabolic activity compared to bulk soil (Anderson *et al.*, 1993).

Microbial populations are known to affect the mobility of heavy metals and availability to the plant through the release of chelating agents, acidification, phosphate solubilization and redox changes (Abou-Shanab *et al.,* 2003; Smith and Read, 1997). Especially some plant growth-promoting bacteria associated with plant roots may also exert some beneficial effects on plant growth and nutrition through a number of mechanisms such as N_2 fixation, production of phytohormones and siderophores and transformation of nutrient elements when they are either applied to seeds or incorporated into the soil (Glick, 1995; Glick *et al.*, 1995; Kloepper *et al.*, 1989). The use of rhizobacteria in combination with plants is expected to provide high efficiency for phytoremediation (Abou-Shanab *et al.*, 2003; Whiting *et al.,* 2001). Therefore, the potential and the exact mechanism of rhizobacteria to enhance phytoremediation of soil and heavy metal pollution has recently received some attention (de Souza *et al.*, 1999; Whiting *et al.,* 2001). Burd *et al.* (1998) observed that both the number of Indian mustard seeds that germinated in nickel-contaminated soil, and the attainable plant size increased by 50%-100% by the addition of *K. ascorbata*

SUD165/26, an associated plant growth-promoting rhizobacteria, to the soil in preliminary field trials. De Souza *et al.* (1999) investigated phytoremediation of Se and Hg in constructed wetlands, and found that the accumulation of Se and Hg was enhanced by rhizobacteria in wetland plant tissues. Potential for phytoremediation depends upon the interactions among soil, heavy metals, bacteria, and plants. These interactions are affected by several factors, such as characteristics and activity of plant and rhizobateria, climatic conditions and soil properties, etc.

The roots of plants interact with a large number of different microorganisms that are present in soil and help in phytoremediation process (Glick, 1995). The functioning of associative plant-bacterial symbiosis in heavy metal polluted soil can be affected from the side of both the micropartner (plant-associated bacteria) and the host plant. Soil microbes play a significant role in recycling of plant nutrients, maintenance of soil structure, detoxification of noxious chemicals and control of plant pests and plant growth (Elsgaard *et al.*, 2001; Filip, 2002; Giller *et al.*, 1998). Thus, bacteria can augment the remediation capacity of plants or reduce the phytotoxicity of the contaminated soil. In addition, plants and bacteria can form specific associations in which the plant provides the bacteria with a specific carbon source that induces the bacteria to reduce the phytotoxicity of the contaminated soil. Alternatively, plants and bacteria can form non-specific associations in which normal plant processes stimulate the microbial community, which in the course of normal metabolic activity degrades the contaminants in soil. The biochemical mechanisms increase the remediation activity of bacteria associated with plant roots. To sum up, the adaptation capabilities of both partners of the associative symbiosis as well as the bioremediation potential of the microsymbiont (association of rhizobacteria with higher plants) are of importance in minimizing the detrimental effect of heavy metal pollution. Rhizobacteria have been shown to possess several traits that can alter heavy metals bioavailability (Lasat, 2002; McGrath *et al.,* 2001; Whiting *et al.*, 2001) through the release of chelating substances, acidification of the microenvironment and by influencing changes in redox potential (Smith and Read, 1997). (Abou-Shanab *et al.*, 2003) reported that the addition of *Sphingomonas macrogoltabidus*, *Mycobacterium liquefaciens* and *Mycobacterium arabinogalactanolyticum* to *Alyssum murale* grown in serpentine soil significantly increased the plant uptake of Ni compared with the un-inoculated control as a result of soil pH reduction.

Rhizosphere microorganisms, which are closely associated with roots, have been termed plant growth promoting rhizobacteria (PGPR) (Glick *et al.*, 1995). Plant growth promoting rhizobacteria include a diverse group of free-living soil bacteria that can improve host plant growth and development in heavy metal contaminated soil by mitigating toxic effects of heavy metals on the plants (Belimov *et al.*, 2004). It is well known that heavy metals can even be toxic for metal-accumulating and metal-tolerant plants if the concentration of metals in the environment is sufficiently high. This is partly attributable to iron deficiency in a range of different plant species. (Römheld and Marschner, 1986; Mishra and Kar, 1974; Wallace *et al.*, 1992) in heavy metal contaminated soil. Furthermore, the low iron content of plants, which are grown in the presence of high levels of heavy metals, generally results in these plants becoming chlorotic since iron deficiency inhibits both chloroplast development and chlorophyll biosynthesis (Imsande, 1998). However, microbial iron-siderophore complexes can be taken up by plants and thereby serve as an iron source for plants (Bar-Ness *et al.*, 1991; Reid *et al.*, 1986; Wang *et al.*, 1993). It was therefore reasoned that the best way to prevent plants from becoming chlorotic in the presence of high levels of heavy metal was to provide them with an associated siderophore-producing bacterium. This suggests that some plant growth promoting bacteria can significantly increase the growth of plants in the presence of heavy metals including nickel, lead and zinc. (Burd and Glick, 2000), thus allowing plants to develop longer roots and get better establishment during early stages of growth (Glick *et al.*, 1998). Once the seedling is established, the bacterium can also help the plant to acquire sufficient iron for optimal plant growth. Similarly, chromium-resistant pseudomonads isolated from paint industry effluents were able to stimulate seed germination and growth of *Triticum aestivum* in the presence of potassium dichromate. In this case, the bacterial enhancement of seedling growth was associated with reduced chromium uptake. The effect of adding *K. ascorbata* SUD165, a plant growth-promoting bacterium, to canola or tomato seeds before the seed germination was also examined in the presence of inhibitory concentrations of Ni^{2+}. The result of these experiments showed that at all concentrations of nickel tested (1 to 6 mmol/L Ni^{2+}) using both a low-level and a high-level bacterial cell treatment (cell suspension absorbance of 0.025 or 0.50 respectively) with canola and tomato plants, with roots and shoots, and in both pouches and pots, the addition of *K. ascorbata* SUD165 significantly decreased the toxicity of added nickel (Glick *et al.*, 1998).

Some rhizobacteria release secretions, such as antibiotics (including the antifungals), phosphate solubilizers, hydrocyanic acid, indoleacetic acid (IAA), siderophores, 1-aminocyclopropane-1-carboxylic acid (ACC) that increase the root absorption of heavy metals, such as Fe and Mn, as well as non-essential metals such as Cd (Salt *et al.*, 1995) that enhance tolerance of host plants by improving the P absorption (Davies *et al.*, 2001; Liu *et al.*, 2000) and promoting plant growth (Budzikiewicz, 1997; Burd *et al.,* 2000; Duffy and Défago, 1999; Ellis *et al.*, 2000; Meyer, 2000).

Abou-Shanab *et al.* (2005) investigated the relation between metal resistance and metal mobilization abilities of rhizobacteria. The highest incidence metal resistance was recorded for phosphate solubilizers with Cr, Zn and Pb (92.5%, 82.2% and 68.2% respectively), then for siderophore producers with Cr, Zn and Pb (78.5%, 71.02% and 61.6% respectively) and finally for acid producers with Cr, Zn and Pb (63.5%, 53.3% and 42.9% respectively).

Rhizobacteria secretion may play a major role among the mechanisms of phytoremediation assisted by rhizobacteria. Indirect mechanisms include preventing phytopathogens from inhibiting plant growth and development, while direct mechanisms include nitrogen fixation, synthesis of siderophores that can solubilize and sequester iron from the soil, production of phytohormones such as auxins and cytokinins, which can enhance plant growth and solubilization of minerals such as phosphorus (Glick, 1995; Glick *et al.*, 1999; Kloepper *et al.*, 1989; McGrath *et al.*, 1995). Rhizobacteria produce metal-chelating agents called siderophores, which have an important role in the acquisition of several heavy metals (Leong, 1986). These organic substances have the effect of scavenging Fe^{3+} and significantly enhancing the bioavailability of soil bound iron (Kanazawa *et al.*, 1994). It has also been recognized that plants grown in metal-contaminated soils are often iron deficient. The production of siderophores by plant growth-promoting bacteria may help plants to obtain sufficient iron (Burd *et al.*,2000; Wallace *et al.*,1992).

Microbial siderophores are used as iron chelating agents that can regulate the availability of iron in the rhizosphere (Bar-Ness *et al.*, 1992). It has been assumed that competition for iron in the rhizosphere is controlled by the affinity of siderophore for iron and ultimately decides the rhizosphere population structure. The important factors that participate are concentration of various types of siderophore, kinetics of exchange and availability of Fe-complexes to microbes as well as plants. Interestingly, the binding affinity of phytosiderophores for iron is less than the affinity of microbial siderophores, but plants require a lower iron concentration for normal growth than microbes (McGrath *et al.*, 2001).

The presence of heavy metals in water bodies causes several health problems. Heavy metals such as mercury, cadmium and chromium can accumulate and enter the food chain and biomagnify to toxic levels. Several fungal species have developed a high resistance to heavy metals and developed a variety of mechanisms to remove ions such as cell surface biomass of *Aspergillus niger* to remove Zn^{2+} and Cd^{2+}, as the low affinity of the resident Ca^{2+} and Mg^{2+} ions of the biosorbent makes them excellent counter ions for the heavy metals that form more stable complexes. Filamentous soil fungi like *Aspergillus terreus, Cladosporium cladosporioides, Fusarium oxysporum, Gliocladium roseum, Penicillium* spp. and *Trichoderma koningii have been* isolated from industrially polluted sediments for the removal of cadmium. The fungus *Penicillium frequentans* has been found effective to remove phenanthrene in soil. The synthesis of lignin degrading enzymes in various microorganisms occurs via secondary metabolism; they are produced in limited amount using sufficient quantity of lignolytic enzymes. Lignin is a complex, variable, hydrophobic, cross linked, three-dimensional aromatic polymer of p-hydroxyphenylpropanoid units connected by C-C and C-O-C links. Lignin is extremely resistant to chemical and enzymatic degradation.

Biological degradation is achieved mainly by fungi, and most efficiently by white-rot basidiomycetes and also by certain ascomycetes. These polymer compounds are degraded only by microorganisms, which can produce enzymes capable of penetrating the substrate deeply. Lignin is degraded by many genera of actinomycetes and eubacteria (Buswell and Odier, 1987). Actinomycetes degrade lignin as primary metabolic activity at high nitrogen level compared to white rot fungi, which degrade lignin through secondary metabolism. In the soil, lignin is degraded by some species of *Streptomyces* and *Nocasdia* (Haider and Trojanowaski, 1980). Mainly white-rot fungi degrade lignin by means of oxidative enzymes (Hatakka, 1994). They produce the extracellular enzymes lignin peroxidase (LiPs), manganese peroxidase (MnPs) and laccases for lignin degradation.

Different white-rot fungi produce different grouping of enzyme, some producing LiP and MnP, some producing MnP and laccases, some producing Lip and laccases and some fungi which are neither producing LiP, MnP and laccases (Hatakka, 1994). Several fungi belonging to the LiPMnP and the MnP-laccases group are effective lignin degrader, while LiP- laccases group have much lower lignin degradation capability (Hatakka, 1994). So MnP plays an essential role in lignin degradation. This ligninolytic system of white-rot fungi is directly involved in the degradation of various xenobiotic compounds and dyes. *Phanerochaete chrysosporium*, a major wood rotting fungus, is capable enough to degrade a wide range of recalcitrant xenobiotic compounds including azo dyes. *Phanerochaete chrysosporium* degrades a wide variety of structurally diverse organopollutants through its non-specific H_2O_2 dependent extracellular lignin degradation enzyme system.

Mechanism

The genes responsible for microbial metal resistance mechanisms are organized in operons and are usually found in plasmids carried by the resistant organisms (Ramanathan *et al.*, 1997; Bruins *et al.*, 2000). The expression of the resistance genes is tightly regulated and induced by the presence of specific metals in the cellular environment (Ramanathan *et al.*, 1997). Because of the specificity of this regulation, the promoters and regulatory genes from these resistance operons can be used to construct metal-specific biosensors (promoter-reporter gene fusions). By using metal specific bacterial sensors, in addition to chemical analysis, it is possible to distinguish the bioavailable metal concentration from the total metal concentration of the samples. Reaction of the fungus, *Fusarium oxysporum*, with the aqueous heavy-metal ions $Pb^{2+}$and Cd^{2+} results in the one-step formation of the corresponding metal carbonates. The metal carbonates are formed by the reaction of heavy-metal ions with CO_2 produced by the fungus during metabolism, and thus provide a completely biological method for production of crystals of metal carbonates. The $PbCO_3$ and $CdCO_3$ crystals thus produced have interesting morphologies that are shown to arise because of interaction of the growing crystals with specific proteins secreted by the fungus during reaction. An additional advantage of this approach is that the reaction leads to detoxification of the aqueous solution and could have immense potential for bioremediation of heavy metals. Under the conditions of this study, the metal ions are not toxic to the fungus that readily grows after exposure to the metal ions.

Bioremediation is a usual procedure and is consequently evident by the public as a appropriate desecrate management practice for infected substance such as soil. Microbes able to degrade the toxic waste raise in figures when the pollutant is degraded, and the biodegradative population declines. The residues of the management are generally not dangerous products and consist of carbon dioxide, water, and cell biomass. This eliminates the possibility of future responsibility related with management and removal of infected material. As an alternative of transferring contaminants from one environmental medium to another, for example: from land to water or air, the whole devastation of mark pollutants is attainable. Bioremediation can be regularly carried out on site without causing any major trouble in normal actions. This also eliminates the prerequisite of transport quantities of desecrate off site and the possible threats to human health and the environment that can take place during carrying. Bioremediation is cheaper than other technologies that are used for clean-up of hazardous waste.

TECHNOLOGIES USED IN BIOREMEDIATION PROCESS

Technologies using bioremediation treatment include bioaugmentation, biofilters, bioreactors, biostimulation, bioventing, composting and landfarming.

Bioaugmentation

Bioaugmentation refers to the introduction of specially selected or genetically engineered strains of microbes to a contaminated site. If site assessments reveal that the species of indigenous microorganisms are unable to degrade target contaminants, exogenous microorganisms with the required biochemical capabilities can be introduced to successfully degrade specific waste compounds.

Biodegradation

Biodegradation refers to the degradation of organic contaminants in soil and/or groundwater by indigenous or transplanted/acclimated microorganisms, primarily bacteria and fungi. Organic contaminants are converted into carbon dioxide, water, and microbial cell mass under aerobic conditions (in the presence of oxygen). Under anaerobic conditions (in the absence of oxygen), methane, small quantities of carbon dioxide and hydrogen, and occasionally intermediate species, which may be less, equally, or more hazardous that the metabolized compound, are produced. Biodegradation can be used to degrade environmental pollutants such as pentachlorophenol (PCP), lindane (hexachlorocyclohexane), dichlorodiphenyl trichloroethane (DDT), and 2, 4-dichlorophenol. Fungi such as *Fusarium oxysporium* and *Phanerochaete chrysosporium*, as well as bacteria, such as *Pseudomonas cepacia* and *Pseudomonas putida*, are used to degrade these pollutants.

Biostimulation

Biostimulation refers to thc addition of oxygen and/or inorganic nutrients to indigenous microbial populations in soils and groundwater. *In situ* or *ex situ* methods can be employed to stimulate biodegradation of contaminants. It is of two types.

Table 7.1 Microbes in bioremediation

S.No.	Microorganisms	Process
1.	*Geobacter metallireducens*	Degradation of uranium
2.	*Pseudomonads, various Corynebacteria, Mycobacterium and some yeasts*	Degradation of petroleum
3.	*Pseudomonads*	Chromium resistant
4.	*K. ascorbata SUD165(Plant Growth Promoting Bacteria)*	Nickel removal
5.	*Some anaerobic bacteria and fungi*	Degradation of dyes
6.	*Aspergillus niger*	Remove Zn^{2+} and Cd^{2+}
7.	*Aspergillus terreus, Cladosporium cladosporioides, Fusarium oxysporum, Gliocladium roseum, Penicillium* spp.and *Trichoderma koningii*	Removal of cadmium
8.	*Penicillium frequentans*	Remove phenanthrene
9.	*White-rot fungi*	Degradation of various xenobiotic compounds and dyes
10.	*Phanerochaete chyrosporium*	Degrade a wide range of recalcitrant xenobiotics compound, including azo dyes.

Bioventing

Bioventing is a process of motivating the natural *in situ* biodegradation of contaminants in soil by providing air or oxygen to the existing soil microorganisms. Oxygen is most commonly supplied through direct air injection into residual contamination in soil. In addition to degradation of adsorbed fuel residuals, the volatile compounds are biodegraded as vapours move slowly through biologically active soil. Bioventing is applicable to any chemical that can be aerobically biodegraded. It is successfully used to remediate soils contaminated by petroleum hydrocarbons, non-chlorinated solvents, some pesticides, wood preservatives, and other organic chemicals.

Lagoon Treatment

Lagoon treatment is an *in situ* bioremediation process that degrades a mixture of organic and inorganic hazardous substances in a lagoon. It requires a combined treatment, both aerobic and anaerobic biodegradation methods, depending on contaminant characteristics. For wastes containing volatile chlorinated hydrocarbons, anaerobic processes are applied followed by an aerobic phase. Solid distribution and slurry mixing techniques including air sparging, pumping, mechanical and dredging must be used in the lagoon treatment in order to maintain high bioremediation rates. Lagoon treatment can remediate galvanizing wastes, phenols, pickling acids, polychlorinated biphenyl (PCB), heavy metals, polycyclic aromatic hydrocarbons (PAHs), and benzene, toluene, ethylbenzene, and xylene (BTEX). This method has been effectively used to treat hazardous substances discharged into lagoons by industrial or other sources. Lagoon treatment requires less cost than alternate technologies.

Bioreactors

Bioreactors represent highly controlled methods of treating contaminated soils and groundwater. Since temperature, pH, nutrient levels and agitation can be controlled in constructed batch- or continuously-fed reactors, microbial activity, and thus contaminant degradation can be optimized.

Compost-based Reactors

A compost-based reactor is a biological approach to convert biodegradable hazardous materials to harmless and stabilized byproducts by using microorganisms under elevated temperature. The increased temperature, typically 122° F to 158° F, results from heat released by microorganisms during the degradation of organic materials. Aerobic composting is used to degrade sewage sludge, whereas anaerobic processes are more suitable for hazardous waste treatment. Composting technology can be applied to municipal sludge, soils and lagoon sediments contaminated with biodegradable organic compounds. It has been demonstrated that composting is suitable for pentachlorophenol (PCP), refinery sludges insecticides contained in cannery wastes, explosive-contaminated soil, ethylene glycol contained in landfill sludge and polycyclic aromatic hydrocarbons (PAHs).

Slurry-based Reactors

Slurry-phase biological treatment is used to remediate a mixture of water and excavated soil. The slurry contains between 5 and 40% solids by weight depending on the nature of the biological reactor. The soil is suspended in a reactor vessel and mixed with nutrients and oxygen. Microorganisms may be added depending on treatment requirements. When biodegradation is complete, the soil slurry is dewatered. Biological treatment in slurry-phase reactors has been successfully used to remediate soils, sludge and groundwater contaminated by hydrocarbons, petrochemicals, solvents, pesticides, wood preservatives, and other organic chemicals.

Land-based Treatments

Land-based treatment, or solid-phase remediation of contaminated soil usually involves *ex situ* remediation methods.

Composting

Composting is a controlled biological process to convert biodegradable hazardous materials to harmless and stabilized byproducts by using microorganisms under elevated temperature. The increased temperature results from the heat released by microorganisms during the degradation of organic materials in the waste. Aerobic composting is used to degrade sewage sludge, and anaerobic processes are more suitable for hazardous waste treatment. The composting of contaminated soil utilizes a bulking agent, such as saw dust, animal waste, or the like, to increase porosity of the media. The composting efficiency is impacted by moisture content, pH, oxygen, temperature, and C:N ratio. The composting technology can be applied to municipal sludge, soils, and lagoon sediments contaminated with biodegradable organic compounds. It has been demonstrated that composting is suitable for pentachlorophenol (PCP), refinery sludges, insecticides in cannery wastes, explosive contaminated soil, ethylene glycol in landfill sludges and polycyclic aromatic hydrocarbons (PAHs).

Land Farming

Land farming is a bioremediation treatment process that is performed in the upper soil zone or biotreatment cells. Contaminated soils, sediments, or sludges are incorporated into the soil surface and occasionally twisted over to aerate the mixture. This technique has been successfully used for years in the management and disposal of oily sludge and other petroleum refinery wastes. These land farming activities cultivate and enhance microbial degradation of hazardous compounds.

Fungal Remediation

The white-rot fungus, *Phanerochaete chrysosporium*, can bind to, and in some instances, mineralize a wide array of organic pollutants, including polychlorinated biphenyls (PCBs), polycyclic aromatic hydrocarbons (PAHs) and the predominant conventional explosives viz., TNT, RDX, and HMX. The lignin-degrading, or wood-rotting enzymes produced by white rot fungus have been reported to be the key to its degradation capabilities.

White-rot Fungus

Fungal remediation refers to the use of fungi to remediate organic soil contaminants, primarily hydrocarbons. One group of fungi *Phanerochaete chrysosporium* or white-rot fungus produces a family of enzymes called lignin peroxidases or ligninases, which has extensive biodegradative properties. White-rot fungus is known to degrade polyaromatic hydrocarbons (PAHs), chlorinated aromatic hydrocarbons (CAHs), polycyclic aromatics, polychlorinated biphenyls, polychlorinated dibenzo(p)dioxins, the pesticides DDT and lindane, and some azo dyes (Cookson, 1995). Degradation of PAHs, which include benzo(a)pyrene, pyrene, fluorene, and phenanthrene, is favored at nitrogen-limiting conditions and low pH (about 4.5) (Suthersan, 1997). It has been documented that white-rot fungus is able to mineralize tri-, tetra- and pentachlorophenol (PCP), and a group of microbes in soil can completely mineralize PCP(Suthersan, 1997). Degradation of cyclodiene insecticides, including chlordane, by white-rot fungus has been demonstrated (Suthersan, 1997). White-rot fungus has been observed to degrade TNT in laboratory-scale studies (using pure cultures).

CONCLUSION

Bioremediation provides a method for crackdown contamination by enhancing the identical biodegradation processes that occur in nature. By increasing the perceptive of microbial populations and their reaction to the natural surroundings and pollutants, escalating the information of the genetics of the microorganisms to enhance capabilities to degrade pollutants, conducting field studies of innovative bioremediation techniques, which are cost efficient, and dedicating sites set away for long phrase study purpose. These opportunities recommend for future prospects and advances of microbial remediation process.

REFERENCES

Abou-Shanab, R.A., Angle, J. S., Delorme, T. A., Chaney, R. L., van Berkum, P., Moawad, H., Ghanem, K. and Ghozlan, H.A. (2003). *N Phytol.*; **158(1):** 219-224.

Abou-Shanab, R.A., Delorme, T. A., Angle, J. S., Chaney, R. L., Ghanem, K., Moawad, H., Ghozlan, H. A. (2003). *Int. J. Phytoremediation.* **5(4):** 367-379.

Alkorta, I. and Garbisu, C. (2001). *Bioresour Technol.* **79(3):** 273-276.

Anderson, T.A., Guthrie, E.A. and Walton, B.T. (1993) *Environ Sci Technol.* **27(13):** 2630-2636.

Barber, S.A. and Lee, R. B. (1974). *N. Phytol.* **73(1):** 97-106.

Bar-Ness, E., Chen, Y., Hadar, Y., Marchner, H. and Romheld, V. (1991). *Plant Soil.* **130(1-2):** 231-241.

Bar-Ness, E., Hadar, Y., Chen, Y., Shanzer, A. and Libman, J. (1992). *Plant Physiol.* **99(4):** 1329-1335.

Belimov, A. A., Kunakova, A. M., Safronova, V. I., Stepanok, V.V., Yudkin, L.Y., Alekseev; Y.V. and Kozhemyakov, A. P. (2004). *Microbiology (Moscow).* **73(1):** 99-106.

Bingham, F.T., Pereyea, F.J. and Jarrell, W.M. (1986). *Metal Ions Biol Syst.* **20:** 119-156.

Bogardt, A. H. and Hemmingsen, B.B. (1992). *Appl. Environ. Microbiol.* **58(7):** 2579-2582.

Bruins, M.R., Kapil, S. and Oehme, F.W. (2000) *Ecotoxicol and Environ Safety.* **45:** 198-207.

Budzikiewicz, H. (1998). *Nat Foresche.* **52C:** 413-420.

Burd, G.I., Dixon, D.G. and Glick, B.R. (1998). *Appl. Environ. Microbiol.* **64(3):** 3663-3668.

Burd, G.I., Dixon, D.G. and Glick, B.R. (2000) *Can. J. Microbiol.* **46(3):** 237-245.

Buswell, J.A. and Odier, E. (1987). *J. Applied. Biochem.* **7:** 371-387.

Chaney, R.L., Brown, S.L. and Li, Y.M. (2000). *US-EPA "Phytoremediation: State of Science", 2000 May 1-2.* Boston, MA: 2000. Progress in Risk Assessment for Soil Metals, and *In-situ* Remediation and Phytoextraction of Metals from Hazardous Contaminated Soils.

Cheng, S., Grosse, W., Karrenbrock, F. and Thoennessen, M. (2002). *Ecol Eng.* **18(3):** 317-325.

Cookson, J.T. (1995). Bioremediation Engineering: Design and Application, McGraw-Hill, New York, NY.

Cunningham, S.D. and Berti, W.R. (1993) *In Vitro Cell Dev Biol.* **29(4):** 207-212.

Cunningham, S.D., Berti, W.R. and Huang, J.W. (1995). *Trends Biotechnol.* **13(9):** 393-397.

Cunningham, S.D. and Ow, D.W. (1996). *Plant Physiol.* **110(5):** 715-719.

Davies, F.T. Jr., Puryear, J.D. and Newton, R.J. (2001). *J. Plant Physiol.* **158(6):** 777-786.

De Souza, M.P., Chu, D., Zhao, M., Zayed, A.M., Ruzin, S.E., Schichnes, D. and Terry, N. (1999). *Plant Physiol.*; **119(2):** 565-573.

De Souza, M.P., Huang, C.P., Chee, N. and Terry, N. (1999). *Planta.* **209(2):** 259-263.

Duffy, B.K. and Défago, G. (1999). *Appl. Environ. Microbiol.* **65(6):** 2429-2438.

Ellis, R. J., Timms-Wilson, T.M. and Bailey, M.J. (2000). *Environ Microbiol.* **2(3):** 274-284.

Elsgaard, L., Petersen, S.O. and Debosz, K. (2001). *Environ Toxicol Chem.* **20(8):** 1656-1663.

Filip Z. (2002). *Agric. Ecosyst. Environ.* **88(2):** 689-712.

Foy, C.D., Chaney, R.L. and White, M.C. (1978). *Annu Rev Plant Physiol.* **29(1):** 511-566.

Garbisu, C., Hernandez-Allica, J., Barrutia, O., Alkorta, I. and Becerril, J.M. (2002). *Rev Environ Health.* **17(3):** 173-188.

Garbisu, C. and Alkorta, I. (2001). *Bioresour Technol.* **77(3):** 229-236.

Giller, K.E., Witter, E. and McGrath, S.P. (1998). *Soil Biol Biochem.* **30(10-11):** 1389-1414.

Glick, B.R. (1995). *Can. J. Microbiol.* **41:**109-117.

Glick, B.R. (2003). *Biotechnol Adv.* **21(5):** 383-393.

Glick, B.R., Patten, C.L. and Holguin, G. (1999). *Biochemical and Genetic Mechanisms Used by Plant Growth-Promoting Bacteria.* London: Imperial College Press.

Glick, B.R., Karaturovic, D.M. and Newell, P.C. (1995). *Can. J. Microbiol.* **41(6)**:533-536.

Glick, B.R., Penrose, D.M. and Li, J.P. (1998). *J. Theor. Biol.* **190(1):** 63-68.

Haider, K. and Trojanowaski, J. (1980). *In: Lignin Biodegradation: Microbiology,Chemistry and Applications. (*Eds. Kirk, T.K., Higuchi, T., Chang, H.M.) *Vol.1*, CRCPress, USA, pp. 111-134.

Hatakka, A.(1994). *FEMS Microbiol. Rev.,* **13:** 125-135.

Imsande, J. (1998). *Physiologia Plantarum.* **103(1):** 139-144.

Kabata-Pendias, A. and Pendias, H. (1989) *Trace Elements in the Soil and Plants.* Boca Raton, FL: CRC Press.

Kanazawa, K., Higuchi, K., Nishizawa, N.K., Fushiya, S., Chino, M. and Mori, S. (1994). *J Exp Bot.* **45(12):** 1903-1906.

Kloepper, J.W., Lifshitz, R. and Zablotowicz, R.M. (1989). *Trends Biotechnol.* **7(2):** 39-44.

Kumar, P.B.A., Dushenkov, V., Motto, H. and Raskin, I. (1995). *Environ Sci Technol.* **29(5):** 1232-1238.

Lasat, H.A. (2002). *J. Environ. Qual.* **31(1):** 109-120.

Leong J. (1986). *Annu. Rev. Phytopathol.* **24(1):** 187-209.

Liu, A., Hamel, C., Hamilton, R.I., Ma, B. L. and Smith, D.L. (2000). *Mycorrhiza.* **9(6):** 331-336.

Loper, J.E. and Henkels, M.D. (1999). *Appl. Environ. Microbiol.* **65(12):** 5357-5363.

Ma, J.F. and Nomoto, K. (1993). *Physiologia Plantarum.* **89(2):** 331-334.

McGrath, S.P. (1994). *In: Toxic Metals in Soil-Plant Systems.* Ross S.M., New York: Wiley: pp. 247-273.

McGrath, S.P., Chaudri, A.M. and Giller, K.E. (1995). *J. Ind. Microbiol.* **14(2):** 94-104.

McGrath, S.P., Zhao, F.J. and Lombi, E. (2001). *Plant Soil.* **232(1-2):** 207–214.

Meyer, J.M. (2000). *Arch Microbiol.* 174(3):135-142.

Mishra, D. and Kar, M. (1974). *Bot Rev.* **40:** 395-452.

Patten, C.L. and Glick, B.R. (2002). *Appl. Environ. Microbiol.* **68(8):** 3795-3801.

Ramanathan, S., Ensor, M. and Daunert, S. (1997). *Trends in Biotechnol.* **15:** 500-506.

Reid, C.P., Szaniszlo, P. J. and Crowley, D.E. (1986). *In:* Iron Siderophores and Plant Diseases. Swinburne TR., New York, Plenum Press, pp. 29-42.

Römheld, V. and Marschner, H. (1986). *Adv Plant Nutr.* **2:** 155-204.

Salt, D.E., Blaylock, M., Kumar, N.P.B.A., Dushenkov, V. Ensley, B. D., Chet, I. and Raskin, I. (1995). *Biol Technol.* **13(5):** 468-474.

Sanità di Toppi, L. and Gabrielli, R. (1999). *Environ. Exp. Bot.* **41(2):** 105-130.

Saxena, P. K., Krishnaraj, S. and Dan, T. (1999). *In: Heavy Metal Stress in Plants: from Molecules to Ecosystems.* Prasad, M.N.V., Hagemeyer, J., Berlin, Springer, pp. 305-329.

Smith, S.E. and Read, D.J. (1997). *Mycorrhizal Symbiosis.* San Diego: Academic Press Inc.

Suthersan, S. (1997). Remediation Engineering Design Concepts, CRC Press, Boca Raton, FL.

Wallace, A., Wallace, G.A. and Cha, J.W. (1992). *J. Plant Nutr.* **15(2):** 1589-1598.

Wang, Y., Brown, H.N., Crowley, D.E. and Szaniszlo, P. J. (1993). *Plant Cell Environ.* **16(5):** 579-585.

Weber, O., Scholz, R.W., Bvhlmann, R. and Grasmuck, D. (2001). *Risk Anal.* **21(5):** 967-977.

Wenzel, W.W., Lombi, E. and Adriano, D.C. (1999). *In: Heavy Metal Stress in Plants: from Molecules to Ecosystems.* Prasad, M.N.V., Hagemeyer, J. Berlin: Springer, pp.273-303.

Whiting, S.N., de Souza, M.P. and Terry, N. (2001). *Environ. Sci. Technol.* **35(15):** 3144-3150.

8

Microbial Removal of Arsenic: An Overview

Umesh P. Dhuldhaj[1], Naveen K. Sharma[2] and Surendra Singh[1]

[1] *Department of Botany, Banaras Hindu University, Varanasi (UP)-221 005, India*

[2] *Department of Botany, Postgraduate College, Ghazipur (UP)-233 001, India*

E-mail: surendrasingh.bhu@gmail.com

In recent years, chronic intake of groundwater with high levels of arsenic has caused severe health concern in many parts of the world. Arsenic is a known toxic metalloid, with its trivalent [As(III)] and pentavalent [As(V)] ionic forms having adverse effects on humans and other organisms. As(III) is more toxic and mobile compared to that of As(V). In natural environments, microbial redox processes greatly transform highly toxic As(III) into less harmful As(V), which influences the arsenic cycling, and its accumulation in soils and groundwaters. This article discusses various aspects of arsenic such as its nature, speciation, soil and water contamination, global scenario of arsenic problem and resultant human health problems. We have also described biochemical (arsenite oxidation, cytoplasmic arsenate reduction, respiratory arsenate reduction, and arsenite methylation) and molecular strategies adopted by microbes to cope up with arsenic stress.

INTRODUCTION

Arsenic (As) is a metalloid element belonging to group V (period 4, block P) of the periodic table with atomic number 33 and atomic weight 74.92 g mol^{-1}, having a single naturally occurring isotope AS^{75} (Rensing and Rosen, 2009). It occurs primarily in four oxidation states, viz. arsenate [As(V)], arsenite [As(III)], elemental arsenic [As(0)] and arsenide [As(-III)]. The term 'arsenic' is derived from the Persian word '*zarnikh*', which means 'yellow orpiment' (As_2S_3) (Rensing and Rosen, 2009). Arsenic compounds have no biological roles. Historically, arsenic has been used in medicine; one could find numerous references extensively cited in the materia medica of ancient cultures (Datta *et al.,* 1979). Arsenic has also been used in cosmetics industry and agriculture, especially as an insecticide, desiccant, rodenticide and herbicide. However, in recent past, the element has attracted substantial global attention for its toxicity to the humans. The agency for Toxic Substances and Disease Registry (ATSDR) has included arsenic in the list of 'Twenty Most Hazardous Substances' (Singh, 2008). Toxicity of arsenic owes to its similarity with phosphate (H_3AsO_4, arsenate). Since the resulting sugar and nucleotide arsenates are less stable than phosphate sugar and nucleotide (Rensing and Rosen, 2009). Arsenite [As(III)], arguably the most toxic form of arsenic, binds with sulfur thiolates and also forms complex with glutathione (GSH), resulting in depletion of GSH pool leading to generation of free radicals. Further, it binds strongly to the enzyme pyruvate dehydrogenase, thus inhibiting oxidative metabolism. The consumption of arsenic contaminated groundwater is found to be responsible for the health hazards such as arsenicosis, dermatological disorders, neuropathy and obstetrics outcomes (Ahamed *et al.*, 2006).

ENVIRONMENTAL FATE OF ARSENIC

Arsenic is widely distributed in the earth's crust, with an average concentration of 2 mg kg^{-1} (or 1 ppm; ranking 20th in abundance). It occurs in trace quantities in all rocks, soils, water and air. Arsenic is found as a main component of nearly 200 minerals, most notably as arsenopyrite (FeAsS). The free metal is uncommon. It has been estimated that about one-third of the atmospheric flux of arsenic is of natural origin. Volcanic activities and hydrothermal sources (e.g., geysers, fumaroles etc.) are the most important sources of arsenic followed by low-temperature volatilization. Mining, copper smelting, coal burning, and other combustion processes also bring arsenic into the environment. In soils, the most often encountered arsenic forms are inorganic As(III) (arsenite) and As(V) (arsenate) (Cullen and Reimer, 1989; Masscheleyn *et al.*, 1991; Pantsar-Kallio and Korpela, 2000; Balasoiu *et al.*, 2001). Anthropogenic sources of arsenic include herbicides, insecticides, rodenticides, wood preservatives, animal feeds, paints, dyes and semiconductors (Rensing and Rosen, 2009). In USA, the sodium and calcium salts of monomethylarsenate (MMA) and dimethylarsenate (DMA) are widely used as herbicides and pesticides (Bhattacharjee and Rosen, 2007; Rensing and Rosen, 2009). According to World Health Organization (WHO), nearly 70% of global arsenic production is used in timber treatment (as copper chromate arsenate), 22% in agricultural chemicals and the rest in glass, pharmaceuticals and non-ferrous alloy industry (WHO, 2001). Ross (1994) categorized anthropogenic sources of arsenic contamination of soil as metalliferous mining and smelting, industry, atmospheric deposition and agriculture. Inorganic arsenic of geological origin reaches groundwater, which is often used for drinking in several parts of the world. The solubility of arsenic depends on the pH and ionic composition of the environment. Elemental arsenic is produced by the reduction of arsenic trioxide (As_2O_3) with charcoal, which is a by-product of copper smelting operations. Arsenic (arsenoopyrite) is also associated with copper and gold, commonly observed during the roasting of ores (Ng *et al.*, 2003). Figure 8.1 shows the arsenic cycle operating in global ecosystems.

Microbes play an important role in the environmental fate of arsenic (Mukhopadhyay *et al.*, 2002; Bhattacharjee and Rosen, 2007). They transform the different forms of arsenic in an ecosystem. Inorganic arsenic forms [As (III) and As(V)] undergo microbially-mediated oxidation and reduction. Microbial activities can result in volatilization of arsenic to gaseous arsines (AsH_3). Further, certain microbes methylate inorganic forms into MMAA (monomethyl arsonic acid), DMAA (dimethyl arsinic acid) and TMAO (trimethyl arsine oxide), respectively, whereas, demethylating microbes re-convert methylated species back to inorganic forms. Methylated forms are further oxidized to MMA (methylarsine), DMA (dimethylarsine) and TMA (trimethylarsine). Figure 8.2 illustrates the role of microbes as well as environmental factors in transformation of different arsenic species. Methylated species such as monomethyl arsonic acid (MMAA), dimethyl arsenic acid (DMAA) and trimethyl arsine oxide (TMAO) dominate in biomass, but have also been detected in soils (Buchet and Lauwerys, 1982; Leonard, 1991; Turpeinen, 2002).

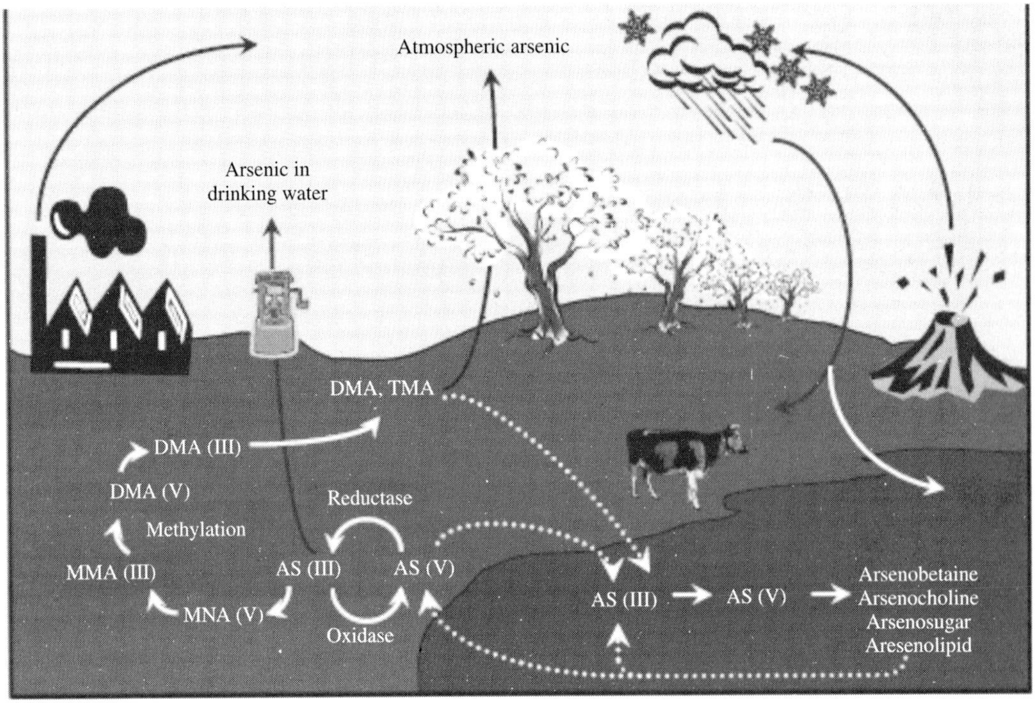

Fig. 8.1 The arsenic biogeochemical cycle (After Bhattacharjee and Rosen, 2007).

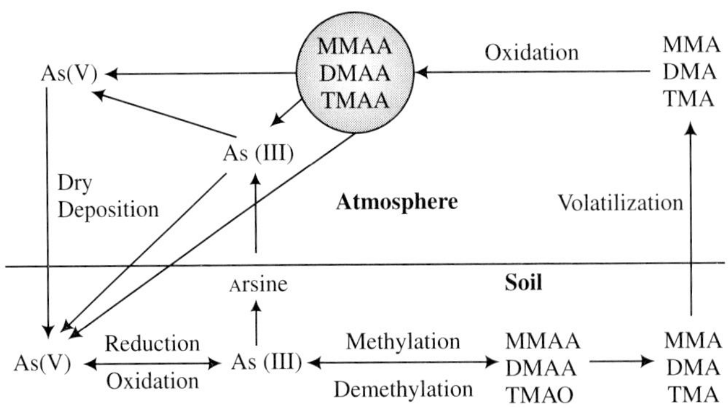

Fig. 8.2 Microbial (⟶) and abiotic (⟶) transformations of arsenic in soils. See text for detail (adapted from Turpeinen, 2002).

EXPOSURE ROUTE AND RISKS

Soluble inorganic arsenic is acutely toxic. Consumption of arsenic contaminated water is the principal route of exposure. In recent times, arsenic problem is created mainly because of drinking of arsenic contaminated water in many parts of the world. However, exposure to arsenic is also possible via consumption of contaminated food (Table 8.1) and inhalation. The concentration of arsenic in air varies in rural and urban areas. Average arsenic concentration in rural air ranges from 0.02-4 μgm^{-3} and 3-200 μgm^{-3} in urban air. A much higher concentration (> 1000 μgm^{-3}) has been reported in the vicinity of industrial areas. Table 8.2 provides the putative natural level of arsenic in different environments. However, the exact concentration varies with environmental factors operating in the area, geology and proximity to the human settlements.

Table 8.1 Chemical names and structures of some typical arsenic species found in seafood samples (adapted from Wuilloud *et al.*, 2006)

Chemical Name	*Structure*	*MW*
Arsenous acid [As(III)]	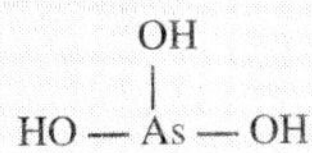	126
Arsenic acid	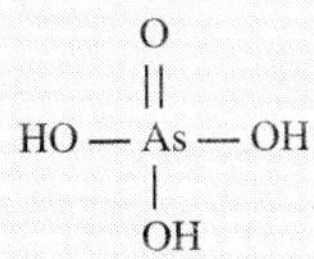	142
Monomethylarsenic acid [MMA]	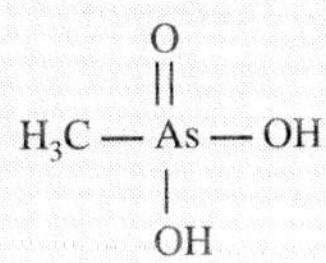	140
Dimethylarsenic acid [DMA]	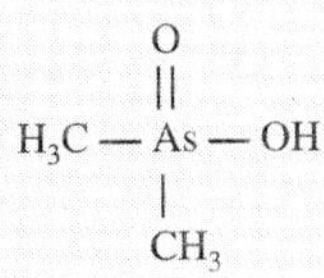	138
Arsenobataine [AsB]	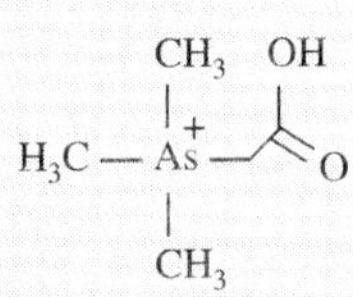	179
Tetramethylarsonium ion [TMA]	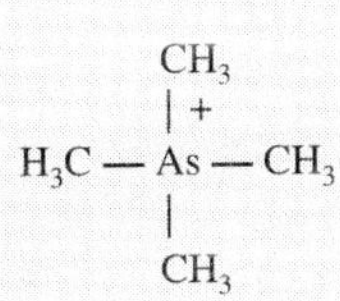	135
Trimethylarsine oxide [TMAO]	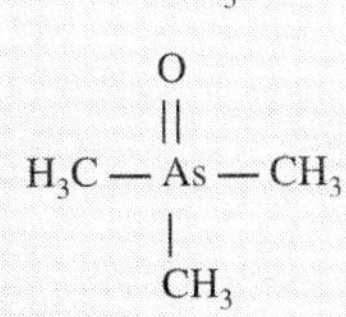	136
Arsenosugars	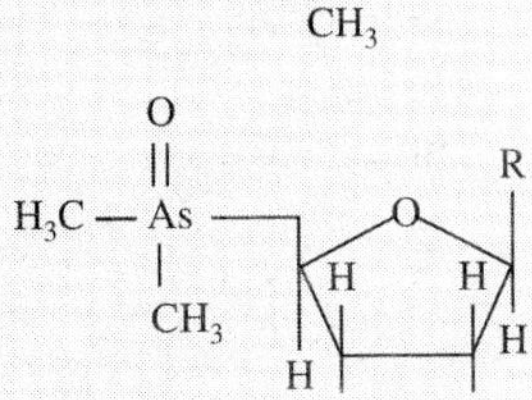	

Contd.

Contd.

5-dimethylarsinoyl-B-ribofuranose [Arsenosugar-H]	R = H	238
3-[5′-deoxy-5′-5-(Dimethylarsinoyl) β-ribofuranosyloxy]-2-hydroxypropylene glycol [Arsenosugar-OH]	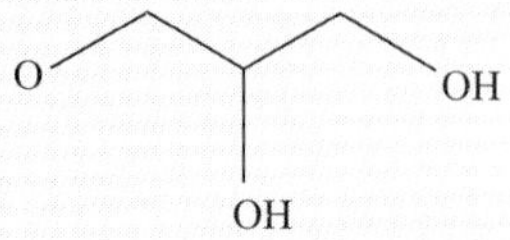	328
3-[5′-deoxy-5′-5-(Dimethylarsinoyl) β-ribofuranosyloxy]-2-hydroxypropane sulphonic acid [Arsenosugar-SO_3]	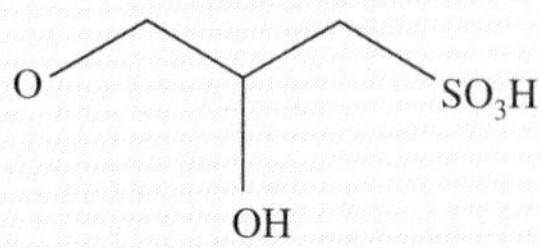	392
3-[5′-deoxy-5′-5-(Dimethylarsinoyl) β-ribofuranosyloxy]-2-hydroxypropyl hydrogen sulfate [Arsenosugar-SO_4]	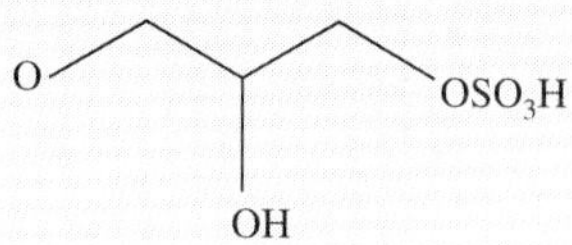	408
3-[5′-deoxy-5′-5-(Dimethylarsinoyl) β-ribofuranosyloxy]-2-hydroxypropyl-2,3 hydroxypropyl phosphate [Arsenosugar-PO_4]	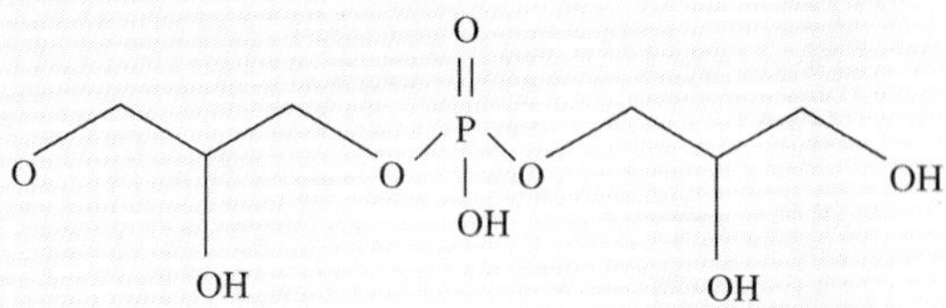	482

Table 8.2 Natural limit of arsenic in different environments (WHO, 2001)

Environment	*Natural Level*
Open-ocean water	1.2 μgL^{-1}
Fresh surface waters (river, lakes, etc.)	< 10 μgL^{-1}
Groundwater (exp. areas with volcanic rocks and sulphide deposits)	1 – 2 μgL^{-1}
Sediment	5 – 3000 $mgkg^{-1}$ (higher at contaminated reas)
Soil	Background conc. 1 – 40 $mgkg^{-1}$ Mean value 5 $mgkg^{-1}$

At contaminated industrial sites, inorganic arsenic species are present in the form of arsenate, arsenite, arsenic sulfide, elemental arsenic and arsine gas forms. Organisms vary in their sensitivity to different arsenic forms, which depend upon the concentration and the kind of arsenic species (oxidation state, as trivalent arsenic is 100 times more toxic than the pentavalent derivatives) as well as time of exposure. In general, inorganic forms are more toxic than organoarsenicals, and arsenite is more toxic than arsenate. Cumulative exposure increases the risk manifolds. Acharyya *et al.* (1999) reported that in humans, sensitivity to arsenic varies from individual to individual, possibily due to the differential expression of genes involved in the synthesis of enzymes AQP9 (the liver isoform).

As(III) is primarily responsible for the biological effect of arsenic. The toxicity of arsenite is due to its affinity for closely spaced cysteine thiolates. It inactivates enzymes and receptors by binding to active site cysteine residue, formation of disulfide bonds, and production of reactive oxygen species by binding to reduced glutathione (Bhattacharjee *et al.,* 2008). Binding to protein sulfhydryl group leads to membrane degradation and cell death (Gebel, 2000). As(V) is a toxic analog for inorganic phosphate in phosphorylation metabolism (Cervantes, 1994; Turpeinen, 2002). It competes with phosphate and acts as a uncoupler of oxidative phosphorylation. Methylated species such as MMAA and DMAA are less toxic than inorganic forms owing to their low solubility and reduced affinity to tissues (Leonard, 1991; Turpeinen, 2002). Gaseous arsines combine with hemoglobin, resulting in severe swelling of the cells and affected tissues (Turpeinen, 2002). The first case of arsenic problem was reported from the families living in the border areas of Bangladesh and West Bengal (India) in the year 1922 (Dhar *et al.,* 1997).

In India, the first report of arsenic contamination in groundwater came from Chandigarh and different villages of Punjab and Himachal Pradesh, in 1976 (Datta and Kaul, 1976). According to Water Resource Ministry, Government of India, several districts of West Bengal, Bihar, Terai regions of Uttar Pradesh and Uttarakhand are under severe threat of arsenic poisoning. Figure 8.3 shows the arsenic affected regions of the world.

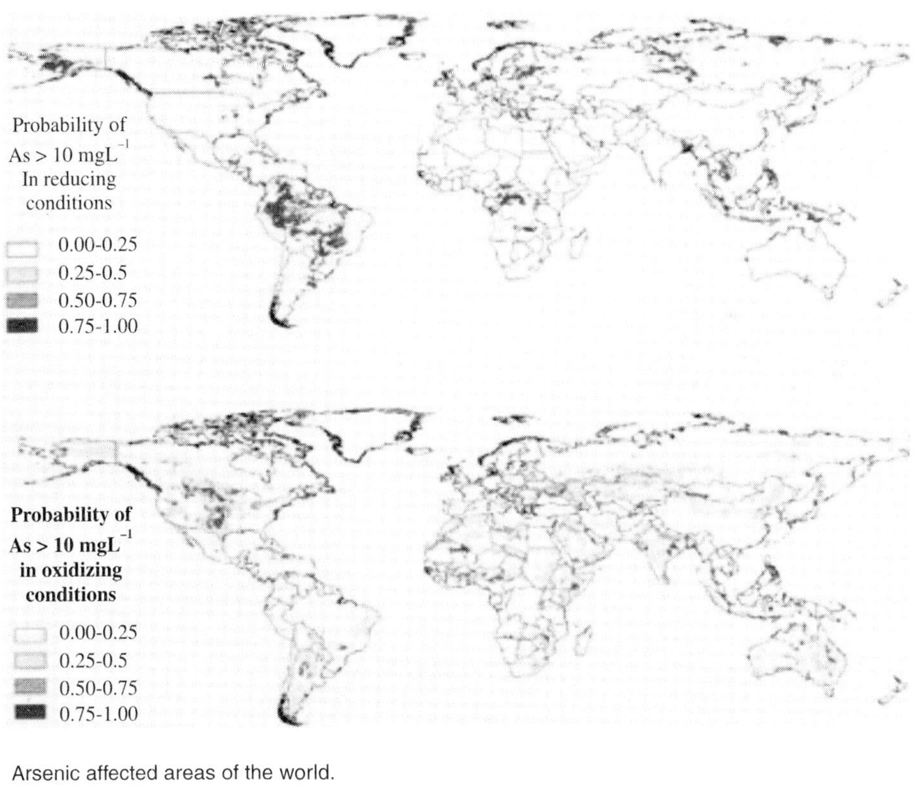

Fig. 8.3 Arsenic affected areas of the world.

Acute as well as long-term exposure to arsenic compounds is related to increased risk of different type of cancers. Evidences indicate that inhaled or ingested inorganic arsenic can injure pregnant women and their unborn babies, as it can cross the placenta and has been reported from the fetal tissues. Further, arsenic has been reported from breast milk, though, at low levels. In animals, exposure to organic arsenic has resulted in low birth weight, fetal malformations and death. Exposure to arsenic in early life (including gestation and early childhood) increases the mortality. The incidence of arsenicosis is found to be much higher in the children (Rahmann *et al.,* 2001; Guo *et al.*, 2001; Guha Mazumdar, 2006).

There appears to be a relationship between arsenic sensitivity and nutrition. Expression of AQP9 has been shown to be elevated by nutritional restriction (Carbrey *et al.,* 2003). Villagers in West Bengal and Bangladesh often have poor diets, which leads to elevation of AQP9 in the liver and hence higher rates of uptake of arsenite. Thus, these individuals are more sensitive to arsenite than inhabitants of cities who have better nutrition. Arsenic trioxide (Trisenox) is used clinically as a chemotherapeutic agent for the treatment of acute promyelocytic leukemia (Soignet *et al.,* 1998; Soignet, 2001). Expression of AQP9 in leukemia cells sensitizes the cells to Trisenox, leading to the proposal that differential expression of AQP9 in leukemia patients could lead to variable effectiveness of Trisenox (Bhattacharjee *et al.*, 2004). The deficiency of calcium, foliate, animal proteins and other vitamins in diet enhances the chances of arsenic susceptibility (Mitra *et al.,* 2008). Besides cancers, arsenic is mainly involved in dermatological, neurological and metabolic pathways disorders.

Dermatological Problems

Exposure to arsenic results in darkening of skin, diffuse melanosis, white and black spots, leucomelanosis, mucus membrane melanosis, spotted and diffuse keratosis, hyperpigmentation marked by rain drop-shaped discolored spots (Guha Mazumdar, 2007). Other symptoms include palpable nodules in dorsum of hands, feet, dorsal keratosis, conjuctional congestion, oedema, gangrene, Bowen's disease (Ahmed *et al.,* 2006), loss of normal hair (Arnold *et al.*, 1990) hepatomegaly and portal hypertension (Guha Mazumdar, 2003).

Neurological Problems

Arsenic poisoning hampers the intelligence (IQ) (Siripitakunkit *et al.*, 1999; Wasserman, 2004; Poddar, 2005). It was found that schoolchildren drinking arsenic contaminated water have low academic achievements. The chief neurological problem is neuropathy showing distal paresthesis, limb pains and distal hypothesias (Ahmed *et al.,* 2006).

Metabolic Disorders

Liver plays an important role in arsenic metabolism and detoxification. Ingested arsenic is first absorbed in the gastrointestinal tract. Upon reaching the liver, arsenate is reduced to arsenite (Gregas and Nemeti, 2002). Further, liver methylates arsenic with the help of the enzyme methyl transferase (Thomas, 2007). The methylation capacity of arsenic is found to be weak in the patients suffering from liver diseases (Buchet *et al.*, 1984; Gaubel *et al.,* 1988). In addition, liver glutathione (an antioxidant) also helps in arsenic detoxification (Liu *et al.*, 2001). Arsenic induced liver cirrhosis was found to be the primary cause of high death rate in the Gazhou, China (Liu *et al.,* 1992; Zhou *et al.*, 2002). Long-term exposure to arsenic leads to liver, gall bladder (arsenic + tobacco) and lung cancers (Chen *et al.*, 1992; Centeno *et al.*, 2002; Chiu *et al.*, 2004; Zhou *et al.*, 2002). Inhalation of arsenic leads to intestinal fibrosis, mild bronchitis

(Rosenberg, 1974), chronic cough and liver fibrosis (Guha Mazumdar, 2005; Santra *et al.*, 1999). In animals, chronic exposure to arsenic damages endothelia and parenchyma cells (Straub *et al.*, 2007).

METAL CONTAMINATION AND MICROBES

Metals play an important role in various life processes of microbes, for example, as micronutrients, in redox processes, molecular stability through electrostatic interactions; are components of various enzymes; and regulate osmotic balance. However, there are many metals (silver, aluminium, cadmium, arsenic, etc.) that have no biological function (non-essential) and some of them (aluminium, arsenic) are toxic to microbes, although at high concentration, both essential and non-essential metals can cause damage to the cells (Bruins *et al.*, 2000). Toxicity of non-essential metals occurs through the displacement of essential metals from their native binding sites or through ligand interactions (Bruins *et al.*, 2000). Developing efficient and environment-friendly technologies to remove toxic metals from natural resources is of great importance. Often, the use of microbes for metal removal has been shown to be more efficient than chemical and physical methods. Microbes have evolved different resistance mechanisms to avoid metal toxicity. On the other hand, they transform the metals to reduce (even increase) its availability for themselves as well as other organisms.

Arsenic Uptake by Microbes

In order to exert their toxic effects, metals have to enter the microbial cells. Often, the structure of metals or their cations and anions show structural resemblance that may fool the uptake system of organisms (e.g., arsenate and phosphate). Usually, microbes have two types of uptake system. One is rapid, non-specific, and driven by the chemiosmotic gradient across the membrane. Since, the mechanism is used by a variety of substrates, it is constitutively expressed (Nies, 1999). The second system is highly substrate specific, which is slow, often uses ATP as an energy source, and is therefore operated by the cell only in need (Nies and Silver, 1995). Because of the first system (i.e., non-specific system), microbes often accumulate toxic concentration of non-essential metal ions inside the cells. In solution, As(V) is available as arsenate (H_3 As O_4), an analogue of phosphate, therefore, it is taken up via phosphate transporters. In *E. coli*, As(V) enters into the cell via ATP-coupled Pst pumps. During the exclusion of arsenic from the cell, As(V) is reduced to As(III) via the enzyme arsenate reductase. As(III) is exported through an exclusive system composed of a single efflux protein, which cannot export As(V) (Fig. 8.4).

As(III) is dissolved to form the undissociated acid $As(OH)_3$ at neutral pH. However, at alkaline pH, it is present as the anion arsenite. There are two transporters for As(III) uptake—in *E. coli* (prokaryote), GlpF (glycerol facilitator, a member of aquaporin (AQP) superfamily) whereas, in eukaryotes, Fps1p (the yeast homologue of GlpF), and LmAOP1 in *Leishmania major*. Yeast (*Saccharomyces cerevisiae*) has another arsenic uptake system i.e., Hxt glucose transporter. In the presence of glucose, which competitively inhibits arsenite uptake by Hxts, most of the arsenite is taken up by Fps1p (Rensing and Rosen, 2009).

In many cases, arsenic toxicity is avoided by minimizing the uptake of arsenic into the cell. For example, *E. coli* possesses two different phosphate transport systems: the Pit and the Pst systems. The Pit system has low phosphate specificity, therefore it also transports arsenate, while the Pst system shows high phosphate specificity (Rosenberg *et al.*, 1977). Therefore, it can be presumed that organisms lacking the Pit system have increased resistance to arsenate (Cervantes *et al.*, 1994; Jackson *et al.*, 2003; Bhat, 2007) compared to those utilizing the Pst system.

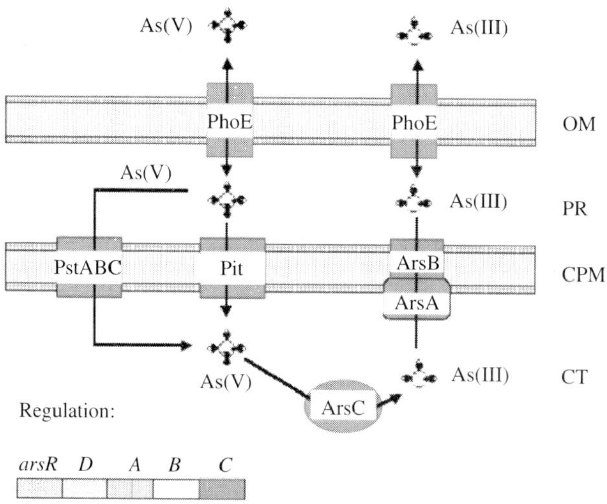

Fig. 8.4 Import and export of arsenic in *E. coli*. As(V) enters the periplasmic space through the outer membrane porin (PhoE protein), and is transported into the cytoplasm by the **Pit** protein or **Pst** system. Within the cell, As(V) is reduced to As(III) by the **ArsC** protein and As(III) is pumped out of the cell by the **ArsAB** efflux ATPase. The *arsRDABC* operon is regulated by the **ArsR** repressor protein and **ArsD** co-regulator protein. (OM = outer membrane, PR = periplasmic space; CPM = cytoplasmic membrane, CT cytoplasmic space (adapted from Nies and Silver, 1995).

Studies indicate that arsenate uptake and resulting toxicity can be reduced by increasing the amount of phosphate in the environment (Abedin *et al.*, 2002; Jackson *et al.*, 2003; Bhat, 2007).

MICROBIAL TRANSFORMATION OF ARSENIC

Biotransformation of toxic metals is an approach adopted by microbes to get rid off such metals. It is an important component of biogeochemical cycles of metals, and is exploited for bioremediation of metal contaminated soils. Microbes transform metals by two ways: redox conversion of inorganic forms and conversion of inorganic form to organic forms and *vice versa* (e.g., methylation and demethylation). Arsenate reducer *Bacterium arsenreducens* and an arsenite oxidiser *B. arsenoxydans* were first identified by Green in 1918. Under anaerobic growth, arsenate is reduced to arsenite by accepting electron (as terminal electron acceptor). The reaction is catalyzed by the enzyme arsenate reductase (Arr). In *Chrysiogenes arsenatis*, acetate serves as electron donor, and the enzyme ArrAB (Dimmer; ArrA and ArrB) is located in the periplasm. However, ArsC arsenate reductases involved in arsenic detoxification are located in cytosol (Niggemyer *et al.*, 2001; Rensing and Rosen, 2009). The *arrAB* genes are expressed anaerobically at nanomolar arsenate or arseinite concentration (Rensing and Rosen, 2009). Although from thermodynamic viewpoint, reduction of arsenate could provide enough energy for microbial growth (Laverman *et al.*, 1995), but overall toxicity of arsenic is likely to restrict the distribution of this process amongst bacteria (Jackson *et al.*, 2003).

Arsenite oxidation is catalyzed by a periplasmic arsenite oxidase (*aox*), with release of energy (Oremland and Stolz, 2003). This enzyme has been reported from both heterotrophic and chemotrophic bacteria (Jackson *et al.*, 2003). In *Agrobacterium tumefaciens*, the arsenite oxidase gene contains sensor kinase system *aoxS* (sensor) and *aoxR* (response regulator). The enzyme has two subunits encoded by the genes *aoxA/aroB/asoB* and *aoxB/aroA/asoA*, respectively (Silver and Phung, 2005). The *aoxB* genes are specific for the arsenite-oxidizing bacteria. Strains containing both arsenite oxidase gene (*aoxB*) and arsenite transporter gene (*ACR3 or arsB*) displayed a higher arsenite resistance level than those possessing only arsenite transporter gene (Cai *et al.*, 2009).

MECHANISMS OF ARSENIC DETOXIFICATION

There are six possible mechanisms that help microbes in developing resistance (metal resistance system) against metal toxicity viz., exclusion by permeability barrier, intra- and extracellular sequestration, active efflux pumps, enzymatic reduction and reduction in the sensitivity of cellular targets (Ji and Silver, 1995; Nies and Silver, 1995; Nies, 1999; Bruins *et al.*, 2000; vide Turpeinen, 2002). A large number of microbes show resistance against the toxic effects of arsenic (Table 8.3).

Table 8.3 Arsenic resistant microbes

Organisms	*References*
E. coli	Xu *et al.*, 1996
	Anderson and Cook, 2004
Trypanosoma equipedrum	Eagle *et al.*, 1944
Stenotrophomonas maltophilia SA Ant 15	Botes *et al.*, 2007
Serratia marcescens	Botes *et al.*, 2007
Pseudomonas putida strains OS-3	Chang *et al.*, 2008
Pseudomonas putida strains -18	Chang *et al.*, 2008
Pseudomona spp.	
	Anderson and Cook, 2004
	Cai *et al.*, 2009
β-proteobacteria or Flavobacteria	Jackson *et al.*, 2005
Exiguobacterium	Anderson and Cook, 2004
Aeromonas	Anderson and Cook, 2004
Bacillus	Anderson and Cook, 2004
	Bhatt, 2007
Acinetobacter	Anderson and Cook, 2004; Cai *et al.*, 2009
Spirochaeta pallida	Klauder, 1924
Leptospirillum ferriphilum	Tuffin *et al.*, 2006
Acidithiobacillus caldus	Kotze *et al.*, 2006
Streptomyces sp. Strain FR-008	Wang *et al.*, 2006
Agrobacterium	Cai *et al.*, 2009
Arthrobacter	Cai *et al.*, 2009
Rhodococcus	Cai *et al.*, 2009
Stenotrophomonas	Cai *et al.*, 2009
Acidithiobacillus ferrooxidans	Dave *et al.*, 2008
Bacillus licheniformis	Clausen, 2004
Synechocystis sp. Strain PCC 6803	Li *et al.*, 2003
Corynebacterium glutamicum ATCC 13032	Ordonez *et al.*, 2005
Scenedesmus abundans	Jahan *et al.*, 2006

The *ars* Operon

Arsenic resistance genes are organized in operons present on the chromosome as well as in the plasmids of bacteria (Bruins *et al.*, 2000). These operons generally consist of either three (*arsRBC*) or five (*arsRDABC*) genes organized into a single transcriptional unit (Silver and Phung, 1996). In *E. coli*, the *ars* operon of pR7773 plasmid consists of five genes *arsA, arsB, arsC, arsD and arsR*. The *arsA* and *arsB* genes encode the pump protein that export As(III); arsC the enzyme arsenate reductase, and *arsR* the protein that regulate the expression of the *ars* operon. In three-gene operon system, *arsR* encodes the arsenic transcriptional repressor, *arsB* arsenite permease and *arsC* the arsenate reductase (Gotz *et al.*, 1983; Diorio *et al.*, 1995; Cai *et al.*, 1998). In contrast to plasmid-borne *ars* operon, the chromosomal *ars* operon contains neither the *arsD* nor *arsA* cistron (Diorio *et al.*, 1995). The ArsR regulatory proteins are the members of ArsR family of arsenic responsive repressors. The first identified member of the family was 117-residue As(III)-responsive ArsR repressor of the *arsRDABC* operon of plasmid R773. Till date, over 200 homologues have been identified in bacteria and archaea (Rensing and Rosen, 2009). For detailed information about the structure of ArsR repressors, readers are requested to consult Rensing and Rosen (2009). Disruption of the chromosomal *ars* operon by *MudI* insertion increased the sensitivity of *E. coli* to sodium arsenite and sodium arsenate by approximately 10-100-fold (Silver *et al.*, 1981).

In highly reducing environment (e.g., inside the cell), arsenite is the most (rather than arsenate) dominant form. In bacteria, at least two different families of arsenite permeases have been discovered viz., ArsB (encoded by the R773 *arsRDABC* operon) and Acr3. ArsB can also be coupled with ArsA-ATPase to form the pump, and confers more arsenite resistance than ArsB alone (vide Rensing and Rosen, 2009). Acr3p, another family of arsenite transport protein, shows analogy (functional similarity) to ArsB, but differs in sequences. Acr3p appeared to be more specific and transports only arsenite (Cai *et al.*, 2009). However, in *Synechocystis,* Acr3p was able to transport both arsenite and antimonite (Lopez-Maury *et al.*, 2003).

The promoters and regulatory genes of these operons can be used to construct the arsenic specific biosensors. For example, Tauriainen *et al.* (1997) developed an arsenic detecting biosensor by controlling the expression of firefly luciferase (*lucFF*) reporter gene by regulatory unit (*ars* promoter + repressor protein ArsR) of *ars* operon of plasmid pR733 in recombinant plasmid pTOO31, with *E. coli* as a host strain. In the absence of As(III), expression of *lucFF* is repressed, while transcription of the promoter is induced in its presence. Consequently, luciferase is produced in a concentration corresponding to that of arsenic present in the environment. Corbisier *et al.* (1993) and Cai and DuBow (1998) used bacterial luciferase (*luxAB*) reporter gene in their studies (Turpeinen, 2002).

The Ycf1p (yeast cadmium factor) of yeast also plays an important role in arsenite detoxification. It catalyzes the vacuolar sequestration of arsenic (III) as glutathione conjugates (Rensing and Rosen, 2009). Recently, a 120-residue polypeptide (encoded by *arsD* gene) showed arsenic chaperons like function, as it delivered arsenite to the ArsAB arsenite translocating ATPase (Rensing and Rosen, 2009).

Cytosolic arsenate reductases (encoded by *ars* operon) confer resistance to arsenate. There are three independent and unrelated families of arsenate reductase. First, ArsCs (e.g., *E. coli* plasmid R773) uses glutaredoxin (Grx) and GSH as reductant. Second includes *S. aureus* plasmid p1258 and *B. subtilis* chromosomal ArsC, which uses thioredoxin as reductant. The third family is found primarily in eukaryotic microbes (e.g., AcrP2 of yeast) (Rensing and Rosen, 2009). Bacterial methylation is also a process of arsenic detoxification. Expression of *E. coli* containing *arsM* gene (isolated from soil bacterium *Rhodopseudomonas palustris*) showed resistance against As(III). Though controversial, an

NADPH-FMN reductase (ArsH) has also been reported to confer resistance against arsenic, however, the mechanism is not clear (Rensing and Rosen, 2009).

Role of Microbes in Arsenic Removal

In soils, arsenic toxicity depends upon its chemical form and bioavailability. Hydrated ions are considered to be more toxic than complex ion and species associated with colloidal particles (Ruseva, 1995; La Forece *et al.*, 2000). Conditions such as waterlogging, pH, redox conditions, other elements, soil and site hydrology, and biotic influences affect the adsorption capacity of soils (Turpeinen, 2002). In general, iron oxides/hydroxides are most commonly involved in the adsorption of arsenic in both acidic and alkaline soils (Polemio *et al.*, 1982; Turpeinen, 2002). Also, arsenic becomes progressively less soluble and bioavailable when time passes (Alexander, 2000). Several techniques such as reverse osmosis, filtration, adsorption, ion exchange, chemical precipitation and distillation have been used for removing arsenic from contaminated water (Mohapatra *et al.*, 2007).

Bioremediation is the use of microorganisms, green plants or their enzymes to reclaim the natural environment altered by contaminants. For example, bacteria such as *Pseudomonas arsenitoxidans, Thermos aquaticus* and *T. thermophilus* oxidize (detoxify) As(III) to As(V) (Ilyaletdinov and Abdrashitova, 1981; Gihring *et al* ., 2001). In contrast, *Sulfurospirillum barnesii, Desulfotomaculum auripigmentum, Bacillus arsenicoselenatis, Crysiogenes arsenatis, Sphingomonas Pseudomonas* and *Wolinella* spp reduce As(V) to As(III). In a strain of *Thermus*, both As(III) oxidation and As(V) reduction mechanisms operate (Gihring and Banfield, 2001;Turpeinen, 2002 and references within). However, microbial transformation of arsenic is inhibited by the presence of phosphate (Huysmans and Frankenberger, 1991) and antimony (Andrewes *et al.*, 2000), but enhanced by molybdate (Oremland *et al.*, 2000). It also depends upon soil properties such as pH, texture, temperature and organic matter content (Turpeinen, 2002).

Fixation of As(III) on the iron oxides is an important method for arsenic removal. Accordingly, when a coagulant is added, arsenic can either co-precipitate or be adsorbed on forming iron. In biological treatment, the iron oxides are not produced by chemical coagulation/precipitation, but by the bacterial activity. In this, microbes deposit iron oxides in the filtering media, therefore offering a large surface area for reaction. Arsenic gets concentrated in the sludge continuously produced by the biological activity. In the last ten years, a number of full-scale plants for the bacterial leaching of refractory gold ores have been commissioned (Harvey and Crundwell, 1996). Refractory gold ores contain arsenic, usually in the form of arsenopyrite (FeAsS), and bacterial leaching of ores results in the formation of arsenite [As(III)] and arsenate [As(V)] in solution. Arsenite is oxidized to arsenate by ferric ions only in the presence of bacteria. During bacterial leaching, a substantial amount of arsenic in the solution is precipitated as ferric arsenate ($FeAsO_4$) (Harvey and Crundwell, 1996). Katsoyiannis *et al.* (2004) used fixed-bed up-flow bioreactors for arsenic removal from groundwater by using iron oxidizing bacteria. Results indicated that As(III) was partially oxidized to As(V) enabling high arsenic removal efficiency (Katsoyiannis *et al.*, 2004). Beceiro-Gonzalez *et al.* (2000) has reviewed the accumulation of arsenic species by microbes such as algae and bacteria. Currently, the emphasis has been on whether a microbe/ biological substrate accumulates the total element or just one of its forms.

Shaheen *et al.* (2007) analyzed the survival of different genera/species of cyanobacteria in composite culture amended with different concentrations of arsenic. Results showed that at 0 ppm level of As in culture medium, the dominant genera of cyanobacterial species were *Aphanothece* (unicellular) *Phormidium* (non-heterocystous filamentous) and *Nostoc, Cylindrospermum, Anabaena, Calothrix* (heterocystous and filamentous). At high concentration (1000 ppm) of As, *Aphanothece* and *Cylindrospermum* died, however, genera/species such as *Phormidium*, *Nostoc* spp, *Anabaena* and *Calothrix* survived without cell damage. With further increase in the concentration, *Phormidium*, *Nostoc* spp, *Anabaena* were able to grow at 5000 ppm level, whereas species of *Nostoc* and *Phormidium* survived even at 10,000 ppm of As in the medium (Table 8.4).

Table 8.4 Tolerance of different concentrations of arsenic (As) in liquid culture medium by the composite cyanobacterial genera of Gotera soil (adopted from Shaheen *et al.*, 2007)

Concentration of arsenic (in ppm) in Chu-10+N culture medium	*Cyanobacterial community composition (genera/species)*
0	*Phormidium* sp., *Nostoc* spp., *Anabaena* sp., *Cylindrospermum* sp., *Calothrix* sp., *Aphanothece* sp.
1000	*Nostoc* spp, *Colothrix* sp.
5000	*Phormidium* sp., *Nostoc* spp., *Anabaena* sp.
10,000	*Phormidium* sp.

CONCLUSION

Since microbes play a key role in controlling the speciation and cycling of arsenic in soils, it is important to have a better understanding of the way microbes transform arsenic in natural environments, mechanisms of their tolerance and environmental and other factors that link their activities to the biogeochemistry of arsenic. There is a need to construct microbial biosensors that can be used to detect and assess the bioavailability of arsenic in natural systems. Despite ample information, till date, microbes have not been used for bioremediation of arsenic under natural field conditions. Also efforts are being made to identify arsenic detoxification genes, which can be used in constructing the arsenic resistant transgenic plants.

REFERENCES

Abedin, M.J., Feldman, J. and Meharg, A.A. (2002). *Plant Physiol.*, **128:**1120-1128.

Acharyya, S.K., Chakraborty, P., Lahiri, S., Raymahashay, B.C., Guha, S. and Bhowmik, A. (1999) *Nature*, **401:** 545-547.

Ahamed, S., Sengupta, M.K., Mukherjee, A., Hossain, M.A., Das, B., Nayak, B., Pal, A., Mukherjee, S.C., Pati, S., Dutta, R.N., Chatterjee, G., Mukherjee, A., Srivastava, R. and Chakraborti, D. (2006). *Sci. Total Environ.*, **370:** 310-322.

Alexander, M. (2000). *Environ. Sci. Technol.*, **34:** 4259-4265.

Anderson, C.R. and Cook, G.M. (2004). *Curr. Microbiol.*, **48:** 341-347.

Andrewes, P., Cullen, W. and Polishchuk, E. (2000). *Environ. Sci. Technol.*, **34:** 2249-2253.

Arnold, H.C., Odom, R.B. and James, W.D, (1990). Andrew's disease of the skin clinical dermatology. 8th edn, Saunders, Philadelphia.

Balasoiu, C., Zagury, G. and Deshenes, L. (2001). *Sci. Total Environ.*, **280:** 239-255.

Beceiro-Gonza´lez, E., Taboada-de la Calzada, A., Alonso-Rodrı´guez, E., Lo´pez-Mahı´a, P., Muniategui-Lorenzo, S. and Prada-Rodrı´guez, D. (2000). *Trends Anal. Chem.*, **19:** 475-480.

Bhat, N.S. (2007). Ph.D. Thesis, School of Biological Sciences, University of Wollongong.

Bhattacharjee, H., Carbrey, J., Rosen, B.P. and Mukhopadhay, R. (2004). *Biochem. Biophysic. Res. Commun.*, **322:** 836-841.

Bhattacharjee, H. and Rosen, B.P. (2007). *In:* Molecular Microbiology of Heavy Metals (Eds. Nies, D.H. & Simon, S.). Springer-Verlag, Heidelberg/New York, pp. 371–406.

Bhattacharjee, H., Mukhopadhyay, R., Thiyagarajan, S. and Rosen, B.P. (2008). *J. Biol.*, 7: 33.

Botes, E., van Heerden, E. and Litthauer, D. (2007). *South Afr. J. Sci.*, **103:** 279-281.

Bruins, M.R., Kapil, S. and Oehme, F.W. (2000). *Ecotox. Environ. Safety*, **45:** 198-207.

Buchet, J.P. and Lauwerys, R. (1982). *In:* Analytical Techniques for Heavy Metals in Biological Fluids (Ed. Facchetti, S.), Elsevier, Amsterdam, pp. 75-89.

Buchet, J.P., Gaubel, A., Pauwel, S., Mahieu, P. and Lauwareys, R. (1984). *Arch. Toxicol.*, **55:**151-154.

Cai, J., Salmon, K. and DuBow, M. S. (1998). *Microbiology*, **144:** 2705-2713.

Cai, L., Liu, G., Rensing, C. and Wang, G. (2009). *BMC Microbiol.*, **9:** 4.

Corbisier, P., Ji, G., Nuyts, G., Mergeay, M. and Silver, S. (1993). *FEMS Microbiol. Lett.* **110:** 231-238.

Carbrey, J.M., Gorelick-Feldman, D.A., Kozono, D., Praetorius, J., Nielsen, S. and Agre, P. (2003). *Proc. Natl. Acad. Sci. USA*., **100:** 2945-2950.

Centeno, J.A., Mallick, F.G., Martinez, L., Page, N.P., Gibb, H., Longfellow, D., Thompson, C. and Laddich, E.R. (2002). *Environ. Health Perspect.*, **110:** 883- 886.

Cervantes, C., Ji, G., Ramirez, J.L. and Silver, S. (1994). *FEMS Microbiol. Rev.*, **15:** 355-367.

Chang, J.S., Kim, Y.H. and Kim, K.W. (2008). *Appl. Microbiol. Biotechnol.*, **80:**155-165.

Chen, C.J., Chen, C.W., Wu, M.M. and Kuo, T.L. (1992). *Br. J. Cancer*, **66:** 888- 892.

Chiu, H.F., Ho, S.C., Wang, L.Y., Wu, T.N. and Yang, C.F. (2004). *J. Toxicol Environ. Health*, **67:** 1494-1500.

Clausen, C.A. (2004). *Waste Management*, **24:** 407-411.

Cullen, W.R. and Reimer, K.J. (1989). *Chem. Rev.*, **89:** 713-764.

Datta, D.V. and Kaul, M.K. (1976). *J. Asso. Phys. India.*, **24:** 599-604.

Datta, D.V., Mitra, J.K., Chhautani, P.N. and Chakravati, R.N. (1979). *Gut*, **20:** 378:384.

Dave, S.R., Gupta, K.H. and Tipre, D.R. (2008). *Bioresource Technol.*, **99:** 7514-7520.

Dhar, R.K., Biswas, B.K., Samanta, G., Mandal, B.K., Chakraborty, D., Roy, S., Jafar, A., Islam, A., Ara, G., Kabir, S., Khan, A.W., Ahmed, S.A. and Hadi, S.A. (1997). *Curr. Sci.*, **73:** 48-59.

Diorio, C., Cai, J., Marmor, J., Shinder, R. and DuBow, M.S. (1995). *J. Bacteriol.*, **177:** 2050-2056.

Eagle, H., Magnuson, H.J., Musselman, A.D. and Watson, E.B. (1944). *J. Pharmacol. Environ. Therapeut.*, **82:** 137-151.

Gaubel, A.P., Mairlot, M.C., Buchet, J.P., Dive, C. and Lauwerys, R. (1988). *Int. J. Clin. Pharmacol. Res.*, **8:** 117-122.

Gebel, T. (2000). *Toxicol.*, **144:** 155-162.

Gihring, T.M. and Banfield, J.F. (2001). *FEMS Microbiol. Lett.*, **10169:** 1-6

Gihring, T.M., Druschel, G.K., McCleskey, R.B., Hamers, R.J. and Banfield, J.F. (2001). *Environ. Sci. Technol.*, **35:** 3857-3862.

Götz, F., Zabielski, J., Philipson, L. and Lindberg, M. (1983). *Plasmid*, **9:**126-137.

Green, H.H. (1918). *South Afr. J. Sci.*, **14:** 465-467.

Gregas, Z. and Nemeti, B. (2002). *Toxicol. Sci.*, **70:**13-19.

Guha Mazumdar, D.N. (2003). *In:* Arsenic exposure and health effects. (Eds. Chappell, W.R., Abernathy, C.O., Calderon, R.L.and Thomas, D.J.) Elsevier, London, pp. 117-134.

Guha Mazumdar, D.N. (2005). *Toxicol. Appl. Pharmacol.*, **206:** 169: 175.

Guha Mazumdar, D.N. (2006). A mission report to ministry of health and ministry of rural development of Cambodia on detection, confirmation and management of arsenicosis. A WHO Consultansy Project Report.

Guha Mazumdar, D.N. (2007). *Indian Pediatrics,* **44:** 925-927.

Guo, X.J., Fujono, Y., Kaneko, S., Wu, K.G., Xia, Y.J. and Yashimura, T. (2001). *Mol. Cell. Biochem.,* **222:** 137-140.

Harvey, P.I. and Crundwell, F.K. (1996). *Mineral Eng.*, **9:** 1059-1068.

Huysmans, K.D. and Frankenberger, W.T. (1991). *Sci. Total Environ.,* **105:** 13-28.

Ilyaletdinov, A.N. and Abdrashitova, S.A. (1981). *Mikrobiologiya,* **50:** 197-204.

Jackson, C.R., Jackson, E.F., Dugas, S.L., Gamble, K. and Williams, S.E. (2003). *Recent Res. Develop. Microbiol.,* **7:** 103-118.

Jackson, C.R., Horrison K.G. and Dugas, S.L. (2005). *Syst. Appl. Microbiol.,* **28:** 727-734.

Jahan, K., Mosto, P., Mattson, C. and Frey, E. and Derchak, L. (2006). *Water, Air, Soil Pollut.,* **6:** 71-82.

Ji, G. and Silver, S. (1995). *J. Ind. Microbiol.,* **14:** 61-75.

Katsoyiannis, I.A., Zouboulis, A.I. and Jekel, M. (2004). *Ind. Eng. Chem. Res.*, **43:** 486-493.

Klauder, J.V. (1924). *Arch. Dermatol.,* **9:** 446-458.

Kotze, A.A., Tuffin, M.I., Deane, S.M. and Rawlings, D.Y. (2006). *Ars. Microbiol.,* **152:** 3551-3560.

La Forece, M.J., Hansel, C.M. and Fendorf, S. (2000). *Environ. Sci. Technol.* **34:** 3937-3943.

Laverman, A.M., Switzer Blum, J., Schaefer, J.K., Philips, E.J.P., Lovley, D.R. and Oremland, R.S. (1995). *Appl. Environ. Microbiol.,* **61:** 3556-3561.

Leonard, A. (1991). *In:* Metals and their compounds in the environment. (Ed. Merian, E.), VCH, Weinheim, pp. 751-772.

Li, R., Haile, J.D. and Kennelly, P.J. (2003). *J Bacteriol.,* **185:** 6780-6789.

Liu, D.N., Lu, X.Z., Li, B.L., Zhou, D.X., Li, F.X., Zheng, D.H. and Wang, K.H. (1992). *Clin. J. Med.,* **31:** 560-562.

Liu, J., Chen, H., Miller, D.S., Sauvedra, J.E., Keefer, L.K., Johnson, D.R., Klaassen, C.D. and Waalkes, M.P. (2001). *Mol. Pharmacol.,* **60:** 302-309.

Lopez-Maury, L., Florencio, F.J. and Reyes, J.C. (2003). *J. Bacteriol.*, **185**: 5363-5371.

Masscheleyn, P.H., Delaune, R.D. and Patrick, W.H. (1991). *Environ. Sci. Technol.,* **25:** 1414-1419.

Mitra, S.R., Guha-Muzumdar, D. N., Basu, A., Block, G., Haque, R., Samanta, S., Ghosh, N., Mohapatra, D., Mishra, D., Chaudhury, G.R. and Das, R. P. (2008). *Soil Sediment Contaminat.,* **17:** 301-311.

Mohapatra, D., Mishra, D., Rout, M. and Chaudhury, G.R. (2007). *J. Environ. Sci. Health: Part A,* **42:** 81-88.

Mukhopadhyay, R., Rosen, B.P., Phung, L.T. and Silver, S. (2002). *FEMS Microbiol. Rev.,* **26:** 311-325.

Ng, J. C., Wang, J.P. and Shraim, A. (2003). *Chemosphere,* **52:** 1353-1359.

Nies, D.H. and Silver, S. (1995). *J. Ind. Microbiol.,* **14:** 186-199.

Nies, D.H. (1999). *Appl. Microbiol. Biotechnol.,* **51:** 730-750.

Niggemyer, A., Spring, S., Stackebrandt, E. and Rosenzweig, R.F. (2001). *Appl. Environ. Microbiol.,* **67:** 5568-5580.

Ordonez, E., Letek, M., Valbuena, N., Gil, A.J. and Mateos, L.M. (2005). *Appl Environ. Microbiol.,* **71:** 6206-6215.

Oremland, R.S. (2000). *In:* Encyclopedia of Microbiology. Ledenberg, J., 2nd ed. Academic Press, NY, pp. 238-247.

Oremland, R.S. and Stolz, J.F. (2003). *Science,* **300:** 939-44.

Pantsar-Kallio, M. and Korpela, A. (2000). *Anal. Chimica Acta,* **410:** 65-70.

Poddar, S. (2005). Ph.D. Thesis in Applied Psychology, University of Calcutta, India.

Polemio, M., Senesi, N. and Bufo, S.A. (1982). *Sci. Total Environ.,* **25:** 71-79.

Rahmann, M.M., Chowdhury, U.K., Mukherjee, S.C., Mandal, B.K., Paul, K., Lodh, D., Biswas, B.K., Chanda, C.R., Basu, G.K., Saha, K.C., Roy, S., Das, R., Palit, S.K., Quamruzzaman, Q. and Chakraborti, D. (2001). *J. Toxicol. Clin. Toxicol.,* 39: 683-700.

Rensing, C. and Rosen, B. (2009). *In:* Encyclopedia of Microbiology. (Ed. Schaeter, M.) Elsevier, Oxford, pp. 205-219.

Rosenberg, H. (1974). *Arch. Pathol.,* 360: 365.

Rosenberg, H.R., Gerdes, R.G. and Chegwidden, K. (1977). *J. Bacteriol.* **131:** 505-511.

Ross, S. (1994). Toxic Metals in Soil-Plant Systems. John Wiley & Sons, Chichester, UK.

Russeva, E. (1995). *Anal. Lab.* **4:**143-148.

Santra, A., Das-Gupta, J., De, B.K., Roy, B. and Guha Muzumdar, D.N. (1999). *Indian. J. Gut.,* **20:** 378-384.

Shaheen R.R., Mahmud, R. and Sen, J. (2007). *J. Soil .Nature,* **1:** 23-29.

Silver, S., Budd, K., Leahy, K.M., Shaw, W.V., Hammond, D., Novick, R.P., Willsky, G.R., Malamy, M.H. and Rosenberg, H. (1981). *J. Bacteriol.,* **146:** 983-996.

Silver, S. and Phung, L.T. (1996). *Annul. Rev. Microbiol.,* **50:** 753-789.

Silver, S. and Phung, L.T. (2005). *Appl. Environ. Microbiol.,* **71:** 599-608.

Singh, S. (2008). Removal of arsenic using cyanobacteria: an experimental study. M. Tech. dissertation, Department of Civil Engineering, Institute of Technology, Banaras Hindu University, Varanasi.

Siripitakunkit, U., Vishudhiphan, P., Pradipasen, M. and Vorapongrathron, T. (1999). *In:* Arsenic exposure and health effects. (Eds., Chappell, W.R., Abernathy, C.O. and Calderon, R.L.) Elsevier, UK, pp. 141-149.

Soignet, S.L., Maslak, P., Wang, Z.G., Jhanwar, S., Calleja, E., Dardashti, L.J., Corso, D., DeBlasio, A., Gabrilove, J., Scheinberg, D.A., Pandolfi, P.P. and Warrell Jr., R.P.J. (1998). *N. Engl. J. Med.,* **339:** 1341-1348.

Soignet, S.L. (2001). *The Oncologist,* **6:** 11-16.

Straub, A.C., Stolz, D.B., Ross, M.A., Hernandez-Zavala, A., Soucy, N.V., Klie, L.R. and Barchowsky, A. (2007). *Hepatology,* **45:** 205:212.

Tauriainen, S., Karp, M. and Virta, M. (1997). *Appl. Environ. Microbiol.,* **63:** 4456-4461.

Thomas, D.J. (2007). *Toxicol. Appl. Pharmacol.,* **222:** 365:373.

Tuffin, I.M., Hector, S.B., Deane, S.M. and Rawling, D.E. (2006). *Appl. Environ. Microbiol.,* **72:** 2247-2253.

Turpeinen, R. (2002). Interactions between metals, microbes and plants: bioremediation of arsenic and lead contaminated soils. A dissertation in Environmental Ecology, Faculty of Science, University of Helsinki, Neopoli, Lahti.

Wang, L., Chen, S., Xiao, X., Huang, X., You, D., Zhou, X. and Deng, Z. (2006). *Appl. Environ. Microbiol.,* **72:** 3738-3742.

Wasserman, G.A. (2004). *Arch. Environ. Health.,* **4:** 223-224.

WHO (2001). Arsenic in Drinking water, Fact sheet No. 210, Revised Edition (http://www.who.int/mediacentre/factsheet/fs21).

Wuilloud, R.G., Altamirano, J.C., Smichowski, P.C. and Heitkemper, D.T. (2006). *JAAS* **21:** 1214-1223.

Xu, C., Shi, W. and Rosen B.P. (1996). *J. Biol. Chem.,* **271:** 2427-2432.

Zhou, Y.S., Du, H., Chen, M.L., Liu, J., Zhang, X.J. and Xu, L. (2002). *Chin. J. Epidemiol.,* **21:** 484-486.

9

Response of Ectomycorrhizal Pine Seedlings to Heavy Metal Pollution in Soil

T. Ajungla[1], G.D. Sharma[2] and M.S. Dkhar[3]

[1]*Dept. of Botany, Nagaland University, Nagaland. 798 627. India.*

[2]*Pro. Vice-chancellor, Assam University, Silchar-788 011, India.*

[3]*Dept. of Botany, NEHU, Shillong-22, Meghalaya, India.*

E-mail: gduttasharma@yahoo.com

The interactions between heavy metals and mycorrhiza have been studied with respect to toxicity on the functioning of the ectomycorrhiza. Four mycorrhizal forming ectomycorrhiza with Khasi pine (Pinus kesiya Royle ex Gordon) were selected. Six heavy metals namely 0 (control), 10, 50, 100, 200 and 500 ppm of Zn, Cd, Ni, Pb, Cu and Al were treated (10 ml each) separately to the mycorrhizal and non-mycorrhizal seedlings. The study was continued for one year. The fungal colonization was maximum in seedlings treated with lower concentration of metals compared to higher concentration. High concentration of heavy metals were specifically toxic to the external mycelium, which ultimately resulted in reduction of ectomycorrhizal development. All the four ectomycorrhizal fungi could withstand the heavy metal toxicity up to 50 ppm. It was observed that non-mycorrhizal pine seedlings were more sensitive to the toxic effect of heavy metals than the ectomycorrhizal ones. The accumulation of metals in the mycelium and protecting pine root against metal toxicity was an important factor. Significantly greater quantity of heavy metals was analyzed in non-mycorrhizal roots than in mycorrhizal ones. The response of ectomycorrhizal fungi to heavy metals varied and that the response dependant on the ectomycorrhizal fungal species and the metal concentrations. The growth of mycorrhizal seedlings without any heavy metal treatments were vigorous as compared to that of seedlings exposed to heavy metals. Inoculation of pine seedlings with ectomycorrhizal fungi consistently showed an increase in shoot height, number of needles, needle length, seedlings volume, root collar diameter, lateral root length and mycorrhizal infection throughout the growing season. A trend in decrease in nutrient concentration of seedlings applied with different concentrations of heavy metals was observed. The concentration of nutrients as a whole was restricted by the presence of heavy metals. The study revealed that the ectomycorrhizal fungi increased the tolerance of pine seedlings to heavy metals thereby allowing the root to retain its normal growth.

INTRODUCTION

Most of the world's terrestrial ecosystems are dominated by plants that require association with mycorrhizal fungi to achieve optimum productivity. Such mutualistic symbiotic association has been recognized for more than a century. Recently, methods have been developed to employ them in forestry and agriculture. Ectomycorrhiza are characteristics of woody perennials in families such as betulaceae, fagaceae, dipterocarpaceae, myrtaceae, pinaceae and salicaceae. These families account for much of the world's wood production. Mycorrhizal fungi act as highly efficient extensions of the host root systems to explore the soil for nutrients and water absorption and translocate them to the host. The host, in turn, provides energy to the fungi in the form of photosynthetates.

The present scantiness of understanding of the complex array of interactions, mechanism and strategies retard the optimal use of mycorrhiza in efforts to improve forest productivity. The physical and chemical characteristics of the soil influence both the fungus and host plant roots in establishing their mycorrhizal association. More information is to be gathered about the ecology and physiology of different mycorrhizal fungi to better predict when and where a specific fungus-host is likely to meet the objective of each mycorrhizal management programme. Ectomycorrhizal basidiomycetes constitute an important element of forest fungal communities (Villeneuve *et al.*, 1989; Vogt *et al.*, 1991), and their unique characteristics as symbionts make them an interesting subject for study on population ecology. Their mycelia maintain a close physiological link to host tree feeder roots (Read, 1992). Conidia are absent among most species (Hutchinsons, 1989), with only a few forming chlamydospores (Agerer, 1991). These fungi therefore rely upon basidiospores, mycelial fragmentation and occasionally sclerotia (Molina *et al.*, 1992) as their principal means of dispersal and reproduction. These fungi have been demonstrated to possess substantial intraspecific variability for a number of traits, including the morphology of ectomycorrhizal roots (Wong *et al.*, 1989; Gardes., *et al.*, 1990) and their influence on the host plant growth and mycorrhizal development (Kropp, 1990b; Marx, 1991).

In addition to its symbiotic functions (Read, 1991), mycorrhizal mycelium also furnishes inoculum available root system (Brown lee *et al.*, 1983; Flemming, 1983) and potentially establishes interplant connections (Read, 1992). Ectomycorrhiza include a great diversity of association. An estimated 2000 fungi can form ectomycorrhiza with Douglas fir alone (Trappe, 1977), and similar number can be postulated for other host genera, such as pines, oaks and beeches. The majority of mycorrhizal fungi are ascomycetes that fruit as mushrooms, truffles or cup fungi (Trappe, 1962). The mycorrhizal fungi show various degrees of host specificity; some hosts show more selectivity towards mycorrhizal fungi than others. Genera in the pinaceae form mycorrhiza with many wide ranging as well as host specific fungi (Molina and Trappe, 1982b).

The Khasi pine (*Pinus kesiya*) that is dominant in higher altitude harbors ectomycorrhizal association (Sharma, 1981b; Kumar, 1990 and Jha, 1990), which helps in establishment, survival and growth of pine seedlings (Koide and Lu, 1995). The selection of suitable ectomycorrhizal fungi for seedling inoculation can enhance the success of forestation programmes (Harley and Smith, 1983). Many tree species including conifers are able to grow in poor soil conditions due to their extensive root system (Koide and Lu, 1995). Ectomycorrhizal association is specially adapted to nutrient stress condition. Their beneficial role in absorption of inorganic nutrients, production and supply of growth regulators, decreasing of soil toxicity and increasing resistance to extreme soil temperatures is known (Heinrich *et al.*, 1989). In the absence of mycorrhiza, tree species become stunted and yellow or they may even die (Sharma 1981b). Ectomycorrhizal fungi modify the morphology of roots, and this change is correlated with the production of cytokinin and other growth regulators that increase the physiological process of the roots. Non-mycorrhizal seedlings, however, fail to survive in natural planting sites, specially during the period of environmental stress (Anderson and Rygwiewiez, 1991). Hence, mycorrhizal fungi can enhance the success of afforestation programmes.

Climatic factors may affect the growth and development of ectomycorrhizal fungi. The studies carried out in laboratory conditions on ectomycorrhizal fungi may, however, show some difference in response to the natural environmental conditions due to complexity and interaction between soil, climatic and biological components (Jha, 1990). Some species, however, have high capacity to absorb and retain pollutants under natural and artificially exposed conditions (Deora *et al.*, 2005). Heavy metals are hazardous as they are accumulated by vegetation and known to interfere with the quality of environment (Bindhu *et al.*, 2005). Heavy metals like cadmium are generated from smelting industries, burning of diesel, heating oil and use of fertilizers and pesticides (Bindhu *et al.*, 2005). Though studies on mycorrhizae have received enough attention during the past few years, however, their interaction in relation to environmental factors needs careful investigation, particularly in relation to the soil pollution caused by heavy metals.

THE EFFECT OF HEAVY METALS ON THE STRUCTURE OF MYCORRHIZA

Heavy metals like Ni, Pb, Cd, Cu and Al, when exposed to pine seedlings, were found to increase vacuolation and inhibition of fungal hyphae penetration into the cortical cells. The effect of heavy metals on the ultrastructure and anatomy of roots is still poorly known. The cytological characteristics of the mycorrhizal fungus altered as the concentration of heavy metals increased. The fungal cytoplasm appeared to be more disrupted at 200 and 500 ppm and above (Plates 9.3 and 9.4). The hyphae penetrated the root directly, with comparatively few infection points, between the anticlinal walls of epidermal cells.

In our study, observation of ectomycorrhiza and non-mycorrhizal short roots by electron microscopy showed variation in the cells due to high concentration of metals. However, in the seedlings roots treated with 50 ppm and below, the hyphae penetrated the root directly. Dense fungal structures are formed mainly in the inner layer forming branches penetrating into deeper cortex (Plate 9.2). White fungal patches, interwoven strands were formed extending out from mycorrhizal mantle (Plate 9.1). Several fruiting bodies were formed and hyphal strands were clearly visible. The effect of heavy metals on the mycorrhizal fungi was variable. In some seedlings, mycelium was able to persist and recover somewhat, whereas in others, the condition of the mycelium did not ameliorate the toxicity of the metals.

Ouzounidou *et al.* (1992) found that Cu-treatment of the root of *Thalspi ochroleucum* cause drastic structural effects like plasmolysis and disintegration of cell component. Denny and Wilkins (1987) also argued that the extrametrical mycelium played a key role in retention of high amount of Zn ions. The cellular and structural changes in the root of pine seedlings treated with heavy metals appeared at higher concentrations in both mycorrhizal and non-mycorrhizal roots, which could be due to the breakdown of cytoplasmic structure, disruption of cell walls and cortical cells and accumulation of dense compounds. The cytological changes observed in metal-stressed pine roots were similar to those that occurred in seedlings in which nutrient deficiency was induced deliberately (Fink, 1991). Fungal cell walls are

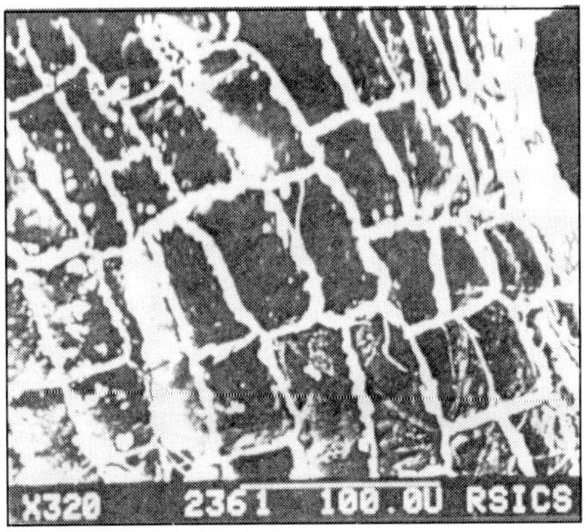

Plate 9.1. Infected with *Boletus* sp. & treated with Cd 10 ppm showing mantle (M) & Harting net (H).

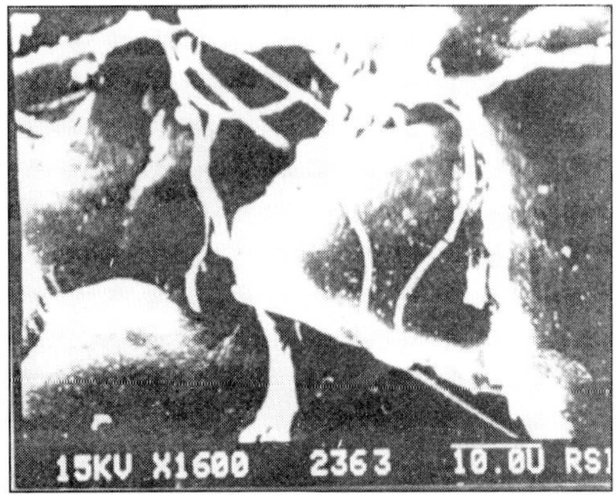

Plate 9.2. Infected with *Seleroderma auranium* treated with Cu 10 ppm showing mycelia.

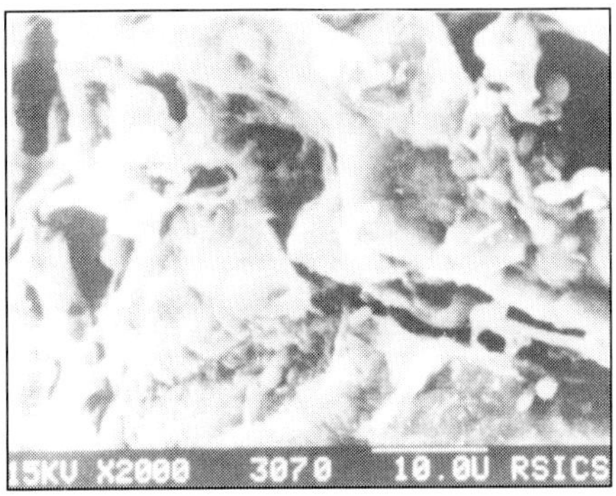

Plate 9.3. Infected with *Cenococcum graniforme* treated with Ni 500 ppm. showing distorted cytoplasm.

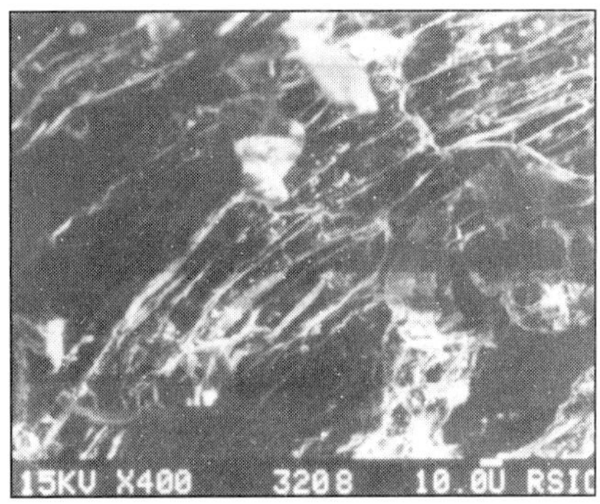

Plate 9.4. Non-mycorrhizal exposed to Pb 500 ppm showing damage by Pb toxicity.

known to have strong affinities for metallic cations (Ashida *et al.*, 1975), which provide much greater concentration of fungal material in the root. Elaborate hyphal coils occupy most of the cortical cells of pine roots with lower concentrations of metals through which absorptions occurs, and these would provide a greatly increased surface for retention of metal ions.

HEAVY METALS ACCUMULATION IN MYCORRHIZAL SEEDLINGS

The use of heavy metals has increased in various forestry practices in the form of fungicides, pesticides and application of municipal and industrial discharges. Atmospheric input of heavy metals can lead to their accumulation in the soil of forest ecosystem, especially of Cd and Pb (Zottl, 1985; Kahle *et al.*, 1992). However, many fungi show remarkable ability to survive and grow in high concentrations of heavy metals (Table 9.1). Toxic metals are numerous and vary in their action (Gadd, 1993). Metal ions can be bound to wall polymers at the cell wall such as chitin or melanin, and inside the fungal cells they might be rendered harmless to complexation, compartmentation or volatilization. There is evidence that ectomycorrhizal fungi can evolve metal tolerance (Colpaert and Van Assche, 1993; and Egerton-Warburton *et al.*, 1995).

Intra- and inter-specific variation may exist in the metal sensitivity of ectomycorrhizal fungi (Brown and Wilkins, 1985; Colpaert *et al.*, 1987; Hartley *et al.,* 1997). Zinc is an essential element required at all levels by all fungi (Carlile and Watkinson, 1994). By contrast Cd and Pb are non-essential elements, which can be toxic above the threshold concentrations (Smith and Read, 1997). Studies have been conducted to evaluate the accumulation of cadmium and chelation of metal ions occurring in the vicinity of plant roots (Naidu and Harter, 1998).

Table 9.1 Concentration of heavy metal (ppm) in the root tissue of mycorrhizal and non-mycorrhizal pine roots

Element concentration (ppm) in soil	*Concentration of heavy metals in different mycorrhizal roots*				
	M1	M2	M3	M4	NM
Zn 10	3.4	2.4	2.4	3.0	5.0
Zn 50	24.5	23.7	25.0	20.0	35.0
Zn 100	42.0	39.0	37.0	40.0	45.0
Zn 200	47.0	61.0	55.0	62.0	67.0
Zn 500	95.0	69.0	75.0	85.0	97.0
Ni 10	2.0	2.0	2.0	2.0	3.0
Ni 50	8.0	12.0	13.0	10.0	15.0
Ni 100	22.0	21.0	20.0	30.0	35.0
Ni 200	32.0	29.0	35.0	41.0	44.0
Ni 500	47.0	47.0	40.0	48.0	57.0
Al 10	2.9	2.4	2.1	2.8	5.2
Al 50	3.4	3.5	4.5	5.2	12.0
Al 100	20.0	14.0	13.0	18.0	28.0
Al 200	28.0	28.0	31.0	29.0	35.0
Al 500	52.0	52.0	43.0	40.0	55.0
Cd 10	2.0	1.0	1.0	1.0	3.0
Cd 50	3.0	3.0	2.0	2.0	4.0
Cd 100	7.1	7.0	5.4	4.9	8.1
Cd 200	15.0	9.0	8.3	8.3	15.8
Cd 500	20.0	21.0	17.0	12.0	30.0
Cu 10	5.1	5.0	5.3	4.9	6.1
Cu 50	19.0	10.0	21.0	13.0	27.0
Cu 100	30.0	24.0	23.0	21.0	37.0
Cu 200	39.0	26.0	27.0	26.0	45.0
Cu 500	61.0	45.0	45.0	40.0	85.0
Pb 10	1.6	1.6	1.5	1.4	2.1
Pb 50	2.4	4.0	4.0	2.9	7.0
Pb 100	4.5	10.0	10.0	8.0	12.0
Pb 200	14.0	15.0	15.0	17.0	20.0
Pb 500	30.0	20.0	22.0	20.0	38.0

M1 = *Scleroderma aurantium*, M2 = *Boletus* sp., M3 = *Cenococcum graniforme*, M4 = *Suillus leutus* NM = Non-mycorrhizal

The translocation and accumulation of heavy metals may be concentrated in tissues. The accumulation of pollutants on the plant surface is a contributing factor to the forest decline, and it is very important to understand the early growth and development of tree seedlings (Simmleit *et al.*, 1986). Plant roots produce stimulatory exudates (volatile and non-volatile) when mycorrhizal fungus penetrates and colonizes the plant host roots (Allen, 1992); mycorrhizal fungi also produce the same substances. Heavy metals are non-volatile compounds which could be important mediators in the host plant root.

Colpaert and Van Assche (1992) found an ameliorating effect in case of Zn toxicity, and clearly indicated that several ectomycorrhizal fungi can protect their host at its elevated concentration in soil. Atmospheric input of heavy metals and mobilization of metals in soil plant system (Srivastava *et al.*, 1999b) can lead to their accumulation in the soil of forest ecosystem. It is generally agreed that metal toxicity is one of the factors responsible for forest decline.

MYCORRHIZAL SEEDLING ESTABLISHMENT, SURVIVAL AND GROWTH IN HEAVY METAL POLLUTED SOIL

Several mycorrhizal fungi may effect the survival of plants and protect them against metal contamination in soil by influencing the uptake and accumulation of toxic ions (Jones and Hutchinsons, 1986, 1988b). However artificial inoculation of host plants with specific mycorrhical fungus depends upon the efficiency of mycobiont to improve the growth of host under varied ecological conditions (Browning and Whitney, 1993). Forest trees and ectomycorrhizal fungi have evolved together by adopting to natural and man made stresses. Heavy metals may reduce root growth, and alter the distribution of cations in the plants (Godbold *et al.*, 1988; Kahle *et al.*, 1992). Higher concentration of certain metals such as Cu, Pb and Zn act as environmental stress factors, as their influence may bring about physiological reactions in the host plant (Levitt, 1980) resulting in reduction in vigor and growth, reproduction and, in the extremes, even death. The survival of seedlings on contaminated sites determines their sensitivity to metal toxicity. Mycorrhizal fungi may bind metals and thus detoxify them. High concentration of dissolved Al has resulted in the screening of many forest tree species for Al sensitivity (Anderson, 1988; Shaedle *et al.*, 1989). Mycorrhizal fungi may affect the response of trees to Al (Harley and Smith, 1983).

The present investigation revealed that mycorrhizal seedlings had better survival and growth than non-mycorrhizal ones (Tables 9.2 and 9.3). Inoculation of pine seedlings with ectomycorrhizal fungi such as *Boletus* sp., *Cenococcum graniforme, Scleroderma aurantium* and *Suillus leutus* consistently stimulated shoot height, needle length, number of needles, root length, root collar diameter and seedlings volume as compared to non-mycorrhizal seedlings. Macfall and Slack (1991) also noted significant increase in pine (*Pinus resinosa* Ait) seedlings, root and shoot dry weights inoculated with ectomycorrhizal fungi as compared to non-mycorrhizal ones. Similarly, Gbdesgesin (1990) observed better survival and growth of pine (*Pinus oocarpa*) seedlings with *Pisolithus tinctorius* in field conditions after a period of four years. The better growth, establishment and survival of mycorrhizal seedlings indicated that these were more tolerant to the toxic effect of heavy metals. The severity of growth inhibition in metal treated non-mycorrhizal seedlings suggested that metal accumulation is primarily responsible for the damage of seedlings. Baar *et al.*, (1994) also observed the reduction in growth of seedlings due to low mycorrhizal level. The presence of growing fungus appeared to reduce the toxicity of Cd, Pb, Zn, Ni, Cu and Al. The toxicity symptoms remain in non-inoculated plants. Our results indicated the inhibition of root elongation at higher concentration (100 ppm and above) of heavy metals. The plant roots were most susceptible to metal damage than other growth parameters (Plates 9.5 and 9.6). The fungus showed rapid colonization and growth so that the toxic effects brought about by the metals were reduced quickly, thereby allowing the root to retain its normal growth. Initially, plant roots became dark, short and thick, and these symptoms were attributed to metal toxicity (Mengal *et al.*, 1982). However, mycorrhizal roots grew normally when compared to brown, short and stubby roots observed in non-mycorrhizal plants.

Table 9.2 Effect of heavy metal toxicity on survival (%) of mycorrhizal pine seedlings

Metals concentration (ppm)	*Survival (%)*				
	M1	M2	M3	M4	NM
Zn 10	76.0	93.0	76.0	83.0	70.0
Zn 50	76.0	86.0	70.0	80.0	66.0
Zn 100	73.0	83.0	66.0	80.0	63.0
Zn 200	70.0	80.0	63.0	73.0	60.0
Zn 500	60.0	70.0	60.0	73.0	58.0
Ni 10	86.0	86.0	93.0	86.0	90.0
Ni 50	80.0	86.0	86.0	80.0	80.0
Ni 100	80.0	83.0	73.0	80.0	73.0
Ni 200	76.0	80.0	73.0	73.0	73.0
Ni 500	73.0	73.0	66.0	73.0	64.0
Al 10	86.0	80.0	90.0	86.0	86.0
Al 50	86.0	80.0	80.0	86.0	80.0
Al 100	80.0	80.0	80.0	84.0	76.0
Al 200	80.0	76.0	73.0	80.0	73.0
Al 500	76.0	73.0	73.0	76.0	70.0
Cd 10	93.0	86.0	86.0	86.0	90.0
Cd 50	93.0	80.0	8.0	80.0	80.0
Cd 100	86.0	80.0	80.0	80.0	76.0
Cd 200	80.0	76.0	80.0	80.0	73.0
Cd 500	80.0	73.0	73.0	76.0	70.0
Cu 10	86.0	93.0	86.0	86.0	86.0
Cu 50	86.0	86.0	80.0	80.0	80.0
Cu 100	80.0	76.0	80.0	80.0	73.0
Cu 200	80.0	80.0	73.0	80.0	73.0
Cu 500	73.0	80.0	73.0	73.0	80.0
Pb 10	93.0	86.0	86.0	86.0	80.0
Pb 50	86.0	80.0	73.0	80.0	80.0
Pb 100	86.0	80.0	73.0	80.0	73.0
Pb 200	73.0	73.0	70.0	73.0	70.0
Pb 500	72.0	73.0	66.0	73.0	60.0

M1 = *S. luteus*, M2 = *Boletus* sp, M3 = *S. aurantium*, M4 = *C. graniforme*. NM = Non-mycorrhizal.

Table 9.3 Effect of heavy metals on the growth of pine seedlings

Metals root conc. length (ppm) (cm)	*Shoot height (cm)*	*Needle length (cm)*	*No. of needles*	*Seed-lings vol. (cm^3)*	*Root collar dm (cm)*
0 30.5	14.0	5.3	167	0.590	0.25
Zn 10 27.1	6.6	3.8	113	0.319	0.22
Zn 50 20.8	5.5	3.5	89	0.266	0.22
Zn 100 16.1	5.4	2.5	78	0.194	0.19
Zn 200 14.8	5.2	2.5	57	0.168	0.18
Zn 500 10.6	5.0	2.4	54	0.162	0.18
Ni 10 26.0	9.5	3.8	146	0.418	0.21
Ni 50 21.1	8.2	3.0	112	0.296	0.19
Ni 100 15.8	7.9	2.7	102	0.252	0.19
Ni 200 15.1	6.1	2.6	92	0.156	0.16
Ni 500 14.8	5.9	2.4	87	0.132	0.15
Al 10 16.1	9.1	3.8	136	0.481	0.23
Al 50 16.0	8.5	3.6	78	0.411	0.22
Al 100 15.6	6.0	2.0	77	0.290	0.22
Al 200 15.0	5.8	2.8	74	0.209	0.18
Al 500 14.5	5.5	2.7	58	0.178	0.18
Cd 10 16.3	9.5	3.5	120	0.419	0.21
Cd 50 16.3	5.8	3.0	119	0.255	0.21
Cd 100 15.4	5.4	2.7	91	0.138	0.16
Cd 200 14.8	5.0	2.5	83	0.128	0.16
Cd 500 14.6	4.5	2.3	66	0.064	0.12
Cu 10 26.4	8.2	3.5	116	0.361	0.21

Contd.

Contd.

Cu 50 23.0	6.8	3.4	106	0.174	0.16
Cu 100 16.0	6.0	3.1	105	0.150	0.14
Cu 200 15.0	5.5	3.1	105	0.079	0.12
Cu 500 13.8	5.4	2.5	85	0.077	0.12
Pb 10 18.9	7.0	4.5	111	0.308	0.21
Pb 50 18.0	6.5	3.7	98	0.286	0.21
Pb 100 17.1	6.1	3.2	81	0.156	0.16
Pb 200 17.0	5.8	2.8	76	0.148	0.16
Pb 500 15.9	5.7	2.7	59	0.082	0.12

With time it appeared either that the plant itself or the inoculated fungus was able to bind the metals, mediate the rhizosphere pH or that the substrates or the root exudates complex the available metals so that the element was no longer a toxic. However, additional researches into understanding of the mechanism of protection of roots against metal toxicity are required.

A major benefit of mycorrhizal association is that it aids the host tree in survival and growth by managing the stress (Bendangmenla *et al.*, 2005). Currently there are opportunities to apply the ectomycorrhizal technology to seedling production and reclamation and reforestation programmes.

HEAVY METALS TOXICITY ON METABOLIC ACTIVITIES

The activity of any particular enzyme in soil is a composite of activities associated with various biotic and abiotic factors (Tiwari *et al.*, 1987a). Dehydrogenase activity in soil provides correlative information on the biological activity and microbial population. Microbial biomass and their dehydrogenase activity have been observed to be influenced by rhizosphere of the host plant (Speir *et al.*, 1980). Urease activity generally correlates with organic matter content. Various factors such as pH, moisture content, temperature and number of microorganisms affect the urease activity in soil (Jha *et al.*, 1992). Phosphatase is thought to be directly related to the level of organic phosphorus in the soil. Therefore the activity of this enzyme is significant in P-cycling and plant nutrition. Phosphatases are also produced by ectomycorrhizal fungi (Dighton, 1983). Acid phosphatase activity and fungal mantle mycelium hydrolyse the complex organic phosphorus, which improves the nutrient uptake. Root surface phosphatase may be more important in organic phosphorus mobilization, making it available to the plants (Antibus *et al.*, 1992). The root surface phosphatase activity has its relationship with mycorrhizal association and P-uptake (Dodd *et al.*, 1987).

The number of mycorrhizal rootlets and fungal mycelium associated with them as determined by the specific mycobiont is important. Variation in the efficiency of mycorrhiza for metabolic activities and NPK uptake may depend on the specific mycorrhizal fungi. Heavy metals like Zn and Pb are found inhibitory to microbial growth and decomposition (Joshi, 1993). However, many fungi show remarkable ability to survive and grow in high concentrations of heavy metals.

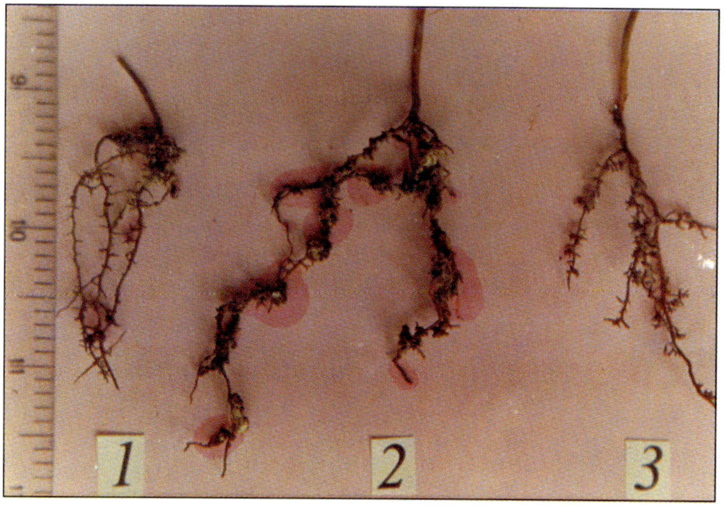

Plate 9.5: Mycorrhizal roots treated with (1) Ni 200 ppm (2) Cd 10 ppm (3) Al 50 ppm.

Plate 9.6: (1) Mycorrhizal roots without heavy metal treatment.
(2) Treated with Ni 10 ppm.

In our experiment, results showed that the enzyme activity was subjected to seasonal variation. The effect of heavy metals on urease, phosphatase and dehydrogenase activity differed considerably. Dehydrogenase activity was apparently less at high concentrations of Zn, Cu, Cd, Pb Ni and Al. The inoculation of ectomycorrhizal fungi into the seedlings increased the activity of dehydrogenase. Highest activity of dehydrogenase was observed during summer and minimum activity was observed during winter (Figs. 9.1 and 9.2). The seasonal fluctuation followed a divergent pattern during the year. During summer months, dehydrogenase activity remained almost constant, but after September it decreased considerably and reached its minimum. During this period, soil temperature and moisture content of the soil were also lowest. It could be inferred that adverse effect due to heavy metals was severe and prolonged. The non-mycorrhizal roots and their rhizospheric soil showed high percentage of inhibition of dehydrogenase activity (Figs. 9.3 and 9.4). It was observed that in the absence of ectomycorrhiza, the added metals drastically reduced the enzyme activity, especially at higher concentration of metals. Possibly the presence of ectomycorrhizal fungi enabled the seedlings to increase their metabolic activities. Jha (1991) correlated the high concentration of various enzymes like urease, dehydrogenase and phosphatase to the high microbial population in soil.

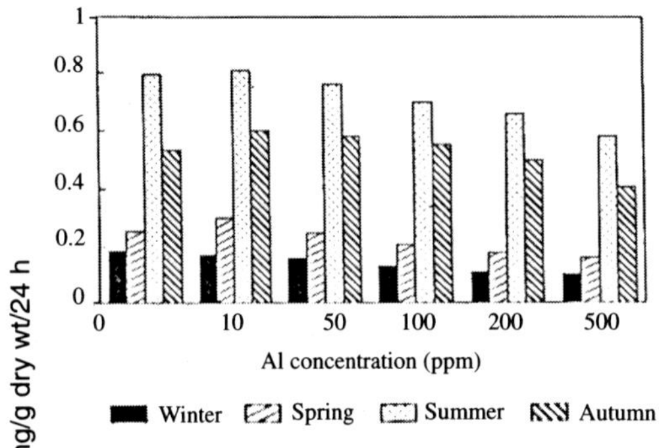

Fig. 9.1

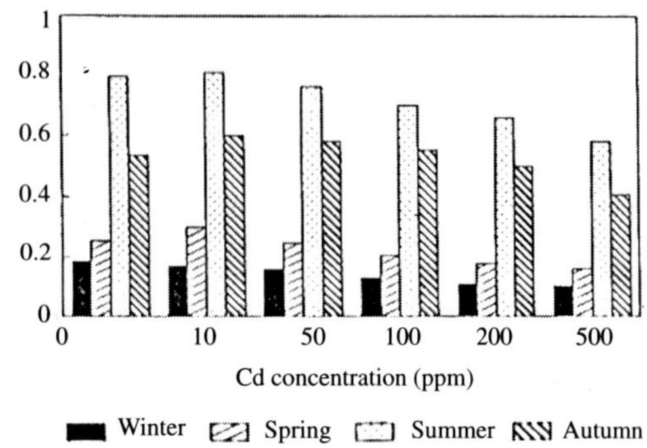

Fig. 9.2

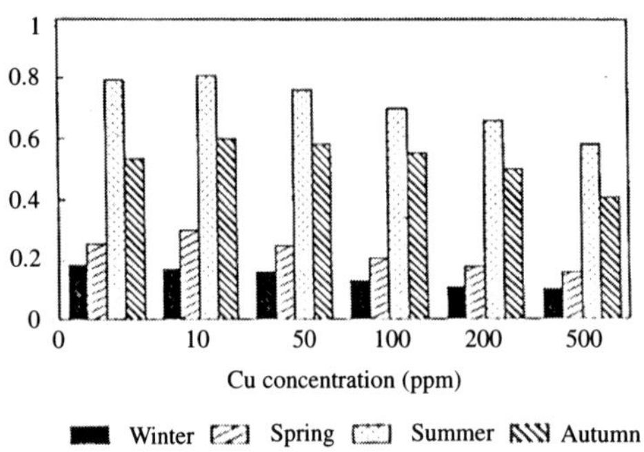

Fig. 9.3

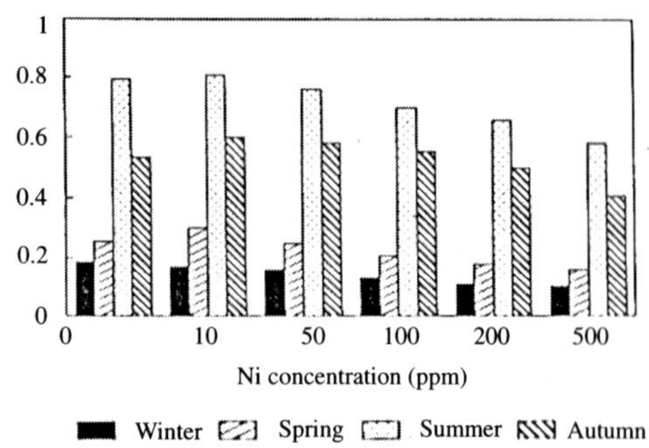

Fig. 9.4

Figs. 9.1-9.4 Dehydrogenase activity on root surface inoculated with *Boletus* sp.

Inoculation of ectomycorrhizal fungi harboured increased activity of urease enzyme than uninoculated ones. The urease activity was apparently less at 100 ppm and above of added metals. During spring to summer, urease activity remained almost constant, but after September, the activity started to increase gradually (Figs 9.17-9.22) and reached its peak in autumn. Among the six metals studied, Al, Cu and Zn were less inhibitory for urease activity as compared to Cd, Ni and Pb. Metals like Ni and Cd were more toxic than the rest of metals (Figs 9.23-9.28). The seasonal variation of enzyme activities appears to be dependent on factors such as aeration, soil moisture and soil microflora (Burns, 1978). The results indicated that there was a decrease in phosphatase, urease and dehydrogenase activity when treated with high concentration of heavy metals. The degree of inhibition is dependent on the amount of metals added, and the intensity of inhibition among the factors may be enhanced due to low amount of organic matter.

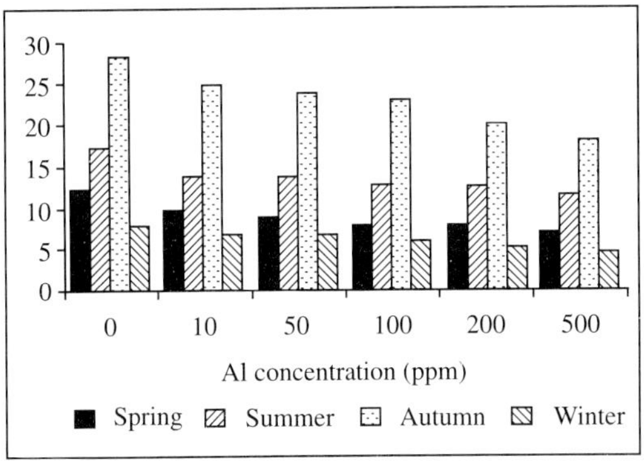

Fig. 9.5

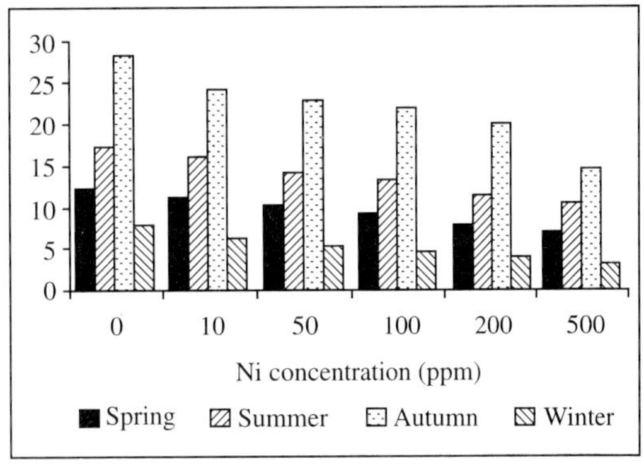

Fig. 9.6

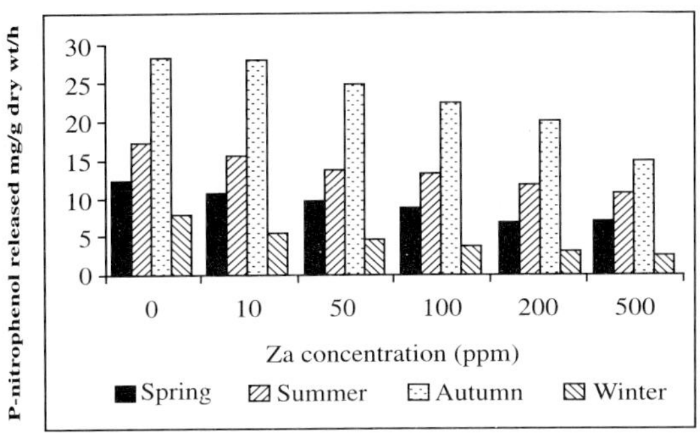

Fig. 9.7

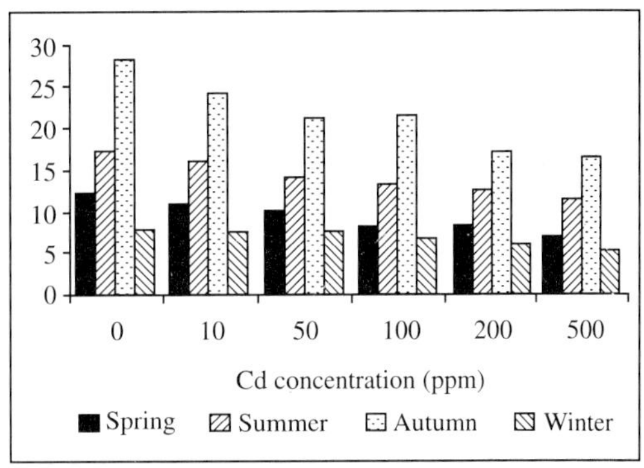

Fig. 9.8

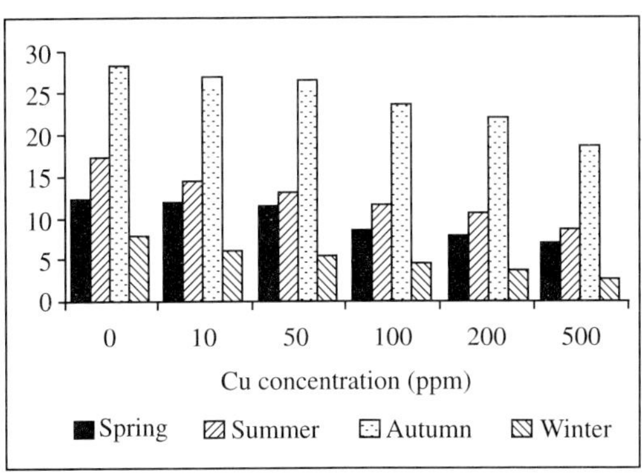

Fig. 9.9

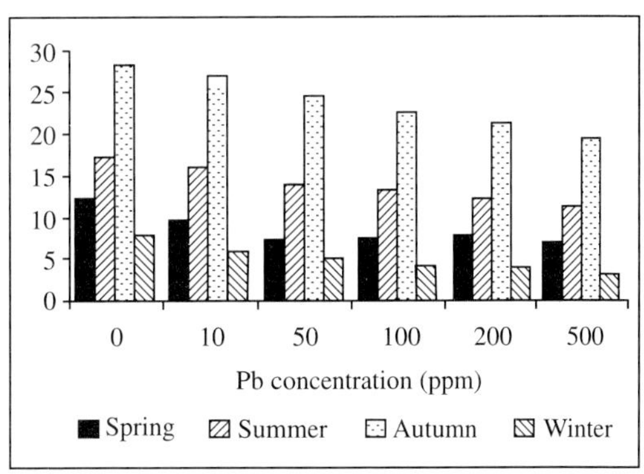

Fig. 9.10

Figs. 9.5-9.10 Phosphatase activity on rhizospheric soil inoculated with mixed mycobionts.

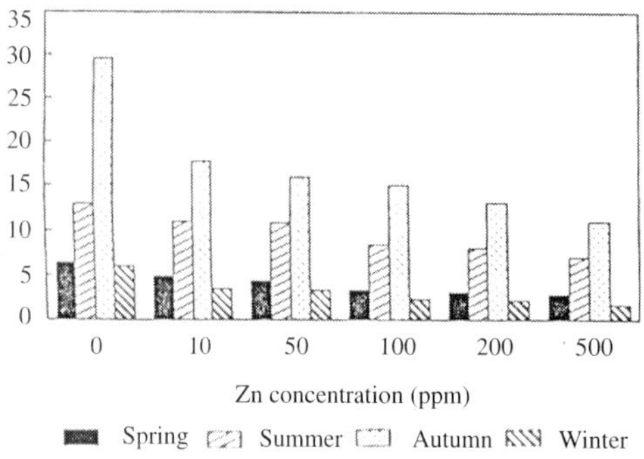

Fig. 9.11

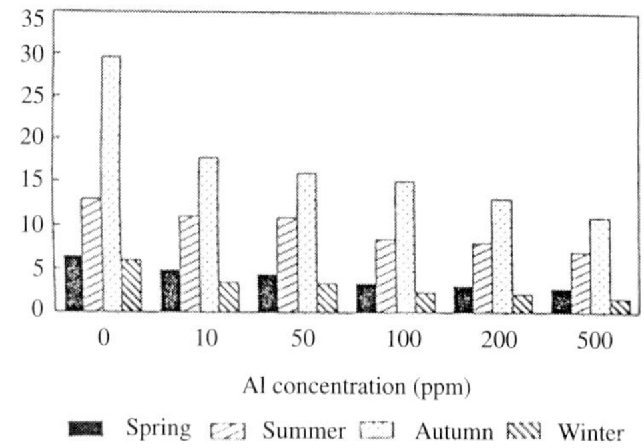

Fig. 9.12

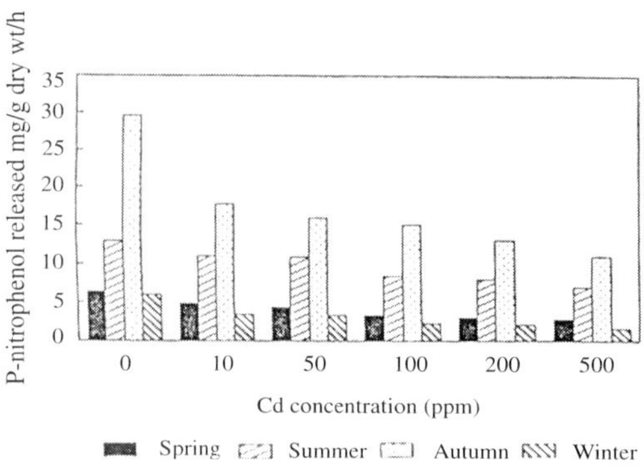

Fig. 9.13

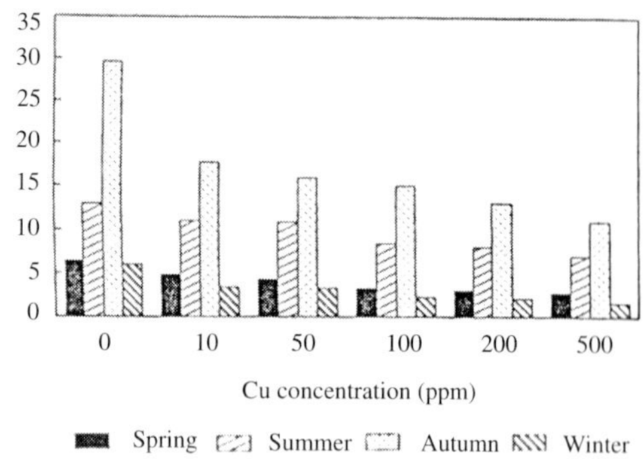

Fig. 9.14

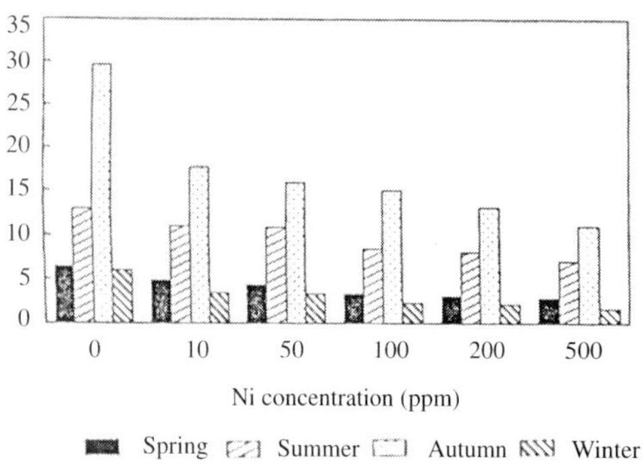

Fig. 9.15

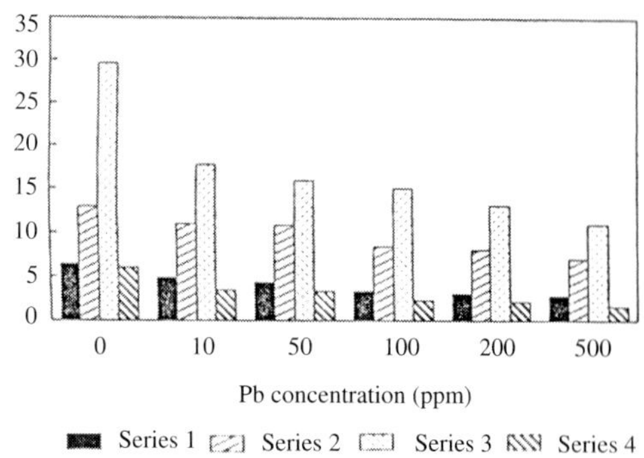

Fig. 9.16

Figs. 9.11-9.16 Phosphatase activity in non-mycorrhizal rhizospheric soil.

Soil organic matter is able to form complex metallic compound by cation exchange, adsorption or chellation. Inhibition of enzyme activity of phosphatase by Cu and Zn cations has been reported (Tabatabai *et al.*, 1977). The microorganisms on the root surface and in rhizosphere region may differ in their sensitivity to metal toxicity. High concentration of metal exposure may also cause death of cells due to disruption of membrane, resulting in the change in viability or competitive ability of the microbes.

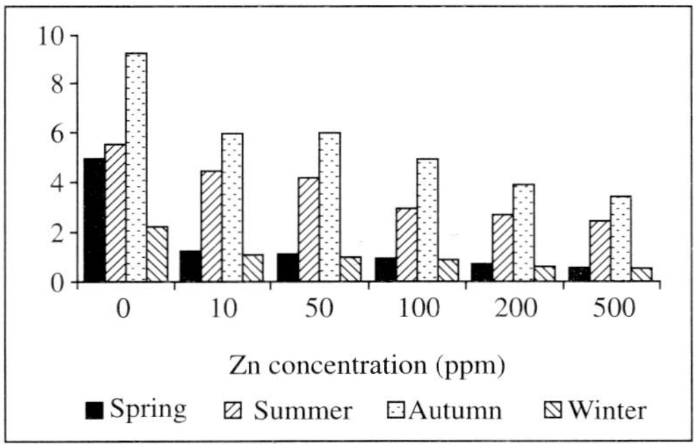

Fig. 9.17

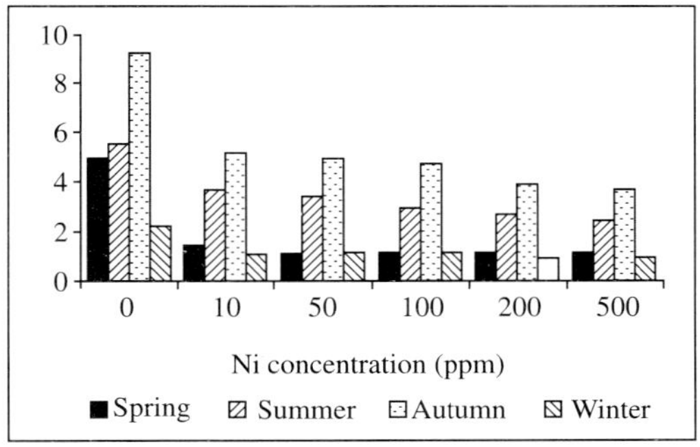

Fig. 9.18

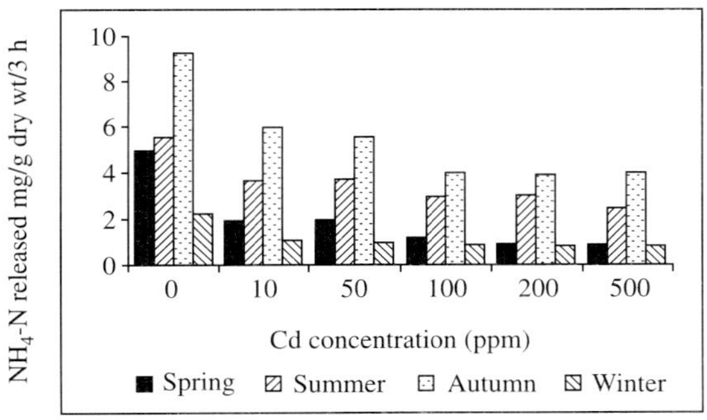

Fig. 9.19

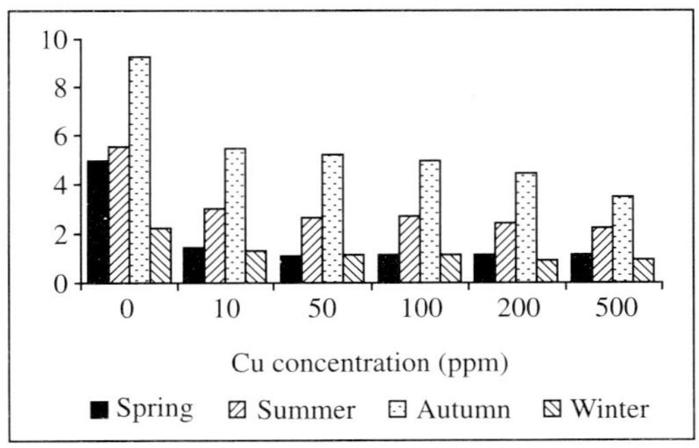

Fig. 9.20

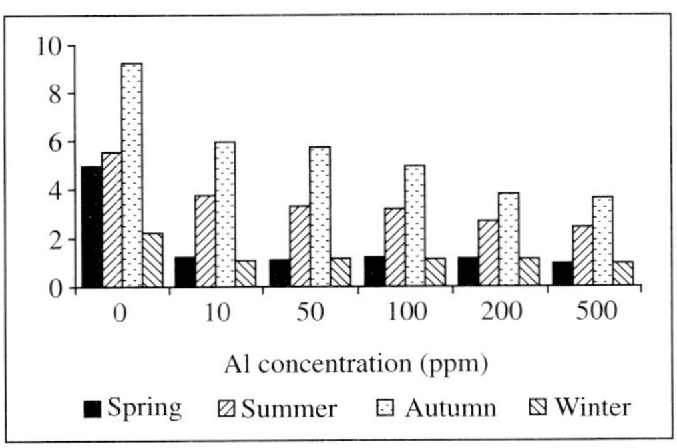

Fig. 9.21

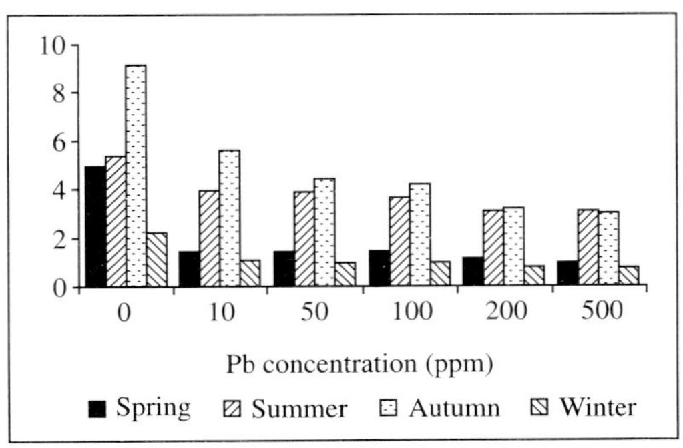

Fig. 9.22

Figs. 9.17-9.22 Urease activity on non-mycorrhizal rhizospheric soil.

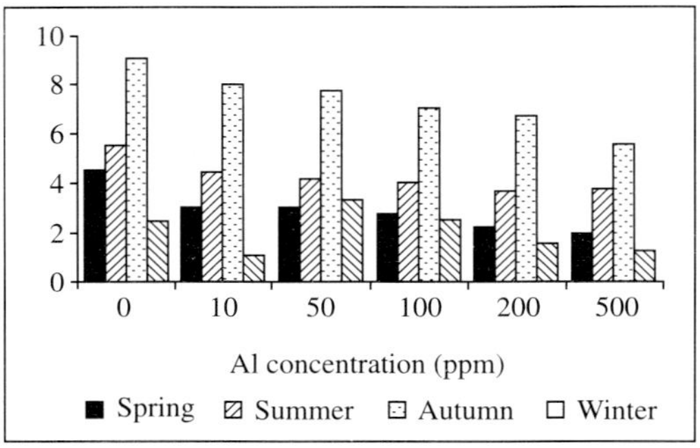

Fig. 9.23

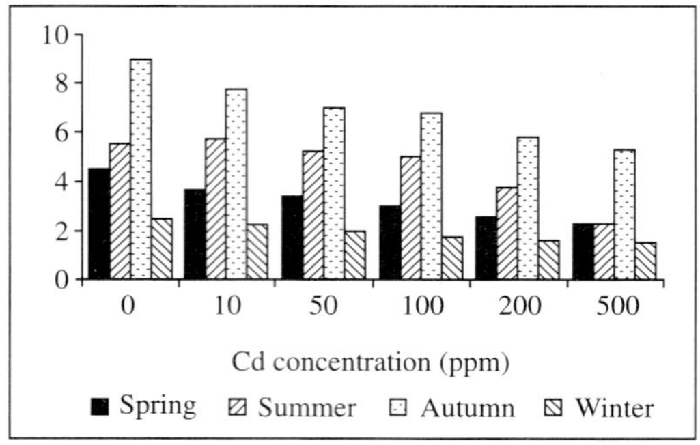

Fig. 9.24

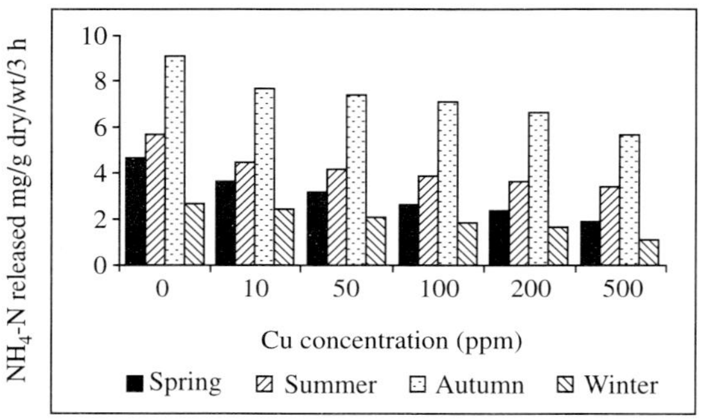

Fig. 9.25

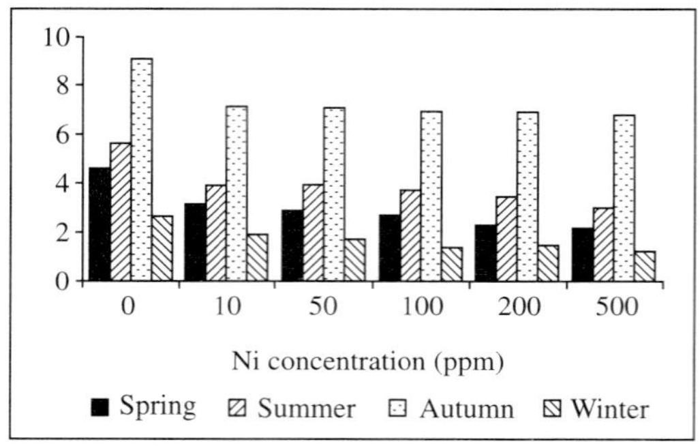

Fig. 9.26

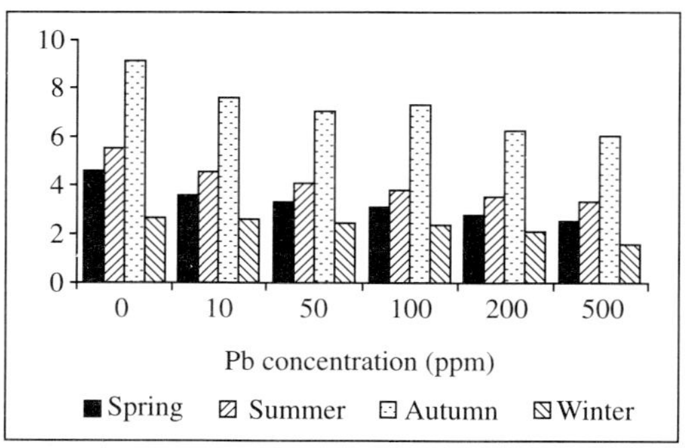

Fig. 9.27

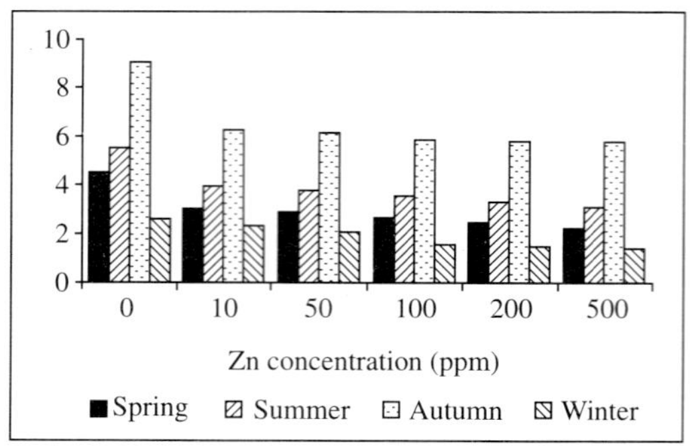

Fig. 9.28

Figs. 9.23-9.28 Urease activity on rhizospheric soil inoculated with mixed mycobionts.

Increased inhibition of phosphatase activity was observed at higher concentration of Pb, Cu, Ni, Cd, Zn and Al treated seedlings. Phosphatase activity was highest in autumn, but from November onward it started to decline and remained constant during the winter months. The activity of phosphatase was higher in case of mixed mycobionts inoculated root and rhizosphere soil (Figs. 9.5-9.10). In case of non-mycorrhizal seedlings, the phosphatase activity was less and inhibition rate was high (Figs. 9.11-9.16). There was a negative correlation between heavy metals concentration and the activity of urease, phosphatase and dehydrogenase activity. A positive correlation was also found between mycorrhizal infection (Table 9.4) and the activity of enzymes ($P < 0.05$ and $P < 0.01$ level). There was a significant variation between sampling periods of phosphatase, urease and dehydrogenase ($P < 0.05$) in both rhizosphere soil as well as root region (Table 9.5) and also between mycorrhizal and non-mycorrhizal ($P < 0.01$ level).

Table 9.4 Correlation coefficient (r) values of mycorrhizal infection with enzyme activities of pine seedling

Parameters		*Mycorrhizal infection*					
		M1	*M2*	*M3*	*M4*	*NM*	*MMF*
Phosphatase	1.	0.91*	0.89*	0.88*	0.80**	NS	0.90**
	2.	0.92*	0.93*	0.96*	0.95*	NS	0.98*
Dehydrogenase	1.	0.87*	0.81**	0.91*	0.89*	NS	0.91*
	2.	0.96*	0.97*	0.93*	0.90*	NS	0.93*
Urease	1.	0.98*	0.91*	0.87*	0.80**	NS	0.92*
	2.	0.90*	0.94*	0.96*	0.86*	NS	0.90*

M1 = *C. graniforme*, M2 = *S. luteus*, M3 = *Boletus* sp, M4 = *S. aurantium*.
NM = Non-mycorrhizal. MMF = Mixed mycorrhizal fungi.
* = significant at $p < 0.01$ level, ** = significant at $p < 0.05$ level, NS = not significant.
1 = root surface. 2 = rhizospheric soil

Table 9.5 Analysis of variance (F) values with the sampling periods, mycorrhizal and non-mycorrhizal with various parameters in pine seedlings

Source of variance		*Variation between sampling periods and roots*	*Mycorrhizal and non-mycorrhizal*
Phosphatase	1.	13.32**	10.84**
	2.	7 .3*	7.91*
Urease	1.	3.5*8	7.9*
	2.	3.43**	3.13*
Dehydrogenase	1.	7.59*	6.33**
	2.	6.71*	6.28**

1 = root surface, 2 = rhizospheric soil, * = significant at $p < 0.01$ level, ** = significant at $p < 0.05$ level

The dehydrogenase activity considerably decreased in the rhizosphere soil as well as on the root surface with high metal doses. Reddy and Faza (1989) also reported decreased dehydrogenase activity in soils containing heavy metals. The root growth was normally low in winter, which lead to the assumption that along with high metals, low temperature added to the reduced microbial activity. The appreciable decrease in urease activity in rhizospheric soil, which received high metal concentration, suggested that it is derived from living cells in low quantity. Gianfreda *et al.* (1994) reported that the application of Cu in the form of fungicides altered the urease activity in soil. The greater inhibition of enzymes in the presence of heavy metals could be due to inhibition of enzyme sites that were not available for catalysis. Stott *et al.* (1985) reported that the metals like Cd, Zn, Ni, Cu and Pb may inhibit enzyme reaction by complexing the substrate, or reaction with enzyme substrate complex. The mode of inhibition is dependent on the type of reaction or complexation produced. Tyler (1981) also observed that heavy metals inhibited a variety of microbial enzymes, indicating that the nature and type of inhibition varies among the metals used and the enzyme studied. However, little information is available on the inhibition of these enzymes on the root surface and in rhizosphere soils by metal ions. It was found that the degree of inhibition of urease, dehydrogenase and phosphatase activity on root surface and rhizosphere soil of pine seedlings by heavy metals is much smaller in mycorrhizal roots than non-mycorrhizal ones. This could be due to binding of metal ions by fungal mycelium, which consisted of mantle and Hartig net. This would explain why mycorrhizal plants had lesser inhibition compared to non-mycorrhizal ones. Denny and Wilkins (1987) also measured lower contents of Zn in the cortex of mycorrhizal than non-mycorrhizal plants.

HEAVY METALS EFFECT ON THE UPTAKE OF NUTRIENTS BY MYCORRHIZAL SEEDLINGS

Mycorrhizal association is specially adapted to nutrient stress condition. Their beneficial role in the absorption of inorganic nutrients, production and supply of growth regulators, decreasing of soil toxicity and increased resistance to extreme soil temperature is known (Heinrich *et al.*, 1989). It has been found that tree seedling lacking mycorrhiza show severe nutrient deficiency until mycorrhiza are formed (Trappe and Strand, 1969). The fungi play a vital role in nutrient cycling, productivity and plant succession in the ecosystem.

Heavy metals disturb nutrient mineralization in soil (Berg, 1991) leading to low nutrient availability. Malfunctioning of organic P compound and P assimilation in plants under Al stress has been reported (Foy, 1988).

The treatment of heavy metals adversely affected the total contents of N, P and K in seedlings. More than 50 ppm of heavy metals doses appeared to have suppressive effects (Table 9.6). Analysis of mineral nutrients in seedlings of pine suggested that the growth was greater in the mycorrhizal seedlings than non-mycorrhizal ones, which could be due to the increased uptake of nutrients, especially N and P. Contents of N in ectomycorrhizal seedlings were more than twice than in non-mycorrhizal ones at each metal treatment level. The cause of growth reduction in non-mycorrhizal plants may be due to their N status, since any change in N uptake and transport would alter the growth of plant. The uptake of nutrients as a whole was restricted by the presence of heavy metals. There is an evidence that Cd and other heavy metals influenced the translocation of essential elements (Smith and Brennan, 1984). Cd, Ni and Pb are considered extremely toxic metals in plants causing disorders in photosynthetic machinery even at relatively low concentration, resulting in the growth reduction of seedlings (Tinker, 1981).

Table 9.6 Effect of heavy metal toxicity on N, P and K uptake in mycorrhizal and non-mycorrhizal pine seedlings

Metals conc.	*Nitrogen (%)*		*Phosphorus (%)*		*Potassium (%)*	
(ppm)	*M*	*0*	*M*	*0*	*M*	*0*
Zn 10	2.31	1.91	0.96	0.79	1.14	0.88
Zn 50	2.25	1.82	0.84	0.70	1.03	0.87
Zn 100	2.20	1.74	0.80	0.62	0.97	0.76
Zn 200	1.78	1.32	0.70	0.65	0.91	0.65
Zn 500	1.62	1.09	0.67	0.50	0.80	0.59
Ni 10	2.49	1.28	0.91	0.80	1.02	0.92
Ni 50	1.98	1.21	0.80	0.69	0.96	0.90
Ni 100	1.91	1.16	0.71	0.60	0.92	0.83
Ni 200	1.84	1.08	0.69	0.51	0.87	0.80
Ni 500	1.69	1.00	0.56	0.40	0.73	0.60
Al 10	2.48	1.85	0.89	0.71	0.95	0.89
Al 50	2.40	1.80	0.81	0.67	0.90	0.83
Al 100	2.33	1.75	0.78	0.59	0.89	0.73
Al 200	1.92	1.58	0.63	0.56	0.71	0.63
Al 500	1.75	1.32	0.59	0.40	0.69	0.61
Cd 10	2.29	1.92	0.93	0.74	1.07	1.00
Cd 50	2.21	1.82	0.79	0.70	1.05	0.95
Cd 100	1.89	1.10	0.73	0.67	0.83	0.76
Cd 200	1.81	1.08	0.70	0.62	0.79	0.75
Cd 500	1.68	1.04	0.60	0.42	0.66	0.60
Cu 10	2.07	1.16	0.90	0.81	1.04	1.24
Cu 50	1.98	1.05	0.86	0.69	1.07	0.85
Cu 100	1.70	1.01	0.80	0.70	0.98	0.62
Cu 200	1.67	0.97	0.73	0.61	0.93	0.61
Cu 500	1.02	0.87	0.62	0.43	0.86	0.57
Pb 10	1.61	1.18	0.94	0.85	1.17	1.10
Pb 50	1.47	1.18	0.86	0.76	1.11	1.02
Pb 100	1.39	1.08	0.80	0.70	0.81	0.78
Pb 200	1.34	1.01	0.75	0.50	0.78	0.71
Pb 500	1.34	0.99	0.67	0.35	0.73	0.70

M = Mycorrhizal, 0 = Non-mycorrhizal

The greater root development in the seedlings treated with 50 ppm and below of heavy metals might have accounted for higher N, P and K accumulation. The benefit of mycorrhiza for improving the nutrient status of trees is largely related to hyphal net of extrametrical mycelia in the soil providing a large surface area for uptake of nutrients (Rousseau *et al.*, 1994). A significant effect on the growth of mycorrhizal inoculated seedlings can be attributed to increased absorptive surface area due to extensive network of fungal mycelium resulting in increasing uptake of water and nutrients from the soil. Variation in the growth of host plant may be due to the efficacy of mycobionts in nutrient and water absorption and the amount of ectomycorrhiza formed during the growing season (Baar *et al.*, 1994). Such differential response in growth due to inoculation of different fungal species is also supported by Marx, (1991) who concluded that not all species of fungi that form ectomycorrhizal have equal benefits to their host under specific conditions and some are more effective than others.

Reduced mineral availability to the plants was due to the reduced surface area of the mycorrhiza caused by pollution, which may result in rapid decline of forest (Dighton *et al.*, 1990). Similar decrease in nutrient concentration in seedlings has been reported due to Ni toxicity (Cataldo *et al.*, 1978). The main causes of reduced nutrient content of the seedlings was the high concentration of added metals in soil, which restricted the mycorrhizae in the root system. Mycorrhiza absorbs nearly most of the minerals, but the effect of mycorrhizal infection on P-uptake is well documented (Kahle *et al.*, 1992). Mycorrhizal association is especially adapted to nutrient stress conditions (Heinrich *et al.*, 1989). It may be possible that under these circumstances, ectomycorrhizal roots and their mycelia function as mineral source-sink than non-mycorrhizal ones. The reduced growth of extramycelium resulting from high concentration of heavy metals is likely to reduce the potential of the fungus to take up minerals and water and transfer them to the seedlings. Mycorrhizal development might be a more important factor than soil nutrient availability for determining nutrient levels especially for P due to its low mobility in the soil. Phosphorus is a key plant nutrient required in optimum amount for proper plant growth. Mycorrhizal inoculation improves plant productivity especially in soil with low nutrient condition and metal polluted soil (Ajungla *et al.*, 2003). Heavy metals disturb nutrient mineralization process in soil (Berg, 1991), leading to low nutrient availability. Ni toxicity also reduces nutrient uptake and plant metabolism (Ajungla *et al.*, 2006).

The effect of heavy metal contamination can be delayed when the metal binds to hyphal cells constituent or is chemically converted into inactive or insoluble compounds. Al often interferes with phosphorus nutrition, which may reduce its uptake by plants.

The nutrient concentration in the seedlings has shown that the lower levels of heavy metals were able to sustain the growth of non-mycorrhiza and mycorrhizal seedlings. The main effect of metal treatment in non-mycorrhizal seedlings was directly correlated to the nutrient availability. At high levels of metals, however, inhibition of nutrient contents may be due to complexing ability. In these circumstances, the presence of an ectomycorrhizal fungal symbiont could be of considerable importance.

There have been extensive studies in relation to the potential use of mycorrhiza in terms of uptake of nutrients like phosphorus, nitrogen and potassium (Jha *et al.*, 1990). The tolerance of heavy metals may be significantly influenced by accumulation of toxic ions in root cell (Tinker, 1981). Cd toxicity often results in water stress (Schlegel *et al.*, 1992).

Mycorrhizal fungi can dramatically increase host plant absorption of mineral nutrients from soil, particularly immobile nutrients such as phosphorus.

CONCLUSION

The mycorrhizal fungi increased the tolerance of seedlings to heavy metals. The ability of mycorrhizal fungi to grow in the presence of heavy metals, though to a lesser extent, is an important factor. At high levels of metals, however, inhibition of root extension and hence complexing ability occurred. Mycorrhizal fungi indirectly influenced the transport of heavy metals in the plants. The whole biomass in sporophore, the extrametrical mycelium as well as the mantle mycelia, can complex a considerable amount of added metals and thus strongly reduced the availability of the toxic ion to the seedlings.

In this study, differential metal uptake may be associated with the development of fungal mantle. The greater root development in the seedlings treated with 50 ppm and below of metals might have accounted for higher P accumulation. The enhanced metal accumulation in non-mycorrhizal roots may be partially responsible for poor root development (Trappe *et al.*, 1969). The metals primarily acted on the mycelium. The fungal tissue might also provide the host with protection against heavy metals depending upon the metal accumulation capacity of the mycelium (Ajungla *et al.*, 2003). Cd, Ni and Pb are considered extremely toxic metals in plants causing disorders in photosynthetic machinery even at relatively low concentration, resulting in growth reduction of seedlings (Tinker, 1981). Therefore, a better understanding of heavy metal sources, their accumulation in soil and their effect on the plant systems seem to be an important issue of the present-day research.

The present result suggests that the greater root development in the seedlings treated with 50 ppm and below might have accounted for higher N, P and K uptake. The enhanced metal accumulation in non-mycorrhizal roots may be partially responsible for the development of poor root (Tan *et al.*, 1990b), which may lead to less exploitation of minerals nutrients. The relation between heavy metal and mycorrhiza is quite complicated. Reduction of fine roots and cell wall was found to be pre-requisite for mycorrhization (Munzenberger *et al.*, 1995).

The interaction between various contaminants and plants with respect to toxicity has been studied (Symenoidis and Karataglis, 1992). However, information on the heavy metal toxicity to the mycorrhizal system is still scarce.

REFERENCES

Agerer, R. (1991). *Mycorrhizae*. **1:** 20-30.

Ajungla, T. and Sharma. G.D. (2003). *NURJ*. **1:**14-17.

Ajungla, T., Sharma, G.D and Dkhar, M.S. (2006). *Environ. Biol. and Cons*. **11:** 15-18.

Allen, M.J. (1992). Mycorrhiza functioning: an integrative plant fungal process. Chapman and Heavy Hall, New York.

Antibus, R.K., Sinsabaugh, R.L and Linkins, A.E. (1992). *Can. J. of Bot*. **70:** 794-804.

Anderson, M. (1988). *Water, Air Soil Pollution*. **39:** 439-462.

Anderson, C.P and Rygiewiecz, P.T. (1991). *Environ. Pollution*. **73:** 217-224.

Ashida, J., Higashi, N and Kikuchi, T. (1975). *Protoplasma*. **57:** 27-32.

Baar, J., Ozinga. W.A and Kuyper, T.W. (1994). *Mycol. Res*. **98:** 725-728.

Berg, A. (1991). Ectomycorrhizal in coniferous forest structure and dynamics and populations communities. Ph. D. thesis Swedish university of Agricultural Sciences. Uppsala, Sweden.

Bendangmenla., Ajungla, T. and Jamir, N.S. (2005). *NURJ*. **3:** 80-83.

Berg, A. (1991). Ectomycorrhizal in coniferous forest structure and dynamics and population communities. Ph. D. Thesis. Swedish University of Agricultural Sciences. Uppsala, Sweden.

Bindhu, S.J., Pati, M.K and Bera, A.K. (2005). *Environ. Biol and Conservation*. **10:** 11-12.

Brownlee, C., Duddridge, A., Malibari, A and Read, D. J. (1983). *Plant Soil*. **71:** 433-443.

Brown, M. T and Wilkins, D.A. (1985). Zn tolerance of *Amanita* and *Paxillus transactiuos* of the British. Mycological Society. **84:** 367-369.

Browning, M.H.R and Whitney, R.D. (1993). *Can. J. For. Res*. **23:** 330-333.

Burns, R.G. (1978). Soil Enzymes. Academic Press. London.

Cataldo, D.A., Garland, T.R and Wildung, R.E. (1978). *Plant Physiol*. **62:** 563-565.

Carlile, M.J and Watkinson, S.C. (1994). The fungi. London. Academic Press Ltd.

Colpaert, J.V and Van Assche, J.A. (1987). *Functional Ecology.* **1:** 415-421.

Colpaert, J.V and Van Assche, J.A. 1992. *Plant Soil.* **145:** 237-243.

Colpaert, J.V and Van Assche, J.A. (1993). *New Phytol.* **123:** 325-333.

Denny, H.J and Wilkins, D.A. (1987). *New Phytol.* **106:** 535-544.

Deora, G.S., Leena Sharma and Chandrakala Suhalka. (2005). *Environ. Biol and Conservation.* **10:** 5-10.

Dighton, J. (1983). *Plant Soil.* **71:** 455-462.

Dighton, J and Jansen, S.E. (1990). Effect of air pollutants on ectomycorrhizal. Air Pollution Res. Report. 30. EEC. Brussels.

Dodd, J.C., Burton, C.C., Burns, R.G and Jefferies, P. (1987).

Egerton-Warburton, L.M., Griffin, B.J. (1995). *Can. J. Bot.* **73:** 1229-1233.

Fink, S. (1991). *Fert. Res.* **27:** 23-27.

Flemming, L.V. (1983). *Plant Soil.* **71:** 263-267.

Foy, C.D. (1988). *Soil Sci. Plant Anal.* **19:** 959-987.

Gardes, M., Wong, K.K.Y and Fortin, J.A. (1990). *Symbiosis.* **8:** 233-250.

Gadd, G.M. (1993). *New Phytol.* **124:** 25-60.

Gbdegesion, R.A. (1990). *For. Ecol. Manage.* **37:** 303-307.

Gianfreda, L., Sannino, F., Ortega, N and Nannipieri, P. (1994). *Soil. Biol. Biochem.* **26:** 777-784.

Godbold, D.L., Fritz, E and Hutterman, A. (1988). Aluminium toxicity in forest decline. Proceedings of the National Academy of Sciences. U.S.A. **85:** 3888-3892.

Heinrich, P.A., Mulligan, D.R and Patrick, J.W. (1989). *Plant and Soil.* **109:** 147-149.

Harley, J.L and Smith, S.E. (1983). Mycorrhizal Symbiosis. Academic Press. London.

Hartley, J., Cairney, J.W.G and Meharg, A.A. (1997). *Plant and Soil.* **189;** 303-319.

Heinrich, P.A., Mulligan, D.R and Patrick, J.W. (1989). *Plant and soil.* **109:** 147-149.

Hutchinson, L.T. (1989). *Trans. Br. Mycol. Soc.* **91:** 346-347.

Jha, B.N., Sharma, G.D and Mishra, R.R. (1990). Effect of pH on the growth of ectomycorrhizal fungi *in vitro*. Proc. Natn. Con. Mycorrhizae, Haryana Agric. Univ. Hisar (Ed. B.L. Jalal and H. Chand). 66-67.

Jha, D.H., Sharma. G.D and Mishra, R.R. (1991). *Soil Biol. Biochem.* **24:** (8) 761-767.

Jones, M.D and Hutchinsons, T.C. (1986). *New Phytol.* **102:** 429-442.

Jones, H.M and Scheffield, E. (1988b). A field survey of *P. aquilinum* (Dennstaedtiaceae pteridophyta) mycorrhizae, Gazette. **31:** 225-230.

Joshi, S.R. (1993). Ecological studies on the effect of air pollution on the leaf surface microorganism and litter decompositions. Ph.D. Thesis, North-Esatern Hill Univ. Shillong.

Kahle, H and Breckle, S. W. (1992). Bleiund Cadmium-Zietbombe in Unseren Waldboden. Biologie in Unserer Ziet. **22:** 21-27.

Koide, R.T and Lu, X. (1995). *New Phytol.* **131:** 435-441.

Kropp, B.R. (1990b). *Mycol. Res.* **94:** 412-415.

Kumar, R. (1990). Ecological investigation on ectomycorrhizae of Khasi pine (*Pinus kesiya* Royle ex. Gordon) in different soil conditions. Ph.D. Thesis, North-eastern Hill University, Shillong.

Levitt, J. (1980). Response of plants to environmental stresses 2, second Ed. New York. Academic Press.

Marx, D.H. (1991). The practical significance of ectomycorrhizae in forest establishment. P-54-90. in Ecophysiology of ectomycorrhizae of forest trees. Proceedings of the 7th Marcus Wallenburg Foundation Symbosia. The Marcus Wallenberg Foundation, Stockholm, Sweden.

Macfall, J.S and Slack, S.A. (1991). *Can. J. For. Res.* **21:** 482-488.

Mengel, K and Kirby, E.A. (1982). Principals of plant nutrition, 3rd edn. Bund AG, Bern.

Molina, R., Massicotte, H and Trappe, J. (1992). Specificity phenomena in mycorrhizal symbiosis community-ecological consequences and practical implications. In mycorrhizal functioning an integrative plant-fungal process. Edited by M.F. Allen. Routlege, Chapamn and Hall Inc., New York. 357-423.

Munzenberger, B., Kottke, I and Obberwinkler, F. (1995). *Tree Physiol.* **15:** 191-196.

Naidu, R and Harter, R.D. (1998). Effect of different organic ligands on cadmium absorption by the extractability from soils. Soil Sciences Society of American Journal. **62(3):** 644-650.

Ouzounidou,G., Eleftheriou, E.P and Karataglis, S.(1992). *Can. J. Bot.* **70:** 947-957.

Reddy, G.B and Faza, A. (1989). *Soil Biol. Biochem* **21:** 327.

Read, D.J. (1991). *Experentia.* **47:** 376-391.

Read, D.J. (1992). The mycorrhizae in mycelium. In: Allen, M.F (Ed). Mycorrhizal functioning: an integrative fungal-plant process. Routlege, Chapman and Hall, New York. 102-133.

Rousseau, J.V.D., Sylvia, D. M and Fox, A.G. (1994). *New Phytol.* **128:** 638-644.

Schaedle, M., Thorton, F.C., Raynal, D.J and Tepper, H.B. (1989). *Tree Physiol.* **5:** 337-356.

Schlegel, H.G., Meyer, M., Schmidt, T., Stoppel, R.D and Pickhardt, M. (1992). A community if Ni resistant bacteria under Ni hyper-accumulating in plants. (Eds. A. J. M Baker , J. Proctor and R.D. Reeves). Intercept Andover. 315-517.

Simmliet, N., Rump, H.H and Schulten, H.R. (1986). Staubreinhaltung der luft. **46:** 256.

Sharma, G.D. (1981b). *Acta. Mycologia* (Poland). **17:** 45-51.

Smith, G.C and Brennan, E. (1984). *For. Sci.* **30:** 582-586.

Smith, S.E and Read, D.J. (1997). Mycorrhizal symbiosis, 2nd Ed. London: Academic Press Ltd.

Spier, J.W., Lee, R., Pansier,E.A and Caims, A. (1980). *Soil Biol. Biochem.* **12:** 289.

Srivastava, S., Prakash, S and Srivastava, M.M. (1999b). *Plant and Soil.* **212:** 203-208.

Stott, D.E., Dick, W.A and Tabatabai, M.A. (1985). *Soil Sci.* B: 112-117.

Symeonidis, L and Karataglis, S. (1992). *Biometals.* **5:** 173-178.

Tan, K and Keltjens, W.G. (1990b). *Plant and Soil.* **124:** 15-23.

Tinker, P.B. (1981). levels, distribution and chemical forms of trace element in food plants. Physiological Transactions of Royal Society. London. **294:** 41-55.

Trappe, J.M. (1962). *Cenoccocum graniforme* and its distribution ecology, mycorrhizae, formation, inherent variation, Ph.D. Thesis, Univ. Wash. Seattle. 148.

Tiwari, S.C., Tiwari, B.K and Mishra, R.R. (1987a). Temporal an depth-wise variations in dehydrogenase and urease activites and bacterial populations in pineapple plantations soils. Proceedings of Indian National Sci. Acad. B53: 173-176.

Trappe, J.M. (1977). *Ann. Revi. Phytophatol.* **15:** 203-222.

Trappe, J.M and Strand, R.F. (1969). *Forest Science.* **15:** 381-389.

Tyler, G. (1981). Heavy metals in soil biology and biochemistry. Soil Biochemistry, 5. E. A. Paul and J. N. Ladd (Ed). Decker, New York. 371-414.

Villeneuve, N. Grantner, N.M and Fortin, J.A. (1989). *Can. J. Bot.* **67:** 2616-2629.

Vogt, K.A., Publicover, D.A and Vogt, D.J. (1991). *Agric. Ecosys. Environ.* **35:** 171-190.

Wong, K.K.Y., Piche, Y., Montpetit, D and Kroppe, B.R. (1989). *Can. J. Bot.* **67:** 1717-1726.

Zottl, H.W. (1985). *Experientia.* **41:** 1104-1113.

10

Exploitation of Actinobacteria in Environmental Bioremediation

D. Dhanasekaran

Department of Microbiology, School of Life Sciences, Bharathidasan University
Tiruchirappalli-620 024
E-mail: dhansdd@yahoo.co.in

Bioremediation is a cost-effective alternative process to clean environmental messes. Enormous quantities of organic and inorganic compounds are released into the environment each year as a result of human activities. In some cases, these releases are deliberate and well regulated (e.g., industrial emissions), while in other cases they are accidental (e.g., chemical or oil spills). Many of these compounds are both toxic and persistent in terrestrial and aquatic environments. The contamination of soil, surface and groundwater is simply the result of the accumulation of these toxic compounds in excess of permissible levels. Whether due to regulatory or legislative requirements, public pressure, insidious side effects on humans or enlightened corporate behaviour, there is growing realisation and movement to clean-up such environmental messes. However, the cost of restoring the burgeoning global inventory of contaminated ecosystems to healthy and acceptable levels is virtually incalculable. As a result, the government, industry and the public have acutely felt the need for more cost-effective alternatives to traditional physical and chemical methods of remediation of these contaminated sites. Actinobacteria are biotechnologically potential microorganisms, which are present in soil, water and all extreme habitats. The extremophilic actinobacteria are used in bioremediation of pollutant in aquatic and terrestrial environment. This chapter describes the application of actinobacteria in bioremediation of pesticides, herbicides, plastics, rubber, hydrocarbon, oil, keratin waste and heavy metals.

INTRODUCTION

Bioremediation consists of using living organisms (usually bacteria, fungi, actinobacteria, cyanobacteria and to a lesser extent, plants) to reduce or eliminate toxic pollutants. These organisms may be naturally occurring or laboratory cultivated. These organisms either eat up the contaminants or assimilate within themselves all harmful compounds from the surrounding area, thereby, rendering the region virtually contaminant free. Generally, these substances are eaten up as organic compounds, while those, which are assimilated within the organism, are heavy metals.

Bioremediation harnesses this natural process by promoting the growth and rapid multiplication of organisms, which can effectively degrade specific contaminants and convert them to nontoxic by-products. Importantly, bioremediation can also be used in conjunction with a wide range of traditional physical and chemical technologies to enhance their efficacy. "Bioremediation is an ecologically sound and state-of-the-art technique that employs natural biological processes to completely eliminate toxic contaminants".

There are two basic types of bioremediation:

Biostimulation

Biostimulation provides nutrients and suitable physiological conditions for the growth of indigenous microbial populations. This promotes increased metabolic activity, due to which microbes degrade the contaminants.

Bioaugmentation

Bioaugmentation means introduction of specific blends of laboratory cultivated microorganisms into a contaminated environment or a bioreactor to initiate the bioremediation process.

The process of developing bioremediation techniques may involve the following steps:

1. Isolating and characterizing naturally occurring microorganisms with bioremediation potential
2. Laboratory cultivation to develop viable populations
3. Studying the catabolic activity of these microorganisms in contaminated material through lab scale experiments
4. Monitoring and measuring the progress of bioremediation through chemical analysis and toxicity testing in chemically contaminated media

Field applications of bioremediation techniques using either/both steps:

(1) *In situ* stimulation of microbial activity by the addition of microorganisms and nutrients and the optimization of environmental factors at the contaminated site itself.

(2) *Ex situ* restoration of contaminated material in specifically designated areas by landfarming and composting methods.

Bioremediation works either by transforming or degrading contaminants. Biotransformation is any alteration in the molecular or atomic structure of the compound, and biodegradation is the breakdown of organic substances into smaller organic or inorganic components through microorganisms. Both types of bioremediation can be used at the site of contamination (*in situ*) or on contamination removed from the original site (*ex situ*).

Some Examples of Bioremediation Technologies

Bioventing (involves the venting of oxygen through soil to stimulate the growth or natural and introduced bioremediation organisms).

Bioaugmentation (the addition of organisms or enzymes to the contaminated material to remove unwanted chemicals).

Biofiltration (removal of organic gases by passing air through compost or soil containing microorganisms that are capable of degrading the gases).

Biostimulation (use of nutrients to stimulate the naturally occurring organisms that can perform bioremediation).

Bioreactor (treatment of a contaminated substance in a large tank containing organisms or enzymes)

Landfarming (use of farming tilling and soil amendment techniques to encourage the growth of bioremediation organisms in a contaminated area).

Composting (involves mixing contaminated materials with compost containing bioremediation organisms).

Actinobacteria are Gram-positive bacteria generally exhibiting branched filamentous growth and contain a high guanine plus cytosine content in their DNA. Metal resistance in actinobacteria has not been investigated thoroughly despite the fact that actinobacteria are metabolically and biosynthetically exceptionally versatile. Because of this versatility, actinobacteria are important in biotechnology and have been employed in bioremediation.

BIODEGRADATION OF PESTICIDES

Actinobacteria have considerable potential for the biotransformation and biodegradation of pesticides. Members of this group of Gram-positive bacteria have been found to degrade pesticides with widely different chemical structures, including organochlorines, *s*-triazines, triazinones, carbamates, organophosphates, organophosphonates, acetanilides, and sulfonylureas. A limited number of these xenobiotic pesticides can be mineralized by single isolates, but often consortia of bacteria are required for complete degradation. Cometabolism of pesticides is frequently observed within this group of bacteria. When compared with pesticide degradation by Gram-negative bacteria, much less information about the molecular mechanisms involved in biotransformations of pesticides by actinobacteria is available. Progress in this area has been seriously hampered by the lack of suitable molecular genetic tools for most representatives of this major group of soil bacteria. Overcoming this constraint would enable a better exploitation of the biodegradation and biotransformation abilities of actinobacteria for applications such as bioremediation and construction of transgenic herbicide-resistant crops.

Biological decomposition of pesticides is the most important and effective way to remove these compounds from the environment. The microorganisms have the ability to interact, both chemically and physically, with substances, leading to structural change or complete degradation of the target molecule (Raymond *et al.*, 2001; Wiren Lehr *et al.*, 2002). Among the microbial communities, bacteria, fungi and actinobacteria are the main transformers and pesticides degraders (Haggblom, 1992; De Schrijver and De Mot, 1999).

In soil the microorganisms metabolize organic pesticides either aerobically or anaerobically. In most cases, the microorganisms degrade the molecules and utilize them as a source of energy and nutrients (Abdelhafid *et al.*, 2000; Topp, 2001; Parales *et al.*, 2002; Getenga, 2003; Boivin *et al.*, 2005), or use them through cometabolism, which occurs when an organic compound is not used by the microorganism for growth, but is metabolized in conjunction with another substrate used for growth (Haggblom, 1992; Kumar *et al.,* 1996; Sanchez *et al.,* 2004). According to Van Eerd *et al.* (2003), the microbial metabolism of pesticides may involve a three-phase process. In phase I, the initial properties of a parent compound are transformed through oxidation, reduction, or hydrolysis to generally produce a more water-soluble and usually a less toxic product than the parent. In phase II, the conjugation of a pesticide or its metabolite is involved to a sugar or amino acid. Conjugation of pesticides often involves utilization of existing enzymatic machinery and is therefore called a cometabolic process. Microbial pesticide conjugation reactions include xylosylation, alkylation, acylation, and nitrosation and can occur intra- or extracellularly. Phase III involves conversion of phase II metabolites into secondary conjugates, which are also nontoxic (Van Eerd *et al.*, 2003).

Enzymes cause microbial decomposition of substances, and this generally occurs after an initial latency period during which the microorganisms adapt to substratum (Dabrowska *et al.*, 2004). The decomposition rate of chemical compounds is a function of availability to microorganisms or enzymatic systems able to degrade those (Van Eerd *et al.*, 2003). Van Eerd *et al.* (2003) presented oxidative transformations where oxygenation is the most frequent first step in the biotransformation of pesticides. Many oxidatives enzymes play an important role in pesticides degradation, for example, peroxidases, laccases, etc. (Duran and Esposito, 2000; Duran *et al.*, 2002; Duran, 2003; Tortella *et al.*, 2005) (Tables 10.1 and 10.2).

Table 10.1 Enzymes and actinobacteria involved in degradation of pesticides

Chemical class	*Enzymes*	*Actinobacteria*
Carbamates (Carbofuran, aldicarb)	Hydrolase[a]	*Rhodococcus* sp.[a]
Acetanilides (Alachlor, metolachlor, propanil)	Glutathione S-transferase	*Streptomyces* sp.[b]
s-Triazines (Atrazine, simazine, ametryne)	Hydrolase[a]	*Nocardioides* sp.[c] *Nocardia* sp.,
Sulfonylurea (chlorsulfuron, ethametsulfuron –methyl, triasulfuron)	P-450 cytochrome, monooxygenase[b]	*Streptomyces griseolus*[b]
Phenoxyacetic (2,4-D, MCPA)	Oxygenase and hydrolase[a]	*Arthrobacter* sp., *Rhodococcus* sp., *Nocardioides* sp.,[b]

a Kumar *et al.* (1996).
b De Schrijver and De Mot (1999).
c Topp (2001).

Table 10.2 Degradation of xenobiotics by isolated enzymes

Pollutant	*Enzymes*	*Actinobacterial source*
Anthracene, Pyrene	Lignin Peroxidase(LiP)	*Nocardia forwardii*
Nitrile compounds	Nitrilase, nitrile hydratase, amidase	*Nocardi*, sp., *Rhodococcus* sp.
Pyrethroids, Parathion, Diazinon	Permethrinase, Parathion hydrolase	*Nocardia* sp.,

(Adapted from Gianfreda and Rao, 2004)

Bioremediation of Polycyclic Aromatic Hydrocarbon (PAH) using Actinobacteria

Polycyclic aromatic hydrocarbons (PAHs) are a class of organic chemicals consisting of two or more benzene rings fused in a linear, angular, or cluster arrangement. Their occurrence in the environment is partly the result of natural processes including forest fires and volcanic eruptions and partly due to anthropogenic activities including the incomplete combustion of fossil fuels, accidental discharge during transport, use and disposal of petroleum products, and incineration of refuse and wastes (Dyke *et al.*, 2003; Fernandez *et al.*, 2002; Beck *et al.*, 1996). Thus, in areas of high population density and industrial activity, PAH release in soils and the wider environment have led to higher concentrations of these contaminants than would be expected from natural processes alone. The problem is exacerbated because PAHs have accumulated in soils, sediments, and animals after their release into the environment because of their hydrophobicity. This is a cause for concern because they have been implicated in many adverse effects on wildlife and human health, most notably carcinogenesis (Brandt *et al.*, 2002; Brenner *et al.*, 2002; Yu, 2002). The recalcitrance of PAHs to microbial degradation generally increases with their molecular weight and octanol-water partitioning coefficient. In addition, many high molecular weight PAHs are degraded only with difficulty or not at all due to their low water solubility, high resonance energy, and toxicity (Cerniglia, 1992). The microbial degradation of PAHs has been reviewed (Juhasz and Naidu, 2000; Cerniglia, 1992) (Table 10.3).

Table 10.3 Actinobacteria degrading PAHs

PAH	*Actinobacteria*
Naphthalene	*Streptomyces* sp., *Rhodococcus* sp.
Phenanthrene	*Micrococcus* sp., *Mycobacterium* sp., *Nocardia* sp., *Nocardioides* sp., *Rhodococcus* sp., *Rhodotorula Streptomyces* sp., *S. griseus*,
Fluoranthene	*Rhodococcus* sp.
Pyrene	*Mycobacterium* sp., *Rhodococcus* sp.,
Chrysene	*Rhodococcus* sp.
Benzo[a]pyrene	*Mycobacterium* sp.

Adapted from Cerniglia (1992, 1997) and Kanaly and Harayama (2000).

Biotransformation of 2,4,6-Trinitrotoluene (TNT)

Biotransformation of 2,4,6-trinitrotoluene (TNT) has been reported under both aerobic and anaerobic conditions (Crawford, 1995; Marvin-Sikkema and de Bont. 1994; Michels and Gottschalk, 1995; Preuss and Rieger, 1995; Spain, 1995; Stahl and Aust, 1995), with complete reduction of one or more nitro side groups typically observed. The aerobic release of nitro groups as nitrite from some nitroaromatics has also been reported elsewhere (McCormick, 1976). Under aerobic conditions, polymers with azoxy linkages can form as products of the condensation of intermediates, e.g., hydroxylamino-toluenes, with nitrosotoluenes (Gorontzy, 1994).

Aerobic composting is one system for the bioremediation of TNT-contaminated soil (Osmon, and Andrew, 1978; Roy and Weston, 1989). No mineralization of (McCormick, 1976) TNT was detected in one major study of TNT transformation under simulated composting conditions (Kaplan and Kaplan, 1982). Similarly, a rapid decrease in TNT concentration from an initial 10,000 mg/kg, but no evidence of ring cleavage and only minor amounts of the usual TNT reduction products was found in composts extracted by Isbister *et al.* (1984). In mesophilic aerated static compost piles, TNT was reduced from 1,190 to 50 mg/kg (Williams, 1992). Known reduced nitroaromatic transformation products (2-amino-4,6-dinitrotoluene (2,4DA6NT), 4-amino-2,6-dinitrotoluene (4A2,6DNT), diaminonitrotoluenes) increased in concentrations for the first several weeks but decreased thereafter.

Actinobacteria are important decomposers in composts (Goodfellow, 1984), but only a few studies have reported on their potential as TNT-transforming microorganisms (Funk, 1994; Kaplan and Kaplan,

1982; Klausmeier *et al.,* 1974). The tolerance of actinobacteria cultures from both TNT-contaminated and uncontaminated environments, for different concentrations of TNT were isolated, determined how selected isolates transform TNT, and examined whether such TNT transformations were constitutive or induced by exposure to TNT. TNT and U-14C-ring-labeled TNT (0.25 mCi/mg) were synthesized as described elsewhere; purity was 99%. Streptomycetes isolated from uncontaminated sites were *Streptomyces viridosporus* T7A (ATCC 39115) (Sinden, 1979); *Streptomyces* strain SR-10, a protoplast fusion recombinant derived from a cross between *S. viridosporus* T7A and *Streptomyces setonii* 75Vi2 (Pettey and Crawford, 1984); *Streptomyces badius* 252 (Phelan *et al.,* 1979); and 12 Kenyan strains isolated from termites (Pasti and Belli, 1985), *Streptomyces chromofus* cus A2, A6, A8, A11, and A20; *Streptomyces chromogenus* A7; *Streptomyces diastaticus* A3, A12, and A13; and *Streptomyces rochei* A4, A10, and A14. Sixteen actinobacteria (explosive-contaminated soil actinobacteria; ESA 1 to ESA 16) were isolated from TNT contaminated soil.

One gram of soil from 20 grams of total sample was vortexed in a tube with 9 ml of water until the sample was dispersed. The tube was then serially diluted to 1026. Spread plate isolations were performed with water yeast extract agar (WYE) and yeast extract Casamino dextrose agar (YCED) (Crawford, 1993), at initial pHs of 6.0, 7.0, and 8.0. Plates were incubated at 37°C. When growth appeared, 16 isolates were chosen, purified by restreaking, and stored on sporulation agar plates of pH 7.1. To test TNT tolerance of the isolates, two sets of plates containing 25, 50, 75, or 100 mg of TNT per liter were used with two media: brain heart infusion agar (BHI), containing Bacto brain heart infusion broth solidified with 2.0% (wt/vol) Bacto agar; and yeast malt extract agar (YMA), containing yeast extract (4 g), malt extract (10 g), Bacto peptone (5 g), glucose (10 g), and agar (20 g) in 1.0 liter of distilled water. Final pH was adjusted to 7.1 before autoclaving. Inoculated plates and inoculated control plates (no TNT) were incubated at 37°C for 1 week. No significant difference was seen in TNT tolerance of actinobacteria isolated from TNT-contaminated or TNT-free soils.

Previous work indicated that TNT tolerance of soil organisms was not a function of the TNT content of their native soil, but the concentrations of TNT (50 mg/liter) prevented or severely limited the growth of most fungi, yeasts, actinobacteria, and Gram-positive bacteria. On YMA agar, only a few of the actinobacteria grew at 75 ppm (parts per million) and only 2 of 31 strains, *S. chromofuscus* A11 and actinobacteria ESA 1, grew at 100 ppm. However, on the richer BHI agar, all the isolates grew up to the maximum tested TNT concentration of 100 ppm. None of the 31 actinobacteria grew when TNT was supplied as a sole carbon and nitrogen source in any medium (25, 50, 75, and 100 mg/liter final concentrations), indicating that a nutrient-rich growth environment can help overcome the toxicity or inhibitory effects of TNT towards actinobacteria. Whether nutritional conditions are sufficient to overcome the inhibition in composts is unknown.

Whether TNT transformation was inducible in *S. chromofuscus* A11 and ESA 1 was determined by measuring the time required to remove 25 ppm of TNT in TNT-preexposed and nonpreexposed cells of strains A11 and ESA 1. Cells were grown for 24 h in 250-ml flasks containing 50 ml of BHI broth. Cells were equally divided into two sets of flasks, TNT (25-ppm final concentration) was added to one set, and both sets were incubated overnight. Cells were collected by centrifugation, washed twice with BHI, and resuspended in BHI, and up to 25 ppm of TNT was added to both sets of flasks. Samples were taken every 3 h for 24 h. Disappearance of TNT and accumulation of 4A2,6DNT and 2,4DA6NT were monitored by high pressure liquid chromatography (HPLC) with a Hewlett-Packard series LS 1090 liquid chromatograph and an Ultracarb 5 octyldecyl silane column (250 by 4.6 mm). The solutes were eluted from the column with an isocratic mobile phase of 55% (vol/vol) methanol and 45% (vol/vol) water, at a flow rate of 0.5 ml/min, as previously described (25). Judging by the time required to degrade 25 ppm of TNT, TNT transformation in the two strains tested was not inducible, since there were no differences in TNT removal rate or 4A2, 6DNT and 2,4DA6NT production by TNT-preexposed cells or nonpreexposed cells.

Dibenzofuran Utilizing Actinobacteria

Dioxins are extremely hazardous, chemically stable compounds that are highly recalcitrant to biological degradation in natural environments. These chemicals are endocrine disrupting compounds that are non-intentionally produced as by-products through chemosynthesis or combustion of waste, and are dispersed in several natural environments at low concentrations.

In biological treatment of waste for environmental remediation, the isolation and analysis of bacteria capable of degrading dioxins are important. To date, several Gram-positive or Gram-negative bacteria able to mineralize non-halogenated dibenzo-p-dioxin (DD) and dibenzofuran (DF) have been isolated (Bressler and Fedorak, 2000; Halden and Dwyer, 1997). The metabolism of these compounds was determined in *Sphingomonas* sp. HH69 (Fortnagel *et al.*, 1990; Wittich *et al.*, 1992) and *Terrabacter* sp. DPO1361 (Strubel *et al.*, 1991) and DBF63 (Monna *et al.*, 1993) in the metabolism of DF and DD, the first attack of dioxygenase is specific to (Wittich *et al.*, 1992), the so-called angular position. The oxygenated products of DF and DD are spontaneously ring-cleavaged, converted to trihydroxy derivatives of biphenyl or diphenylether, and further converted through the action of dioxygenase and hydrolase to salicylic acid and catechol, respectively. The genes and metabolic enzymes of Gram-negative *Sphingomonas wittichii* RW1 for metabolizing DF and DD were analyzed in detail. The molecular information obtained showed that the enzymes involved in the metabolism of these compounds were phylogenetically distant from those encoded by genes of other species involved in the metabolism of aromatic hydrocarbons.

Interestingly, these metabolic genes for DF and DD degradation were randomly distributed in the genome and they did not form operons, suggesting that the genes encoding the enzymes for metabolizing these substrates were in the early stage of gene evolution. This strain was able to decompose singly and doubly chlorinated dioxins, but it had diffculty in decomposing dioxins with three or more substituted chlorine units (Wilkes, 1996). On the other hand, the genes of Gram-positive bacteria that encode enzymes for metabolizing DF were determined in *Terrabacter* species. The genes encoding extradiol dioxygenase and hydrolase that are probably involved in the catabolism of 2, 2, 3-trihydroxybiphenyl of *Terrabacter* sp. DPO360 (Schmid *et al.,* 1997) and DBF63 (Kasuga *et al.*, 1997) were cloned and analyzed. Both of the gene clusters were closely related, but a slight divergence was observed in nucleotide sequences (72% in nucleotides). Recently, a gene cluster encoding large and small subunits of the terminal dioxygenase of *Terrabacter* sp. DBF63 (dbfA1A2)was reported (Kasuga *et al.*, 2001). This dioxygenase was functionally expressed in *E. coli* with electron-transport systems derived from the host strain, and converted DF to 2, 2, 3-trihydroxybiphenyl, therefore, this enzyme is an angular dioxygenase. The PCB-degrading *Rhodococci* exhibit relatively strong degradation activity and diverse substrate specificity than the Gram-negative strains. (Chung, 1994; Seto *et al.*, 1995; Asturias and Timmis, 1993). Likewise, the degradation activity of DF-degrading bacteria toward chlorinated dioxins is expected to be higher in Gram-positive strains than gram negative bacteria.

Isolation of various DF and DD degrading bacteria and characterization of their genes encoding enzymes for degrading dioxins are important to improve the bioremediation technologies for dioxins. The bacterial strains used belong to the *Rhodococcus, Terrabacter, and Microbacterium* genera and were involved in degradation of dibenzofuran and dibenzo-p-dioxin.

BIODEGRADATION OF HERBICIDE (ALACHLOR)

The herbicide alachlor (2-cloro-N-(methoxymethyl)-N-(2,6-diethylphenyl)-acetamide) is commonly used for pre-emergence control of grasses and weeds in a wide range of commercially important crops in Brazil, including coffee, corn, cotton, peanuts, soybean, and sugar cane. Alachlor is also among the most frequently used chloroacetanilide herbicides in Europe and North America, for both agricultural and noncrop applications (Graham *et al.*, 2000; Aga and Thuman, 2001). This herbicide is applied directly to the soil (Monteiro, 1997) and can reach groundwater and rivers where it can cause serious pollution problems (Inoue *et al.*, 2002). According to USEPA (United State Environmental Protection Agency), alachlor is classified as extremely toxic and potentially carcinogenic to humans (El-Sakka *et al.*, 1999; Hanioka *et al.*, 2002).

Microbial degradation under aerobic and anaerobic conditions is the main form of degradation of alachlor in the environment (Stamper and Tuovinen, 1998). Although complete mineralization has not yet been described, bacteria and fungi can metabolize this herbicide via several catabolic routes, including cometabolic pathways, to yield a series of alachlor-derived compounds (Stamper and Tuovinen, 1998). Actinobacteria represent a group of relatively abundant and metabolically diverse bacteria in soils (Labeda and Shearer, 1990). These bacteria are capable of degrading a wide range of complex molecules and producing extracellular enzymes (McCarthy and Williams, 1992)—features that are desirable for environmental bioremediation. Pesticide-degrading actinobacteria belonging to the genera *Arthrobacter, Brevibacterium, Clavibacter, Corynebacterium, Micromonospora, Mycobacterium, Nocardia, Nocardioides, Rhodococcus,* and *Streptomyces* have been described (De Schrijver and De Mot, 1999), although some taxa were represented by only a single isolate.

Herbicide and Soil Treatment

Alachlor was obtained as a commercial emulsified concentrated formulation (480 g L–1) from Monsanto (Brazil). Diluted aqueous suspensions (2.5%, v/v) were used as stocks for the degradation experiments. Soil treatment consisted of applying alachlor (6 L ha^{-1}) over a delimited experimental plot of garden soil. Six samples were collected from the first 5 cm of top soil over a 4 m^2 area, 20 days after herbicide application. Samples were pooled, homogenized, and dried at room temperature for several days prior to being used for the selective isolation experiments.

Selective Isolation of Actinobacteria

One gram of the pooled dry soil sample was added to sterilized distilled water (9 mL) and the suspension was shaken at 200 rpm for 1 h. Serial dilutions (10^{-2}, 10^{-3}, 10^{-4}) were prepared using sterilized distilled water and 0.1 mL aliquots were inoculated onto Petri dishes containing either mineral agar (Labeda and Shearer, 1990) or starch casein media (Küster and Williams, 1964), supplemented with alachlor (1.4, 14 or 144 mg L–1) and cycloheximide (50 µg mL^{-1}). The plates were incubated at 30°C for up to 10 days. Actinobacteria like colonies were streaked onto modified Bennett's agar (1 g yeast extract, 0.8 g Lab-Lemco, 2.0 g Bacto-casitone, 10 g glucose and 15 g agar per liter of distilled water, pH 7.2) and checked for purity. Suspensions of mycelia and spores were preserved in 20% glycerol at –80°C.

Screening of Herbicide Resistant Actinobacteria

The ability to grow at high concentrations of herbicide was determined by inoculating test strains onto Bennett's agar plates supplemented with commercial alachlor at 240, 480 and 720 mg L–1, respectively.

The plates were incubated at 30°C for 7 days and the resulting growth was compared with that of control plates without herbicide.

In vitro Degradation and HPLC Analysis

Starter cultures were cultivated in 125 mL Erlenmeyer flasks containing 10 mL of mineral salts medium (2 g $NaSO_4$, 0.2 g $MgSO_4$.7 H_2O, 0.65 gK_2HPO_4, 1 g NH_4Cl, 1 g KNO_3, 0.01 g $FeSO_4$.7 H_2O and 0.1% yeast extract in 1 liter of distilled water, pH 7.3), with 0.5% glucose. The flasks were incubated under stationary conditions for 24 h at 30°C, followed by 48 h incubation with shaking (150 rpm). Starter cultures (10 mL) were inoculated into 125 mL Erlenmeyer flasks containing 30 mL of liquid mineral salt medium, supplemented with 72 mg L^{-1} alachlor aqueous solution. The flasks were incubated for 7 days at 30°C with shaking at 150 rpm. All experiments were done in duplicate. The samples were centrifuged (15,000) ***g*** 10 min^{-1} and filtered using cellulose ester membrane (0.22 μm) prior to high performance liquid chromatography (HPLC) analysis. HPLC was done by using an LC-6A Shimadzu chromatograph, fitted with a UV-visible detector (220 nm) and a C18 column (25 cm × 4.6 mm, Varian). The mobile phase contained acetonitrile/water (50:50, v/v) at a flow rate of 1 mL min–1. Aliquots (20 μL) of culture media were injected and run at room temperature, and alachlor degradation was determined relative to the peak area detected in blank control samples.

HEAVY METAL RESISTANCE

Heavy metals comprise the major part of the elements in the periodic table. Many of these metal ions are essential trace elements, but at higher concentrations they become toxic to most microorganisms. However, some bacteria have evolved mechanisms to detoxify heavy metals, and some even use them for respiration. So, microbial interactions with metals have important environmental and health implications. Some implications are useful (the use of bacteria to clean-up metal-contaminated sites) and other implications are not so beneficial (the presence of metal resistance mechanisms may contribute to the increase in antibiotic resistance). To have any physiological or toxic effect, most heavy metal ions have to enter the cell. There are two general uptake systems for heavy metals.

Mercury Resistant Actinobacteria

The environmental mercury cycle is mediated by compounds that are leached from natural sources by weathering of rocks and soil. However, the major sources of environmental contamination of mercury arise from human activities, such as burning coal and petroleum products, use of mercurial fungicides in papermaking and agriculture and mercury catalysts in industry, which can increase local mercury levels several thousandfold above background. Microorganisms in contaminated environments have developed resistance to mercury and are playing a major role in decontamination. Samples from metal contaminated environments are suitable sources for isolation of metal resistant microorganisms.

Mercury resistance was first reported in actinobacteria (Nakahara, 1985) with inducible mercuric resistance in *Streptomyces lividans* 1326, a laboratory strain. Subsequently, Sedlmeier and Altenbuchner (1992) cloned and analyzed the mercuric resistance operon. The mercury resistance genes in *S. lividans* 1326 were encoded by a very large amplicable element, AUD2, which possesses transposon like characteristics with insertion sequence like repeats at its ends, linking mercury resistance to genetic instability (Eichenseer and Altenbuchner, 1994). *S. lividans* 1326 exhibits mercury resistance, mediated by six open reading frames (ORFs) arranged in two divergently transcribed operons.

The regulatory and transport genes form one operon and the mercuric reductase and the organomercurial lyase the second operon. Both operons are under the control of divergent promoters located in the inter-cistronic region (Brunker, 1996). The merB gene encodes an organomercurial lyase, which cleaves the C-Hg bond, releasing Hg^{2+} ions, which are then reduced into volatile elemental mercury (Hg^0) by the product of merA, the mercuric reductase. The combination of both merA and merB confers a broad spectrum mercury resistance to the isolate, as opposed to a narrow-spectrum resistance conferred by merA alone (Sedlmeier and Altenbuchner, 1992).

In general, actinobacteria were considered to be terrestrial microorganisms. Actinobacteria in marine and estuarine sediments have not been extensively investigated, although their ubiquitous presence in the marine sediments has been well documented Goodfellow and Haynes (1984); Takizawa *et al.* (1993); Dhanasekaran *et al.* (2008). The possibility that autochthonous actinobacteria communities exist is suggested by isolation of actinobacteria from deep ocean sediment (Goodfellow and Haynes, 1984; Weyland and Helmke, 1998; Dhanasekaran *et al.* (2009). Moreover, growth characteristics of *Rhodococcus marinonascens* (Weyland and Helmke, 1998) and other actinobacteria isolated from the marine environment (Jensen, 1991) suggest that some actinobacteria may be indigenous to the marine environment. Takizawa *et al.* (1993) demonstrated a diverse actinobacteria community in the Chesapeake Bay. Moran *et al.* (1995) showed that *Streptomyces* spp. is present as actively growing mycelia in marine sediments.

Determination of Mercury Resistance by Agar Diffusion Assay

Sensitivity of the strains to mercury was tested by agar diffusion assay. Discs (6 mm diameter) were saturated with 20 ml $HgCl_2$ or phenylmercuric acetate (PMA) solutions. Discs were placed on the surface of agar plates inoculated with 108 spores of the strain to be tested, and zones of inhibition were measured after incubation at 26°C for 3 days. Sensitive strains showed zones of inhibition of 10 mm, whereas zones of inhibition of resistant strains were 67 mm at 100 nmol $HgCl_2$ or 20 nmol PMA. The growth of strains was compared to the *S. lividans* control strains, TK24 (mercury-sensitive), and *S. lividans* 66 (mercury-resistant).

Extremophilic Actinobacteria in Oil Degradation

One of the most urgent problems of the modern world is environment purification from different toxic residues. Oil hydrocarbons are the principal pollutants of the environment. Today great attention is paid to the working of ecologically safe biological technologies for rehabilitation of soils contaminated with crude oil. Bioremediation of toxicant contaminated soils is generally based on activation of endemic microflora and introduction of environmentally adapted microorganisms (bioaugmentation) into soil (Daane, 2001). In this respect the use of extremophilic microorganisms, among them halophiles, alkaliphiles and thermophiles, adapted to local environment is most effective.

A prospective method for detoxification of soils contaminated with crude oil is the use of preparations in which microorganisms, active destroyers of hydrocarbons, are incorporated. Introduction of pure cultures capable of oxidation of aliphatic, aromatic and other hydrocarbons, into contaminated soils enhances soil detoxification and stabilization of the processes of biological degradation with comparatively lower economical expenses and is of no danger for environment (Nicholson and Fathepure, 2004).

The halophilic, alkalophilic and thermophilic actinobacteria have been isolated from different types of soil of Georgia. Among 405 strains of extremophilic actinobacteria, halophilic, alkaliphilic and thermophilic strains capable of oil hydrocarbons (hexane, benzene, benzpyrene, naphthalene, crude oil) detoxification have been isolated. It has been stated that among the hydrocarbon destroying extremophilic actinobacteria, thermophiles of *Thermoactinomyces* genera are most distinguished (Pataraya *et al.*, 2006; Gurielidze, *et al.*, 2008; Pataraya *et al.*, 2008).

Mono and mixed cultures of extremophilic actinobacteria with capabability of oil detoxification have been selected for introduction into contaminated soil. 1 kg soil was placed into two pots. 7 days later the soil was artificially polluted with oil (0.5%). According to regularities adopted in former USSR countries, 0.1% dose of oil was considered dangerous, but by international rules it must not exceed 0.05%. Wheat, previously germinated and infected with actinobacteria cultures, was planted in oil polluted soil. The initial actinobacteria introduced into soil were *Streptomyces levoris, Streptomyces pruniviolaceus, Streptomyces* spp., *Streptomyces streptomycini, Thermoactinomyces* spp., and *Thermoactinomyces dichotomicus*. A small dose of the mineral fertilizer NPK – 50 g/m^2, was introduced into soil. Fourteen variants were selected for the test, different monocultures of alkaliphilic, halophilic and thermophilic strains *Streptomyces levoris, Streptomyces pruniviolaceus, Streptomyces* spp., *Streptomyces streptomycini, Thermoactinomyces* spp., *Thermoactinomyces dichotomicus*. The following variants as mixed cultures *Streptomyces* spp. + *Thermoactinomyces* spp., *Streptomyces streptomycini* + *Thermoactinomyces dichotomicus*, *Streptomyces levoris* + *Thermoactinomyces dichotomicus*, *Streptomyces levoris* + *Thermoactinomyces* spp., *Streptomyces levoris* + *Streptomyces* spp. + *Thermoactinomyces* spp., *Streptomyces levoris* + *Streptomyces streptomycini* + *Thermoactinomyces dichotomicus*, *Streptomyces levoris* + *Streptomyces levoris* + *Streptomyces* spp. + *Streptomyces streptomycini* have been used. The better growth of seedlings compared to the control was observed in the pot with halophilic monoculture *Streptomyces streptomycini*.

An analogous situation was observed with thermophilic actinobacteria monoculture *Thermoactinomyces dichotomicus*. In the case of mixed cultures the following variants: *Streptomyces streptomycini* + *Thermoactinomyces dichotomicus*, *Streptomyces levoris* + *Thermoactinomyces* spp., *Streptomyces levoris* + *Streptomyces streptomycini* + *Thermoactinomyces dichotomicus* are most distinguished. In these variants, there was always one thermophilic actinobacteria. While observing 16-day-old seedlings, it was found that as a result of the effect of mono and mixed cultures on seedlings, the development was better compared to the control (Gurielidze *et al.*, 2009).

Bioremediation of Hydrocarbons

Attention has been focused on the utilization of hydrocarbons by microorganisms largely through their effects on aircraft fuel systems. They can block filters, cause corrosion of airframes through conversion of the hydrocarbon to CO_2, water, organic acids and shorter chain hydrocarbons. They may also produce emulsifying agents.

The hydrocarbons are a diverse group of chemicals that include straight chain saturated and unsaturated compounds (alkanes, alkenes and alkynes), non-benzoid cyclic hydrocarbons (e.g., cycloalkanes) and aromatic hydrocarbons, often in mixtures. Crude oil is a naturally occurring complex mixture of hydrocarbons with perhaps 200 components. These may include all the alkanes between C_1 and C_{32}; all four branched hexanes; all possible C_8 isomers of alkyl benzene (Gutnick and Rosenberg, 1977).

Hydrocarbon utilizing actinobacteria have been isolated from oil wells, sedimentation ponds, water at the bottom of storage tanks and oil enriched with hydrocarbons. *Arthobacter, Corynebacterium, Mycobacterium* and *Nocardia* utilizing cyanohexane, n-dodecane, n-hexadecane, n-octane and n-pentadecane were found in all samples from an unenriched, upland moorland soil, with most at 20 cm where lipid and hydrocarbon material had accumulated (Jones and Edington, 1968). Jet fuel systems have yielded *Brevibacterium,*

Streptomyces and perhaps, *Rhodococcus rhodochrous* (Edmonds and Cooney, 1967). Rolling mill and other industrial emulsions have yielded *Corynebacterium, Micromonospora, Nocardia, Mycobacterium* and *Streptomyces* isolates (Purkiss, 1972; Genner and Hill, 1981).

Nocardioides simplex grew on medium containing paraffin wax, light oil, kerosene, toluene and xylene, but not on benzene or a commercial mixture of low boiling point hexanes (Bushnell and Haas, 1941). *Nocardia hydrocarbonoxydans* and *Nocardia petroleophila* can grow well in atmospheres containing simple hydrocarbons (Nolof and Hirsch, 1962; Hirsch and Engel, 1956). *Rhodococcus globerulus* showed a limited ability to grow on substituted alicyclic rings, but not on cyclohexane (Donoghue *et al.*, 1976). Fuhs (1961) listed more than 100 microorganisms that could utilize hydrocarbons including bacteria, fungi, yeast and about 30 actinobacteria, comprising species of *Arthrobacter, Corynebacterium, Micromonospora, Mycobacterium, Nocardia, Nocardioides, Rhodococcus* and *Streptomyces* (Kurup *et al.* 1970). *Nocardia hydrocarbonoxydans* incompletely oxidized gaseous aliphatic hydrocarbons from octane to hexadecane and primary n-alcohols ($C_6 - C_{12}$) and also oxidized aldehydes ($C_{12} - C_{12}$), monocarboxylic acids ($C_6 - C_{14}$) and the dicarboxylic acids, sebacic and succinic acids.

Organisms were isolated from soils supplemented with a range of hydrocarbons and media with crude oil as the only carbon source and used to test bituminous products. Isolates included five Actinobacteria and four other bacteria. The Actinobacteria genera represented were *Arthrobacter* (crude oil), *Brevibacterium* (petrol), *Corynebacterium* (from soil supplemented with tar oils), *Mycobacterium* (lubricating oil) and *Nocardia* (asphalt cement). The *Mycobacterium* and *Nocardia* strains produced the greatest effect on bituminous material since they were most like the products used to treat the soil from which they originated.

Saturated aliphatic hydrocarbons are usually oxidized first in the C_1 position by *Brevibacterium erythrogenes*. They are then degraded by the β-oxidation system to give a fatty acid, which is then degraded by the β-oxidation system, but sometimes, as with *Mycobacterium smegmatis*, oxidation in the C_2 position occurs to give a methyl ketone. Also ω-oxidation can occur, as in *Corynebacterium*, to give dicarboxylic acids. In *Brevibacterium erythrogenes*, degradation of pristane (2, 6, 10, 14-tetra methyl-penta decane) to pristanic acid leads, by ω-oxidation, to the formation of pristandioic acid and ultimately to methylpentadioic acid. Trimethyltridecanoic and trimethylundecanoic acids are produced by β-oxidation. Pristane metabolism was inhibited in the presence of hexadecane (Pirnik *et al.*, 1974; Gutnick and Rosenberg, 1977).

Pathways of alkene degradation are not well defined, and even less is known of alkyne metabolism. "*Mycobacterium lacticola*" has been reported to produce acetaldehyde from acetylene, but this has not been confirmed. Non-benzoid cyclic hydrocarbons have also received little attention and Actinobacteria are not implicated in their breakdown. However, benzene, in the presence of a *Nocardia* species, yielded the trans-trans isomer of muconic acid, probably via the intermediate catechol, although *Rhodococcus rhodochrous* accumulates phenol in the medium, re-utilizing it in a manner congruent with the nature of an intermediate product, probably to form catechol. Three different ring fusion mechanisms have been reported in *Rhodococcus rhodochrous* (Traxler and Flannery, 1968). The presence of substitutions on the aromatic ring can force oxidation to the alkyl side chain so that *Nocardia opaca* forms phenyl acetic acid from 3-phenyl eicosane. Cyclohexanol is oxidized more slowly by *Rhodococcus globerulus* than by an *Acenetobacter* species.

The growth on hydrocarbons can affect the cell lipid of *Nocardia* in a manner suggesting β-oxidation of fatty acids. Cultures grown on glucose yield 28% total lipid composed of glycerides, whereas those grown on hexadecane yield 48% total lipid, predominantly cetyl palmitate. Neither hexane nor tridecane permitted wax formation, while alkanes with 13-20 carbon atoms led to the formation of cellular triglycerides and waxes with a similar carbon skeleton to the substrate. Thus n-heptadecane gave cell lipids having predominantly C_{17} acids but also some C_{15} and C_{13}. Hexadecane grown cells gave only even numbered fatty acids, with the predominant palmitic acid (Mc Kenna and Kallio, 1965).

Several Actinobacteria produce extracellular emulsifying agents. *Arthrobacter, Brevibacterium, Corynebacterium* and *Nocardia* species produce a trehalose lipid in the oil phase of culture broths, which consists of one mole of a, a-trehalose and two mole of a-branched-b-hydroxyacid (Gutnick and Rosenberg, 1977). By contrast, the emulsifying agent produced by another oil-degrading *Arthrobacter* isolate was an acidic polysaccharide composed of 2 major sugars (D-galactosamine and unidentified amino uronic acid), a minor sugar (D-glucose) and an unidentified fatty acid esters, giving it a molecular weight of about 106. The emulsifier was produced on hexadecane, ethanol and acetate media and the rate of production was proportional to both hydrocarbons and emulsifier concentration. Light petroleum, diesel and a variety of crude and gas oils were emulsified well, but not kerosene and gasoline. However, the addition of aromatic compounds, e.g., 2-methyl naphthalene, improved the emulsification of kerosene and gasoline (Rosenberg *et al.,* 1979; Zuckerberg *et al.,* 1979). *Rhodococcus rodhochrous* can also produce an emulsifying agent on n-decane (Holdom and Turner, 1969).

BIOREMEDIATION OF RUBBER WASTE

Natural rubber latex is obtained by tapping the trunk of *Hebea brasiliensis*. It is then coagulated and placed in boiling water. Subsequent air drying gives "Pale sheet", while drying in heated smoke houses to retard mould developments gives "Smoked Sheet". The basic polymer in natural rubber is cis-1, 4-polyisoprene. Chemicals may be added for vulcanization and fillers to enhance the basic properties, together with plasticizers, pigments and processing aids. Polyisoprene can also be manufactured synthetically and there is a range of other synthetic rubbers, including cis-polybutadiene, styrene butadiene, polychoroprene (Neoprene), nitrile rubber (co-polymers of butadiene acrylonitrile), buty 1-rubber, polysulfide rubber, silicone rubber and fluorinated rubber.

Both natural and synthetic rubbers are subject to biodeterioration, which may be modified by some of the additives used. Actinobacteria were first implicated in the deterioration of natural rubber, when Sohangen and Fol (1914) found *Streptomyces* species causing considerable disintegration of natural and vulcanized rubber inoculated with soil. Later, Spence and Van Niel (1936) showed that *Streptomyces* species could clear latex agar plates, indicating dissolution of the rubber globules. Kalinenko (1938) isolated further rubber-degrading organisms, one of which was able to perforate a thick film of purified natural rubber, while Zyska *et al.,* (1972) isolated Actinobacteria from one of the eleven rubber, cable samples in which they formed 3% of the microorganisms isolated (Tables 10.4 and 10.5).

Table 10.4 Actinobacteria causing deterioration of natural rubber

Rubber Type	*Species*	*References*
Guayule latex	*Streptomyces* species	Spence and Van Niel (1936)
Hevea latex	*Streptomyces* species	Spence and Van Niel (1936)
Natural	*Streptomyces aurantiacus, S. coelicolor, S. elastica, S. fuscus, S. longispororuber*	Kalinenko (1938)

Contd.

Contd.

Purified, Natural	*Streptomyces albus,*	
	S. fuscus,	
	Micromonospora species,	Zobell and Beckwith (1944)
	Nocardia species,	
	Streptomyces species	
Vulcanized natural	*Streptomyces* species	Taysum (1966);
		Cundell and Mulcock (1976)
	Rhodococcus ruber	
	Nocardia and	
	Streptomyces species	
	Nocardia asteroids	
	Streptomyces fulvoviriis	
	S. litmani	Orchanrd and Goodfellow (1980)
Natural rubber (NR)	*Gordonia species*	Linos and Steinbuchel (1998)

Based on Hookey (1983).

Table 10.5 Actinobacteria colonizing synthetic rubber

Rubber Type	*Species*	*References*
Neoprene	*Streptomyces* species	Leeflang (1968); Hills (1967)
	Unidentified	
Nitrile	*Streptomyces* species Unidentified actinobacteria	Leeflang (1968); Hills (1967)
Styrene-butadiene	Unidentified actinobacteria	Leeflang (1968); Cundell and Mulcock (1976)
Silicone	*Streptomyces acidophilus,*	Calderon and Staffeldt (1965)
	S. albus, S. rochei,	
	S. globisposus,	
	S. novaecaesareae	
Isoprene rubber (IR)	*Gordonia species*	Linos and Steinbuchel (1998)

Based on Hookey (1983).

BIOREMEDIATION OF PLASTICS

Plastics are composed of one or more polymers mixed with a variety of additives to modify their properties. The polymers may be made up of one or more monomers in a repeating series. There are more than 40 generic types of polymer, including polyolefins, nylons, vinyls and urethanes, within which there may be a variety of resins with similar chemical structures. The additives include plasticizers to give flexibility; fillers to give strength, antioxidants, antistatic agents, colourants, flame retardants, heat stabilizers, biocides and ultraviolet radiation stabilizers. Many of these are organic compounds with smaller molecular weights than the polymers. The greatest bulk of additives are formed by the plasticizers, which may consist of natural or modified vegetable oils, esters of organic acids, polyesters and chlorinated hydrocarbons.

Biodeterioration of plastic may lead to opacity and loss of strength, flexibility and electrical conductivity characteristics, the development of varied odours and the appearance of unwanted pigments. Reports of biodeterioration of plastics are numerous and, in some of these, actinobacteria have been implicated. However, it is usually not the polymer that is attacked but the plasticizer (Klausmeier and Andrews, 1981).

Poly (tetramethylene succinate) (PTMS), a high melting point (T*m* D 113°C), biodegradable aliphatic polyester composed of 1, 4-butanediol and succinic acid, has good mechanical properties similar to those of conventional plastics. Among the four kinds of commercial biodegradable plastic, poly (caprolactone) (PCL) and poly (3-hydroxyalkanoate) (PHA) are easily degraded by microorganisms, and the distributions of PCL and PHA degraders in the environment are higher than those of PTMS- and poly (lactide) (PLA) degraders (Mergaert and Swings, 1996; Pranamuda *et al.*, 1997). In addition, we observed that the abiotic hydrolysis of PTMS was slower than PLA at high temperatures (Pranamuda *et al.*, 1999). Thermophilic microorganisms play an important role in the composting process. During composting, a high temperature develops which is one of the key technologies for treatment of biodegradable plastic wastes (Tokiwa *et al.*, 1992). Hence, thermophilic microorganisms that are able to degrade PTMS at high temperatures are especially required. The clear zone technique has been found to be a powerful and practical method for studying plastic degradation (Pranamuda *et al.*, 1997, 1999). Clear zone method is useful to select an active PTMS degrading actinobacteria strain Nishida and Tokiwa (1993). Among the twelve strains obtained from the culture collections, four tested strains, namely, *Microbispora rosea* subsp. Aerate IFO 14046, *M. rosea* subsp. aerata IFO 14047, *Excellospora japonica* IFO 14486 and *E. viridilutea* JCM 3398 showed clear zones around their colonies on emulsified PTMS agar plates (Table 10.6). *M. rosea* subsp. aerata IFO 14046 distinctly showed the highest clarity of clear zones formed around the colonies on the fourth day after inoculation. The clear zone appearance was observed after 1 day of colony forming on PTMS-emulsified plate. It is likely that the colonies formed released extracellular enzymes (Jarerat and Tokiwa, 2001).

Degradation of PTMS on PTMS-emulsified Agar Plates

The thermophilic actinobacteria strains were streaked on emulsified PTMS/agar plates (Pranamuda *et al.*,1999), grown for 30 days at its optimum temperature, and degradation ability was determined by the formation of clear zone around the colonies.

Degradation of PTMS and Other Polyester Films

Ten ml of seed culture (0.4 mg dry cell) was inoculated in duplicate 250 ml Erlenmeyer flasks containing 100 ml basal medium and 100 mg PCL, PHB, PTMS or PLA films. The polymer films were previously sterilized with 5% (w/v) sodium hypochlorite for 10 s. The flasks were incubated on a rotary shaker (180 rpm) at 50°C. Before the extraction of residual polyester films, 5 ml culture media was taken for analysis of water-soluble total organic carbon concentration (TOC) and pH. TOC was measured with a TOC-5000 analyzer (Shimadzu Co. Ltd.). Residual films were recovered directly from the culture broth by extraction with 100 ml chloroform and evaporation on a rotary evaporator. The recovered polymers were dried in a vacuum at 80°C (Table 10.7).

Table 10.6 Clear zone forming ability of thermophilic actinobacteria obtained from the culture collections on agar plates emulsified with PTMS[a]

Strain[b]	*Cultivation temperature (°C)*	*Colony formation time (days)*	*Clear zone formation time (days)*
Microbispora rosea subsp. *aerata* IFO 14046	50	3	4/+++[c]
M. rosea subsp. *aerata* IFO 14047	45	7	10/++[c]
Excellospora japonica IFO 14486	45	3	4/+[c]
E. viridilutea JCM 3398	45	3	7/+[c]
Actinomadura rubrobrunea (Streptomyces peucetius subsp.caesius IFO 14622)	50	5	– c
A. fastidiosa (*Microtetraspora fastidiosa* IFO 14337)	45	2	– c
Saccharopolyspora rectivirgula IFO 12991	50	2	– c
Thermomonospora curvata JCM 3096	50	10	– c

[a]The strains were streaked on agar plate with emulsified poly(tetramethylene succinate) (PTMS).

[b]The strains were obtained from the culture collections.

[c]Clear zone forming ability: –, clear zone not formed

Table 10.7 Degradation of various polymers by *M. rosea* subsp. aerata IFO 14046[a]

Polymer film[b]	*Film pH loss (mg)*[d]	*Weight (mg)*[d]	*TOC*[c]	*Dry cell weight (mg)*[d]
PTMS film				
Film control (no inoculation)	0.4 ± 0.2	4.0 ±0.1	6.9	
Culture of strain IFO 14046	50.8 ± 0.2	19.3 ± 1.2	6.8	6.7 ± 0.2
PCL film				
Film control (no inoculation)	1.0 ± 0.3 3	3.8 ± 0.5	6.9	
Culture of strain IFO 14046	100.0 ±_ 0.2	22.9 ± 0.1	6.5	7.8 ± 0.3
PHB film				
Film control (no inoculation)	0.5 ± 0.1	3.8 ±0.1	6.9	
Culture of strain IFO 14046	1.2 ± 0.2	2.4 ± 0.1	6.9	2.0 ±0.3
PLA film				
Film control (no inoculation	0.9 ± 0.2	3.9 ± 0.5	6.9	
Culture of strain IFO 14046	1.9 ±0.5	2.5 ± 0.2	6.9	2.5 ± 0.2
Cell control (no film)		2.3 ± 0.1	7.0	0.6 ± 0.2

[a]*M. rosea* subsp. *aerata* IFO 14046 was cultivated in 100 ml basal medium containing 100 mg polymer film on a rotary shaker (180 rpm) at 50°C for 7 days with 0.4 mg cell inoculum.

[b]Polymer film: PTMS, poly(tetramethylene succinate); PCL, poly("-caprolactone); PHB, poly(hydroxybutyrate); PLA, poly(lactide).

[c]TOC: Water soluble total organic carbon.

[d]Values are means standard errors of duplication.

Polyethylenes

Polyethylenes are widely used plastics belonging to the class of synthetic polymers known as polyolefins. Most biodeterioration problems involved fungi, but Liu and Schwartz (1961) used an inoculum of four strains of *Pseudomonas aeruginosa*, a *Nocardia* species or a *Brevibacterium* species. Polymers with a molecular weight of 17,000 or less, allowed bacterial populations to increase 100-fold during the first week, but after that they declined. Water-soluble nutrients could not be extracted, suggesting that the growth was most likely due to the presence of low molecular weight oligomers in the plastic. After growth, the 'spent' medium supported further growth if new plastic was added, but cleaning, washing the polyethylene and adding it to new medium supported growth on inoculation only if the molecular weight was 4,800, the smallest tested.

Degradation of thermally degraded, air-oxidized, low-density, polyethylene (average M.W. 2200) in soils allowed the isolation of *Arthrobacter* with a variety of other bacteria (Spencer *et al.,* 1976). Tests of polyethylene and polypropylene preparations and backings showed that most were not attacked by '*Streptomyces rubrireticuli*' or an unidentified actinobacteria. However, a polypropylene, acrylic backing supported growth, while complex tapes containing polyethylene and polypropylene allowed growth only because of non-polymeric constituents, especially bitumen (Pankhurst *et al.,* 1972).

Polyvinyls

Actinobacteria have been implicated chiefly in the discolouration of vinyl plastics. The causal organism has been identified as *Streptoverticillium rubrireticuli, Streptoverticillium waksmanii* (Yeager, 1962) and this organism has subsequently been used in biodeterioration testing of PVC wrappings and coatings (Pankhurst *et al.,* 1975). Tests with '*Streptomyces rubrireticuli*', and an unidentified actinobacteria (Pankhurst *et al.,* 1972) showed that PVC polymers, copolymers and simple unplasticized formulations supported little or no growth, but backings and laminated tapes containing plasticizers and other additives supported growth of the actinobacteria.

Polyesters

Polyester polymers have been reported to form good substrates for some fungi, but Actinobacteria do not appear to have been implicated in their deterioration.

Polyurethanes

Polyurethanes tend to be more susceptible to microbial degradation than many polymers through degradation of the remaining free isocyanate groups, the splitting of urea and amide groups, the breaking off of urethane groups and, finally, the cleavage of the rings of the isocyanuric acid units. In favourable cultural conditions, degradations may be detectable within 30 days (Filip, 1986). Again, Actinobacteria have been mainly implicated, but *Streptomyces violaceoruber* (frequently), together with *Streptomyces parvullus, Streptomyces plicatus, Nocardia autotropica* and *Nocardiopsis orientalis* have been isolated from degraded polyester polyurethane (Pommer and Lorenz, 1986).

Acrylic and Styrene Resins

Growth of *'Streptomyces rubrireticuli'* and an unidentified actinobacteria occurred on polystyrene, polyester resin, propylin, acrylic resin and on a polystyrene, polyester encapsulant (Pankhurst *et al.,* 1972).

Plasticizers

Many plasticizers can serve as microbial nutrients, even when incorporated into plastic formulations. They often become colonized by fungi but sometimes also by actinobacteria, especially *Brevibacterium* and *Nocardia species* (Klausmeier and Andrews, 1981). Another 28 unidentified actinobacteria, probably all streptomycetes, were found able to grow on at least one of the six plasticizers (Klausmeier and Osmon, 1976). Plasticizers differ in their ability to support microbial growth. Although iso-octyl-epoxy-stearate and di-iso-octyl phthalate, both alone and together, and di-iso-decyl phthalate supported growth of *Aspergillus niger* and *fumigatus,* only iso-octyl-epoxy-stearate alone and mixed with di-iso-octyl phthalate suppoted actinobacteria growth (Pankhurst *et al.,* 1972).

Biodegradation of Keratin Waste

Keratinolytic microorganisms and their enzymes may be used to enhance the digestibility of feather keratin. They may have important applications in processing keratin-containing wastes from poultry and leather industries through the development of non-polluting methods (Onifade *et al.,* 1998). Generally, an increase in keratinolytic activity is associated with thermophilic organisms, which require high energy, inputs to achieve maximum growth and the decomposition of keratin wastes (Friedrich and Antranikian, 1996; Nam *et al.,* 2002). The Actinobacterial isolates can degrade raw feathers and are therefore useful to develop efficient processes involving keratin substrates. Subhasish and Dhanasekaran, (2010) isolated keratinolytic Actinobacteria from feather dumping soil in Tiruchirappalli, Nammakkal, Tamil Nadu, and India. The degradation process was taking long time and all these three isolates achieved complete degradation of feather between 20 and 25 days, and they used feather as the sole organic source for carbon, sulfur and energy.

Primary Screening of Keratinolytic Actinobacteria

Milk agar medium containing the following ingredients (in grams per liter) was used for the primary screening of keratinolytic Actinobacteria (Riffel and Brandelli, 2006): Peptone, 5.0; Yeast Extract, 3.0; Dextrose, 1.0; Skim Milk Powder, 10.0, Agar 15.0 and pH was maintained at 7.2. All the ingredients of Milk agar medium were sterilized in autoclave except skim milk powder. Skim milk powder was added separately once the medium reached the tolerable temperature (45°C), and the medium was poured in sterile Petri dishes. Suspected Actinobacterial isolates, which were already maintained in ISP1 medium, were inoculated in Milk agar plates. The plates were incubated at room temperature and examined for clear zone formation after 4 days (Figs. 10.1 and 10.2).

Before Treatment

After Treatment

Before Treatment

After Treatment

Before Treatment

After Treatment

Fig. 10.1 Enrichment of soil sample.

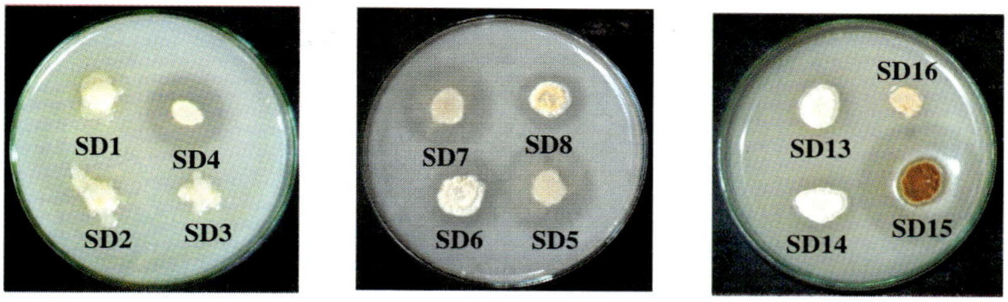

Fig. 10.2 Primary screening of keratinolytic actinobacteria.

Secondary Screening of Keratinolytic Actinobacteria

All positive isolates obtained from the primary screening were subjected to perform the secondary screening in order to isolate the feather degrading Actinobacteria. Modified Basal Liquid medium supplemented with raw chicken feather was used for the secondary screening. $MgSO_4$, $7H_2O$ 0.2 g/lit; K_2HPO_4 0.3 g/lit; KH_2PO_4 0.4 g/lit; $CaCl_2$ 0.22 g/lit and Yeast extract 0.1 g/lit were used to prepare the Modified Basal Liquid medium (Mona, 2008). Whole fresh raw feather was collected from chicken processing shop. Feathers were washed properly with tap water to remove the blood and other dust particles followed by washing with distilled water. Washed, cleaned, white chicken feather was dried in room temperature. 25 ml of Modified Basal Liquid medium was taken in each boiling test tubes and one cleaned, dried medium size chicken feather was added to each boiling tube. The medium was sterilized and the isolates inoculated once the medium became cool. Selected isolates were chosen based on their zone forming capability on Milk Agar medium. The boiling tubes were incubated at room temperature and examined weekly for four weeks (Figs. 10.3 and 10.4).

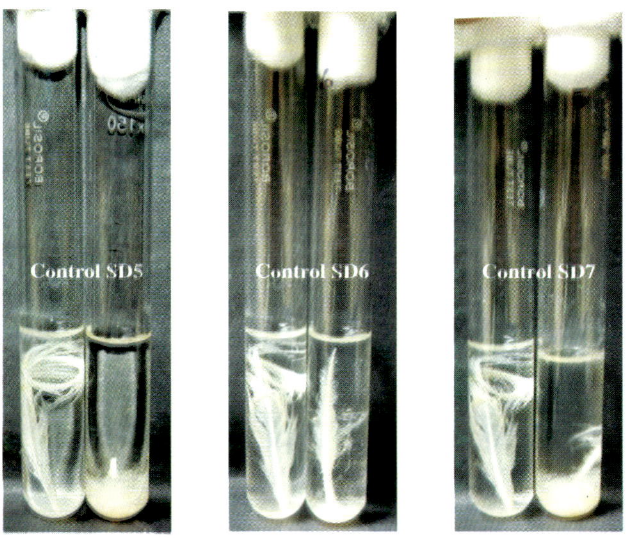

Fig. 10.3 Secondary screening of keratinolytic actinobacteria.

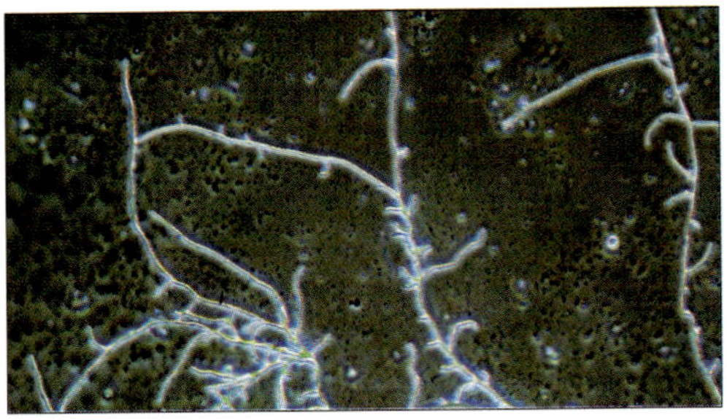

Streptomyces sp SD5

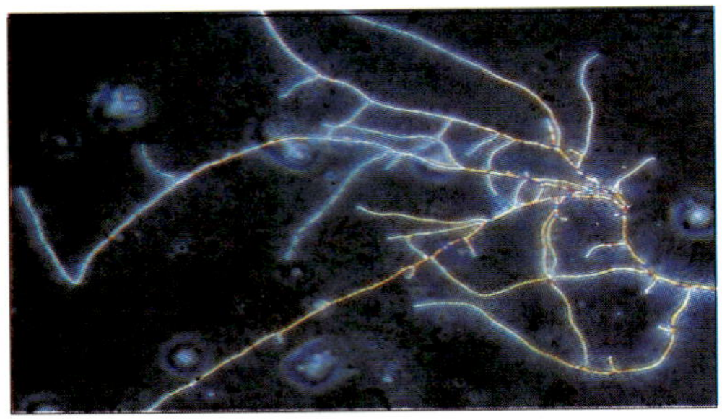

Streptomyces sp SD6

Fig. 10.4 Microscopic view of keratinolytic actinobacterial isolates.

General Guidelines may be Helpful in the Selection of a Bioremediation Technique

The age of the pollutant mixture, as well as the type and concentration of pollutants, may influence the rate and the extent of the bioremediation treatment. The performance of bioremediation and the behavior of pollutants are usually site specific. It can be difficult to generalize from one case to another. When there is scaling up from small-to large-scale studies, contradictory data can be obtained with great diversity in the removal yield of pollutants among the different scales of studies. Well-designed experiments and statistical analysis are required to determine the efficacy of a bioremediation process. For clean-up of polluted environments, bioremediation is a promising technology due to its low cost compared to physical and chemical approaches. Actinobacteria can be the potent microoorganisms in bioremediation of environmental pollutants such as pesticides, herbicides, heavy metals, plastics, rubber and kertin waste.

REFERENCES

Abdelhafid, R., Houot, S. and Barriuso, E. (2000). *Biol. Biochem.* **32:** 389-401.

Aga, D.S. and Thurman E.M. (2001). *Environ. Sci. Technol.* **35:** 2455-2460.

Asturias J.A. and K.N. Timmis. (1993). *J. Bacteriol.* **175:** 4631.

Beck, A.J., Johnson, D.L. and Jones, K.C. (1996). *Sci.Total Environ.* **185:**125-149.

Boivin, A., Amellal, S., Schiavon, M. and Genuchten, T. (2005). *Environ. Pollut.* **138:** 92-99.

Brandt, C.A., Becker, J.M. and Porta, A. (2002). *Environ. Toxicol. Chem.* **21:** 1638-1643.

Brenner, R.C., Magar, V.S., Ickes, J.A., Abbott, J.E., Stout, S.A., Crecelius, E.A. and Bingler, L.S. (2002). *Environ. Sci. Technol.* **36:** 2605-2613.

Bressler D.C. and Fedorak, P.M. (2000). *Can. J. Microbiol.* **46:** 397.

Brunker, P., Rother, D., Sedlmeier, R., Klein, J., Mattes, R. and Altenbuchner, J. (1996). *Mol. Gen. Genet.* **251:** 307-15.

Bushnell, L.D. and Hass, H.F. (1941). *J. Bacteriology* **41:** 653-673.

Calderon, O.H. and Staffeldt, E.E. (1965). International Biodeterioration Bulletin **1:** 33-37.

Cerniglia, C.E. (1992). Biodegradation. **3:** 351-368.

Cerniglia, C.E. (1997). *J. Ind. Microbiol. Biotechnol.* **19:** 324-333.

Chung, S.Y., M. Maeda, E. Song, K. Horikoshi. and Kudo, T.(1994). *Biosci. Biotech. Biochem.* **58:** 2111.

Crawford, D.L., J.M. Lynch, J.M. Whipps. and Ousley, M.A. (1993). *Appl. Environ. Microbiol.* **59:** 3899-3905.

Crawford, R.L. (1995). In J.C. Spain (ed.), Biodegradation of nitroaromatic compounds. Plenum Press, New York, pp. 87-98

Cundell, A. and Mulcock, A.P. (1976). *New Zealand J. of Science*. **19:**291-295.

Daane, L.L., I. Harjono, G.J. Zylstra. and Haggblom, M.M. (2001). *Appl. Environ. Microbiol*. **7:** 2683-2690.

Dabrowska, D., Kot Wasik, A, and Namieoenik, J. (2004). *Pol. J. Environ. Stud*. **13:** 617-626

De Schrijver A. and de Mot R. (1999). *Critic. Rev. Microbiol*. **25:** 85-119.

Dhanasekaran, D., Panneerselvam, A. and Thajuddin, N. (2008). *J. of Culture Collections*. **6:**10-20.

Dhanasekaran, D., Selvamani, S., Panneerselvam, A. and Thajuddin, N. (2009). *African J. Biotechnol*. **8 (17):** 4159-4162.

Donoghue, N.A., Griffin, M., Noris, D.V. and Trudgill, P.W. (1976). In : Proceedings of the Third International Biodegradation Symposium (Eds. J.M. Sharpley and A.M. Kaplan), Applied Science Publishers, London, pp.43-56.

Duran, N. and Esposito, E. (2000). *Appl. Catal. B Environ*. **28:** 83-99.

Duran, N., Rosa, M., D'Annibale, A. and Gianfreda, L. (2002). *Enzyme Microb. Technol*. **31:** 907-931.

Duran, N. (2003) In:Wastewater Treatment using Enzymes (Ed. A. Sakurai), Research Signpost, Kerala, India, pp. 41-51.

Dyke, P.H., Foan, C. and Fiedler, H. (2003). Chemosphere. **50(4):** 469-480.

Edmonds, P. and Cooney, J.J.(1967). *Applied Microbiology*. **11:** 411-416.

Eichenseer, C. and Altenbuchner, J. (1994). *J. Bacteriol*. **176:** 7107-12.

El Saca, S., Salen Eel, D. and Andel Rahman M.S. (1999). *J. Appl. Toxicol*. **22**: 31-35.

Fernandez, P., Grimalt, J.O., and Vilanova, R.M. (2002). *Environl. Sci. Technol*. **36(6):** 1162-1168.

Filip, Z. (1986). In: Biodeterioration and biodegradation of plastics and polymers (Ed. K.J. Seal), Biodeterioration Society Occasional Publication. **1:** 51-55.

Fortnagel, P., Harms, H., Wittich, R., Krohn, S., Meyer, H., Sinnwell, V., Wilkes, H. and Francke, W.(1990). *Appl. Environ. Microbiol*. **56:** 1148.

Friedrich, A.B. and Antranikian, G. (1996). *Appl. Environ. Microbiol*. **62:** 2875-2882.

Fuhs, G.W. (1961). *Archv fur Microbiologie*. **39:** 374-422.

Funk, S.B., Pasti-Grigsby, M.B., Felicione, E.C. and Crawford, D.L. (1994). In: R.E. Hinchee, D.B. Anderson, F.B. Metting, Jr., and G.D. Sayles (Eds.), Applied biotechnology for site remediation. Lewis Publishers, Boca Raton, Fla.

Genner, C. and Hill, E.C. (1981). In: Microbial biodeterioration (Ed. A.H. Rose), Economic Microbiology **6:** pp. 259-306. Academic Press, London.

Getenga, Z. and Kengara, F. (2004). *Bull. Environ. Contam. Toxicol*. **72:** 266-275.

Gianfreda, L. and Rao, M.A. (2004). *Enzyme Microb. Technol*. **35:** 339-354.

Goodfellow, M., Mordaski, M. and Williams, S. T. (1984). The biology of the actinomycetes. Academic Press, Inc., New York.

Goodfellow, M. and Haynes, J.A. (1984). In: Biological, Biochemical, and Biomedical Aspects of Actinomycetes (Eds. Ortiz-Ortiz, L., Bojalil, L.F. and Yakole, V.), Academic Press, Orlando, FL, pp. 453-472.

Gorontzy, T., Drzyzga, O., Kahl, M. W., Bruns-Nagel, D., Breitung, J., Von Loew, E. and Blotevogel, K.H. (1994). *Crit. Rev. Microbiol*. **20:** 265-284.

Graham D.W., Miley M.K., Denoyelles F., Smith V.H., Thurman E.M. and Carter R. (2000). *Wat. Res*. **34:** 4054-4062.

Gurielidze, M., T. Berishvili, N. Cholokava, et al. (2008). *Proc. Georg. Acad. Natl. Sci. Biol. Ser*., B.6, **3-4:** 53-57.

Gurielidze, M., Berishvili, T., Cholokava, N., Pataraya., D. and Nutsubidze, N. (2009). *Microbiology. Bull. Georg. Natl. Acad. Sci.* **3(3):**118-121.

Gutnick, D.L. and Rosenberg, E. (1977). *Ann. Revi. Microbiol.* **31:** 379-396.

Haggblom, M. (1992). *FEMS Microbiol. Rev.* **103:** 29-71, 1992.

Halden R. and D. Dwyer. (1997). *Bioremediat. J.* **1:** 11.

Hanioka N., Watanabe K., Yoda R. and Ando M. (2002). *Drug. Chem. Toxicol.* **25:** 25-37.

Hirsch, P. and Engel, H. (1956). *Bericht der Deutschen botonischen Gesellschaft.* **69:** 441-454.

Hills, D.A. (1967). *Rubber Journal.* **149:** 12-18.

Holdom, R.S. and Turner, A.G. (1969). *J. Applied Bacteriol.* **34:** 448-456.

Hookey, J.V. (1983). Ph.D. Thesis, University of Newcastle-upon-Tyne, UK.

Inoue M.H., Oliveira J.R., Constantin J., Reginato J.B. and Tornisielo V.L. (2002). In: XXIII Congresso Brasileiro da Ciência das Plantas Daninhas, Análise do potencial de contaminação ambiental dos herbicidas utilizados no estado do Paraná, pp. 183.

Isbister, J.D., Anspach, G.L., Kitchens, J.F. and Doyle, R.C. (1984). Microbiologies. **7:** 47-73.

Jarerat, A. and Tokiwa, Y. (2001). *Biotechnology Letters.* **23:** 647-651.

Jensen, P.R., Dwight, R. and Fenical, W. (1991) *Appl. Environ. Microbiol.* **57:** 1102-1108.

Jones, J.G. and Edington, M.A. (1968). *J. Gen. Microbiol.* **52:** 381-390.

Juhasz, A.L., and Naidu, R. (2000). *Int. Biodeter. Biodegr.* **45:** 57-88.

Kalinenko, V.O. (1938). *Mikrobiologya.* **17:** 119-128.

Kanaly, R.A., and Harayama, S. (2000). *J. Bacteriol.* 182(8), 2059-2067,

Kaplan, D.L.and Kaplan, A.M. (1982). *Appl. Environ. Microbiol.* **44:**757-760.

Kasuga, K., Nojiri, H.,Yamane, H., Kodama, T. and Omori, T. (1997). *J. Ferment. Bioeng.* **84:** 387.

Kasuga, K., Habe, H., Chung, J., Yoshida, S T., Nojiri, H., Yamane, H. and Omori, T. (2001). *Biochem. Biophys. Res. Commun.* **283:** 195.

Klausmeier, R.E., Osmon, J.L. and Walls, D.R. (1974). *Dev. Ind. Microbiol.* **15**:309-317.

Klausmeier, R.E. and Osmon, J.L. (1976). In: Proceeding of the Third International Biodegradation Symposium (Eds. J.M. Sharply and A.P. Kaplan), Applied Science Publisher, London, pp. 815-818.

Klausmeier, R.E. and Andrews, C.C. (1981). In: Microbial Biodeterioration (Ed. A.H. Rose), Economic Microbiology Academic Press, London, 6, 431-474.

Kumar, S., Mukerji, K. and Lal, R. (1996). *Crit. Rev. Microbiol.* **22:**1-26.

Kurup, P.P. Randhawa H.S. and Mishra S.K. (1970). *Mycopathologia et Mycologia Applicata.* **40:** 362-367.

Küster E. and Williams S.T. (1964). *Nature.* **202:** 928-929.

Labeda D.P. and Shearer M.C.(1990). In: Labeda D.P. ed., Isolation of Biotechnological Organisms from Nature. McGraw-Hill Publishing Company, New York, USA, pp.1-19.

Leeflang, K.W.H. (1968). *J. the American Water Works Association.* **60:** 1070-1076.

Linos, A. and Steinbuchel, A. (1998). *Kautsch. Gummi Kunstst.* **51:** 496-499.

Liu, J.H. and Schwartz, A. (1961). *Kunstoffe.* **51:** 317-319.

Marvin Sikkema, F.D. and De Bont, J.A.M. (1994). *Appl. Microbiol. Biotechnol.* **42:** 499-507.

McCarthy A.J. and Williams S.T. (1992). *Gene.* **115:** 189-192.

McCormick, N.G., Feeherry, F.E. and Levinson, H.S.(1976). *Appl. Environ. Microbiol.* **31:** 949-958.

Mc Kenna, E.J. and Kallio, R.E. (1965). *Annual Review of Microbiology.***19:** 183-208.

Mergaert, J. and Swings, J.(1996). *J. Ind. Microbiol. Biotechnol.* **17:** 463-469.

Michels, J. and Gottschalk, G. (1995). In J.C. Spain (ed.), Biodegradation of nitroaromatic compounds. Plenum Press, New York, pp. 135-149.

Mona, E.M. (2008). *World J. Microbiol. Biotechnol.* **24:** 2331-2338.

Monna, L., Omori, T. and Kodama, T. (1993). *Appl. Environ. Microbiol.* **59:** 285.

Monteiro R.T. (1997). In: (Eds. Melo I.S. and Azevedo J.L.) Microbiologia Ambiental. EMBRAPACNPMA, Jaguariúna SP, Brasil, pp. 107-124.

Moran, M.A., Rutherford, L.T. and Hodson, R.E. (1995). *Appl. Environ. Microbiol.* **61:** 3694-3700.

Nakahara, H., Schottel, J.L., Yamada, T., Miyakawa, Y., Asakawa, M., Harville, J. and Silver, S. (1985). *J. Gen. Microbiol.* **131:** 1053-1059.

Nam, G.W., Lee, D.W., Lee, H.S., Lee, N.J. Kim, B.C. Choe, E.A, Hwang, J.K., Suhartono, M.T. and Pyun, Y.R. 2002. *Arch. Microbiol.* **178:** 538-547.

Nicholson, C.A. and Fathepure, B.Z. (2004). *Appl. Environ. Microbiology.***70(2):**1222-1225.

Nishida H, and Tokiwa, Y. (1993). *J. Environ. Polym. Degrad.* **1:** 227-233.

Nolof, G. and Hirsch, P. (1962). *Archive fur Mikrobiologie.* **44:** 278-297.

Onifade, A.A., Al-Sane, N.A., Al-Musallan, A.A. and Al-Zarban, S. (1998). *Bioresour. Technol.* **66:** 1-11.

Osmon, J.L. and Andrew, C. C. (1978). U.S. National Technical Information Service ADE400073. U.S. National Technical Information Service, Spring- field, Va.

Orchard, V. and Goodfellow, M. (1980). *J. Gen. Microbiol.* **118:** 295-312.

Pankhurst, E.S., Davies, M.J. and Blake, H.M. (1972). In: Biodeterioration of Materials Volume 2 (Eds. A. H. Walters and E. H. Hueck Van der Plas), Applied Science Publisher, London, pp. 76-90.

Pankhurst, E.S., Nicholle, H.G.M. and Allan, K. (1975). In: Microbial Aspects of the Deterioration of the Material (Eds. R.J. Gilbert and D.W. Lovelock), Academic Press, London, pp. 135-151.

Parales, R., Bruce, N., Schmid, A., and Wackett, L. (2002). *Appl. Environ. Microbiol.* **68:** 4699-4709.

Pasti, M.B., Pometto, A.L, Nuti, M.P. and Crawford, D.L. (1990). *Appl. Environ. Microbiol.* **56:** 2213-2218.

Pataraya, D., M. Gurielidze, T. Berishvili, *et al.,* (2006). *J. Biological Physics and Chemistry.* **6(4):** 149-154.

Pataraya, D., M. Gurielidze, T. Berishvili, N. Cholokava, P. (2008). Proceedings of IV Congress of Microbiologists of Uzbekistan, Tashkent, pp. 12-13.

Pettey, T.M. and Crawford, D.L. (1984). *Appl. Environ. Microbiol.* **42:** 290-296.

Phelan, M.B., Crawford, D.L. and Pometto, A.L.(1979). *Can. J. Microbiol.* **25:** 1270-1276.

Pirnik, M.P., Atlas, R.M. and Bartha, R.(1974). *J. Bacteriol.* **119:** 868-878.

Pommer, E.H. and Lorenz, G. (1986). In: Biodeteriorationa and Biodegradation of Plastics and Polymers (Ed. K.J. Seal), Biodeterioration Society Occasional Publication 1, 77-86.

Posada, D. and Crandall, K.A. (1998). Bioinformatics. **14:** 817-818.

Pranamuda, H, Tokiwa, Y. and Tanaka, H. (1997). *Appl. Environ. Microbiol.* **63:** 1637-1640.

Pranamuda, H., Chollakup, R. and Tokiwa, Y. (1999). *Appl. Environ. Microbiol.* **65:** 4220-4222.

Preuss, A. and Rieger, P.G. (1995). In: J.C. Spain (Ed.), Biodegradation of nitroaromatic compounds. Plenum Press, New York.

Purkiss, B.E. (1972). In : Biodeterioration of Materials Volume 2 (Eds. A.H. Walters and E.H. Hueck/Van der Plas), pp. 91-102. Applied Science Publishers, London.

Raymond, J., Rogers, T., Shonnard, D. and Kline, A. (2001). *J. Hazard. Mater.* **84:** 189-215.

Riffel, A. and Brandelli, A.(2006). *Braz. J. Microbiol.* **37:** 395-399.

Rosenberg, E., Zuckerberg, A., Rubinovitz, C. and Gutnick, D.L. (1979). *Applied and Environmental Microbiology.* **37:** 402-408.

Roy, F., Weston, I. (1989). U.S. Army Toxic and Hazardous Materials Agency, Aberdeen Proving Ground, Aberdeen, Md.

Sanchez, M., Estrada, I., Martinez, O., Martin-Villacorta, J., Aller, A., and Moran, A. (2004). *Chemosphere.* **57:** 673-679.

Schmid, A., Rothe, B., Altenbuchner, J., Ludwig, W. and. Engesser, K. H. (1997). *J. Bacteriol.* **179 :** 53.

Sedlmeier, R. and Altenbuchner, J. (1992). *Mol. Gen. Genet.* **236:** 76-85.

Semple K.T., Reid B.J. and Fermor T.R. (2001). *Environ. Pollut.***112:** 269–283.

Seto, M., Kimbara, K., Shimura, M., Hatta, T., Fukuda, M. and Yano, K. (1995). *Appl. Environ. Microbiol.* **61:** 3353.

Sinden, D.L. (1979). M.S. thesis. University of Idaho, Moscow.

Sohangen, N.L. and Fol, J.G. (1914).Zentrablatt fur Bakteriologie, Parasitenkunde, Infektionskrankheiten und Hiygiene. 1 Abteilung **49:** 87-89.

Spain, J.C. (1995). In: (Eds. J.C. Spain), Biodegradation of nitroaromatic compounds. Plenum Press, New York.

Spence, D. and van Niel, C. B.(1936). *Industrial Engineering Chemistry* **28:** 847-850.

Spencer, L., Heskins, M. and Guillet, J.E. (1976). In: Proceedings of Third International Biodegradation Symposium (Eds. J.M. Sharpley and A.M. Kaplen), Applied Science Publisher, London, pp. 753-763.

Stahl, J.C., and Aust, S. (1995). In: (Ed. J.C. Spain), Biodegradation of nitroaromatic compounds. Plenum Press, New York.

Stamper D.M. and Tuovinen O.H. (1998). *Crit. Rev. Microbiol.* **24:** 1-22.

Strubel,V.,. Engesser, K.H Fischer, P. and Knackmuss, H.J. (1991). *J. Bacteriol.* **173:** 1932.

Subhasish. S and Dhanasekaran, D. (2010). *Current Research Journal of Biological Sciences.* **2(2):** 124-131.

Swofford D.L. (2000). Phylogenetic Analysis Using Parsimony and Other Methods Sinauer Associates, Sunderland, MA, USA.

Takizawa, M., Colwell, R.R. and Hill, R.T. (1993). *Appl. Environ. Microbiol.* **59:** 997-1002.

Taysum, D.H. (1966). In: Microbiological Deterioration in the Tropics (Eds. N.J. Butler and H.O.W. Eggins,), Society of Chemistry and Industry monography 23,105-120.

Tokiwa, Y., Iwamoto, A., Koyama, M., Kataoka, N., Nishida, H. (1992). Macromol. Chem., Macromol. Symp. **57:** 273-279.

Topp, E.A. (2001). *Biol. Fertil. Soils.* **33:** 529-534.

Tortella, G., Diez, M., and Dur´an, N. (2005). *Crit. Rev. Microbiol.* **31:** 197-212.

Traxler, R.W. and Flannery, W.L. (1968). In: Biodeteriration of Materials (Eds. A.H. Walters and J.J. Elphick), Elsevier, Amsterdam, pp. 44-54.

Van Eerd, L., Hoagland, R., Zablotowicz, R., and Hall, C. (2003). Pesticide metabolism in plants and microorganisms, Weed Sci. 51.

Weyland, H. and Helmke, E.(1988). In: The Biology of the Actinomycetes '88. Proceedings of the 7th International Symposium on the (1998) 177-184 Biology of Actinomycetes (Eds. Okami, Y., Beppu, T. and Ogawara, H) Japan Scientific Society Press, Tokyo, pp. 294-299.

Wilkes, H., Wittich, R., Timmis, K., Fortnagel, P. and Francke, W. (1996). *Appl. Environ. Microbiol.* **62:** 367.

Williams, R.T., Ziegenfuss, P.S. and Siks, W.E. (1992). *J. Ind. Microbiol.* **9:**137-144.

Wiren Lehr, S., Scheunert, I. and Dorfler, U. (2002). *Geoderma.* **105;**351–366, 2002.

Wittich, R.M. Wilkes, H. Sinnwell, V. Francke, W. and Fortnagel, P.(1992). *Appl. Environ. Microbiol.* **58:** 1005.

Yeager, C.C. (1962). Pink staining in polyvinyl chloride. Plastics World. **20:** 14-15.

Yu, H.T. (2002). *J. Environ. Sci. Health C.* **20(2):** 149–183.

Zuckerberg, A., Diver, A., Peeri, Z., Gutnick, D.L. and Rosenberg, E. (1979). *Applied and Environ. Microbiol.* **37:** 414-420.

Zobell, L.E. and Beckwith, J.D. (1944). *J. of the American Water Workers Association.* **46:** 39-56.

Zyska, B.J., Rytych, B.J., Zankowicz, L.P. and Fudalej, D.S. (1972).In: Biodeterioration Materials Volume 2 (Eds. A. H. Walters and E.H. Huek-van der Plas), Applied Science Publisher, London, pp. 256-267.

11

Ex situ and *in situ* Bioremediation of Petroleum Contaminated Sites: An Integrative Approach Through Microbial Technology

Reena Das and Bhupendra N. Tiwary*

School of Biotechnology, Guru Ghasidas University, Bilaspur (C.G.)-495-009

**Corresponding author Phone: + 91 940 6034535*

E-mail: tiwarybn2@yahoo.co.in

Petroleum hydrocarbons, due to their large-scale usage, are one of the main potential sources of environmental contamination leading to pollution and health hazards. Most of its elements are proven carcinogens and immuno-toxicant. Accidental spillage of petroleum products has proved to be a serious threat to the environment. Various physico-chemical technologies have been reported for decontaminating petroleum contamination. However, being less effective and costly, interest is rapidly growing for biological approach of remediation of petroleum contaminated sites. Bioremediation is a technological process whereby biological systems, such as, microorganisms and plants are harnessed to effect the clean-up of the polluted environment. The important determinant of bioremediation is the bioavailability of hydrocarbons. Many biotic and abiotic factors are the important postulates to improve bioavailabilty and enhance hydrocarbon bioaccumulation/bioremediation processes. The environmental fate of hydrocarbon detoxifying microbes and their ecological consequences of intervention constitute other important descriptors for the efficiency and sustainability of bioremediation processes. The scope of bioremediation has been extended by developing and cultivating microbes for use under varied conditions for restoring heavily contaminated sites. Advancement in technological and growing economy is bringing in great progress in research and development in bioremediation as a natural solution. This review pays attention to detailed integrative approaches in *ex situ* and *in situ* bioremediation of petroleum hydrocarbons contamination to reduce the toxicity to a safe and acceptable level, metabolic mechanisms underlying hydrocarbon interaction with microbes and plants, key factors that affect the efficiency of the hydrocarbons bioremediation, ecotoxicity and successful monitoring of bioremediation, and future developments in the bioremediation technology. It also demonstrates the recent advanced tools to develop genetically engineered microorganisms (GEMs) to optimize and control *ex situ* and *in situ* bioremediation.

INTRODUCTION

Modern society continues to rely on the use of petroleum hydrocarbons for its energy needs. Despite recent technological advances, accidental spills of crude oil and its refined products occur on frequent basis during the routine operations of extraction, transportation, storage, refining, and distribution (Khan *et al.,* 2006). Accidental and deliberate crude oil spills have been, and still continue to be, a significant source of environmental pollution, and pose a serious environmental problem due to the possibility of air, water and soil contamination (Trindade *et al.*, 2005; Vazquez *et al.*, 2009; Rosenberg and Ron, 1996; Head and Swannell, 1999). The fate of petroleum hydrocarbons in the environment from various actual environmental oil contamination incidents has now been examined. For example, approx. 6*107 barrels of oil was spread over 2*107 m^3 soil, and 320 oil lakes were created across the desert during the first Gulf War in Kuwait (Al-Saleh and Obuekwe, 2005). The data from last 20 years include oil spills of over 7 tonnes from tankers, combined carriers and barges. Although the data suggest a reduction in oil spills, the trend may only represent a temporary downward fluctuation that is part of erratic cycling over the long term (Etkin and Welch, 1997).

In the chemical and petroleum industries, considerable volumes of oily sludge are unavoidably generated. These inevitably result in the contamination of soil and groundwater. In large concentrations, the hydrocarbon molecules that make up crude oil and petroleum products are highly toxic to many organisms, including humans. Petroleum products contain many hazardous organic chemicals such as benzene, toluene, naphthalene, and benzopyrene, some of which are recognized as carcinogens (Soriano *et al.*, 1998; Levine *et al.*, 2009; Goldstein, 2008; Cook *et al.*, 2001).

Gasoline and fuel oil are complex mixtures of hydrocarbons that include n-alkanes, branched alkanes, cycloalkanes and aromatic compounds. The approximate composition of gasoline and fuel oil is 60% aliphatic-40% aromatic and 80% aliphatic-20% aromatic respectively. GCMS scan illustrates the complex range of petroleum hydrocarbon compounds in commercial use (Fig. 11.1).

Polycyclic aromatic hydrocarbons (PAHs) are a large group of compounds exhibiting similar characteristics. They are large, high molecular weight compounds with low water solubility, and two to five condensed aromatic rings. Common PAH's include anthracene, benzo-(a) pyrene, chrysene, naphthalene and pyrene. Most PAH's exhibit moderate to good biodegradation by surfactant enhanced remediation. Some PAH compounds are present in gasoline and fuel oils (Ivey, 2001).

Petroleum contains aromatic hydrocarbons, which could be a health risk on exposure over a period of time (Viswanathan, 1999). The major effect of exposure to petroleum hydrocarbons is the central nervous system depression and polyneuropathy. Studies have shown that repeated exposure of laboratory animals to high concentrations of whole gasoline vapours at 67, 262 and 2056 ppm has caused kidney damage and cancer of kidney in rats and liver cancer in mice. IARC (International Agency for Research on Cancer) has listed gasoline as possible carcinogenic (2B) to humans (with sufficient experiments in animals and inadequate evidence in humans). NIOSH (National Institute for Occupational Safety and Health) lists gasoline as carcinogen with no further classification (MSDS). Among the components of gasoline, N-heptane and cyclohexane are known to cause nercosis

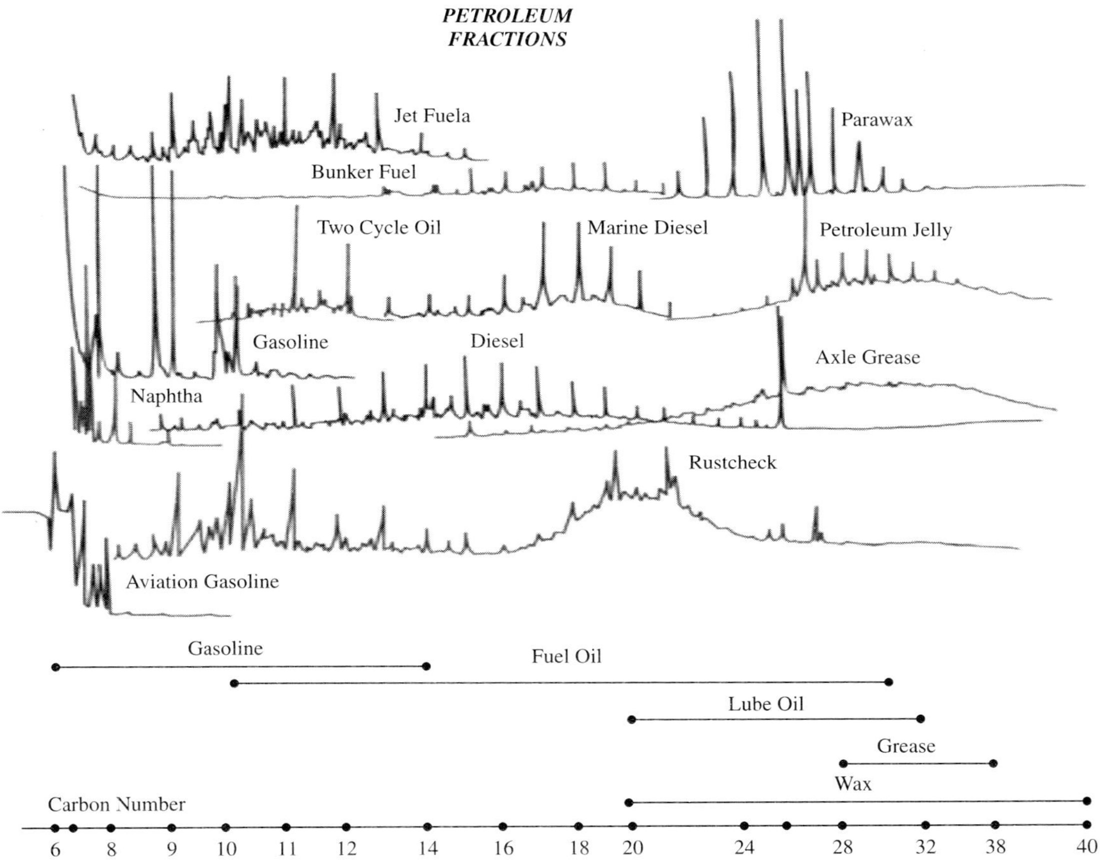

Fig. 11.1 GCMS scan illustrating the complex range of petroleum hydrocarbon compounds in commercial use (Adapted from Ivey, 2000).

and irritation of eyes and mucous membranes. Cyclohexanes have been reported to cause changes in liver and kidney functions in rabbits (US-EPA). n-heptane have been reported to cause polyneuritis following prolonged exposure (Goel *et al.*, 1982). ACG1H (American Conference of Government Industrial Hygienists), NTP (National Toxicology Program) and OSHA (Occupational Safety and Health Administration) lists benzene as a human carcinogen with an assigned TL V of 0.5 ppm 8 hour TW A and a STEL of 2.5 ppm (http://www.health-report.co.uk/benzene-toxic-chemical.htm). Petroleum contains trace amounts of sulfur and nitrogenous compounds, which are dangerous by themselves and can react with the environment to produce secondary poisonous chemicals. It also contains aromatic hydrocarbons, which could be a health risk on exposure over a period of time. Many health effects are of concern, including anemia, which might even increase the risk of cancer, damage to the neural system and vital organs like kidney and liver (Viswanathan, 1999). Methyl tertiary-butyl ether (MTBE), an additive in unleaded petrol as an oxygenate, known to dissolve and spread rapidly in groundwater system, is a potential human carcinogen (Viswanathan, 1999). MTBE does not significantly adhere onto soil particles, and it does not appear to readily biodegrade in the environment. MTBE persist both in aerobic and anaerobic conditions; it has an unpleasant odor. Trimethylbenzene may cause nervousness, tension, anxiety and asthmatic bronchitis. Toluene causes impairment of coordination and momentary loss of memory at exposures of 200-500 ppm, and palpation's at 500-1500 ppm (Faust, 1994).

The contamination by hydrocarbons emphasizes the need for environmental restoration by restricting and managing their usage and effective clean-up of the contaminated sites. As physico-chemical methods are neither feasible nor economically viable (Roberts, 1998), bioremediation, i.e., the use of biological methods to restore contaminated areas, especially by the addition of bacteria and other microorganisms that consume or neutralize contaminants, has become an attractive alternative for the remediation of polluted sites. Bioremediation is the enhancement of live organisms such as fungi, bacteria and plants to absorb and metabolically breakdown hydrocarbon and organic contaminants (Hildebrandt and Wilson, 1991; Vidali, 2001; Diaz, 2008). It involves the application of organisms and nutrients such as phosphate and nitrogen to the contaminated soil/water. Nitrate and phosphate supplements enhance the biodegradation of oil (Atlas and Bartha, 1992). Bioremediation involves the use of microorganisms for the transformation of complex or simple chemical compounds into non-hazardous forms by biological agents, resulting in materials of a higher nutritive value or simply reducing the final bulk of the product (Grady, 1985) (Fig. 11.2). This then gives rise to a variety of products, most of which are more water-soluble than the parent hydrocarbon. Bacteria can live and multiply in most hostile circumstances and are able to detoxify poisonous chemical substances such as carbon dioxide and water, utilizing most times the energy released in the process (Viswantahan, 1999). Bioremediation is one of the primary mechanisms through which petroleum hydrocarbons and other organic pollutants are removed from the environment; the self-cleaning capacity of the nature is high.

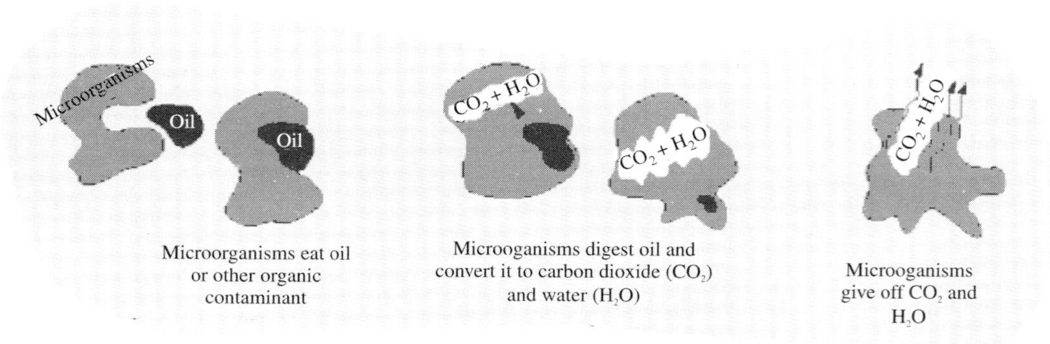

Fig. 11.2 Schematic diagram of aerobic biodegradation of oil in soil (EPA, 1996).

This chapter pays attention to detailed integrative approach in *ex situ* and *in situ* bioremediation of petroleum hydrocarbons contamination to reduce the contamination to a safe and acceptable level, key factors that affect the efficiency of hydrocarbons, bioremediation and successful monitoring of the bioremediation and future development in the bioremediation technology. This review also demonstrated recent advanced tools to develop genetically engineered microorganisms (GEMs) to optimize and control *ex situ* and *in situ* bioremediation.

BIOREMEDIATION STRATEGIES

In conventional bioremediation, enzymes released by the microbes can only attack one surface of the contaminant. This leads to slower, less effective remediation, whereas in enhanced bioremediation, a patented combination of surfactants and emulsifiers break the contaminant down into tiny pieces, which can then be surrounded by enzymes and quickly digested. Bioremediation accelerates what would occur naturally by "biodegradation" or the conversion of spilled oil by naturally occurring oil-degrading microbes into carbon dioxide, water and biomass. This process can be enhanced by the addition of nutrients (biostimulation) such as nitrogen and phosphorus and seeding the area with additional microbes (bioaugmentation). Bioremediation can be used at the site of contamination *(in situ)* or on contamination removed from the original site *(ex situ)*. *In situ* techniques involve processes like biostimulation, bioaugmentation and intrinsic bioremediation, and do not require excavation of the contaminated soils. So, these are less expensive, create less dust, and cause less release of contaminants than *ex situ* techniques. *Ex situ* bioremediation involves removing the contaminated soil or water and treating it with microbes and nutrients to mineralize the contaminant.

Ex situ Bioremediation

Ex situ techniques can be faster, easier to control, and used to treat a wider range of contaminants and soil types than *in situ* techniques. However, they require excavation and treatment of the contaminated soil before and, sometimes, after the actual bioremediation step. The *ex situ* techniques include *slurry-phase bioremediation and solid phase bioremediation.*

The *ex situ* approach to hydrocarbon bioremediation is carried out aboveground by physically extracting the impacted medium. It is commonly applied to dissolved-phase contamination via pumping and treatment with aboveground bioreactors. Soils are treated aboveground via land-farming, biopiling and composting. The primary advantage of *ex situ* technique is the degree of control that can be exerted over the processes being used to manipulate the system (Pavel *et al.*, 2008). Generally, the primary disadvantage is the expense and disruption associated with removal, treatment, and disposal or replacement of the impacted medium. *Ex situ* bioremediation of petroleum contaminated sites involves various treatments.

Slurry-phase bioremediation: Contaminated soil is combined with water and other additives in a large tank called a "bioreactor" and mixed to keep the microorganisms, which are already present in the soil, in contact with the contaminants in the soil (Fig. 11.3). Nutrients and oxygen are added, and conditions in the bioreactor are controlled to create the optimum environment for the microorganisms to degrade the contaminants. Upon completion of the treatment, the water is removed from the solids, which are disposed of or treated further if they still contain pollutants. Slurry-phase biological treatment can be a relatively rapid process compared to other biological treatment processes, particularly for contaminated clays. The success of the process is highly dependent on the specific soil and chemical properties of the contaminated material. This technology is particularly useful where rapid remediation is a high priority. (EPA, 2003; Hyman and Dupont, 2001).

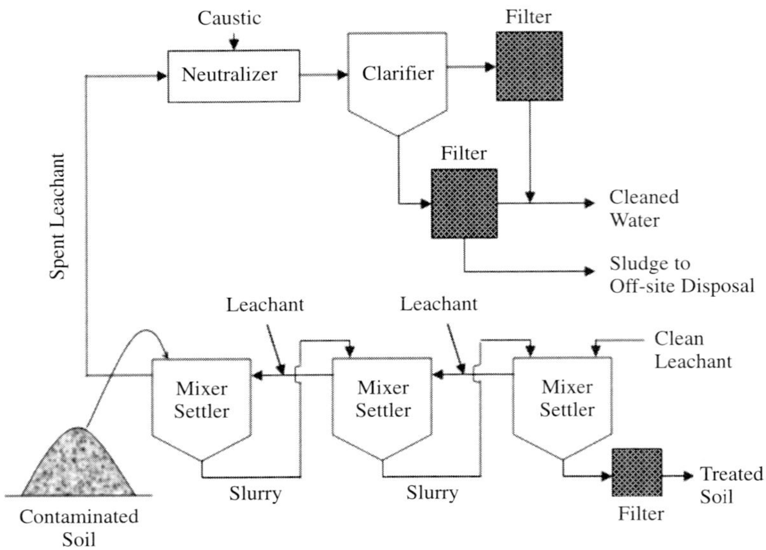

Fig. 11.3 Slurry-phase bioreactor (FRTR, 2000).

Solid-phase bioremediation: Solid-phase bioremediation is a process that treats soils in aboveground treatment areas equipped with collection systems to prevent any contaminant from escaping the treatment. Moisture, heat, nutrients, or oxygen are controlled to enhance biodegradation for the application of this treatment. Solid-phase systems are relatively simple to operate and maintain, require a large amount of space, and clean-ups require more time to complete than with slurry-phase processes. Solid phase soil treatment processes include *landfarming, soil biopiles,* and *composting* (Hyman and Dupont, 2001).

Landfarming: In this relatively simple treatment method, contaminated soils are excavated and spread on a pad with a built-in system to collect any "leachate" or contaminated liquids that seep out of contaminant-soaked soil (Fig. 11.4). The soils are periodically turned over to mix air into the waste. Moisture and nutrients are controlled to enhance bioremediation. The length of time for bioremediation to occur will be longer if nutrients, oxygen or temperature are not properly controlled. In some cases, reduction of contaminant concentrations may be attributed more to volatilization than biodegradation. When the process is conducted in enclosures controlling escaping volatile contaminants, volatilization losses are minimized. (Rubinos *et al.*, 2007).

Soil biopiles: In this the contaminated soil is piled in heaps several meters high over an air distribution system. Aeration is provided by pulling air through the heap with a vacuum pump (Fig. 11.5). Moisture and nutrient levels are maintained at levels that maximize bioremediation. The soil heaps can be placed in enclosures. Volatile contaminants are easily controlled since they are usually part of the air stream being pulled through the pile (EPA, 2003).

Composting: Biodegradable waste is mixed with a bulking agent such as straw, hay, or corn cobs to make it easier to deliver the optimum levels of air and water to the microorganisms. Three common designs are *static pile composting* (compost is formed into piles and aerated with blowers or vacuum pumps), *mechanically agitated in vessel composting* (compost is placed in a treatment vessel where it is mixed and aerated), and *windrow composting* (compost is placed in long piles known as windrows and periodically mixed by tractors or similar equipment) (Cunningham, 2000).

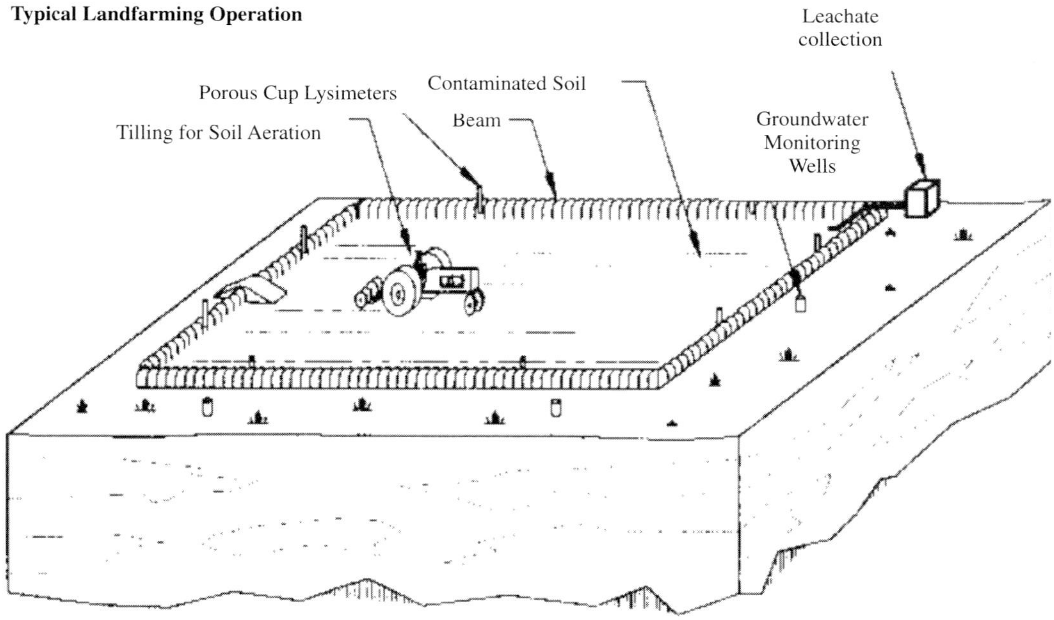

Fig. 11.4 Landfarming (FRTR, 2000).

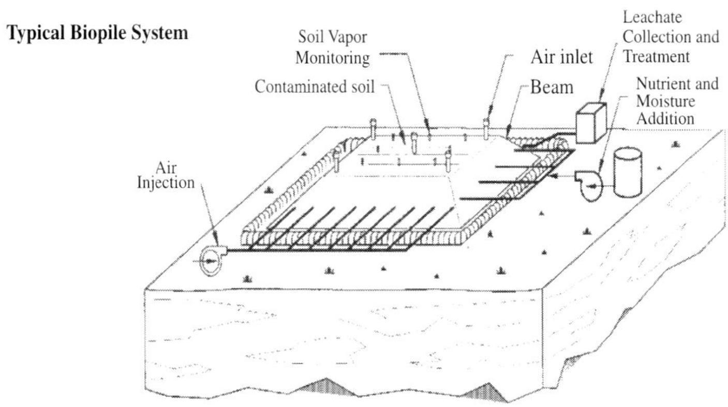

Fig. 11.5 Biopile system (FRTR, 2000).

Ex situ Phytoremediation

Phytoremediation has been applied to a number of contaminants in small-scale field and/or laboratory studies. These contaminants include heavy metals, radionuclides, chlorinated solvents, petroleum hydrocarbons, PCBs, PAHs, organophosphate insecticides, explosives, and surfactants (Khan, 2007). Certain species of higher plants can accumulate very high concentrations of hydrocarbons in their tissues without showing toxicity. Plant treatments included Scots Pine (*Pinus sylvestris*), Poplar

(*Populus deltoides x Wettsteinii*), a grass mixture (Red fescue, *Fesuca rubra*; Smooth meadowgrass, *Poa pratensis* and Perennial ryegrass, *Lolium perenne*) and a legume mixture (White clover, *Trifolium repens* and Pea, *Pisum sativum*) (Palmroth *et al.*, 2002) fescue (*Lolium arundinaceum* Schreb) – ryegrass (*Lolium multiflorum* L.) bermudagrass *(Cynodon dactylon* (L.) Pers.*)*. For this clean-up method to be feasible, the plants must (1) extract large concentrations of hydrocarbons into their roots; (2) translocate the hydrocarbons into the surface biomass; and (3) produce a large quantity of plant biomass. In addition, remediative plants must have mechanisms to detoxify and/or tolerate high PAH's concentrations accumulated in their shoots.

Integrative Approach in *ex situ* Bioremediation (Physico-Chemical and Biological)

The studies on the integration of physico-chemical and biological methods to decontaminate hydrocarbons to a safe and acceptable level are a new approach in bioremediation and need the attention of scientists. Slurry-phase processes and solid-phase soil treatment processes including landfarming, soil biopiles, and composting are successfully detoxifying the hydrocarbon contamination. To further enhance the *ex-situ* bioremediation, an integrative approach of soil, microbes and plants is used to decontaminate the heavily contaminated sites. The specificity of the plant-bacteria interaction is dependent upon soil conditions, which can alter the contaminant bioavailability, root exudate composition, and nutrient levels. In addition, the metabolic requirements for hydrocarbon remediation may also dictate the form of the plant-bacteria interaction i.e., specific or nonspecific. Along with toxicity, there are often additional factors that limit the plant growth in contaminated soils including arid conditions, lack of soil structure, low water supply and nutrient deficiency.

In situ Bioremediation

In situ techniques do not require excavation of the contaminated soils, so they are less expensive, create less dust, and cause less release of contaminants than *ex situ* techniques. Also, it is possible to treat a large volume of soil at once. *In situ* techniques, however, may be slower than *ex situ* techniques, difficult to manage, and most effective at sites with permeable (sandy or uncompacted) soil. The goal of aerobic *in situ* bioremediation is to supply oxygen and nutrients to the microorganisms in the soil. Aerobic *in situ* techniques can vary in the way they supply oxygen to the organisms that degrade the contaminants. Such methods are *biostimulation* and *bioaugmentation.* Oxygen can be provided by pumping air into the soil above the water table (bioventing) or by delivering the oxygen in liquid form as hydrogen peroxide. *In situ* bioremediation may not work well in clays or highly layered subsurface environments because oxygen cannot be evenly distributed throughout the treatment area. *In situ* remediation often requires years to reach clean-up goals, depending mainly on how biodegradable specific contaminants are. Less time may be required with easily degraded contaminants (EPA, 1996).

Biostimulation: It involves the modification of the environment to stimulate existing bacteria capable of bioremediation. This can be done by addition of various forms of rate limiting nutrients, phosphorus, nitrogen, oxygen, or carbon (e.g., in the form of molasses) and electron acceptors/donors (acetate, nitrate, sulphate, glutamate etc) and gaseous formulations to contaminated environment (Garcia-Blanco *et al.,* 2007; Tongarun *et al.*, 2008). Alternatively, pollutant removal rates have also been stimulated by generating an optimal balance of physical factors such as aeration, temperature and buffering of environmental pH by altering the redox state and electrokinetics state of contaminated samples (Brusseau *et al.*, 1999). Additives are usually added to the subsurface through injection wells, although injection well technology for biostimulation purposes is still emerging. Removal of the contaminated material is also an option, albeit an expensive one. Biostimulation can be enhanced by bioaugmentation. This process, overall, is referred to as bioremediation and is an EPA-approved method for reversing the presence of oil or gas spills. Biostimulation is more effective if it is used in combination with bioaugmentation methods (Silva *et al.*, 2004; Olaniran *et al.*, 2009). While evaluating the performance of biostimulation methods in comparison with bioaugmentation and natural attenuation, the kinetic efficiency of biostimulation was found to be relatively slow as compared to bioaugmentation process (Hamdi *et al.*, 2007; Salinaz-Martinez *et al.*, 2008).

Bioaugmentation: Bioaugmentation is a rational rearrangement of microbial richness leading to dominion of microbial group(s) with specific catabolic traits, which are necessary for cleaning up of pollutants (Dejonghe *et al.*, 2001). The important advantage of bioaugmentation is that it enhances the performance of indigenous bacteria several fold through the addition of bacterial strains with specific activities over a relatively short time scale (Yu *et al.*, 2005). Conventionally, bioaugmentation studies have focused on exogenous introduction of efficient pollutant degrading strain(s) or bacterial consortium to contaminated site for decontamination purpose. Interestingly, few studies have attempted to evaluate the *in situ* biodegradation performance. Hydrocarbon contamination can delay or inhibit microbial degradation of organic pollutants, so for an effective *in situ* biodegradation, bioaugmentation is necessary. Additionally, this study evaluated the ability of bioaugmentation to enhance organic degradation in these co-contaminated soils. Finally, it was determined whether enhanced degradation was due to survival of the introduced organism (cell bioaugmentation) or plasmid transfer to indigenous microbial populations (gene bioaugmentation). *Escherichia coli* D11, which lacks chromosomal genes necessary for complete 2, 4-D mineralization, was used for gene bioaugmentation in Madera soil. Significant gene transfer of the plasmid to the indigenous populations was observed, and the rate of 2, 4-D degradation was enhanced relative to that of controls. Cell bioaugmentation was further demonstrated when *Comamonas testosteroni* was used to enhance the biodegradation of 3-CB in Madera soil. In this case no transfer of plasmid pBRC60 to indigenous soil recipients was observed. For the Madera soil, non-bioaugmented samples ultimately showed complete 2, 4-D degradation. In contrast, non-bioaugmented Brazito soils showed incomplete 2, 4-D degradation. These studies are unique in showing that both cell bioaugmentation and gene bioaugmentation can be effective in enhancing organic degradation in co-contaminated soils. Ultimately, the bioaugmentation strategy may depend on the degree of contamination and the time frame available for remediation. Apart from the above methods, quite a few other variants of bioaugmentation have also been developed and implemented successfully for remediation purpose. "Co-bioaugmentation" is one such variant wherein the process is rendered effectively by exogenous introduction of multiple microbial strains with different metabolic potentials (Roane *et al.*, 2001). Bioaugmentation is a straightforward approach, yet the use of this technology has not become common largely due to the limited success with isolation of efficient pollutant degrading microorganisms. Further the bioaugmentation process needs to address several other issues such as optimization of the process before its application.

BIOTIC AND ABIOTIC FACTORS FOR ENHANCEMENT OF BIOREMEDIATION

Various biotic and abiotic factors, which influence the weathering, including biodegradation of oil, also influence the rates of microbial growth and enzymatic activities, and the rate of petroleum hydrocarbon degradation. The persistence of petroleum pollutants depends on the quantity and quality of the hydrocarbon mixture and the properties of the affected ecosystem (Atlas, 1981).

Biotic Factors

Bacterial Chemotaxis

Microorganisms exhibit wide behavioural adoptions that can be of great significance for *in situ* bioremediation purposes. Chemotaxis is one of the most important adoptions, because it allows increased bioavailability of the pollutants, and thereby helps in maximization of pollutant degradation (Pandey and Jain, 2002). A few bacteria belonging to diverse groups have been identified that exhibit chemotaxis towards environmental pollutants such as petroleum associated hydrocarbons, explosive, nitroaromatic compounds, and polycyclic aromatic hydrocarbons (Bhusan and Jain, 2000; Gordillo *et al.*, 2007). Common soil bacteria such as *Rhizobium* sp., *Bradyrhizobium* sp., *Pseudomonas* sp., and *Azospirillum* sp. have been shown to be chemotactically attracted towards different aromatic hydrocarbons. Many of these compounds are present in soils, sediments, and rhizosphere, and they serve as sources of carbon and energy for the microorganisms. Aromatic acids such as benzoate, *p*-hydroxybenzoate (PHB), methylbenzoates, *o*-, *m*-, and *p*-toluates, salicylate, DL-mandelate, β-phenylpyruvate, and benzoylformate have been reported to be attractants for *Pseudomonas putida* PRS2000 (Pandey and Jain, 2002). Based on the metabolism, chemotaxis is divided into two subcategories—metabolism-dependent and metabolism-independent chemotaxis. The first one is associated with pollutants that are used as a source of metabolic energy. The second one is associated with pollutants that are co-metabolically transformed to generate lesser toxic products (Grimm and Harwood, 1997; Pandey and Jain, 2002). Electron donors/acceptors act as important components of the metabolic machinery. Therefore, bacterial moments towards electron acceptors/donors may be called metabolism-dependent chemotaxis. Generally microbiologists consider positive chemotaxis for detoxification of hydrocarbons (Lovely *et al.*, 1975; Parales *et al.*, 2000). Negative chemotaxis phenomenon, therefore could be utilized to explore the alternative methods for control of the microbial fouling by coating surfaces with less universal toxic chemical at non-lethal concentrations, which prevent fouling by repelling a potential primary microbial film. In a case studied by Young and Mitchell (1973), the effect of negative chemotaxis response to sublethal concentration of hydrocarbon compounds, chloroform, ethanol, benzene, and toluene has been reported. The results suggested that the hydrocarbons were significantly inhibited by the microbial fraction up to 96%. This study suggested that positive chemotaxis could be used to enhance the *ex situ* bioremediation. However, negative chemotaxis may be utilized for developing new approaches for controlling the non-specific microbial fouling. Bacterial chemotaxis behavior has focused on the phenotypic characterization of chemotactic responses in an *in vitro* environment, based on assays (drop plate, swarn plate, and capillary assay) that have been used successfully for qualitative determination of chemotaxis (Shonnard *et al.*, 1992; Armitage *et al.*, 1997). Further, it has been suggested that the development of assays for quantification of chemotactic response may bring a significant improvement in the determination of chemotactic behavior as well as the development of bioremediation technology (Pedit *et al.*, 2002). The development of assays for qualitative and quantitative chemotactic responses is expected to improve the *in situ* bioremediation methods significantly. It is being realized that the distribution of chemotaxis-related genetic elements is much wider than initially expected (Li *et al.*, 2007).

Biofilm

Formation of a 'biofilm' is one of the adaptive responses that can be successfully implemented for *in situ* bioremediation process (Johnsen and Karlson, 2004). Most of the organisms release a slimy material, which gets adhered to a matrix or substrate. This slimy coating is identified as 'microbial biofilm' (Costerton *et al.*, 1999; Guerrero *et al.*, 2002). Initial studies have indicated the role of microbial biofilms in microbial pathogenesis, wherein biofilms were reported to act for bacterial survival against the host's defense mechanism (Gristina and Costerton, 1985; Passerini *et al.*, 1992). However, later, this phenomenon was found to be associated with *in situ* microbial activities (Ward *et al.*, 2006). Microbes adhere to the environmental surfaces, and their association with these surfaces involves the synthesis of extracellular homo- or heteropolymers of sugars called exopolysaccharides (EPS). These extracellular polymers are fabricated and extended from the cells to the surfaces in a very organized manner forming a tangled and channelized network of polymeric fibres (Potera, 1996). The whole assemblage including the resident microbes and the channelized network of the EPS is termed *Biofilm*. Because of its polyelectrolyte nature, the microbial biofilms are highly absorptive and can collect significant quantities of silt, clay hydrocarbons and other detritus from their immediate environment (Characklis and Cooksey, 1983). Thus, their unique physical, biological and chemical properties make them a very useful tool for environment cleanliness. Hence, the microbial biofilms are implicated in the natural and modulated environmental cleanliness systems for purification of the drinking water, detoxification of the oil spills, removal of heavy metals and biodegradation of the hazardous xenobiotics in the contaminated waters and the soils, as well as environmental monitoring biosensor fabrications (Capone and Bauer, 1992; Brayers, 1993).

Biosurfactants

Another microbial feature that has been identified to strongly influence the *in situ* bioremediation of chemical and metal pollutants is the 'production of biosurfactants'. Biosurfactants are microbial-derived surface active agents that can lower surface and interfacial tension of liquids (Georgiou *et al.*, 1992). The word surfactant is a contraction of SURFace ACTive AgeNT. Biosurfactants are produced by a variety of microorganisms belonging to *Pseudomonas* sp., *Flavobacterium* sp., *Bacillus* sp., *Rhodococcus*, *Nocardia*, *Corynebacterium*, *Candida*, *Mycobacterium* and *Arthrobacte*r (Bodour *et al.*, 2003). They are amphiphilic molecules with hydrophilic and hydrophobic domains, thereby facilitating the uptake of hydrocarbons into living cells. Owing to their surface active properties, microbial surfactants can accumulate at interfaces, form micelles, lower surface tension, and enhance the solubilization of poorly soluble compounds in water (Kuiper *et al.*, 2004).

1. Bioavailability enhancement mechanism using biosurfactants

The mechanism of PAHs bioavailability enhancement using surfactants is as follows:

(a) direct uptake of the PAH from the partial micelle (Fig. 11.6A)
(b) uptake for PAH from aqueous phase after release from partial micelle (Fig. 11.6B)
(c) facilitated direct uptake of PAH via cell-surfactant- PAH contact (Fig. 11.6C)
(d) hypothesized non-micellular biosurfactant enhancement of PAH solubilization (Fig. 11.6D) (Schippers *et al.*, 2000).

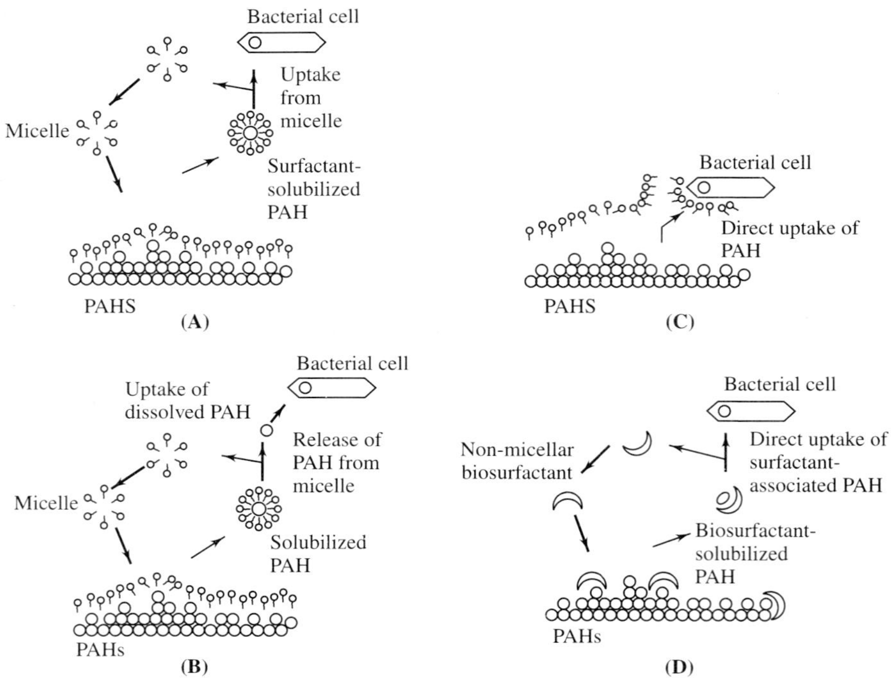

Fig. 11.6 Biosurfactant's mechanism enhancing the bioavailability of PAH (adapted from Ivey, 2000).

Genetically Modified Bioremediators

Biotechnology can transfer the ability to manufacture detoxifying proteins from one type of organism to another. One organism that was so modified has earned the distinction of being the first microorganism to be patented. Called the "oil-eater," the microorganism was actually a naturally occurring bacterium that had been given four plasmids, which were also naturally occurring. It was the combination of the four transferred plasmids in a single bacterial cell that was novel and therefore patent-worthy. The four plasmids in the oil-eater gave the bacterium the ability to degrade four components of crude oil. It was invented by Ananda Chakrabarty at General Electric in 1980 (Drobnik, 1999).

Today, transgenic technology creates designer bioremediators. A transgenic organism contains a gene from another type of organism in all of its cells. The altered organism then manufactures the protein that the transgene encodes. The technology works because all organisms use the same genetic code. In other words, the same DNA and RNA triplets encode the same amino acids in all species.

The use of Genetically Engineered Microorganisms (GEMs) is being considered for *in situ* bioremediation. Applications of genetically engineered microorganisms (GEM) in bioremediation have received a great deal of attention, but have largely been confined to laboratory environments. This has been due to regulatory risk assessment concerns and to a large extent the uncertainty of their practical impact and delivery under field conditions. There are at least four principal approaches to GEM development for bioremediation application. These include:

(1) modification of enzyme specificity and affinity;

(2) pathway construction and regulation;

Table 11.1 Microbial strains which have undergone modification of bioremediation pathways. (Junker *et al.*, 2001)

Genetic Engineering for Biodegradation of Contaminants

Microorganism	*Modification*	*Contaminants*
Pseudomonas sp. B 13	pathway	mono/dichlorobenzoates
P. putida	pathway	4-ethylbenzoate
P. putida KT2442	pathway	toluene/benzoate
Pseudomonas sp. FR1	pathway	chloro-,methylbenzoates
C. testosteroni VP44	substrate specificity	o-, p-monochlorobiphenyls
Pseudomonas sp. LB 400	substrate specificity	PCB
E. coil JM 109 (pSHF1003)	substrate specificity	PCB, benzene, toluene
P. pseudoalcealigenes KF707-D2	substrate spedificity	TCE, toluene, benzene
E. coil FM5/pKY287	regulation	TCE, toluene

(3) bioprocess development, monitoring, and control; and

(4) bioaffinity bioreporter sensor applications for chemical sensing, toxicity reduction and end point analysis.

The development of effective and cost-efficient bioremediation processes is the goal of environmental biotechnology. The combination of microbiological and ecological knowledge, biochemical mechanisms, and field engineering designs are essential elements for successful *in situ* bioremediation using GEM. (Viswanthan, 1999).

Many microbial strains have been identified for biodegradation of contaminants, with slight modification done in their metabolism pathway (Table 11.1). One of the earliest genetically modified microbial strain is *Pseudomonas flourescens,* which is studied extensively. *Pseudomonas stutzeri, Escherichia coli,* and other species of *Pseudomonas* are studied extensively for their ability to mutate in accordance to their living environment. These microbes are considered potential for genetic engineering. The TOL plasmid pathway of *Pseudomonas putida* has been manipulated extensively to expand its catabolic capability on different branched compounds. Ramos *et al.* (1987) modified the TOL metabolic pathway to use 4-ethylbenzoate as a substrate. These restructured strains were mutants isolated by either altering a pathway regulator XylS (Ramos *et al.*, 1986) or by modifying substrate specificity of enzymes (catechol-2, 3-dioxygenase). A WbpL mutant of *Pseudomonas putida* DOT-T1E strain, which lacks the O-antigenic side chain of lipopolysaccharides, was found to be tolerant to a number of toxic compounds, including chelating agents, organic acids, detergents, and aromatic hydrocarbons (Junker *et al.*, 2001).

However, the deliberate release of GEMs in the environment is a subject of great concern. This has led to the construction of biological contaminants system by which bacteria are killed in a controlled suicide process. The use of GEMs took a long time before actually being implemented due to the fear of accidental release, unintended effect, and potential human hazard. This led to the search of naturally occurring bacterial strains that could perform some of the, if not all, biodegradation that would ultimately lead to the bioremediation of the contaminants (Viswanathan, 1999).

Abiotic Factors

Abiotic factors play an important role in the majority of environmental phenomena (Jia *et al.*, 2005). The metabolic reaction involved in the bioremediation of hydrocarbons also follows the principle of 'enzyme catalysis', and therefore they exhibit optimal performance only over a very narrow range of physico-chemical parameters.

Temperature

Biodegradation of hydrocarbons can occur over a wide range of temperatures. Many psychrotrophic, mesophilic, and thermophilic hydrocarbon-utilizing microorganisms have been isolated. In an earlier study, Zo Bell (1973) and Traxler (1973) reported hydrocarbon degradation below 0°C. On the other hand, Klug and Markovetz (1967) and Mateles *et al.* (1967) reported hydrocarbon degradation at 70°C. Mulkins-Philips and Stewart (1974) found that 9 months after the spillage of Bunker C fuel oil into Chedabucto Bay, the bacterial population isolated from contaminated areas showed rates of degradation at 5°C, which were 21 to 70% less during 14 days of incubation than during 7 days at 10°C. Atlas and Bartha (1973) found that higher number of hydrocarbon utilizers capable of growth at 5°C were present in Raritan Bay, N.J., during winter than other seasons. The evidence suggests a seasonal shift to a microbial community capable of low temperature hydrocarbon degradation.

Atlas and Bartha (1973) also found that the effects of temperature differ, depending on the hydrocarbon composition of a petroleum mixture. Low temperature retards the rates of volatilization of low molecular weight hydrocarbons, some of which are toxic to microorganisms. The presence of such toxic components was found to delay the onset of oil biodegradation at low temperatures (Atlas *et al.*, 1973). At 20°C, lighter oils had greater abiotic losses and were more susceptible to biodegradation than heavier oils. Rates of oil mineralization for the heavier oils were significantly lower at 20°C than for the lighter ones. The light crude oils, however, had toxic volatile components that evaporated only slowly, inhibiting microbial degradation of these oils at 10°C. A significant lag phase before the onset of biodegradation was found for the lighter oils. No toxic volatile fractions associated with the heavy oils were tested. Paraffinic, aromatic and asphaltic fractions were also subjected to biodegradation.

Nutrients

When considering an oil slick, there is a mass of carbon available for microbial growth within a limited area. Since microorganisms require nitrogen and phosphorus for incorporation into biomass, the availability of these nutrients within the same area as the hydrocarbon is critical. The rates of diffusion may be inadequate to supply sufficient nitrogen and phosphorus to establish optimal C/N and C/P ratios for microbial growth and metabolism. Researchers examining the fate of large oil spills have thus concluded in many cases that concentrations of N and P are limiting with respect to rates of hydrocarbon biodegradation.

Ward and Brock (1976) reported that during summer nutrient deficiencies limited oil biodegradation in temperate lakes. Higher rates of oil biodegradation could be obtained by the addition of nitrogen and phosphorus.

Atlas and Bartha (1973) have described an oleophilic nitrogen and phosphorus fertilizer, which could overcome limitations of nitrogen and phosphorus, stimulating petroleum biodegradation. The fertilizer consisting of paraffinized urea and octylphosphate supported degradation of oil. Optimal C/N and C/P ratios were 10:1 and 100:1, respectively. Dibble and Bartha (1979) studied the effect of landfarming i.e., disposal by biodegradation in soil of oily sludges generated in the refining of crude oil, and found that oil sludge biodegradation was optimal at a soil water-holding capacity of 30-90%, a pH of 7.5 to 7.8, temperature above 20°C, a C/N ratio of 60:1, and a C/P ratio of 800:1. These studies indicate that rates of nutrient replenishment are generally inadequate to support rapid biodegradation of large quantities of oil. The nitrogen and phosphorus containing fertilizers can be used to stimulate microbial hydrocarbon degradation.

Physical State of Oil Pollutants

The physical state of petroleum hydrocarbons has a marked effect on their biodegradation. The degree of spreading of the oil spill determines in parts the surface area of oil available for microbial colonization by hydrocarbon degrading microorganisms (Berridge *et al.*, 1968). The degree of spreading is reduced at low temperatures because of the viscosity of the oil. In soils, petroleum hydrocarbons are absorbed by plant materials and soil particles, limiting its spreading.

Liquid aromatic hydrocarbons are utilized by bacteria at the water-hydrocarbon surface, whereas solid aromatic hydrocarbons are not metabolized. At 30°C, diphenylmethane is a liquid and can be degraded easily, but at 20°C, it is in a solid form and cannot be utilized by *Pseudomonas* sp. Similarly, naphthalene cannot be utilized in the solid form, but can be utilized if dissolved in liquid hydrocarbon (Wodzinsky *et al.*, 1977).

Availability of increased surface area accelerates biodegradation (Gatellier, 1971). Hydrocarbon degrading microorganisms can be observed growing over the entire surface of an oil droplet; growth does not appear to occur within the oil droplets.

After extensive weathering, petroleum hydrocarbons often occur in the environment as tar balls, becoming quite resistant to microbial degradation. The surface area-to-volume ratio of a tar ball is not favourable for microbial growth. Tar balls often accumulate on areas where microbial activities are limited by available water, which is needed to support microbial growth and enzymatic hydrocarbon-degrading activities. Thus, dissolution and emulsification of hydrocarbons appear to have positive effects on degradation rates.

Salinity and Pressure

These two factors are specific features of particular ecosystems such as saline lakes and deep seas (high hydrostatic pressure), which represent specialized environment where petroleum contamination can occur.

Ward and Brock (1978) have examined hydrocarbon degradation in hypersaline environments. When hydrocarbons were added to natural samples of various salinities (ranging from 3.3 to 28.4%) from salt evaporation ponds of Great Salt Lake, Utah, rates of metabolism of these compounds decreased with increase in the salinity. Microorganisms in saline waters containing more than 20% of salinity could not use mineral oil as a sole source of carbon and energy, thus proving that biodegradation is not possible in hyper-saline environment.

Schwarz *et al.* (1975) examined the growth and utilization of hydrocarbons at ambient and *in situ* pressure for deep sea bacteria, which was found to be significantly less than the rates found under the conditions of ambient temperatures and atmospheric pressure. It appears that oil, which enters deep ocean environments, will be degraded very slowly and persist for long.

Oxygen

The reports of the existence of microorganisms, which are capable of anaerobic hydrocarbon metabolism in nature, have been provided by many researchers, including the reports of some microorganisms that are capable of alkane dehydrogenation (Chouteau *et al.*, 1962; Iizuka *et al.*, 1969). These microorganisms have an enzymatic mechanism, which permits the addition of water across the double bond, forming a secondary alcohol, and therefore permitting anaerobic growth. In the case of *Pseudomonas* strain studied by Senez and Azoulay (1961), the organisms consumed oxygen while growing on heptane, even though it had an *n*-heptane dehydrogenase enzyme.

Hambrick *et al.* (1980) found that at pH values of 5 and 8, mineralization of hydrocarbons in estuarine sediments was highly dependent on oxygen availability. The rates of hydrocarbon degradation decreased with decreasing oxygen reduction potential, i.e., with increasing anaerobiosis. They concluded that hydrocarbons would persist in reduced sediments for longer periods of time than in aerated surface layers. The importance of oxygen in hydrocarbon degradation is indicated by the fact that the major degradative pathways for both the saturated and aromatic hydrocarbons involve oxygenases and molecular oxygen. The theoretical oxygen demand is 3.5 g of oil oxidized per gm of oxygen (Floodgate, 1976).

MECHANISM OF *IN SITU* BIOREMEDIATION

Petroleum is an extremely complex mixture of hydrocarbons. Among the hundreds of individual components, several classes, based on related structures, can be recognized. Studies have been performed to determine the metabolic pathways for degradation of these compounds, and there have been a number of reviews on this subject (Donoghue *et al.*, 1976; Foster, 1962; Gibson, 1968; Hopper, 1978).

Hydrocarbon Structure and Biodegradation

The structure of a hydrocarbon compound plays an important role in its biodegradation. The n-alkanes (straight chain) and n-alkyl-aromatics (substituted aromatic) in the C_{10} to C_{22} range are considered to be of low toxicity and most biodegradable (Bossert and Bartha, 1984). Hydrocarbons above C_{22} have lower toxicity and are generally considered less biodegradable due to their physical characteristics, which include low water solubility, sorption onto surfaces, and a solid to semi-solid state at 35°C.

Compounds in the C_1 to C_4 range are gaseous and considered to be biodegradable, but this is not the typical mechanism employed to remove them. Counterparts in the C_5 to C_9 range have high solvent-membrane toxicity to microorganisms, but in low concentration they are considered to be easily biodegradable.

Branched n-alkanes and cyclo-alkanes are less biodegradable as their tertiary and quaternary carbon atoms inhibit the β-oxidation step required for degradation. Aromatic hydrocarbons are biodegradable, but the bioavailability of high molecular weight compounds such as PAH's decreases dramatically as the number of condensed rings increases. These compounds exhibiting lower biodegradability due to surface absorption and low solubility are commonly referred to as recalcitrants or xenobiotics.

1. N-alkane

The biological degradation pathway for n-alkane (straight chain) and branched alkanes has been well established and reported extensively in literature. The biodegradation pathway for n-alkane is shown below (Grubbs & Molnaa, 1987).

Typically, the degradation pathway (Fig. 11.7) consists of the following steps:

- Initial enzyme catalyzed oxidation to produce primary fatty alcohol
- Sequential oxidation of the alcohol to fatty acid
- Oxidation of the β-carbon to produce a ß-keto acid
- Decarboxylation to produce a degraded alkane

Clearly all resultant intermediates in this mineralization process should possess a low to very low toxicity, since only naturally occurring fatty acids are being produced.

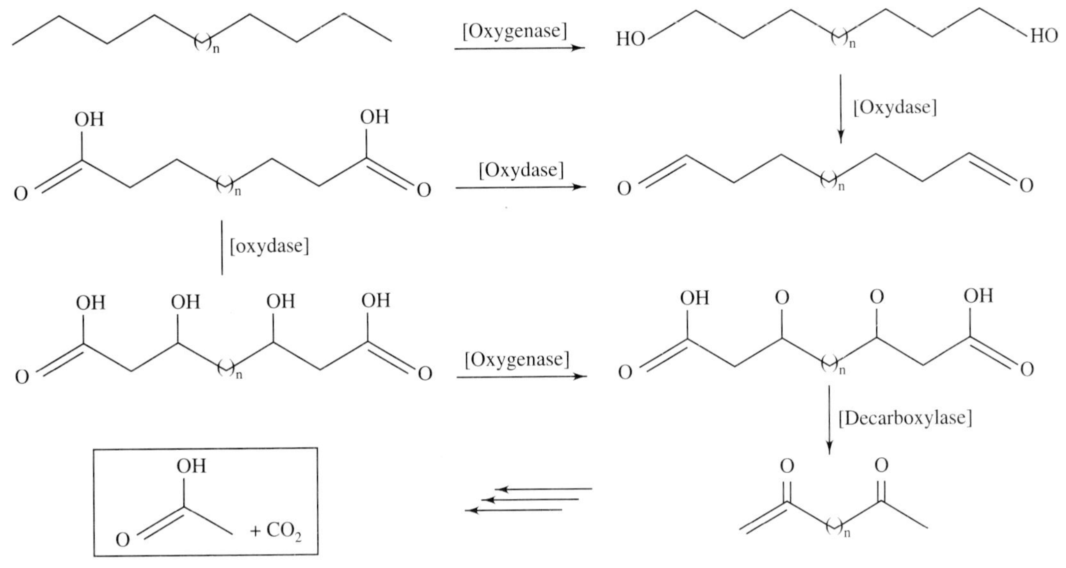

Fig. 11.7 Degradation pathway of n-alkane (adapted from Ivey, 2000).

2. *Cyclic alkanes*

Even though cyclic alkanes are very similar in structure to n-alkanes, their biodegradation pathway appears to be fundamentally different (Fig. 11.8).

Although not fully characterized, it has been reported that the following steps are required (Bartha, 1986):

- Sequential enzyme mediated oxidation of the ring to form a cycloalkanone
- Baeyer-Villiger type oxidation of the cyclic ketone by an as yet uncharacteristic second oxygenase enzyme to produce a lactone
- Hydrolysis, resulting in ring fission, to generate what amounts to an oxidized n-alkyl fatty acid that can be further degraded by the mechanism outlined in the n-alkane pathway.

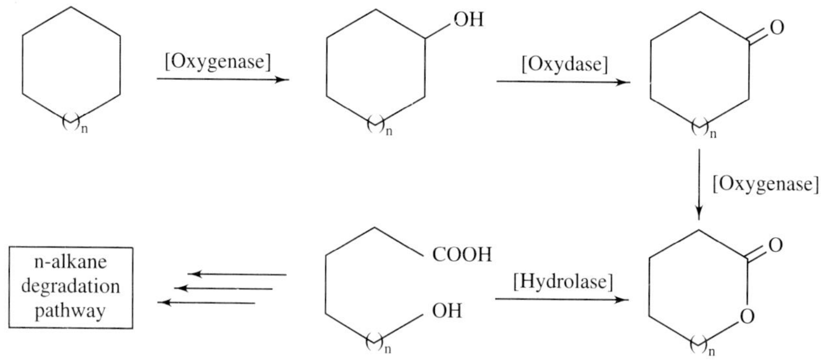

Fig. 11.8 Biodegradation pathway for cyclic alkanes (adapted from Bartha, 1986).

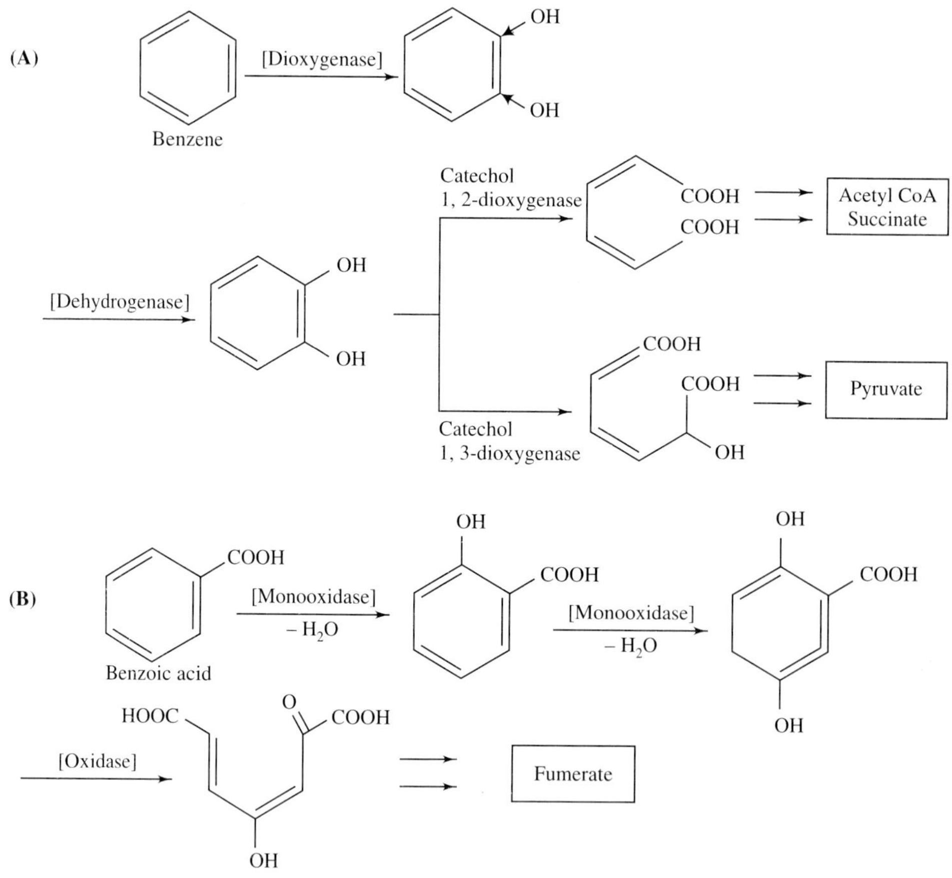

Fig. 11.9 Biodegradation of simple aromatics, **(A)** the catechol pathway, and **(B)** the gentisate pathway (adapted from Leisinger and Burner, 1987).

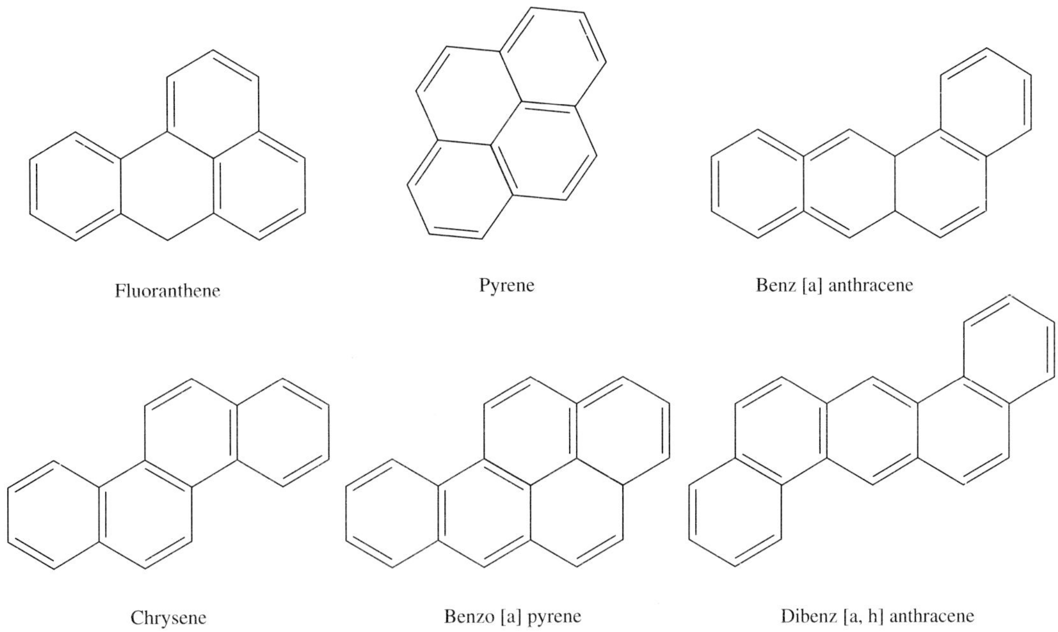

Fig. 11.10 Typical high molecular weight PAH compounds (adapted from Ivey, 2000).

3. Aromatics

Simple aromatic or "benzenoid type" compounds generally pose no resistance to microbial degradation for a large variety of microorganisms (Fewson, 1981). The key factor in the degradation of aromatic compounds by these ring fission enzymes is their ability to destroy the resonance contained within the ring. This can be accomplished, however, only by the initial positioning of at least two hydroxyl groups, either ortho or para, relative to each other.

The biodegradation of aromatic compounds (Fig. 11.9) proceeds via two well-established pathways: (a) catechol and b) gentisate (Leisinger & Burner, 1987). In both the pathways, ring activation is followed by ring cleavage and the subsequent transformation of the fission products.

The degradation of substituted aromatics, such as ethyl-benzene and toluene, would also proceed via an analogous pathway. These products, once generated, would then follow a similar microbial mineralization as outlined in the n-alkane pathway.

4. Polycyclic aromatic hydrocarbons (PAH)

Polycyclic aromatic hydrocarbons (PAHs) are organic compounds with multiple benzene rings. PAHs are typical components of asphalts, fuels, oils, and greases. They are also called polynuclear aromatic hydrocarbons. The bacterial degradation of PAHs with more than three rings (Fig. 11.10), often referred to as high molecular weight (HMW) PAHs, is often challenging to be mineralized by microorganisms. This is related to their low solubility and high affinity to solid surfaces and organic liquids, which generally limits their bioavailability to the microorganisms present in soils (Ortega-Calvo, 2004). Surfactant-enhanced bioremediation of soils containing low soluble hydrocarbons is a promising biodegradation technique (Jaffe, 2000).

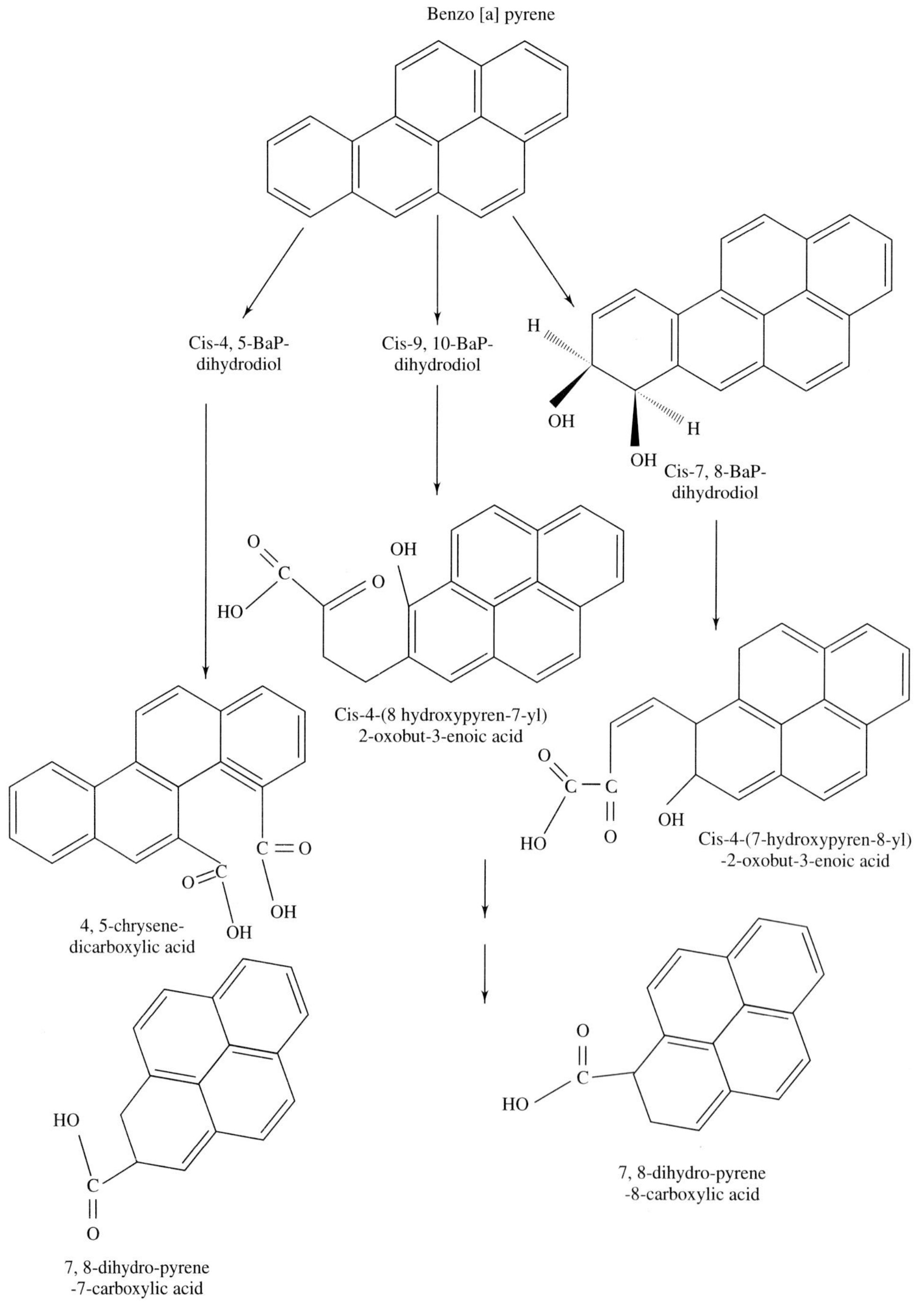

Fig. 11.11 Biodegradation pathway for Benzo[a] pyrene (adapted from Ivey, 2000).

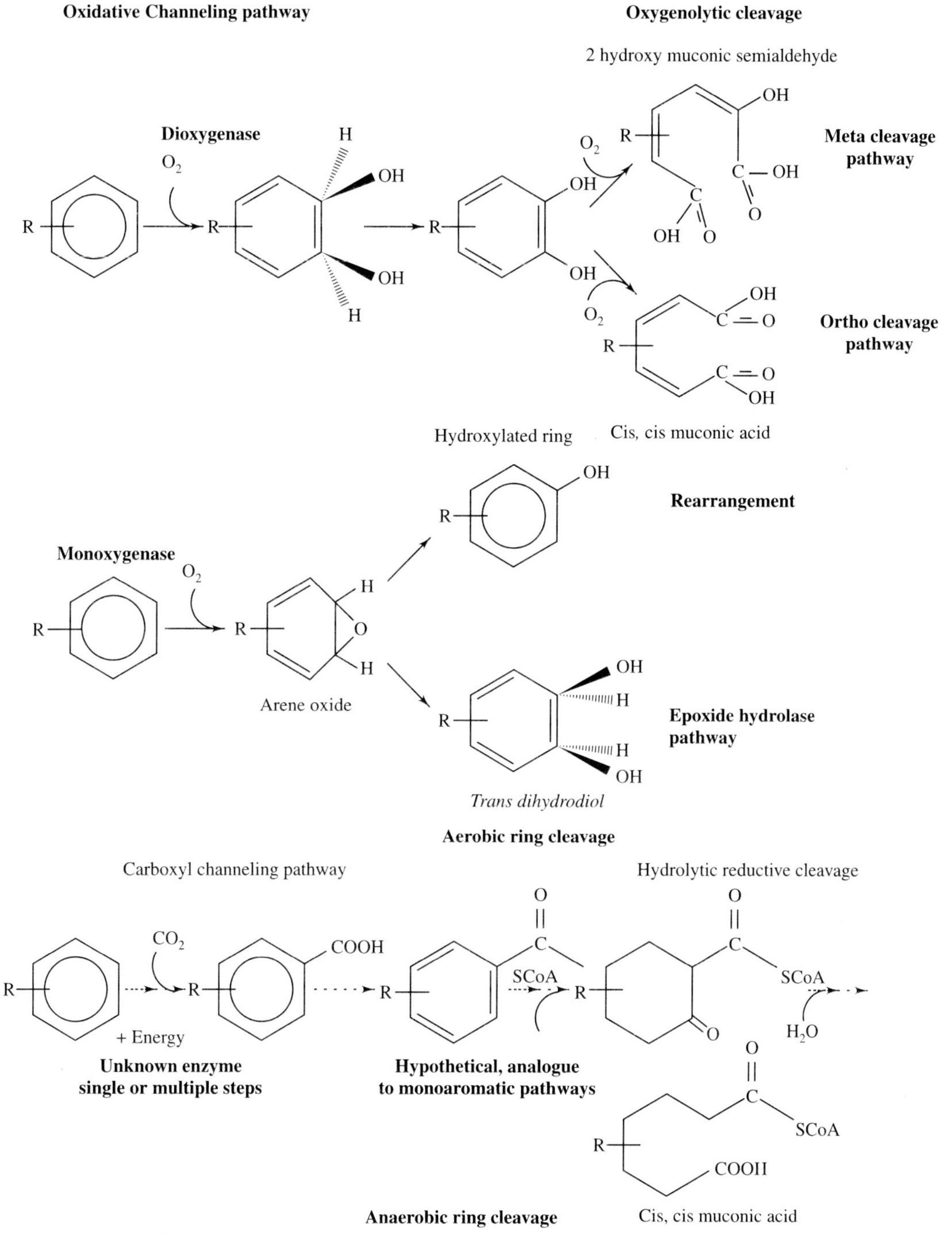

Fig. 11.12 Aerobic and anaerobic ring cleavage.

The biodegradation of high molecular weight PAH aromatic compounds has been well described (Meckenstock *et al.*, 2002). The initial step in the aerobic catabolism of a PAH molecule occurs via oxidation of a PAH to a dihydrodiol (Fig. 11.11) by a multi-component enzyme system. The dihydrodiol intermediates may then proceed through either an ortho cleavage type pathway or a meta cleavage pathway, leading to central intermediates such as protocatechuates and catechols, which are further converted to tricarboxylic acid cycle intermediates (van der Meer *et al.*, 1992). The mechanism for PAH ring cleavage under aerobic and anaerobic conditions has been described (Fig. 11.12).

MONITORING *IN SITU* BIOREMEDIATION

The efficiency of most of the *in situ* bioremediation processes has been evacuated in the form of time dependent and endpoint measurement of complete disappearance of the target pollutant(s) (Hageman *et al.*, 2004). Approaches to monitoring and verifying enhanced *in situ* biodegradation have included measurement of changes over time in the (a) concentration of hydrocarbons, (b) temperature, (c) number of hydrocarbon degrading microorganisms, (d) ratio of fast degrading hydrocarbons, and (e) metabolic intermediates. Measurements of oxygen consumption over time and elevated carbon dioxide concentrations in soil gas have been used as indicators of hydrocarbon degradation. One method to substantiate biodegradation is to measure stable carbon isotope ratios in the soil gas, carbon dioxide. Stable carbon isotope ratio analysis is inexpensive and commercially available. Carbon dioxide produced by hydrocarbon degradation may be distinguished from that produced by other processes based on carbon isotopic compositions characteristic of the source material and/or fractionation accompanying microbial metabolism (Aggrawal *et al.*, 1991). A measurement of the stable carbon isotope ratios ($\delta^{13}C$) of microbial metabolic end products presents a promising method for monitoring *in situ* bioremediation of petroleum hydrocarbons. Differences between the $\delta^{13}C$ values of hydrocarbons and indigenous carbon sources (e.g., plant matter, soil carbonates) can be exploited to trace the origins of metabolic end products. However, in zones of methanogenesis and/or where the $\delta^{13}C$ values of endogenous plant matter overlap those of hydrocarbons, $\delta^{13}C$ measurements can produce ambiguous results. In such cases, simultaneous measurement of the radiocarbon (^{14}C) contents of metabolic end products can be used to determine their sources (Conrad *et al.*, 1997).

Organisms that are capable of utilizing benzene, toluene, ethylbenzene, xylene, alkanes and polycyclic aromatic hydrocarbons have been studied extensively and their mechanism of compounds degradation has been elucidated. Knowledge of the metabolic pathways used by anaerobic bacteria to break down hydrocarbon has allowed identifying unique intermediate compounds that can be used as biomarkers for *in situ* activity. One of these intermediates is 2-methlybenzylsuccinate, the product of fumarate addition to o-xylene by the enzyme responsible for toluene utilization. This compound has been found to be a reliable indicator of anaerobic toluene degradation. Field studies have confirmed that the biomarker is detectable in field samples and its distribution corresponds to areas where active biodegradation is predicted. For naphthalene, three biomarkers have been identified [2-naphthoic acid (2-NA), tetrahydro-2-NA, and hexahydro-2-NA] which can be used in the field to identify areas of active *in situ* degradation (Phelps and Young, 2005).

The potential of functional gene array analysis to monitor changes in the amount of functional marker genes as indicators of PAH's biodegradation has also been investigated. A prototype functional gene array has been developed for targeting key functions in the biodegradation of naphthalene, toluene and xylenes. Internal standard probe based normalization was introduced to facilitate comparison across multiple samples. Coupled with one-colour hybridization, the signal normalization improved the consistency among replicate hybridizations resulting in better discrimination for the differences in the amount of target DNA. During the naphthalene biodegradation in a PAH-contaminated soil slurry microcosm, the normalized hybridization signals in naphthalene catabolic gene probes were shown to be in good agreement with the amount of naphthalene-degradation genes and the production of $^{14}CO_2$. Gene arrays provide efficient means for the monitoring of contaminant biodegradation in the environment (Nyyssonen *et al.*, 2007).

One more technique that has proved to be a good predictor of monitoring the rate of biodegradation is push-pull test. In a push-pull test, reactants along with a conservative tracer are injected or "pushed" into a well (petroleum reservoir) and allowed to incubate for a prescribed length of time. Samples are then withdrawn or "pulled" from the same well as a function of time. Analytes are measured in the extracted water to determine breakthrough curves for each compound under investigation and interpretations are made relative to the unreactive tracer. Breakthrough curves for the reactants, products, and the tracer can then be used to calculate mass balances and ultimately the biotransformation rates. While quantifying the loss of parent hydrocarbon and formation of the daughter metabolite, a conservative *in situ* rate constant can be delineated (Ollivier *et al.*, 2000).

The kinetics based *in situ* hydrocarbon bioremediation has been considerably aided by advancements in different analytical methods such as atomic absorption spectroscopy (AAS), colorimetry, inductively coupled plasma atomic emission spectroscopy (ICP-AES), polarography, selective ion electrodes, X-ray fluorescence, energy dispersive analysis via X-rays (EDAX), and electron microprobe analysis etc to simple field portable instruments. The current TPH detection systems are generally limited to spectrophotometric chemical test kits. These offer the convenience of field analysis but have several important limitations such as speciation is not achieved, only total content is determined, chemical and physical interferences to measured signal can be dramatic, still require a high degree of user competence. Thus, data are poor to determine trends in pollution and to contribute to a proper risk assessment. A more attractive approach should accomplish for a proper solution of the above limitations to implement the advanced analytical techniques to monitor the *in situ* bioremediation of hydrocarbons.

The effective monitoring of microbial bioremediation under *in situ* conditions is rather poor because in many cases the decrease in pollutant concentration may be observed as an outcome of absorbance of the pollutant to the environment matrix. The majority of methods for pollutants extraction from the environmental samples are based on the chemical nature of the target pollutant(s). On the basis of the chemical nature of the extraction treatment, the methods may be classified as organic solvent extraction, chemical-oxidation extraction, super fluid extraction and aqueous sample extraction (Semple *et al.*, 2007). These workers have recently provided a comprehensive data of the different extraction methods indicating their functional classification, target contamination, working principle, weaknesses and strengths. The recent studies indicate that efficient pollutant extraction target the physio-chemical nature (soil adsorption, hydrophobic, water solubility, etc.) of the pollutant for developing efficient extraction methods (Szolar *et al.*, 2004). Advancement in the technological methods for qualitative and quantitative estimation of chemical pollutants and their speciation, along with improvement in the extraction methods, has led to efficient and accurate pollutants degradation kinetics. Further development in these techniques would lead to increased success of *in situ* bioremediation.

ASSESSMENT OF ECOTOXICITY OF PETROLEUM HYDROCARBONS

An ideal bioremediation process should result in overall reduction of ecotoxicity of the target environment on its completion. Most of the initial *in situ* bioremediation processes did not perform the ecotoxicity test of the target pollutants. Initially, the term 'ecotoxicity' was used to explain the hazardous effect of chemicals on different diversity of life and environment (Migliore *et al.*, 1996). Later it was used with respect to the hazardous environmental and industrial samples (e.g., industrial effluent samples etc.) (Baun *et al.*, 2008). It is mandatory to measure the toxic effects of the hazardous pollutants on the members of different levels of trophic chain i.e., producer (blue green algae), primary consumers (crustaceans, amphibians etc.), secondary consumers (fishes) and microorganisms (Licht *et al.*, 1996). Alternative approach selects one specific organism rather than assessing the toxicity on diversity of microorganisms. One good example is luminescent bacteria viz. *V. fisheri*. These methods detect the comparative quantitation of bioluminescence in the presence and absence of test pollutants (Richardson and Johnson, 1993). Some other alternative methods to assess the ecotoxicity are the use of some animal models like amphibian larva, arthropods and shrimps. Most biological assays used chronic fish test, acute crustacean test and fish 96hLC50 test to monitor the toxicity of the target pollutants. In an experiment, Salanitro *et al.* (1997) used earthworm and plant toxicity as assessment parameters for assessing the levels of TPH. Hydrocarbon bioremediation in artificially weathered oily soils usually followed first-order removal rates in which 50-75% and 10-90% of the total petroleum hydrocarbons (TPH) were degraded in 3-4 months for the low and high organic soils, respectively. Gas chromatographic profiles (simulated boiling point distillation of saturates and aromatic compounds) showed that after bioremediation, hydrocarbons in oily soils decreased from 70 to 90%, 40 to 60%, and 35 to 60% for those carbon number species in the range of $C_{11} - C_{22}$, $C_{23} - C_{32}$, and $C_{35} - C_{44}$, respectively. Genetically modified microbial (GMM) biosensors have been used as good agents for soil ecotoxicity. The advantages of using genetically modified microbial (GMM) biosensors for soil ecotoxicity testing include their sensitivity and speed of detection. The potential of GMM biosensors involving its *lux* gene reporting of overall metabolic activity of *Pseudomonas fluorescens* and *Rhizobium leguminosarum* biovar. *trifolii* for soil ecotoxicity testing has been observed (Paton *et al.,* 1997).

Advantages of Bioremediation

- Minimal exposure of on site workers to the contaminant
- Long-term protection of public health
- The cheapest among all methods of pollutant removal
- The process can be done on site with a minimum amount of space and equipment
- Eliminates the need to transport hazardous material
- Uses natural process
- Transforms pollutants instead of simply moving them from one media to another
- Performs the degradation in an acceptable time frame

Disadvantages: Potential Problems

- Poor management
- Unable to estimate the length of time it's going to take, it may vary from site. It can take a few months to as long as a few years.
- Not all organic compounds are biodegradable

CONCLUSION

The quest for a cheap source of energy coupled with the extensive rate of industrialization has expanded the frontiers of petroleum hydrocarbon exploration with its unavoidable negative consequence, i.e., the pollution of the environment. Oil or fuel can harm the marine environment by smothering marine life or acting as a toxin to both marine and coastal flora and fauna. It can also bioaccumulate in organisms and thus affect organisms higher in the food chain. Sea animals and birds can be harmed when their feathers or fur are coated with oil. Chemical contaminants within the oil can also impair reproduction in sea animals and birds. When petroleum spills on the soil, it quickly migrates into the groundwater causing pollution of local groundwater by organics, threatens the safety of potable water, limits the use of groundwater, causes enormous economic loss and ecological disaster and also affects agricultural production. Several remediation alternatives have been in use for the restoration of polluted systems. Bioremediation, which exploits the biodegradative abilities of live organisms and/or their products, has proven to be the preferred alternative in the long-term restoration of petroleum hydrocarbon polluted niche, with the added advantage of cost efficiency and environmental friendliness. Scientists have extended the scope of bioremediation by developing and cultivating microbes for use under varied conditions. Certain strains of microorganisms can digest highly poisonous materials such as dioxins, polychlorinated biphenyls, toluene, asphalt products and phenol. Bioremediation has successfully employed these microbes to eliminate petroleum contaminants and degrade them into carbon dioxide, water and salt. Due to possible risks associated with the release of these microorganisms into the environment, containment in this specialized area is necessary. At present, bioremediation is the method of choice because of economic and ecological concerns. It is, and will continue to expand and provide environmental engineers the cutting edge technology for treatment of petroleum contamination to clean-up the polluted environment.

REFERENCES

Aggarwal, P.K. and Hinchee, R.E. (1991). *Environ. Sci. Technol* **25** (**6**): 1178-1180.

AL-Saleh, E.S. and Obuekwe, C. (2005). *Intl. Biodeter. Biodegrad.* **56:** 1-7.

Armitage, J.P. and Schmitt, R. (1997). *Microbiology,* **143:** 3671-3682.

Atlas, R.M. and Bartha, R. (1973). *Environ. Pollut.* **4:** 291- 300.

Atlas, R.M. and Bartha, R.C. (1992). *Adv. Microbial. Ecol.* **12:** 287-338.

Atlas, R.N. (1981). *Microbiol. Rev.* **45:** 180-209.

Bartha, R. (1986). *Microbiol. Ecol.* **12:** 155-172.

Baun, A., Hartmann, N.B., Grieger, K. and Kusk, K.O. (2008). *Ecotoxicol.* **17**(**5**): 387-395.

Berridge, S.A., Dean, R.A., Fallows, R. and Fish, A. (1968). *In:* Scientific aspects of pollution of the sea by oil. (Ed. P. Hepple). Institute of Petroleum, London, pp. 2-11.

Bhushan, B., Samanta, S.K., Chauhan, A., Chakraborti, A.K. and Jain, R.K. (2000). *Biochem. Biophys. Res. Commun.* **275:** 129-133.

Bodour, A.A., Dress, K.P. and Maier, R.M. (2003). *Appl. Environ. Microbiol.* **69:** 3280-3287.

Bossert, I. and Bartha, R. (1984). *Petrol. Microbiol.*, MacMillan Publishing Co., New York.

Brayers, J.D. (1993). *J. Appl. Bacteriol.* **74:** 98-109.

Brown, D.W., Ramos, L.S., Fiedman, A.J. and Macleod, W.D. (1969). *In: Trace organic analysis: a new frontier in analytical chemistry.* Special Publication no. 519. Natural Bureau of Standards. Washington D.C. pp. 161-169.

Brusseau, M.L., Sabatini, D. and Gierke, J. (1999). Introduction in: Innovative Subsurface Remediation: Field Testing of Physical, Chemical, and Characterization Technologies, (Eds. Brusseau ML, Sabatini DA, Gierke JS and Annable MD), *American Chemical Society*, Washington DC.

Capone, D.G. and Bauer, J.M. (1992). *Environ. Microbiol.* 191-237.

Characklis, W.G. and Cooksey, K.E. (1983). *Adv. Appl. Microbiol.* **29:** 93-138.

Chouteau, J., Azoulay, E. and Senez, J.C. (1962). *Nature* (London). **194:** 576-578.

Conrad, M.E., Paul, D.F., Fischer, M.L., Buchanan, B.B., Leighton, T. and Kashgarian, M. (1997). *Environ. Sci. Technol.* **31(5):** 1463-1469.

Cook, S.V., Chu, A. and Goodman, R.H. (2002). *Water, Air and Soil Poll.* **133:** 297-314.

Costerton, J.W., Stewart, P.S. and Greenberg, E.P. (1999). *Science* **284:** 1318-1322.

Cunningham, C.J. and Philip, J.C. (2000). Comparison of Bioaugmentation and Biostimulation in ex situ Treatment of Diesel Contaminated Soil, Land Contamination and Reclamation, University of Edinburgh, Scotland.

Díaz, E. (2008). Microbial Biodegradation: Genomics and Molecular Biology (1st ed.*)*. Caister Academic Press.

Dibble, J.T. and Bartha, R. (1976). *Soil Sci.* **158:** 58-60.

Donoghue, N.A., Griffin, M., Norris, D.G. and Trudgill, P.W. (1976). *Environ. Poll* **154(2):** 192-202.

Drobník, J. (1999). *Inl. Biodet. Biodeg.* **44(1):** 3-6.

EPA (1996). A Citizen's Guide to Bioremediation. *Solid Waste and Emergency Respons*e. (5102G).

EPA (2003). *Underground Storage Tanks*. www. epa. Gov /swerust1 /ustsystm /erpdoc.pdf

Etkin, D.S. and Welch, J.(1997). Proceedings of the 1997 International Oil Spills Conference. American Petroleum Institute. Washington DC: 949-952.

Faust, R.A. (1994). Toxicity summary for toluene Oak ridge reservation environmental restoration program.

Foster, J.W. (1962). *J. Microbiol. Serol.* **28:** 241- 274.

FRTR (2000). *In-situ BiologicalTreatment.* Remediation technologies screening matrix and reference guide, Version 4.0. Federal Remediation Technologies Roundtable.

Garcia-Blanco, S., Venosa, A.D., Suidan, M.T., Lee, K., Cobanli, S. and Haines, J.R. (2007). *Biodegradation.* **18:**1-15.

Gatellier CR (1971). *Chim. Ind.* (Paris). **104:** 2283-2289.

Georgiou, S., Lin, S.C. and Sharma, M.M. (1992). In: Abstract papers, 3rd European Congress of Biotechnology, *Verlagchemie Weinheim.* **1:** 79-83.

Gibson, D.T. (1968). *Science.* **161:** 1093-1097.

Goel, S.K., Rao, G.S. and Pandya, K.P. (1982). *Toxicol Lett.***14(3-4):**169-74.

Goldstein, R.J. (2008). Toxicity Hydrocarbons, eMedicine Specialties Pediatrics: Cardiac Disease and Critical Care Medicine.

Gordillo, F., Chávez, F.P. and Jerez, C.A. (2007). *FEMS Microbiol. Ecol.* **60(2):** 322-328.

Grady, F. (1985). *Biotechnol. Bioeng.* **27:** 660-671.

Grimm, A.C. and Harwood, C.S. (1997). *Appl. Environ. Microbiol.* **63:** 4111-4115.

Gristina, A.G. and Costerton, J.W. (1985). *J. Bone Joint Surg. Am.* **67(2 suppl A):** 264-273.

Grubbs, R.B. and Molnaa, B.A. (1987). *In-situ* Biological Treatment of Troublesome Organics, presented at Frensno Conference Centre, Frenso, California.

Guerrero, R., Piqueras, M. and Berlanga, M. (2002). *Int. Microbiol.* **5:** 177-188

Hageman, K.J., Field, J.A., Istok, J.D. and Semprini, L. (2004). *J. of Cont. Hydrol.* **75(3-4):** 281-296.

Hambrick, G.A, DeLaune, R. and Patrick, Jr. W.H. (1980). *Appl. Environ. Microbiol.* **40:** 365-369.

Hamdi, H., Benzarti, S., Manusadžianas, L., Aoyama, I. and Jedidi, N. (2007). *Soil Biol. Biochem.* **39 (8):** 1926-1935.

Head, I.M. and Swannell, R.P. (1999). *Curr. Opin. Biotechnol.* **10:** 234-239.

Hildebrandt, W.W. and Wilson, S.B. (1991). *J. Petrol. Techn*: 18-22.

Hyman, M. and Dupont, R.R. (2001). Groundwater and Soil Remediation. Process Design and Cost Estimating of Proven Technologies, ASCE Press.

Ivey, G.A. (2000). Surfactant Enhanced Remediation (SER) Using Ivey-sol® Surfactant Technology Improving Pump and Treatment, Bioremediation, Chemical Oxidation and Reduction Technologies.

Izuka, H., Ilida, M. and Fujita, S. (1969). *Z. Allg. Mikrobiol.* **9:** 223-226.

Jaffe, P.A. (2000). Assessment of Surfactant-Enhanced Bioremediation for Soils/Aquifers Containing PAH.

Jia, B.R., Zhou, G.S., Wang, F.Y., Wang, Y.H., Yuan, W. and Zhou, L. (2005). *Soil Biol. Biochem.* **38:** 653-660.

Johnsen, A.R. and Karlson, U. (2004). *Appl. Microbiol. Biotechnol.* **63(4):** 452-459.

Junker, F., Rodríguez-Herva, J.J., Duque, E., Ramos-González, M.I., Llamas, M. and Ramos, J.L. (2001). *Extremophiles.* **5:** 93-99.

Khan, A.G. (2007). *Methods in Biotechnol.* **23:** 89-97.

Khan, K., Naeem, M., Arshed, J. M. and Asif, M. (2006). *J. of Appl. Sci.* **6(10):** 2302-2306.

Klug, M.J. and Markovetz, A.J. (1967). *Nature* (London). **215:** 1082-1083.

Kuiper, I., Ellen, L., Lagendijk, R.P., Jeremy, P.D., Gerda, E.M.L., Jane, E.T., Ben, J.J.L. and Guido, V.B. (2004). *Mol. Microbiol.* **51(1):** 97-113.

Leisinger, T. and Burner, W. (1987). Poorly Degradable Substances, Mikrobiologisches Institute Eidgenossische Technische Hochschule, Zurich, Switzerland.

Levine, M.D. and Gresham, I.I.I.C. (2009). Toxicity Hydrocarbons, eMedicine Specialties.

Li, Y., Hu, Y., Fu, W., Xia, B. and Jin, C. (2007). *Biochem. Biophy. Res. Comm.* **360:** 863-867.

Licht, D., Ahring, B. and Arvin, E. (1996). *Biodegradation,* **7:** 83-90.

Lovely, P.S. and Dahlquist, F.W. (1975). *J. Theor. Biol.* **50:** 477-496.

Meckenstock, R.U., Morasch, B., Kästner, M., Vieth, A. and Richnow, H.H. (2002). *Water, Air and Soil Pollution: Focus* **2(3):** 141-152.

Migliore, L., Brambilla, G., Casoria, P., Civitareale, C., Cozzolino, S. and Gaudio, L. (1996). *Agri., Ecosys. & Env.* **60(2-3):** 121-128.

Mulkins- Philips, G.J. and Stewart, J.E. (1974). *Appl. Microbiol.* **28:** 915-922.

Nyyssönen, M., Piskonen, R. and Itävaara, M. (2008). *Environ. Poll.* **154:** 192-202.

Olaniran, A.O., Balgobind, A. and Pillay, B. (2009). *J. Env. Sci.* **21(5):** 661-666.

Ollivier, B., Magot, M. and Patel, B.K.C. (2005). *Antonie Leeuwenhoek.***77:** 103:116.

Ortega-Calvo, J.J. (2004). Microbial Physiology of PAH Biodegradation Under Bioavailability Restrictions.

Palmroth, M.R., Pichtel, J. and Puhakka, J.A. (2002). *Bioresour Technol.* **84(3):** 221-28.

Pandey, G. and Jain, R.K. (2002). *Appl. and Environ. Microbiol.* **68(12):** 5789-5795.

Parales, R. E., Ditty, J.L. and Harwood, C.S. (2000). *Appl. Environ. Microbiol.* **66:** 4098-4104.

Passerini, L., Lam, K., Costerton, J.W. and King, E.G. (1992). *Crit. Care Med.* **20:** 665-673.

Paton. G.I., Rattray. E.A.S., Campbell. C.D., Cresser. M.S., Glover. L.A., Meeussen. J.C.L. asnd Killham, K. (1997). *In:* Biological indicators of soil health and sustainable productivity. (Eds. Pankhurst, C., Doube, B., Gupta, V). CAB International, Wallingford. 397-418.

Pedit, J.A., Marx, R.B., Miller. C.B. and Aitken, M.D. (2002). *Biotechnol. Bioeng.* **78:** 626-634.

Pepper, I.A., Gentry, T.J., Newby, D.T., Roane, T.M. and Josephson, K.L. (2002). *Environ. Health Persp. Suppl.*110 (S6).

Potera, C. (1996). *Science* **273:** 1795-1797.

Richardson, G.E. and Johnson, B.E. (1993). *Semin. Oncol.* **20:** 105-127.

Roberts, E.R. (1998). Bioremediation of petroleum contaminated soils, biological, chemical and physical processes; Lewis Publishers. Boca Raton. Florida.

Rosenberg, E. and Ron, E.Z. (1996). *In:* Bioremediation. Principles and Applications, (Eds. Crawford, R.L. and Crawford, D.L.) *Biotechnology Research Series 6*, University Press, Cambridge. pp. 100-124.

RSEI: US EPA. (2001). Office of Pollution Prevention and Toxics. *Risk-Screening Environmental Indicators Model: Version 2.0 (1988-2000 TRI reporting data).*

Rubinos, D., Villasuso, R., Muniategui, S., Barral, M. and Díaz- Fierros, F. (2007). *Water, Air, and Soil Poll.* **181:** 385-399.

Salanitro, J.P., Dorn, P.B., Huesemann, M.H., Moore, K.O., Rhodes, I.A., Jackson, L.M.R., Vipond, T.E., Western, M.M. and Wiseiewski, H.L. (1997). *Environ. Sci & Technol.* **31(6):** 1769-1776.

Salinas-Martínez, A., Santos-Córdova, M., Soto-Cruz, O., Delgado, E., Pérez-Andrade, H., Háuad-Marroquín, A. and Medrano-Roldán, H. (2008). *J. of Env. Manag.* **88(1):** 115-119.

Satyawali, Y., Van Roy, S., Dejonghe, W., Vangeel, S. and Gemoets, J. (2009). Fate of heavy metals after *in situ* bioprecipitation induced by sulfidogenesis: A study on stability of metal precipitates, *Goldschmidt Conference Abstracts.* 1(Flemish Institute for Technological Research, VITO,

Schippers, C., Gessner, K., Muller, T. and Scheper, T. (2000). *J. Biotechnol.* **83:** 189:198.

Schwarz, J.R., Walker, J.D. and Colwell, R.R. (1975). *Can. J. Micdrobiol.* **21:** 682-687.

Semple, K.T., Morris, A.W. and Paton, G.I. (2003). *Eur. J. Soil Sci.* **54:** 809-818.

Senez, J.C. and Azoulay, E. (1961). *Biochem. Biophys. Acta.* **47:** 307-316.

Shonnard, D.R., Taylor, I.R.T., Tompson, A. and Knapp, D.R.B. (1992). *Appl. and Env. Microbiol.* 2737-2743.

Silva, E., Fialho, A.M., Sá-Correia, I., Burns, R.G. and Shaw, L.J. (2004). *Environ Sci Technol.* **38(2):** 632-37.

Soriano, F., Roblas Fernandez, Calvo, R. and Calvo G. (1998). *Antimicrob. Agents Chemother.* **42:** 1028-1033.

Szolar, O.H.J., Rost, H., Hirmann, D., Hasinger, M., Braun, R. and Loibner, A.P. (2004). *J. Environ. Qual.* **33:** 80–88.

Tongarun, R., Luepromchai, E. and Vangnai, A.S. (2008). *Curr Microbiol.* **56:** 182- 188.

Traxler, R.W. (1973). *In:* The microbial degradation of oil pollutants. (Eds. Ahearn D.G. and Meyers S.P.) Publication no. LSU-SG-73-01, Centre for Wetland Resources, Louisiana State University. Baton Rouge, pp. 163-170.

Trindade, P.V.O., Sobral, L.G., Rizzo, A.C.L., Leite, S.G.F. and Soriano, A.U. (2005). *Chemosphere.* **58:** 515-522.

van der Meer, J.A. (1992). Molecular mechanisms of genetic adaptation to xenibiotic compounds.

Vázquez, S., Nogales, B., Ruberto, L., Hernández, E., Christie-Oleza, J., Lo Balbo, A., Bosch, R., Lalucat, R. and Mac Cormack, W. (2009). *Microb. Ecol.* **57:** 598-610.

Vidali, M. (2001). *Pure Appl. Chem.***73(7):** 1163-1172.

Ward, D.M. and Brock, T.D. (1976). *Appl. Environ. Microbiol.* **31:** 764-772.

Ward, O.P., Qin, W.M., Dhanjoon, J., Ye, J. and Singh, A. (2006). *Adv. Appl. Microbiol.* **58:** 1-75.

Wodzinsky, R.S. and LaRocca, D. (1977). *Appl. Environ. Microbiol.* **33:** 660-665.

Young, L.Y. and Mitchell, R. (1973). *Appl Environ Microbiol.* **25(6):** 972-975.

Young, L.Y. and Phelps, C.D. (2005). *Environ Health Perspect.* **113(1):** 62-67.

Yu, N.V. (2006). Methods of sequential extraction of heavy metals from soils: New approaches and the mineralogical control (a review). **39:** 1074-1083.

ZoBell, (1973). *In:* The microbial degradation of oil pollutants. (Eds. Ahearn D.G. and Meyers S.P.) Publication no. LSU-SG-73-01, Centre for Wetland Resources, Louisiana State University. Baton Rouge, pp.153-161.

12

Microbial Degradation of Keratin and Keratinases

Itisha Singh[1] and R.K.S. Kushwaha

Department of Botany, Christ Church College, Kanpur-208 001

[1]Department of Applied Microbiology and Biotechnology, Dr. H.S. Gour University, Sagar-470003

E-mail kushwaharks@vsnl.net

Keratinous solid waste is accumulating in the environment at an increasing rate in the form of feathers, hairs, horns, hooves, nails, etc. It is degraded only by keratinolytic microorganisms, which produce keratinases. The present article reviews keratin degradation by fungi and bacteria and production of fungal and bacterial keratinases including keratinases of dermatophytes. Some specific requirements such as substrate and temperature have also been mentioned. Additionally, fungal degradation of various types of keratinous substrates is illustrated for the first time. The possible industrial importance of microbial keratinases has been reviewed and elaborated.

INTRODUCTION

Keratin is an insoluble macromolecule requiring the secretion of extracellular enzymes for biodegradation to occur. Keratin comprises long polypeptide chains, which are resistant to the activity of non-substrate-specific proteases. Adjacent chains are linked by disulphide bonds thought responsible for the stability and resistance to degradation of keratin (Safranek and Goos, 1982). The degradation of keratinous material is important both medically as well as agriculturally (Shih, 1993; Matsumoto, 1996). Secretion of keratinolytic enzymes is associated with dermatophytic fungi, for which keratin is the major substrate (Matsumoto, 1996). However, the production of such enzymes is not exclusive to dermatophytes, since geophilic species have demonstrated keratinase production (Kushwaha and Nigam, 1996). World-wide poultry processing plants produce millions of tonnes of feathers as a waste product annually (Santos *et al.*, 1996), which consist of approximately 90% keratin; the keratin is largely responsible for their high degree of recalcitrance.

The keratinous waste is increasingly accumulating in the environment mainly in the form of feathers, hair, horns, hooves and nails generated from various industries. The sewage and bottom sediments of rivers and canals contain an enormous amount of hidden keratinous waste as a result of daily shaving habits in metros. Today, it is also becoming a part of solid waste management and is difficult to degrade. Recycling of such wastes is increasing attention. Keratin forms a major component of the epidermis and its appendages viz. hair, feathers, nails, horns, hooves, scales and wool. On the basis of secondary structural confirmation, keratins have been classified into α and β (Voet and Voet, 1995; Akhtar and Edwards, 1997). The keratin fibrils in both the configurations are twisted in a parallel manner to form micro and macro fibrils that warrant stability to the fiber (Kreplak *et al.*, 2004; Zerdani *et al.*, 2004). Keratins are also grouped into hard and soft keratins according to the sulfur content. Hard keratins found in appendages like feathers, hair, hooves and nails have high disulfide bond content and are tough and inextensible. Whereas, soft keratins like skin have low content of disulfide bonds and are more pliable (Voet and Voet, 1995; Schrooyen *et al.*, 2001). Keratin wastes can be efficiently degraded by bacteria, actinomycetes and fungi due to keratinases (Onifade *et al.*, 1998). Keratinases known to date cannot completely solubilize native keratin (Ignatova *et al.*, 1999; Ramnani *et al.*, 2005). Nonetheless, keratinases in nature have been continuously contributing to valorization of voluminous keratin containing wastes in the form of hair, feathers, dead birds and animals (Onifade *et al.*, 1998; Farag and Hassan, 2004). Keratinases from dermatophytic fungi have long been well known due to their notorious pathogenic nature (Sohnle and Wagner, 2000). These enzymes have only recently gained biotechnological importance. Their growing importance is mainly contributed to the isolation of keratinases from non-pathogenic microorganisms and their ability to degrade keratin into economically useful keratin product (Onifade *et al.*, 1998; Lin *et al.*, 1999; Riffel *et al.*, 2003), nitrogenous fertilizers, biodegradable films, glues and foils (Friedrich and Antranikian, 1996; Schrooyen *et al.*, 2001; De Tonit *et al.*, 2002).

However, they also represent a potentially valuable source of protein as animal feedstock if keratinolysis can be achieved (Shih, 1993). Keratinolytic enzymes have been studied from a variety of fungi and, to a lesser extent, bacteria. However, current research is centered on the potential use of keratinases of bacterial origin for the industrial treatment of keratin-containing compounds, e.g., serine proteases produced by *Bacillus licheniformis* (Lin *et al.*, 1997; Evans *et al.*, 2000). Such interest results from the broad substrate range of these bacterial enzymes, their rates of activity towards keratin-containing compounds and their thermostability.

Filamentous fungi synthesize a variety of hydrolytic enzymes. Several species are used for the production of industrially important enzymes such as different proteases, carbohydrases and lipases. These are the key enzymes in fungal invasion of skin and skin formations, and have been mostly studied for dermatophytes such as *Trichophyton* (Yu *et al.*, 1968) and *Microsporum* as well as the yeast *Candida*, which also causes skin infections. Keratinolytic enzymes are also involved in microbial bioconversion of keratinous waste. For this purpose, enzymes of *Streptomyces* (Bockle *et al.*, 1995) and *Bacillus* spp. (Lin *et al.*, 1992, 1995) have been investigated. Noval and Nickerson (1955) tested 15 bacteria, 21 actinomycetes and 18 fungi for keratinolytic activity, and found that *Streptomyces* was most effective in the degradation of sheep wool. Among the 34 fungi tested for keratin hydrolysis, the most active in peacock feathers were *Verticillium tenuipes, Trichophyton equinum* and *T. mentagrophytes.* In another study among 21 fungi tested for degrading chicken feathers, *Trichophyton simii* was the most effective. In test on different keratins, 16 dermatophytes were tested. The hair of guinea pig was degraded by *T. mentagrophytes, T. verrucosum* and *Keratinomyces ajelloi,* while only *T. gallinae* was able to degrade chicken feathers (Warwrzkiewicz *et al.*, 1991).

FUNGAL KERATINASE

Acremonium, Alternaria radicina, Aspergillus flavus, Cladosporium cladosporoides, Curvularia inequalis, Fusarium culmorum, Geotrichum sp. Gliomastrix murorum, Monodactys castannea, Myrothecium verrucaria, Pacecilomyces variotii, Penicillim raistrckii, Stachybotrys atra, Trichurus spiralis and *Ulocladium botrytis* were studied by Fredrich *et al.* (1999) for the keratinase production.

Scott and Untereiner (2004) screened the following fungi for their ability to produce keratinase employing keratin azure method. *Arthroderma curreyi, A. gypseum, A. incurvatus, A. otae, A. quadrifidum, A. silverae, Chrysosporium vallenarense, Ctenomyces serratus, Epidermophyton floccosum, Milochevitch Microsporum canis, M. cookei, M. persicolor, Trichophyton krajdenii, T. mentagrophytes, T. mentagrophytes, T. mentagrophytes, T. mentagrophytes, T. raubitschekii, T. rubrum, T. simii, Arachniotus ruber, Arachnomyces minimus, Gymnascella aurantiaca, Gymnoascoideus petalosporus, Gymnoascus reessii, Amauroascus aureus, A. mutatus, A. niger, A. purpureus, Aphanoascus fulvescens, A. mephitalis, A. terreum, Apinisia graminicola, Ascocalvatia alveolata, Auxarthron californiense, A. zuffianum, Chrysosporium keratinophilum, C. tropicum, Nannizziopsis vriesii, Neogymnomyces demonbreunii, Onygena equina, Polytolypa hystricis, Renispora flavissima, Shanorella spirotricha, Spiromastix grisea, S. tentaculatum, S. warcupii, S. warcupii, Uncinocarpus reesii, Aspergillus alliaceus, A. niger, and Byssochlamys nivea.* The most keratinolytic group among fungi belongs to fungi imperfectii including the following genera: *Chrysosporium, Aspergillus, Alternaria, Trichurus, Curvularia, Cladosporium, Fusarium, Geomyces, Gleomastis, Monodictys, Myrothecium, Paecilomyces, Stachybotrys, Urocladium, Scopulariopsis, Sepedonium, Penicillium, and Doratomyces.*

Four fungal species including two dermatophytes and two saprophytes were isolated from sewage sludge samples. They were tested for their degradative ability towards three types of keratin substrates (human hair, chicken feathers and wool). The rate of keratin degradation was expressed as weight loss over three weeks of incubation using a liquid culture medium. Human hair had the highest degradation rate by colonization of *Chrysosporium pannicola* and *Microsporum gypseum* at 62% and 4% respectively. Chicken feathers were highly degraded by *Aspergillus flavus* (32%) while wool degradation was highest by *C. pannicola* (45.5%) and *Trichophyton mentagrophytes* var. *erinacei* (38%). There was a significant difference ($p < 0.001$) in keratin substrate degradation rates by the examined fungi. Keratinase activity was highest for *C. pannicola* and *M. gypseum* in the culture medium baited with human hair. *Aspergillus flavus* revealed the highest activity of this enzyme in cultures amended with chicken feathers, while *T. mentagrophytes* var. *erinacei* showed highest keratinase activity in cultures with wool substrate. The amount of protein released into the culture medium varied among the tested fungi. The alkalinity of the medium's increased over incubation time from 6.5 to 7.8. Microscopic examination showed maceration of the keratin substrates by the fungi.

Fungal involvement in keratin degradation and keratinase production has been shown by many workers. (Evans and Hose, 1975; Safranek and Goos, 1982; Nigam and Kushwaha, 1992; Kushwaha and Nigam, 1995; Kushwaha, 1995, 2000). Extracellular and cell bound keratinases of *T. mentagrophytes* were studied by Yu *et al.*, 1967, 1971. Calvo *et al.*, 1991 tested 300 strains of *Chrysosporium* for keratinase and other proteases. Keratin degradation ability of *Aspergillus quercinus, Chrysosporium tropicum, Microsporum fulvum* and *Trichophyton mentagrophytes* was determined by Kushwaha and Agrawal (1981). Feather and leather degradation by 5 *Chrysosporium,* 4 *Aspergillus,* 2 *Penicillium* and 2 each of *Acremoniun* and *Fusarium* was monitored by Nigam *et al.* (1994). Recently, Singh and Kushwaha (2007) illustrated the hair penetration by keratinophilic fungi. *Chrysosporium georgii* has also been able to produce intracellular and extracellular keratinases.

KERATINASE AND DERMATOPHYTES

The dermatophytes are a group of fungi that can invade the keratinized tissues of human and animals. The ability of these fungi to produce various enzymes has been implicated in the pathogenicity of the host skin (Matsumata, 1996). Keratinase is the major enzyme involved in the pathogenesis process (Howard, 1983), and noteworthy information is available on the keratinase production by different species of dermatophytes (Wawarzkiez, 1991). Among the dermatophytes, different species of *Trichophyton* were reported as exocellular enzyme producers (Samadani *et al.*, 1995; Ibrahim-Granet; 1996). It is of interest to study the enzyme patterns of dermatophytes, particularly the keratinase, as this plays an important role in the breakdown of keratin substrate. Since keratin is the main component of the skin, hair and nails, the breakdown of this substrate by dermatophytes requires the secretion of a specific enzyme. The present study demonstrated that keratinase produced by *Trichophyton mentagrophytes* var. *erinacei*can actively digested guinea pig hair and fibrous protein as substrates. Thus this dermatophyte is highly capable to invade the keratinized tissues. A comparison of keratinase released by *Trichophyton mentagrophytes* with other related species showed a great similarity in the enzyme characterization with that of *T. schoenlenii,* as both dermatophytes have a MW of 38 000 dalton. However, the activity of keratinase produced by *T. schoenlenii* was found to be increased against guinea pig hair in culture medium amended with Fe. Brasch *et al.* (1991) showed that when keratin is supplied into the medium, seven different enzymes are released by *T. rubrum,* which indicated that the activity of extracellular enzymes is dependent on the nutrients supplied into the growth medium. The optimal keratinase activity was detected at pH 5.5 and stability at 55°C, indicating that the high activity of the enzyme occurred at an acidic medium as previously stated. It is recommended that the enzyme assay should be established under certain pH and temperature. Nevertheless, the high activity of keratinase in guinea pig hair and fibrous protein can be related to its substrate specificity or the removal of some accessory proteins that are capable of splitting the disulphide bonds present in keratinized protein during the purification process. On the other hand, inhibition of the enzyme activity by PMSF and less inhibition by NEM may explain that the purified keratinase 125 belongs to the acidic protein group as suggested before (Simpany and Baxter, 1996). A recent study on proteinase produced by *Trichophyton entagrophytes* var. *erinacei* showed that this enzyme belongs to a serine group (Aubaid and Mushin, 1998). Purified keratinase showed no inhibition in the presence of the serine protease inhibitor PMSF. However, inhibition was demonstrated in the presence of EDTA, indicating that the keratinase is a metalloprotease. The majority of the keratinases reported in the literature have been shown to be serine proteases. A metalloprotease was reported to be produced extracellularly by *Streptomyces pactum* (Bocckle *et al.*, 1995). However, a serine protease produced in conjunction with the metalloprotease was largely responsible for keratinolytic activity in this strain.

Among the potential virulence factors of dermatophytes, secreted proteases and especially keratinolytic ones have been investigated the most. They could provide the fungus with nutrients, by degrading keratin into easily assimilable metabolites (Apodaca and McKerrow, 1989a), and allow the invasion of keratinized structures (Apodaca and McKerrow, 1989b). Furthermore, keratinolytic proteases could be involved in the control of host defense mechanisms (Grappel and Blank, 1972; Collins *et al.*, 1973). Keratinolytic proteases have been isolated from different species of dermatophytes including *Trichophyton rubrum* (Meevootisom and Niederpruem, 1979; Asahi *et al.*, 1985; Lambkin *et al.*, 1996), *Trichophyton mentagrophytes* (Yu *et al.*, 1968,1971), and *M. canis* (Brouta *et al.*, 2001). Despite the presumed role of these keratinases in pathogenesis, very few studies have dealt with their *in vivo* expression. A well-characterized 31.5 kDa keratinolytic subtilisin-like serine protease was previously shown to be secreted by *M. canis* as the major component, *in vitro*, in a minimal medium enriched with cat keratin. Moreover, the *in vivo* expression of this keratinase was demonstrated in the hair of both *M. canis* naturally infected cats and experimentally infected guinea pigs, suggesting its role in the pathogenesis of this dermatophytic infection. The role of this protease, thought to be an essential *M. canis* virulence factor, should be further investigated, however, no dermatophyte keratinolytic protease has been characterized so far at the molecular level. Such a characterization would therefore be an important step towards the understanding of the pathogenesis of dermatophytic infection.

The amino acid sequence of *M. canis*-secreted SUBs also showed high percentages of identity with secreted proteases from the filamentous fungi *T. rubrum* (Woodfolk *et al.*, 1998), *A. fumigatus* (Jaton-Ogay *et al.*, 1992), *A. oryzae* (Tatsumi *et al.*, (1988), *A. flavus* (Ramesh *et al.*, (1994), and *A. nidulans* (Katz *et al.*, 1994). Other sequence homologies between *M. canis* and *Aspergillus* spp. proteases have already been reported. Indeed, the N-terminal extremity sequence of the 43.5 kDa *M. canis* keratinolytic metalloprotease (Brouta *et al.*, 2001) disclosed marked similarities with those of metalloproteases from *A. fumigatus* and *A. oryzae* (Doumas *et al.*, 1999). Moreover, the recent molecular characterization of the 43.5 kDa *M. canis* keratinase gene showed that it was homologous to genes encoding the latter metalloproteases (Brouta *et al.* unpublished). These results strengthen the hypothesis (Brouta *et al.*, 2001) according to which *M. canis* and *Aspergillus* spp., both members of the *Onygenales* family, would share fundamental similarities in their proteolytic system, even though they produce proteinases with different specificities related to the substrates they hydrolyze and the tissues they invade.

BACTERIAL KERATINASES

Keratinolytic enzymes are widespread in nature and are elaborated by numerous microorganisms isolated from different habitats and sources. A vast variety of bacteria, actinomycetes and fungi are able to degrade keratin. Among the bacteria, degradation is mostly confined to Gram-positives, including *Bacillus, Lysobacter, Nesternokia, Kocurica* and *Microbacterium.* However, a few strains of Gram-negative bacteria, viz. *Vibrio, Xanthomonas, Stenotrophomonas* and *Chryseobacterium* (Sangali and Brandelli, 2000; De Toni *et al.*, 2002; Yamamura *et al.*, 2002; Lucas *et al.*, 2003) have also been recently reported. In addition, a few thermophiles and extremophiles belonging to the genera *Fervidobacterium, Thermoanaerobacter, Bacillus* and *Nesternokia* have also been described (Friedrich and Antranikian 1996; Rissen and Antranikian, 2001). Actinomycetes from the Streptomyces group, viz. *S. fradiae* (Novel and Nickerson, 1959), *Streptomyces* sp. (Mukhopadhyay and Chandra, 1990), *S. pactum* (Bockle *et al.*, 1995), *S. albidoflavus* (Letourneau *et al.*, 1998), *S. thermoviolaceus* (Chitte *et al.*, 1999) and *S. graminofaciens* (Szabo *et al.*, 2000), and the *Thermoactinomyces* group, viz. *T. candidus* (Ignatova *et al.*, 1999) and another *Thermoactinomyces* sp. (Gousterova *et al.*, 2005), are also reported as keratin degraders. However, only a few have reached commercial exploitation. Keratinases from *Bacillus* sp., particularly *B. licheniformis* and *B. subtilis* have been extensively studied due to their effectiveness in terms of feather degradation (Manczinger *et al.*, 2003; Thys *et al.*, 2004). *B. licheniformis*, a source of the Versazyme, is the first commercial keratinase developed by Shih and coworkers at North Carolina. Industrial trials are ongoing and the product is expected to reach the market shortly (Gregg, 2002).

Keratin serves as the inducer, however, soy meal is also known to induce enzyme production (Gradisar *et al.*, 2000). Most of the reports available on keratinases group them as inducible enzymes, however, few constitutive keratinases have also been reported (Manczinger *et al.*, 2003). Microbial keratinases are predominantly extracellular when grown on keratinous substrates, however, a few cell-bound (Friedrich and Antranikian, 1996; Onifade *et al.,* 1998; Rissen and Antranikian, 2001; Nam *et al.,* 2002) and intracellular keratinases have also been reported (El-Naghy *et al.,* 1998; Onifade *et al.,* 1998).

In most of the reports on constitutive keratinases, the nature of the enzyme is based on their caseinolytic rather than keratinolytic activity. It appears that keratinolytic activity is mostly inducible. Further, simple sugars such as glucose have been reported to suppress the synthesis of keratinase due to catabolic repression (Santos *et al.,* 1996; Ignatova *et al.,* 1999; Mohamedin, 1999; Singh, 1999; Wang and Shih, 1999; Yamamura *et al.,* 2002; Bernal *et al.,* 2003; Suntornsuk and Suntornsuk, 2003; Thys *et al.,* 2004), which is a well known phenomenon of microbial proteases (Gupta *et al.,* 2002). However, the comparison of keratinolytic titers of various microorganisms is difficult due to the variety of substrates and the definitions of keratinase units employed. As far as physical parameters for production are concerned, they are species-specific and thus vary with respect to the organism (Williams *et al.,* 1990; Friedrichand Antranikian, 1996; El-Naghy *et al.,* 1998; Sangali and Brandelli, 2000; Vidal *et al.,* 2000; Rissen and Antranikian, 2001; Rozs *et al.,* 2001; Yamamura *et al.,* 2002; Riffel *et al.,* 2003; Thys *et al.,* 2004). Alkaline pH from 6 to 9 supports keratinase production and feather degradation in many cases. Temperature for keratinase production ranges from 28 to 50°C for most bacteria, actinomycetes and fungi, to as high as 70°C for *Thermoanaerobacter* and *Fervidobacterium* spp. (Friedrichand Antranikian, 1996; Rissen and Antranikian, 2001; Nam *et al.,* 2002). Psychrotrophic production of keratinase has also been reported for *Stenotrophomonas* sp. (Yamamura *et al.,* 2002). Keratinase has been produced under submerged shaking conditions, except for a few thermophilic bacteria (Friedrich and Antranikian, 1996; Nam *et al.,* 2002; Rissen and Antranikian, 2001) and fungi (Kaul and Sumbali 1999; Singh 1999) where static submerged fermentation has been reported. Parihar and Kushwaha (2001) studied protein release from feathers during solid state fermentation.

Keratin is used as an inducer. All fermentations leading to keratinase production are also accompanied by subsequent degradation of keratin substrate. Kinetics of keratinase production and keratin degradation were explained by Ramnani and Gupta (2005). They also indicated that keratinolysis cannot serve as a marker for keratinase production and vice versa. This is also indicated by Williams *et al.,* 1990; Sangali and Brandelli, 2000; Vidal *et al.,* 2000; Kim *et al.,* 2001; Ramnani and Gupta, 2005; Thys *et al.,* 2004). Keratinase degradation takes 24 h to several days (Ramnani and Gupta, 2005, Kaul and Sambali, 1999).

TEMPERATURE AND SUBSTRATE REQUIREMENT

The enzyme from *Chrysosporium keratinophilum* (Dozie *et al.,* 1994) and thermophile *Fervidobacterium islandicum* (Nam *et al.,* 2002) showed exceptionally high temperature optima of 90 and 100°C, respectively, with a half-life of 30 and 90 min, respectively. Thermal stabilization of the enzyme in the presence of divalent cations such as calcium has also been reported (Mukhopadhyay and Chandra, 1990; Dozie *et al.,* 1994; Bressollier *et al.,* 1999; Chitte *et al.,* 1999; Ignatova *et al.,* 1999; Rissen and Antranikian, 2001; Nam *et al.,* 2002; Riffel *et al.,* 2003; Farag and Hassan, 2004). Keratinases have a broad substrate specificity and are active against both soluble and insoluble proteinaceous substrates. Among the soluble proteins, they possess the ability to hydrolyze casein, gelatin, bovine serum albumin and hemoglobin, whereas among insoluble proteins, they hydrolyze feathers, wool, silk, collagen, elastin, horn, stratum corneum, hair, azokeratin and nail. Many keratinases have not been sequenced, but sequence homologies of some known keratinases indicate that they belong to subtilisin family of serine proteases.

INDUSTRIAL INVOLVEMENT OF KERATINASE

Keratinases from microorganisms have attracted a great deal of attention in the recent decade, particularly due to their multitude of industrial applications such as in the feed, fertilizer, detergent, leather and pharmaceutical industries. Currently, the most promising application of keratinases and keratinolytic microorganisms is the production of nutritious, cost-effective, environmentally benign feather meal for poultry. Besides their use in traditional industrial sectors like detergent, medicine, cosmetics, leather and feed (Farag and Hassan, 2004), they also find application in newer fields like prion degradation for the treatment of the dreaded mad cow disease (Langeveld *et al.,* 2003), biodegradable plastic manufacture and feather meal production, and thus can be aptly called "modern proteases". Although many applications of keratinases are still in the stage of infancy, a few have found way to commercialization, particularly the use of Bioresource International's Versazyme for feather meal production (Gregg, 2002). Despite the availability of several reports on keratinolytic microorganisms, which are increasing day by day, there is only one extensive review by Onifade *et al.* (1998) available on keratinases, which emphasizes their biotechnological potential with respect to feather meal production. Further, the mechanism of keratinolysis is highly complex and not yet well understood. Since the keratinases of many microorganisms, particularly fungi, have not been exploited, it is therefore need of the hour to exploit them. Other potential uses of keratinases include the anaerobic digestion of poultry waste to generate natural gas for fuel (Brutt and Ichida, 1999), modification of fibers such as silk and wool (Rissen and Antranikian, 2001), in medicine and pharmaceuticals for elimination of acne or psoriasis, elimination of human callus for preparation of 30 vaccines for dermatophytosis, and additives in skin-lightening agents as they stimulate keratin degradation (Vignardet *et al.,* 2001).

The new research, which tested the effects of a bacterial enzyme keratinase on brain tissues from cows and sheep, showed that when the tissue was pretreated in the presence of a detergent, the enzyme fully degraded the prion, rendering it undetectable. The researchers now plan another study to test the effectiveness of the enzyme on the treated prions in mice and effectiveness in decontaminating equipment that processes animal by-products. Many scientists believe that mad cow disease is spread by healthy animals eating feed containing by-products from BSE-infected animals. Using keratinase to gobble up harmful prions on the processing equipment would go a long way in reducing the risk of spreading mad cow disease. Shih hit upon the idea of using keratinase to degrade prions based on his more than two decades of work as a poultry scientist looking for ways to manage poultry waste. He discovered that a bacteria, *Bacillus licheniformis* strain PWD-1 could degrade chicken feathers. Shih isolated and characterized the bacterial enzyme, keratinase, and then isolated and sequenced the gene that encodes keratinase. He was able to develop a way to produce mass quantities of the enzyme. Shih found that keratinase can be added to chicken feed to increase the digestibility and efficiency of the feed, i.e, chickens who eat feed with the enzyme grow to optimal weight quicker and need less feed to grow to that optimal weight. The enzyme can thus provide the same benefit in feed that antibiotics currently provide. Animal producers are looking for safer substitutes to antibiotics, and Shih believes that keratinase can serve that purpose.

ACKNOWLEDGEMENTS

We are thankful to DST for providing financial assistance and to Dr. R. Gupta for literature and discussions on bacterial keratinase.

REFERENCES

Akhtar W. and Edwards, H.G.M. (1997). *Spectrochim. Acta.* **53:**81-90.

Apodaca, G. and McKerrow, J.H. (1989a) *Infect. Immu.* **57:** 3072-3080.

Apodaca, G. and McKerrow, J.H. (1989b) *Infect. Immun.* **57:** 3081-3090.

Aubaid, A.H. and Muhsin, T.M. (1998) *Mycoses* **41:** 163-168.

Bockle, B., Galunsky, B. and Muller, R. (1995) *Appl. Environ. Microbiol.* **61:** 3705-3710.

Bernal, C., Vidal, L., Valdivieso, E. and Coello, N. (2003) *World J. Microbiol. Biotechnol.* **19:** 255-261.

Bockle, B., Galunsky, B. and Muller, R. (1995) *Appl. Environ. Microbiol.* **61:** 3705-3710

Brasch, J., Martins, B.S. and Christophers, E. (1991) *Mycoses* **34:** 365-368.

Bressollier, P., Letourneau, F., Urdaci, M. and Verneuil, B. (1999) *Appl. Environ. Microbiol.* **65:** 2570-2576.

Brouta, F., Descamps, F., Fett, T., Losson, B., Gerday, C. and Mignon, B. (2001) *Med. Mycol.* **39:** 269-275.

Brutt, E.H. and Ichida, J.M. (1999) *US Patent* 5, 877,000.

Calvo, R.M., M.A.Calvo and J. Larrondo (1991) *Mycopathologia* **116:** 177-179.

Chitte, R.R., Nalawade, V.K. and Dey, S. (1999) *Lett. Appl. Microbiol.* **28:** 131-136.

Collins, J.P, Grappel, S.F. and Blank, F. (1973) *Dermatologica* **146:** 95-100.

De Toni, C.H., Richter, M. F, Chagas, J.R., Henriques, J.A.P. and Termignoni. C. (2002) *Can. J. Microbiol.* **48:** 342-348.

Dozie, I.N.S., Okeke, C.N. and Unaeze, N.C. (1994) *World J. Microbiol. Biotechnol.* **10:** 563-567.

Doumas, A., Crameri, R., Léchenne, B. and Monod, M. (1999) *J. Food. Mycol.* **2:** 271-279.

Evans, E.G.V. and Hose, H. (1975) Sabouraudia **13:** 323-328.

Evans, K.L., Crowder, J. and Miller, E.S. (2000) *Canadian J. Microbiol.* **46:** 1004-1011.

El-Naghy, M.A., El-Ktatny, M.S, Fadl-Allah, E.M, and Nazeer, W.W. (1998) *Mycopathologia* **143:** 77-84.

Farag, A.M. and Hassan, M.A. (2004) *Enzyme Microb. Technol.* **34:** 85-93.

Friedrich, A.B, and Antranikian, G. (1996) *Appl. Environ. Microbiol.* **62:** 2875-2882.

Friedrich, J., Gradisar, H., Mandin, D., and Chaumont, J.P. (1999) *Lett. Appl. Microbiol.* **28:** 127-130.

Grappel, S.F. and Blank, F. (1972) *Dermatologica* **145:** 245-255.

Gradisar, H., Kern, S. and Friedrich, J. (2000) *Appl. Microbiol. Biotechnol.* **53:** 196-200

Gregg, R. (2002) *Triangle. Tech. Journal* (http://www.triangle techjournal.com)

Gupta, R., Beg, Q.K, and Lorenz, P. (2002) *Appl. Microbiol. Biotechno.* **59:** 15-32.

Gousterova, A., Braikova, D., Goshev, I., Christov, P., Tishinov, K.,Tonkova, V.E., Haertle, T., and Nedkov, P. (2005) *Lett. Appl. Microbiol.* **40:** 335-340.

Howard, D. (1983) In: *Fungi pathogenic for human and animals; Pathogenicity and detection.* Maecel Dekker, USA., 543.

Ignatova, Z., Gousterova, A., Spassov, G., and Nedkov, P. (1999) *Canadian J. Microbiol.* **45:** 217-222.

Ibrahim-Granet, O., Hernandez, F.H., Chevrier, G., and Dupont, B. (1996) *J. Med. Vet. Mycol.* **34:** 83-90.

Jaton-Ogay, K., Suter, M., Crameri, C., Falchetto, R., Fatih, A. and Monod, M. (1992) *FEMS Microbiol. Lett.* **92:** 163-168.

Katz, M.E., Rice, R.N. and Cheetham, B.F. (1994) *Gene* **150:** 287-292.

Kaul, S. and Sambali, G. (1999) *Mycopathologia* **146:** 19-24.

Kim, J.M., Lim, W.J. and Suh, H.J. (2001) *Process Biochem.* **37:** 287-291.

Kreplak, L., Doucet, J., Dumas. P. and Briki, F. (2004) *Biophys J.* **87:** 640-647.

Kushwaha, R.K.S. and Nigam, N. (1996) *Nat. Acad. Sci. (India) Letters* **19:** 107-109.

Kushwaha, R.K.S. (1995) In: *Biodeterioration of Cultural Property*. (Eds. Eranayanak and Singhasiri). Bangkok, Thailand. pp. 438-442.

Kushwaha, R.K.S. and S.C. Agrawal (1981) *Proc. Nat. Acad. Sci.* **51:** 181-183.

Kushwaha, R.K.S. (2000) In: *Biology of dermatophytes and other keratinophilic fungi,* (Eds. R.K.S.Kushwaha and J. Guarro), Revista Iberoamericana Micologia, Bilbao, Spain, pp. 66-76.

Lambkin, I., Hamilton, A.J. and Hay, R.J. (1996) *FEMS Immunol. Med. Microbiol.* **13:** 131-140.

Langeveld, J.P.M., Wang, J.J, Van de Wiel, D.F.M., Shih, G.C., Garssen, G.J.,Bossers, A., Shih, J.C.H, (2003) *J. Infect. Dis.* **188:** 1782-1789

Lee, G.G., Ferket, P.R. and Shih, J.C.H. (1991) *FASEB J.* **59:** 1312.

Letourneau, F., Soussotte, V., Bressollier, P., Branland, P. and Verneuil, B. (1998) *Lett. Appl. Microbiol.* **26:** 77-80

Lin, X., Lee, C.G., Casale, E.S. and Shih, J.C.H. (1992) *Appl. Environ. Microbiol.* **58:** 3271-3275.

Lin, X., Kelemen, D.W., Miller, E.S. and Shih, J.C.H. (1995) *Appl. Environ. Microbiol.* **61:** 1469-1474.

Lin, X., Wong, S.L., Miller, E.S. and Shih, J.C.H. (1997) *J. Ind. Microbiol. Biotechnol.* **19:** 134-138.

Lin, X., Inglis, G.D., Yanke, L.J, and Cheng, K.J. (1999) *J. Ind. Microbiol. Biotechnol.* **23:** 149-153.

Lucas, F.S., Broennimann, O., Febbraro, I. and Heeb, P. (2003) *Microb. Ecol.* **45:** 282-290.

Matsumata, T. (1996) In: *Principle and practice of clinical mycology,* (Eds. Kibbler, C.C., Mackenzie, D.L. & Odds F.C.) Wiley & Sons Ltd, USA, pp. 103-129.

Manczinger, L., Rozs, M., Vagvolgyi, C,S. and Kevei, F. (2003) *World J. Microbiol. Biotechnol.* **19:** 35-39.

Mohamedin, A.H. (1999) *Int. Biodeterio. Biodegrad.* **43:** 13-21.

Mukhopadhyay, R.P. and Chandra, A.L. (1990) *J. Exp. Biol.* **28:** 575–577.

Nam, G.W., Lee, D.W., Lee, H.S., Lee, N.J., Kim, B.C., Choe, E.A., Hwang, J.K., Suhartono, M.T. and Pyun, Y.R (2002) *Arch. Microbiol.* **178:** 538-547.

Nigam, N., Dhawan, S. and Nair, M.V. (1994) *Internat. Biodegrad. Bideterio.* **33:** 145-152.

Nigam, N. and Kushwaha, R.K.S. (1992) In: *2nd Internat. Conf. Biodeterio. Cult. Prop.* (Eds. Toshi *et al.*), pp. 180-185.

Novel, J.J. and Nickerson, W. (1995) *J. Bacteriol.* **77:** 251-263.

Onifade, A.A., Al-Sane, N.A., Al-Musallam, A.A. and Al-Zarban, S. (1998) *Bioresour. Technol.* **66:** 1-11.

Parihar, Pramila and Kushwaha, R.K.S. (2001) *Mycoscience* **41:** 645-649.

Ramnani, P., Singh, R. and Gupta, R. (2005) *Canadian J. Microbiol.* **51:** 191-196.

Riffel, A., Lucas, F., Heeb, P. and Brandelli, A. (2003) *Arch. Microbiol.* **179:** 258-265.

Rissen, S. and Antranikian, G. (2001) *Extremophiles* **5:** 399-408.

Rozs, M., Manczinger, L., Vagvolgyi. C. and Kevei, F. (2001) *FEMS Microbiol. Lett.* **205:** 221-224.

Sangali, S. and Brandelli, A. (2000) *J. Appl. Microbiol.* **89:** 735-743.

Ramesh, M.V., Sirakova, T. and Kolattukudy, P. E. (1994) *Infect. Immun.* (1994) **62:** 79-85.

Schrooyen, P.M.M., Dijkstra, P.J., Oberthur, R.C., Bantjes, A. and Feijen, J. (2001) *J. Agric. Food. Chem.* **49:** 221-230.

Singh, C.J. (1999) *Mycopathologia* **143:** 147-150.

Sohnle, P.G. and Wagner, D.K. (2000) In: *Encyclopedia of microbiology,* (Ed. Lederberg, J.) 2nd edn. Academic, San Diego, pp. 451-459.

Safranek, W.W. and Goos, R.D. (1982) *Canadian J. Microbiol.* **28:** 137-140.

Santos, R.M.D.B., Firmino, A.A.P., de Sa´, C.M. and Felix, C.R. (1996) *Current Microbiol.* **33:** 364-370.

Shih, J.C.H. (1993) *Poultry Sci.* **72:** 1617-1620.

Samadani, A.J, Dykes, P.J. & Marks, R. (1995) *J. Med. Vet. Mycol.* **33:** 167-170.

Simpany, M. F. and Baxter, M. (1996) *J. Med. Vet. Mycol.* **34:** 31-36.

Singh, Itisha and Kushwaha, R.K.S. (2007) *J. Mycol. Pl. Pathol.* In press.

Scott, D.W., Miller, W.H. and Griffin, C. E. (2001) In: *Small Animal Dermatology*, (Eds. Muller, G.H. & Kirk, R.W.) Philadelphia: Saunders WB pp. 339-361.

Scott, J. A. and Untereiner, W.A. (2004) *J. Med. Vet. Mycol.* **42:** 239-246.

Thys, R.C.S., Lucas, F.S., Riffel, A., Heeb, P. and Brandelli, A. (2004) *Lett. Appl. Microbiol.* **39:** 181-186.

Vidal, L., Christen, P., and Coello, M.N. (2000) *World J. Microbiol. Biotechnol.* **16:** 551-554.

Vignardet, C., Guillaume, Y.C., Michel, L., Friedrich, J. and Millet, J. (2001) *Int. J. Pharm.* **224:** 115-122.

Voet, D., and Voet, J.G. (1995) In: *Biochemistry*, (Ed. Stiefel, J.) 2nd edn. Wiley, New York, pp. 154-156.

Wang, J.J. and Shih, J.C.H. (1999) *J. Ind. Microbiol. Biotechnol.* **22:** 608-616.

Wawrzkiewiez, K., Woski, T. and Lobarzewski, J. (1991) *Mycopathologia* **114:** 1-8.

Williams, C.M., Richter, C.S., Mackenzie, J.M. Jr. and Shih, J.C.H. (1990) *Appl. Environ. Microbiol.* **56:** 1509-1515.

Woodfolk, J.A., Wheatley, L.M., Piyasena, R.V., Benjamin, D.C. and Platts-Mills, T.A.E. (1998) *J. Biol. Chem.* **273:** 29489-29496.

Yamamura, S., Morita, Y., Hasan, Q., Rao, S.R., Murakami. Y., Yokoyama, K. and Tamiya, E. (2002) *J. Biosci Bioeng.* **93:** 595-600.

Yu, R.J., Harmon, S.R. and Blank, F. (1968) *J. Bact.* **96:** 1435-1436.

Yu, R.J., Harmon, S.R., Grappel, S.F. and Blank, F. (1971) *J. Invest. Dermat.* **56:** 27-32.

Zerdani, I., Faid, M. and Malki, A. (2004) *Afr. J. Biotechnol.* **3:** 67-70.

13

Rhizoremediation Mediated by Plant Growth Promoting Rhizobacteria (PGPR)

Avita K. Marihal[2], S.M. Pradeep[2], K.S. Jagadeesh[2] and Sarita Sinha[1]

[1]Ecotoxicology and Bioremediation Group, National Botanical Research Institute, Lucknow-226 001

[2]Dept. of Agricultural Microbiology, University of Agricultural Sciences, Dharwad-580 005

E-mail: jagsbio@gmail.com

With the increasing successful stories of decontamination, different strategies for remediation are gaining importance and popularization. Rhizoremediation is a specific type of phytoremediation which involves both plants and their associated rhizosphere microbes. Rhizosphere interaction between plants and microbial communities, including PGPR, benefits both the organisms. The rhizobacteria receive nutrients from root exudates, and the plants have enhanced nutrient uptake and reduction in the toxicity of soil contaminants. In contrast to the limited studies of rhizoremediation, beneficial plant growth promoting, root-colonizing rhizobacterial strains (PGPR) have been extensively described. Treating the seeds with rhizobacteria has opened up new avenues in the area of rhizoremediation and can contribute to the restoration of polluted sites. The rhizobacteria secrete plant growth promoting substances, siderophores, phytochelators and enzyme ACC deaminase. These enhance the bioavailability of metal and complexation of metals. Screening and selection of rhizobacterial strains with multiple beneficial traits will go a long way in the restoration of polluted agricultural soils. Further, the studies on the selection of efficient rhizobacteria, bacteria-plant combination and effective means to sustain and proliferate the rhizobacteria in the roots will be helpful to formulate appropriate bioremediation strategies. All these aspects are reviewed in this chapter.

INTRODUCTION

Many substances known to have toxic properties have been introduced into the environment through human activities. These substances vary in the degree of toxicity and danger to human health. These include petroleum hydrocarbons, polycyclic aromatic hydrocarbons, halogenated hydrocarbons, pesticides, solvents and heavy metals. These substances either immediately or ultimately come in contact with and/or are sequestered by soil. Conventional methods to remove, reduce, or mitigate toxic substances introduced into soil or groundwater via anthropogenic activities and processes include pump and treat systems, soil vapor extraction, incineration, and containment. These conventional and engineering-based decontamination methods are expensive, partially because of the cost of excavating and transporting large quantities of contaminated materials for *ex situ* treatment (Chaudhry *et al.*, 2005). The increasing costs and limited efficiency of these traditional physico-chemical treatments of soil have spurred the development of alternative technologies for *in situ* applications, particularly those based on biological remediation capabilities of plants and microorganisms (Chaudhry *et al.*, 2005; Singh and Jain, 2003). Bioremediation, which uses materials of microbial and plant origin, has been recognized as an alternate method of environmental clean-up compared to conventional methods. The emerging science and technology of bioremediation offers an alternative method to detoxify contaminants. Bioremediation has been demonstrated and is being used as an effective means of mitigating these pollutants.

Phytoremediation refers to the use of plants for bioremediation. Plants have the inherent ability to absorb and translocate essential and non-essential elements and organic chemicals from the soil through roots. It is often expanded to mean the use of plants and their associated microbes for environmental clean-up (Pilon-Smits, 2005; Singh and Jain, 2003). Phytoremediation is easy to implement, and both the set-up and maintenance are cost-effective. This noninvasive method is also sustainable and can be visually attractive. On the other hand, soil properties and climate can restrict the plant growth. Favorable plant properties for phytoremediation, in general, are fast growth rate, high biomass production, competitiveness, hardiness, and tolerance of pollution. Phytoremediation can be applied to both organic and inorganic pollutants present as solid, liquid, or gaseous substrates (Pilon-Smits, 2005). Depending on their properties, organics may be degraded in the root zone of plants, or may be taken up, followed by degradation, sequestration, or volatilization. Inorganics cannot be degraded, but can be phytoremediated via stabilization or sequestration in harvestable plant tissues (Pilon-Smits, 2005). The main application of phytoremediation has so far been to remove toxic heavy metals from soil (Chaudhry *et al.*, 2005; Salt *et al.*, 1998). However, there is a growing interest in broadening applications of the technology to remove/degrade even organic pollutants in the environment.

RHIZOREMEDIATION: THE USE OF BENEFICIAL PLANT-MICROBE INTERACTIONS FOR ENVIRONMENTAL CLEAN-UP

Without the microbial contribution, phytoremediation alone may not be a viable technology for many hydrophobic organic pollutants (Chaudhry *et al.*, 2005). In many of these studies, an important contribution to the degradation of pollutants is ascribed to microbes present in the rhizosphere of plants used during phytoremediation, or plants that are emerging as natural vegetation on a contaminated site. This contribution of the rhizomicrobial population is referred to as *rhizoremediation* (Anderson *et al.*, 1993; Schwab and Banks, 1994). In some cases, rhizosphere microbes are even the main contributors to the degradation process. A plant can be considered to be a solar-driven biological pump and treatment system, attracting water and accumulating water-soluble pollutants in the rhizosphere leading to degradation or translocation of the pollutant (Erickson, 1997).

The success of a plant species as the spot of rhizoremediation might depend on; (1) highly branched root system to harbor large numbers of bacteria; (2) primary and secondary metabolism; and (3) establishment, survival, and ecological interactions with other organisms (Kuiper *et al.*, 2004). Plant roots can act as a substitute for tilling the soil to incorporate additives (nutrients) and improve aeration (Kuiper *et al.*, 2004).

Various grass varieties and leguminous plants have shown to be suitable for rhizoremediation (Kuiper *et al.*, 2001, 2004). *Populus* sp. and *Salix* sp. have been used successfully for rhizoremediation of PHC contaminated soils probably due to the introduction of oxygen into deeper soil layers through specialized root vessels, parenchyma (Zalesny *et al.*, 2005).

The success of beneficial processes is based on the rhizosphere competence of the microbes, which is reflected by the ability of the microbes to survive in the rhizosphere, compete for the exudate nutrients, sustain in sufficient numbers, and efficiently colonize the growing root system (Kuiper *et al.*, 2004). Usually, several bacterial populations degrade pollutants more efficiently than a single species/strain due to the presence of partners, which use various intermediates of the degradation pathway more efficiently (Kuiper *et al.*, 2004). During rhizoremediation, the degradation of a pollutant has been reported as the result of the action of a consortium of bacteria (Kuiper *et al.*, 2004).

ROLE OF PLANT GROWTH PROMOTING RHIZOBACTERIA (PGPR)

Plant growth-promoting rhizobacteria (PGPR) are free-living soil-borne bacteria that colonize the rhizosphere aggressively and enhance the growth of plants when applied to seed or crops (Kloepper *et al.*, 1980). The rhizosphere is the soil around the roots, which is under the influence of roots. It is a site in which complex interactions occur between the root and associated microorganisms. A variety of plant associated bacteria improve plant growth, and it is estimated that about 2-5% of the rhizosphere bacteria are plant growth promoting rhizobacteria (Antoun and Kloepper, 2001).

In contrast to the limited studies of rhizoremediation (Kuiper *et al.*, 2004), beneficial plant growth promoting, root-colonizing rhizobacterial strains (PGPR) have been extensively described. Bacteria associated with the roots of plants can strongly act on the plant nutrition and plant resistance, thanks to numerous mechanisms involved in mutualistic relationships. Such is the case with PGPR able to modify the plant growth and development in two ways: (i) an indirect way by producing antibiotics to inhibit soil pathogens, and (ii) a direct way by increasing nutrient and water uptake and therefore the plant biomass (Glick *et al.*, 1999; Belimov *et al.*, 2004).

These bacteria belong to diverse genera, including *Acetobacter, Achromobacter, Anabaena, Arthrobacter, Azoarcos, Azospirillum, Azotobacter, Bacillus, Burkholderia, Clostridium, Enterobacter, Flavobacterium, Frankia, Hydrogenophaga, Kluyvera, Microcoleus, Phyllobacterium, Pseudomonas, Serratia, Staphylococcus, Streptomyces,* and *Vibrio*, as well as the well-known legume symbiont *Rhizobium.*

DEVELOPING RHIZOREMEDIATION AS A REMEDIAL STRATEGY FOR ORGANIC CONTAMINANTS

The successful application of rhizoremediation is largely dependent on the capacity of contaminant degraders or plant growth promoting microbes to efficiently colonize growing roots. Both plants and soil microorganisms have some limitations in their individual abilities to remove and breakdown organic compounds. For example, even plants that are relatively tolerant to various environmental contaminants often remain underdeveloped, or grow slowly in the presence of the contaminants. A technology combining plant and microorganisms, mainly PGPR inoculated into the plant roots, may promote a synergistic action, leading to improved plant growth. The net result of adding PGPR to plants is a significant increase in seed germination and increased biomass of plants, making phytoremediation a faster and more efficient process. This may overcome many of the limitations of single organism, and provide a useful and more powerful approach for enhancing remediation of contaminated environments.

Biodegradation of organic compounds is affected by the plant-microbial interactions in the rhizosphere, which offers a favorable environment for co-metabolism of soil-bound and recalcitrant chemicals. The microbial transformation of organic compounds is probably helped by the abundance of energy provided in root exudates. Rhizosphere interaction between plants and microbial communities, including PGPR, benefits both the organisms. The bacteria receive nutrients from root exudates and the plants have enhanced nutrient uptake and reduction in the toxicity of soil contaminants.

Although rhizoremediation occurs naturally, it can also be optimized by deliberate manipulation of the rhizosphere. This can be accomplished by using suitable plant-microbe pairs. These can be either combinations of plants and plant growth promoting rhizobacteria (PGPR), or combinations of plants and contaminant-degrading microbes. For example, a grass species combined with a naphthalene degrading microbe protected the grass seed from the toxic effects of naphthalene, and the growing roots propelled the naphthalene degrading bacteria into soil that would have been too deep to penetrate in the absence of roots (Kuiper *et al.,* 2004). A convergence of phytoremediation and microbial bioremediation strategies led to a more successful approach to remediation of contaminants, particularly organic compounds. Microbe-assisted phytoremediation, with both naturally occurring microbes and deliberately stimulated via seed inoculation, has been investigated in the laboratory, greenhouse and field (Greenberg, 2006; Chaudhry *et al.,* 2005; Banks *et al.,* 2003). A variety of contaminant-degrading enzymes can be found in plants, fungi, endophytic bacteria and root-colonizing bacteria. These include peroxidases, dioxygenases, P450 monooxygenases, laccases, phosphatases, dehalogenases, nitrilases, and nitroreductases (Susarla *et al.,* 2003; Chaudhry *et al.,* 2005). Although there are some organisms that can completely degrade a specific organic contaminant (e.g., *Sphingobium chlorophenolicum* strain ATCC 39723 mineralized pentachlorophenol (Cai and Xun, 2002)), individual species generally do not contain entire degradation pathways.

It has been shown that maize plants exhibited maximum tolerance to PCP compared to other plants tested and a number of predominant bacteria isolated from rhizosphere soils of these PCP tolerant plants (Marihal *et al.,* 2009). When screened for PCP degradation potentials, isolate MAZ2 showed complete degradation of PCP (50 ppm). The experiment has revealed that most of the PCP (50 ppm) was degraded in 30 days, indicating that plants protect themselves from the phytotoxicity effects. The bacteria present in the rhizosphere of these tolerant plants have degraded PCP effectively and protected them against the PCP toxicity, suggesting that both plants and associated microbial communities play a significant role in attenuating the PCP toxicity (Table 13.1).

They further showed that the PCP degrading bacteria belonged to PGPR group (Marihal *et al.,* 2008). They isolated as many as 27 PCP tolerant rhizobacteria and 19 endophytic bacteria and subjected them to plant growth promotional abilities such as phosphate solubilization, IAA production, antagonistic activity against plant pathogens and HCN production. They observed that six rhizobacteria and five endophyic bacteria capable of PCP degradation exhibited all these four characters, indicating that these isolates could be used both as PGPR and bioremediating agents (Tables 13.2 and 13.3).

Table 13.1 Rhizoremediation of PCP using efficient PCP degrading bacteria in maize plants

Treatments	Fresh Biomass (gm/plant)			Dry Biomass (gm/plant)			% PCP degraded in rhizosphere soil (30 DAI)
	Root	Shoot	Total biomass	Root	Shoot	Total biomass	
Control (no PCP)	1.60	4.25	5.85	0.50	1.03	1.53	-
PCP (UIC)	0.83	2.63	3.47	0.33	0.53	0.87	45.29
PCP + Inoculated with MAZ1	0.93	2.75	3.68	0.43	0.67	1.00	100.00
PCP + Inoculated with MAZ2	1.53	3.18	4.72	0.57	0.83	1.40	100.00
PCP + inoculated with MAZ1 + MAZ 2	1.30	2.73	4.03	0.57	0.83	1.33	97.34
SE±	0.14	0.25	0.32	0.04	0.08	0.11	1.49
CD@1 %	0.62	1.11	1.43	0.18	0.34	0.50	6.68

Table 13.2 Plant growth promotional activities of the PCP degrading rhizobacterial isolates

Sl. No.	Code no. of the Isolates	Plant growth promotional activities of the isolates			
		P- solubilization	IAA -Production	HCN Production	Antibiosis
1.	SOY1	–	–	–	+
2.	SOY2	+	+	+	+
3.	SOY3	-	+	+	+
4.	SOY4	+	+	+	–
5.	SOY5	+	+	+	–
6.	SOY6	–	+	+	+
7.	SOY7	+	–	+	+
8.	SOY8	+	+	+	+
9.	SUN1	+	+	–	+
10.	SUN2	+	–	–	+
11.	SUN3	+	–	–	–
12.	SAFF1	–	+	+	+
13.	SAFF2	+	+	+	+
14.	SAFF3	–	+	+	+
15.	SAFF4	–	–	–	+
16.	SAFF5	–	–	+	+
17.	SAFF6	–	–	+	+
18.	SAFF7	–	+	+	+
19.	SAFF8	+	+	+	+
20.	GRN1	–	–	–	+
21.	GRN2	+	–	+	+
22.	GRN3	+	+	+	+
23.	MAZ1	+	+	+	+
24.	MAZ2	+	+	+	+
25.	WHT1	+	+	+	–
26.	WHT2	+	+	+	–
27.	WHT3	+	+	+	–

Note: + = Positive, – = Negative

Table 13.3 Plant growth promotional activities of the PCP degrading endophytic bacterial isolates

Sl. No	Code No. of the Isolates	Plant growth promoting substances by the isolates			
		P- solubilization	IAA-Production	HCN Production	Antibiosis
1.	SOY(root) 1	+	+	–	–
2.	SOY(root) 2	–	+	+	–
3.	SAF(root) 1	–	–	+	–
4.	SAF(root) 2	+	+	+	–
5.	SAF(root) 3	+	+	+	+
6.	SAF(root) 4	+	+	+	+
7.	SUN(root) 1	+	+	+	+
8.	SUN(root) 2	+	–	–	+
9.	SUN(root) 3	–	–	–	+
10.	GRN(root) 1	+	–	+	–
11.	GRN(root) 2	–	–	+	–
12.	GRN(root) 3	–	+	–	–
13.	GRN(root) 4	+	+	+	+
14.	WHT(root) 1	+	+	+	–
15.	SOY(leaf) 1	+	+	+	–
16.	SOY(leaf) 2	+	+	+	+
17.	SAF(leaf) 1	–	+	+	–
18.	GRN(leaf) 1	–	–	–	–
19.	WHT(leaf) 1	+	–	+	–

Note: + = Positive, – = Negative

A total of 125 bacterial isolates with the inherent ability of degrading carbofuran were obtained from a sandy loam soil with a history of pesticide application (Bano and Mussarat, 2004). Out of these 125 isolates, NJ-101 was specifically chosen based on its relatively higher growth efficiency and enhanced tolerance up to 200 ppm carbofuran in mineral salts medium. The data indicated complete transformation of carbofuran within 40 days of incubation at 30°C. The ability of performing multifarious biological activities in tandem suggested the uniqueness of the isolate NJ-101. The ability to produce hydrogen cyanide and siderophore stipulated its role in biological control. Furthermore, the growth inhibition of *Fusarium* sp. validated the antagonistic activity of NJ-101 against the common phytopathogens. Concurrent production of indole acetic acid and solubilization of inorganic phosphate revealed its plant growth promoting potential. Thus, the innate capability of this novel isolate for parallel biodegradation, biocontrol and plant growth promotion has significance in the management of agro-environmental and phytopathological problems.

RHIZOBACTERIA IN METAL BIOREMEDIATION

Rhizobacteria have been used or manipulated with three main objectives for the remediation of metal contaminated soils: a) hyperaccumulation of metals in plants; b) reducing the uptake of metals; and c) *in situ* stabilization of the metals complexes.

Increased metal uptake in hyperaccumulators is aided by changes in the rhizosphere and rhizobacterial secretions. The chemical condition of the rhizosphere differs from bulk soil as a consequence of various

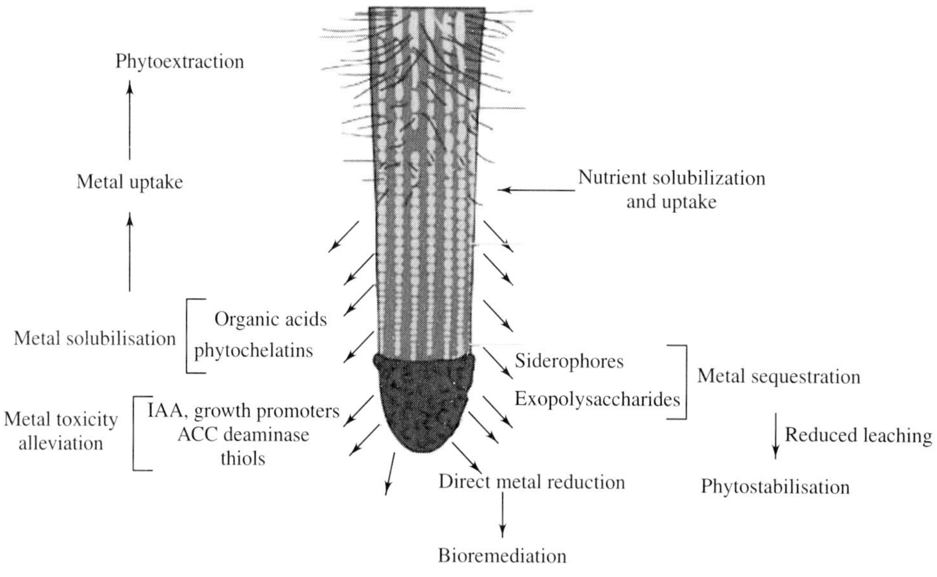

Fig. 13.1 Bacterial activities in the rhizosphere (Marschner, 1995).

processes induced by plants roots as well as rhizobacteria (Marschner, 1995) (Fig. 13.1) like secretion of organic acids followed by reduction in pH, production of siderophores, phytochelains, amino acids and ACC deaminase.

For effective bioremediation of metal contaminated soils, several organisms isolated from varied environments have been utilized (Zhuang *et al.*, 2007). Abou-Shanab *et al.* (2006) studied the effect of rhizobacteria that facilitated the release of nickel accumulation in *Alyssum murale*. In *Brassica napus*, the inoculation of Cd resistant rhizobacteria increased the accumulation of Cd (Sheng and Xia, 2006).

A number of PGPR strains associated with plants grown in metal contaminated soils like *Azotobacter chroococcum* HKN-5, *Bacillus megaterium* HKP-1, *Bacillus mucilaginosus* HKK-1, *Bacillus subtilis* SJ-101, *Brevundimonas* sp. KR013, *Pseudomonas fl uorescens* CR3, *Rhizobium leguminosarum bv. trifolii NZP561, Kluyvera ascorbata* SUD165 (Zhuang *et al.*, 2007) have been used in bioremediation.

Nickel tolerant rhizosphere bacterial isolates belonging to genus *Pseudomonas*, *Bacillus* and *Cupriavidus* from *Rinorea bengalensis* and *Dichapetalum gelonioides* sp. *Andamanicum* were capable of accumulating nickel from aqueous solution. Compared to a single strain, group of bacterial cultures can be very effective. Chen and Cutright (2003) utilized a rhizobial microbial consortium for treating an aqueous solution containing 600 mg/L of Cd, Cr and Ni. The consortium was resistant to metal toxicity and facilitated reduction in aqueous metal concentration with selectivity of Cr > Cd > Ni.

Endophytic bacteria reside within plant hosts without causing disease symptoms. Recently, the benefits of combining endophytic bacteria with plants for increased remediation of pollutants have been successfully tried for the removal of toxic metal from contaminated soils. Further, the metal resistant endophytes are reported to be present in various hyperaccumulator plants growing on heavy metal contaminated soils and play an important role in successful survival and growth of plants. Moreover, the metal resistant endophytes are reported to promote plant growth by various mechanisms such as nitrogen fixation, solubilization of minerals, production of phytohormones, siderophores, and utilization of 1-aminocyclopropane-1-carboxylic acid as a sole N source and transformation of nutrient elements (Mani *et al.*, 2009). Many plant growth promoting endophytes can assist their host plants to overcome contaminant-induced stress responses, thus providing improved plant growth (Nele, 2009).

MECHANISMS OF PGPR INFLUENCING HEAVY METAL ACCUMULATION

Rhizobacteria produce metal-chelating agents called siderophores, which have an important role in the acquisition of several heavy metals (Leong, 1986). These organic substances have the effect of scavenging ferric iron and significantly enhancing the bioavailability of soil bound iron (Kanazawa *et al.*, 1994). It has also been recognized that plants grown in metal-contaminated soils are often iron deficient, and the production of siderophores by plant growth promoting bacteria may help plants obtain sufficient iron (Burd *et al.*, 2000; Wallace *et al.*, 1992). Siderophores have been implicated in the biological control of several soil borne plant pathogens.

Some PGPR contain the enzyme ACC deaminase that helps in reducing the impact of ethylene on root growth (Glick, 1998). In addition, depending on the conditions, plant root growth may also be stimulated by IAA produced by PGPR bound to the seeds or roots (Patten and Glick, 2002). As a matter of fact, low levels of IAA produced by rhizobacteria promote primary root elongation, whereas high levels of IAA stimulate lateral and adventitious root formation (Glick, 1995) but inhibit primary root growth (Xie *et al.*, 1996). Thus, plant growth-promoting bacteria can facilitate plant growth by altering the hormonal balance within the affected plant (Glick *et al.*, 1999). Since the enzyme ACC deaminase, when present in plant growth-promoting bacteria, can act to modulate the level of ethylene in a plant, lower the stress placed on plants by the presence of heavy metals and therefore ameliorate some of the apparent toxicity of heavy metals to plants. Sheng *et al.* (2008) observed increases in biomass production and total lead uptake in *B. napus* after inoculation with *Microbacterium* sp. G16, a bacterial strain that can produce IAA, ACC deaminase and siderophores.

CONCLUSION

Rhizoremediation is a specific type of phytoremediation, which involves both plants and their associated rhizosphere microbes. It can occur naturally, or can be actuated by deliberately introducing specific microbes. These microbes can be pollutant degraders and/or can promote plant growth under stress conditions. Since initial research on phytoremediation showed greater promise as a cost-effective remedial strategy, considerable effort has been devoted to making the transition from the laboratory to commercialization. Treating the seeds with rhizobacteria has opened up new avenues in the area of rhizoremediation and can contribute to the restoration of polluted sites. However, not many reports on the utilization of this technique on a massive scale are available. Screening and selection of rhizobacterial strains with multiple beneficial traits will go a long way in the restoration of polluted agricultural soils. Further, the studies on the selection of efficient rhizobacteria, bacteria-plant combination and effective means to sustain and proliferate the rhizobacteria in the roots will be helpful to formulate appropriate bioremediation strategies.

REFERENCES

Abou-Shanab, R.A.I., Angle, J.S., Chaney, R.L. (2006). *Soil Biol. Biochem.* **38:** 2882-2889.

Anderson, T.A., Guthrie, E.A., and Walton, B.T. (1993). *Environ. Sci. Technol.* **27:**2630-2636.

Antoun, H., and Kloepper, J.W. 2001. *In: Encyclopedia of Genetics.* (Eds. Brenner, S., and Miller, J.F.) pp. 1477-1480. Academic Press.

Belimov, A.A., Kunakova, A.M., Safronova, V.I., Stepanok, V.V., Yudkin, L.Y., Alekseev, Y.V. and Kozhemyakov, A.P. (2004). *Microbiol.* **73:** 99-106.

Bano and Mussarat, (2004). *FEMS Microbiol. Letters* **231**: 13-17.

Burd, G.I., Dixon, D.G., Glick, B.R. (2000). *Can. J. Microbiol.* **46(3):** 237-245.

Cai, M., Xun, L. (2002). *J. Bacteriol.* **184:** 4672-4680.

Chaudhry Q.,M. Blom-Zandstra, Gupta, S. and Joner, E.J. (2005). *Environ. Sci. Pollut. Res.,* **12:** 34–48.

Chen, H. and Cutright, T.J. (2003). *J. Environ. Engrg.* **129:**4-9.

Erickson, L. E. (1997). *Ann. N. Y. Acad. Sci.* **829:** 30-35.

Glick, B.R., Penrose, D.M. and Li, J. (1998). *J. Theor. Biol.* **190:** 63-68.

Greenberg, B.M., (2006). *Can. Reclam.* **1:** 27-29.

Kanazawa, K., Higuchi, K., Nishizawa, N.K., Fushiya, S., Chino, M., Mori, S., (1994). *J. Exp. Bot.* **45(12):** 1903-1906.

Kloepper, J.W., Leong, J., Teintze, M., Schroth, M., (1980). *Nature and Biotechnology* **286:** 885-886.

Kuiper, I., Kravchenko, L., Bloemberg, G. V., and Lugtenberg, B. J. J. (2001). *Mol. Plant-Microbe Interact.* **15:** 734-741.

Kuiper, I., Lagendijk, E.L, Bloemberg, G.V. and Lugtenberg, B.J.J. (2004). *Mol. Plant Microbe Interact.* **17:** 6-15.

Leong, J. (1986). *Annu. Rev. Phytopathol.* **24(1):** 187-209.

Marihal, K. A., Jagadeesh, K.S. and Sinha, S. (2009a). *Internatl. J. Environ. Sci. and Engrng.,* **14:** 189-193.

Marihal, K. A., Jagadeesh, K.S. and Sarita S. (2009b). *First Asian PGPR Congress for Sustainable Agriculture, 21-24, June* 2009, pp. 107.

Marschner, H. (1995). M*ineral Nutrition of Higher Plants.* Academic Press, London, pp. 889.

Mani, Rajkumar, Noriharu, A. and Helena, F. (2009). *Chemosphere,* **6:** 47-49.

Pilon-Smits, E. (2005). *Annu. Rev. Plant Biol.,* **56:** 15-39.

Salt, D.E., Smith, R.D. and Raskin, I. (1998). *Ann. Rev. Plant Phys. Plant Mol. Biol.* **49:** 643-668.

Schwab, A.P. and Banks, M.K., (1994). *In:* Anderson TA, Coats JR, editors. Bioremediation through rhizosphere technology. Washington DC: American Chemical Society;

Sheng, X.F. and Xia, J.J. (2006). *Chemosphere* **64:** 1036-1042

Singh, O.V. and Jain, R.K. (2003). *Appl. Microbiol. Biotechnol.* **63:** 128-135.

Wallace, A., Wallace, G.A., Cha, J.W., (1992). *J. Plant. Nutr.,* **15(2):**1589-1598.

Zalesny, J.R.S., Bauer, E.O., Hall, R.B., Zalesny, J.A., Kunzman, J., Rog, C.J. and Riemenschneider, D.E. (2005). *Int. J. Phytorem.* **7:** 177-197.

Zhuang, X., Chen, J., Shim, H. and Bai, Z. (2007). *Environ Int.,* **33:** 406-413.

14

Cyanobacteria: An Agent of Heavy Metal Removal

Jay Shankar Singh, D.P. Singh and Sonal Dixit
Department of Environmental Science, B.B. Ambedkar University
Raibarely Road, Lucknow-226 025, U.P.
Email: dpsingh_lko@yahoo.com

Cyanobacteria are widespread organisms, with specific properties, such as high nutrient removal capacity and tolerance to highly variable conditions which make them well-suited for toxic heavy metal remediation purposes. Using cyanobacteria to bio-remedy heavy metals-contaminated natural environments has become a practical approach for environmental restoration. Because of its special cell wall structure, high capacity of heavy metal-enrichment, and easy to desorption, cyanobacteria has been considered an ideal biological absorbent. The presence of class II metallothioneins in various strains of cyanobacteria (*Synechococcus* sp.) may participate in the sequestration of toxic metal ions from various contaminated sites. EPS-producing cyanobacteria (*Cyanospira capsulata*, Cyanothece CE 4, *Cyanothece* ET 5, *Cyanothece* VI 22, *Nostoc* PCC 7936, *Cyanothece* VI 13, Cyanothece 16Som 2, *Cyanothece* PE 14 and *Cyanothece* TI 4) remove copper, chromium or nickel, when simultaneously present in aqueous solutions. The cyanobacterium *Gloeothece* sp. strain PCC 6909 and its sheath less mutant were tested for their abilities to remove copper ions from aqueous solutions. Microscopy studies and chemical analyses have revealed that although the mutant of *Gloeothece* sp. does not possess a sheath, it releases large amounts of polysaccharide material (released exocellular polysaccharides [RPS]) into the culture medium. The mutant was more effective in the removal of heavy metal than the wild type. It has been demonstrated that the contribution of sheath to the metal-removal capacity of the wild type is scarce and the RPS of the mutant is more efficient in removing copper. Thus, cyanobacterial sorbents with good metal selectivity may be very useful for building up processes aimed to recover valuable metals from industrial wastewaters.

INTRODUCTION

The pollution of natural environments by heavy metals has become a serious problem not only in industrialized countries but also in developing countries. At present, heavy metals are one of the most widespread causes of pollution, and their continuous accumulation in water bodies and soils constitutes a serious hazard to both the environment and human health (Forster and Wase, 1997; Ledin, 2000). These heavy metal pollutants enter the environment through a variety of human activities, such as mining, refining and electroplating industries (Micheletti *et al.,* 2007). Indeed, the effluents produced by industries contain a variety of heavy metals, such as arsenic, cadmium, copper, chromium, nickel, lead and zinc, which significantly contribute to the increase of the presence of these toxic substances in the environment. The removal of toxic heavy metals has received increasing attention in recent years and various biomaterials, such as bacteria, fungi, and plants have been employed (Kotarba and Ruml, 2000; Hiroyasu *et al.,* 2005; Kiran *et al.,* 2008).

Cyanobacteria are characterized by high tolerance and can exist in various extreme conditions: in hot springs, snow, water rich in salts etc. Simultaneously, they are very sensitive to the pollution by heavy metals. These oxygen-evolving organisms quickly respond and adapt to stress conditions, in general, and heavy metals, in particular (Raveender *et al.,* 2002). They have developed natural methods of resistance towards heavy metals, viz., a reduction in metal intake by extracellular sequestration, localization/compartmentalization inside the cell or energy-dependent efflux (Verma and Singh, 2006). Cyanobacteria account for most of the biologically sequestered heavy metals in terrestrial as well as aquatic environments. Their ability to absorb and metabolize heavy metals is associated with their large surface:volume ratios, the presence of high-affinity, metal-binding groups on their cell surfaces, and efficient metal uptake and storage systems. Cyanobacteria may bind a large of their biomass as metals. In addition to essential trace metals required for metabolism, cyanobacteria can efficiently sequester toxic heavy metals.

The use of cyanobacteria and certain other algae in reducing the heavy metal waste in industrial area has become a trend nowadays, as it could lessen the existing heavy metals in the waste. This waste becomes a major cause of concern due to the health effects related with them. Many have been done to reduce the heavy metals in wastewater by using cyanobacteria. Some reports mentioned that cyanobacteria and certain algae have been used as an absorbent agent in removing heavy metals like Cu, Cd, Pb, Cr etc. (Mehta and Gour, 2005; Anjana *et al.*, 2007; El-Enany and Issa, 2000; Cain *et al.,* 2008).

Accumulation of heavy metals is due to adsorption onto the cell surface (wall, membrane or external polysaccharides) and binding to metallothioneins, exopolysaccharide (EPS), and other intracellular molecules. The presence of metallothioneins in various strains of cyanobacteria may serve as defense mechanisms against metal ion toxicity. Such proteins may be used to develop engineered strains of cyanobacteria with increased metal ion binding ability. *Synechococcus* can eventually be used as a source for a novel approach in using biosystems to remediate contaminants from solution and making those contaminants available to industry through an environment-friendly biofiltration system.

The cyanobacterial exopolysaccharides (EPS; a general term which includes both the polysaccharidic structures that remain intimately associated with the cell, i.e., the sheath and capsule, and those released into the culture medium, i.e., the RPS) exhibit some typical characteristics that distinguish them from the polymers synthesized by other bacteria. They frequently contain two different uronic acids; build a polymer particularly rich in negatively charged groups; possess a larger number of different monosaccharides, which increase the number of possible conformations of the polymer; and contain sulfate groups, a unique feature among prokaryotes and one that is shared by the EPSs produced by *Archaea.* In this context, EPS-producing cyanobacteria appear to be the promising candidates due to the unique characteristics of their polysaccharidic envelopes (Micheletti *et al.,* 2008). The recent study of Demirel *et al.* (2009) demonstrated that the potential of using unicellular cyanobacteria species, isolated from Kucukcekmece Lake, Turkey, for biological iron removal from aqueous solutions. EC_{50} at 96 h was estimated to be 13.92 mg/L for *Synechocystis* sp. E35. Extracellular polysaccharides (EPSs) were clearly seen in SEM images of *Synechocystis* sp. E35 grown at a 10 mg/L metal concentration. The aim of this chapter is to share some information concerning the role of metallothioneins, exopolysaccharide (EPS) and other intracellular molecules present in cyanobacteria for removing the heavy metals from different contaminated sources. This chapter also describes some important factors affecting the uptake and sorption of heavy metals by cyanobacteria and other algae.

BIOMECHANISMS OF HEAVY METAL REMOVAL IN CYANOBACTERIA

Some studies concerning the use of cyanobacteria as a removal agent of heavy metal have been done by many scientists in many fields, especially environmental studies. Cyanobacteria, one of the micro living materials, have good potential for eliminating the heavy metal from freshwater (Inthorn *et al.*, 2002). Anjana *et al.* (2007) studied the bio-absorption of chromium from metal contaminated soil in the premises of textile mill by using the cyanobacterial strains *Nostoc calcicola,* and *Chroococus* sp. The biosorption of Cr was found to be optimum at initial pH 3-4 and 30 minutes contact time. Raungsomboon *et al.* (2008) tried to remove lead from aquatic environment using cyanobacterium strain *Gloeocapsa* sp. Chromium and salt tolerant cyanobacterial strains i.e., *Lyngbya* (*L. putealis* and *L. ceylanica var. constricta*) and *Gloeocapsa* isolated from contaminated sites were investigated along with their metal bioaccumulative potential. These showed greater potential of chromium bioaccumulation, which increased further as both salt and metal concentration increased. In the two species of *Nostoc,* however, bioaccumulative potential improved at higher metal concentration, but was not affected significantly by salt concentration (Kiran *et al.,* 2008). More information about the function of cyanobacteria as removal agent in some sources is given in Table 14.1.

Table 14.1 Some cyanobacteria reported to remove heavy metals from different sources

Cyanobacteria	*Metal removed*	*Source*	*References*
Anacystis nidulans	Cu	Metal solution	Singh and Yadava (1986).
Tolypothrix tenuis	Cd	Aqueous solution	Inthorn *et al.* (1996)
Nostoc muscorum	Cu and Cd	Multimetal solution	Prasad and Pandey (2000)
Spirulina platensis (*Spi*SORB)	Cu	*Coulmanr* reactor system	Vannela and Verma (2006)
Nostoc calcicola and *Chroococus* sp	Cr	Metal contaminated soil	Anjana *et al.* (2007)
Lyngbya and *Gloeocapsa.*	Cr	Contaminated sites	Kiran *et al.* (2007)
Gloeocapsa sp	Pb	Residue of cyanobacteria cell after polysaccharide extraction	Raungsomboon *et al.* (2006, 2008)
Nostoc linckia and *N. rivularis*	Zn and Cd	Sewage water	El-Enany and Issa (2000)
Spirulina platensis and *Aphanothece flocculosa,*	Hg	Wet biomass	Cain *et al.* (2008)
Spirulina sp	Trace element	Copper smelter and refinery effluent	Chojnachkaa *et al.* (2004)
Aulosira fertilissima	Cr and Ni	Free cell condition	Banerjee *et al.* 2004
Nostoc muscorum and *Anabaena subcylindrica*	Cu, Pb, Co and Mn	Sewage and industrial wastewater	El-Sheekh *et al.* (2005)
Gloeothece sp. Strain PCC 6909	Cu	Wastewater	Micheletti *et al.* (2008)

Banerjee *et al.* (2004) reported the scavenging of Ni and Cr toxicity in *Aulosira fertilissima* by immobilization. They described the role of immobilization in ameliorating nickel and chromium toxicity on the enzymes of the nitrogen assimilating pathway in treated and non-treated cells and under free cell conditions. Uptake studies of metals showed higher uptake of both the metals by immobilization. Ni was taken up at higher rates than Cr in *Aulosira fertilissima* (Table 14.2).

Table 14.2 Uptake of nickel and chromium added to the medium as lethal doses after 8 days of growth of free cells and immobilized cells of *Aulosira fertilissima*. (From Banerjee *et al.*, 2004; *Electronic J. Biotech.* Vol. 7 No. 3, Issue of December 15, 2004)

Condition	*Ni*			*Cr*		
	Initial conc. of Ni in the Medium (in mg l^{-1})	Final conc. of Ni in the medium after 8 days (in mg l^{-1})	Percentage uptake	Initial conc. of Cr in the medium (in mg l^{-1})	Final conc. of Cr in the medium after 8 days (in mg l^{-1})	Percentage uptake
Free cells	0.001	0.0003	70%	0.002	0.0015	25%
Immobilized Cells	0.001	0.00011	89%	0.020	0.0009	55%

Role of Cyanobacterial Metal-Binding Proteins (Metallothioneins) in Heavy Metal Removal

Cyanobacteria have developed natural methods of responding to heavy metals such as copper, lead, and cadmium through passive accumulation in cells and through surface binding to various functional groups like metallothioneins (MT)—low molecular weight, cysteine-rich, metal-binding proteins (Klaassen *et al.,* 1999). Metallothioneins can be characterized into three specific classes: class I contains most animal metallothioneins; class II consists of metallothioneins whose cysteine locations in the polypeptide are distantly related to those found in archetypal equine renal metallothioneins; and class III metallothioneins are characterized by atypical non-translationally synthesized metal-thiolate polypeptides. Cyanobacterial metallothioneins belong to class II. They possess approximately 56 amino acids including nine cysteine residues. This number of cysteine residues is less than the 20 cysteine residues out of 60 amino acids for the animal class I metallothioneins and 12 cysteine residues out of 75 amino acids for plant class I metallothioneins (Silver and Ji, 1994).

Until now, a complete study of the uptake of heavy metal ions by the inactivated biomass of cyanobacteria (under batch and flow conditions), specifically *Synechococcus* spp. has not been fully performed. In addition, metallothionein expression by various strains of cyanobacteria is yet to be investigated. For example, *Spirulina platensis*, a cyanobacterium, was shown to contain detectable levels of mercury and lead when grown under contaminated conditions (Slotton *et al.,* 1989), implying that this cyanobacterium was taking up the toxic metal ions from its environment. Further studies confirmed that this cyanobacterium both adsorbs and takes up metal ions (Bender *et al.,* 1994). Reports also indicate that carboxyl groups on algal cell biomass are responsible for binding to various ions (Gardea-Torresdey *et al.,* 1990). Strains of *Synechocystis* spp. have been shown to develop a thickened calyx when exposed to copper-stressed growth conditions (Gardea-Torresdey *et al.,* 1998). *Synechococcus* sp. PCC 7942 was found to possess a copper-transporting P-type ATPase in the thylakoid membrane (Bonilla *et al.,* 1995). *Synechococcus cedrorum* 1191 was shown to be tolerant to heavy metals and pesticides (Gothalwal and Bisen, 1993). Other investigators have studied the biosorption of heavy metals by algal biomass (Volesky and Schiewer, 1997). Such findings show the possibility of manipulating or overexpressing existing resistance mechanisms and the use of such organisms to remove harmful metals from the environment. An important resistance mechanism may be the production of metallothioneins.

Structure and Occurrence of Metallothionein

MTs have been found throughout the animal kingdom—in higher plants, eukaryotic microorganisms, and many prokaryotes (Kojima and Hunziker, 1991). Metallothioneins are low-molecular weight proteins or polypeptides (6,000 – 8,000 amu), which bind metal ions in metal-thiolate clusters. These polypeptides are abundant in cysteine residues (cys) and often possess a characteristic pattern of sulfur containing amino acids (Turner and Robinson, 1995). They are commonly found in association with essential metal ions such as zinc and copper, but they also have been shown to bind toxic metals like cadmium, mercury, and lead. Their metal binding properties are mediated via the abundant cysteine residues and their characteristic organization into – Cys – Cys –, – Cys – X – Cys –, or – Cys – X – X – Cys – sequences (X corresponds to any other amino acid in the protein sequence). Synthesis of metallothioneins has been shown to be prompted by elevated concentrations of some metals (Turner and Robinson, 1995). All cysteines are known to participate in the coordination of 7 mol of Cd or zinc (Zn) per mol of MT (5). Coordination of these cysteine residues results in a high binding affinity for Zn (10^{-18}) and Cd (10^{-22}) (Fig. 14.1).

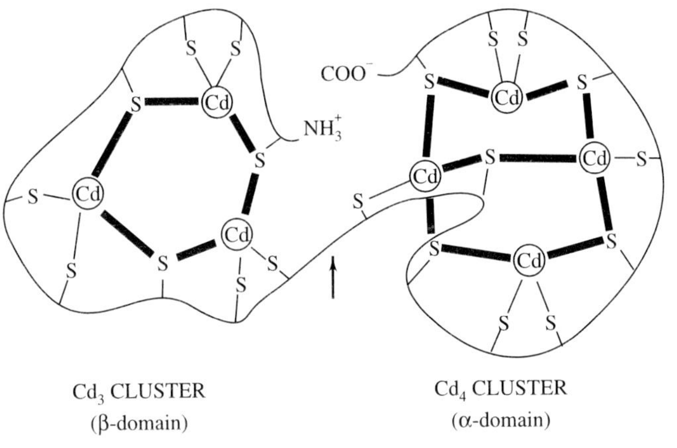

Fig. 14.1 Domain nature of metallothionein. Four and three atoms of cadmium (Cd) are coordinated in alpha and beta domains of metallothionein, respectively. (Klaassen *et al.*, 1999).

Role of Metallothionein (Mt) in Heavy Metal Homeostasis

Zinc: Zinc (Zn) is a physiologically important metal and the most abundant metal bound to constitutive MT. Zn provides essential structural and catalytic functions to a wide variety of proteins. More than 300 different enzymes depend on Zn for proper protein folding and biological function. Zn is also crucial in the regulation of gene expression because numerous transcription factors have "zinc finger motifs" that are maintained by Zn.

Apo-MT (metallothionein with no metals bound) is a Zn acceptor because of the abundance of free sulfhydryl groups and their high affinity for Zn. However the sulfhydryl groups are highly reactive, and Zn, although bound with high affinity, can undergo an exchange reaction, which allows Zn to be transferred from MT to other proteins (Maret and Vallee, 1998). The affinity of sulfhydryl groups for Zn can also make MT an efficient metal ion scavenger. This implies a possible regulatory role of MT in the activation or inactivation of various molecular effectors. Such a possibility was demonstrated by showing that apo-MT can chelate Zn out of the transcription factor IIIA (TFIIIA), a process that inactivates TFIIIA (Zeng *et al.*, 1991). Therefore, it is tempting to speculate that MT might be essential for Zn homeostasis by regulating Zn absorption, or as a donor of Zn to various enzymes and transcription factors during development or protein synthesis.

The role of MT in intestinal Zn absorption was recently reevaluated using both MT-transgenic and MT-null mouse models (Davis *et al.*, 1998). At 2 h after a single oral dose of Zn, serum Zn concentrations were twofold higher in MT-null mice, while in MT-transgenic mice, serum Zn concentrations were only one-third of that of controls, which suggests that MT reduces Zn absorption. Intestinal Zn was higher in MT-null mice but was unchanged in MT-transgenic mice, which suggests that MT does not reduce Zn absorption simply by sequestration of Zn in the mucosa (Davis *et al.*, 1998).

MT has been suggested to provide a biologically important pool of Zn during periods of extreme Zn deficiency, as the teratogenic effects observed in fetuses of dams placed on a Zn-deficient diet were lower in MT-I transgenic mice than in control mice (Dalton *et al.*, 1996). Hepatic concentrations of Zn were 60% less in newborn MT-null mice than in control mice, and kidney development in the MT-null pups was retarded when they were fed a Zn-deficient diet (Kelly *et al.*, 1996). However, these renal abnormalities resolved with time and did not impair kidney function (Palmiter, 1998). When adult MT-null mice were challenged with a toxic dose of Zn, they had a greater incidence of pancreatic acinar cell degeneration compared with controls (Kelly *et al.*, 1996). During endotoxemia, MT-null mice were also less responsive than control mice to hepatic Zn accumulation and reduction in plasma Zn levels (Rofe *et al.*, 1996).

Thus, MT may aid in maintaining Zn homeostasis and protecting against excess Zn-induced toxicity. However, MT-null animals appear "normal," and thus MT does not appear to play the most crucial role in enabling Zn to perform its important roles in growth and development. However, it should be emphasized that the apparent "normal" appearance of MT-null mice could be due to the presence of back-up systems, and thus does not necessarily argue against MT having a physiological role in Zn homeostasis.

Copper: Copper (Cu) is an essential metal for structural and catalytic properties of many enzymes, such as Cu/Zn superoxide dismutase, cytochrome-C oxidase, and copper-responsive transcription factors. However, excess Cu can be toxic, particularly when associated with a deficit in Cu excretion (Bremner, 1998). There are two diseases in humans caused by abnormal transport of Cu: Wilson's disease and Menkes' disease. Wilson's disease is a hypercupremic state, whereas Menkes' disease is a hypocupremic state. Wilson's disease is due to a defect of a P-type ATPase (ATP7B), which is located on autosome 13 in humans and autosome 16 in rats (Suzuki, 1995). As a result of the mutation in the Cu efflux transporter (Bingham *et al.*, 1998), there is an inability to transport Cu across the bile canalicular membrane, and thus Cu accumulates in liver during aging. Menkes' disease gene is located on the X chromosome and is characterized by mutation of a copper efflux ATPase (ATP7A) (Harris and Gitlin, 1996). This results in decreased transport of Cu across the placenta to the fetus, as well as decreased efflux of Cu from the intestine into the blood, thereby creating a copper-deficient state.

Both copper efflux ATPases and MT are important mechanisms affecting copper toxicity (Dameron and Harrison, 1998).

Analysis of Wilson's disease patients suggests that MT is the major Cu binding protein in their liver, and increased liver MT levels assist in the detoxification of the accumulated Cu (Nartey *et al.,* 1987). Thus, the beneficial effects produced by Zn administration to Wilson's patients could be due to induction of MT (Brewer *et al.,* 1990). Indeed, MT-rich cells are resistant to Cu toxicity (Liu *et al.,* 1991). It has been proposed that MT protects against Cu toxicity by sequestration of Cu from critical cellular targets (Dameron and Harrison, 1998). Cu is a transition metal and can exist in three oxidation states: Cu, CuC, and Cu_2C. It appears that MT containing Zn and Cu functions as an antioxidant; however, when MT is saturated with Cu, it becomes a prooxidant and may cause oxidative liver damage (Deng *et al.,* 1998).

The role of MT in Menkes' disease has been studied by crossing MT-I and-II–null mice with mice carrying the Mottled-Brindled allele (Mo-BrJ), a murine model for X-linked Menkes' disease (Kelly and Palmiter, 1996). It is believed that Mo-BrJ males die from Cu-deficiency because of an inability to transport Cu from the intestine into the circulation. Since MT avidly binds Cu, elimination of MT in the intestine might enhance the passage of Cu into the circulation, resulting in prolonged survival. Contrary to expectation, on an MT background, most offspring of Mo-BrJ mice die before gestational day 11. These results suggest that MT protects against Cu toxicity in the embryo (Kelly and Palmiter, 1996).

As Cu is an essential metal that binds to MT, one might anticipate that MT would have an essential role in the normal biological activity of Cu in the body. However, since mice with a targeted deletion of MT appear to be "normal," the results suggest that MT is not essential for Cu homeostasis. However, it does appear that MT can protect against the toxicity of Cu under extreme conditions.

Why Metallothionein was Evolutionarily Conserved

Why MT was highly conserved through evolution? What would have been the selective disadvantage if MTs were lost during the course of evolution? It is well documented in the evolutionary literature that the more functionally constrained a structure, the slower its evolutionary rate (i.e., the functionally important parts of a gene or protein will evolve at a much slower rate than the functionally less or nonimportant parts), particularly if the nonsynonymous substitutions are concerned. This trend can be explained by both natural selection and the neutral theory (Ridley, 1996). The differences in MT gene structure also conform to this rule, as the untranslated regions are a lot more divergent than the coding regions. This further reinforces a question: Why is it necessary for MT structure, in particular the position of cysteines, to be so well conserved through evolution? What selective advantage does MT impart to the survival/perpetuation of the species that has MT? According to the Darwinian view of evolution, appearance of any character (variation) is a random event and is independent of the need. It is the selective advantage of that variation to the species that leads to its fixation in the population and to further adaptive changes during the course of evolution. Thus, MTs might have appeared as a small metal-binding ligand molecule early in the history of life, but it was obviously a characteristic offering selective advantage to life and thus was favored by natural selection. Although the driving force behind the further evolution of MT is subject to speculation, its metal-binding ability appears to have been a major determinant in its subsequent evolution. This is evidenced by the overall structural conservation of MT, particularly the positions of the cysteine residues, and the resulting slow evolutionary rate.

A snapshot of MT structure and function in prokaryotes and lower eukaryotes, mollusks, and mammals offers some clues to its structural and functional evolutionary trend. It appears that early in evolution, the main function of MT (the class II MTs) was to preferentially bind to and be induced by physiologically important metals. For example, studies on the regulation of MT gene from the cyanobacteria *Synechococcus* (Huckle *et al.,* 1993) indicate that in mammals, various metal ions including Cd, Zn, and Cu increase the abundance of the transcript (Huckle *et al.,* 1993). However, unlike mammalian MT, the most potent inducer of *Synechococcus* MT *in vivo* is Zn, followed by Cu and Cd. Similarly, the main function of MT in the lower eukaryote yeast *Saccharomyces* is to detoxify Cu by maintaining low levels of free ion (Hamer *et al.,* 1991). In terrestrial gastropods, there are two distinct structural and functional types of MTs, one that preferentially binds Cu and one that binds Cd. Evidently, these two MT types serve two different functions (Dallinger *et al.,* 1997). The story of mammalian MT is best known and has been discussed in the preceding sections. Thus, MT evolution has made it a perfect metal-binding molecule whose inducibility and metal-binding ability have undergone changes throughout the course of evolution from lower to higher forms. Events such as gene duplication and subsequent evolution of the duplicated genes following split from the ancestral one have led to the structural divergence of species-specific MT genes (Hamer, 1986). Nevertheless, the metal-binding ability of MT protein remains unaltered.

If MT is so well conserved because it is an important protein, why are MT-null mice normal? An answer to this question leads us to think that MT may not have a critical role in normal Zn biology, or there exists a parallel/back-up system to compensate for the loss of MT. In contrast, the increased susceptibility of MT-null mice to Cd reinforces the protective role of MT against Cd toxicity. These explanations are actually in contrast to the long-held belief that the primary function of MT is in maintaining Zn and/or Cu homeostasis, and that protection from Cd toxicity is an adjunct function dictated merely by its structure.

Although the appearance and evolution of MT was probably not dictated by Cd, however with the evolution of higher life forms, it appears that MT became more indispensible for protection against Cd and other heavy-metal toxicity than for performing the other suggested functions. It also appears that additional/alternative mechanisms to compensate for the loss of MT have evolved in mammals, but no such mechanisms have evolved to protect against Cd toxicity. That is why MT-null mice are normal but highly susceptible to Cd toxicity. This thesis, however, does not negate other suggested functions of MT. MT in normal mice may still be among the first line of effector molecules modulating intermolecular Zn transfer, and it may form a significant line of defense against oxidative stress. But as these functions are not impaired in the absence of MT, there is no mechanism to protect the animals from Cd toxicity.

Although the physiological functions of MT are still elusive, and a number of functions have been attributed to it, they are all subject to debate. On the contrary, the only function of MT that has almost been unequivocally established (that has not been contradicted) is its role in protection against Cd toxicity. It has been calculated that 7% of the general population have Cd induced kidney alterations due to chronic Cd exposure (Jarup *et el.,* 1998). Incidents of chronic human Cd exposure in developed as well as developing countries are well documented. In each case, chronic Cd exposure manifested in renal proximal tubular cell damage (Jarup *et al.,* 1998). So what would the significance be if humans did not have MT? If one would examine the human and impose renal dysfunction at one-tenth the amount known to produce renal dysfunction in humans (because Cd produces nephrotoxicity in MT-null mice at one-tenth the dose in control mice), there would be a major overlap in the incidence of Cd exposure and altered renal function. That is to say, a large percentage of the human population would be victims of Cd-induced nephropathy. Thus, MT also appears to be critical for human health for protection from Cd toxicity.

Gardea-Torresdey *et al.* (1998) reported the ability of *Synechococcus* sp. PCC 7942 to uptake copper (II), lead (II), cadmium (II), nickel (II), chromium (III), and chromium (VI) under batch conditions (Table 14.3).

Table 14.3 Metal ion binding capacities of inactivated cells of *Synechococcus* sp. PCC 7942 biomass

Metal tested	*mg metal/g biomass*
Copper (ii)	11.3 ± 0.8
Lead (ii)	30.4 ± 2.2
Nickel (ii)	3.2 ± 0.7
Cadmium (ii)	7.2 ± 2.1
Chromium (iii)	5.4 ± 3.8
Chromium (vi)	0.8 ± 1.0

Note: Each data represents the mean of three replicates. Each experiment was performed at pH 5, and a 95% confidence interval was used to determine error (Gardea-Torresdey *et al.*, 1998).

A genetic investigation was performed to identify genes for class II metallothioneins in *Synechococcus* sp. PCC 7942 and seven other strains of cyanobacteria by Gardea-Torresdey *et al.* (1998). They demonstrated that genes for these proteins are widespread among the various genera and species of cyanobacteria. Polymerase chain reaction showed the presence of class II metallothionein genes in seven species of cyanobacteria. The best established example of this gene from *Synechococcus* sp. PCC 7942 yielded a PCR product of 187 base pairs. Their results suggest that class II metallothionein genes are widespread among the cyanobacteria (Table 14.4). Class II metallothioneins may participate in the sequestration of toxic metal ions by the cyanobacteria (Turner and Robinson, 1995).

Table 14.4 Polymerase Chain Reaction (PCR) product and restriction digestion product sizes (base pairs) obtained for SmtA genes (metallothionein) from DNA isolated from cyanobacterial species

Cyanobacterial Species	*smtA PCR products*	*Hae III*	*Msp I*	*Rsa*	*Taq I*
Anabaena ATCC 22664	220	ND 43 U = 17	160	ND	ND
Fischerella ATCC 27929	20	ND 45 U = 5	170	ND	ND
Synechocystis ATCC 22663	187	125 50 U = 12	134 17 U = 36	95 U = 92	100 U = 87
Nostoc ATCC 29105	187	105 15 U = 67	100 10 U = 77	90 U = 97	97 U = 90
Prochlorothrix hollandica	187	105 60 U = 22	105 20 U = 62	80 U = 107	97 U = 90
Spirulina ATCC 53843	187	106 25 U = 56	120 20 U = 47	90 U = 97	90 U = 97
Synechocystis PCC 6714	187	128 U = 59	128 U = 59	90 U = 97	95 U = 92
Synechococcus PCC 7942	187	112 U = 75	112 U = 75	90 U = 97	100 U = 87

Note: PCR products were digested with *Hae* III, *Msp* I, *Rsa* I, and *Taq* I. PCR products and restriction digestion fragments are given in base pairs. U = Fragment sizes which could not be resolved and ND = no digestion. (Gardea -Torresdey *et al.*, 1998).

Heavy Metal Removal by Extracellular Polymeric Substances (EPS) Producing Cyanobacteria

Extracellular polymeric substances (EPS) of microbial origin are complex mixture of biopolymers comprising polysaccharides, proteins, nucleic acids, uronic acids, humic substances, lipids, etc. Cyanobacterial cells containing a thick capsular polysaccharide structure outside the cell possess large number of binding sites for trapping metal ions and are quite promising in heavy metal removal (Pal and Pal, 2008). The use of EPS-producing cyanobacteria (or isolated EPSs) is a valid alternative to conventional chemical and physico-chemical methods to remove metallic cations from polluted waters (Volesky, 2001). Among eleven unicellular and filamentous RPS-producing cyanobacteria, *Cyanothece* CE 4 and *Cyanospira capsulate* showed quick and effective Cu (II) adsorption (De Philippis *et al.*, 2001). The higher metal removal observed with the cultures of the mutant can be explained by the larger amounts of RPS released into the culture medium than with the wild type. It was reported that the random mutagenesis did not block the synthesis and release of the carbohydrates but only their mobilization for the formation of a structured sheath. In addition, the metal-removal capacity of the RPS solution of the mutant was considerably higher than that of the wild type. Thus it may be said that the higher copper removal capacity observed for the whole cultures of the mutant is due to the release of large quantities of polysaccharidic material, together with better metal-binding properties of its polymer. Live algae possess intracellular polyphosphates which participate in metal sequestration, as well as algal extracellular polysaccharides that serve to chelate or bind metal ions (Zhang and Majidi, 1994). The iron biosorption/bioaccumulation by *Synechocystis* sp. E35 was evaluated by fractionating the Fe content as the remaining metal in supernatant, the adsorbed metal on the cell surface and the intracellular accumulation. *Synechocystis* sp. E35 adsorbed appreciable quantities of iron ions on the cell surface within 5 min. Metal ions were adsorbed onto the surface of cells followed by active uptake resulting in the transportation of the metal ions across the cell membrane and into the cytoplasm. Intracellular metal uptake increased with increasing metal concentrations from 10 to 15 mg/L (Demirel *et al.*, 2009).

This new technology presents advantages such as the use of natural and renewable sources, reduced costs and rapid kinetics of metal removal, the ability to remove metallic ions present at low concentrations, the possibility to treat contaminated waters simultaneously with several different metal ions, and the possibility of recovering valuable metals from the biosorbent (De Philippis *et al.*, 2001, 2007). The fast kinetics of copper removal exhibited by the cultures of both the *Gloeothece* sp. strain PCC 6909 wild type and the mutant (Micheletti *et al.*, 2007) strongly suggest that the metal-binding process was essentially due to an ion-exchange mechanism, in accordance with the hypothesis previously formulated for the metal-removal process carried out by other cyanobacteria (Singh, 1998; De Philippis *et al.*, 2007). The cyanobacterium *Microcystis aeruginosa* fo. *Flosaquae* strain C3-40 produces an extracellular capsule that strongly accumulates metals (Plude *et al.*, 1991). The capsule from strain C3-40 is the only pectin-like polysaccharide reported from a microbe. As such, it may have applications as a texturizer, gelling agent that does not require heating, immobilizer for the localization or timed release of metals, and material that can remove toxic metals from polluted waters. An advantage is that the capsule can bind many metal species at high pH. Parker *et al.* (2000) reported the sorption of cadmium (II), copper (II), lead (II), manganese (II), and zinc (II) by purified capsular polysaccharide from the cyanobacterium *Microcystis aeruginosa* fo. *flos-aquae* strain C3-40 by four methods: equilibrium dialysis, metal removal from solution as detected by voltammetry, metal accumulation by capsule containing alginate beads, and calorimetry (Table 14.5).

The carboxylate groups of uronic acid salts are known to be involved in metal sorption by many acidic polysaccharides (Geddie & Sutherland, 1993). Parker *et al.* (2000) suggested that the galacturonate probably plays some role in metal binding, since it comprises 83% of the capsule by weight and the amounts of bound metal per saccharide subunit are quite large. However, it is also possible that the five neutral sugars in the capsule (Plude *et al.*, 1991) enhance metal binding.

Table 14.5 Metal-binding capacities of capsular polysaccharide from the strain Microcystis aeruginosa fo. flos-aquae C3-40. (Parker *et al.*, 2000)

Metal	*Metal bound at saturation* (*m mol metal* g^{-1} *capsule*)	(*m mol metal equiv.*$^{-1}$ *sugar subunits*)	*pH*	*Method*
Cu(II)	1.7	0.35	pH 9.0	Voltammetry
	3.3	0.68	pH 8.8	Equilib dialysis
	4.1	0.85	pH 8.0	Alginate beads
Cd (II)	1.23	0.25	pH 9.0	Voltammetry
	1.15	0.23	pH 8.0	Equilib dialysis
Mn (II)	1.72	0.35	pH 9.0	Voltammetry
	2.84	0.58	pH 8.0	Alginate beads
Pb (II)	1.36	0.28	pH 9.0	Voltammetry
	1.50	0.30	pH 8.8	Equilib dialysis
Zn (II)	1.23	0.25	pH 9.0	Voltammetry

Metal Sorption and Accumulation by Algae

Algae accumulate high concentrations of metals depending on their concentration in the external environment. The concentration factor for heavy metals varies greatly in different algal species, but it increases as the metal concentration in the water decreases (Kelly, 1988). Since the amount of metal accumulated by algae is related with the concentration of metal in water, it may be possible to use metal content of indigenous algae for biomonitoring of metal pollution in a water body (De Filippis and Pallaghy, 1994). Furthermore, the potential metal accumulation capability of algae could be used to alleviate the burden of toxic metal load, and to recover precious metals from wastewaters.

The accumulation of heavy metals in algae involves two processes: an initial rapid (passive) uptake followed by a much slower (active) uptake (Bates *et al.*, 1982). During the process of passive uptake, metal ions adsorb onto the cell surface within a relatively short span of time (few seconds or minutes), and the process is independent of metabolism. While active uptake is metabolism-dependent, causing the transport of metal ions into the cytoplasm across the cell membrane. In some cases, the transport of metal ions may also occur via passive diffusion owing to metal-induced increase in the cell membrane permeability (Gadd, 1988).

Bates *et al.* (1982) described a simple method for distinguishing adsorbed from intracellular metal in algal cells. The method involves washing cells with 2 mM EDTA, which removes surface-bound metal, leaving behind the intracellular fractions. The intracellular metal can be quantified after digesting the EDTA-washed cells. The measurement of surface adsorbed metal can be done by subtracting intracellular metal from the total metal accumulated by the cell. Several researchers used this common method to distinguish adsorbed from intracellular metal in spite of inevitable removal of a small fraction of intracellular metal during washing of EDTA (Bates *et al.*, 1982). The relative importance of metal adsorption and uptake may vary with algal species and metal ions (Trevors *et al.*, 1986). In general, the adsorption contributes much more, even > 80% (Mehta *et al.*, 2000a), than uptake, to total metal accumulation by algal cells. However, there are a few reports suggesting a greater contribution of uptake than adsorption or almost similar contribution of both the processes to total metal accumulation (Avery *et al.,* 1998). After the first minute of exposure to Cu, > 90% of the total metal content was found adsorbed on the surface of *Scenedesmus subspicatus* (Knauer *et al.,* 1997). With the passage of time, the relative contribution of the surface-bound Cu declined with a concomitant increase in intracellular Cu, thereby suggesting the transport of adsorbed Cu into the cells. Interestingly, surface adsorption has been invoked as an important mechanism in algae for tolerating elevated levels of heavy metals (Lombardi *et al.,* 2002).

The algal cell wall contains many functional groups, such as hydroxyl (-OH), phosphoryl, amino (-NH_2), carboxyl (-COOH), sulphydryl (-SH), etc., which confer negative charge on the cell surface. Since metal ions in water are generally in the cationic form, they are adsorbed onto the cell surface (Grist *et al.,* 1981). Each functional group has a specific pKa (dissociation constant) (Niu and Volesky, 2000), and it dissociates into corresponding anion and proton at a specific pH. These functional groups are found associated with various cell wall components, e.g., peptidoglycan, teichoic acids, polysaccharides and proteins. Since the distribution and abundance of cell wall components vary among different algal groups, the number and kinds of functional group also vary among them. Among different cell wall constituents, polysaccharides and proteins have most of the metal binding sites (Kuyucak and Volesky, 1989a).

Peptidoglycan, having linear chains of N- acetylglucosamine and β 1, 4-N-acetylmuramic acid with peptide chain, is the major component of cell wall of cyanobacteria (blue-green algae), providing mostly carboxylic groups for metal binding (Chojnacka *et al.,* 2005). Lipo-polysaccharides, lipids and membrane proteins are also important in metal binding by cyanobacteria. Phosphoryl groups are mainly associated with lipopolysaccharides, lipids and peptidoglycans of cell wall. Amino groups are associated with membrane proteins and peptide component of peptidoglycan. It has been suggested that carboxyl groups on the cyanobacterial cell wall are the dominant active sites for the binding of metal ions (Chojnackaet *et al.,* 2005). The outer sheath or capsule of many strains of cyanobacteria is made up of polysaccharides. The nature of cyanobacterial capsule is anionic, owing to the presence of uronic acids and/or of other charged groups (De Philippis and Vincenzini, 1998). Because of the anionic properties of cyanobacterial capsule, it shows very high affinity towards metal ions and may offer a promising chelating agent for the removal of heavy metals from wastewaters (De Philippis *et al.,* 2001). A wide difference in metal binding capacity of capsulated and uncapsulated cyanobacterial strains has been demonstrated (Pradhan and Rai, 2000). A cyanobacterial strain with thick capsule showed higher metal binding capacity than the strains devoid of or with a thin layer of capsule (Singh *et al.,* 1998). However, the presence of gelatinous capsule around cyanobacterial cell may slow down the diffusion rate of metal ions into the chelating matrix of cell wall (De Philippis *et al.,* 2003).

The functional groups involved in metal sorption by algae have been identified, but not fully, by FTIR spectroscopy, pH-titration, potentiometric and conductimetric titration techniques, and also after blocking of functional groups with certain chemical agents. FTIR analysis led to suggest the involvement of carboxyl groups in binding of Au (III) on *Chlorella vulgaris* (Ting *et al.,* 1995). Participation of carboxyl groups in adsorption of Cu, Cd and Pb on cyanobacterial cell wall has also been demonstrated (Yee *et al.,* 2004). Seki and Suzuki (1998) showed that biosorption of bivalent metal ions by brown algae, namely, *Macrocystis pyrifem, Kjellmaniella crassiforia* and *Undaria pinnatifida,* was due to binding to carboxyl groups of alginic acid. Furthermore, using FTIR analysis of non-living *S. fluitans,* showed binding of Cd and Pb largely on the carboxyl and to a small extent on sulfonate groups (Fourest and Volesky, 1997). Mehta *et al.* (2002b) demonstrated the involvement of carboxyl groups in adsorption of Cu onto *C. vulgaris.*

Participation of sulfonate, amino and hydroxyl groups in adsorption of various metal ions has been demonstrated, but to a lesser extent than that of carboxyl groups. Potentiometric titration study on *Chlamydomonas reinhardtti* revealed the presence of amino and thiol groups along with carboxyl groups. According to Greene *et al.* (1986), amino group plays an important role in binding of Au to *C. vulgaris,* as pretreatment of the alga with succinic anhydride, which is known to react with amino groups making them unavailable for metal binding, resulted in a significant (50%) decrease in Au binding. On the basis of an IR data, Gong *et al.* (2005) concluded that amino and hydroxyl groups play a predominant role (at high pH) in binding of Pb on *Spirulina maxima.* Ting *et al.* (1995) studied the mechanism of Au (III) sorption by *C. vulgaris* using X-ray photoelectron spectroscopy (XPS) analysis. They found elemental gold on the cell surface, and this led them to suggest the involvement of a reduction process in Au sorption. Greene *et al.* (1986) suggested that sulphydryl groups are not involved in Au binding by *Chlorella vulgaris.*

The above discussion leads to the generalization that carboxyl groups of cell wall polysaccharides play a predominant role in heavy metal sorption by algae and cyanobacteria. Thiol group plays an important role in sorption of metals like Cd at lower pH (> 2) (Sheng *et al.,* 2004). Although various potential fuctional groups have been demonstrated in algae, their mere presence does not guarantee participation in biosorption of metals. Steric hindrance, conformational changes or cross-linking, all of which change with environmental conditions (pH, ionic strength, competing cations or ligands), may prevent some surface functional groups from binding to metal (Adhya *et al.,* 2002). For example, surface charge may be neutralized either by binding with cations or by cross-linking between oppositely charged surface groups.

Several studies reveal that the process of heavy metal biosorption involves mechanisms, such as ion exchange, complexation, electrostatic attraction, and microprecipitation (Volesky and Holan, 1995). Ion exchange has been shown to be the most important mechanism for the biosorption of metal ions by algal biomass (Grist *et al.,* 1990). Greene *et al.* (1987) observed that the binding of Cu^{2+}, Pb^{2+}, Zn^{2+}, Ni^{2+} and Cr^{3+} to *Spirulina platensis* was accompanied by the liberation of protons from the biomass. Release of Mg^{2+} after binding of Cu^{2+} and Zn^{2+} on *Oscillatoria anguistissima* has been reported by Ahuja *et al.* (1999). Williams and Edyvean (1997) observed a concomitant release of Ca^{2+} during biosorption of Ni^{2+} by the brown alga *Ecklonia maxima.* All these studies suggest that heavy metal sorption involves exchange of metal ions with surface bound protons or cations. Ion exchange capacity is highly variable among different algal species. Pirszel *et al.* (1995) reported the maximum ion exchange capacity (in terms of Na^+/H^+ exchange) of five algal species ranging from 41-825 eq g^{-1} dry weight. Large variability in ion exchange capacity of different algal forms may be due to variation in cell wall composition. Unicellular algae generally show a higher ion exchange capacity than filamentous forms due to higher surface/volume ratio (Pirszel *et al.,* 1995). Ion exchange capacity and consequently metal sorption capacity of algal biomass increases with an increase in pH (Mehta *et al.,* 2002). This has been explained as an effect of decreasing competition with protons for the same binding sites (Crist *et al.,* 1994). In view of complexity of the composition of the cyanobacterial membrane surfaces, it is possible that various mechanisms operate simultaneously to varying degrees depending on the algal species and the environmental conditions (Sheng *et al.,* 2004). Aluminum sorption onto algal cells involves a different kind of mechanism. Aluminum ions bind to biomass in the form of polynuclear aluminum species (Bottero *et al.,* 1980). These polymerized aluminum ions prevented other heavy metal ions from accessing to binding site.

It has been demonstrated that once the metals are inside the cell, they may bind to intracellular components or precipitate (Gadd, 1988). Biological macromolecules and enzymes with appropriate functional groups or metal cofactors are impacted by metal activity. In *Ankistrode smus falcatus*, Wong *et al.* (1984) have demonstrated that Sn was about 85% in the cellular polysaccharide fraction, 15% in the protein fraction, and 0.2% in lipid and low molecular weight fractions. Metals may be detoxified by accumulation in polyphosphate bodies and intracellular metal-binding proteins of cyanobacteria and eukaryotic algae (Zhang and Majidi, 1994), and within the vacuoles of some eukaryotic algae (Gadd, 1988). The presence of one metal may change the distribution of others among cellular components. Okamura and Aoyama (1994) have shown that when present in a mixture, Cd and Cr (VI) influence each other's concentration and distribution among membrane, cell wall, and soluble and miscellaneous fractions of *Chlorella ellipsoidea*.

The available literature suggests that Pb is sorbed maximally compared to other metals in a majority of algal species (Davis *et al.,* 2003). Brown algae like *Ascophyllum, Sargassum,* etc., sorb more metal than other algae due to their high alginate content. In general, metal sorption capacity of algae is the least for Ni, although *M. aeruginosa* possesses a very high Ni sorption capability (Pradhan *et al.,* 1998). Lee *et al.* (2000) screened 48 species of red, brown and green marine algae for their Cr (VI) adsorbing potential, and found extraordinarily high selectivity of Cr (VI) sorption in *Pachymeniopsis* sp. (Rhodophyta). This alga was found to be poor in sorbing other heavy metals from water. Metal sorption potential of brown algae has been more thoroughly investigated compared to that of other marine algae and freshwater filamentous algae. Freshwater filamentous diatoms and sheath-forming filamentous blue-green algae, which might bind heavy metals with great efficiency, have somehow failed to receive adequate attention of the researchers.

A considerable potential in adsorbing anionic species of certain metals has been found in algae. For example, algal cells can also adsorb Cr (VI) with considerable ease at low pH values (< 2) (Dnniez and Aksu, 2002). The removal of Cr (VI) takes place by algae in anionic conditions as well as through its reduction to the cationic Cr (III) under strongly acidic conditions. In nature Cr occurs only in these two forms, with Cr (VI) being much more toxic to biota than Cr (III). At low pH, the algal biomass provides protons for the reduction of Cr (VI) to Cr (III). Protonated biomass of *Ecklonia*, brown seaweed, could completely reduce Cr (VI) to Cr (III) (Park *et al.,* 2004). Cr (III) thus formed was present in the solution or as partly bound to the biomass. Cr (VI) reduction was independent of biomass concentration, but increased with decreasing pH. In another paper, Park *et al.* (2004) used prolonged (1 or 10 days) thermal treatment (60-100C) for enhancing the capability of *Ecklonia* biomass in reducing Cr (VI) to Cr (III). However, thermal treatment decreased the number of carboxyl groups by 76%, and this inter alia decreased the efficiency of Cr (III) adsorption. The latter authors suggested a two-stage process for the complete removal of Cr (VI) and Cr (III) using thermally treated biomass for reducing Cr (VI) at lower pH, and subsequently using native biomass for removing Cr (III) at higher pH.

Bioremedial Application of Cyanobacteria for Metal Removal

Research works on the use of algal biomass for removing metal ions from aqueous solutions are still in incipient stage. Although thousands of algal species are known, only a few of them have been investigated for their metal sorption ability and subsequent use in wastewater treatment. Metal biosorption experiments have been conducted with freshwater green algae (e.g., *Chlorella,* spp., *Cladophom* spp., *Scenedesmus* spp., *Chlamydomonas reinhardtii*), brown algae (e.g., *Sargassum natans, Fucus vesiculosus, Ascophyllum nodosum, Laminaria japonica*).

Cyanobacteria like *Microcystis aeruginosa and Oscillatoria* are easy to grow in culture and some algal species are being grown commercially in large quantity. Metal sorption ability of algae varies greatly from species to species and even among strains of a single species for any metal, although this variation may also be due to variable experimental conditions in different studies. A suggestion has also been made that cells grown under different conditions vary with regard to composition of their cell wall, and hence in biosorption characteristics (Chojnackaet *et al.,* 2005). Some strains of cyanobacteria show a high affinity for sorbing a particular metal ion, whereas others do not show such specificity and may sorb several metal ions.

The affinity of various algal species for binding metal ions shows different hierarchies. In general, metal ions with greater electronegativity and smaller ionic radii are preferentially sorbed by algal biomass. The ability of algae to remove metals is comparable and even at times higher than that of other sorbents. Metal removal efficiency of the commonly used ion exchangers and resins is very low at or below 10 mg l^{-1} metal concentration in the solution. Nevertheless, algae may almost completely remove metal ions from solutions having low metal concentrations (Mehta and Gaur, 2001a). Axtell *et al.* (2003) found 97% removal of Pb by the macroalga *Macrospom* from a solution having 39.4 mg l^{-1} initial concentration of Pb. Many times algae have been found to outperform other biosorbents in removing metals from solutions. Algal biomass could be used in the form of biotraps for the removal of heavy metals from industrial effluents. AlgaSORB®, a commercial product, consisting of gel encapsulated algal cell wall, has a remarkable affinity for Hg, Pb, Cd, Cr, Cu, Zn, Ni, Ag, Au, etc. (Darnall, 1989). An important characteristic of AlgaSORB® is that high concentrations of common ions do not interfere with sorption of metal ions. Where synthetic resins are inefficient in removing heavy metals from wastewaters having high concentrations of total dissolved solids (TDS), AlgaSORB® could be used successfully to remove toxic metals (Darnall, 1991). Chitoplex, an insoluble crosslinked chitosan, is another commercial biotrap for detoxification of heavy metal-containing industrial wastewaters (Crusberg *et al.,* 1991).

Factors Affecting Heavy Metal Sorption by Cyanobacteria

Effect of concentration of heavy metals: Heavy metals sorption and removal by algal biosorbents mainly depend on the initial concentration of metals in the solution. It was found that metal sorption initially increases with increase in metal concentration in the solution, and then becomes saturated after a certain concentration of metal (Da Costa and Leite, 1991; Aloysius *et al.,* 1999; Mehta and Gaur, 2001a; Mehta *et al.,* 2002a; Mehta *et al.,* 2002b). Algal cell surface has several kinds of functional groups with varying affinity for an ionic species. Low and high affinity functional groups are involved in sorption of metal ions at high and low concentration of metal ions respectively.

Effect of pH: Several experiments have demonstrated that sorption of metal ions is a function of pH of the solution. Therefore, efforts have been made to find out the optimum pH for maximizing metal removal by algae. There are numerous studies that show increased metal sorption with increasing pH of the solution. Since a majority of metal binding groups of algae are acidic (e.g., carboxyl), their availability is pH dependent. These groups generate a negatively charged surface at acidic pH, and electrostatic interactions between cationic species and the cell surface is responsible for metal biosorption. A decreased metal sorption by algae has been frequently observed at extremely acidic pH (< 2) (Crist *et al.,* 1981; Ozer *et al.,* 1994; Mehta and Gaur, 2001b). There is also a great variability in optimum pH for sorption of a particular metal ion by different algal species. For example, the optimum pH for sorption of Cu by cyanobacteria (*Microcystis aeruginosa* and *Spirulina platensis*) is far greater than that for Cu sorption by green algae (*Cladophora prolifera, Chlorella vulgaris, C. kessleri).* This variability may be related to the differences in chemical composition of cell surface of various algal species. Chojnacka *et al.* (2005) found a distinct relationship between pH of aqueous metal solution and involvement of functional group in binding of Pb onto *Spirulina maxima*. For pH ranges 2-5, 5-9 and 9-12, respectively, the functional groups involved in binding of Pb were carboxyl, carboxyl and phosphate, carboxyl, phosphate and hydroxyl.

Effect of temperature: It has been generally observed that the variation in temperature considerably affects the metal uptake by live cells. Several reports showed significant alterations in metal uptake by live organisms due to change in temperature regime (Skowronski, 1986; Mehta and Gaur, 2001c; Mehta *et al.,* 2002b), with maximum uptake occurring at specific temperature optima. Increased metal sorption with increase in temperature (Tsezos and Volesky, 1981; Kuyucak and Volesky, 1989; Aksu and Kutsal, 1991; Aksu, 2002) suggests that metal biosorption by algae is an endothermic process. On the contrary, some studies indicate exothermic nature of metal sorption by algae (Cruz *et al.,* 2004; Aksu, 2001; Benguell and Benaissa, 2002). Increased biosorption of heavy metals with increasing temperature has been ascribed to bond rupture that perhaps enhances the number of active sites involved in metal sorption or higher affinity of sites for metals. There are also some reports, which show no effect of temperature on metal sorption (Norris and Kelly, 1979; Zhao *et al.,* 1994).

Effect of presence of ions species: Metal sorption by an algal biosorbent is also affected by the presence of anions in the medium. Lowered accumulation of Co and Cu by algae in the presence of carbonate, orthophosphate, sulphate, nitrate, EDTA and chloride ions has been observed (Rai *et al.,* 1981). However, increased accumulation of ionic species like nitrate and ammonium occurred in the presence of Cu and Fe in *Anabaena doliolum* (Rai and Mallik, 1992). The presence of other cations, including metal ions, also significantly affect metal sorption by algae (Mehta and Gaur, 2001c; Mehta *et al.,* 2002a; Mehta *et al.,* 2002b). Industrial wastewaters contain different kind of impurities, which may significantly affect metal biosorption (Ho and McKay, 2000). Among such impurities, light ion exists in most industrial effluent and they can greatly affect metal sorption potential of biosorbents (Lee and Volesky, 1997; Chen and Yiacoumi, 1997; Low *et al.,* 2000). Reduced metal uptake in the presence of light metals is attributed to competition for cellular binding sites, or precipitation or complexation by carbonates, bicarbonates or hydroxides of Ca and Mg (Rai *et al.,* 1981). High concentrations of salts like NaCl in solution also decrease the rate of metal sorption by algae (Cho *et al.,* 1994). Garnham *et al.* (1992) and Corder and Reeves (1994) have shown that Na decreases the accumulation of Ni, Co and Cs by cyanobacteria and some algae. Whereas most of the studies report inhibitory effect of light metal ions on sorption of heavy metals by biosorbent, a few of them show no effect (Pawlik and Skowronski, 1994; Jalali- Rad *et al.,* 2004).

Effect of biomass concentration: Several studies have shown that the biomass concentration considerably affects the recovery of significant amount of metal ion from a solution. Gong *et al.* (2005) reported that increasing biomass of *Spirulina maxima* showed a decrease in Pb sorption capacity per unit cell mass. They found that increasing biomass concentration from 0.1 to 20 g l^{-1} resulted in a significant reduction in Pb sorption capacity of *Spirulina maxima* from 121 to 21 mg g^{-1}. Similarly, Hamdy (2000) has reported a decreased sorption of Cr, Co, Ni, Cu and Cd by different algae with increasing concentration of biomass. This may be due to the limited availability of metal, increased electrostatic interactions, interference between binding sites and reduced mixing at higher biomass concentrations (Meikle *et al.,* 1990; Fourest *et al.,* 1994). However, no straight forward relationship between biomass concentration and metal removal has been noticed. Mehta and Gaur (2001a) reported that increasing the biomass concentration by 100-fold enhanced Ni and Cu removal from 13 to 65% and 10 to 85%, respectively, from solution having 5 mg l^{-1} Ni or Cu. Greater availability of metal binding sites was the main cause of increased metal removal at higher biomass concentration (Mehta and Gaur, 2001a).

Effect of other factors: Metal sorption by algae may be greatly influenced by nutrient level, growth rate and illumination. Subramanian *et al.* (1994) reported that Cu, Cd and Zn uptake by algae increased with increase in concentration of nitrate in the medium. Algal growth increases with increasing light intensity to saturation level, but the influence of light intensity on metal sorption remains largely unknown. Several reports showed inhibition of metal sorption by algal spp. in dark (Garnham *et al.,* 1992; Pawlik and Skowronski, 1994). However, higher Zn uptake has been shown in dark (Subramanian *et al.,* 1994). The growth phase of algal culture also influenced the metal sorption. Variation in growth conditions possibly caused the changes in composition of the cell surface, thereby affecting metal biosorption characteristics of the biomass.

CONCLUSION

Cyanobacteria are unique microbes that have many advantages in our life. They might be used as an agent, which can remove the heavy metal and finally improve the environment quality. Some reports show achievements in reducing the heavy metal from the factory wastewater and environment.

Rice field ecosystems possess a bidirectional natural metal ameliorating system where *Aulosira* mats act as immobilized cells, and decay of *Aulosira* and other cyanobacteria act as natural chelators protecting the rice plants from the deleterious effects of heavy metals. This is significant for India, as the rice fields get their water for irrigation from sources that are often highly contaminated with these two metals as a result of dumping of idols and other effluents from paint, tannery and leather industries. The presence of these metals could have a direct bearing on the nitrogen economy of these fields if the cyanobacteria are adversely affected.

Class II metallothionein proteins present in several cyanobacterial strains may act as defense mechanisms employed by the organism by binding metal ions intracellularly. Future experiments will attempt to over express these genes in engineered strains of cyanobacteria with the idea that these strains would then be capable of binding more metal ions from solution.

The performance of a given EPS-producing cyanobacterium in metal-removal processes depends not only on the amount of EPS produced but also on its quality and molecular structure.

Many algae have enormous capability to absorb metals, and there is an immense potential for using them to decontaminate the wastewater. Algae can also effectively remove metals from multi-metal solutions. Several factors like temperature, pH, different ionic species, biomass concentrations etc. significantly affect the metal uptake and biosorption by algae.

ACKNOWLEDGEMENTS

This work was possible through grants attributed to Dr. Jay Shankar Singh as Senior Research Associate (Scientists' Pool Scheme) by CSIR, HRDG, New Delhi.

REFERENCES

Adhya, J., Cai, X., Sayre, R.T. and Traina, S.J. (2002). *Colloids and Surfaces A: Pysicochem.* Eng. Aspects **210:** 1-11.

Ahuja, P., Gupta, R., and Saxena, R.K. (1999). *Process Biochem.* **34:** 77-85.

Aksu, Z. (2001). *Biochem. Eng. J.,* **7:** 79-84.

Aksu, Z. (2002). *Process Biochem.,* **38:** 89-99.

Aksu, Z., and Donmez, G. (2001). *J. Environ. Sci. Health, Part A* **36:** 367-381.

Aksu, Z., and Kutsal, T. (1991). *J. Chem. Technol. Biotechnol.* **52:** 109-118.

Aloysius, R., Karim, M.I.A. and Arif, A.B. (1999). *World J. Microbiol. Biotechnol.* **15:** 571-578.

Anjana, K., Kaushik., A. Kiran, B. and Nisha, R. (2007). *J. Hazar. Mat.,* **148:** 383-386.

Avery, S.V., Codd, G.A., and Gadd, G.M. (1998). *In :* Wastewater Treatment with Algae, pp. 55-72.

Axtell, N.R., Sternberg, S.P., and Claussen, K. (2003). *Bioresource Technol.* **89:** 41-48.

Banerjee, M., Mishra, S. and Chatterjee, J. (2004). *Electronic J. Biotech.,* **7:** 302-309.

Bates, S.S., Tessier, A., Campbell, P.G.C., and Buffle, J. (1982). *J. Phycol.* **18:** 521-529.

Bender, J., J.P. Gould, J.P., Vatcharapijarn, Y., Young, J.S. and Phillips, P. (1994). *Water Environ. Research,* **66:** 679-683.

Benquell, B. and Benaissa, H. (2002). *Water Res.* **36:** 2463-2474.

Bingham, MJ., Ong, TJ., Summer, KH., Middleton, RB. and McArdle, HJ. (1998). *Am. J. Clin Nutr.* **67(Suppl. 5):** 982-87S.

Bonilla, I., Bolanos, L. and Mateo, P. (1995). *Physiol. Plant.* **94:** 31-36.

Bottero, J.Y., Cases, J.M., Fiessinger, F., and Poirier, J.E. (1980). *J. Phys. Chem.* **84:** 2933-2939.

Bremner, I. (1998). *J. Am. Coll. Nutr.* **9:** 487-91.

Cain, A., Vannela, R. and Woo, L.K. (2008). *Bioresource Technol.* **99:** 6578-6586.

Chen, J.P. and Yiacoumi, S. (1997). *Sci. Technol.* **32:** 51-69.

Cho, D.Y., Lee, S.T., Park, S.W. and Chung, A.S. (1994). *J. Environ. Sci. Health,* Part A **29:** 389-409.

Chojnacka, K., Chojnacki, A. and Gorecka, H. (2004). *Hydrometallurgy.* **73:** 147-153.

Chojnacka, K., Chojnacki, A. and Gorecka, H. (2005). *Chemosphere.* **59:** 75-84.

Corder, S.L. and Reeves, M. (1994). *Appl. Biochem. Biotechnol.,* **45:** 847-859.

Crist, R.H., Martin, J.R., Carr, D., Watson, J.R. and Clarke, H. (1994). *Environ. Sci. Technol.* **28:** 1859-1866.

Crist, R.H., Martin, J.R., Guptill, P.W., Eslinger, J.M. and Crist, D.R. (1990). *Environ. Sci. Technol.* **24:** 337-342.

Crist, R.H., Oberholser, K., Shank, N. and Nguyen, M. (1981). *Environ. Sci. Technol.* **15:** 1212-1217.

Crusberg, T.C., Weathers, P.J. and Baker, E.F. (1991). *In: Innovative Hazardous Wastewater treatment Technology Series* 3.Technomic Publishing Co., Inc., Lanscaster, PA.

Cruz, C.C.V., Da Costa, A.C.A., Henriques, C.A. and Luna, A.S. (2004). *Bioresource Technol.* **91:** 249-257.

Da Costa, ACA. and Leite, SGF. (1991). *Biotechnol. Lett.,* **13:** 359-362.

Dallinger, R., Berger, B., Hunziker, P. and Kagi, JH. (1997). *Nature* **38:** 237-38.

Dalton, T., Fu, K., Palmiter, RD. and Andrews, GK. (1996). *J. Nutr.,* **126:** 825-33.

Dameron, CT. and Harrison, MD. (1998). *Am. J. Clin. Nutr.* **67:** 1091-97S.

Darnall, D.W. (1989). *In: Hazardous Waste treatment:* Biosystems for pollution control, pp. 113-124. Proceeding of 1989 A and WMA/EPA International symposium.

Darnall, D.W. (1991). *In: Hazardous Waste treatment:* Biosystems for pollution control, pp. 113-124. Proceeding of 1989 A and WMA/EPA International symposium. *Innovative Hazardous Wastewater treatment Technology Series.* 3. Technomic Publishing Co., Inc., Lanscaster, PA.

Davis, SR., McMahon, RJ. and Cousins, RJ. (1998). *J. Nutr.,* **128:** 825-31.

Davis, T.A., Volesky, B. and Mucci, A. (2003). *Water Res.* **37:** 4311-4330.

De Filippis, L.F. and Pallaghy, C.K. (1994). *In:* Algae and water pollution, (Eds. Rai, L.C., Gaur, J.P. & Soeder, C.J.), Schweizerbart'sche Verlagsbuchhandlung (Nagele u. Obermiller), Stuttgart, pp. 31-77.

De Philippis, R. and Vincenzini, M. (1998). *FEMS Microbiol. Rev.* **22:** 151-175.

De Philippis, R., Paperi, R. and Sili, C. (2007). *Biodegradation,* **18:**181-187.

De Philippis, R., Paperi, R., Sili, C. and Vincenzini, M. (2001a). *J. Appl. Phycol.* **15:** 155-161.

De Philippis, R., Sili, C., Paperi, R. and Vincenzini, M. (2001b). *J. Appl. Phycol.,* **13:** 293-299.

Demirel, S., Ustun, B., Aslim, B. and Suludere, Z. (2009). *J. Hazard. Materials* (*In Press*).

Deng, DX., Ono, S., Koropatnick, J. and Cherian, MG. (1998). *Lab. Invest.,* **78:** 175-83.

Donmez, G. and Aksu, Z. (2002). *Process Biochem.* **38:** 751-762.

El-Enany, A.E. and Issa, A.A. (2000). *Env. Tox. Pharma.* **8:** 95–101.

El-Sheekh, M.M., El-Shouny, W A., Osman, M E.H. and El-Gammal, E.W.E. (2005). *Env. Tox. Pharma.***19:** 357-365.

Forster, C.F. and Wase, A.J. (1997). *In:* Biosorbents for metal ions, (Eds. Wase, A.J. & Forster, C.F.), Taylor & Francis Ltd., London, United Kingdom, pp. 1-10.

Fourest, E. and Volesky, B. (1997). *Appl. Biochem. Biotechnol.* **67:** 215-226.

Fourest, E., Canal, C. and Roux, J.C. (1994). *Appl. Microbiol. Biotechnol.* **37:** 399-403.

Gadd, G.M. (1988). *In: Biotechnology*. pp. 401-434. Rehm, H.J., Ed., VCH, Weinheim.

Gardea-Torresdey, J.L., Arenas, J.L., Francisco, N.M.C., Tiemann, K.J. and Webb, R. (1998). *J. Hazard. Subst. Res.,* **1:** 1-18.

Gardea-Torresdey, J.L., Becker-Hapak, M.K., Hosea, J.M. and Darnell, D.W. (1990). *Environ. Sci. Technol.,* **19:** 1372-1379.

Garnham, G.W., Codd, G.A. and Gadd, G.M. (1992). *Appl. Microbiol. Biotechnol.,* **37:** 270-276.

Geddie, J.L. and Sutherland, I.W. (1993). *J. Appl. Bact.,* **74:** 467-472.

Gong, R., Ding, Y., Liu, H., Chen, Q. and Liu, Z. (2005). *Chemosphere.* **58:** 125-130.

Gothalwal, R. and Bisen, P.S. (1993). *Biology and Env. Sci.* **6:** 187-194.

Greene, B., Hosea, M., McPherson, R., Henzl, M., Dale, A.M. and Darnall, D.W. (1986). *Environ. Sci. Technol.* **20:** 627-632.

Greene, B., McPherson, R., and Darnall, D. (1987). *In:* Metal Speciation, Seperation and Recovery. (Eds. Patterson, J.W.& Pasino, R.), Lewis, Chelsea, Ml, pp. 315-338.

Hamdy, A.A. (2000). *Curr. Microbiol.* **41:** 232-238.

Hamer, D., Culotta, V., Furst, P., Hackett, R., Hsu, T., Hu S *et al.* (1991). *Annu. Rev. Biochem.* **55:** 913-51.

Harris, ZL. and Gitlin, JD. (1996). *Am. J. Clin. Nutr.,* **63:** 836-41S.

Haung, A. (1967). *Acta Chem. Scand.* **15:** 1794-1795.

Huckle, JW., Morby, AP., Turner, JS. and Robinson, NJ. (1993). *Mol. Microbiol.,* **7:**177-87.

Inthorn, D., Nagase., H., Isaji, Y., Hirata, K and Miyamoto, K. (1996). *J. Ferm. Bioen.,* **6:** 580-584.

Inthorn, D., Silapanuntakul, S. and Incharoensakdi, A. (2002). *Asian J. Microbiol. Biotech. Env. Sci.,* **4 :** 1-6.

Jalali-Rad, R., Ghalocerian, H., Asef, Y., Dalir, S.T., Sahaftipour, M.H. and Gharanjik, B.M. (2004). *J. Hazardous Materials.* **116:** 125-134.

Jarup, L., Berglund, M, Elinder, CG., Nordberg, G. and Vahter, M. (1998). *Scand. J. Work Environ. Health* **24(Suppl.):**1-51.

Kelley, M. 1988. *Mining and the Freshwater Environment.* BP Elsevier Applied Science, London.

Kelly, EJ. and Palmiter, RD. (1996). *Nat. Genet.,* **13:** 219-22.

Kelly, EJ., Quaife, CJ., Froelick, GJ and Palmiter, RD. (1996). *J. Nutr.* **126:** 1782-90.

Khauer, K., Behra, R., and Sigg, L. (1997). *J. Phycol.* **33:** 596-601.

Kiran, B., Kaushik, A. and Kaushik, C.P. (2008). *Process,* **43:** 598-604.

Klaassen, C.D., Liu, J. and Choudhuri, S. (1999). *Annu. Rev. Pharmacol. Toxicol.,* **39:** 267-94.

Kojima, Y. and Hunziker, PE. (1991). *Methods Enzymol.* **205:** 419-21.

Kuyucak, N. and Volesky, B. (1989). *Biotechnol. Bioeng.* **33:** 809-814.

Kuyucak, N. and Volesky, B. (1989). *Biotechnol. Bioeng.* **33:** 219-235.

Ledin, M. (2000). *Earth Sci. Rev.,* **51:** 1-31.

Lee, D.C., Park, C.J., Yang, J.E., Jeong, Y.H. and Rhee, H.I. (2000). *Appl. Microbiol. Biotechnol.* **54:** 597-600.

Lee, H.S. and Volesky, B. (1997). *Water Res.* **31:** 3082-3088.

Liu, J., Kershaw, W.C. and Klaassen, C.D. (1991). *Toxicol. Appl. Pharmacol.* **107:** 27-34.

Low, K.S., Lee, C.K. and Liew, S.C. (2000). *Process Biochem.* **36:** 59-64.

Maret ,W. and Vallee BL. (1998). *Proc. Natl. Acad. Sci., USA* **95:** 3478-82.

Mehta, S.K. and Gaur, J.P. (2001a). *Ecol. Eng.* **18:** 1-13.

Mehta, S.K. and Gaur, J.P. (2001b). *Appl. Microbiol. Biotechnol.* **55:** 379-382.

Mehta, S.K. and Gaur, J.P. (2001c). *Eur. J. Protistol.* **37:** 261-271.

Mehta, S.K., Singh, A. and Gaur, J.P. (2002b). *J. Environ. Sci. Health*, Part A **37**: 399-414.

Mehta, S.K., Tripathi, B.N. and Gaur, J.P. (2002a). *J. Appl. Phycol.* **14:** 267-273.

Meikle, A.J., Gadd, G.M. and Reed, R.H. (1990). *Enzyme Microb. Technol.* **12:** 865-872.

Micheletti, E., Colica, G., Viti, C. Tamagnini, P. and De Philippis, R. (2007). *J. Appl. Microbiol.,* **105:** 88-94.

Nartey, N.O., Frei, J.V. and Cherian, M.G. (1987). *Lab. Invest.* **57:** 397-401.

Niu, H. and Volesky, B. (2000). *J. Chem. Technol. Biotechnol.* **75:** 436-442.

Norris, P.R. and Kelly, D.P. (1979). *J. Gen. Microbiol.* **99:** 317-324.

Okamura, H. and Aoyama, I. (1994). *Environ. Toxicol. Water Qual.* **9:** 7-15.

Ozer, D., Aksu, Z., Kutsal, T. and Caglar, A. (1994). *Environ. Technol.* **15:** 439-448.

Pal, A. and Pal A.K. (2008). *Indian J Microbiol.,* **48:** 49-64.

Palmiter, R.D. (1998). *Proc. Natl. Acad. Sci., USA* **95:** 8428-30.

Park, D., Yun, Y.S., Cho, H.Y. and Park, J.M. (2004). *Ind. Eng. Chem. Res.* **43:** 8226-8232.

Parker, D.L., Schram, B.R., Plude, J.L. and Moore, R.E. (1996). *Appl. envir. Microbiol.* **62:** 1208-1213.

Parker, D.L., Mihalick, J.E., Plude, J.L., Plude, M.J., Clark, T.P., Lynn, E., Joshua, F.J., Rai, L.C. and Kumar, H.D. (2000). *J. Applied Phycology*, **12:** 219-224.

Pawlik, B. and Skowronski, T. (1994). *Environ. Exp. Bot.* **34:** 225-233.

Pirszel, J., Pawlik, B. and Skowronski, T. (1995). *J. Ind. Microbiol.* **14:** 319-322.

Plude, J.L., Parker, D.L., Schommer, O.J., Timmerman, R.J., Hagstrom, S.A., Joers, J.M. and Hnasko, R. (1991). *Appl. Envir. Microbiol.,* **57:** 1696-1700.

Pradhan, S. and Rai, L.C. (2000). *W.J. Microbiol. Biotechnol.* **16:** 579-584.

Pradhan, S., Singh, S., Rai, L.C. and Parker, D.L. (1998). *J. Microb. Biotechnol.* **8:** 53-60.

Prasad, B.B. and Pandey, U.C. (2000). *W.J. Microbiol. Biotech.***16:** 819-827.

Rai, L.C. and Mallick, N. (1992). *World J. Microbiol. Biotechnol.* **8:** 110-114.

Rai, L.C., Gaur, J.P. and Kumar, H.D. (1981). *Biol. Rev. Phil. Soc.* **56:** 99-151.

Raungsomboon, S., Chidthaisong, A., Bunnag, B., Inthorn, D. and Harveya, N.W. (2008). *Bioresource Technol.* **99:** 5650-5658.

Raungsomboona, S., Chidthaisonga, A., Bunnagb, B., Inthornc, D. and Harveya, N.W. (2006). *Water Research,* **40:** 3759-3766.

Raveender, V., Scaria, J. and Verma, S.K. (2002). *Bull. Environ. Contamin. Toxicol.* **69:** 632-637.

Raveender, V. and Verma, S.K. (2006). *Bioprocess Biosys. Eng.*, **29:** 7-17.

Ridley, M. (1996). *Evolution*. Cambridge, UK: Blackwell Sci. 719 pp.

Rofe, A.M., Philcox, J.C. and Coyle, P.C. (1996). *Biochem. J.*, **314:** 793-97.

Romeru-Gonzalez, M.E., Williams, C.J. and Gardiner, P.H. (2001). *Environ. Sci. Technol.* **35:** 3025-3030.

Seki, H. and Suzuki, A. (1998). *J. Colloid. Interface. Sci.* **206:** 297-301.

Seki, H., and Suzuki, A. and Iburi, Y. (2000). *J. Colloid. Interface. Sci.* **229:** 196-198.

Sheng, P.X., Ting, Y.P., Chen, J.P. and Hong, L. (2004). *J. Colloid. Interf. Sci.* **275:** 131-141.

Silver, S. and Ji, G. (1994). *Envir. Health Perspectives,* **102:** 107-113.

Singh, S.P., Pradhan, S. and Rai, L.C. (1998). *Process Biochem.* **33:** 495-504.

Singh, S.P. and Yadava, V. (1986). *Biol. Zentralbl.* **105:** 539-542.

Skowronski, T. (1986). *Chemosphere.* **15:** 69-76.

Slotton, D.G., Goldman, C.R. and Frank, A. (1989). Commercially Grown *Spirulina* Found to Contain Low Levels of Mercury and Lead, Nutrition Reports International, pp. 1165-1172.

Subramanian, V.V., Sivasubramanian, V. and Gowrinathan, K.P. (1994). *J. Environ. Sci.* Health, Part A **29:** 1723-1733.

Suzuki, KT. (1995). *Res. Commun. Mol. Pathol. Pharmacol.* **89:** 221-40.

Ting, Y.P., Teo, W.K. and Soh, C.Y. (1995). *J. Appl. Phycol.* **7:** 97-100.

Trevors, J.T., Stratton, G.W. and Gadd, G.M. (1986). *Can. J. Microbiol.* **32:** 447-464.

Tsezos, M. and Volesky, B. (1981). *Biotechnol. Bioeng.* **23:** 583-604.

Turner, J.S. and Robinson, N.J. (1995). *J. Industrial Microbiol.* **14:** 119-125.

Verma, S.K. and Singh, H.N. (2006). *FEMS Microbiology Letters,* **84:** 291- 294.

Volesky, B. (2001). *Hydrometallurgy,* **59:** 203-216.

Volesky, B. and Schiewer, S. (1997). *Env. Sci. Technol.* **31:** 1863-1871.

Volesky, B. and Holan, Z.R. (1995). *Biotechnol. Prog.* **11:** 235-250.

Wong, P.T.S., Manguire, R.J., Chau, Y.K. and Kramar, O. (1984). *Can. J.Fish, Aquat. Sci.* **41**: 1570-1574.

Yee, N., Benning, L.G., Phoenix, Y.R., and Ferris, F.G. (2004). *Environ. Sci. Technol.* **38:** 775-782.

Zeng, J., Vallee, B.L. and Kagi, J.H. (1991). *Proc. Natl. Acad. Sci., USA* **88:** 9984-88.

Zhang W. and Majidi, V. (1994) *Environ. Sci. Technol.* **28:** 1577-1581.

Zhao, Y., Hao, Y. and Ramelow, G.J. (1994). *Environ. Monit. Assess.,* **33:** 61-70.

15

Unravelling the Potentiality of Microbial Inoculants in Phytonematode Management

Rakesh Pandey, Aakansha Gupta, Arun Mishra and Alok Kalra

Central Institute of Medicinal and Aromatic Plants
(Council of Scientific and Industrial Research),
P.O. CIMAP, Lucknow-226 015, India
E-mail: rakeshpandey66@hotmail.com

Nematodes are parasites of plants, algae, bacteria, fungi, other nematode species (as predators or even parasites), almost all vertebrates including fishes and invertebrates like insects and spiders. In soil an unseen and hidden enemy pest which silently spreads from nursery to nursery and field-to-field, attacking and causing enormous damage to almost major agricultural crops, worldwide is plant parasitic nematode. To manage the nematode problem in agricultural crops, various methods are available including chemical nematicides, but the adverse effect of nematicides on environment and human health compelled the researchers to use alternate nematode management tactics. Several non-chemical methods are available like organic amendments, fallow, flooding, changes in time of sowing/planting material, tillage practices, crop rotations, use of antagonistic crop, trap crop/cover crop, use of nematode free planting materials or seeds, solarization and biological control. Due to economic pressure and ever increasing world population, it becomes necessary to consider more profitable and environment-friendly methods for phytonematode management in agricultural crops. Exploring the potentiality of microbial inoculants, especially rhizospheric bacteria, to manage plant parasitic nematodes on agri crops has become one of the most important, feasible, environment-friendly and sustainable approaches. The present article summarizes the disease managing potentiality of the rhizospheric bacterial microbes and influence of various biotic and abiotic factors affecting the antagonistic activity against a variety of plant parasitic nematodes.

INTRODUCTION

Root rhizosphere is an active and densely populated area in which the roots interact with different components like invading root systems of other plant species for space, water, and mineral nutrients, and with millions of soil microbes, including bacteria, fungi, and nematodes. Thus, host, microbes and different abiotic factor interactions occur continuously in such biologically active zone of plants. Such type of interaction can either be positive or negative. The positive interaction occurs with useful microbes like mycorrhizal fungi, nitrogen-fixing bacteria, siderophores producers and phosphate solubilizers, and similarly the negative interaction occurs mostly with pest and pathogens. Therefore, the root rhizosphere is a hot spot of interacting microbes. In soil environment, the plant roots are exposed to a variety of microbes, resulting in the secretion of root exudates that include amino acids, organic acids, sugars, phenolics, and various other secondary metabolites. Root exudates serve as a major source of nutrient for microbes inhabiting such intensive zone. Most of the plants utilize these microbes to meet their hormonal and nutritional demands. Root exudates also play a significant role as attractant or repellent to different soil microbes.

The major soil-borne pest and pathogens are adapted to grow and flourish in the agricultural soil, but the root rhizosphere is considered a playground and infection court where the pathogen establishes a parasitic relationship with the host (Fig. 15.1). The rhizosphere is also a battlefield where the complex rhizosphere community, both microflora and microfauna, interacts with pathogens and influences the outcome of pathogen infection (Fig. 15.2). Various microbes that adversely affect crop health and yield are pathogenic fungi, bacteria and nematodes, whereas microorganisms that are beneficial include nitrogen-fixing bacteria, endophytes, AMF, and plant growth-promoting rhizobacteria (PGPR). The fluctuation in the population of different microbes has a direct effect on plant health.

Diseases caused by a variety of pathogens present in root rhizosphere pose a serious challenge and economic threats to different agricultural crops all around the world. It has been evidenced that despite the wide use of chemical pesticides in crop production, the losses due to pests and pathogens are significant. Plant parasitic nematodes are cosmopolitan in nature and parasites of major agricultural crops all around the world. Different types of plant parasitic nematodes, viz., migratory ectoparasites, migratory endoparasites, sedentary semi-endoparasites, sedentary endoparasites and above-ground parasites (Winslow, 1960) occupy the root rhizosphere and adversely affect the plant growth and yield (Luc *et al.,* 2005).

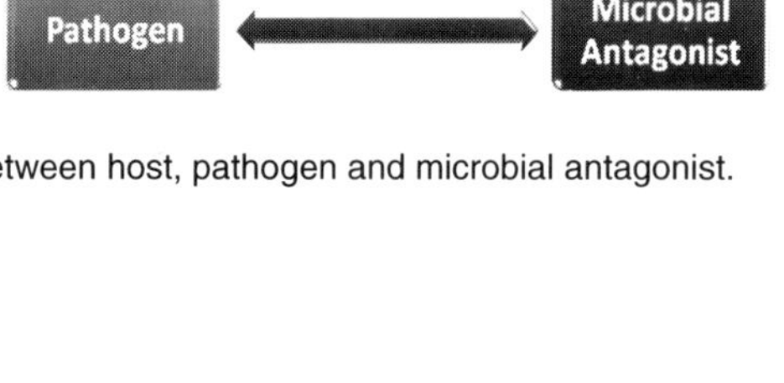

Fig. 15.1 Possible interaction between host, pathogen and microbial antagonist.

The most economically important nematodes in agriculture are the sedentary and migratory endoparasites, mainly root-knot nematodes, *Meloidogyne* spp., cyst nematodes, *Heterodera* spp, lesion nematode *Pratylenchus* spp. and burrowing nematode, *Radopholus similis*. In general, the major agricultural crops have been plagued by various plant parasitic nematodes that feed on different plant parts viz. roots, rhizome, sucker, tubers, seedlings, stem, leaves, buds and crowns (Gupta and Pandey, 2009). These nematodes make major hurdle like disrupting the ability of plant roots to take up water and nutrients from the soil. Several non-chemical methods are available like organic amendments, fallow, flooding, changes in time of sowing/planting material, tillage practices, crop rotations, use of antagonistic crop, trap crop/cover crop, use of nematode free planting materials or seeds, soil solarization and biological control, but due to economic pressure and ever increasing world population, it becomes necessary to consider more profitable methods for phytonematode management in a variety of crops. Although chemical nematicides have proved useful in protecting crops from plant parasitic nematodes, the major crops severely affected by these pests are vegetables, fruits, sugarcane, sugar beet, cotton, oil seed, pulses, tobacco, tea, coffee, cereals, spices, medicinal and aromatic plants. It is difficult to assess the exact loss caused by phytonematodes on each crops, but based on extensive survey data (Sasser and Freckman, 1987; Koenning *et al.*, 1999) it has been estimated that overall yield loss averages 12.3% annually. This figure approaches even more on selected crops like vegetables, fruits, medicinal and aromatic plants. In monetary terms the worldwide figure exceeds $US100 billion annually. Another way to consider the impact of plant-parasitic nematodes is through the management strategies employed in their control. In 1982, 50,000 tonnes of nematicide active ingredient were applied to crops in the United States at a cost exceeding $US1 billion (Landels, 1989), and between 1986 and 1990 in The Netherlands, nematicide application was more than three times the combined total of chemicals needed to combat insects, fungi and weeds on experimental, sustainable farms (Lewis *et al.*, 1997). Nowadays due to adverse impact of nematicides on environment, human and animal health, and detection of residues in food and underground water, the effective nematicides have been withdrawn from the world market and tight restriction has been imposed on the rest of chemical nematicides.

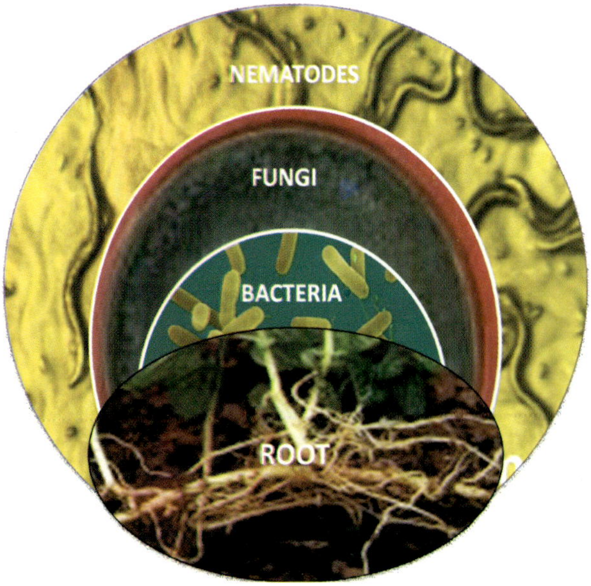

Fig. 15.2 Relationship between root and its major rhizospheric interactors.

NEED FOR MICROBIAL MANAGEMENT OF PHYTONEMATODES

Concern over chemical nematicides has led to an increased endeavour towards more environment friendly method of nematode management, and microbial nematode management has got momentum to reduce the population of important plant parasitic nematodes. Initially major research on the biocontrol of phytonematodes concentrated on the identification and biology of microbial agents. Even the management of phytonematodes achieved through microbes was often slow acting, less potential and more species specific. Despite some constraints in the microbial management of phytonematodes, several successes have been made to develop and formulate large number of microbes against major nematode species. In recent years more efforts have been directed towards the use of microbes to minimize the phytonematodes population, and to make soil more suppressive to nematode diseases (Sharon *et al.*, 2001; Gupta and Pandey 2009; Pandey *et al.*, 2009). In most cases, the microbial management of plant parasitic nematodes has been very effective under laboratory conditions, but field results have shown varying degrees of success (Stirling, 1991; Pandey *et al.*, 2000; Giannakou *et al.*, 2004; Dong *et al.*, 2006, Kumar *et al.*, 2009). It is widely accepted that the use of microbial pesticides is broad spectrum, target specific and does not pose a threat of resistance development and environmental hazard.

Microbes are more abundantly present in soil (Fig. 15.2), and some of them have shown more potential for lowering the plant parasitic nematode population in soil (Siddiqui *et al.*, 2007; Olivera *et al.*, 2004; Kumar *et al.*, 2009). In the phytonematode management, major emphasis should be given to improve soil health and gain economic benefits. Soil health is the capacity of a soil to function within the ecosystem boundaries to sustain biological productivity, maintain environmental quality, and promote plant health (Doran *et al.*, 1996). A healthy soil possesses high microbial biodiversity and provides relief from pests or pathogens, and most importantly, improves plant health and productivity (Compant *et al.*, 2005). The development of effective nematode control with soil microbes should be based on:

- development of efficient and sensitive isolation techniques favoring rhizosphere competence;
- formulation of screening techniques based on mechanisms of action that lead to detection of isolates with biological activity towards specific nematode behavior patterns;
- regulation of biotic and abiotic factors in favor of the nematode management system; and
- development of acceptable formulations for seed and planting material.

The presence of bacterial antagonists in the root has adverse effect on nematode population development through the production of some secondary metabolites when interacted with the roots. The effect of management depends on the interaction among host-microbes-environmental interaction. Thus, phytonematode management can be achieved through simultaneously promoting the growth of plant (Mittal *et al.*, 1995; Duponnois *et al.*, 1999; Whipps and Davies, 2000; Siddiqui and Shaukat, 2002, 2004) or beneficial organisms (Mittal *et al.*, 1995), facilitating the antagonistic activity (Duponnois *et al.*, 1999) or rhizosphere colonization of the microbial antagonists (Meyer and Roberts, 2002; Meyer, 2003), while antagonizing nematode. Aside from stable virulence towards target nematode, some other features of microbial strains must also be met before the development of these microbes for nematode management:

- strains should be: non-pathogenic to non-target organisms including humans, livestocks, birds, and other terrestrial and aquatic organisms;
- good colonizers of the host rhizosphere, establishing and reproducing in the soil;
- biologically competitive with other soil organisms;
- adaptable to variable environmental conditions;

- compatible with other pathogen control methods;
- compatible with other management practices and commercialization methodology; and
- conducive to plant growth and soil health.

TYPES OF BACTERIAL ANTAGONISTS

Different types of bacteria are involved in decreasing the nematode population in soil. On the basis of their mode of action, these bacteria may be considered as obligate parasite, opportunistic, rhizospheric, cry protein forming, endophytic and symbiotic bacteria, as few are parasitic to nematodes and others are indirectly involved to reduce the nematode infestation in plants (Fig. 15.3).

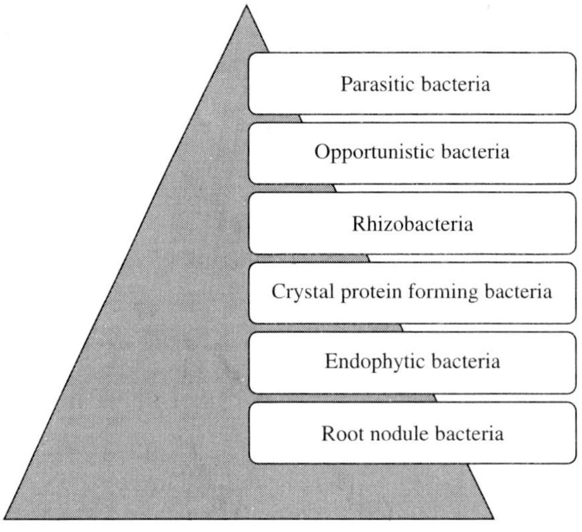

Fig. 15.3 Types of nematode antagonistic bacteria.

Parasitic Bacteria—*Pasteuria penetrans*

Pasteuria penetrans is a Gram-positive, obligate hyperparasite, endospore forming nematode parasitic bacteria (Fig. 15.4), which has a great potential to control different genera of plant parasitic nematodes on a variety of crops. *P. penetrans* is highly diverse in nature and has been reported all around the world on a variety of phytonematodes. This bacterium has been reported in 51 countries on 323 nematodes species belonging to 116 genera, including both plant parasitic nematodes and free living nematode species (Chen and Dickson, 1998). Majority of plant parasitic nematodes are parasitized by these bacteria (Pandey *et al.*, 2000; Bird *et al.*, 2003). The host range and morphological differences of *Pasteuria* vary in their parasitism from species to species (Sayre and Wergin, 1977). The non-motile endospores produced by *P. penetrans* attach with the cuticle of moving nematode (Fig. 15.4) in soil (Davies *et al.*, 2005). The germ tube of the germinating endospore penetrates inside the nematode cuticle, which then grows and within a few days the whole nematode body is full with large number of endospores of *P. penetrans*. Various factors are responsible for the attachment of spores to the nematode species (Stirling *et al.*, 1986, Persidis *et al.*, 1991, Davies and Danks, 1993; Davies and Redden, 1997; Bekal *et al.*, 2001; Preston *et al.*, 2003; Davies and Oppermann, 2006). In general, the bacteria infected nematode larvae, feed, moults and reaches the adult stage, but fecundity is greatly reduced or completely blocked (Sayre and Starr, 1985; Oostendrop *et al.,* 1991). On the completion of the bacterial life cycle, the nematode body disintegrates in the soil and large number of bacterial endospores are released into the soil. These endospores again attach to the motile nematode and complete their life cycle, which leads to the reduction in the nematode population in the soil. It has been reported that more than two million spores may be present in the body of one female root-knot nematode (Dabire and Mateille, 2004). *Pasteuria* spores may survive adverse conditions and persist for a longer period under the sandy soil. Clay soil and soil with high organic matter may interfere with the movement of the endospore with the percolating water. The major abiotic factors that influence the effectiveness of *Pasteuria* are soil moisture and temperature.

The major five species of *Pasteuria* infecting different plant parasitic nematodes are *Pasteuria penetrans*, *P. thornei*, *P. nishizawae*, *Pasteuria usage*, and *P. hartismeri.*

The endospores of the important species of *Pasteuria,* in general, possess narrow host range, as individual spores of this bacteria do not adhere or recognize all species of nematodes. In general, *P. penetrans* infect root knot nematode (*Meloidogyne* spp.) (Sayre and Starr, 1985, *P. thornei* infect root lesion nematode (*Pratylenchus* brachyurus.) (Sayre *et al.*, 1988); *P. nishizawae* infect the cyst nematode, *Heterodera* spp., *Globodera* spp. (Sayre *et al.*, 1991; Atibalentja *et al.,* 2000); *P. usage* infect *Belonolaimus longicaudatus* (Giblin-Davis *et al.*, 2003) and *P. hartismeri* infect *Meloidogyne ardensis* (Bishop *et al.*, 2008). *P. penetrans* has also been reported as parasite of *Caenorhabditis elegans* (Gives *et al.,* 1999). The molecular approaches have also been made to sequence the whole genome of *P. penetrans* (Bird *et al.,* 2003; Davies, 2005), and markers have been developed to identify different species of *Pasteuria* (Mouton *et al.*, 2007; Mouton and Ebert, 2008).

Various experiments have been carried out on various aspects of *P. penetrans* infection on nematode species. *P. penetrans* proved to be an efficient microbe in suppressing the plant parasitic nematode population on a variety of crops (Davies *et al.*, 1990; Giblin-Davis *et al.*, 1990; Stirling, 1984; Brown 1985; Bhattacharya and Swarup, 1988; Oostendorp *et al.*, 1991; Weibelzahl-Fulton *et al.*, 1996; Chen *et al.*, 1996; 1997; Chen and Dickson, 1998; Trudgill *et al.*, 2000). Concentration of 10^5 to 10^6 spores/g soil was found to be sufficient to check many nematode larvae on entering inside the root (Stirling *et al.* 1991).

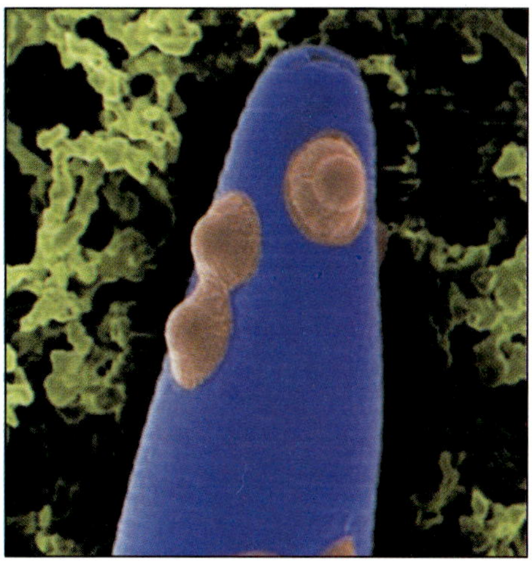

Fig. 15.4 Association of *Pasteuria penetrans* spores on body of nematode (permission obtained from Keith G. Davies, Plant Pathology and Microbiology, Rothamsted Research, Harpenden, United Kingdom).

In general, beyond doubt, *P. penetrans* is an effective biological control agent of phytonematodes, but its practical use is limited by the lack of efficient methods for mass production of endospores. The efficacy and implementation of biocontrol of nematodes through *P. penetrans* was considerably influenced by a variety of environmental factors like soil types, texture, soil moisture, temperature etc. The efficacy of *P. penetrans* greatly differs from one soil type to another (Dabiré and Mateille, 2004). With respect to management, the intensive irrigation of vegetables in the areas infested by root-knot nematodes could lead to the loss of *P. penetrans* spore populations, either native to these areas or introduced as bio-nematicides. Irrigation must be used only to improve plant growth, but its proper management (volume and application) is essential so as to allow the development of microbial antagonists of plant-parasitic nematodes. In laboratory experiments it was confirmed that intensive irrigation leached the spores down the soil profile and decreased the percentage of infected *Meloidogyne* juveniles (Kounbobr *et al.,* 2005).

Lack of an appropriate technology for mass production of endospore for inundative or augmentative release is the major hurdle in the management of phytonematodes through this bacterium. In this context, Pasteuria Bioscience LLC, Florida, has developed a media in which it is possible to grow vegetative stages of *Pasteuria* (Hewlett *et al.*, 2004).

Opportunistic Parasitic Bacteria

Some of the bacteria other than obligate parasite live saprophytically and target nematodes, as one of the food sources for their growth and proliferation. These bacteria are also able to penetrate the cuticle of the nematode and may kill the pest on the advent of adverse conditions. Such types of bacteria are known as opportunistic bacteria like *Brevibacillus laterosporus*, *Bacillus laterosporus* (Haung *et al.*, 2005). Various isolates of *B. laterosporus* have been reported to kill a number of nematode species (Oliveira *et al.,* 2004). During the infection of nematode by opportunistic bacteria, hydrolytic enzymes play a critical role in the degradation of nematode cuticle (Cox *et al.,* 1981; Decraemer *et al.,* 2003; Niu *et al.*, 2005, 2006; Tian *et al.,* 2006, 2007). Several bacterial proteases have also been reported to be involved in the infection process against the nematode. Most of the work on this group of bacteria is in progress using free living nematode as a target to develop potential agent for nematode management.

Rhizobacteria

Beneficial plant-microbe interactions in the rhizosphere are the determinants of plant health and soil fertility. In the era of sustainable agricultural production, the interactions in the rhizosphere play a pivotal role in transformation, mobilization, solubilization, etc. from a limited nutrient pool in the soil and subsequent uptake of essential plant nutrients by the crop plants to realize full genetic potential of the crop. Soil microorganisms are very important in the biogeochemical cycles of both inorganic and organic nutrients in the soil and in the maintenance of soil health and quality. Thus, the need of the hour is to enhance the efficiency of the meager amount of external inputs by employing the best combinations of beneficial microbes for sustainable agricultural production. Beneficial free-living soil bacteria isolated from the rhizosphere, which have been shown to improve plant health or increase yield, are usually referred to as plant growth-promoting rhizobacteria (PGPR) (Kloepper and Schroth, 1981) or plant health promoting bacteria (Sikora, 1988, 1991).

The root colonization is a process whereby bacteria survive inoculation to seed or in to soil, multiply in the spermosphere in response to seed exudates, which are rich in carbohydrates and amino acids (Kloepper and Schroth, 1981; Oostendrop and Sikora, 1990; Kloepper *et al.,* 1991, 1992; Kloepper, 1993; Spiegel *et al.,* 1991), attach to the root surface and colonize the developing root system. During the past several decades, many researchers have studied various PGPR strains for their capacity to increase the plant growth and yield, and to control the plant pathogens including plant pathogenic nematodes under greenhouse and field conditions (Becker *et al.,* 1988; Weller, 1988; Leeman *et al.,* 1995; Sikora, 1992; Jayakumar *et al.,* 2002). Therefore, rhizobacteria are considered efficient rhizosphere competitors in the rhizosphere, which displace the native microorganisms (Kloepper *et al.,* 1981; Hoffmann Heargarten *et al.,* 1997). Aerobic endospore forming bacteria, mainly *Bacillus* spp. and *Pseudomonas* spp., are among the dominant populations in the root rhizosphere, which antagonize the phytonematode population (Rovira and Sands, 1977; Kloepper *et al.,* 1992; Madamba *et al.,* 1999; Insunza *et al.,* 2002; Li *et al.,* 2005). *Pseudomonas* spp. have been reported to exhibit nematode suppressive effect against a variety of nematode species through the production of antibiotic and induction of systemic resistance (Spiegel *et al.,* 1991; Kloepper *et al.,* 1992; Kluepfel *et al.,* 1993; Cronin *et al.,* 1997a; Samaliev *et al.,* 2000; Siddiqui and Saukat, 2004; Kokalis-Burelle *et al.,* 2006). Several genera of other rhizobacteria that have shown antagonistic activities against plant parasitic nematodes are *Actinomycetes, Agrobacterium, Arthobactor, Alcaligenes, Aureobacterium, Azotobacter, Beijerinckia, Burkholderia, Chromobacterium, Clavibacter, Clostridium, Comamonas, Corynebacterium, Curtobacterium, Desulforibtio, Enterobacter, Flavobacterium, Gluconobacter, Hydrogenophaga, Klebsiella, Methylobacterium, Phyllobacterium, Phingobacterium, Rhizobium, Serratia, Stenotrotrophomonas* and *Variovorax* (Jacq and Fortuner, 1979; Kloepper *et al.,* 1991, 1992; Racke and Sikora, 1992; Guo *et al.,* 1996; Kluepfel *et al.,* 1993; Cronin *et al.,* 1997a, b; Duponnois *et al.,* 1999; Neipp and Becker, 1999; Jonathan *et al.,* 2000; Tian and Riggs 2000; Tian *et al.,* 2000; Meyer *et al.,* 2001; Mahdy *et al.,* 2001; Hallmann *et al.,* 2002; Mena and Pimentel, 2002; Meyer, 2003; Siddiqui *et al.,* 2007).

The induction of resistance mediated by rhizobacteria (ISR) has been reported to be active against nematode pests (Van Loon *et al.*, 1998; Ramamoorthy *et al.*, 2001). Resistance can be induced by deposition of callose, accumulating phenols and cell wall thickening. When the plant is attacked by the pathogen or pest, rhizobacteria promote the synthesis of some defence chemicals viz. PR proteins, increase the chitinase and peroxidase activity and also help to synthesise phytoalexins and other important secondary metabolites. (Van Loon *et al.*, 1998; Siddiqui and Mahmood, 1999; Ramamoorthy *et al.*, 2001). Bacterial determinants of ISR include lipopolysaccharides (LPSs), siderophores and salicylic acid (SA) (Van Loon *et al.*, 1998; Ramamoorthy *et al.*, 2001). A potent antihelminthic and insecticidal compound, avermectin is produced by *Streptomyces avermitilis.* One such avermectin named, abamectin, is reported to be successful in controlling *Meloidogyne incognita* root-knot nematode infection (El-Nagdi and Youssef, 2004). Several rhizobacteria produce metabolic by-products, which directly or indirectly reduce nematode population at large around the root rhizosphere (Fig. 15.5). For example, ammonia produced by ammonifying bacteria during the decomposition of nitrogenous organic materials reduces nematode population in soil. *Pseudomonas* reduces nematode population at significant level by the production of antibiotic such as 2, 4 diacetylphloroglucinol (DAPG) (Cronin *et al.* 1997a; Siddiqui and Saukat, 2002). Similarly, Mena and Pimentel (2002) reported that *Corynebacterium pauronetabolum* produces hydrogen sulphide and chitinase, which directly inhibit the nematode egg hatching. It was reported that up to 10% of rhizobacteria showed antagonistic activities against major parasitic nematodes (Oostendorp and Sikora, 1986; Kloepper *et al.*, 1992; Westcott and Kluepfel, 1993) including cyst (*Globodera* and *Heterodera* spp.) and root-knot (*Meloidogyne* spp.) nematodes.

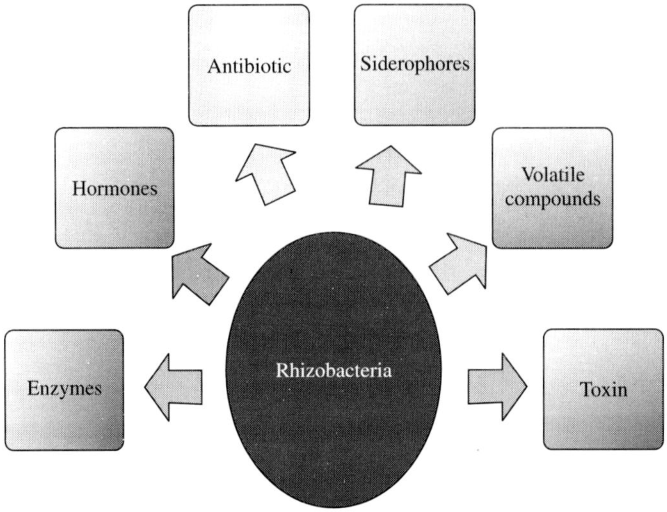

Fig. 15.5 Mode of action of rhizobacteria.

Some bacteria based products like Bio Yield™, Gustafson LLC based on *Paenobacillus macerans* and *Bacillus amyloliquefaciens* are available in the market for the management of a variety of plant parasitic nematodes (Meyer, 2003). Other product, Deny, based on *Burkholderia cepaci* was found very effective in reducing egg hatching and juvenile mobility in soil (Meyer and Roberts, 2002). BioNem is also used to manage the root-knot nematode infestation in vegetable crops in Israel based on *Bacillus firmus* (Giannakou and Prophetou-Athanasiadou, 2004; Marleny *et al.,* 2008). Wheat mash, as an organic amendment in combination with the 200-ml culture of the actinomycete, *Streptomyces costaricanus* sp. nov. (ATCC 55274), gave a higher shoot weight and responses than their individual use.

MECHANISM OF NEMATODE CONTROL

The mechanisms of PGPR-mediated enhancement of plant growth and yields of many crops are due to the production of several enzymes, hormones, antibiotics, volatile compounds, siderophores and phosphate solubilising activities (Fig. 15.5). However, the possible explanations include the following:

- The ability to produce ACC deaminase to reduce the level of ethylene in the roots of the developing plants, thereby increasing the root length and growth (Jacobson *et al.*, 1994; Glick *et al.*, 1998; Li *et al.*, 2000; Penrose and Glick, 2001).
- Ability to produce hormones like indole acetic acid (IAA) Patten and Glick, 2002), gibberellic acid (Mahmoud *et al.*, 1984) and cytokinins (Tien *et al.*, 1979).
- Asymbiotic nitrogen fixation (Kennedy *et al.*, 1997).
- Antagonism against phytopathogenic microorganisms by producing siderophores, β-1,3-glucanase, chitinases, antibiotics, fluorescent pigment and cyanide (Scher and Baker, 1982; Voisard *et al.*, 1989; Renwick *et al.*, 1991; Catellan *et al.*, 1999; Pal *et al.*, 2001).
- Solubilization of mineral phosphates and mineralization of other nutrients (De Freitas *et al.*, 1997).

- Antibiotics produced by the rhizobacteria directly or indirectly induce resistance and hence reduce nematode population. (Sikora and Hoffmann Heargarten, 1993; Oostendrop and Sikora, 1990; El-Nagdi and Youssef, 2004).
- Disrupts the nematode-host recognition and thus regulate the nematode behavior.
- They compete with nematode for nutrients.
- Rhizobacteria promote plant growth and therefore nematodes could not attack the healthy roots easily.

CRY PROTEIN PRODUCING BACTERIA

Bacillus thuringiensis (Bt), an aerobic Gram-positive bacterium, remains the focus of research on biopesticides. Crystal protein, a pore forming toxin produced by this bacteria is known to be toxic to a narrow range of insect species all around the world (Leyns *et al.,* 1995; Schenpe *et al.,* 1998, Maagd *et al.,* 2001), leaving vertebrate, beneficial organisms unaffected. Some Cry proteins are also toxic to other invertebrates such as nematodes, mites and protozoans (Bottjer *et al.,* 1986; Bowen *et al.* 1986a, b; Feitelson *et al.,* 1992). It was found that six Cry proteins, viz., Cry5, Cry6, Cry12, Cry13, Cry14 and Cry21 are toxic to a variety of nematodes (Crickmore *et al.,* 1998; Marroquin *et al.,* 2000; Pandey *et al.,* 2000; Wei *et al.,* 2003; Crickmore, 2005). The purified thermostable exotoxin was reported to be toxic to *Meloidogyne* eggs and larvae *in vitro* at 1:10 concentration (Prasad and Tilak, 1972), whereas with *Panagrellus redivivus*, a LC 50 was obtained with 175ng/ml of a solution containing 10.7% active Thuringienisn-A. Cry protein exerts its effects by forming lytic pores in the cell membrane of gut epithelial cells after the ingestion of toxin by target nematode larvae, the crystals dissolve within the gut of the nematode, and this is followed by proteolytic activation (Crickmore, 2005). Cry toxicity is directed against the intestinal epithelial cells of the midgut and leads to vacuole and pore formation, pitting, and eventual degradation of the intestine (Marroquin *et al.*, 2000). A large number of works has been published about the *B. thuringiensis* bacteria and their target host (Huffmann *et al.*, 2004; Crickmore, 2005).

ENDOPHYTIC BACTERIA

Bacteria that reside inside the living tissues without harming or gaining benefit are known as endophytic bacteria. (Hallmann *et al.,* 1997; McInory and Kloepper, 1995; Azevedo *et al.,* 2000; Hallmann 2001; Surette *et al.,* 2003). These bacteria can accelerate seedling emergence, promote plant growth under adverse conditions and reduce the disease severity caused by a variety of plant pathogens (Sturz and Matheson, 1996; Hallmann *et al.,* 1997, 1999; Munif *et al.,* 2000; Saukat *et al.,* 2002; Sturz and Kimpinski, 2004). Inspite of different ecological niches, root rhizobacteria and endophytic bacteria showed some of the same mechanisms for plant growth promotion and inhibition of phytopathogens (Kobayashi and Palumbo, 2000; Pandey *et al.,* 2000). Competition for ecological niche, substrate, produce inhibitory chemicals and induce systemic resistance in the host plant is shown by both the groups of bacterium. It has been suggested that bacterial endophytes, when introduced at an early stage during plant development, are able to circumvent the phytopathogens (Sturz and Nowak, 2000; Sturz *et al.,* 2000). It has been reported that bacterial lipopolysaccharides of *Rhizobium etli* strain G12 act as inducer of systemic resistance in potato towards infection by the cyst nematode *Globodera pallida.* (Reitz *et al.,* 2000). Bacterial endophytes that act as microbial bioinoculants can be divided in two groups:

- Extensive colonizers of the internal plant tissues, which suppress the pathogens by niche occupation, antibiosis, or both.
- Primary colonizers which occupy the root cortex where they elicit plant defense/resistance mechanisms.

In general, the mutualistic endophytes are considered a major nematode managing tool because both the organisms inhabit the same niche and are present in the cortex of the plant, are good root colonizers and can also be applied to tissue culture plantlets or suckers through multiplication.

ROOT NODULATING BACTERIA

The plant-nematode relationship has adverse effects on plant growth. As a result of nematode infection, the nodulation and nitrogen fixation has been reported to be suppressed (Hussaini and Seshadri, 1975), stimulated (Hussey and Barker, 1976), or remain unaffected. Root-nodule bacteria are reported to produce toxic metabolites inhibitory to many plant pathogens (Hague and Gaffar, 1993). Antibiotics and phytoalexins produced by rhizobia probably reduce damage from nematodes and other pathogens. Apart from their nitrogen fixing capabilities, some rhizobia also benefit economically important crops by protecting them from various soil-borne plant pathogens including root-knot nematodes (Siddiqui and Shaukat, 2002). The control mechanisms include suppression of juvenile survival. *Microbacterium esteramaticum* and *Kocuria varians* have been reported to possess activity against root-lesion nematode (*Pratylenchus penetrans*); they suppress the nematode population without yield reduction. (Munif *et al.*, 2000).

FACTORS INFLUENCING THE ROOT COLONIZATION BY RHIZOBACTERIA

No matter how well suited a nematode antagonist is to a target nematode *in vitro*, rational management decision can be made only by analyzing the interactions naturally occurring among "host plant – nematode target –soil microbes environment". The colonization of plant roots by rhizobacteria is affected by a number of biotic and abiotic factors (Fig. 15.6) like host plant species, soil pH, soil temperature, soil types and other soil microbes (Andreogloua *et al.*, 2003).

Host Plant

Exudates from roots of the plant serve as the source of nutrient to the bacteria present in the rhizosphere. These exudates have direct impact on the growth and development of the rhizospheric bacteria. These exudates may have positive or negative impact on the rhizospheric microbial community. Sometimes root exudates have deleterious impact on the microbes and, on other hand, microbes utilize these exudates for their growth and multiplication. Therefore plant species, cultivars and growth stage of the plant can affect the root colonization by rhizobacteria (Sikora, 1988). Cultivar selection also influences the level of biological control of the potato cyst nematode caused by *Agrobacterium radiobactor* (Hackenberg and Sikora, 1992). Variations in cultivar-bacterial interactions are probably caused by differences in the composition of the hatching factor, the amount produced and the time of release.

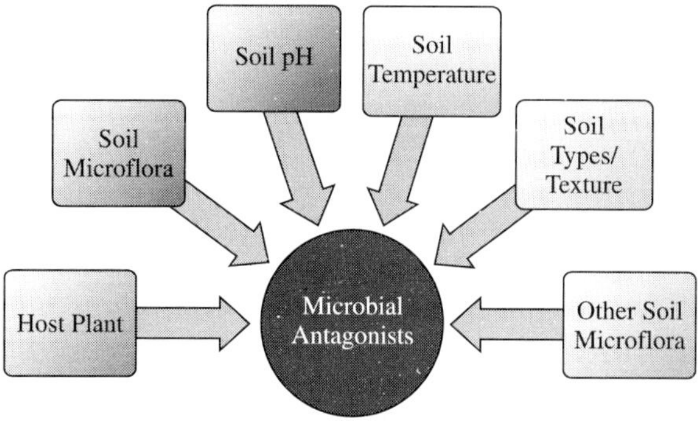

Fig. 15.6 Factors influencing the growth and development of microbial antagonists.

Soil Microflora

Natural soil restricts plant root colonization indicating that the soil microflora has profuse effect on the process of colonization by introduced strains of rhizobacteria. Root colonizing bacteria show interactions like competition, mutualism, and antagonism in the rhizospheric soil. Soil microflora have been reported to produce secondary metabolites like antibiotics, toxins, lytic enzymes, growth factors and various hormones, which out compete the deleterious microbes and promote plant health.

Abiotic Factors

The growth, development and distribution of root colonizing bacteria gets considerably influenced by abiotic conditions prevailing in the soil. Rhizobacterial plant root colonization is greatly influenced by soil pH, soil temperature, soil types, and soil texture (Bensalim *et al.*, 1998; Andreogloua *et al.*, 2003). It has been reported that soil moisture influences the control mechanism of *Heterodera schachtii* by *Pseudomonas fluorescens* (Oostendrop and Sikora, (1989). However, in one of the experiments, Sikora (1992) reported that temperature and soil moisture have less effect on the biocontrol of *Globodera pallida* through *Agrobacterium radiobactor*. Phytonematode population can only be managed by effective establishment of rhizobacteria. This can be achieved by the following ways:

- Efficient and effective isolation technique for rhizosphere competent bacteria.
- Development of quick and suitable *in vitro* screening techniques for efficient rhizobacteria against phytonematodes.
- Manipulation of rhizobacteria, which should be resistant to different biotic and abiotic factors as these factors negatively affect the growth and development of rhizobacteria.
- Screening of rhizosphere competent rhizobacteria.
- Development of formulation techniques with effective and efficient application to planting materials/sites towards management of phytonematode population.

ATTRIBUTES OF EFFECTIVE BIOCONTROL STRATEGY

The final and the ultimate goal of plant-parasitic nematode control is to improve soil health and gain economic benefits. Healthy soil is biologically and chemically active zone with high biological distribution and diversity. There are probably many naturally occurring microorganisms that play a crucial role in reducing the nematode population in the rhizosphere. Some of the desirable attributes of a successful biocontrol agent are as follows:

- It must not be pathogenic to plants, humans, or other animals, i.e., it should be non-pathogenic to non-target organisms.
- A successful biocontrol candidate must reduce or suppress nematode population in large quantities, so that after a given period the nematode population has been reduced to a level below the damage threshold.
- The biocontrol agent must be able to adapt in the varying soil environment and must be durable for longer period.
- It must out compete the pre existing parasites and predators in the host ecosystem.
- It must have sufficient infective propagules with high reproductive potential to maintain high population.
- The propagules or the infective units should be able to germinate and grow rapidly so that they are effective in invading and killing their competitor.
- The biocontrol agent should have the capability of producing various effective secondary metabolites like antibiotics, toxins, enzymes, etc., which limit the growth and proliferation of the nematode.
- A successful biocontrol agent should be readily and inexpensively mass produced and must have effective commercial production.
- It must exhibit compatibility with other fertilizers, pesticides, and agricultural practices.
- The application of the biocontrol agent should not only suppress the nematode population, but also result in increased crop yield.

LIMITATIONS OF MICROBIAL INOCULANTS

With such advancement in the microbial management strategies, the commercialization of these microorganisms lags far behind their less performance in the field. Despite appreciable results in the laboratory, rational management decision can be made only by analysing the interaction between microbes, host and soil environment. Various factors are also responsible for limiting the active use of microbes for nematode management like physical, chemical and biological characteristics of soil, presence of other microbial agents in soil, improper distribution and delivery problems and limited performance of many microbial inoculants in colonizing host root rhizosphere.

FUTURE PROSPECTS

The potential of unraveling microbial inoculants against plant parasitic nematodes is of immense important, though it is yet to be exploited to its full strength. The lack of spectacular results in comparison to the chemical nematicides has limited its use. It is important to recognize that the suppression of nematode population with microbial inoculants will take time and will slowly be manifested over a period of time. Therefore, we should have patience to replace the other management tactics with such methods. We must keep in mind that microbial inoculants constitute only a small portion of the overall nematode management strategies. The potential use of microbial inoculants against plant pathogens can move significantly beyond the present status provided resident antagonists are maintained as natural communities through cultural practices and may involve major changes in the screening of these beneficial organisms. Call of the hour is to work more intensively and extensible in the field of microbial ecology. However, the integrated approach of plant parasitic nematode management has considerably reduced our dependence on chemical nematicides. Suppression of nematode population by the utilization of microbial inoculants is a very challenging problem. This goal can only be achieved by the removal of obstacle through pouring in lots of persistent hard work, dedication and properly understanding the soil microbe nature and their interactions.

ACKNOWLEDGEMENTS

Authors are grateful to Director CIMAP, Lucknow for providing facilities and Dr. Keith G. Davies, Department of Plant Pathology and Microbiology, Rothamsted Research, Harpenden, UK, for providing photograph.

REFERENCES

Andreogloua, F.I., Vagelasa, I.K., Woodb, M., Samalievc, H.Y. and Gowena, S.R. (2003). *Soil Biol. Biochem,* **35:** 1095–1101.

Atibalentja, N., Noel, G.R. and Domier, L.L. (2000). *Int. J. Syst. Evol. Micr.* **50:** 605-613.

Azevedo, J.L., Maccheroni, W. Jr., Pereira, J.O. and Luiz, de Araújo, W. (2000). *Electronic J. Biotechnol.* **3:** 40-65.

Becker, J.O., Zavaleta-Mejia, E., Colbert, S.F., Schroth, M.N., and Weinhold , A.R .(1988). *Phytopathol.* **78:**1466-69.

Bekal, S., Borneman, J., Springer, M.S., Giblin-Davis, R.M. and Becker, J.O. (2001). *J. Nematol.* **33:** 110-115.

Bensalim, S., Nowak, J. and Asiedu, S. (1998). *Am. Pot. J.*, **75:** 145-152.

Bhattacharya, D., and Swarup, G. (1988). *Indian J. Nematol.* **18:** 61-70.

Bird, D.M., Opperman, C.H. and Davies, K.G. (2003). *Int. J. Parasitol.* **33:** 1269-1276.

Bishop, A.H., Gowen, S.R., Pembroke, B., and Trotter, J.R. (2008). *J. Invert. Pathol.* **96:** 28-33.

Bottjer, K.P., Bowen, L.W. and Gill, S.S. (1986). *Exp Parasitol.* **60:** 239-244.

Bowen, L.W., Bottjer, K.P. and Gill, S.S. (1986b). *Exp Parasitol.* **60:** 314-322.

Bowen, L.W., Bottjer, K.P. and Gill, S.S. (1986a). *Exp Parasitol.* **62:** 247-253.

Brown, S.M. (1985). *Soil Biol. Biochem.* **17**: 483-486.

Catellan, A.J., Hartel, P.G., and Fuhrmann, J.J. (1999). *Soil Sci. Soc. Am. J.* **63**: 1670-1680.

Chen, Z.X., and Dickson, D.W. (1998). *J. Nematol.* **30:** 313-340.

Chen, Z.X., Dickson, D.W., and Mitchell, D.J. (1997). *J. Nematol.* **29:** 1-8.

Chen, Z.X., Dickson, D.W., McSorley, R., Mitchell, D.J. and Hewlett, T.E. (1996). *J. Nematol.* **28:** 159-168.

Chen, Z.X. and Dickson, D.W. (1998). *J Nematol.* **30:** 313-340.

Compant, S., Duffy, B., Nowak, J., Clement, C. and Barka, E.A. (2005). *Appl. Environ. Microbial.* **71:** 4951-4959.

Cox, G.N., Kusch, M. and Edgar, R.S. (1981). *J. Cell Biol.* **90:** 7-17.

Crickmore, N. (2005). *Trends Microbiol.* **13:** 347-350.

Crickmore, N., Zeigler, D.R., Feitelson, J., Schnepf, E., Rie, J.V., Lereclus, D., Baum, J. and Dean, D.H. (1998). *Microbiol. Mol. Biol. Rev.*, **62:** 807-813.

Cronin, D., Moenne-Loccoz, Y., Dunne, C. and O'Gara, F. (1997b). *Eur. J. Plant Pathol.* **103:** 433-440.

Cronin, D., Moenne-Loccoz, Y., Fenton, A., Dunne, C., Dowling, D.N. and O'gara, F. (1997a). *Appl. Environ. Microbio.* **63:** 1357–1361.

Dabiré, K.R. and Mateille, T. (2004). *Soil Biol. Biochem.* **36(3):** 539-543.

Davies K.G. and Redden, M. (1997). *J. Appl. Microbiol.* **83:** 227-235.

Davies, K.G and Danks, C. (1993). *J. Nematol.* **39:** 53-64.

Davies, K.G. (2005). *Adv. Appl. Microbiol.* **57**: 53-78.

Davies, K.G. and Opperman, C.H. (2006). *In: Multitrophic Interactions in the Soil, IOBC/wprs Bulletin*, Vol. 29 (Eds. Raaijmakers JM and Sikora R.A.), pp. 11-16.

Davies, K.G., Flynn, C.A., Laird, V., and Kerry, B.R. (1990). *Rev. Nematol.* **13:** 303-309.

De Freitas, J.R., Banerjee, M.R. and Germida, J.J. (1997). *Biol. Fertl.*, Soils **24:** 358-364.

Decraemer, W., Karanastasi, E., Brown, D .and Backeljau, T. (2003). *Biol. Rev.* **78:** 465-510.

Dong, L.Q. and Zhang, K.Q. (2006). *Plant Soil* **288:** 31-45.

Doran , J.W., Sarrantonio, M. and Liebig, M.A .(1996). Soil health and sustainability. *Adv Agron.* **56:** 1-54.

Duponnois, R., Ba, A.M. and Mateille, T. (1999). *Nematol.* **1:** 95-101.

El-Nagdi, W.M.A. and Youssef, M.M.A. (2004). *J. Pest. Sci.* **77:** 75-78.

Feitelson, J.S., Payne, J. and Kim, L. (1992). *Bio/Technol*, **10:** 271-275.

Giannakou, I.O. and Prophetou-Athanasiadou, D. (2004). *Appl. Soil Ecol.* **26:** 69-79.

Giblin-Davis, R.M., McDaniel, L.L., and Bilz, F.G. (1990). *J. Nematol.* **22:** 750-762.

Giblin-Davis, R.M., Williams, D.S., Bekal, S., Dickson, D.W., Brito, J.A., Becker, J.O. and Preston, J.F. (2003). *Int. J. Sys. Evol. Microbiol.* **53:** 197-200.

Gives, P.M. Davies, K.G., Morgan, M. and Behnke, J.M. (1999). *J. Helminthol.* **73:** 67-71.

Glick, B.R,. Penrose, D.M., and Li, J. (1998). *J. Theor. Biol.* **190:** 63-68.

Guo, R.J., Liu, X.Z .and Yang, H.W. (1996). *Chinese Biol Control*, **12:** 134-137.

Gupta, A. and Pandey, R. (2009). Mycorrhiza: The saviour of plants from Phytonematodes in Microbes, Applications and effects (Ed. Trivedi P.C., Jaipur pp:143-157

Hackenberg, C. and Sikora, R.A. (1992). *J. Nematol.*, **24:** 594.

Hallmann, J., Rodriguez-Kabana, R. and Kloepper, J.W. (1999) *Soil Biol. Biochem.* **31:** 551-560.

Hallmann, J., Faupel, A., Krachel, A. and Berg, G. (2002). *Fund. Appl. Nematol.* **21:** 511-517.

Hallmann, J., Quadt-Hallmann, A., Mahaffee, W.F. and Kloepper, J.W. (1997). *Can. J. Microbiol.* **43:** 895-914.

Hallmann, J., Quadt-Hallmann, A., Miller, W.G., Sikora ,R.A. and Lindow, S.E. (2001). *Phytopathol.* **91:** 415-422.

Haque, S.E. and Gaffar, A. (1993). *Phytopathol.* **138:** 157-63.

Hewlett, T.E., Gerber, J.F., and Smith, K.S. (2004). In: ''Nematology Monographs and Perspectives.'' (Eds. Cook and Hunt), *Proc. Fourth Int. Congr. Nematol.* **2:** 175-185.

Hoffman-Hergarten S., Keuken, O., Gulatin, M. and Sikora R. A. (1997). *In:* Plant growth promoting rhizobacteria - present status and future prospects. *Proc. Int.Workshop Plant-Growth-Promot. Rhizobacteria.* (Eds. A Ogoshi, K Kobayashi, Y Homma, F Kodama, N Kondo and S Akino.) pp. 364-367. 4th Jpn.-OECD Joint Workshop, Sapporo. JPN.

Huang X.W., Tian, B.Y., Niu, Q.H., Yang, J.K., Zhang, L.M. and Zhang, K.Q .(2005). *Res. Microbiol.* **156:** 719-727.

Huffman, D.L., Bischof, L.J., Griffitts J.S. and Aroian, R.V. (2004). *Int. J. Microbiol.* **293:** 599-607.

Hussaini, S.S. and Seshadri, A.R. (1975). *Indian J. Nematol.* **5:** 189-99.

Insunza, V., Alstrom, S. and Eriksson, K.B . (2002). *Plant Soil* **241:** 271-278.

Jacq, V.A .and Fortuner, R. (1979). *Revue Nématol.* **2:** 41-50.

Jayakumar, J., Ramakrishnan, S. and Rajendran, G. (2002). *Pesttol.* **26:** 45-46.

Jonathan, E.I., Barker, K.R., Abdel-Alim, F.F., Vrain T.C. and Dickson, D.W. (2000). *Nematropica,* **30:** 231-240.

Kennedy, I.R., Pereg-Gerk, L.L., Wood, C., Deaker, R., Gilchrist, K. and Katupitiya, S., (1997). *Plant Soil* **194:** 65-79.

Kloepper J.W. (1993). *In:* Meeting, F. B., Jr. (Eds.). *Soil Microbial Ecology* pp. 25-274. Dekker, New York.

Kloepper, J.W. and Schroth, M.N. (1981). *Phytopathol.* **71:** 642-644.

Kloepper, J.W., Rodriguez-Kabana R., Mcinroy, J.A. and Young, R.W. (1992) *Plant Soil* **139:** 75-84.

Kloepper, J.W., Rodriguez-Kabana, R., Mclnroy, J.A. and Collins, D.J. (1991). *Plant Soil* **136:** 95-102.

Kluepfel, D.A., Mclnnis, T.M. and Zehr, E. (1993). *Phytopathol.* **83:** 1240-1245.

Kobayashi, D.Y. and Palumbo, J.D. (2000). Bacterial endophytes and their effects on plants and uses in agriculture. In: *Microbial Endophytes.* (Eds. CW Bacon and J F White Jr). pp. 199-233. Marcel Dekker, New York, USA.

Koenning, S.R., Overstreet, C., Noling, J.W., Donald, P.A., Becker, J.O. and Fortnum, B.A. (1999). *J. Nematol.* **31:** 587-618.

Kokalis-Burelle, N., Kloepper, J.W. and Reddy M.S. (2006). *Applied Soil* **31:** 91-100.

Kounbobr, R.D., Saliou, N., Jean-Luc, C. Sabine, F., Mamadou, T.D. and Thierry M. (2005). *Biol. Fertil. Soils* **41:** 205-211.

Kumar, T., Wahla, V., Pandey P., Dubey, R.C. and Maheshwari, D.K. (2009). *W.J. Microbiol. Biotechnol.* **25:** 277-285.

Landels, S. (1989). Fumigants and nematicides. Chemical Economics Handbook, Stanford Research Institute International, California.

Leeman M, van Pelt, J.A., Den, O.F.M., Heinsbroek, M., Bakker. P.A.H.M. and Schippers, B. (1995). *Euro. J. Plant Pathol.* **101:** 655-664.

Lewis, W.J., van Lenteren, J.C., Phatak, S.C. and Tumlinson, J.H. III (1997). *Proc. Natl. Acad. Sci.* USA **94:** 12243-12248.

Leyns, L., Borgonie, G., Arnaut, G. and DeWaele, D (1995). *Fundam. Appl. Nematol.* **18:** 211-218.

Li, B., Xie, G.L., Soad, A. and Coosemans, J. (2005). *J. Zhejiang. Univ. Sci.* **6B:** 496-501.

Li, J., Daniel, H., Charles, T.C. and Glick, B.R. (2000). *Curr. Microbiol.* **41:** 101-105.

Luc, M., Sikora, R.A. and Bridge, J.(2005). Plant Parasitic Nematodes in Subtropical and Tropical Agriculture, 2nd ed., 871 p., CABI, Bioscience, Egham, Surrey, U.K.

Maagd, R.A., Bravo, A. and Crickmore, N. (2001). *Trends Genet.* **17:** 193-199.

Madamba, C.P., Camaya, E.N., Zenarosa, D.B. and Yater, H.M. (1999). *The Philippine Agriculturist* **82:** 113-122.

Mahdy, M., Hallmann, J. and Sikora, R.A. (2001). *Meded Rijksuniv Gent Fak Landbouwkd Toegep Biol Wet*, **66:** 655-662.

Mahmoud, S.AZ., Ramadan, E.M., Thabet, F.M., and Khater, T.(1984). *Zentralbl. Mikrobiol.* **139:** 227-232.

Marleny, B.C., Nancy, K.B., Lawrence, K.S., Edzard van S. and Kloepper, J.W. (2008). *Biological Control,* **47(1):** 55-59.

Marroquin, L.D., Elyassnia, D., Griffitts, J.S., Feitelson, J.S. and Aroian, R.V. (2000) . *Genet* **155:** 1693-1699.

Mclnory, J.A. and Kloepper, J.W. (1995). *Plant Soil* **173:** 337-342.

Mena, J. and Pimentel, E. (2002). *Nematol* **4:** 287.

Meyer, S.L.F. (2003). *Pest Manag. Sci.,* **59:** 665-670.

Meyer, S.L.F. and Roberts, D.P. (2002). *J. Nematol.* **34:** 1-8.

Meyer, S.L.F., Roberts, D.P., Chitwood, D.J., Carta, L.K., Lumsden, R.D. and Mao, W. (2001). *Nematropica* **31:** 75-86.

Mittal, N., Saxena, G. and Mukerji, K.G. (1995). *Crop Prot.* 1**4:** 647-651

Mouton, L., and Ebert, D. (2008). *Curr. Microbiol.* **56:** 447-452.

Mouton, L., Nong, G., Preston, J.F., and Ebert, D. (2007). *Appl. Environ. Microbiol.* **73:** 3715-3718.

Munif, A., Hallmann, J. and Sikora R.A. (2000). *Mededelingen Faculteit Landbouwkundige, Universiteit Gent* **65:** 471-480.

Neipp, P.W. and Becker, J.O. (1999). *J. Nematol.* **31:** 54-61.

Niu, Q.H., Huang, X.W., Tian, B.Y., Yang, J.K., Liu, J., Zhang, L. and Zhang, K.Q. (2005). *Appl Microbiol Biotechnol* **69:** 722-730.

Niu, Q.H., Huang, X.W., Zhang, L., Li, Y.X., Li, J., Yang, J.K. and Zhang, K.Q. (2006). *Arch. Microbiol.* **185:** 439-448.

Oliveira, E.J., Rabinovitch, L., Monnerat, R.G., Passos, L.K.J. and Zahner, V. (2004). *Appl. Environ. Microbiol.* **70:** 6657-6664.

Oostendorp, M. and Sikora, R.A. (1986). *Rev. Nematol.* **9:** 304.

Oostendorp, M. and Sikora R.A. (1989). *Rev. Nematol.* **12:** 77-83.

Oostendorp, M. and Sikora, R.A. (1990). *Rev Nematol.* **13:** 269-274.

Oostendorp, M., Dickson, D.W. and Mitchell, D.J. (1991). *J. Nematol.* **23**: 58-64.

Pal, K.K., Tilak, K.V.B.R., Saxena, A.K., Dey, R, Singh, C.S. (2001). *Microbiol. Res.* **156**: 209-223.

Pandey, R., Singh, H.B. and Kalra, A. (2000). *Int. J. Tropical Plant Disease* **18:** 1-23.

Pandey, R., Gupta, A., Haider, R. and Kalra, A. (2009). *J. Mycol. Plant Pathol.* **39 (1):** 86-89

Pandey, R., Singh, H.B and Kalra, A. (2000). *Internat. J. Tropical Plant Disease* **18:** 1-23.

Patten, C.L., Glick, B.R. (2002). *Appl. Environ. Microbiol.* **68:** 3795-3801.

Penrose, D.M. and Glick, B.R. (2001). *Can. J. Microbiol.* **47:** 368-372.

Persidis, A., Lay, J.G., Manousis,T., Bishop, A.H. and Ellar, D.J. (1991). *J. Cell Sci.* **100:** 613-622.

Prasad, S.S.S.V. and Tilak K.V.B.R. (1972). *J. Invertebr. Pathology* **20:** 377-378.

Preston J.F., Dickson, D.W., Maruniak, J.E., Nong, G., Brito, J.A., Schmidt, L.M .and Giblin-Davis, R.M. (2003). *J Nematol* **35:** 198-207.

Racke, J. and Sikora, R.A. (1992). *Soil Biol. Biochem.* **24:** 521-526.

Ramamoorthy, V., Viswanathan, R., Raguchander, T., Prakasam, V. and Samiyappan, R. (2001). *Crop Prot.* **20:** 1-11.

Reitz, M., Rudolph K., Schröde, r L., Hoffmann-Hergarten, S., Hallmann, J. and Sikora, R.A. (2000). *Appl. Environ. Microbiol.* **66:** 3515-3518.

Renwick, A.R., Campbell, A., and Coe, S. (1999). *Plant Physiol.* **40:** 524-532.

Rovira, A.D. and Sands, D.C. (1977). *J Appl Bacteriol.* **34:** 253-259.

Samaliev, H.Y., Andreoglou, F.I., Elawad, S.A., Hague, N.G.M. and Gowen, S.R. (2000). *Nematol.* **2:** 507-514.

Sasser, J.N., Freckman, D.W. (1987). *In:* Veech, J.A., Dickson, D.W. (Eds.), Vistas on Nematology, Society of Nematology Inc, Hyattsville, MD.

Sayre, R. M. and Wergin, W.P. (1977). *J. Bacteriol.* **129:** 1091-1101.

Sayre, R.M. and Starr, M.P. (1985). *Proc. Helminthol. Soc. Wash.,* **52**: 149-165.

Sayre, R.M., Starr, M.P., Golden, A.M., Wergin, W.P. and Endo, B.Y.(1988). *Proc. Helm. Soc. Wash.* **55:** 28-49.

Sayre, R.M., Wergin, W.P, Schmidt, J.M and Starr, M.P. (1991). *Res. Microbiol.* **142:** 551-564

Schenpe, E., Crickmore, N., Rie, J.V., Lereclus, D., Baum, J., Feitelson, J., Zeigler, D.R. and Dean, D.H. (1998). *Microbiol. Mol. Biol. Rev.,* **62:** 775-806.

Scher, F.M. and Baker, R.(1982). *Phytopathol.* **72:** 1567-1573.

Sharon, E., Bar-Eyal, M., Chet, I., Herrere-Estrella, A., Kleifeld O., and Spiegel, Y., (2001). *Phytopathol.* **91:** 687-693.

Shaukat, S.S., Siddiqui , I.A,. Hamid, M., Khan, G.H. and Ali, S.A. (2002). *Pakistan J. Biol. Sci.* **5:** 669-671.

Siddiqui, I. A. and Shaukat, S.S. (2003). *Soil Biol. Biochem.* **35:** 1615-1623.

Siddiqui, I.A. and Shaukat, S.S. (2002). *J Phytopathology-phytopathologische Zeitschrift* , **150:** 469-473.

Siddiqui, I.A. and Shaukat, S.S. (2004). *J Phytopathol.* **152:** 48-54.

Siddiqui, Z.A .and Mahmood, I. (1999). *Biore Technol* **69:** 167-179.

Siddiqui, Z.A., Baghel, G. and Akhtar, M.S. (2007). *W. J. Microbiol. Biotechnol.* **23**: 435-441.

Sikora, R.A. (1991). The concept of using plant health promoting rhizobacteria for the biological control of plant parasitic nematodes. Proc. Int. Workshop Plant Growth-Promoting Rhizobacteria, 2nd. Interlaken, Switzerland. WRRS Bull. XIV.

Sikora, R.A. and Hoffmann-Hergarten, S. (1993). Biological control of plant parasitic nematodes with plant-health promoting rhizobacteria. *Biologically based technology* (Eds. Lumsden PD and Vaugh JL), pp. 166-172. ACS Symposium series, USA.

Sikora, R.A. (1988). *Med. Fac. Landbouwwet. Rijksuniv. Gent.* **53:** 867-78.

Sikora, R.A. (1992). *Annu. Rev. Phytopathol.* **30:** 245-270.

Spiegel, Y., Cohn, E., Galper, S., Sharon, E. and Chet, I. (1991). *Biocontrol Sci Technol,* **1:** 115-125.

Stirling, G.R. (1984). *Phytopathol.* **74**: 55-60.

Stirling, G.R. (1991). *Biological Control of Plant Parasitic Nematode: Progress, Problems and Prospects.* CAB International, Wallington, UK.

Stirling, G.R., Bird, A.F. and Cakurs, A.B. (1986). *Revue Nematol.* **9:** 251-260.

Sturz, A.V. and Kimpinski, J. (2004). *Plant Soil,* **262:** 241-249.

Sturz, A.V. and Matheson, B.G. (1996). *Plant Soil* **184:** 265-271.

Sturz, A.V. and Nowak, J. (2000). *App. Soil Ecol.* **15:**183-190.

Sturz, A.V. and Christie, B.R. (2003). *Soil Tillage Res* **72:** 107-123.

Sturz, A.V., Christie, B.R. and Nowak, J. (2000). *CRC Crit. Rev. Plant Sci.* **19:** 1-30.

Surette, M.A., Sturz, A.V., Lada, R. R. and Nowak, J. (2003). *Plant Soil* **253:** 381-390.

Tian H and Riggs RD (2000). *J. Nematol.* **32:** 377–388.

Tian, B.Y., Yang, J.K., Lian, L.H., Wang, C.Y. and Zhang, K.Q. (2007). *Appl. Microbiol. Biotechnol.* **74:** 372-380.

Tian, B.Y., Li, N., Lian, L.H., Liu, J.W., Yang, J.K. and Zhang, K.Q. (2006). *Arch. Microbiol.* **186:** 297-305.

Tian, H., Riggs, R.D. and Crippen, D.L. (2000). *J. Nematol.* **32:** 370-376.

Tien, T.M., Gaskins, M.H., and Hubbell, D.H. (1979). *Appl. Environ. Microbiol.* **37:** 1016-1024.

Trudgill, D.L., Bala, G., Blok, V.C., Daudi, A., Davies, K.G., Fargette, M., Gowen, S.R., Madulu, J.D., Mateille, T., Mwageni, W., Netscher, C., Phillips M.S. (2000). *Nematology* **2:** 823-845.

Van Loon L.C., Bakker P.A.H.M. and Pieterse C.M. (1998). *Annu Rev Phytopathol* **36:** 453-483.

Voisard, C., Keel, C., Haas, D. and Defago, G.(1989). *EMBO J.* **8:** 352-358.

Wei, J.Z, Hale, K., Carta, L., Platzer, E., Wong, C., Fang, S.C. and Aroian, R.V (2003). *PNAS* **100:** 2760-2765.

Weibelzahl-Fulton, E., Dickson, D.W., and Whitty, E.B. (1996). *J. Nematol.* **28:** 43-49.

Weller, D.M. (1988). *Ann. Rev. Phytopathol.* **26:** 379-407

Westcott, S.W. and Kluepfel, D.A. (1993). *Phytopathol.* **83:** 1245-1249.

Whipps, J.M. and Davies, K.G. (2000). *Biological control: measures of success* (Eds. Gurr, G. and Wratten, S.), pp. 231–269. Kluwer Academic Publishers, Dordecht, The Netherlands.

Winslow, R.D. (1960). *In:* ''Nematology, Fundamentals and Recent Advances with Emphasis on Plantparasitic and Soil Forms.'' (Eds. Sasser and Jenkins), pp. 341-415. University of North Carolina Press, Chapel Hill.

16

Microbial Bioremediation of Azo Textile Dye

S.P. Gautam, A. Bose and S. Tiwari

Yeast and Mycorrhiza Biotechnology Laboratory, Department of Biosciences, R.D. University, Jabalpur (M.P.)

E-mail: hodbiosrdvv@yahoo.co.in

Pollution has become a worldwide concern; control of water pollution is gaining increasing importance in recent years. Presence of organic compound in water bodies imparts them aesthically unacceptable. Effluent discharged from textile and dye stuff industries to neighboring water bodies makes them polluted. Wastewater treatment is currently causing significant health concern to environment regulator agencies. The presence of very small amount of dye (> 1ppm for some dyes) in water is highly visible and affects water transparency and gas solubility in lakes, rivers and other water bodies. Therefore, government legislation is forcing the textile industries to treat their wastewater to a high standard. Present effluent treatment methods are physico-chemical methods, which are costly and less effective. The ability of microorganism to carry out dye decolorization has received much attention. Involvement of microbial biotechnology in wastewater treatment systems is cost-effective. This review discusses about the harmful effect of dyes, current available technique of dye removal from wastewater and involves reports on progress of microbial decolorization of dye used in textile industries.

INTRODUCTION

One of the very pressing environmental problem of textile industries is the removal of colour from effluent, prior to its discharge into local sewage. Colour is the first contaminant to be recognized in wastewater, and brightly coloured water-soluble dyes are problematic as they pass unaffected through conventional sewage treatment systems (Kausar *et al.*, 2000). Textile industries consume substantial volume of water and chemicals for wet processing of textile. These chemicals are used for designing, souring, bleaching, dying, printing and finishing. They range from element, inorganic compound, polymer and organic compounds. There are more than 8000 chemical products associated with dying process listed in the colour index (Society of Dyers and Colorists, 1976). Approximately over 1,00,000 commercially available dye exist with over 7×10^5 metric tonnes of dye stuff products annually (Meyer, 1981; Zollinger, 1987).

Azo Dye

In textile industries various colorant materials are used for dying. Chemically they belong to various groups like acidic dye, reactive dye, basic, disperse dye, azo dye and anthroquinone-based metal complex, etc. Among these, azo dyes are commercially the most important group, making about half of the total stuff used Maximo *et al.*, 2003). Azo dye, the largest chemical class of dye with the greatest variety of colours, has been used extensively for textile dying, leather dying and paper printing. These dyes are highly water-soluble. These soluble reactive azo dyes, which are being used in large quantities, are known to hydrolyze during application, which may result in 30-50% of the dye being discharged. This is why in textile and paper coloration industries, aromatic dyes from residual dye bath result into colored water stream (Easton, 1995).

ENVIRONMENT AND HEALTH CONCERN

The pollution causing potential of textile dyes has been a primary concern to environment. Heavy metal ions from textile effluents have also been reported to be at high concentration in both algae and higher plants exposed to such effluents (Shrivastava and Prakash, 1991), because some disperse dyes have a tendency of bioaccumulation (Anilker, *et al.,*1981; Baughman and Perenich, 1988). Dyes can be detrimental to microbial population present in such treatment works, and may lead to decrease in the efficiency of plant and cause treatment failure (Ogawa *et al.,* 1989). Similar adverse effect has also been detected in aquatic microbial populations and the aquatic environment, in general, (Richardson, 1983; Michaels and Lewis, 1985) or in laboratory cultures exposed to such dyes (Ogawa *et al.,* 1989). Three hundred ppm of dye, which is a regular concentration used in industries, completely eliminates the growth of bacteria (El-Rahim *et al.,* 2003).

Majority of these dyes are either toxic or mutagenic and carcinogenic (Chung, 1982; Hu, 2001) and pose a potential health hazard to all forms of life. Some azo dyes have been identified as most problematic compounds in textile effluent, as they are difficult to remove due to their high water solubility and low exhaustion (Carliell *et al.*, 1995). The major affect of azo dye is the carcinogenic potential of aromatic amine, which enters the environment either as a by-product of manufacturing or as metabolic intermediate from reductive cleavage of azo linkage. Generally, these dyes are recalcitrant to biodegradation because of: *(i)* poor membrane permeability of sulfonated constituents, *(ii)* production of aryl sulfonates that are often toxic to microbes, *(iii)* limited substrate specificity of microbial system, and *(iv)* absorption of dyes to sediments and other environmental compartments Loper, (1995).

Azo dyes are also widely used as colorants due to the degree of industrialization in the society. Approximately 1.5×10^6 pounds (0.068×10^6 kg) of the dye Amaranth were used each year in over 60 countries (Collins and Laughlin, 1972). Since intestinal cancer is more common in highly industrialized society, a possible connection between these tumors and the use of azo dyes has been investigated (Breg *et al.*, 1973, 1974; Wynder, 1974; Wolff and O'ehme, 1974). Azo dye compounds are linked to bladder cancer in humans and hepatocarcinoma and nuclear abnormalities in intestinal epithelial cells in mice (Manning *et al.*, 1995; Medvev *et al.*, 1988; Percy *et al.*, 1989). Azo dyes are degraded by azo reductase present in intestinal microorganisms *in vivo* (Jones *et al.*, 1964; Larson *et al.*, 1976; Roxon *et al.*, 1967), and to a lesser extent by the enzymes of cytosolic and microsomal fractions of liver to produce aromatic amines, which are known human carcinogens and have been found in the urine of dye stuff workers and test animals following the administration of azo dyes. Thus, a number of azo dyes have been classified as carcinogenic (Hartman, 1978). Food colorant, Amaranth has been shown to be toxic to rat fetus and carcinogenic to rats (Andrianova, 1970; Collina *et al.*, 1975, 1973).

A report prepared by Laboratory of Government Chemist (LGC) European Commission on "Risk of cancer due to textile and leather goods coloured with azo dye" was expressed at 7th CSTEE (Scientific Committee for Toxicology, Ecotoxicology and Environment) plenary meeting Brussels, on 18 Jan 1999. The committee found that the total exposure of an adult resulting from leaching of dye from fabrics, over a life time use of garment covering the whole body is calculated as 723 μg/kg, while that of a small child, who receives oral exposure by sucking a piece of garment is calculated as 13 mg/kg. The committee recommended that the use of azo dye should be restricted. Other findings and recommendations of the report are: (a) the use of azo dye, which has the potential to give rise to 14 aromatic amines classified as category 1 to 2 carcinogens according to directive 76/769/EEC should be restricted to lowest possible, or completely eliminated; (b) the main routes of human exposure to azo dye are identified as (i) oral ingestion—mainly referring to the sucking of textile clothes by babies and young children; (ii) dermal absorption—The rate of primary concern for consumers wearing azo compound dyed product as well as for workers in dye production plants; and (iii) inhalation—a route of concern for workers in dye production industry as well as those handling newly dyed products.

WASTEWATER TREATMENT

The government legislation is becoming more stringent in developed countries regarding the removal of dyes from industrial effluents of textile industries. This means that for most textile industries, developing on site or in plant facilities to treat their own effluent before discharge is a fast approaching actuality. Recently state and federal agencies in USA have been requiring lower effluent colour limits i.e., < 200 units of American Dye Manufactures Institute, ADMI (Mc Curdy *et al.*, 1992). But the removal of colour from wastewater is not an easy job, because dyes are difficult to treat because of their synthetic origin and mainly complex aromatic molecular structures. Such structures are often constructed to resist fading on exposure to sweat, soap, water, light or oxidizing agents (Poots *et al.,* 1976a,b; Mc Kay, 1979), and this renders them more stable and less amenable to biodegradation (Fewson, 1988; Sheshadri *et al.*,1994).

DECOLORIZATION TECHNIQUES

This review illustrates the use of microorganisms for textile industrial wastewater treatment, but prior to this a critical study of the most widely used methods of dye removal from dye containing effluent is also done along with disadvantages of each. Basically three types of methods are employed in industrial wastewater treatment plants: (1) physico-chemical methods, (2) physical methods, (3) biological treatment methods.

1. Physico-chemical Methods

Oxidative processes: H_2O_2 is used which is required to be activated by UV light or other means. But this method results in the formation of wastewater, which is resistant to biological treatment or is poisonous to live biomass (Solkar and Le Marchel, 1997). Another agent is H_2O_2 + Fe(II) salt

(Fentos reagents). One major disadvantage is the sludge generation through the flocculation of the reagent and dye molecule.

Ozonation: It can be applied in gaseous state, therefore, it does not increase the sludge volume. A disadvantage of ozonation is its short halflife (20 min) that can be further shortened if dyes are present. Its decomposition is accelerated under alkaline conditions, therefore, careful monitoring of effluent pH is required (Solkar and Le Marchel, 1997). In all it is not suitable because continuous ozonation is required due to its short life and high cost (Xu and Leburn, 1999).

Photochemical: It degrades dye molecule to CO_2 and H_2O by UV treatment in the presence of H_2O_2, by production of high concentration of hydroxyl radicals. Its advantage is no sludge production, and disadvantage is that it is costly and inconvenient in industrial scale application (Yang *et al.*, 1998).

Sodium hypochloride (NaOCl): This method attacks the amino group of dye molecule by Cl^- and accelerates azo bond cleavage, but its disadvantages are that it is unsuitable for disperse dye, by-products are released in waterways and causes the release of aromatic amines, which are more toxic (Banat *et al.*, 1999; Solkar and Le Marchel, 1997).

Cucurbituril: It forms insoluble cucurbituril dye cation aggregates, since adsorption occurs reasonably fast. Its disadvantage is the cost, because to be industrially feasible, cucurbituril would need to be incorporated in fixed bed sorption filters (Karcher *et al.*, 1999 a, b; Bushmann, 1992).

Electrochemical destruction: No sludge build up occurs in this technique. The breakdown metabolites are also non-hazardous. The cost of electricity is comparable to the price of chemicals (Ogutveren and Kaparal, 1994; Pelegrini *et al.*, 1999).

2. Physical Treatment Methods

Adsorption: This technique has gained much favour recently due to its efficiency in the removal of pollutants. Decolorization by physical methods is the result of two processes—adsorption and ion exchange. The following methods work upon adsorption principle.

Activated carbon: This is very effective for adsorbing cationic, mordant and acid dye and to a slightly lesser extent dispersed direct, vat, pigment and reactive dye. It is the most commonly used method for dye removal. Its only disadvantage is that the activated carbon is expensive and needs to be reactivated; reactivation results in 10-15% loss of sorbant (Raghavacharya, 1997).

Peat: It is widely available and used in countries like Ireland and UK. It has the ability to absorb transition metals and polar organic compounds from dye containing effluent. It requires no activation and cost is also much less (Poots and Mc Kay, 1976 a), but availability is limited.

Wood chips: They show good adsorption capacities for acid dye, although disadvantages are their hardness and longer contact time fraction (Poots and Mc Kay, 1976 b; Nigam *et al.*, 2000).

Fly ash and coal (Mixture): The ratio used is 1:1. A high ash concentration increases the adsorption rates of mixture, but causes generation of sludge Gupta *et al.* (1990).

Silica gel: An effective material for removing basic dye, although air binding and air fouling with particulate matter prevents it being used commercially.

Other materials: Natural clay, corncobs, and rice hub are advantageous for dye removal due to their widespread availability and cheapness (Nigam *et al.,* 2000; Nawar and Doma, 1989; Nasser and El-Geundi, 1991).

Membrane: Membrane separates dye continuously from the effluent, which is resistant to temperature, adverse chemical environment and microbial attack. Disadvantage is that the concentrated residue left after filtration causes disposal problems, high capital cost, etc. (Mishra and Tripathy, 1993; Xu and Leburn, 1999).

Ion exchange: It is not used widely because ion exchange cannot accommodate large number of dye containing effluent (Solkar and Le Marshal, 1997).

Irradiation: The dissolved oxygen is consumed rapidly during irradiation, so a constant and adequate supply is required. This has a effect on cost. Some dyes can be oxidized effectively only at laboratory scale (Honsono *et al.*, 1993).

Electrokinetic coagulation: It involves the addition of ferrous sulphate and ferric chloride, allowing excellent removal of direct dyes from wastewater. Its disadvantage is that it is not very effective for acid dyes, and the cost of chemicals is also high (Mishra and Tripathi, 1993).

3. Biological Treatment Methods

The ability of microorganisms to decolorize and metabolize dyes has long been a matter of research, and it has been suggested that only biotechnological approach can offer complete degradation of dye with a co-reduction in BOD and COD. Mc Kay (1979) concluded that "decolorization through biological systems would receive increased attention in the future". Among the many biological systems available are: (i) aerobic activated sludge or rotating biofilm reactors (Shaul, *et al.*, 1991; Jiang and Bishop, 1994); (ii) aerobic-anaerobic packed bed reactors (Schiliephake, *et al.*, 1993; Lin and Liu, 1994); (iii) aerobic-anaerobic fluidized-bed reactors Sheshadri, *et al.*, (1994); (iv) aerobic-anaerobic sequential batch or continuous flow reactors (Loyd, *et al.*, 1992, Ganesh, *et al.*, 1994; Oxsring, *et al.*, 1996); and (v) aerobic batch reactors Carliell *et al.*, (1995).

(a) Decolorization with fungal culture

White-rot fungus has been explored for its dye decolorizing ability since long. Bumps *et al.* (1989) investigated the feasibility using white-rot fungus to treat contaminated soil sediments and wastewater, including polycyclic aromatic compounds and triphenyl methane dye that could be degraded to carbon dioxide and water. Wood rotting fungi *Phanerochaete chrysosporium, Trametes* sp. and *Aspergillus* sp. have been found to effectively degrade a variety of azo dyes under aerobic conditions (Kandelbauer and Gubitz), (in press). Microbial decolorization of pulp and paper effluent water and azo dye with simultaneous production of lignolytic enzyme has been studied in detail in *Phanerochaete chrysosporium* and *Streptomyces chromofuscus* (Paszczynski *et al.*, 1992). *Phanerochaete chrysosporium* was also shown to biodegrade the azo and heterocyclic dyes orange II, Tropaeofin O, Congo Red and Azure B. The extent of colour removal varied depending on the dye complexity, nitrogen availability in media and lignolytic activity in culture (Cripps *et al.,* 1990). Capalash and Sharma (1992) tested the biodegradation of 18 azo dyes using *Phanerochaete chrysosporium* and only eight were degraded with 40% – 70% colour removal.

The *Phlebia tremellosa* fungal strains decolorized eight synthetic textiles to 96% in 14 days under stationary incubation conditions (Kirby *et al.,* 2000). The fast decolorization of diazo linked dye was also reported (Knapp and Newby, 1995). *Neurospora crassa* was able to decolorize diazo dye up to 89% - 91% within 24 h. When the concentration of dye Vermelho Reanil P8B ranged up to 20 mg /l^{-1} Corso *et al.* (1981), strains of *Myrothecium verrucaria* and *Ganoderma* sp. showed up to 99% decolorization after 48 h. incubation. The mechanism was found to be adsorption to the fungus mycelium. *Myrothecium* showed a very strong binding affinity to some azo dyes, which were recoverable with methanol, suggesting a hydrophobic-hydrophilic interaction in dye binding mechanism (Braimi-Horn *et al.,* 1992).

Other facultative anaerobic fungi that are capable of growth on dyes as sole carbon source have been reported, however, they do not seem to carry out decolorization (Marchant *et al.*, 1994; Nigam *et al.,* 1995 a, 1995 b). They appear to cleave some of the bonds in these dyes to use as a carbon source, but do not affect the chromophore center of the dye. This capacity might be of significance in degrading the dye containing effluent when other decolorizers are present. Report on various fungi capable of decolorizing dyes is given in Table 16.1.

Table 16.1 Decolorizing efficiencies of some fungi

Culture	*Dye and concentration*	*Percent removal/time*	*Mechanism*	*Reference*
Aspergillus sojae B-10′	Amaranth (10 mg/1)	97.8% (5 days)	NR	Ryu & Weon (1992)
	Sudan III (10 mg/1)	97.4% (5 days)	NR	
	Congo Red (10 mg/1)	93.0% (5 days)	NR	
Myrothecum sp.	Orange II (100 mg/1)	25-91% (24 h)	Adsorption	Mou *et al.* (1991)
	10B (Blue)	58-98% (24 h)	Adsorption	
	RS Red (100mg/1)	81-98% (24 h)	Adsorption	
Pycnoporus cinnabarinus	Pigment plant effluent (unknown concentration)	90% (3 days)	Extracellulr oxidases	Schliephake *et al.* (1993)
Trichoderma sp. effluent	Hardwood extraction (unknown concentration)	85% (3 days)	ligninolytic enzymes	Prasad & Joyce (1991)
Candida sp.	Procyon Blue MX2G (100 mg/1)	96.8% (2 h)	Adsorption	De Angelis & Rodrigues (1987)
	Procyon Red HE7B (100 mg/1)	98.9% (2 h)	Adsorption	

NR = Not reported

(b) Decolorization with algal culture

There has been only one report of algae capable of degrading azo dyes through an induced form of an azoreductase (Jinqi and Houtian, 1992). Several species of *Chlorella* and *Oscillatoria* were capable of degrading azo dyes to their aromatic amines and further to simpler organic compounds or CO_2. Some were even capable of utilizing a few azo dyes as their sole source of carbon and nitrogen. Such algae were proposed by the authors for use in stabilization ponds, as they can play a role in aromatic amine removal.

(c) Decolorization with bacterial culture

Several actinomycete strains have been reported with a capability to decolorize reactive dyes, including anthraquinone, phthalocyanine and azo through the adsorption of dyes to the cellular biomass without any degradation. Other Cu-based azo dyes such as formazan-copper complex dyes were completely decolorized through degradation, (Zhou and Zimmermann, 1993). In bacterial cultures, azo reductase enzyme was responsible for the initiation of degradation of orange II dye by these strains, and substituting any of the group near the azo group's chemical structure hindered the degradation (Zimmermann *et al.,* 1982). Haug *et al.* (1991) described a bacterial consortium capable of mineralizing the sulfonated Mordant Yellow. An alternation from anaerobic to aerobic condition was required to achieve complete degradation, because different members of consortium needed different conditions for optimum reaction and main azo-bond cleavage. Ilgi *et al.* (2000) studied the decolorization of textile dye stuffs DRIMAREN ORANGE K-GL, EVERZOL RED and EVERDIRECT SUPRA yellow PG by mixed bacterial consortium, and they found that sucrose and lactose enhanced the decolorization efficiency as compared to glucose. Nigam *et al.* (1996) demonstrated the use of bacteria for azo dye biodegradation. These microbial systems have a drawback of requiring a fermentation process, and are therefore unable to cope up with large volume of textile effluents. Zissi *et al.* (1997) showed that *Bacillus subtilis* could be used to break down p-amino azobenzene, which is a specific azo dye. Reports on bacterial cultures involved in dye deodorizations are given in Table 16.2.

Table 16.2 Degradation efficiency of some bacterial cultures

Culture	*Dye and concentration*	*Percent removal/time*	*Mechanism*	*Reference*
Aeromonas hydrophila var 24B	Various azo dyes (0.2 mmol/l)	40-100% (24 h)	Azoreductase (cell free extract)	Yatome *et al.* (1987)
Bacillus subtilis IFO 13719	2-carboxy 4′ dimethyleamino benzene	100% (20 min)	Azoreductase in growing cells	Yatome *et al.* (1991)
Klebsiella pneumoniae RS-13	Methyl Red (MR) (100 mg/l)	100% (24 h)	Azoreductase	Wong & Yuen (1996)
Pseudomonas cepacia 13 NA	Orange I (0.045 mmole)	= 90% (10 h)	Azoreductase (in growing cells and cell free extract)	Yatome *et al.* (1991)
Pseudomonas cepacia 13NA (immobilized system)	p-aminoazobenzene (10 mg/l)	60-80% (10 h RT)	Azoreductase	Ogawa & Yatome (1990)
	Red G (100 mg/l)	37.4% (2 days)	Azoreductase	
Pseudomonas luteola	RP_2B (100 mg/l)	92.4% (2 days)	Azoreductase	Hu (1994)
Pseudomonas stutzeri	Various azo dyes (0.1 mmol/l)	90% (8-20 min)	Azoreductase (cellular extract)	Yatome *et al.* (1990)
Pseudomonas stutzeri IAM 12097	Orange I (0.045 mmol/l)	= 80% (20 h)	Azoreductase (cell free extract)	Yatome *et al.* (1991)
	Orange II (0.045 mmole)	= 80% (20 h)	Azoreductase (cell free extract)	
Streptomycetes BW130	Azo-reactive Red 147 (150 mg/l)	29.0% (14 days)	Adsorption	
	Anthraquinone Blue 114(280 mg/l)	27.0% (14 days)	Adsorption	Zhou & Zimmermann (1993)
	Phthalocyanine Blue 116 (200 mg/l)	39.0% (14 days)	Adsorption	

(d) Decolorization of azo dyes by yeast culture

In natural environment, azo dye can be transformed or degraded by a variety of microorganisms, including aerobic-anaerobic bacteria and fungi. However, the long growth cycle and moderate decolorization rate limit the performance of fungal system (Banat *et al.,* 1996; Swamy and Ramsay, 1999). Three hundred ppm concentration of dye, which is a regular concentration used in industries, completely eliminates the growth of test bacteria (El-632Rahim *et al.,* 2003). In contrast to fungi, bacteria can reduce the colour intensity more satisfactorily, but individual bacterial strain could not degrade azo dye completely (Hung *et al.,* 1991; Caughlin *et al.,* 1997), and the intermediate products are carcinogenic aromatic amines that need to be further decomposed. Mixed culture studies may be more appropriate for decolorization of azo dyes (Nigam *et al.,* 1996).

Yeast is surely one of the promising organisms for bioremediation and water pollution control, with its versatility in function. The use of naturally occurring yeast represents a potentially promising means of destroying polluting chemicals in wastewater treatment system or soil. Some yeasts isolated from all types of water, for example *Aureobasidium* and *Rhodotorula* that are normally associated with foliage and soil, probably enter water with run-off (Hagler and Aheam, 1987). The actual contribution of yeast in biodegradation of hydrocarbons in the environment may be more important than previously expected, considering the metabolic diversity demonstrated for yeasts (Midelhoven, 1993; Sampaio, 1999). Yeasts belonging to genera *Candida, Debaryomyces, Aureobasidum, Geotrichum, Pichia, Rhodotorula, Tremella, Hanseniaspora* and *Cryptococcus* have been isolated from stressed environment of a gold extraction liquid circuit in which the cyanide concentration varies from 150-300 ppm, supporting the diversity of yeast in all environmental conditions (Rezende *et al.,* 1999). Different kinds of dried yeasts (*Saccharomyces cerevisiae, Schizosaccharomyces pombe, Kluyveromyces marxianus, Candida sp, C. tropicalis, C. lipolytica, C. utilis, C. quilliermendii* and *C. membranefaciens*) have showed good biosorption capabilities and rates in aqueous solution of a reactive azo dye, Remazol Blue with 250 mg/g cells (Aksu and Donmez, 2003). Trindade and Angelis (1995) refer to azo dye removal by *Rhodotorula* yeast, presumably by an adsorptive interaction with fully grown cells, and Luo and Liu (1996) used a yeast strain, isolated from dye contaminated soil, in the decolorization and degradation of direct orange. *Candida zelylanoides* and *Issatehenkia occidentalis* contain azo reductase enzyme system, which mediates dye decolorization of several structurally related azo dyes, methyl orange (orange 52) and acid orange (orange II) to produce sulfonated amines (Ramalho *et al.,* 2002, 2004; Martins *et al.,* 1999).

Although references of yeast in literatures of biodegradation of dyes are very limited, yeast strains with their diversity in occurrence, membrane biosorptive capacities, potential enzyme system, open a path for biodegradation of related phenolic or aromatic compounds for use in industrial effluent treatment and decontamination in natural areas. Treatment of textile wastewater by purely biological process may be possible by biosorption, biodisintegration, biotransformation, biocatalysis, and biodegradation.

MECHANISMS INVOLVED IN DECOLORIZATION OF DYE

Biosorption

"Adsorption by living/dead microbial biomass". The uptake or accumulation of chemicals by microbial mass has been termed biosorption (Hu, 1992, 1996; Tsezos and bell, 1989; Kumar *et al.,*1998). Dead bacteria, yeast and fungi have been used for the purpose of decolorizing dye containing effluent. Textile dyes vary greatly in their chemical structure, therefore, their interaction with the microorganisms depends upon the specific chemistry of microbial biomass and chemical structure of dye. The binding affinity and rates also vary greatly. It has been observed that the biomass derived from the thermotolerant ethanol-producing yeast strain *K. marxianus* IMB3, exhibited a relatively high affinity for heavy metals (Riordan *et al.,* 1997; Bustard and Mc Hale, 1998; Riordan and Mc Hale 1998). Bustard *et al.,* (1998) showed that this type of biomass has a widened spectrum and high affinity for dye removal.

This method is advantageous if the dye containing effluent is very toxic and all other methods are not effective. It is effective when the conditions are not always favorable for the growth and maintenance of microbial population. Adsorption by biomass also occurs by ion exchange (Hu, 1992). Actinomyces act as an adsorbent for decolorization of effluents containing anthroquinone, phalocynine and azo dyes (Zhou and Zimmerman, 1993). Biosorption occurs in a few minutes in algae and in a few hours in bacteria (Hu, 1996). In addition to heat killed *Funalia trogii,* pellets were also tested (Yesilad *et al.,* 2002) for their ability to decolorize ASTRAZON red dye. These pellets adsorbed the dye and 55% decolorization was obtained in 24 h. Chao and Lee (1994) found that the fungal strains of *P. chrysosporium* pre-cultured in a high nitrogen medium were able to enhance the decolorization of two azodyes. El-Rahim and Mowad (2003) obtained the highest biomass dry weight accumulation with *Aspergillus orchrocous* strain 5 and *Aspergillus niger* strain 31 associated with decolorization of dye. Decolorization of several dyes was also studied by Novotny *et al.* (1997) and Dey *et al.* (1994). They found that decolorization reached 99% of congo red in 9 days in nitrogen limited media.

ENZYMATIC SYSTEM: TOOL FOR DEGRADATION OF AZO TEXTILE DYE

Microbial enzymes have been explored to a great extent in various forms and produced industrially for use in industrial effluent treatment and dye degradation. Few of these are enzymes are azoreductase, laccase, catalase, some peroxidases, etc.

Azoreductase (EC 1.7.1.6)

An intracellular azoreductase or azobenzene reductase is responsible for decolorizing activity of bacteria and yeast. One of the key steps of dye degradation is aerobic/anaerobic reduction of azo bond, where azo chromophore is broken down to produce corresponding amine (Gingell and Walker, 1971; Roxon *et al.,* 1967; Wuhrmann *et al.,* 1980).

The azo bond is reduced and cleaved by azo reductase under anaerobic conditions to form corresponding amines, which is a key step in decolorization of azo dyes (Tan *et al.,* 1999; O' Neill *et al.,* 2000). Although decolorization can occur under anaerobic conditions, the activity of azo reductase from *Pseudomonas* was very high under static conditions, which removed 90% of Direct fast scarlet 4-BS within 36 h, but the activity was suppressed partly in the presence of oxygen under shaking condition (He Fang *et al.*, 2004). Genomic DNA fragments have been isolated from azo reducing bacterial species and expressed in non-decolorizing species (Rafii and Coleman, 1999; Suzuki *et al.,* 2001). Methyl red was treated with crude azo reductase solution (bacterial cell lysate) aerobically in the presence of β NADPH. Molecular cloning and characterization of the gene coding for azoreductase from *Bacillus sp.* OY1-2 was done, and the gene was expressed in *E. coli*. Recombinant azoreductase gave ten times greater reducing activity towards azo dyes than the original *Bacillus sp.* (Suzuki *et al.,* 2001).

In the mechanism, reductase dye acts as an oxidizing agent for reduced nucleotide of microbial electron chain and gets itself reduced and decolorized, concurrently with re-oxidation of reduced nucleotide. In order for this to occur, additional carbon is required to allow decolorization to occur at a viable rate.

This additional carbon is converted to methane and carbon dioxide, releasing the electron. In lab scale, glucose has been added to provide a source of carbon (Carliell *et al.*, 1996).

The most generally accepted mechanism of azo reduction involves the participation of redox mediators, acting as electron shuttles between extracellular dye and the intracellular reductase (Fig. 16.1). The azo bond reduction thus occurs extracellularly. Anthro hydroquinone sulfonate (Keck *et al.*, 1997; Kudlich *et al.*, 1997), riboflavin and benzyl viologen (Samde *et al.*, 1998) are examples of redox mediators, which have been shown to accelerate azo bond reduction by intact cells. This mechanism also accounts for the reduction of highly polar azo dyes, which cannot usually cross the cell membrane. Recently it was shown that the naphthalene sulfonate-degrading *Sphingomonas* species strain BN6 converted 2 naphthol sulfonate to some kind of redox mediators. It was suggested that these redox mediators enable the strains, under anaerobic conditions, to transfer redox equivalent to azo dyes (Chung *et al.*, 1978; Fieser *et al.*, 1931; Stahl *et al.*, 1995; Tratmyek *et al.*, 1989).

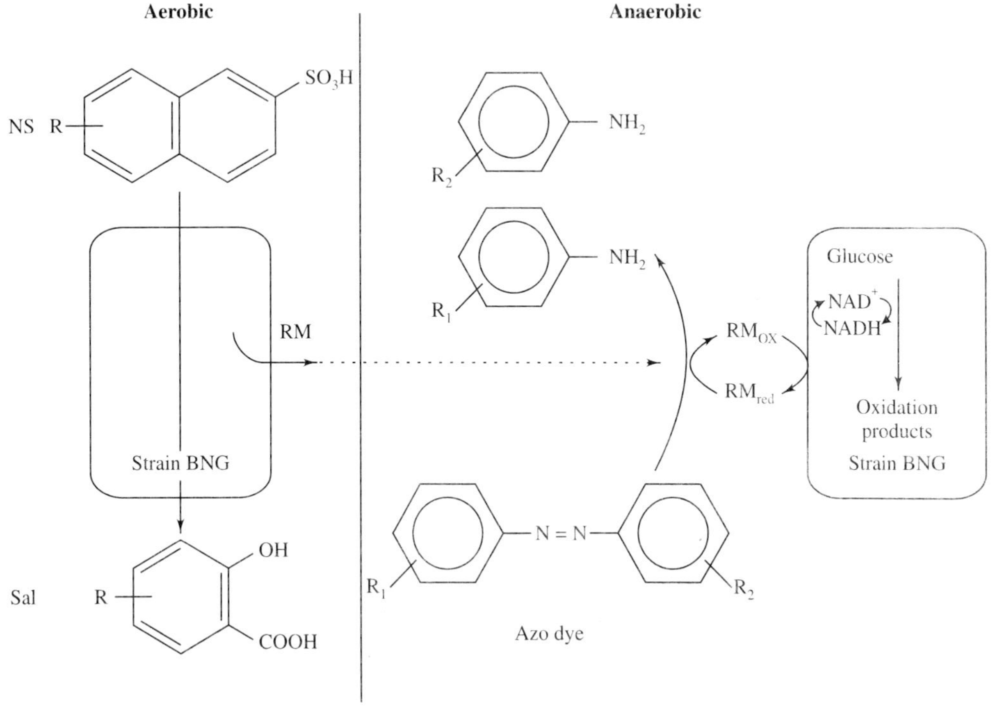

Fig. 16.1 Proposed mechanism for the redox mediator (RM) dependent reduction of azo dyes by strain BN6 (the catabolic pathways of different naphthalene sulfonate to salicylate (Nortemann *et al.*, 1994).

The cellular extracts generally showed much higher rate of anaerobic reduction of azo dyes than the preparation of resting cells. This has been explained by low permeability of the cell membrane for highly polar sulfonated azo compounds. A different model for nonspecific reduction of azo dyes by bacteria, which does not require transport of azo dye or reduced flavin through cell membrane, was recently suggested for *Sphinomonas xenophage* BN6 (Nortemann *et al.*, 1994). It was proposed that in this system quinines act as redox mediators (Lovely *et al.*, 1996). It was previously suggested that the presence of redox mediator could enhance the rate of bacterial azo dye reduction of intestinal bacteria under anaerobic conditions. Therefore, the whole cell of strain BN6 was incubated under anaerobic conditions with sulfonated azo dye amaranth in the presence of a well known redox mediator AQS. Thus, it was found that AQS significantly increases the rate of azo dye decolorization. It was noted that the rate of azo dye decolorization was dependent on the concentration of mediator added (Brown, 1981; Kopeakova and Kopeak, 1990).

Decolorization of azo dyes by yeast is less studied than the homologous process mediated by bacterial species. Few ascomycetes yeast strains and *I. occidentalis* are capable of reducing several mono azo dyes to the corresponding amines, and therefore promote their decolorization through cleavage of azo bonds. (Ramalho *et al.*, 2002, 2004). The mechanism of azo dye decolorization by yeast strain is same as the hypothesis proposed as early in 1975 in a study describing the decolorization of azo dyes by *Proteus vulgaris*. In yeast, azo dye reduction occurs in the presence of living matter and outside the cell, because the sulfonic azo dyes are impermeant to the cell membranes, and intracellular NAD(P)H, which is the primary source of electrons, is also impermeant to the cell membrane. Therefore, there is involvement of an externally directed reductase activity in the plasma membrane that is capable of transferring reducing equivalent to acceptor species in extracellular medium. Here azoreductase has intracellular location, therefore a redox mediator could facilitate the transfer of reducing equivalent from intracellular NAD(P) H to substrate dye, which is a terminal electron acceptor (Ramalho *et al.*, 2004). Redox mediators are usually quinoid compounds that are formed as by-products of degradation mechanism, which has already been described previously.

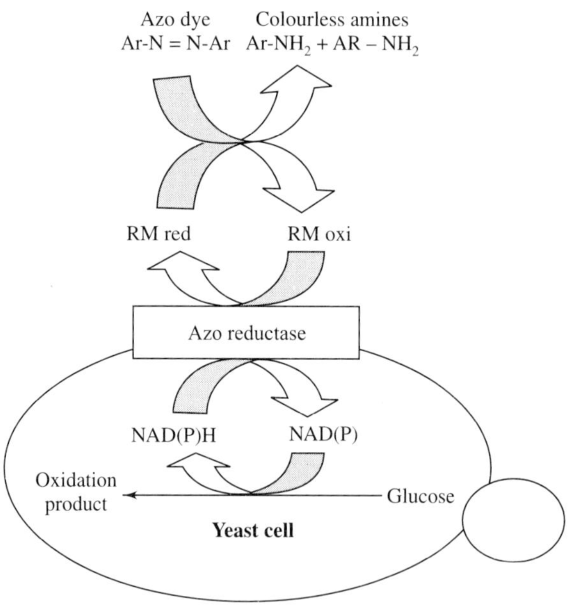

Fig. 16.2 In yeast azo dye reduction decolorization occurs In aerobic conditions in the presence of additional carbon source by intact cells. Martins *et al.* (1999).

Laccase (Polyphenol Oxidase) EC (1:10.3.2)

Laccase (benzenediol: oxygen oxidoreductase comprising a family of multicopper oxidizes, is an enzyme which has been found in many organisms and catalyses the oxidation of large variety of a organic (phenolic and non-phenolic) substrates (Mayer, 1987). Laccase is a multi-copper oxidizer enzyme, which reduces molecular oxygen to water and simultaneously performs one electron oxidation of various aromatic substrates (diphenol, methoxy-substituted monophenols, aromatic amines). Fungal laccases are involved in various processes in nature, and their applications in detoxification of various aquatic and terrestrial pollutants and in the wastewater has been suggested. Laccases are also involved in oxidation of various phenolic and non-phenolic substrates, and also in lignin degradation and degradation of polyaromatic compounds. Laccases have been found in many white-rot fungi and some basidiomycetes and ascomycetes fungi (Thurston, 1994; Majcher Czyk, 1998; Messerchmidt, 1997; Gianfredal, 1999; Smith *et al.,* 1997; Leonowicz *et al.,* 2001; Bollag *et al.,*1988). Most laccases reported so far are the extracellular enzymes. Laccase has broad substrate specificities ranging from iodide to phenols. In addition to oxidizing phenols with higher redox potentials, laccases were also found to be able to oxidize other organic compounds with higher redox potentials (Xu, 1996). In terms of degradation of phenolic lignin model compounds by laccase, much work has been done by Higuchi and co-workers (1985). Laccase is able to catalyze Cα - Cβ cleavage followed by β-O-4 ether cleavage, thus generating a new phenolic hydroxyl group. Laccase can also cause aromatic ring cleavage and demethoxylation of a phenolic lignin model compound (Kawai *et al.,* 1988 a and 1988 b).

In later years it was demonstrated that laccase is able to oxidize non-phenolic lignin substructures in the presence of a low molecular weight organic compound acting as a mediator. This discovery resulted in new uses of laccase in pulp bleaching and degradation of dye in textile industry (Bourbonnais and Paice; 1992; Pedersen and Schmidt, 1992). Since laccase can be easily produced in large quantities at a relatively low price, research on application of laccase for pulp bleaching has been advancing rapidly especially since the discovery that certain low molecular weight organic compounds enable laccase to oxidize non-phenolic lignin model compound Bourbonnais and Paice (1992).

Catalase (EC 1.11.1.6)

Hydrogen peroxide: hydrogen peroxide oxidoreductase

$$2H_2O \xrightarrow{\text{Catalase}} 2H_2O + O_2$$

Catalase preparations are used to destroy peroxides (by-product of degradation metabolism) in cell culture. Catalase activity in fungal cultures was studied during the decolorization of textile dye. Catalase was secreted in abundant quantities on 2nd day of incubation by all the fungi. The activity of this enzyme in fungal isolates varied from 2 to 3.2 units. In *A. niger* maximum catalase production 5.0 unit was found (Kausar *et al.,* 2000).

Peroxidase

Doner: H_2O_2 Oxidoreductase E.C.- 1.11.1.7

Peroxidase (POD) includes a group of specific enzyme (NAD peroxidase, fatty acid peroxidase, etc.) as well as a group of non-specific enzyme from different sources. It catalyses the dehydrogenation of a large number of organic compounds such as phenols, aromatic amines, hydroquinone, etc. It occurs in animals, higher plants and many other organisms (Sadashivam and Manickam, 1992). The mechanism of action of peroxidase is:

$$\text{Substrate} + H_2O_2 \xrightarrow{\text{POD}} \text{Oxidized substrate} + 2\,H_2O_2$$

The ability of fungi to degrade azo dye is also related to the ability to synthesize lignin degrading exo enzyme such as lignin peroxidase and Mn peroxidase (Maximo *et al.* 2003; Swamy and Ramsay, 1999; Paszcynski *et al.*, 1992). Kuhwara *et al.* (1984) indicated that manganese peroxidase participates in lignin degradation and decolorization of artificial polymeric dye complex. Michel *et al.* (1991) demonstrated that purified lignin peroxidase and manganese peroxidase were effective in the decolorization of Kraft bleach plant effluent, and Sayadi *et al.* (1995) observed decolorization of olive mill wastewater by these two purified enzymes.

PRESENT RESEARCH

The studies are undergoing at author's laboratory on biotransformation of azo textile dye using yeast. It has resulted in isolation of 50 dye degrading yeasts isolates from Jabalpur (local dyers soil); Kanpur (leather industry waste) and Ahmedabad (textile industry waste). One strain *Pichia rebaulensis* has been found to be the most promising strain and is able to decolorize the dyes amaranth, acid orange and methyl orange up to 100% in 24 h under optimized laboratory conditions. Involvement of azoreductase and polyphenol oxidase was found in decolorization mechanism, and metabolites were studied using HPLC. Yeast strains were also modified genetically to obtain the desired decolorization of azo dyes.

CONCLUSION

Microbial and biotechnological approach for treatment of industrial wastewater appears to be the most practical method over available conventional methods. A major advantage of anaerobic microbial system, apart from decolorization of soluble dye, is the production of biogas which can be reused to provide heat and power and will reduce energy cost. Initially such biological process could be adopted as pre-treatment decolorization step, combined with conventional treatment system. Concerted efforts are still required to establish biological decolorization system industrially but microbial biotechnology has great potential in this vital area of environmental protection.

REFERENCES

Aksu, Z. and Donmez, G. (2003) *Deprt of chem. Eng*. Hacettepe University, Ankara. Pub Med-123-175.

Andrianova, M. M. (1970) *Vopr. Pitan* **29:** 61-65.

Anliker , R.(1979) *J. Ecotoxicol. Environ. Safety* **3:** 59-74.

Banat,I.M.; McMullan, G.; Mechan, C.; Kirby, N; Nigam, P.; Smytgh, W.F.; Merchant, R.(1999) In *proceeding of the Industrial waste technical; conference*, Indian apoliis, USA pp. 1-16.

Banet, I.M.; Nigam, P.; Singh, D.; Marchant, R. (1996): *Biores. Technol.* **58:** 217-227.

Baughman, G.L. and Perenich, T.A (1988) *Bull. Environ. Contam. Toxicol.* **40:** 545-552.

Berg, J.W. and Howell, M.A. (1974) **34:**807-814.

Berg, J.W.; Haeszel, W. and De Vesa, S.S. (1973) *In proceedings of the seventh National cancer conference.* J.B. Lippincott, Philadelphia pp. 459-464.

Bollag, J.M.; Shuttleworth, K.L. and Anderson, D.H. (1988) *Appl. Environ. Mocrobiol.* **54:** 3086-3091.

Bourbonnais Rand Paice, M.G. (1992) *Appl. Mocrobiol. Biotechnol.* **36:** 823-827.

Brahimi-Horn, M.C.; Lim, K.K.; Liany, S.L. and Mou, D.G. (1992) *J. Ind. Microbiol* **10:** 31-36.

Brown, J.P. (1981) *Appl. Environ. Mocrobiol.* **41:** 1283-1286.

Bumpus, J.A.; Ferando, T.; Jurek, M.A. and Aust, S.D. (1989) *Biotechnology application in hazardious waste treatement* :363-381.

Buschmann, H.J. (1992) *Inorg. Chem. Acta.* **193:** 93-97.

Bustard, M. and McHale, A.P. (1998) *Bioprocess Eng.* **19:** 351-353.

Bustard, M.; McMullan, G. and McHale, A.P. (1998) *Bioprocess Eng.* **19:** 427-430.

Capalash, N. and Sharma, P. (1992) *World J. Microbial. Biotechnol.* 309-312.

Carliell, C.N.; Barclay, S.J.; Naidoo, N.; Buckley, C.A. (1996) *Water S.A. (Pretoria)* **22:** 225-233.

Carliell, C.N.; Barclay, S.J.; Naidoo, N.; Buckley, C.A.; Mulholland, D.A. and Senior, E. (1995) *Water S.A. (Pretoria)* 21:61-69.

Chao, W.L. and Lee, S.L. (1994) *World J. Microbiol. Biotechnol.* **10:** 556-559.

Chung, K.T. (1982) *Mut. Res.* **114:** 269-81.

Chung, K.T.; Fulk G.E. and Egan M.(1978) *Appl. Environ. Mocrobiol.* **35:** 558-562.

Collina, T.F.X,; Mc Laughlin, J. (1973) *Cosmet Toxicol* **11:** 355-3654.

Collina, T.F.X,; Black, T.N.; Ruggles, D.L And Gray, G.C. (1975) *Toxicology* **3:** 129-118.

Collina, T.F.X. and Mc Laughlin, J. (1972) *Food Cosmet. Toxical.***10:** 619-624.

Corso, C.R.; De Angelis, D.F.; De Oliveira, J.E. and Kiyanc (1981) *Eur. J. of Appl. Microbial Biotechnol.* **13:** 64-66 .

Coughlin, M.F.; Kinkle, B.K,; Tepper, A. and Bishop, P.L. (1997) *Water Science Technol.* **36:** 215-220.

Cripps, C.; Bumpus, J.A. and Aust, S.D.(1990) *Applied and Envirionmental microbiology* Apr:1114-1118.

De Angelis, F.E. and Rodrigues, G.S. (1987) *Arquiros de Biologis E. Technologia (Curritiba)* **30:** 301-309.

Dey, S.; Maiti, T.K. and Bhattacharya, B.C. (1994) *Appl. Environ. Microbiol.* **60:** 4216-4218.

Easton, J.R. (1995) *In the cooper P(Ed)* in develop effluent .

Fewson, C.A. (1988) *Trends. Biotechnbol.* **6:** 148-153.

Fieser, L.F. and Peters, H.A. (1931) *J. Am. Chem. Soc.* **53:** 793-805.

Ganesh, R.; Boardmann, G.D. and Michelsen, D. (1994) *Water Res.* **28:** 1367-1376.

Gianfreda, L,; Xu, F.; Bollag, J.M. (1999) *Bioremediation J.* **3:** 1-25.

Gingell, R. and Walker, R. (1971) *Xenobiotica* **I:** 231-239.

Gupta, G.S.; Prasad, G. and Singh, V.H. (1990) *Water Res.* **24:** 45-50.

Hagler A..N and Ahearn D.G (1987) In the yeasts 2nd ed. Vol (Ed. Rose A.H. and Haniron, J.S.) Academic Press London pp. 181-205.

Hartman, C.P.; Fulk, G.E and Andrews, A.W. (1978) *Mutant Res.* **58:** 125-132 .

He Fang, Hu W. and Li, Y .(2004) Chemosphere **57:** 293-301.

Higuchi, T. (1985) In: *Biosynthsis and biodegradation of wood components*, (Higuchi T., Ed.) Academic Press, pp. 557-576.

Hosono, M.; Arai, H.; Aizawa, M.; Yamamoto, I.; Shimizu, K.; sufiyama, M. (1993) *Appl. Rad. Iso.* **144:** 1199-1203.

Hu, T.L (1992) *Water Science Technol.* **26:** 357-366.

Hu, T.L (1994) *Biores. Technol.* **49:** 47-51.

Hu, T.L (1996) *Water Science Technol.* **34:** 89-95.

Hu, T.L (2001) *Water Science Technol.* **43:** 261-9.

Hung, W.; Schmidt, A.; Nartemann, B.; Hempel, D.C.; Stoiz, A.; Knachmuss, H.J. (1991) *Application environment microbial.* **57:** 3144-3149.

Idaka, E. and Ogawa, Y. (1978) *J. Soc. Dyers and Colourists* **94:** 91-94.

Ilgi, K. K.; Fikret, K.; Mc Mullan, G. and Marchant, R. (2000) *Biotech Letters* **22:** 1179-1181.

Jiang, H. and Bishop P.L. (1994) *Water Science Technol.* **29:** 525-530.

Jinqi, H. and Houtian, L. (1992) *Environ. Poll.* **75:** 273-278.

Jones R.; Ryan, A.J. and Wright, S.E (1964) *Cosmet. Toxicol* **2:** 447-452.

Kandelbauer, A. and Gubitiz, G.M (In press) In *Bioremediation for decolourisation of textile dyes, a review* (Eds. Licthfouse, V.; Dudd, S. and Robert, D). Enviournment Chemistry, Spinger Verlag, Heiddberg, Germany.

Karcher, S.; Kornmuller, A. and Jekel, M. (1999 a) *Actahydrochim* **27:** 38-42 .

Karcher, S.; Kornmuller, A.; Jekel, M. (1999 b) *Water Sci. Technol.* **40:** 425-433.

Kausar, N.; Seshikala, D. and Singara Charya, N.A. (2000) *Indian J Microbiol.* **40:** 191-197.

Kawai, S.; Umezawa, T. and Higuchi, T. (1988 a) *Arch. Biochem. Biophys.***262:** 99-110.

Kawai, S.; Umezawa, T.; Shimada, M. and Higuchi, T. (1988) *FEBS Lett.* **2:** 309-311.

Keck, A.; Klein, J.; Kudlich. M.; Stolz, A.; Knackmuss, H.J. and Mattes, R. (1997) *Appl. Environ. Mocrobiol.* **63:** 3684-90.

Kirby, N.; Marchant, R. and Mc Mullan, G. (2000) *FEMS Microbiol. Lett.* **188:** 93-96.

Knapp, J. S. and Newby, P.S. (1995) *Water Research Oxford* **7:** 1807-1809.

Kopeckova, P. and Kopece, K. (1990) *Macromol. Chem.* **191:** 2037-2045.

Kudlich, M.; Keeck, A.; Klein, J. and Stolz, A. (1997) *Appl. Environ. Mocrobiol.* **63:** 3691-4.

Kumar, M.N.V.R.; Sridhari, T.R.; Bhavani, K.D. and Dutta, P.K. (1998) *Colorage* **40:** 25-34.

Kuwara, M.; Glenn, J.K.; Morgan, M. and Gold, M.H. (1984) *FEBS Lett.* **169:** 147-150.

Larsen, L.C.; Eyer, T.M. and Scheline, RR (1976) *Acta Pharmacol Toxical* **38:** 353-357

Leonowic, Z.A.; Cho, N.S.; Luterek, J.; Wilkolazka, A.; Wojtaswasilewska, M.; Matuszwska, A.; Hofrichter, M.; Wesenberg, D. and Rogaiski, J. (2001) *J. Basic Microbiol.* **41:** 185-227.

Levine, W.G. and Raza, H. (1988) *Drug Metab. Dispos.* **16:** 441-448.

Lin, S.H. and Liu, W.Y. (1994) *J. Environment Eng.* (NY) **120:** 437-446.

Loper, J.C. (1995) *1994-1995 Research Progress,* University of Cincinnati.

Lovely, D.R.; Coates, J.D.; Blunt-Haris, E. L.; Phillips, E.J.P. and Woodward, J.C. (1996) *Nature* **382:** 445-448.

Loyd, C.K.; Goardman, G.D. and Michelsen, D.L. (1992) *Hazard. Ind. Waste* **24:** 593-601.

Luo, Z. and Liu, M. (1996) *Zhongguo Jishui Paishui* **12(4):** 12-13.

Machuca, A. and Duran, N. (1993) *Appl. Biochem.* **43:** 37-44.

Majcherczyk A.; Johannes, C, and Huttermann, A. (1998) *Enzyme Micro. Technol.* **22:** 336-341.

Manning, B.W.; Cerniglia, C.E. and Fcderle, T.W. (1985) *Appl. Environ. Microbiol.* **50:** 10-15.

Marchant, R.; Nigam, P. and Banat, I.M. (1994) *Mycol. Res.* **98:** 757-760.

Martins, M.A.M.; Cardoso M.H.; Queizroz, M.J.; Ramalho, M.T. and Campos, A.M. O.(1999) *Chemosphere* **38(11):** 2455-2460.

Maximo, C.; Maria, T.P.A. and Ferreira, M.C. (2003) *Enzyme Microbial. Technol.* **32:** 145-151.

Mayer, A.M. (1987) *Phytochemistry* **26:** 11-20.

Mc Curdy, M.W.; Boardman, G.D.; Michelson, D.L. and Woodby, B.M. (1992) In *46th Proc. Purdue Industrial Waste Conf.* Lewis Publishers, pp. 229-234.

Mc Kay, G. (1979) *Am. Dye Stuff Reporter* **68:** 29-36.

Medvev, Z.A.; Crowne, H. M. and Medvedeva, M.N. (1988) *Mech. Ageing. Dev.* **46:** 159-174.

Michaels, G.B and Lewis, D.L.(1985) *Environ. Toxicol. Chem.***4:** 45-50.

Michel, F.C.; Dass, S.B.; Grulke, E.A and Reddy, C.A. (1991) *Applied Environ. Microbiol.* **57:** 2368-2375.

Middelhoven, W.J. (1993) *Antonie Van Leeuwenhoek*, **63:** 125-144.

Mishra, G. and Tripathi, M. (1993) *Colourage* **40:** 35-38.

Mou, D.G.; Lim, K.K. and Shen, H.P. (1991) *Biotechnol. Adv.* **9:** 613-622.

Nasser, N.M. and El-Geundi (1991) *J. Chem. Technol. Biotechnol.* **50:** 257-264.

Nawar, S.S. and Doma, H. A. (1989) *Sci. Tot. Environ.* **79:** 271-279.

Nigam, P., Singh, D., Marchant, R. (1995b) In: *Environmental Biotechnology: Principal and Applications*, (Eds. MooYoung, M.), Kluwer Academic, The Netherlands pp. 278-292.

Nigam, P.; Armour, G.; Banat, I.M.; Singh, D. and Marchant, R. (2000) *Bioresource Technol.* **72:** 219-226.

Nigam, P.; Banat, I.M.; Oxspring, D.; Marchant, R.; Singh, D. and Smyth, W.F. (1995a) *Microbios* **84:** 171-185.

Nigam, P.; Banat, I.M.; Singh, D. and Marchant, R. (1996) *Process Biochem.* **31:** 431-442.

Nortemann, B.; Kuhon, A. E.; Knackmuss, H.J. And Stolz, A. (1994) *Arch. Microbiol.* **161:** 320-327.

Novotny, C.; Vyas, B. R.; Erbanova, P.; Kubatova, A. and Sasek, V. (1997) *Folia Microbol. (Praha)* **42:** 136-140.

O'Neill, C.; Haekes, F.R.; Hawkes, D.L.; Esteve, S.S. and Wilcox, S.J. (2000) *Appl. Microbiol. Biotechnol.* **53(2):** 249-254.

Ogava,T., Fugi, F.; Kawal, K.; Yatomi, C. and Idaka, E.(1989). *Bull. Environ. Contam Toxical.* **42:** 402-408.

Ogawa, T. and Yotome, C. (1990) *Bull. Environ. Contam. Toxicol.* **44:** 561-566.

Ogawa, T., Yotome, C., Idaka, E. and Kamiya, H. (1986) *J. Soc. Dyers and Colorists* **2:** 12-14.

Ogutveren, U.B. and Kaparal, S. (1994) *J. Environ. Sci. Health* **29:** 1-16.

Oxspring, D.A., McMullan, G., Smyth, W. F. and Marchant, R. (1996) *Biotechnol Lett.* **18:** 527-530.

Paszczynski A., Pasti Grigsby, M.B., Goszcynski, S., Crawford, R.L. and Crawrord, D.L. (1992) *Appl. Environ. Microbiol.* Nov: 3598-3604.

Pedersen, G. and Schmidt, M. (1992) *International Patent* 9218687.

Pelegrini, R.; Peralto-Zamora, P.; DeAndrade, A.R.; Reyers, J. and Duran N. (1999) *Appl Catal. B. Environ.* **22:** 83-90.

Percy, A.J.; Moore, N. and Chipman, J.K. (1989) *Toxicology* **57:** 217-223.

Poots, V.J.; Mc.Kay, G. and Heakt, J.K. (1976 a) *Water Res.* **10:** 1061-1066.

Poots, V.J.; Mc.Kay, G. and Heakt, J.K.(1976 b) *Water Res.* **10:** 1067-1070.

Prasad, D.Y. and Joyce, T.K. (1991) *Tappi. J.* (Jan) 165-169.

Raffi F. and Coleman T. (1999) *J. Basic Microbiol.* **39:** 39-35.

Raghwacharya, C. (1997) *Chem. Eng. World* **32:** 53-54.

Ramalho, P.A.; Cardoso, M.H.; Cavaco-Paulo, A. and Ramalho, M.T. (2004) *Appl. Envion. Microbiol.* **76:** 2279-2288.

Ramalho, P.A.; Scholze, H.; Cardoso, M.H.; Ramalho, M.T. and Oliveira- Campos, A.M. (2002) *Enzyme Microbiol. Technol.* **31:**848-854.

Rezende R.P.; Dias J. C.T.; Rosa C.A. and Linardi, V.R. (1999) *J. Appl. Microbiol.* **45:** 185-192.

Richardson, M.L. (1983) *J. Soc. Dyers Colourists* **99:** 198-200.

Riordan, C. and McHale, A.P. (1998) *Bioprocess Eng.* **19:** 277-280.

Riordan, C.; Bustard, M.; Putt, R. and McHale, A.P. (1997) *Bioprocess Eng.* **19:** 385-387.

Roxon, J.J.; Rayan, A.J. and Wright, S.E. (1967) *Food Cosmet. Toxicol.* **5:** 367-369.

Roxon, J.J.; Rayan, A.J. and Wright, S.E. (1967) *Food Chem. Toxic* **5:** 645-656.

Ryu, B.H. and Weon, Y.D. (1992) *J. Microbial. Biotechnol.* **2:** 215-219.

Sadashivam, S. and Manickam, A. (1992) In *Biochemical methods*, 2nd Ed, Wiley Eastorn Limited. New Delhi, pp. 106-107.

Sampio, J.P. (1999) *Can. J. Microbiol.* **45:** 491-512.

Sayadi, S. and Ellouz, R. (1995) *Appl. Environ. Microbiol.* **61:** 1098-1103.

Schliephake, K.; Lonergan, G.T.; Jones, C.L. and Mainwaring, D.E. (1993) *Biotechnol Lett.* **15:** 1185-1188.

Semde, R.; Pierre, D.; Geukens, G.; Devleeshouwer, M. and Moes, A.J. (1998) *Int. J. Pharma.* **161:** 45-54.

Seshadri, S.; Bishop, P.L. and Agha, A.M. (1994) *Waste Mgmnt.* **15:** 127-137.

Shaul, E.M.; Holdsworth, T.J.; Dempsey, C.R. And Dostall, K.A. (1991) *Process Chemosphere* **22:** 107-119.0220.

Shrivastava, P.N and Prahash, A.(1991) *J. Ind .Poll . Control Fed* 25-30

Smith, M.; Thrston, C.F. and Wood, D.A. (1997) In *Multicopper oxidases (A. Messerchmidt, Editor)* World Sci. Singapore, pp. 201-224.

Society of Dyes and Colourists (1976) *colour index*, 3rd Edn. Society of dyers and colourists,Yorkshire , N.K.

Solkar, Y.M. and Le Marshel, A.M. (1997) *Dyes Pigments* **37:** 335-356.

Stahl, J.D.; Rasmussen S.J. and Aust, S.D. (1995) *Arch. Biochem. Biophysics.* **322:** 221-227.

Suzuki, Y.; Yoda, T.; Rhul, A. and Sugira, W. (2001) *J. Biol. Chem.* **276:** 9059-9065.

Swamy, J. and Ramsay, J.A. (1999) *Enzyme. Microbial. Technol.* **24:** 130-137.

Tan, N.C.G.; Prenafestbould, F.X.; Opsteeg, J.L.; Lettinya, G. and Field, J.A. (1999) *Appl. Microbial. Biotechnol.* **51:** 865-871.

Thurston, C.F. (1994) *Microbiology* **140:** 19-26.

Tratnyek, P.G. and Mccalady, D.L. (1989) *J. Agric. Food. Chem.* **37:** 248-254.

Trindade, R.C. and Angelis, D.F. (1995) In *7th Symposium on Microbial Eco.* (Santos, S. Paulo) Brazil, 27, Aug-Sep, pp. 24-86.

Tsezos, M. and Bell J.P. (1989) *Water Res.* **23:** 561-568.

Wolf, A.W. and Oehme, F.W. (1974) *J. Am. Med. Asso.* **164:** 623-629.

Wong, P.K. and Yuen, P.K. (1996) *Water Res.* **30:** 1736-1744.

Wuhrmann, K.K.; Mecher and Kappeler, T. (1980) *Appl. Microbial. Biotechnol.* **9:** 325-338.

Wynder, E.L. and Reddy, B.S. (1974) *Cancer* **34:** 801-806.

Xu, F. (1996) *Biochemistry* **35:** 7608-7614.

Xu, Y. and Lebrun, R.E. (1999) *Separ Sci. Technol.* **34:** 2501-2519.

Yang, Y.; Wyatt II, D.T. and Bahorsky, M. (1998) *Text. Chem. Colour* **30:** 27-35.

Yatome, C.; Ogawa, T.; Hayashi, H. and Ogawa, T. (1991) *J. Environ. Sci. Health* A**26:** 471-485.

Yatome, C.; Ogawa, T.; Hishida, H. and Taguchi, T. (1990) *J. Soc. Dyers Colorists* **106:** 280-282.

Yatome, C.; Ogawa, T.; Itoh, K.; Sugiyama, A. and Idaka, E. (1987) *J. Soc. Dyers Colorists* **3:** 389-395.

Yesilada, O.; Cing, S. and Asma, D. (2002) *Bioresour. Technol.* **81:** 155-157.

Zhou, W. and Zimmerman W. (1993) *FEMS Microbiol. Lett.* **107:** 157-162.

Zimmerman, T.; Kulla, H.G. and Lesinger, T. (1982) *Eur. J. Biochem.* **129:** 197-203.

Zollinger, H. (1987) VCH Publishers, NewYork, pp. 92-100.

17

Eco-friendly and Economically Viable Integrated Nutrient Management for Sustainable Agriculture

Sandeep Kumar, Pankaj Kumar, R.C. Dubey and D.K. Maheshwari

Department of Botany and Microbiology

Gurukul Kangri University, Haridwar

E-mail: maheshwaridk@gmail.com

Soil health has become a major concern for sustainable agriculture in the new millennium. Intensive agricultural practices, rapid industrialization and an increase in imbalanced usage of nutrient supply have led to soil degradation and decline in soil fertility. The available statistics reveal an alarming situation. Nowadays, heavy fertilization (60-300 kg/ha) is required to achieve optimal yield and protein content. Excessively applied mineral nutrients end upto a large extent in groundwater, where they reduce drinking water quality and cause eutrophication with disastrous effects on soil microbial ecology and aquatic ecosystem. Judicious use of fertilizers with biofertilizers is required to sustain an ecofriendly and economically viable agriculture to meet the rising food demand in future from a limited production area. Two decades ago, plant growth-promoting rhizobacteria (PGPR) were introduced as microbial inoculants for biofertilization, phytostimulation, biopesticides and some time for bioremediation. A large-scale application of PGPR to crops as inoculants seems to be attractive as it would substantially reduce the use of chemical fertilizers and pesticides. In addition, the application of PGPR will increase crop yield, thereby helping to feed the growing world population. Beneficial plant-microbe interactions in the rhizosphere are the determinants of plant health and soil fertility. Soil-plant-microbe interactions are complex, and there are many ways in which the outcome can influence the plant health, productivity and soil fertility. Hence, the present review summarizes the various studies with an aim to evaluate the integrated effect of PGPR and inorganic fertilizers on different crops and their health-supporting rhizobacteria.

INTRODUCTION

Fertilizers have played a key role in making the green revolution possible in India. They are essential components of modern agriculture because they provide essential nutrients to the plant for their growth and yield. However, overuse of chemical fertilizers has resulted in unanticipated environmental impacts (Adesemoye *et al.,* 2009). In intensive cropping system, supplementing the soil with all nutrients through chemical fertilizer is considered inevitable for obtaining optimum crop yield. But it has been supported by many workers that continuous use of fertilizers may affect soil ecosystem and may lead to adverse impact on soil productivity. Hence, for sustainable agriculture, all the efforts should be streamlined to protect and maintain soil health. Nowadays, biofertilizers are gaining importance in agriculture (Paul and Savithri, 2003), which may help in enhancing the crop yield quality and play a role in imparting resistance to environmental stress such as drought, extreme heat, early frost, pests and pathogen problems (Kumar *et al.,* 2006). Plant growth-promoting rhizobacteria (PGPR) in the form of biofertilizer (Cakmakci, *et al.,* 2006) and biopesticides (Arora *et al.,* 2008) have been proved for use in agricultural crops. During the last three decades or so, plant growth promotion and biological control of pest and pathogen has been widely applied, well established, intensively investigated and used commercially in different countries worldwide in agriculture, silviculture, horticulture and environmental remediation (Jeffries *et al.,* 2003; Reed and Glick, 2004; Fravel, 2005).

Application of PGPR with traditional inorganic fertilizers in field has proved to be an effective means to increase the solubility of insoluble phosphorous ions and other minerals to plants with simultaneous reduction in disease incidence. They take systemic and simultaneous account of environmental aspects, quality of the produce and profitability of agriculture (Luc, 2000). Alternatively, substitution of chemicals with bacterial fertilizers and biopesticides, especially blending of chemical fertilizers with chemical adaptive PGPR is a promising approach to obtain sustainable fertility of the soil and plant growth (Joshi *et al.,* 2006). Various groups of PGPR are reported to solubilize insoluble phosphate into soluble form of phosphorus (Vassilev *et al.,* 2006) to secrete plant growth hormones such as gibberellins, auxin and cytokinins (Etesami *et al.,* 2009a,b) and other metabolites besides producing antibiotics and siderophores. Such characteristics of PGPR provide the benefits to support plant health. There are several PGPR currently commercialized whose growth-promoting activity in crop plants has been demonstrated in several ways including production of iron-sequestering siderophores and antimicrobial compounds that hinder colonization of hosts by phytopathogens (Weller, 1998), induction of host systemic disease resistance, solubilization of precipitated mineral nutrients and production of phytohormones, thereby enhancing the ability of plants to take up nutrients from soil and increasing the yield (Glick, 1995).

Degradation of soil reflected by decline in the yield of major crops, and increasing disease and pest incidences under conventional agriculture are the common global problems. The reduced crop productivity in conventional agriculture has been caused by indiscriminate use of chemical inputs (fertilizers and agrochemicals) and intensive cropping, which has made soil sick (Narwal, 2006), leading to depletion of beneficial microbial communities (Seneviratne, 2009). Continuous usage of chemical fertilizers subvert the soil ecology, disrupt environment, degrade soil fertility and consequently exhibit harmful effects on human health (Ayala and Rao, 2002) and contaminate groundwater (Joshi *et al.,* 2006).

Microbial diversity has profound effect on the function of soil ecosystem. Decomposition of organic matter, nutrient cycling, bioremediation of toxic pollutants, and management of infectious diseases are some key positive aspects for action of microbes in the ecosystems. Soil bacteria are more sensitive to the application of chemical N fertilizer during the plant growth cycle (Seneviratne, 2009). Further, temporal changes in bacterial function have been observed to disappear in the conventional cultivation with chemical inputs (Papatheodorou *et al.,* 2008). This leads to the accumulation of allelopathic compounds resulting in reduced crop productivity. In conventional agriculture, chemical fertilizers and herbicides affect negatively the potential for topdown control of above ground pests (Birkhofer *et al.,* 2008), possibly due to reduced microbial diversity. They also change interactions within and between below ground and above ground components, ultimately promoting negative environmental impacts of agriculture by reducing internal biological cycles and pest control.

Beneficial plant-microbe interactions in the rhizosphere are the determinants of plant health and soil fertility. In the era of sustainable agricultural production, the interactions in the rhizosphere play a pivotal role in transformation, mobilization, solubilization, etc. from a limited nutrient pool in the soil and subsequent uptake of essential plant nutrients by the crop plants to realize full genetic potential of the crop. Soil microorganisms play a crucial role in biogeochemical cycling of both inorganic and organic nutrients in the soil and in the maintenance of soil health and quality (Jeffries *et al.,* 2003). Thus, the need of the hour is to enhance the efficiency of meager amount of external inputs by supplementing with beneficial microorganisms so as to achieve the maximum production without any adverse effect on soil ecosystem.

The history of PGPR application spans more than 100 years. For many years, PGPR strains isolated from soil have been used for microbial inoculation in the plant rhizosphere. During the last few decades, the Soviet Union, the United States, European countries and China have all initiated practical programmes to develop microbial applications in agriculture at large scale (Jagnow *et al.,* 1991). There are a number of limiting factors. One of the main problems of microbial introduction in practice is that the applied microorganisms sometimes do not survive, or do not execute their specific function (van Veen *et al.,* 1997). Nor does successful introduction of a PGPR strain to one soil-plant environment guarantee its survival in another soil sample or host plant genotype (Pillay and Nowak, 1997). Similar problems are also reported for hydroponic and soilless systems of plant growth (Paulitz and Belanger, 2001). Thus, results of experiments in which selected PGPR strains are introduced in rhizospheres of different plant species or in different soil environments are difficult to interpret, because of the natural complexity of the rhizosphere as a biological system (Horwath *et al.,* 1998; Edge and Wyndham, 2002).

Beneficial microorganisms (such as *Alcaligens, Agrobacterium, Azoarcus, Azospirillum, Azotobacter, Arthrobacter, Bacillus, Clostridium, Enterobacter, Gluconacetobacter, Pseudomonas, Burkholderia, Rhizobium, Serratia, Xanthomonas,* etc.) introduced in rhizosphere are affected by a large number of abiotic and biotic factors, each potentially producing an unfavourable effect. It is known that abiotic factors such as soil temperature (Pillay and Nowak, 1997), soil pH (Bashan *et al.,* 1995), oxygen availability (Hojberg *et al.,* 1999), availability of nutrients, soil water content (Mawdsley and Burns, 1994), soil type (Horwath *et al.,* 1998), soil clay content (Bashan *et al.,* 1995), and soil texture and micropore structure (van der Hoeven *et al.,* 1996) affect the survival of PGPR. The abundance of microorganisms in the rhizophere induced by the availability of plant produced organic substrates leads to intense biotic interactions including predation by protozoa and nematodes (Brimecombe *et al.,* 1999), bacteriophage activity (Ashelford *et al.,* 2000), microbial competition for resources (Kravchenko and Makarova, 1993), and direct interspecific microbial interactions. Interspecific interactions include negative interactions through inhibition of microbial activity by antibiotic production, and positive interactions through synergisms or increased nutrient availability (van Veen *et al.,* 1997). The method of PGPR inoculation also affects the survival in rhizosphere: important parameters are inoculum density (Pillay and Nowak, 1997), initial dose, physiologic state of the introduced microorganisms and the target plants (Lugtenberg *et al.*, 2002), the technique of PGPR inoculation into the soil and the addition of fertilizers (Duquenne *et al.*, 1999).

CURRENT AND FUTURE CONSUMPTION OF FERTILIZERS

The mid-sixties to mid-seventies were known for achieving Green Revolution wherein the role of fertilizers was significant, contributing to 50-60% increase in food grain production. India also witnessed a significant increase in cropping intensity till the 1980's. But within 3-4 years, a decline with the growth rate of food-grain production with respect to productivity (i.e., per hectare crop yields) and fertilizer input (N, P & K) response or productivity was observed. This is an alarming situation based on the annual report (2005-2006) of the Department of Fertilizers, Ministry of Chemical and Fertilizers, Govt. of India. According to the report, the annual consumption of fertilizer nutrients (N, P & K) increased from 1.0 kg per hectare to 96.7 kg per hectare. Productivity enhancement should concurrently address the conservation and improvement of soil, water, biodiversity, atmosphere, renewable energy sources, etc. Keeping these in focus, the goal of Evergreen Revolution in productivity advancement in perpetuity without ecological harm has been developed (Kesavan and Swaminathan, 2006).

The high price of fertilizers in mid-2008 encouraged some farmers to use greater amounts of organic nutrient sources, which could have long-term impact on crop nutrition practices (Heffer and Prud'homme, 2009).

Table 17.1 World fertilizer consumption

Mt nutrients	2008	2009 (e)	2013 (f)
Nitrogen, N	99.3	101.0	110.4
Phosphorous, P_2O_5	35.9	37.2	43.9
Potassium, K_2O	24.8	25.0	31.0
Total	160.0	163.2	185.3

(e) Estimated; (f) forecast. *Source: P. Heffer, IFA, May 2009*

World fertilizer demand in 2008-2009 came down by 5.1% with the previous year from 168.1 to 159.6 million metric tonnes (Mt). However, nitrogen (N) has been much less affected as farmers cannot afford drastic cuts in N fertilizer application rates without immediate yield penalties, contrary to the situation with P and K fertilizers. N, P and K fertilizer demand was estimated as down 1.6, 7 and 14%, respectively. Global demand in 2013-2014 is expected to get increased as 2.3% annually on an average as compared to that in 2006-2007 and 2008-09. Global fertilizer demand in the year 2008 was estimated to be about 160 Mt nutrients and is hoped to reach 185.3 Mt in the year 2013 (Table 17.1); although, each type of fertilizer including chemical fertilizer has its advantages and disadvantages. (Table 17.2)

AGROCHEMICALS

Agrochemicals including the chemical fertilizers reduce the population of beneficial microorganisms at high concentration, due to inhibitory effect on bacterial growth (Smiley, 1981). The abnormal morphological changes in *Rhizobium meliloti* cells have been observed by Strzeleowa (1970) by growing *R. meliloti* on Throton's agar medium containing 2.5 mg ml^{-1} urea. Excessive nitrogenous fertilization increased the generation time and disrupted protein synthesis in *Acetobacter diazotrophicus* (renamed as

Table 17.2 Advantages and disadvantages of chemical fertilizers

Advantages • They are easily available everywhere and no special condition is required for storage. • Nutrients present in chemical fertilizers are soluble and easily available to the plant system, and in this way their effect is fast. • The price is affordable to both small and big farmers. • The nutrient level is high, although the required nutrient for plant is lower than that supplied through chemical fertilizers. • Unlike biofertilizers, there is no need of further modification in chemical fertilizer before applying it in the field. • They are not live products, hence, can be transported easily.
Disadvantages • Only a portion of the applied nutrients is taken up by plants. • Excessive and imbalanced use of chemical fertilizers adversely affects the soil, causing decrease in organic carbon, reduction in microbial flora of soil, increasing acidity, alkalinity and hardening of soil. • Over-application of N causes softening of plant tissues, which makes the plants more sensitive to diseases and pests. • Some chemical fertilizers/pesticides are not biodegradable. • Fertilizer components such as nitrogen and phosphorus eutrophication may cause death of aquatic animal life. • Production of chemical fertilizers adds to the pollution.

Gluconoacetobacter diazotrophicus) as visualized by Becking (1995). Muthukumarasamy *et al.* (2002) examined higher population of *G. diazotrophicus* from low fertilized soil in rhizosphere as compared to excessive N-fertilized soil. Such effects of different chemicals on microbes have been documented by a number of workers (Saraf and Sood, 2002; Joshi *et al.,* 2006). Similarly, the application of pesticides on oil seed crop resulted in the accumulation of their residues in seeds, oil and oilcake (Bhatnagar and Gupta, 1998). Gricher *et al.* (2001a) reported a reduction in height of sesame up to 66% and plant stand (biomass) 8-98%, after the application of different herbicides as compared to control. The seedling damage and reduction in the crop stand due to application of various chemicals including fungicides, weedicides and pesticides have been reported by Gricher *et al.* (2001b).

Biological methods have demonstrated a number of environment-friendly and economic advantages over chemical based control application. On the other hand, the exact biocontrol mechanisms are still unknown in many microorganisms (Vassilev *et al.*, 2006). Few workers have reported that many plant growth promoters used for inoculation in cropping systems promote plant growth directly or indirectly via production of phytohormones, enhancement of the nutrient uptake, or biocontrol of dreaded pathogens (Gupta *et al.,* 2006; Pandey *et al.,* 2005; Chandra *et al.,* 2008; Kumar *et al.,* 2009; Adesemoye *et al.,* 2009) Arora *et al.* (2009) have reported that biological formulations containing fast growing *Sinorhizobium meliloti* RMP5 and slow growing *Bradyrhizobium* BMP1 enhanced the process of symbiotic nitrogen fixation in soil supplemented with Mo and Fe.

SOIL NUTRIENTS

Fertilizers are the carrier of poisonous heavy metals like lead, cadmium, etc. Some of the synthetic fertilizers may contribute a significant quantity of heavy metals to the soil due to their use for a long time. Consequently, the amounts of heavy metals in soil ecosystem may build up to toxic levels for plants, animals and human health (Ram, 1994).

For maintenance and enhancement of soil fertility, appropriate sustainable technology is required in order to replenish the nutrients so as to maintain and build up the soil nutrient status. Long-term studies carried out at several locations on different cropping systems (Shrotriya *et al.*, 2005) indicated that the application of all the chemical fertilizers has deleterious effect on soil health, leading to unsustainable yield. On the other hand, biofertilizers in combination with chemical fertilizers (NPK) or alone have been reported to improve the growth and yield of *Brassica* crop (Vyas, 2003).

SOIL PATHOGENS

Soils can become suppressive to diseases caused by soil-borne phytopathogens under intensive cropping with retention of crop residues. Soil-borne pathogens have later increased in the first 2-4 years of converting to intensive cropping with retention of residues and then declined until the soil became disease suppressive after 10 years (Roget, 1995). Wiseman *et al.* (1996) determined that the soil suppressive to Rhizoctonia root rot, take-all disease and Fusarium crown rot was due to soil microorganisms. It is not clearly defined that which groups of organisms are dominant and responsible for creating suppressive soil; therefore, it is difficult to resolve the problem. Suppression may be due to more than one mechanism or involvement of certain microorganisms/biological group which are involved in the interaction between different biotic groups.

In order to manage or enhance the development of disease suppression, by reducing or avoiding the initial disease peak and reducing the time required to build up suppression, it is desirable to understand how farm practices (crop cultivars, crop rotations, nitrogen-nutrient inputs, direct drill-cultivation, herbicides) impact the ecology of the system. Central to this is an understanding of the organisms directly responsible for the suppression of disease and how farm management practices impact on the populations or functions of the relevant organisms (Barnett and Ryder1, 2003).

SOIL MANAGEMENT/IMPROVEMENT

The beneficial effect of combined application of urea, farmyard manure (FYM) with phosphobacteria and rhizobia on nutrient uptake and post-harvest soil nutrient availability has been reported by numerous workers (Ramamoorthy *et al.,* 1994). Thaunanthan *et al.* (2001) observed that the combined use of fly ash, FYM, and inorganic fertilizer (N, P & K) enhanced the growth and yield of crops. Deshmukh *et al.* (2002) obtained highest seed yield through the integrated use of organic and inorganic fertilizers.

The bacteria useful to plants are of two general types: symbiotic bacteria and free-living ones often found in soil and near the root, on or even within the plant tissues (Kloepper *et al.,* 1988). PGPRs have been introduced as microbial inoculants for biofertilization, phytostimulation, biopesticides and sometimes as bioremediation (Bloemberg and Lugtenberg, 2001; Khan *et al.,* 2009). Large-scale application of PGPR to crops as inoculants seems to be attractive as it would substantially reduce the use of chemical fertilizers and pesticides (Singhal *et al.,* 2003).

ADOPTION OF CULTURAL PRACTICES

Instead of spending money on commercial fertilizers, farmers can adopt cultural practices to improve the soil quality and get a better harvest. The green manure method and organic farming composting are important cultural practices of sustainable agriculture.

Green Manuring

Green manuring has been well practiced in India since 14th century B. C. In this method, legume plants are grown in field to accumulate nutrients and ploughed to release accumulated nutrients to be used by other economically important crops. Upon decomposition, these plants deliver nutrients and support the infiltration of water into the soil. The contribution of organic matter to the soil from a green manure crop is comparable to the addition of 9 to 13 tonnes per acre (0.4 ha) of farmyard manure. Microsymbionts of leguminous plants fix nitrogen from the air and release into the soil. This nitrogen enriches the soil and feeds all plants in the area. The portion of green manure-nitrogen available to crop plants is usually about 40 to 60% of the total amount of nitrogen contained in the legume. For example, a purple vetch crop that accumulated 90 kg of nitrogen per acre prior to ploughing will contribute approximately 45 kg of nitrogen per acre to the succeeding grain or vegetable crop. Lesser amounts are available for the second or third crop following a legume, but increased yields are apparent for two to three growing seasons. When they have built up maximum biomass, they work into the surface soil. They are usually cut before flowering; growing a green manure is thus different from growing a legume crop in the rotation. Once worked into the soil, the fresh plant material releases nutrients quickly and will be fully decomposed within a short period of time. Old or coarse material (e.g., straw, twigs) will decompose at a slower rate than fine material such as leaves and contributes to the build up of soil organic matter. Green manure is thus an inexpensive way to improve the soil fertility and nutrition of the main crops. Advantages and important aspects of green manure are given in Table 17.3.

Table 17.3 Advantages and important aspects of green manure

Advantages:

- The plants penetrate the soil with their roots, make it more friable, and bind nutrients, which would otherwise be washed away.
- They suppress weeds and protect the soil from erosion and direct sunlight.
- If legume plants are used, nitrogen is fixed from the air into the soil.
- Some green manures can be used as fodder plants or even to provide food for human consumption (e.g., beans and peas).
- When green manures decompose, they release all kinds of nutrients in correct mixture for the main crops to utilize, thus improving their yield.
- The incorporated plant material encourages the activity of soil organisms and builds up organic matter in the soil. This improves soil structure and water holding capacity.

Important aspects:

- Labour is required for tillage, sowing, cutting and incorporation of plants into the soil.
- If green manures are intercropped with the main crops, they compete for nutrients, water and light.
- When old or coarse plant material is incorporated into the soil, nitrogen may be temporarily unavailable for plant growth (see nitrogen immobilisation above).
- If food and space are in short supply, it may be more appropriate to grow a food crop rather than a green manure and recycle the crop residues, or to intercrop a green manure crop with the main crop.
- Benefits of green manure occur over the long term and are not always visible immediately.

Alternative to Green Manure: An alternative to green manure crop in the field is to collect fresh plant material from elsewhere and work it into the soil, i.e., trees and/or shrubs growing alongside crops in an agro-forestry system may provide a large quantity of green material, which can be used as green manure or for mulching.

Organic Farming

Organic farming system is not new in India and is being followed since ancient times. It is a method of farming system, which is primarily aimed at cultivating the land and raising crops in such a way as to keep the soil alive and in good health by the use of organic wastes (crop, animal and farm waste, aquatic waste) and other biological materials along with beneficial microbes (biofertilizers) to release nutrients for increased sustainable production in an eco-friendly and pollution-free environment.

The initial effort made by Sir Albert Howard (father of organic farming) has paid off, metamorphosing into a practice that sustains soil health and ecosystems by relying on biodiversity, ecological processes and the progress of innovative health sciences. Organic farming to be more profitable than conventional farming especially when it has many non-business benefits like improved soil health, safer food and a better environment. It does not realize that food security is not just about production and availability of food but also about access to relevant food in a hygienic food preparation and consumption environment for a healthy life (*The Tribune*, 15 Jan, 2009).

Recently, Ramesh *et al.* (2010) did a survey on certified organic farms in our country to ascertain the real benefits and feasibility of organic farming in terms of the production potential, economics and soil health in comparison to the conventional farms and found that organic farming, in spite of the reduction in crop productivity by 9.2%, provided higher net profit to farmers by 22.0% compared to conventional farming.

According to the global survey of organic farming, it is practiced in 120 countries covering a total of 31 MH and the trade of organic food has crossed 4.40 billion. The United States has emerged as the largest consumer of organic products in 2007 at $ 21.2 billion including $ 20 billion alone on organic food and drinks (*Financial Express*, 8 Dec, 2008).

India has produced around 3,96,997 MT of certified organic products, which includes all varieties of food products, namely, Basmati rice, pulses, honey, tea, spices, coffee, oilseeds, fruits, processed foods, cereals, herbal medicines and their value-added products. India exported 86 items in 2007-2008 with the total volume of 37533 million US $.

Organic farming is a holistic production system that avoids the use of synthetic fertilizers, pesticides and Genetically Modified Organisms (GMOs), minimizing air, soil and water pollution. This type of agriculture benefits from the recycling and use of natural products. Extensive use of dried foliage and kitchen compost not only reduces the investment overheads, but also ensures the growth of crops that are devoid of synthetic interference. The technique is characterized by the use of green manure, biological pest control methods and special cultivation techniques to maintain soil productivity. Limiting the use of synthetic fertilizers or completely doing away with them reduces the risk of exposure to ailments that arise on account of synthetic pesticides, ingrained plant growth regulators and the presence of genetically modified organisms in organic food products. Today, organic farming caters to a major and preferred industry worldwide. Organically grown food products have a huge market catered to, by farmlands covering approximately 10% of the total world-farmland cover. Organic agriculture is definitely more sustainable in the long-term, improving soil fertility and terrain drought-resistance greatly. These farming practices completely waive off external costs incurred due to investment in chemical pesticides and nutrient runoff, and a number of health issues that result from agro-chemical residues. Following are the advantages of organic farming:

(i) It reduces water usage, nutrient-contamination by pesticides, soil erosion and carbon emissions and increases the biodiversity.

(ii) It produces the same crop variants as those produced via conventional farming methods, but incurs 50% lower expenditure on fertilizer and energy, and retains 40% more topsoil.

(iii) This type of farming effectively addresses soil management. Even damaged soil, subject to erosion and salinity, is able to feed on micronutrients via crop rotation, inter-cropping techniques and the extensive use of green manure.

(iv) It enables farmers to get rid of irksome weeds without the use of any mechanical and chemical applications. Practices such as hand-weeding and soil enhancement with mulch, corn gluten meal, garlic and clove oil, table salt and borax not only get rid of weeds and insects, but also guarantee crop quality.

(v) The use of green pesticides such as neem, compost tea and spinosad is eco-friendly and non-toxic. These pesticides help in identifying and removing diseased and dying plants in time and subsequently increasing the crop defence systems.

PLANT GROWTH PROMOTING RHIZOBACTERIA (PGPR)

Research on PGPRs has been progressing at an ever increasing rate since the introduction of the term used by Kloepper and coworkers in the late 1970 (Kloepper and Schroth, 1978). Suslow (1982) further coined the term "rhizobacteria" for those bacteria in the rhizosphere that aggressively colonized the root system. The premier examples of such bacterial genera include *Actinoplanes, Agrobacterium, Alcaligenes, Amorphosporangium, Arthrobacter, Azotobacter, Bacillus, Burkholderia, Cellulomonas, Enterobacter, Erwinia, Flavobacterium, Gluconacetobacter, Micromonospora, Pseudomonas, Rhizobia, Serratia, Streptomyces, Xanthomonas,* etc. as stated by a number of workers (Glick *et al.*, 1995, 1997; Lucy *et al.*, 2004). Recently, a novel PGPR, *Delftia tsuruhatensis* HR4 has been reported both as a diazotroph as well as a biocontrol agent against various plant pathogens (Han *et al.*, 2005).

Symbiotic bacteria (rhizobia) are capable of eliciting and invading root and stem tissue forming nodules on leguminous plants where they undertake symbiotic nitrogen fixation. Although symbiotic bacteria are associated with leguminous crops, recently their growth promotion in certain non-legumes has also been reported (Antoun *et al.*, 1998). Both, dicot as well as monocot plants show growth enhancement by the application of rhizobacteria (Peng *et al.*, 2002). Such enhancement mainly involved rhizobacterial-mediated growth promoting characteristics (Mc Inroy and Kloepper, 1995).

NITROGEN-FIXING RHIZOBACTERIA

Biofertilization accounts for approximately 6.5 % of the nitrogen supply to crops worldwide (Bloemberg and Lugtenberg, 2001). Biological nitrogen fixation is esteemed to contribute 180×10^6 metric tonnes/year globally (Postgate, 1998), of which 80% comes from symbiotic associations and the rest from free-living or associative systems (Graham, 1988). Symbiotic nitrogen fixers include rhizobia and *Frankia*. The most efficient nitrogen fixing bacterial strains belong to the genera *Rhizobium, Azorhizobium, Mesorhizobium, Allorhizobium, Bradyrhizobium, Methylobacterium* and *Sinorhizobium*.

Free-living nitrogen-fixing rhizobacteria is known to be of great agronomic significance. The non-symbiotic nitrogen fixers include *Acetobacter, Azospirillum, Azotobacter, Azoarcus* and *Herbaspirillum*. The limitation of non-symbiotic nitrogen fixation is the availability of energy and carbon source for extensive nitrogen fixation process. This limitation can be compensated by moving closer to or inside the plants viz., diazotrophs present in rhizosphere, rhizoplane or those growing endophytically

(Tilak *et al.,* 2005). The most familiar genera of the family Fabacease, i.e., rhizobia, play a role as an important bioinoculant. They also help in remediation of contaminated soil as they grow slowly for long period in soil, but infect compatible legumes hosts. They can grow rapidly, and successful infection by a single bacterium can lead to the formation of nitrogen-fixing nodule on the roots. Moreover, once the symbiosis is established, nodules may accumulate the metal. This would be an alternative and less expensive method to remove metals from the soil (Khan *et al.,* 2009).

PHOSPHATE SOLUBILIZERS

Phosphate (P) deficiency is common in almost all the soils and crops in different countries of the world. For sustaining high growth in agriculture, the current thrust is on the use of new or alternative phosphorus sources including improved fertilization techniques and phosphorus solubilizing microbes (Raju *et al.,* 2005). The phosphatic biofertilizers improve the situation and definitely supplement plant P requirements (Kang *et al.,* 2004; Kumar *et al.,* 2005; Pandey and Maheshwari, 2007). Most agricultural soils contain large reserves of phosphorus, a considerable part of which has accumulated as a consequence of regular applications of P-fertilizers, but a large portion of soluble inorganic phosphate applied to the soil as chemical fertilizer is rapidly immobilized after application and becomes unavailable to plants. Large amounts of phosphoric fertilizers added to soil enhance agro productivity on a regular basis, but most of this remains immobilized in large quantity and hence is not available to plants (Sridevi and Mallaiah, 2009). The maintenance of available phosphorus remains a major challenge. The biogeochemical cycle of phosphorus is influenced by various microorganisms, which affect phosphorus metabolization in soil. The precipitated inorganic phosphate is solubilized by the action of minerals and organic acids produced by soil bacteria (Seshadri *et al.,* 2000). Organic compounds containing phosphorus are decomposed and mineralized by bacteria (Aaronson and Patni, 1996) and other groups of microorganisms. Fluorescent pseudomonads, rhizobia and few other bacteria have shown phosphate solubilizing activity (Gupta *et al.,* 1999, 2001, 2002; Arora *et al.,* 2001; Deshwal *et al.,* 2003; Kumar *et al.,* 2005a, b), which has helped in the enhancement of growth and productivity of crops such as sunflower (Reddy *et al.,* 2005), peanut (Parasuram and Mani, 2003; Dey *et al.,* 2004) and mustard crops (Penrose and Glick, 2003; Joshi *et al.,* 2006).

Bacteria bear the ability to solubilize inorganic or organic P from soil after their inoculation in soil or plant seeds (Gerretsen, 1948; Kloepper *et al.,* 1988; Gaur and Ostwal, 1972; Datta *et al.,* 1982; Kumar *et al.,* 2005) resulting in enhanced plant growth. Inoculation with two strains of *R. leguminosarum* selected for their P-solubilization ability showed an improvement in root colonization, plant growth promotion and increased P concentration in lettuce and maize (Chabot *et al.,* 1996). Lifshitz *et al.* (1987) reported that *P. putida* stimulated the growth of root and shoot and increased ^{32}P-labeled phosphate uptake in canola. Inoculation of rice seeds with *A. lipoferum* strain 34H increased P ion content and resulted in significant improvement of root length, fresh and dry shoot weight (Murthy and Ladha, 1988). Simultaneously, an increase in P uptake and crop yields has also been observed after inoculation with *B. firmus* (Datta *et al.,* 1982), *B. polymyxa* (Gaur and Ostwal, 1972) and *B. cereus* (Fernandez *et al.,* 1984). Application of phosphorus and phosphate-solubilizing bacteria (PSB) has been reported promising in seed yield, oil content and oil yield in sunflower as compared to uninoculated control (Patel and Thakur, 2003).

POTASSIUM SOLUBILIZERS

Potassium (K) is the third important nutrient after nitrogen (N) and phosphorus (P) for plant growth and development and plays an essential role in enzyme activation, protein synthesis and photosynthesis. Bertsch and Thomas (1985) demonstrated that in most of the soil K exists in the form of silicate minerals. K can be available to plant when the minerals are slowly solubilized or weathered. Lin Qi-mie *et al.* (2002) reported that a few bacteria may produce acids, alkalies or chelators to enhance the release of elements from potassium containing minerals. Silicate dissolving bacteria increased 70% in rhizosphere soil, and 20% in non-rhizosphere soil, respectively. Recently, Sugumaran and Janarthanam (2007) reported that the number of potassium solubilizing bacteria such as *Bacillus mucilaginous* MCRCp1 increased by more than 500 times. Due to phosphorus and potassium, the nutritional status of the soil is markedly improved through inoculation of this bacterium. Plant dry matter and oil content of groundnut increased by 125% and 35.41%, respectively through the inoculation of MCRCp1. Grovdev (1987) reported that the production of exopolysaccharides by bacteria seems to be the main mechanism of releasing K from silicates.

Potassium released from mica to water-soluble and poor exchangeable pools of K due to inoculation of mica with potassium solubilizing strain *B. mucilaginosus* increased biomass, yield uptake and K recoveries in sudan grass (*Sorghum vulgare*) (Basak and Biswas, 2009). Vandevivere *et al.* (1994) proposed that *B. mucilaginosus* increases the dissolution rate of silicate and alumino-silicate minerals and releases the K^+ and SiO_2 from the crystal lattice primarily by generating organic acids. However, this hypothesis is controversial because *B. mucilaginosus* is also thought to accelerate the dissolution of a variety of silicates by the production of extracellular polysaccharides (EPS). The dispute about the mechanism by which *B. mucilaginosus* decomposes silicate minerals and releases K^+ and SiO_2 may have severely limited the use of the organism in agriculture as a form of biological K fertilizer (Girgis *et al.*, 2008). Liu *et al.* (2006) proved that EPS strongly adsorbed the organic acids and attached to the surface of the mineral, resulting in accumulation of high concentration of organic acids near the mineral, which indicates that EPS adsorbed SiO_2 affected the equilibrium between the mineral and fluid phases leading to the reaction toward SiO_2 and K^+ solubilization.

INTEGRATED NUTRIENT MANAGEMENT

Nutrient management is the key issue in sustainable soil fertility. Various sources of nitrogen, phosphorus, and potassium and gypsum fertilization have been recommended for a high economic return of the investment through optimized yield and quality. The basic concept underlying integrated plant nutrition system is the maintenance and possible increase of soil fertility for sustaining enhanced crop productivity through optimal use of all nutrients, particularly inorganic fertilizers (Duhoon *et al.*, 2001). Integrated use of N, P and K together gave better seed yield in sunflower as compared to their individual application (Rao and Soren, 1991). The balanced dose of fertilizer alone increased about 50% of rice production (Muntasir *et al.*, 2001). Fertilization pattern of N, P, K and S has been developed for sunflower and a higher yield with application of N_{80} $P_{17.5}$ $K_{33.5}$ (Mandal *et al.*, 2003) is observed.

Integrated use of organic and inorganic fertilizers in a balanced proportion for sustainable crop production has been emphasized (USDA report, 1980). Alagawadi and Gaur (1992) reported inoculation of rhizobia with reduced doses of nitrogen for reduction in the nitrogen-fertilization. Valladares *et al.* (2002) reported low fertilizer and rhizobial inoculants for achieving high quality seedlings. The integrated use of organic, inorganic and biofertilizers not only sustained productivity by improving soil physical conditions, but also reduced the need of costly inorganic fertilizers (Duhoon *et al.*, 2001).

Integrated nutrient supply seems to be essential not only for increasing the crop productivity but also for the maintenance and possibly improvement of soil fertility for sustainable crop productivity (Shrotriya, 2005). Results from various cropping systems showed positive interaction of the integrated use of mineral fertilizers, organic manures, and biofertilizers for maintaining the growth throughout the crop duration (Wu *et al.,* 2005). The addition of biofertilizers not only helps in the proliferation of beneficial microbes in soil, but also provides residual effect on subsequent crops (Deshwal *et al.,* 2006), helps in decomposition of organic matter (Patersion, 2003), and availability of nutrients to plants (Cakmakci *et al.,* 2006). Microbial inoculants as a source of biofertilizers have become a hope for most countries as far as economical and environmental viewpoints are concerned (Singhal *et al.,* 2003; Kloepper, 2003; Kumar *et al.,* 2006).

BIOFERTILIZERS AND CROP IMPROVEMENT

The commercial history of biofertilizers began in 1895 with the launch of 'Nitragin' by Nobbe and Hiltner, a laboratory culture of Rhizobia, followed by the discovery of *Azotobacter* and then the blue green algae and a host of other microorganisms. *Azospirillium* and Vesicular-Arbuscular Mycorrhizae (VAM) are fairly recent discoveries. In India, the first study on legume- *Rhizobium* symbiosis was conducted by N.V. Joshi and the first commercial production started as early as 1956. However, the Ministry of Agriculture initiated the real effort to popularize and promote the input with the setting up of the National Project on Development and Use of Biofertilizers (NPDB) (*www.ieg.nic.in*).

Kapur and Naik (2004) studied the effect of mixed culture liquid formulation of biofertilizers along with pure culture of *Azotobacter* and phosphate solubilizing bacteria. A significant improvement has been observed in the N, P and chlorophyll content of leaves of chickpea and available P in soil. Elkoca *et al.* (2008) have reported the influence of nitrogen fixing and phosphorus solubilizing bacteria on the nodulation, plant growth, and yield of chickpea. The effect of integrated nutrient management with biofertilizers has been examined in peanut and horse gram (Parasuraman and Mani, 2003). Dey *et al.* (2004) reported that isolates of fluorescent *Pseudomonads* increased the growth and yield of peanut (*Arachis hypogaea*) upto 18-28%. Shehata and El-khawas (2003) examined the effect of two biofertilizers on sunflower (*Helianthus annus* cv. Vedock) and showed the increased seed yield, nutrient content of seeds, nitrogen and all nitrogenous compound, mineral and seeds oil contents and decreased saturated fatty acids such as palmitic and stearic, while increase in main unsaturated fatty acid (oleic, linoleic and linolinic) and induced synthesis of two new protein of low molecular weight (2.1 kDa for biogien and 14.9 kDa for microbien) were reported.

Application of biofertilizers (*Azospirillum* and *Phosphobacterium*) along with inorganic fertilizers nutrient sources (NPK) resulted in higher growth, stalk and seed yield in sunflower as compared to sole application of nutrient sources (Reddy *et al.,* 2005). Integrated use of *Rhizobium* and phosphorous solubilizing microorganisms (PSM) along with recommended dose of inorganic fertilizer showed the maximum dry matter, seed oil content and seed yield of soybean (Lanje *et al.,* 2005). Microbial inoculants not only increased the nutritional assimilation but also improved soil properties, such as organic matter content and total N in soil (Wu *et al.,* (2005). Experimental findings revealed the functional and structural soil microbial property influenced by organic and inorganic fertilization (N, P & K) in long term field experiments. Tufenkci *et al.* (2006) found that the application of phosphorus and nitrogen with and without *Rhizobium* inoculation gave better and significant results over the control.

Penrose and Glick (2003) obtained bacterial strains that could utilize 1-aminocyclopropane-1-carboxylate (ACC) as sole source of nitrogen from the soil. Ahmed *et al.* (2004) reported that seed inoculation of wheat with PGPR contained ACC deaminase (EC: 4.1.99.4) activity in combination with NPK (inorganic fertilizer) significantly increase the weight and elongation of root, number of tillers, straw and grain yield with the uptake of NFP and K over the control. All these PGPR strains induced root elongation in canola seedling under the gnotobiotic conditions. Pandey *et al.* (2005) isolated *Burkhulderia* MSSP strain having ACC deaminase activity. In addition, Glick *et al.* (2007) reported the plant growth promotion by bacterial ACC deaminase.

Several studies have shown that growth promotion effects are seen early in plant development and subsequently translate into higher yield (Glick *et al.,* 1997; Polyanaskaya *et al.,* 2000). Commercial preparations using free-living PGPRs are also available to administer various crops and bacterial inoculants for biocontrol of various diseases of economic agricultural crops (Tables 17.4 and 17.5). Two major breakthroughs in plant inoculation technology occurred in the late 1970s by involvement of the use of biocontrol agents, mainly *P. fluorescens* and *P. putida* groups (Kloepper and Scroth, 1981; Glick *et al.,* 1995). In recent years, various other bacterial genera such as *Bacillus, Flavobacterium, Acetobacter, Azospirillum* and some fungi such as *Trichoderma, Gliocladium,* etc. have also been evaluated as commercial bioinoculants (Kloepper, 1993; Maheshwari *et al.,* 2001; Bhatia *et al.,* 2005; Kumar *et al.,* 2005). The desirable results of plant inoculation can be obtained by the use of both soils as well as seed application procedures (Arora *et al.,* 2001; Bhatia *et al.,* 2003; Kumar *et al.,* 2005). In India there are a lot of companies involved in the production of biofertilizers (Table 17.6).

Table 17.4 Commercially available inoculants using free-living plant growth promoting rhizobacteria (Glick *et al.,* 1999; Chet and Chertnin, 2002)

Bacterial strains	*Product*	*Intended crop*
Agrobacterium radiobacter	Diegall Galltrol-A Nogall Norbac 84 C	Fruit, nut, ornamental nursery stock and trees
Azospirillum brasilense	Azo-Green	Turf and forage crops
Azospirillum brasilense Cd	Zea-Nit	Maize
Azospirillum lipoferum Br-17 *Azospirillum lipoferum* CRT1	AZOGREEN-m	Maize
Bacillus amyloliquefaciens GB99 *Bacillus subtilis* CG 122	Quantum 4000 Bio Yield^{TM}	Broccoli, cabbage, canthaloupe, cauliflower, celery, cucumber, lettuce, ornamentals
Bacillus subtilis	Epic, HiStick N/T, Kodiak, Rhizo-Plus, Serenade, Subtilix, System 3	Barley, beans, cotton, legumes peanut, pea, rice, and soybean
Burkholderia cepacia	Blue Circle, deny, Intercept	Alfalfa, barley, beans, peas, sorghum, cotton, maize, vegetables and wheat
Pseudomonas fluorescens	Blight Ban A506, Conquer, Victus	Almond, apple, cherry, mushroom, peach, pear, potato, strawberry and tomato
Pseudomonas syringae	Bio-save10	Citrus and poam fruit
Streptomyces griseovirdis K61	Mycostop	Field, ornamental and vegetable crops

Table 17.5 Commercially available bacterial inoculants for the protection of economic agricultural crops

Antagonist	*Product*	*Target pathogen*	*Intended crop*	*Country of origin*
A. radiobacter K 84	Diegal Galltrol *Agrobacterium*	*A. tumefaciens* Galltrol,	Crown gall of several crops *Agrobacterium radiobacter*	Fruit Growers Cchemical Co. NZ. Ag biocheimal Inc. CA, USA. Trees, shrubs Ag Biochem, Inc. Norbac 84-C *tumefaciens*
Urinda CA (USA)				
Agrobacterium radiobacter	Bakuterohzu	Crown gall disease	Rose	Japan
B. cepacia	Deny	*Pythium* sp.	Damping-off of several crops	CCT Crop Carlsbad, USA
B. subtilis GB07	Epic	*R. solani, P. ultimum*	Damping-off of	Gustafson Inc. TX, USA
B. subtilis GB07	Kodiak		legumes and cotton	
Bacillus subtilis	Epic	*Rhizoctonia solani, Fusarium* sp.	Cotton, legumes	Gustafson Inc, Dallas (USA)
Bacillus subtilis	Kodiak	*Pythium ultimum, Rhizoctonia solani*	Cotton, legumes	Gustafson, Inc. Dallas TX (USA)
Bacillus subtilis	Biotok	*Coriticum invisium, C. theae*	Tea	Tockalia Exoerimental Station, Tea Research Association, Jorhat (Assam)
P. fluorescens	Bioshiel		Cereals, pulses and vegetables	Anu Biotech International Ltd. Faridabad (Hariyana)
P. fluorescens	Pant Biocontrol Agent - 3	Causative pathogens of soil borne diseases	Pulses and vegetables CROPS	G.B.Pant University, PantNagar (Uttaranchal)
P. fluorescens WCS 374r	Biocoat	*F. oxysporum* f. sp. *Raphani* *F. oxysporum* f. sp. *dianthi*	Fusarium wilt Carnation wilt	S & G Seeds, BV, Netherlands
Pseudomonas cepacia	Blue circle	*Rhizoctonia solani,Pythium sp.*	Vegetable crops	Stine Microbials, Madison WI (USA)
Pseudomonas fluorescens	Dagger G	*Rhizoctonia solani, Pythium ultimum*	Cotton	Ecogen Inc, Langhorne PA (USA)
Pseudomonas fluorescens	Bio Coat	*Fusarium* sp.	Radish	Australia
Pseudomonas fluorescens bv 5	Victus	*Phytopthora tolaasii*	Mushrooms	Sylvan, Kattanning, PA (USA), Millar, FC; Sylvan, PC)
S. griseoviridis	Mycostop	*F. oxysporum* f. sp.*dianthi* A. brassicicola	Damping-off of crucifers	Kemira Agro oy, Finland
Streptomyces griseovirides	Myostop	*Alternaria* sp., *Fusarium* sp.	Vegetable, ornamentals	Kermira Biotech, Helsinki, (Finland)

Table 17.6 List of biofertilizer production units in different states of India

States	*Production Units*
Andhra Pradesh	Sri Aurbindo Institute of Rural Development (SAIRD), Nalgonda Bacterial Culture Production Lab., Hyderabad Biofertiliser Unit-Vijayawada, Madras Fertilizers Limited, Chennai Acharya N.G. Ranga Agriculture University, Agriculture Research Station, Amaravathi Godavari Fertilizers and Chemicals Limited, Kakinada
Assam	Hindustan Fertilizer Corporation Ltd. (FP & ARD), Parbatpur North East Green Tech Pvt. Ltd., Guwahati Microbiology Laboratory, Assam Agro Industries Development Corporation Limited, Guwahati Assam Agricultural University, Jorhat
Bihar	Hindustan Fertilizer Corporation Limited, Begusarai M/s Pyrites, Phosphates & Chemicals Limited, Rohtas
Gujarat	National Agricultural Research Project Biofertilizer Project Gujarat Agriculture University, Anand Gujarat State Fertilizers and Chemicals Limited, Vadodara Gujarat State Co-operative Marketing Federation Ltd., Ahmedabad
Haryana	Regional Biofertilizer Development Centre, Hissar Ganpati Bio Organic Limited, Safidon
Himachal Pradesh	Central Laboratory, Shimla
Jharkhand	Hindustan Fertilizer Corporation Ltd., Sindri
Karnataka	West Coast Herbochem Ltd., Bangalore Regional Biofertiliser Development Centre, Bangalore Biofertilizer Unit- Bangalore, Madras Fertilizer Limited, Chennai Karnataka Biofertilisers, Bijapur Kadur Agro, Bangalore Samrath Bio-Tech Ltd., Hubli Shakthi Bio-Tech (P) Ltd., Vijaywada Karnataka Agro Industries Corporation Limited, Bangalore University of Agricultural Sciences, Bangalore Karnataka Compost Development Corporation Limited, Bangalore Rhizobium Culture Production Laboratory, Bangalore University of Agricultural Sciences, Dharwad
Kerala	Biofertilizer Production Unit, Ramanathapuram, Ramanathapuram The Fertilisers and Chemicals Travancore Ltd., Kochi Soil Testing Laboratory, Pattambi, Palakkad Agro Bio-Tech Research Centre Ltd., Kottayam
Madhya Pradesh	Regional Biofertiliser Development Centre, Jabalpur Samridhi Bioculture Pvt. Ltd., Indore Bio-Tech Research Centre, M.P. State Co-operative Oil-seed Growers' Federation Ltd., Dhar Hindustan Fertilizer Corporation Ltd., Bhopal Trupti Bio-Tech Laboratory, Balaghat The M.P. State Agro Industries Development Corporation, Biofertiiser Plant, Bhopal Narmada Bio-Tech Limited, Barwaha Nafed Biofertilizer, Indore National Fertilizers Limited, Indore
Maharashtra	Regional Biofertiliser Development Centre, Nagpur Sainath Agro Vet Industries Pvt. Ltd., Ahmed Nagar BAIF Development Research Foundation, Pune Samruddhi Agrotech, Pune Maharashtra Research & Development Centre, Solapur Kumar Krishi Mitra Bio Products (I) Pvt. Ltd., Pune Vasantdada Sugar Institute, Pune Biofertiliser Production Unit Sahakar Maharshi Shankarrao Mohite-Patil Sahakari Sakhar Karkhana Ltd., Solapur Institute of Natural Organic Agriculture (INORA), Pune K-Ferts Lab, Nanded Nirmal Seeds Pvt. Ltd., Jalgaon Rashtriya

Contd.

Contd.

	Chemicals & Fertilizers Limited, Mumbai Nomain Agri-Bio Pvt Ltd., Pune Nilayam Bio-Fertiliser Production Unit, Wardha Kisan Agro Chem, Naded Nav Maharshta Chakan Oil Mill Ltd., Sangli Environmental Protection Research Foundation, Sangli Arun Biofertilizers, Kolhapur Mahatama Phule Krishi Vidyapeeth, Pune Mauli Biotech, Pune Bio Agro Fertilisers, Pune M/s Niku Bio-Research Lab, Pune
Manipur	Regional Biofertiliser Development Centre,Imphal
Mizoram	Biofertilizer Production Unit, Neihbawi, Department of Agriculture, Aizawl
New Delhi	Indian Agriculture Research Institutre (IARI), New Delhi Indian Farmers Fertiliser Cooperative Limited, New Delhi
Orissa	Regional Biofertiliser Development Centre, Bhubneshwar Orissa Agro Industries Corporation Ltd., Bhubneshwar Deputy Director of Agriculture (PP), Bhubneshwar Hindustan Fertiliser Corporations Limited, Bhubneshwar State Bio Chemist, Bhubneshwar
Pondicherry	Pondicherry Agro Service and Industries Corporation Limited (PASIC), Pondicherry
Punjab	Biofertiliser Production Unit, Ludhiana
Rajasthan	Nafed Biofertilizer, Bharatpur Rhizobia Scheme Agriculture Department, Jaipur
Tamilnadu	Department of Agricultural Microbiology, Agriculture College and Research Institute, Tamil Nadu Agricultural University, Madurai Biofertilizer Production Unit, Department of Agriculture, Govt. of Tamil Nadu, Cuddalore Biofertilizer Production Unit, Department of Agriculture, Govt. of Tamil Nadu, Thantavur Biofertilizer Production Unit, Department of Agriculture, Govt. of Tamil Nadu, Trichy KRIBHCO, Chennai Regional Research Station, Tamil Nadu Agricultural University, Piyur Monarch Bio-Fertilisers and Research Centre, Chennai Lakshmi Bio-Tech, Cuddalore Marygreen Afrotech (P) Ltd., Chennai Tamil Nadu Agricultural University, Coimbatore T Stanes & Company Limited, Coimbatore Esvin Advanced Technologies Limited, Chennai Southern Petrochemical Industries Corporation Limited, Chennai Biofertiliser Unit-Manali, Madras Fertilizers Limited, Chennai Biofertilizer Production Unit, Salem Biofertilizer Production Unit, Kudumiamalai Main Biocontrol Research Laboratory, Chengalpattu The SIMA Cotton Development and Research Association, Coimbatore
Uttar Pradesh	National Biofertiliser Development Centre, Ghaziabad Myodelphia Chemicals Company (Pvt.) Ltd., Ghaziabad M/s Kanhaiya Agrotech (Pvt.) Ltd., Mathura Motilal Nehru Farmers Training Institute, Allahabad Krishak Bharati Cooperative Limited, Noida
West Bengal	Amit Biotech, Kolkata West Bengal Forest Development Corporation Ltd., Kolkata Eastern Enterprises, Kolkata Micro Bac India, North 24-Parganas Excel Bio-Tech Pvt. Ltd., Kolkatta Nimpit Ashram, South 24-Parganas Green Tech Farms & Agro Pvt. Ltd, Kolkata Nodule Research Laboratory, Nadia Hindustan Fertilizer Cooperation Ltd., Kolkata Process Development and Analytical Control Research Laboratory, Kolkata Nitrofix Laboratories, Kolkata

Source: *National Biofertiliser Development Centre, Govt. of India, Ministry of Agriculture* (http://dacnet.nic.in/ncof/productionunit.htm)

The principal goal of agriculture is the production of quality, safe, and affordable food for ever-increasing worldwide population. Agricultural growers and producers have the additional constraints of economic profitability and sustainability with the increasing problems associated with the use of synthetic chemicals in agriculture. There has been an ever-increasing interest in the use of native and non-native beneficial microorganisms to improve plant health and productivity while ensuring safety for human consumption and protection of the environment. Scanty information is available regarding the nature of biochemical changes that occur due to application of Integrated Nutrient Management (INM), growth hormones and biofertilizers. A reduction in dose of chemical fertilizers in combination with PGPR has been reported by several workers in different crops.

REFERENCES

Aaronson, S., and Patni, N.J. (1996) *Limnol. Oceaeanogr.* **21**: 838-645.

Adesemoye, A.O., Torbert, H.A., and Kloepper, J.W. (2009) *Plant Microbe Interact.* DOI 10.1007/s00248-009-9531-y.

Ahmed, W., Shahroona and Zahir, Z.A., Arshad, M. (2004) *Pak. J. Agri. Sci.* **41(3-4)**:119-124.

Alagawadi, A.R., and Gaur, A.C. (1992) *Trop. Agric.* **69**: 347-350.

Antoun, H., Beauchamp, C.J., Gaussard, N., Chabot, R., and Lalande, R. (1998) *Plant and Soil* **204**: 57-67.

Arora, N.K., Kang, S.C., and Maheshwari, D.K. (2001) *Curr. Sci.* **81**: 673-677.

Arora, N.K., Khare, E., Oh, J.H., Kang, S.C. and Maheshwari, D.K. (2008) *World J. Microbiol. Biotechnol.* **24**:581–585.

Arora, N.K., Khare, E., Singh, S., Maheshwari, D.K. (2009) *World J. Microbiol. Biotechnol.* DOI 10.1007/s11274-009-0237-6.

Ashelford, K.E., Norris, S.J., Fry, J.C., Bailey, M.J. and Day, M.J. (2000) *Appl. Environ. Microbiol.* **66**: 4193-4199.

Barnett, S.J. and Ryder1, M.H. (2003) *In*: 6th International PGPR Workshop, 5-10 October 2003, Calicut, India.

Basak, B.B. and Biswas, D.R. (2009) *Plant Soil* **317**: 235-255.

Bashan, Y., Puente, M.E., Rodriguezmendoza, M.N., Toledo, G., Holguin, G., Ferreracerrato, R., Pedrin, S. (1995) *Appl. Environ. Microbiol.* **61**: 1938-1945.

Becking, J.H., (1995) *In*: *Azospirillum* III Genetics Physiology Ecology. (Ed. Klingmuller, W.), Springer-Verlag, Berlin, Heidelberg, pp. 243-262.

Bertsch, P.M. and Thomas, G.W. (1985) *In*: Potassium in agriculture. (Ed. Munson, R.D.). ASA, CSSA and SSSA, Madison, WI, pp. 131-162.

Bhatia, S., Bhaita, S., Dubey, R.C. and Maheshwari, D.K. (2003) *Ind. J. Expt. Biol.* **41**: 1442-1446.

Bhatia, S., Dubey, R.C. and Maheshwari, D.K. (2005) *Ind. Phytopathol.* **58**: 17-24.

Bhatnagar, A. and Gupta, A. (1998) *Bull. Envirn. Contam. Toxicol.* **60**: 569-600.

Birkhofer, K., Bezemer, T.M., Bloem, J., Bonkowski, M., Christensen, S., Dubois, D., Ekelund, F., Fließbach, A., Gunst, L., Hedlund, K., Mader, P., Mikola, J., Robin, C., Setala, H., Tatin-Froux, F, Van der Putten, W.H. and Scheu, S. (2008) *Soil Biol. Biochem.* **40**: 2297-2308.

Bloemberg, G.V. and Lugtenberg, B.J.J. (2001) *Curr. Opin. Plant Biol.* **4(4)**: 343-350.

Brimecombe, M.J., De Leij, F.A. and Lynch, J.M. (1999) *Microb. Ecol.* **38**: 387-397.

Cakmakci, R., Donmez, F., Adyin, A. and Sahin, F. (2006) *Soil Biol. Biochem.* **38**: 1482-1487.

Chabot, R., Antoun, H. and Cescas, M.P. (1996) *Plant Soil* **184**: 311-321.

Chandra, S., Choure, K., Dubey. R.C., and Maheshwari, D.K., *Braz. J. Microbiol.* **38**: 124-130, 2007.

Datta, M., Banish, S. and Gupta, R.K. (1982) *Plant Soil* **69**: 365-373.

Deshmukh, M.R., Jain, H.C., Duhoon, S.S. and Goswami, U. (2002) *J. Oilseeds Res.* **19**: 73-75.

Deshwal, V.K., Dubey, R.C. and Maheshwari, D.K. (2003) *Curr. Sci.* **84**: 443-448.

Deshwal, V.K., Kumar, T., Dubey, R.C. and Maheshwari, D.K. (2006) *Curr. Sci.* **91(4)**: 423-424.

Dey, R., Pal, K.K., Bhatt, D.M. and Chauhan, S.M. (2004) *Microbiol. Res.* **159 (4)**: 371-394.

Duhoon, S.S., Jain, H.C., Deshmukh, M.R. and Goswami, U. (2001) *J. Oilseeds Res.* **18(2)**: 178-180.

Duquenne, P., Chenu, C. Richard, G. and Catroux, G. (1999) *FEMS Microbiol. Ecol.* **29**: 331-339.

Edge, T.A. and Wyndham, R.C. (2002) *Can. J. Microbiol.* **48**: 717-727.

Elkoca, E., Kantar, F. and Sahin, F. (2008) *J. Plant Nutr.* **31**:157–171.

Etesami, H., Alikhani, H.A. and Akbari, A.A. (2009a) *World App. Sci. J.* **6(12)**: 1629-1633.

Etesami, H., Alikhani, H.A., Jadidi, M. and Aliakbari, A. (2009b) *World App. Sci. J.* **6(11)**: 1576-1584.

Fernandez, A.O., Carpena, A.O. and Cadakia, L.C. (1984) *Anal. Edaf. Agrobiol.* **43**: 235-245.

Fravel, D.R. (2005) *Annu. Rev. Phytopathol.* **43**: 337-359.

Gaur, A.C. and Ostwal, K.P. (1972) *Ind. J. Exp. Biol.* **10**: 393-394.

Gerretsen, F.C. (1948) *Plant Soil.* **1**: 51-81.

Girgis, M. G. Z., Heba, M.A., Khalil, and Sharaf, M.S. (2008) *Aust. J. Basic and App. Sci.* **2(1)**: 68-81.

Glick, B.R. (1995) *Can. J. Microbiol.* **47**: 109–117.

Glick, B.R., Karaturo, D.M. and Newell, P.C. (1995) *Can. J. Microbiol.* **41**: 553-536.

Glick, B.R., Liu, C., Ghosh, S., and Dumbroff, E.B. (1997) *Soil Biol. Biochem.* **29**: 1233-1239.

Glick, B.R., Todorovic, B., Czarny, J., Cheng, Z., Duan, J. and McConkey, B. (2007) *Crit. Rev. Plant Sci.* **26**:227-242.

Graham, P.H. (1988) Principles and application of Soil Microbiology, pp. 322-345.

Gricher, W.J., Sestak, D.C., Brewer, K.D., Besler, B.A., Stichler, R.C. and Smith, D.T. (2001a) *Crop Protect* **20(5):** 389-394.

Gricher, W.J., Sestak, D.C., Brewer, K.D., Besler, B.A., Stichler, R.C. and Smith, D.T. (2001b) *Crop Protect* **20(8)**: 389-394.

Gupta, C.P., Kumar, B., Dubey, R.C., and Maheshwari, D.K., (2006) *Biocontrol.* 51: 821-835.

, C.P., Dubey, R.C. and Maheshwari, D.K. (2002) *Biol. Fert. Soils* **35**: 399-405.

Gupta, C.P., Sharma, A., Dubey, R.C. and Maheshwari, D.K. (1999) *Cytobios* **99**: 183-189.

Gupta, C.P., Sharma, A., Dubey, R.C. and Maheshwari, D.K. (2001) *Ind. J. Exp. Biol.* **39**: 1318-1321.

Heffer. P. and Prud'homme, M. (2009) Fertilizer outlook 2009-2013. 77th IFA Annual Conference Shanghai (China), 25-27 May, 2009.

Hojberg, O., Schnider, U., Winteler, H.V., Sørensen, J. and Haas, D. (1999) *Appl. Environ. Microbiol.* **65**: 4085-4093.

Horwath, W.R., Elliott, L.F. and Lynch, J.M.(1998) *Lett. Appl. Microbiol.* **26**: 87-92.

Jagnow, G., Hoflich, G. and Hoffmann, K.H. (1991) *Angew. Bot.* **65**: 97-126.

Jeffries, P., Gianinazzi, S., Perotto, S., Turnau, K. and Barea ,J.M. (2003) *Biol. Fertil. Soils* **37**: 1–16.

Joshi, K.K., Kumar, V., Dubey, R.C. and Maheshwari, D.K. (2006 *Kor. J. Env. Agric.* **25(3):** 228-235.

Kang, J.G., Shin, S.Y., Kim, M.J., Bajpai, V., Maheshwari, D.K. and Kang, S.C. (2004) *J. Antibiot.* **57**: 1-6.

Kapur, R.M. and Naik, R.M. (2004) *J. Soils Crops* **14(1):** 22-25.

Kesavan, P.C. and Swaminathan, M.S. (2006). *Curr Sci* **90(2)**: 145-146.

Khan, M.S., Parvaze, A. Z., Mohammad, O. (2009) *Environ Chem Lett* **7**:1-19

Kloepper, J.W. (1993) *In*: soil microbial ecology. (ed. Metter, F.B.) Marcl Dekkar, Inc, New York, pp. 255-274.

Kloepper, J.W. (2003) 6th International PGPR workshop. 81-90. Indian Institute of Spices Research, Calicut, India.

Kloepper, J.W., Lifshitz, K. and Zablotowicz (1988) ISI Atlas Sci Anim Plant Sci 60-64.

Kloepper, J.W. and Schroth, M.N. (1978) *In*: Proc. 4th Int. Conf. Plant Pathology Bacteria, Vol. 2, staion de pathologie, (ed. Angers INRA), Gibert-Clary, Tours, France, pp. 879-882.

Kloepper, J.W. and Schroth, M.N. (1981) *Phytopathol.* **71**: 642-644.

Kravchenko, L.V. and Makarova, N.M. (1993) *Microbiol.* **62**: 324-327.

Kumar, B., Dubey, R.C. and Maheshwari, D.K. (2005) *In*: Microbial Diversity: Current Perspectives and Potential Applications, (eds. Satyanarayana, T. and Johri, B.N.), IK International Pvt Ltd, New Delhi, pp. 471–492.

Kumar, P., Tripathi, N. and Verma, O. (2006) *Agri. Update* **1(3)**: 45-47.

Kumar, S., Pandey, P. and Maheshwari, D.K. (2009) *Eur. J. Soil. Biol.* **45**: 334-340.

Kumar ,T., Bajpai, V.K., Maheshwari, D.K. and Kang, S.C. (2005b) *Agric. Chem. Biotechnol.* **48**: 79-83.

Kumar, T., Kang, S.C. and Maheshwari, D.K. (2005a) *Agric. Chem. Biotechnol.* **48(4)**: 161-166.

Lanje, P.W., Buldeo, A.N., Zade, S.R. and Gulhane, V.G. (2005) *J. Oilseeds Res.* **15(1)**: 132-135.

Lifshitz, R., Kloepper, J.W., Kozlwski, M., Cacison, J., Tipping, E.M. and Zalestha, I. (1987) *Can J Microbiol* **33**: 390-395.

Lin Qi-mei Rao, Z., Sun Yan-Xing Yao, J. and Xing, L. (2002) *Agric. Sci. China* **1**: 81-85.

Liu, W., Xu, X., Wu, X., Yang, Q., Luo, Y. and Christie, P. (2006) *Environ. Geochem. Health.* **28**: 133-140.

Luc M Maene, (2000)10th World Food Prize Congress, Washington DC, pp. 169–171.

Lucy, M., Reed, E. and Glick, B.R. (2004) *Antonie van Leeuwenhek* **86**: 1-25.

Maheshwari, D.K., Dubey, R.C. and Sharma, V.K. (2001) *Ind. J. Microbiol.* **41**: 251-256.

Mandal, B.K., Mandal, B.B., Murmu, N.N., Tudu, B.C. and Khanda, C.M. (2003) *Ind. J. Plant Physiol.* **8**: 103-105.

Mawdsley, J.L. and Burns, R.G. (1994) *Soil Biol. Biochem.* **26**: 849-859.

Mc Inroy, J.A. and Kloepper, J.W. (1995) *Plant Soil* J **73**: 337-342.

Muntasir I.M., Tauhiduzzaman, S. and Ishaque, M. (2001) *Ind. J. Agric. Chem.* **34**: 15-21.

Murthy, M.G. and Ladha, J.K. (1988) *Plant Soil* **108**: 281-285.

Muthukumarasamy, R., Revathi, G. and Loganathan, P. (2002) *Plant Soil* **243**: 91-102.

Narwal SS (2006) *In*: Allelopathy: A physiological process with ecological implications (Eds. Reigosa MJ, Pedrol N, Gonzalez L) Springer. The Netherlands. pp. 537-564.

Pandey, P., Kang, S.C., Gupta, C.P., and Maheshwari, D.K. (2005) *Curr. Micontrol* 51: 303-309.

Pandey, P., Kang, S.C. and Maheshwari, D.K. (2005) *Curr. Sci.* **89**: 177-180.

Pandey, P. and Maheshwari, D.K. (2007) *Curr. Sci.* **92(8)**: 1137-1142.

Papatheodorou, E.M., Efthimiadou, E. and Stamou, G.P. (2008) *Eur. J. Soil Biol.* **44**: 429-436.

Parasuraman, P. and Mani, A.K. (2003) *Ind. J. Agro.* **48(2)**: 82-85.

Patel, S.R. and Thakur, D.S. (2003) *J. Oilseeds Res.* **20(1)**: 153-154.

Patersion, E. (2003) *Eur. J. Soil Sci.* **54**: 741-750.

Paul, K.I., and Savithri, K.E. (2003) *J. Tropic. Agricul.* **4**: 47-49.

Paulitz, T.C. and Belanger, R.R. (2001) *Annu. Rev. Phytopathol.* **39**: 103-133.

Peng, G.X., Tan, Z.Y., Wang, E.T., Reinhold-Hurek, B., Chen, W.F. and Chen, W.X. (2002) *Int. J. Syst. Evol. Microbiol.* **52**: 457-462.

Penrose, D.M and Glick, B.R. (2003) *Physiol. Plant.***118**: 10-15.

Pillay, V.K. and Nowak, J. (1997) *Can. J. Microbiol.* **43**: 354-361.

Polyanaskaya, L.M., Vedina, O.T., Lysak, L.V. and Zvyagintev, D.G. (2000) *Microbiol.* **71**: 109-115.

Postgate, J. (1998) Nitrogen fixation, Cambridge University Press, Cambridge 3rd edn. 112.

Raju, R.A., Subba Rao, A. and Rupa, T.R. (2005) *Ind. J. Fert.* **1(8)**: 25-28.

Ram, N. (1994) *Ind. Far. Dig.* 27(2): 14-15.

Ramamoorthy, K., Vairavan, K., Vijayalakshmi, R. and Jehangir, K.S. (1994) *Ind. J. Pulses Res.* **7(1)**: 84-85.

Ramesh, P., Panwar,N. R., Singh, A. B., Ramana,S., Sushil, K. Y. Shrivastava, R. and Subba Rao, A. (2010) *Curr. Sci.* **98 (9)**: 1190-1194.

Rao, S.V.C.K. and Soren, G. (1991) *Ind. J. Agron.* **36**: 95-98.

Reddy, P.M., Reddiramu, Y. and Ramakrishna, Y. (2005) *J. Oilseeds Res.* **22(1)**: 59-62.

Reed, P.M. and Glick, B.R. (2004) *Anton. Van Leeuwenhoek* **86**: 1-25.

Roget, D.K. (1995) *Aust. J. Exp. Agric.* **35**: 1009-1013.

Saraf, M. and Sood, N. (2002) *J. Ind. Bot. Soc.* **81**: 154-157.

Seneviratne, G. (2009) *Curr. Sci.* **96(5)**: 633.

Seshadri. S., Muthukukarswami, R., Lakshminarasimhan, C. and Ignacimuthu, S. (2000) *Curr. Sci.* **79**: 565-567.

Shehata, M.M. and El-khawas, S.A. (2003) *Pak. J. Biol. Sci.* **6(4)**: 1257-1268.

Shrotriya, G.C. (2005) *Ind. J. Fert.* **1 (2)**: 31-38 & 41-43.

Singhal, V., Pratibha and Sengar, R.S. (2003) *Ind. Farm.* ***April***: 11-12.

Sridevi, M. and Mallaiah, K.V. (2009) *Ind. J. Microbiol.* **49**: 98-102.

Strzeleowa, A. (1970) *Acta. Microbiol. Polan.* **2**: 23-24.

Sugumaran, P. and Janarthanam, B. (2007) *World. J. Agric. Sci.* **3(3)**: 350-355.

Suslow, T.V. (1982) *In*: Phytopathogenic Prokaryots, (Eds. Mount, M.S. and Lacy, G.H.), London: Academic Press.

Thaunanthan, K., Imayavarambarn, V., Singaravel, R., and Kandasamy, S. (2001) Sesame and sunflower Newsletter No.16.

Tilak, K.V.B.R., Ranganayaki, N., Pal, K.K., De, R., Saxena, A.K., Nautiyal., C.S., Mittal, S., Tripathi, A.K., and Johri, B.N. (2005) *Curr. Sci.* **89(1)**: 136-150.

Tufenkci, S., Erman, M., Sonmez, F. (2006) *Ind. J. Agri. Sci.* **75(5)**: 261-264.

Valladares, F., Salvador, P.V., Dominguez, S., Fernandez, M., Penuelas, J.L. and Pugnaire, F.I. (2002) *Plant Soil* 240: 253-262.

van der Hoeven, N., van Elsas, J.D., Heijnen, C.E., (1996) *Ecol. Model.* **89**: 161-173.

van Veen, J.A., van Overbeek, L.S., and van Elsas, J.D. (1997) *Microbiol. Mol. Biol. Rev.* **61**:121-135.

Vassilev, N., Vassileva, M., and Mikelaeva, I. (2006) *Appl. Microbiol. Biotechnol.* **71**: 137-144.

Vyas, S.P. (2003) *Fert. News* **48(7)**: 49-51.

Weller, D.M. (1998) *Ann. Phytopathol.* **26**: 379–407.

Wiseman, B.M., Neate, S.M., Ophel-Keller, K., and Smith, S.E. (1996) *Soil Biol. Biochem.* **28:** 727-732.

Wu, S.C., Cao, Z.H., Li, Z.G., Cheung, K.C., and Wong, M.H. (2005) *Geoderma* **125**: 155–166.

www.http://dacnet.nic.in/ncof/productionunit.htm

www.*ieg.nic.in*

Index